KU-579-436

ROAD ATLAS
EUROPE

1st edition November 1990
© The Automobile Association 1990

This edition is exclusive to W.H. Smith Ltd, Greenbridge Road, Swindon
SN3 3LD.

All rights reserved. No part of this publication may be reproduced, stored in a
retrieval system, or transmitted in any form or by any means — electronic,
mechanical, photocopying, recording or otherwise, unless the permission of the
publisher has been obtained beforehand.

Published by The Automobile Association, Fanum House, Basing View,
Basingstoke, Hampshire RG21 2EA

ISBN 0 7495 0077 8

Produced by the Cartographic Department of The Automobile Association.

Printed by Graficromo SA,Cordoba, Spain

The contents of this book are believed correct at the time of printing.
Nevertheless, the publisher can accept no responsibility for errors or
omissions or for changes in the details given.

A CIP catalogue record for this book is available from the British Library.

JOURNEY PLANNING MAP

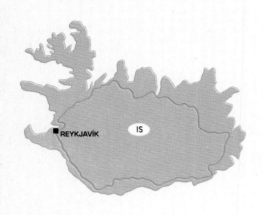

IS

REYKJAVÍK

IRL

GB

DUBLIN

LONDON

E ROUTES

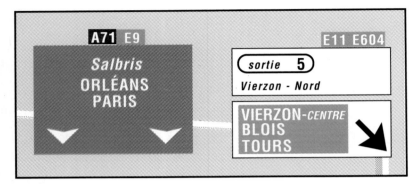

Roadsign identifying E Route, France

The new European Agreement on Main International Traffic Arteries came into force on 15 March 1983. This followed several earlier agreements dating back to 1950, and provides a co-ordinated plan for the construction standard and development of roads of international importance, collectively the European international network.

The network consists of a grid system of roads with even numbers for routes running east to west and, generally, odd numbers for routes running north to south. In addition, there are intermediate roads located between the main routes.

The contracting parties have agreed on a plan to sign the roads of the 'E' road network with 'E' numbers identified by green and white signs with the 'E' prefix. Not all European countries are signatories to this agreement and of those who are, not all have implemented the 'E' road numbering system. On traffic signs in Belgium, for instance, nearly all motorways are part of the European international network, displaying only 'E' numbers in preference to the 'A' numbers shown on the remainder. Some countries display on signposts both the 'E' road number and the national

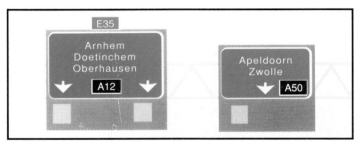

Roadsign identifying E Route, Netherlands

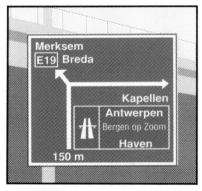

Roadsign identifying E Route, Belgium

number (see examples). Other countries (eg Sweden) signed an earlier agreement but have not signed the latest one, and are therefore not showing the latest 'E' road numbers on their signs.

After forty years under the auspices of UNESCO, with the EEC keeping a watching brief on developments, the introduction of a European International network is far from complete.

MAP SYMBOLS

A4	Motorway - dual carriageway
A7	Motorway - single carriageway
A1	Toll motorway - dual carriageway
A6	Toll motorway - single carriageway
	Motorway junction
	Motorway junction - restricted access
	Motorway service area
	Motorway under construction
	Primary route
	Main road
	Secondary road
	Other road
D600 E57 N59	Road numbers
	Dual carriageway or four lanes
	Road in poor condition

	Scotland: narrow A roads with passing places
	Under construction
TOLL Toll	Toll road
	Transit route (G.D.R.)
	Scenic route
)========(	Road tunnel
	Car transporter (rail)
68	Distances (km)
70	Distances (miles) in G.B. and Ireland
10-6 970	Mountain pass (height in metres) with closure period
	Gradient 14% and over. Arrow points uphill
	Gradient 6% - 13% Gradient 20% and over in G.B.
X	Frontier crossing with restricted opening hours
N Ireland Rep Ireland	Frontier crossing
AA	AA shop

AA	AA port shop
IBIZA V	Vehicle ferry
	Hovercraft ferry
	Airport
	International boundary
	National boundary
	Viewpoint
	Motor racing circuit
3560 SNOWDON	Mountain/spot height (heights in G.B. and Ireland in feet, elsewhere in Europe in metres)
	Mountain railway
	Urban area
	River, lake and canal
■ Jockfall	Place of interest
64	Overlaps and numbers of continuing pages

1

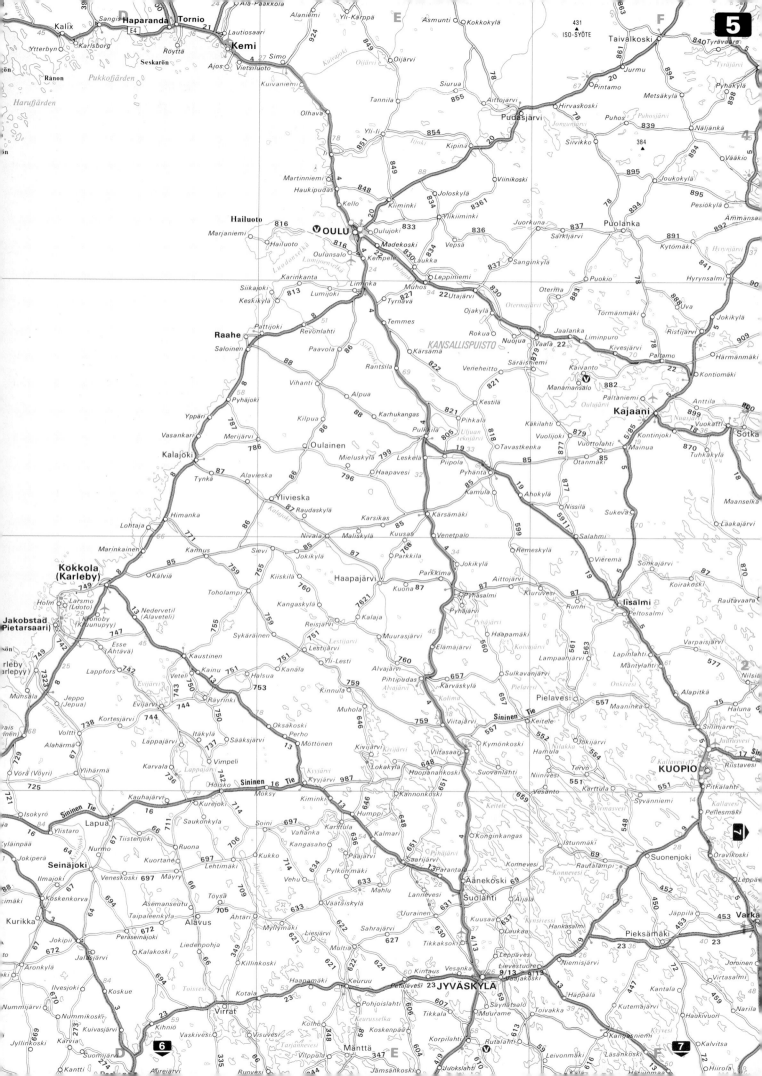

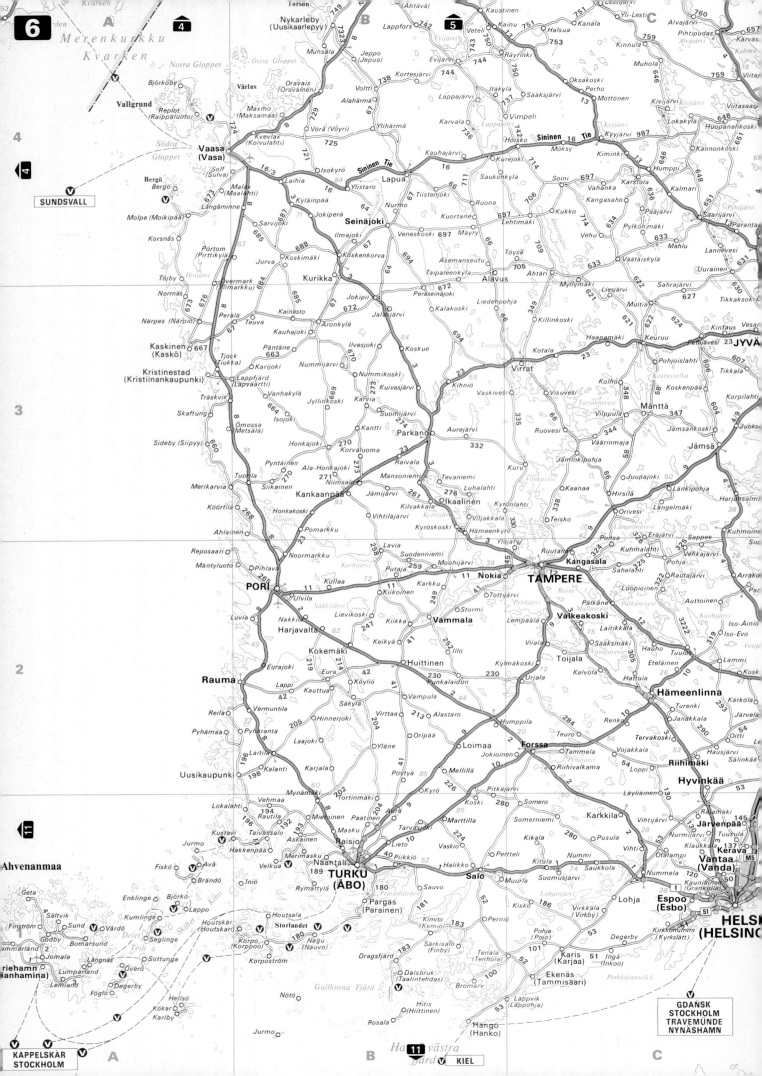

Lampaanjärvi · Lapinlahti · Juuka · Nunnanlahti · Vuonislahti
Mäntylahti · 577 · Nilsiä · Säyneinen · Koli · Jaakonvaara · Naarva · Pihlajavaara
Pielavesi · 557 · Alapitkä · 570 · Viitaniemi · Polvela · Ahmovaara · Ukko-Koli · Ukkola · Kivilahti · Huhus · Korentovaara · Hattuvaara
Onkivesi · Maaninka · 75 · Haluna · 569 · Juankoski · Kaavi · Sivakkavaara · Luikonlahti · Martonvaara · Uimaharju · Tyrjänsaari · 520 · 514
Keitele · 552 · Jokijärvi · 554 · Siilinjärvi · 17 · Sininen · 566 · 573 · Polvijärvi · Kontiolahti · Eno · Luhtapohja · Ilomantsi · KANSALLISPUISTO
KUOPIO · Riistavesi · Tuusjärvi · 572 · Maariänvaara · Kokonvaara · 502 · Jakokoski · 73 · Kovero · Marjovaara · 500
Kallavesi · Pitkälahti · 17 · Kuusjärvi · Outokumpu · Kontkala · JOENSUU · Heinävaara · Tuupovaara · Mutalahti
Tervo · 551 · Syvänniemi · Pellesmäki · 542 · Viinijärvi · 17 · 476 · 41 · Kiihtelysvaara · 496
Karttula · Virmasvesi · Ruskila · Palokki · 95 · Liperi · Pyhäselkä · Hammaslahti · Öllölä · Hollola
Istunmäki · Suonenjoki · Oravikoski · Juojärvi · Karvio · Särvikumpu · Leppälahti · Tutjunniemi · 482 · 500
Rautalampi · 452 · Leppävirta · Heinävesi · 477 · Vihtari · Oravisalo · Rääkkylä · Tohmajärvi · Uusi-Värtsilä · Vyartsilya
Konnevesi · 450 · 453 · Jäppilä · Varkaus · Kangaslampi · 468 · Koivumäki · Kerma · 470 · Pöllakkä · 474 · Orivesi · 490 · Värtsilä
Pieksämäki · 23 · Kangaslampi · Viljolahti · Savonranta · Kitee · Ozero Yaniservyri · Suystamo
Niemisjärvi · Joroinen · Tiemassaari · Ahvensalmi · Oravi · Enonkoski · 471 · Kesälahti · Lyaskelya
Leivonmäki · Virtasalmi · Rantasalmi · 464 · Juvola · Varparanta · Makkola · Kerimäki · Puhos · Sortavala
Hankasalmi · Kantala · 459 · Narila · 464 · Parkumäki · Kallislahti · 71 · Puruvesi · Pyhäjärvi
Toivakka · Kutemajärvi · Haukivuori · 14 · 64 · Savonlinna · Kulennoinen · 479 · Hiukkajoki · Akonpohja
Kangasniemi · Kalvitsa · Juva · Pihlajalahti · 437 · 435 · Rauhaniemi · Putikko · 14 · Särkisalmi
Läsänkoski · Hiirola · 434 · Sulkava · 435 · Kiviapaja · Vuoriniemi · 406 · Parikkala · Simpelejärvi
Mikkeli · Harjunmaa · Kaskii · Ryhälä · 438 · Lohikoski · Särkilahti · Simpele · Kurkijoki · Ladozhskoye Ozero
Otava · 431 · Anttola · Puumala · Pohja-Lankila · Lahko · Khiitola
Hirvensalmi · Hietanen · 62 · 434 · Syyspohja · 406 · Rautjärvi · Priozersk
Ruorasmäki · 427 · Ristiina · Hurissalo · 62 · Virmutjoki · Borodinskoye · Melnikovo
Hartola · 428 · Toivola · 416 · Pellosniemi · Ruokolahti · Khiitola
Pertunmaa · 426 · Vihantasalmi · Saimaa · Virolahti · Imatra · Vesiputout · Svetogorsk · Priozersk
Sysmä · 413 · Mäntyharju · 419 · Suomenniemi · Partakoski · Imatra · Svetogorsk
Onkiniemi · Varpanen · 381 · 409 · Savitaipale · 408 · Joutseno · Lesogorskiy · Kamennogorsk
Nikkaroinen · 610 · Nurmaa · Kiesila · Taipalsaari · 392 · Nuijamaa · Kamennogorsk · Sosnovo
Heinola · 60 · Hühdasjärvi · Heituinlahti · Lappeenranta · Hytti · Brusnichnoe · Viborg
Vesivehmaa · 313 · Vuolenkoski · 377 · Tuohikotti · 378 · 36 · Jurvala · Ylämaa · Sovetskiy · Kamenka · Pervomaisk
Vierumäki · 363 · Jaala · Valkeala · Taavetti · 367 · Muurola · 384 · Primorsk · Polyany · Zelenogorsk
Pyhäntaka · 362 · Iitti · Utti · Kaipiainen · Muurikkala · Torfyanovka (Yulya Urpala) · Kamenka
Nastola · 12 · Kuusankoski · Koria · 61 · Pyhältö · Miehikkälä · Vaalimaa · Sovetskiy · Pervomaisk
Orimattila · 167 · 360 · Kouvola · Myllykoski · Anjalankoski · Metsäkylä · Paijäri · Virojoki · Virolahti
Artjärvi · Elimäki · 354 · Anjala · 351 · Hamina · Summa · Klamila · Primorsk · Polyany
Myrskylä (Mörskom) · Lapinjärvi (Lappträsk) · 357 · Karhula · Kotka · Mussalo · Ostrov Berezovyy · Repino · Sestroretsk · Vsevolozhsk
Lovisa (Loviisa) · Pyhtää (Pyttis) · Kronshtadt · 57
Porvoo Borgå · 157 · Perna · Valko (Valkom) · Kirkonmaanselkä · Haapasaari · Lomonosov · LENINGRAD
Ebbo (Epoo) · Kabböle · Ostrov Sur Sari · Ostrov Seyskari · Uste · Petrodvorets · Kolpine
Tolkis (Tolkkinen) · Tirmo · Kernovo · Krasnoye Selo · Pushkin
Pellinge (Pellinki) · Ostrov Moshchnyy

STOCKHOLM

Begunitsy · Gatchina · Ust'-Luga · Volosovo · Vyra · Siverskiy

Narva · Sillamäe · Kingisepp

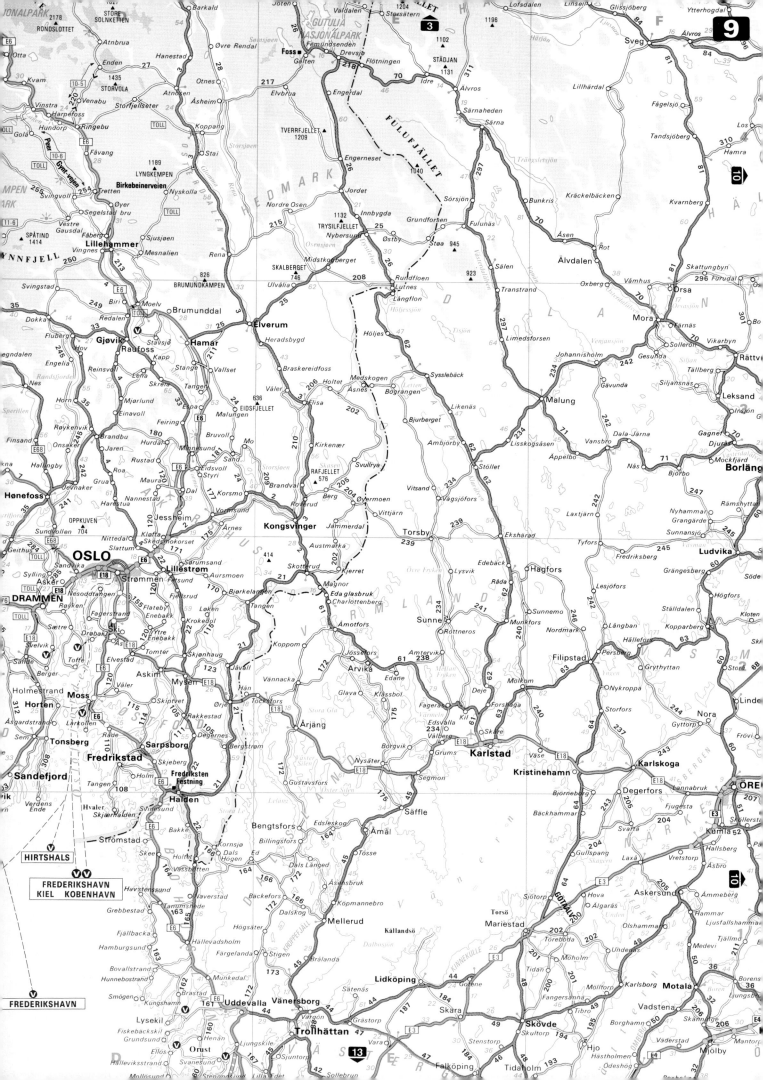

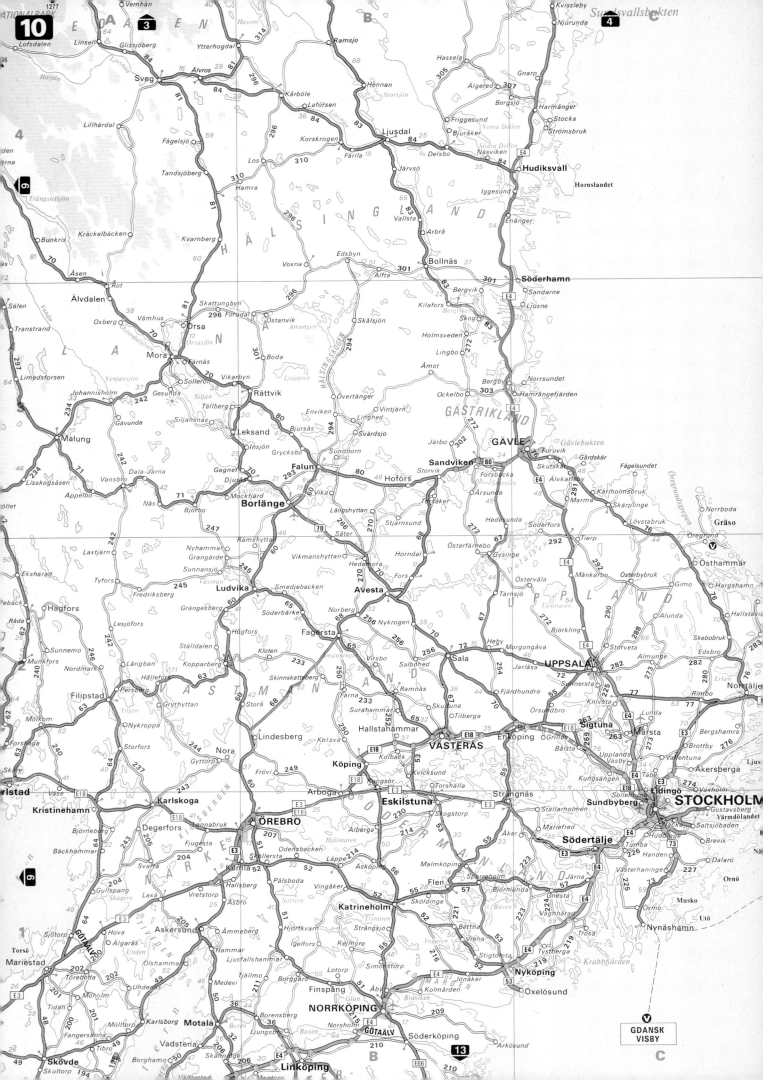

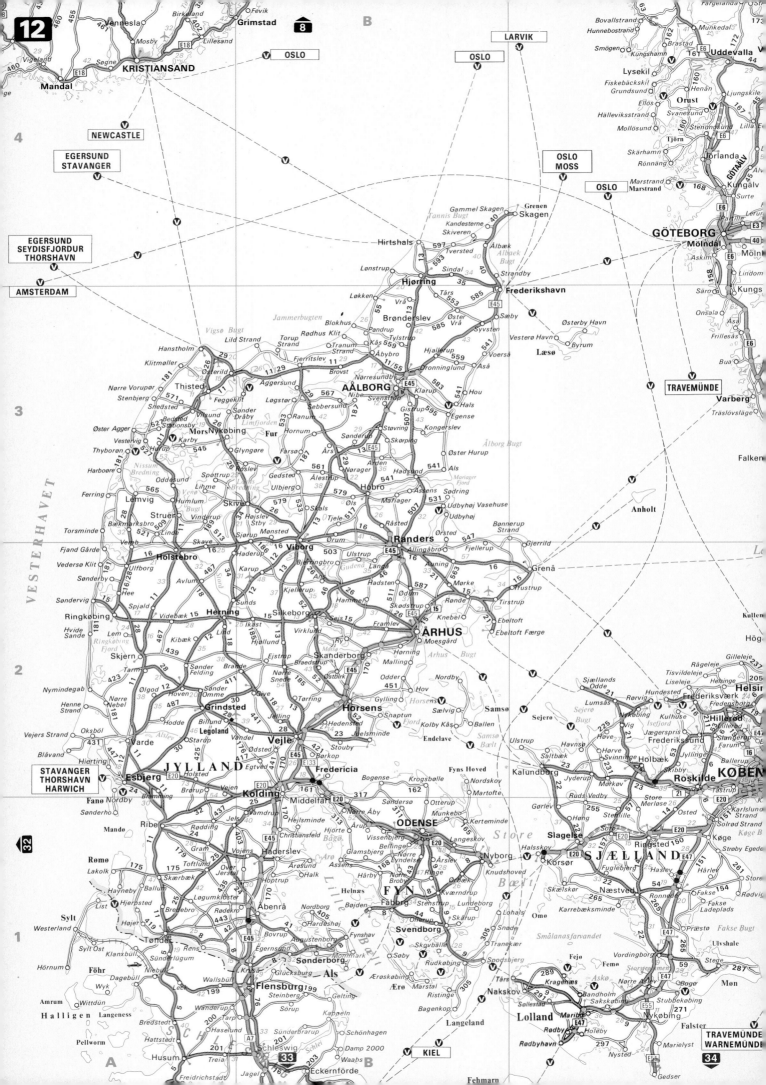

A   B   C

4

3

Tory Island   Fanad Head

Tory   Sound

Horn Head   Rosapenna

Bloody Foreland   Dunfanaghy

R257   N56   Cresslough   R245

Gola   R258   Milford   R245

Island   R259   ▲2466   R251   Kilmacrenan   R245

ERRIGAL

Aran Island   R260   Crolly   R254   Letterkenny

R259   (Croithli)   R250

R259   Dungloe   N56   R236

R252

Gweebarra Bay   R250   R252   Stranorlar   N15

R250   Ballybofey

R261   ▲2219   Castlederg

Glenties

Rossan Point   Glencolumbkille   Ardara   R262

Malin More   (Gleann Cholm   Lough

Cille)   Eske   Mount   Donegal

1972   Carrick   Charles

SLIEVE LEAGUE   (An Charraig)   Lough

Kilcar   Killybegs   Dunkineely   R232   Derg

(Cill Charthaigh)   Ballintra   Dru

St John's Point   N15   R231   Pettigo

Ballyshannon   Kesh   A35

Bundoran   Belleek   Irvinestown

Inishmurray   R279   Rosscor   Lower Lough   B82

Cliffony   Kinlough   Garrison   Derrygonnelly

Grange   R280   Scribbagh   R281   B80

1722   Manorhamilton   Enniskillen

Erris Head   Broad   Downpatrick Head   BENBULBEN

Haven   46   Rosses Point   R286   Belcoo   Lisbella

Belmullet   R314   Ballycastle   Easky   N15   Glenfarne   N16   A509

(Beal an Mhuirhead)   R314   Killala   Dromore   Strandhill   R292   Sligo   Blacklion   Upper Lough

Bunnahowen   Bay   West   R291   R287   Dowra   R207   R206

Inishkea   R313   Killala   Enniscrone   N59   Ballysadare   R290   R200

Bangor Erris   Colloony   R289   Drumkeeran   R260   IRON

Duvillaun More   N59   N59   Bunnyconnellan   OX   R294   N17   Swanlinbar   MTS

Blacksod Bay   Crossmolina   R136   MTS   Ballymote   N4   Lough   R202

2204   ▲2369   Ballina   Tobercurry   R296   Ballyfarnan   Allen   R205

SLIEVE MORE   R312   R310   R293   Keadue   R208   Ballinamore   R199

Achill Head   Keel   2646   N57   Curry   R284   Ballinafad   Leitrim   R209   Fenagh   Killashandra

Achill Island   R319   NEPHIN   Foxford   Charlestown   R367   Boyle   Carrick-   R201   Carriga

N59   R315   N57   Carracastle   R294   Grallagh   on-Shannon

Lough   R317   Swinford   N5   Drumsna   N4

Feeagh   R312   Turlough   R310   Kilkelly   R325   R361   Mohill   Drumod   Roosky   Drumlish

Clare   Newport   R311   Castlebar   N5   Ballaghaderreen   N61   Elphin   R202   Farnaght   R198

Clew Bay   N60   Kiltimagh   Frenchpark   R369   N4   Longford

Westport   R335   N60   Knock   N17   R325   Loughglinn   Tulsk   Strokestown   N5   Ballinalee   Grana

Louisburgh   R324   Balla   N83   Castlerea   R367   Castleplunkett   Newtown   N4

Caher   CROAGH PATRICK   R330   Ballyhean   R323   Ballinlough   Scramoge   Forbes   Cloondara

Inishturk   2510   Claremorris   Ballyhaunis   R327   Ballintober   R371   Killashee   R393

N59   R335   Lough   N60   R327   Ballymoe   N60   Lanesborough   N63   Rathowen

Inishbofin   Partry   Carra   R331   Ballindine   R328   R362   R364   Roscommon   Keenagh

Inishshark   Ballinrobe   Kilmaine   R332   Dunmore   Glenamaddy   Fuerty   R366   Knockcroghery   R397

Cruagh   Leenene   Lough   Neale   16   Creggs   R362   N63

Letterfrack   R344   Mask   Kilmaine   Clonbur   R345   2239

R335   R331

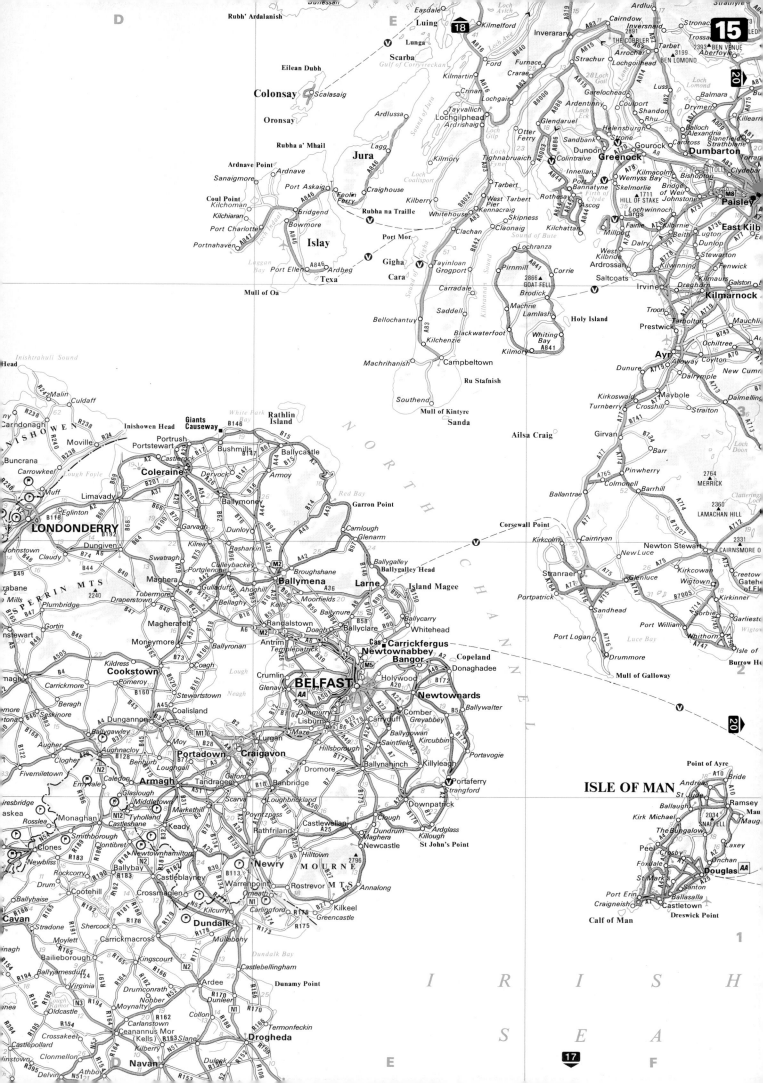

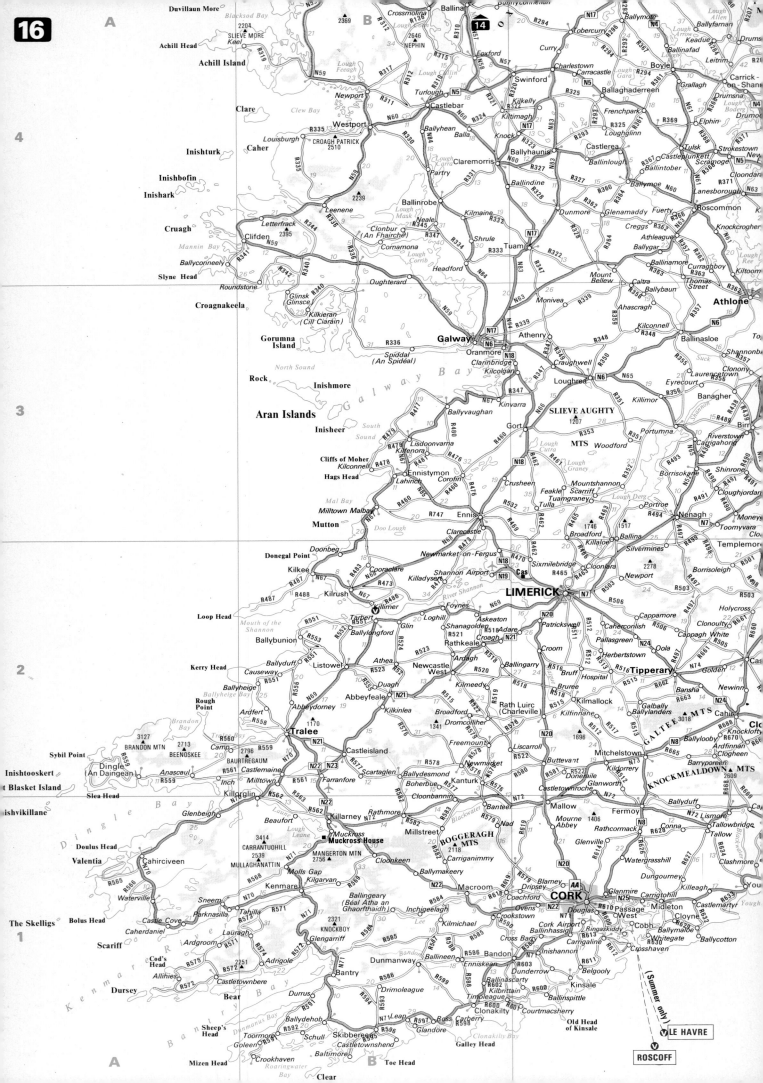

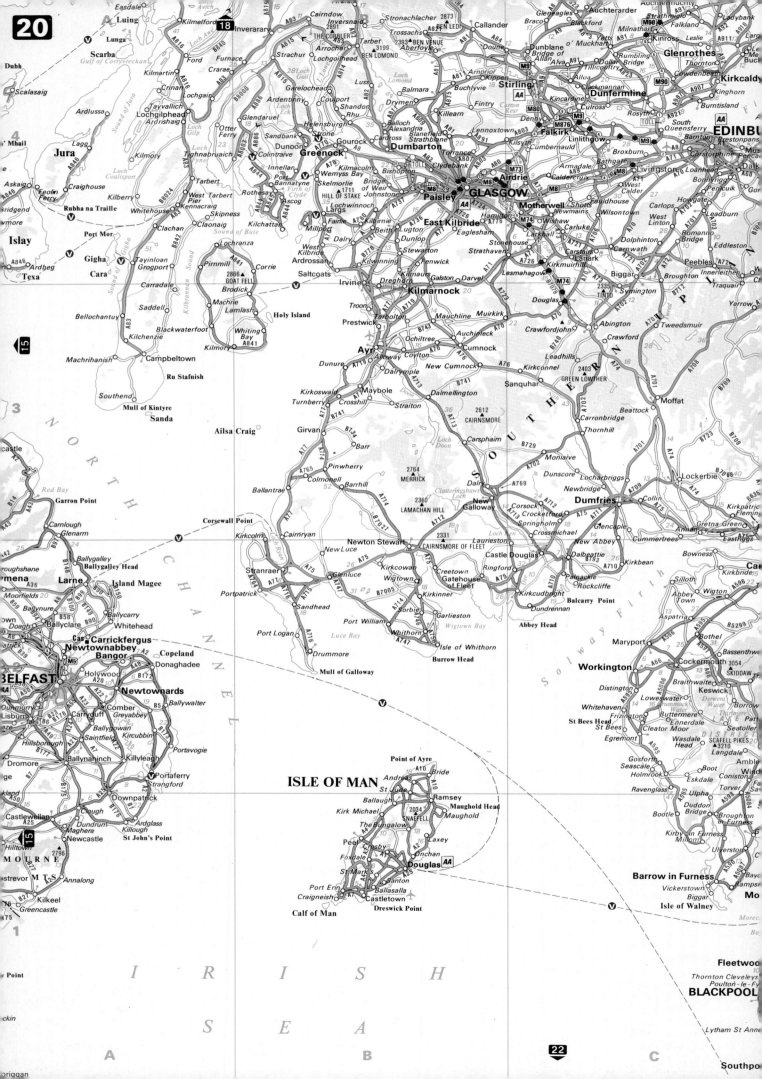

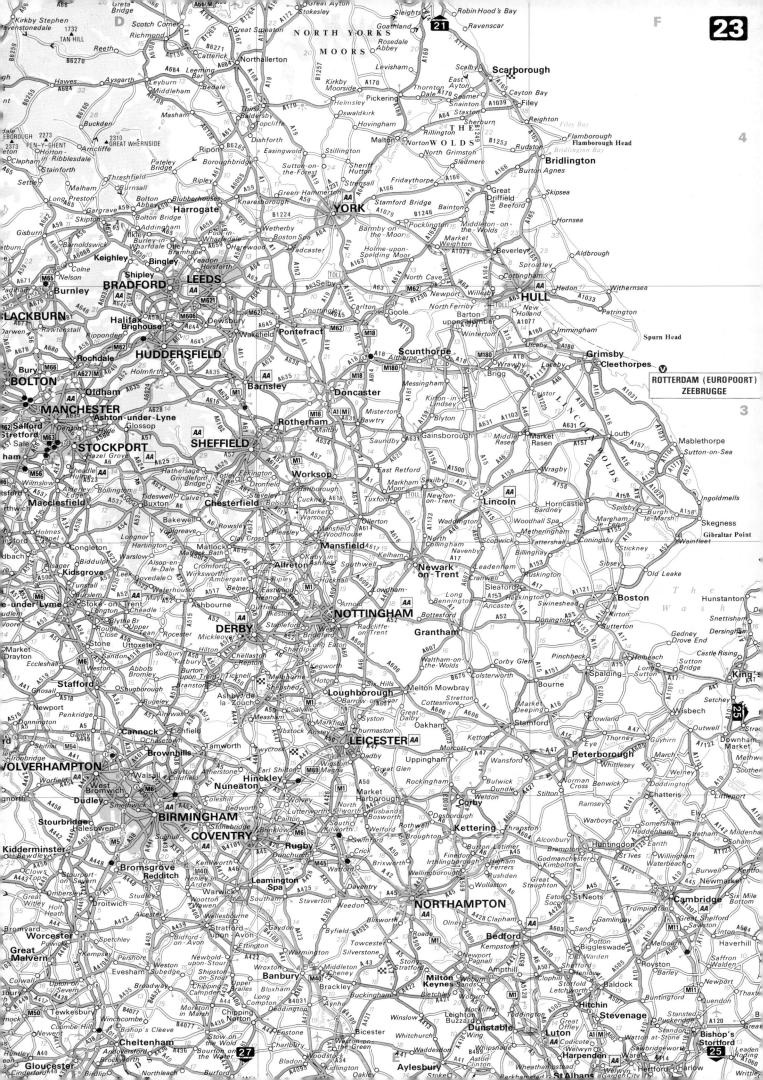

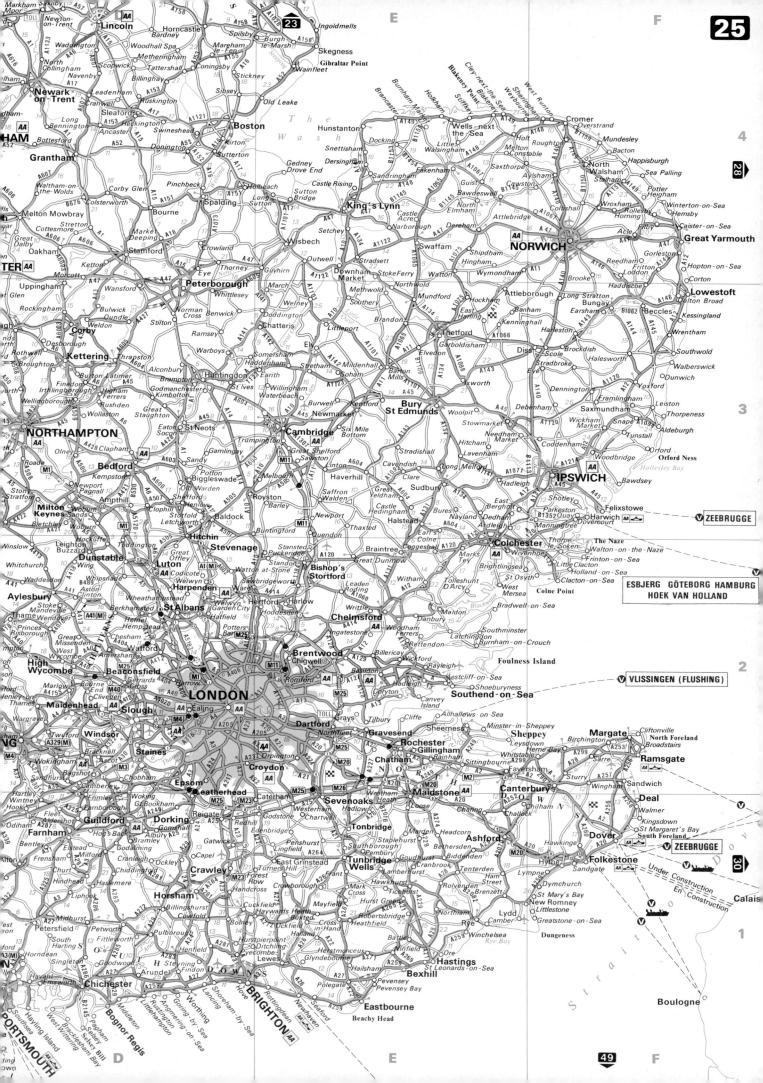

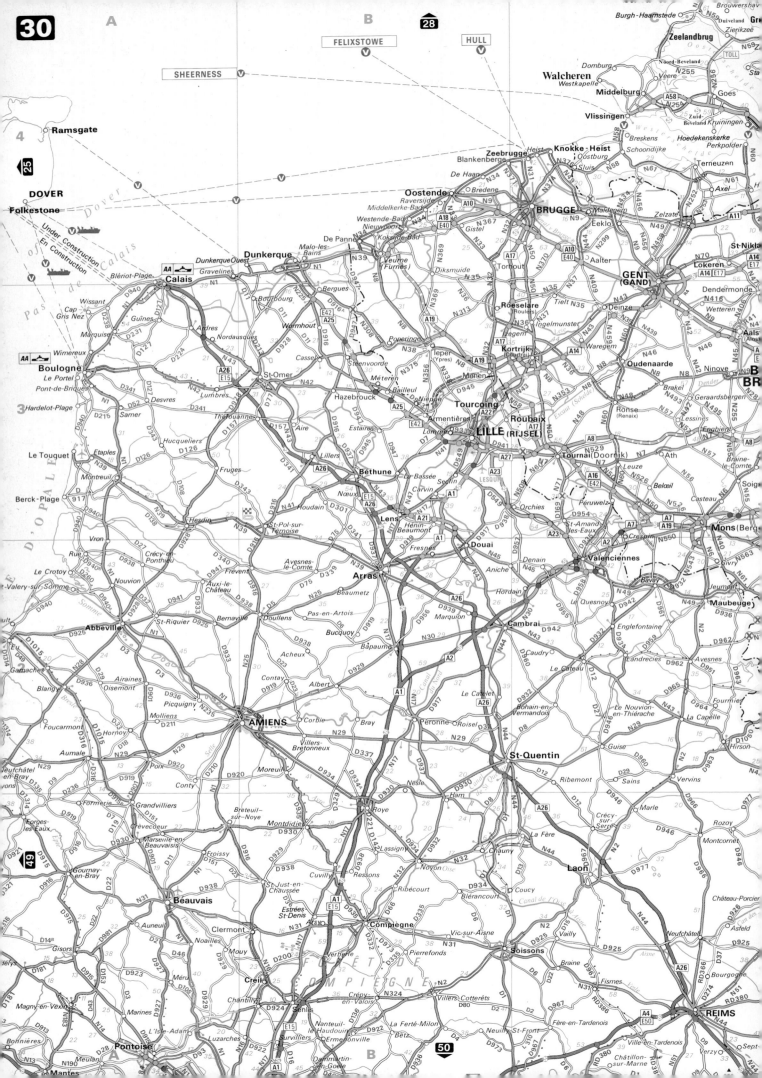

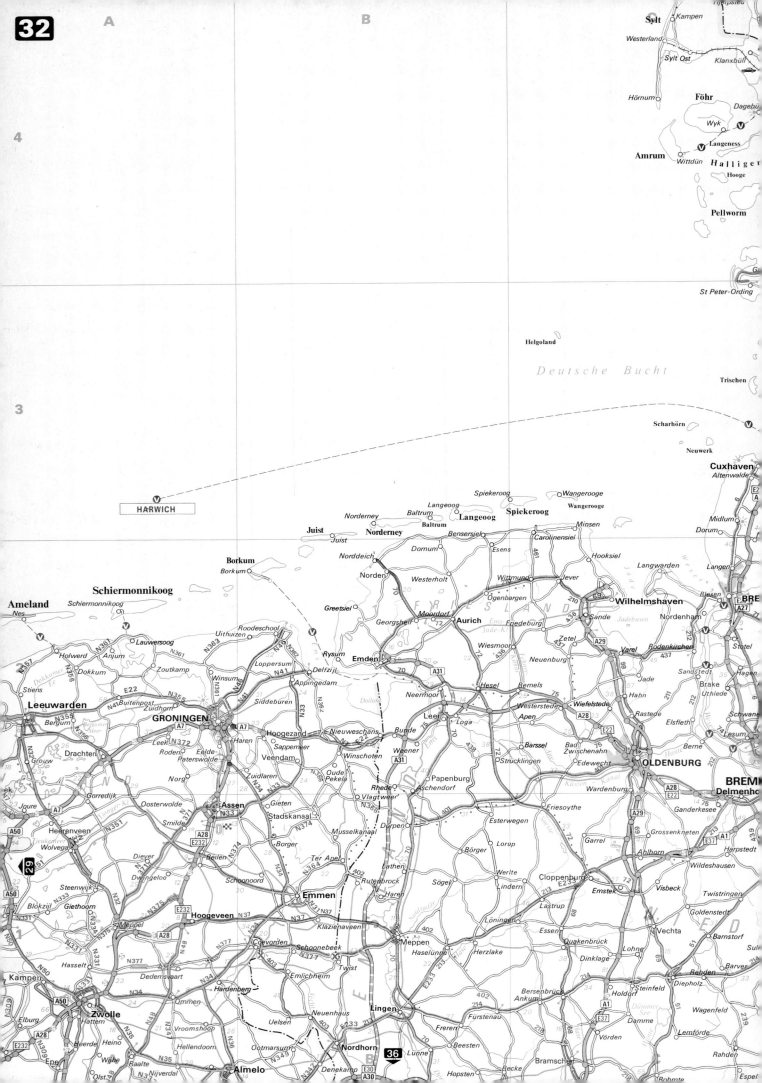

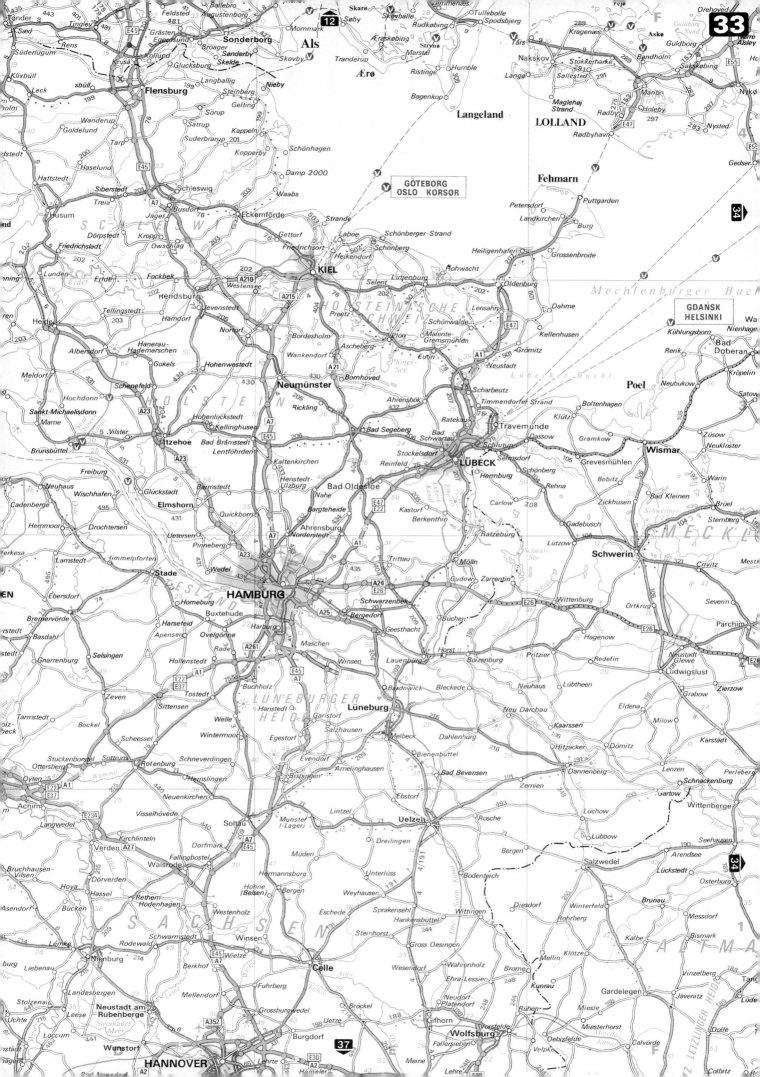

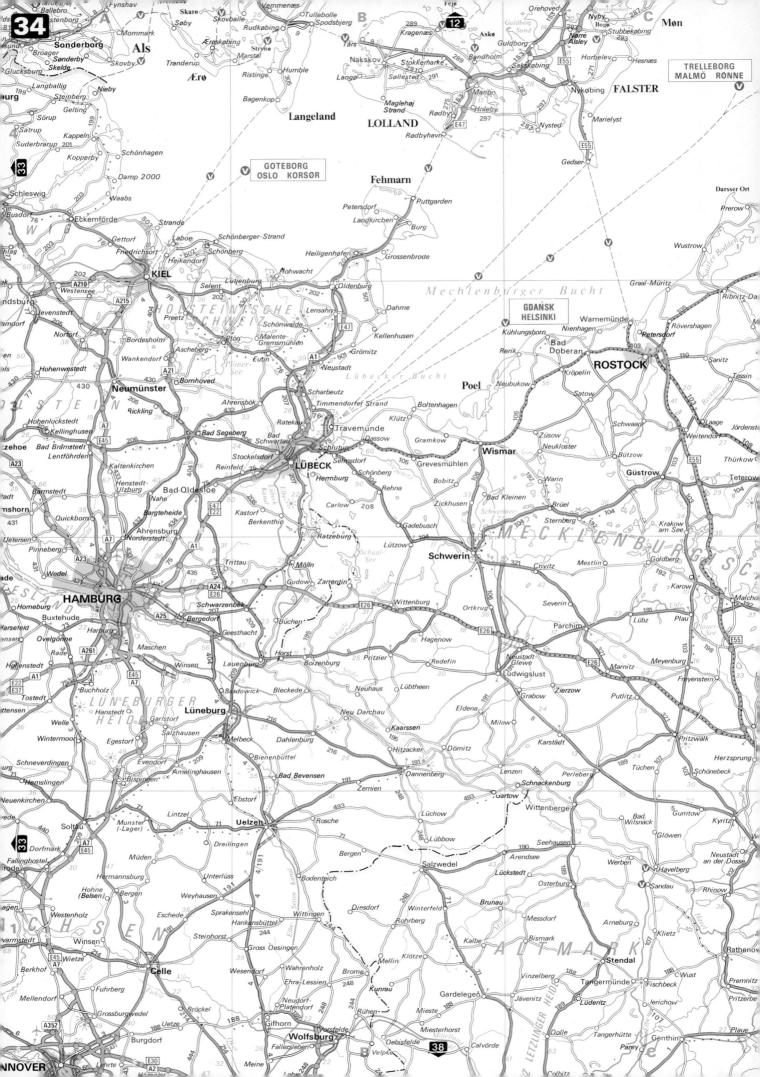

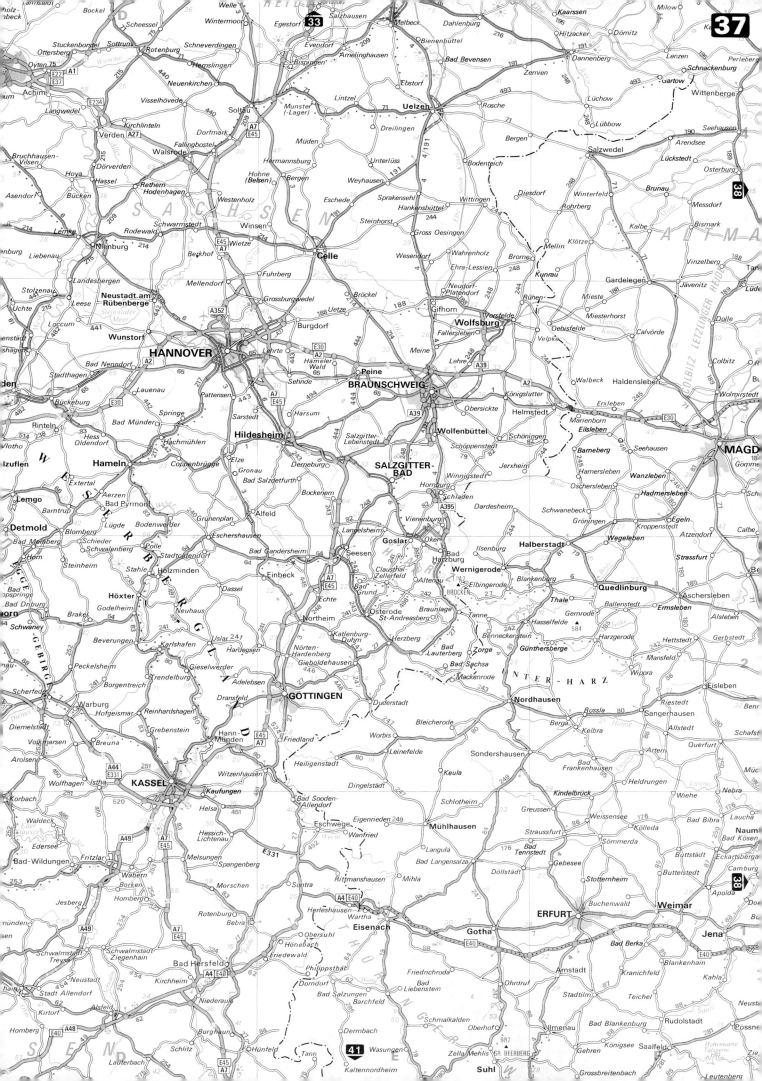

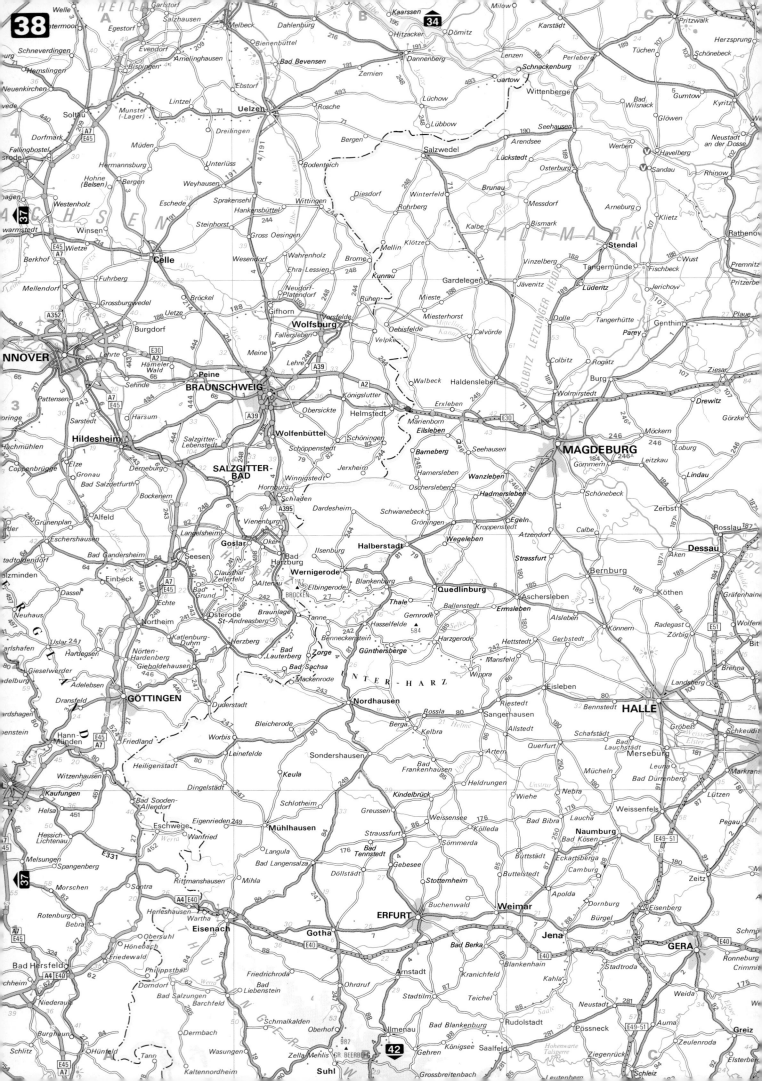

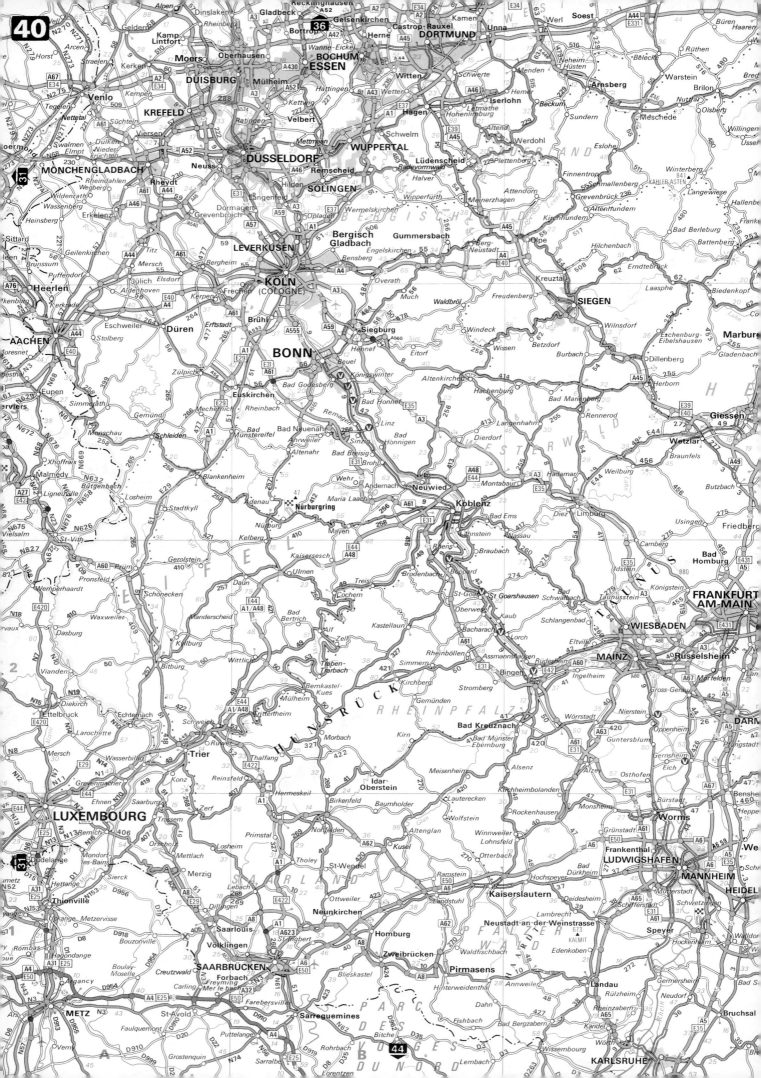

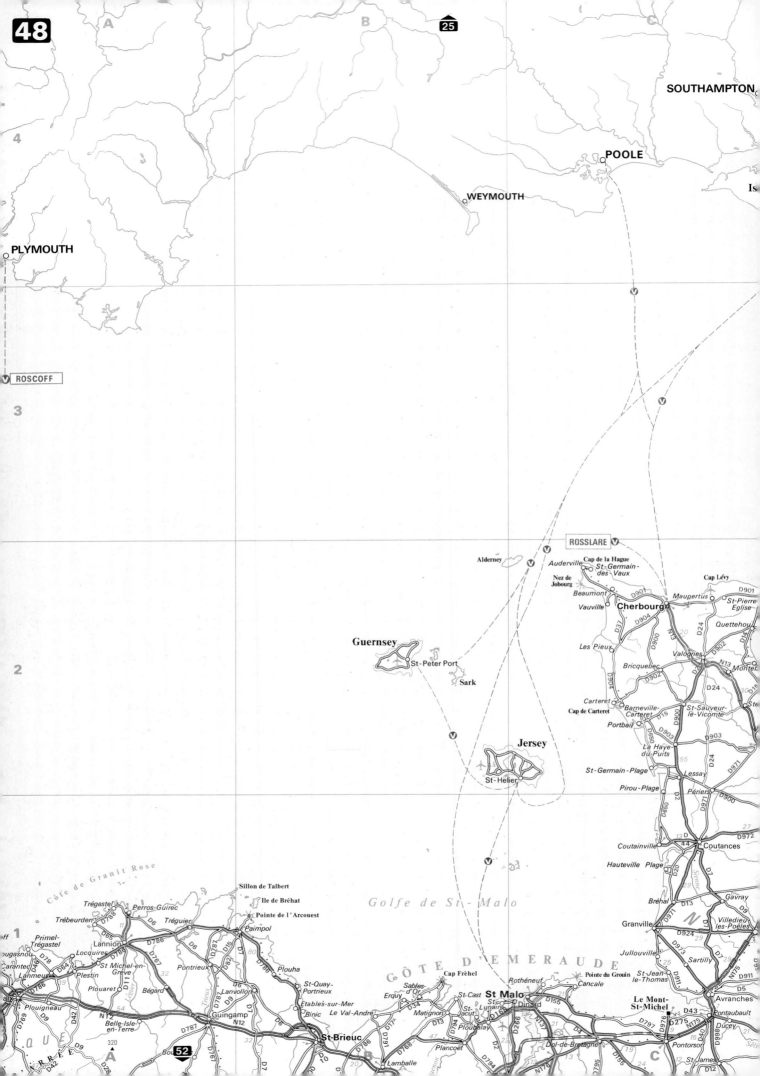

48

SOUTHAMPTON,

POOLE

WEYMOUTH

Is

PLYMOUTH

ROSCOFF

ROSSLARE

Alderney
Auderville • Cap de la Hague
St-Germain-
des-Vaux
Cap Lévy
Nez de
Jobourg
D901
Maupertus
St-Pierre
Eglise
D901
Beaumont
D901
Vauville
Cherbourg
D904
Quettehou
D37
N13
D24
Les Pieux
D900
Valognes
D902
N13
Montel
Bricquebec
D902
D24
Guernsey
St-Peter Port
Sark
Carteret
Barneville-
Carteret
St-Sauveur-
le-Vicomte
Ste
Cap de Carteret
D16
D900
Portbail
D903
D650
La Haye-
du-Puits
D903
D24
D971
Jersey
St-Germain - Plage
55
Lessay
St-Helier
Pirou-Plage
D650
D2
D971
Périers
D900
Coutainville
13 D
44
D972
Coutances
Hauteville Plage
D7
D20
Bréhal
D971
D13
Gavray
Côte de Granit Rose
Sillon de Talbert
Ile de Bréhat
Golfe de St - Malo
Granville
D924
Villedieu
les-Poêles
Trégastel
Perros-Guirec
Pointe de l'Arcouest
Trébeurden
D788
Tréguier
Paimpol
N
Primel-
Trégastel
Lannion
D786
Jullouville
D973
Sartilly
D175
D911
ougasnou
Locquirec
D767
D786
Plouha
St-Jean-
le-Thomas
25
N175
D911
aranted
St Michel-en-
Grève
D6
D787
D15
80
St-Quay-
Portrieux
Cap Fréhel
Pointe du Grouin
Cancale
D911
Lanhmeur
Plestin
D786
Pontrieux
Lanvollon
Etables-sur-Mer
Rothéneuf
Le Mont-
St-Michel
D5
Plouaret
Bégard
D787
D9
Binic
Le Val-André
St-Cast
St Malo
Avranches
Plouigneau
N12
Belle-Isle-
en-Terre
D787
N12
D6
Sables-
d'Or
Erquy
Matignon
St-
Jacut
St-
Lunaire
Dinard
D155
N176
D43
Pontaubault
D797
Ducey
Plouignean
D169
D9
D42
320
Guingamp
D791
Ploubalay
D2
D266
D795
D155
Pontorson
D976
D975
St-Brieuc
D786
Plancoët
Dol-de-Bretagne
D794
D12
St-James
QUE
D9
52
D167
Lamballe
D794

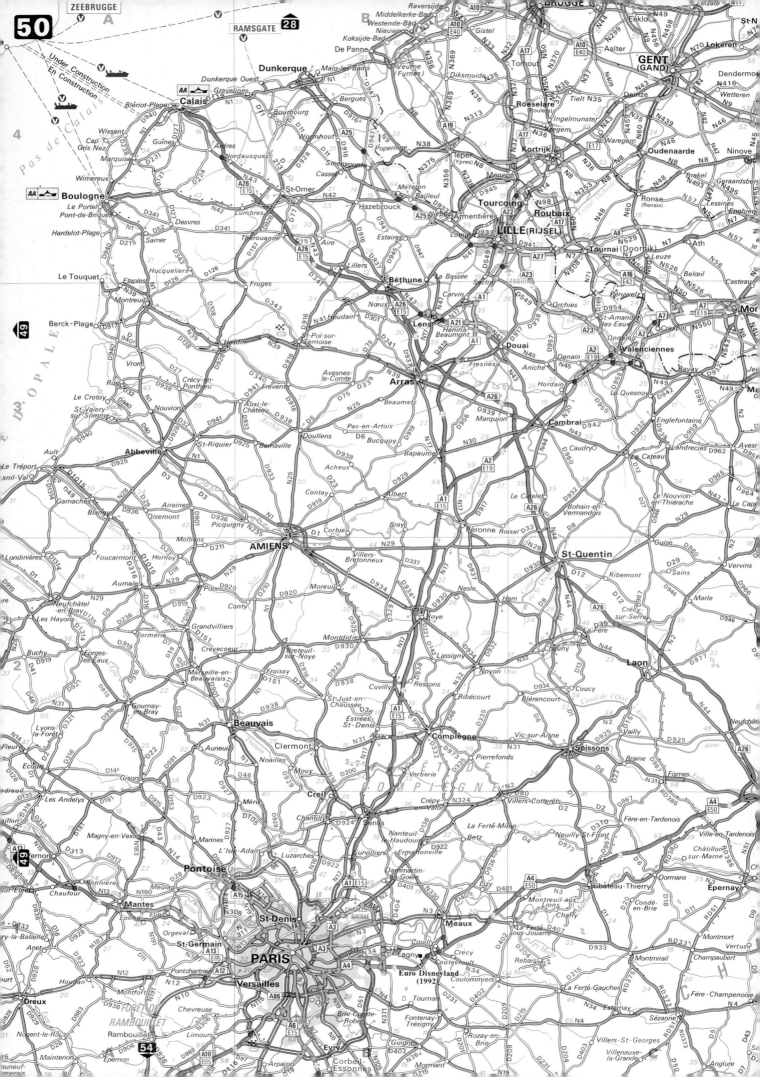

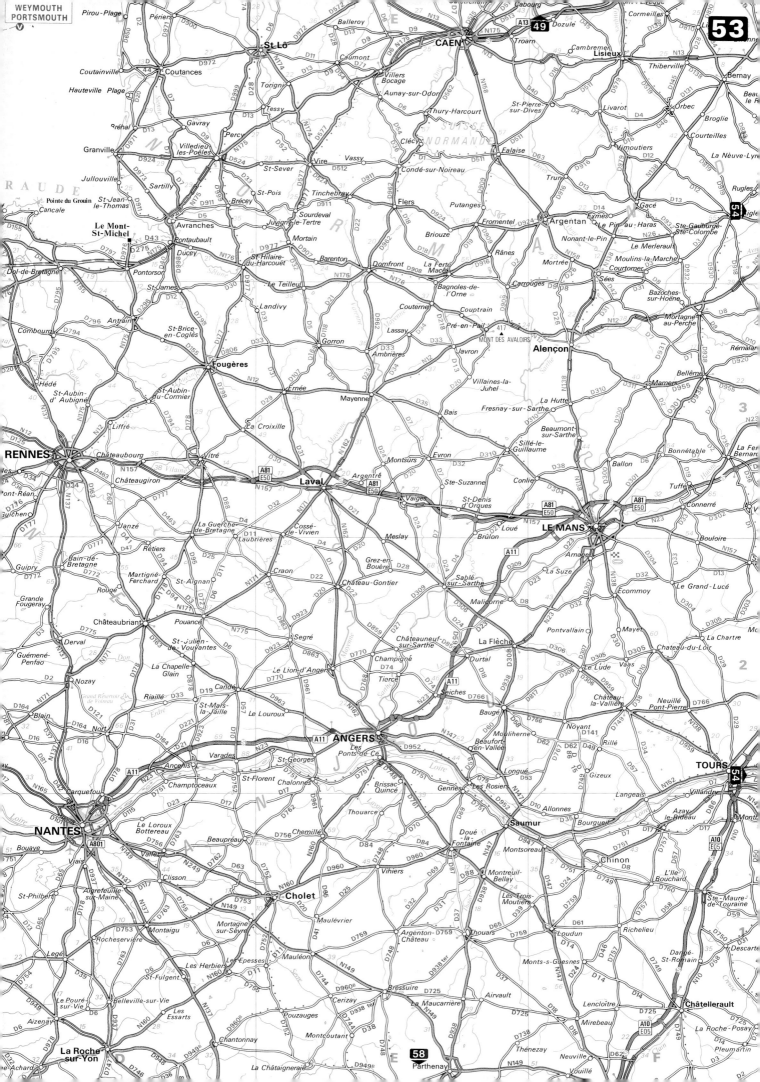

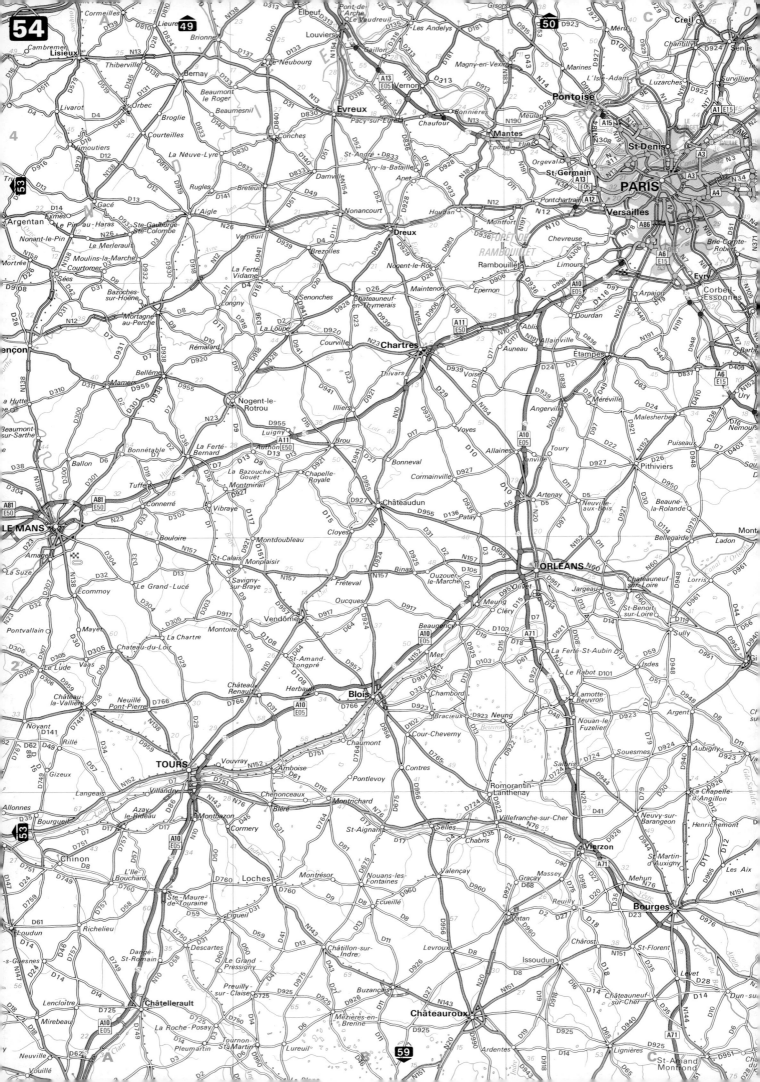

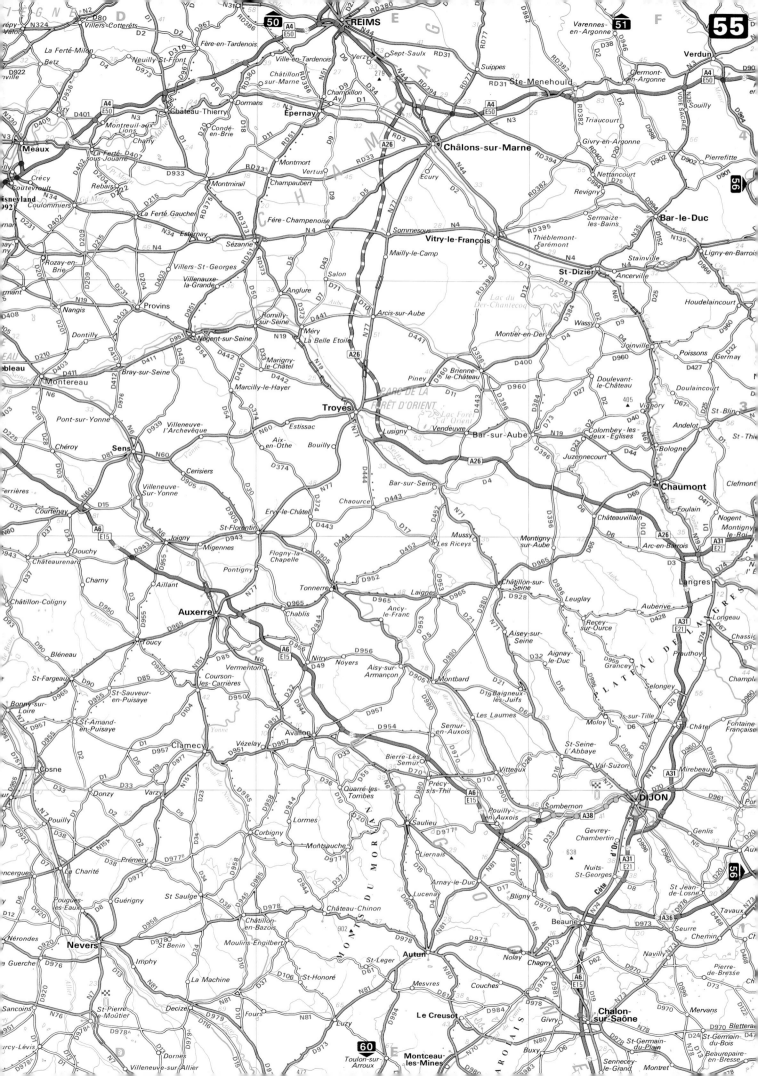

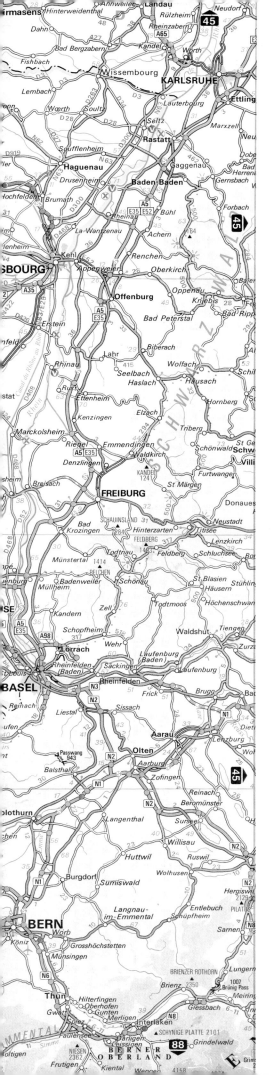

CORSE

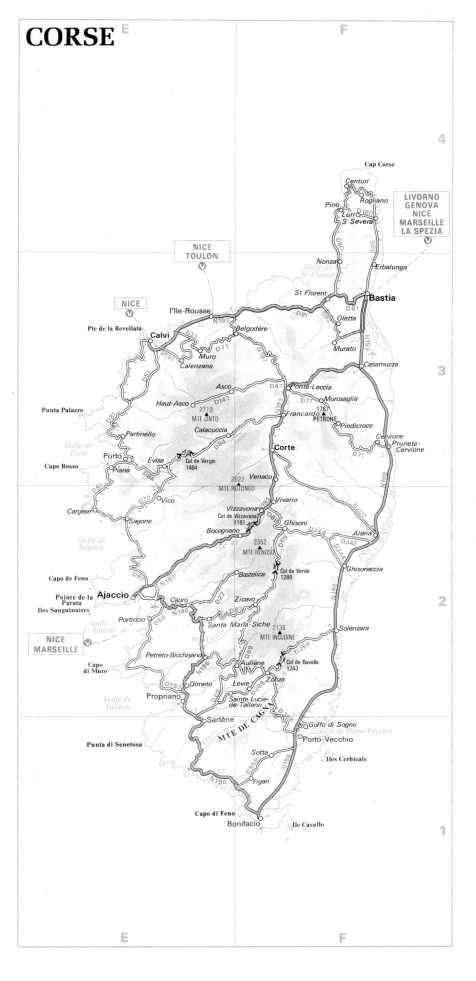

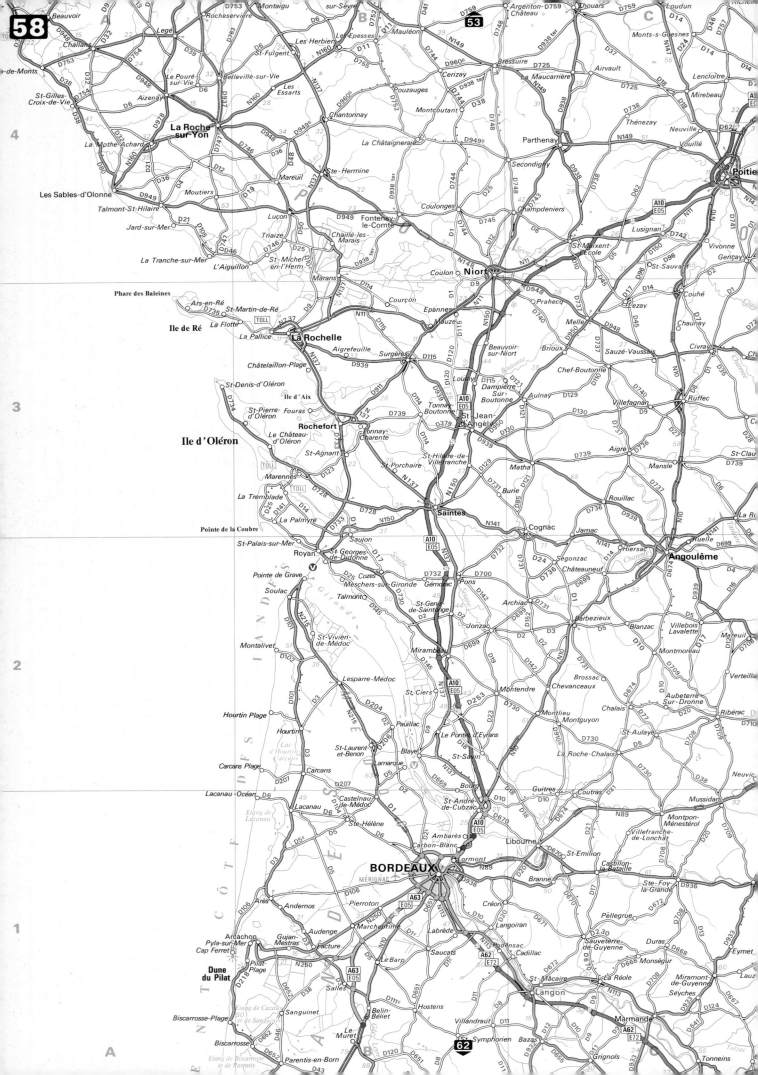

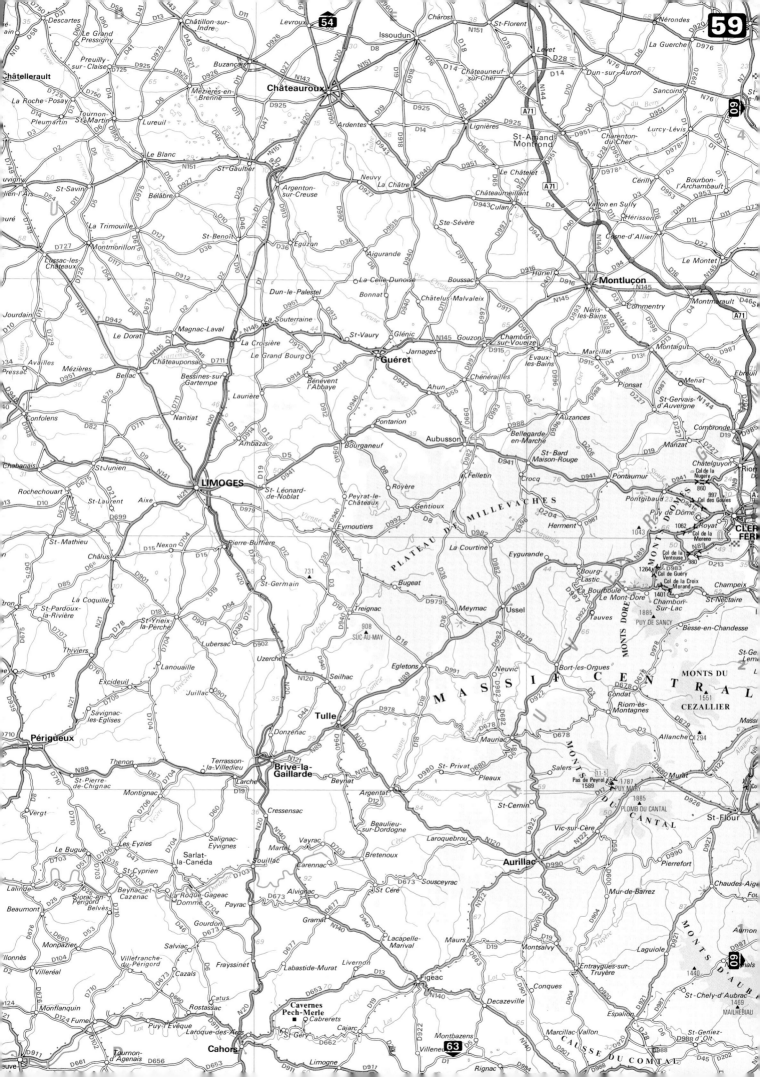

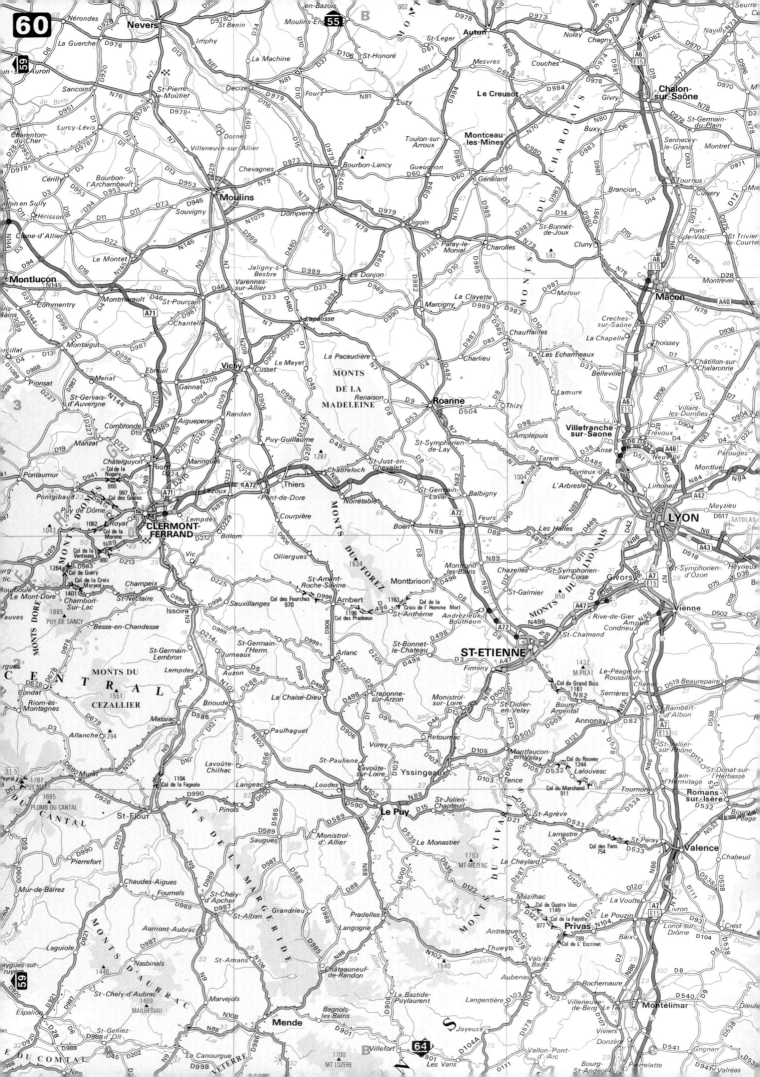

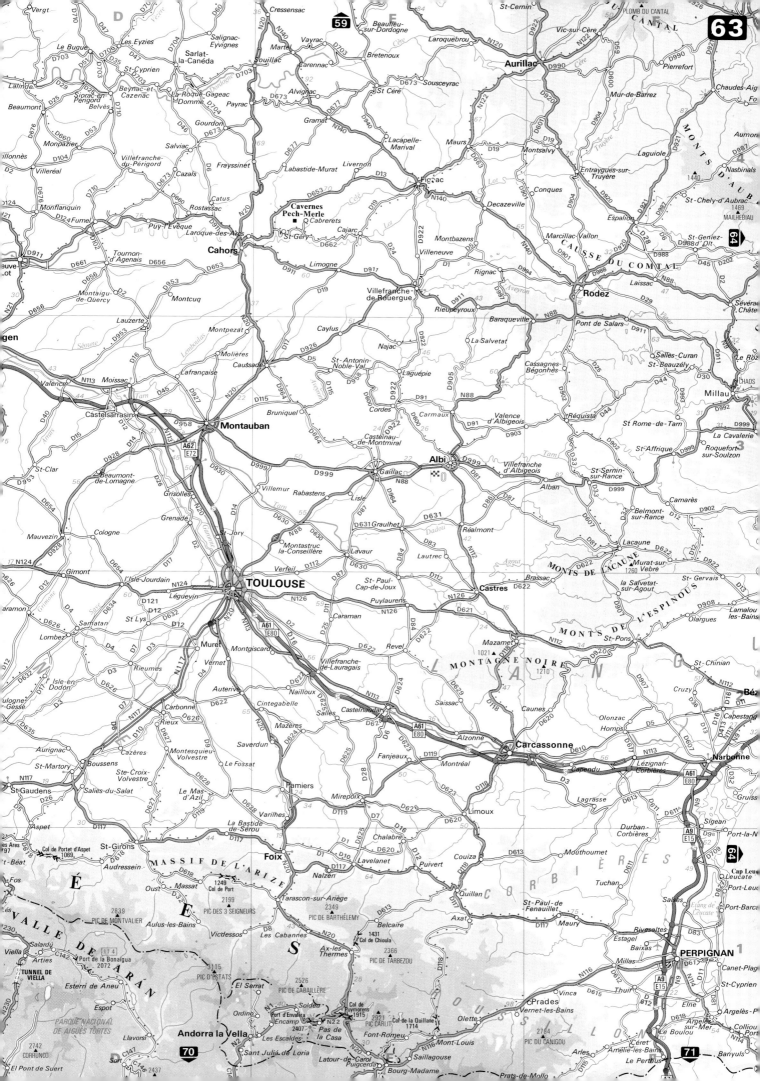

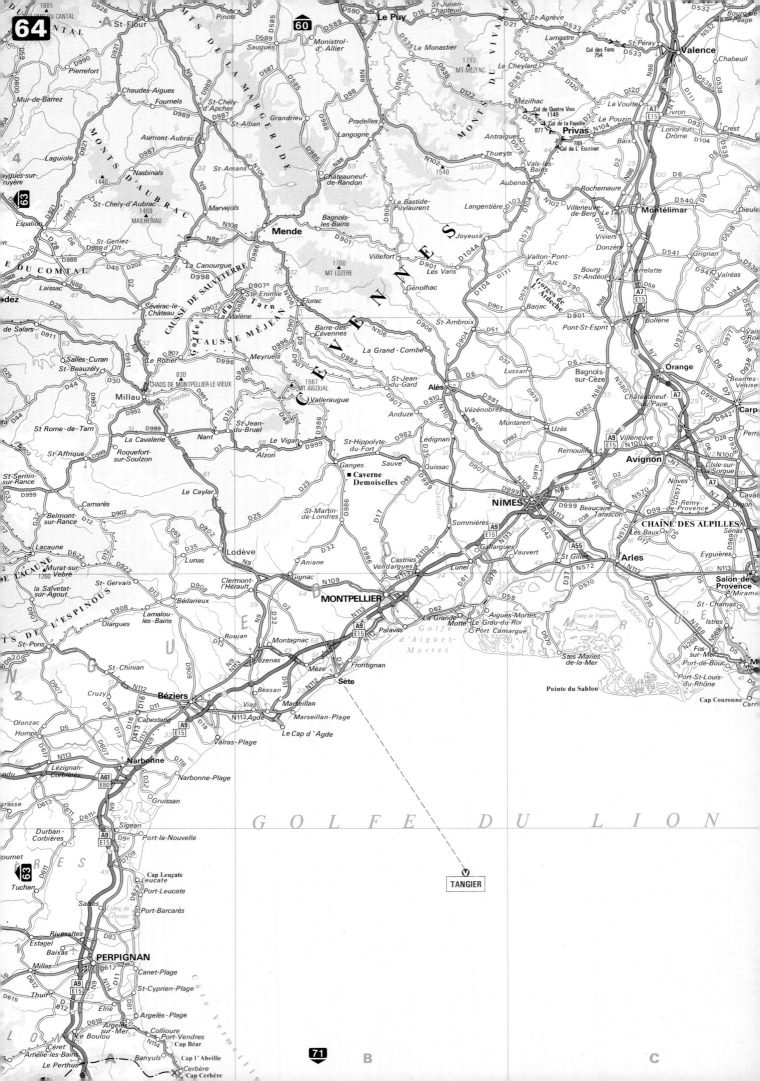

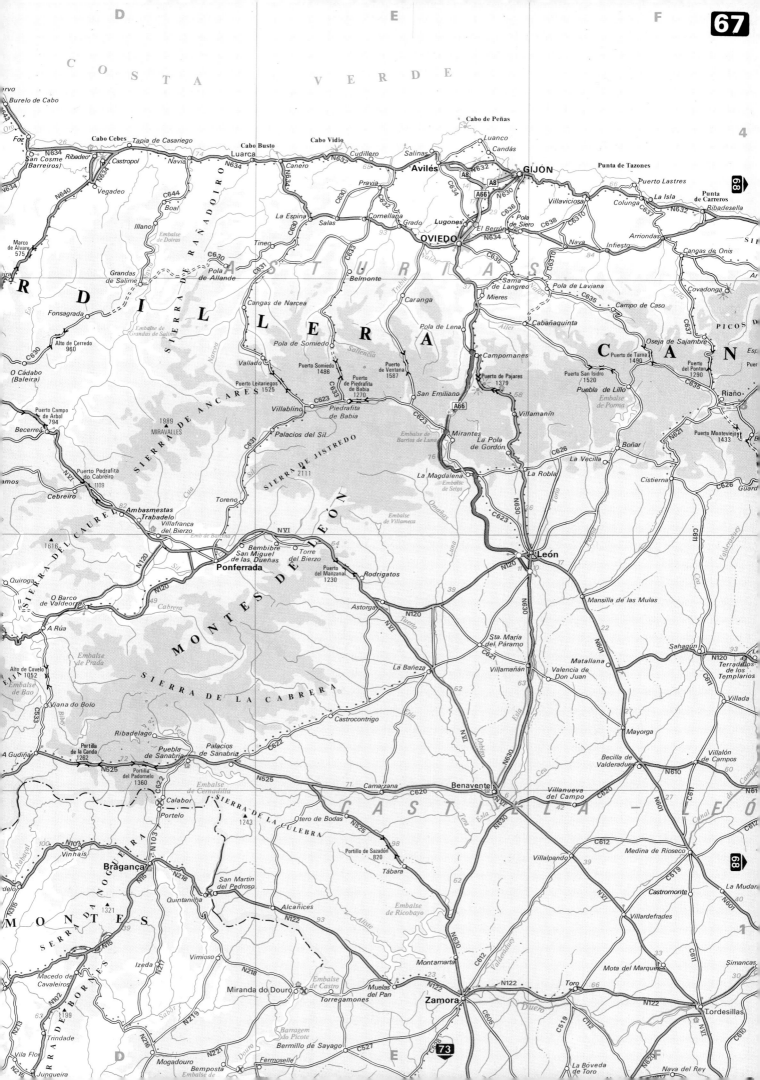

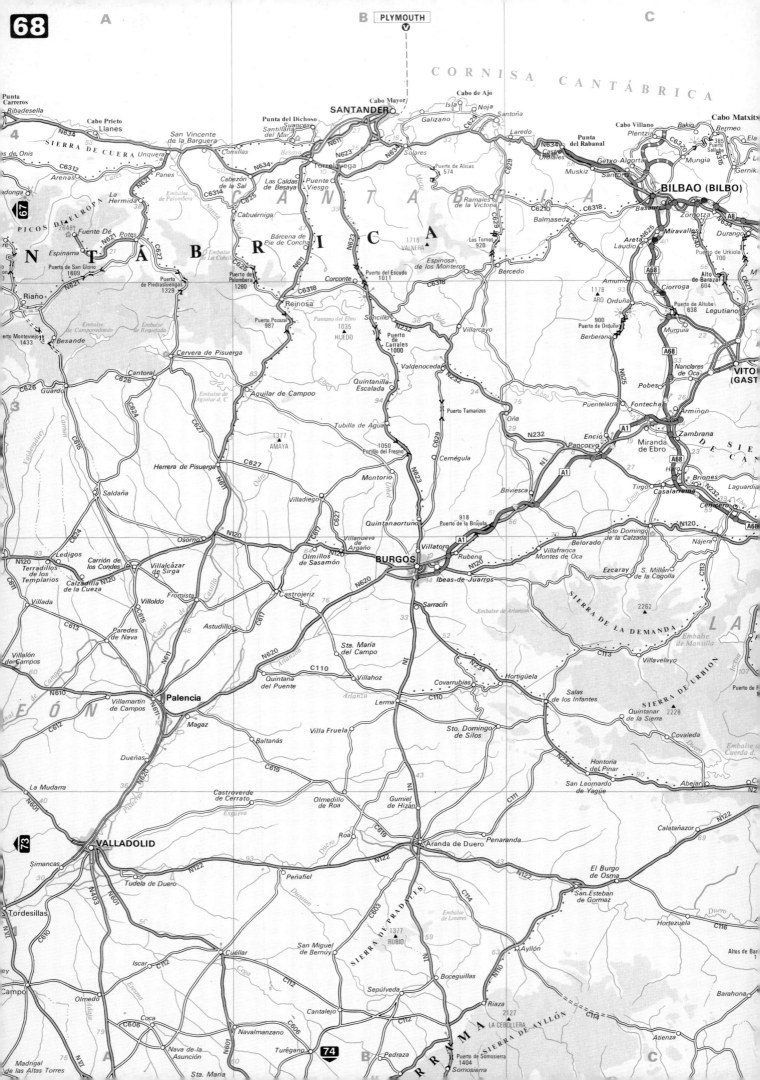

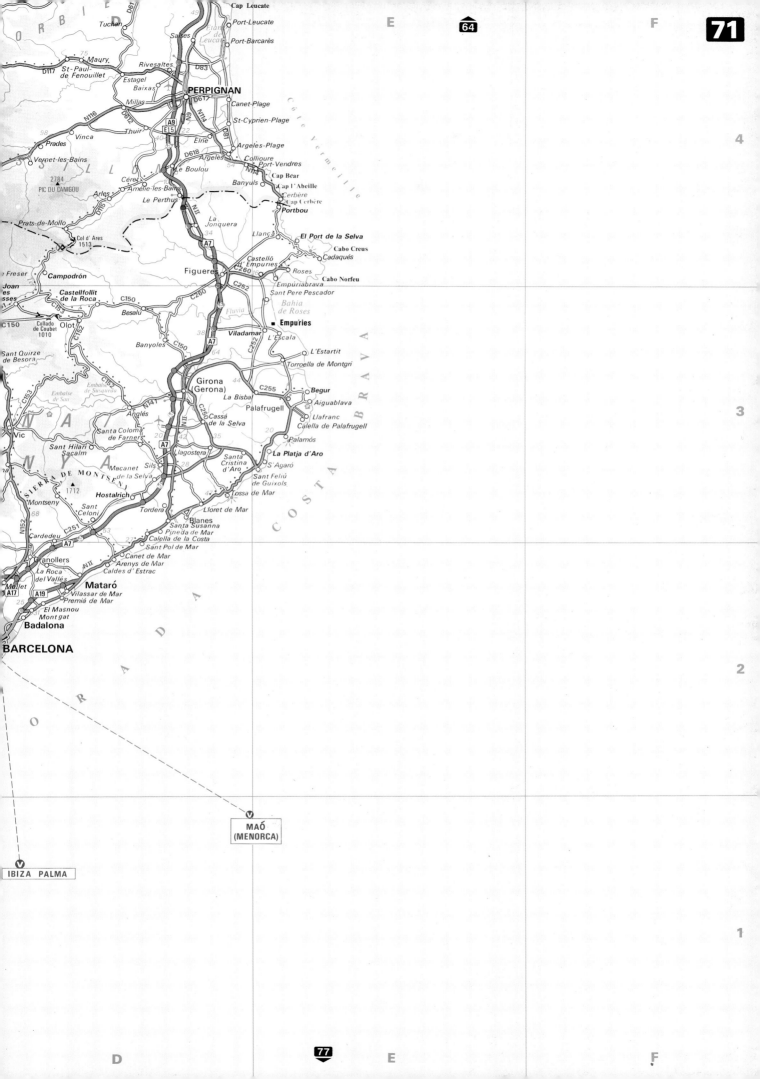

ORBIE
Tuchan
D61
Cap Leucate
Port-Leucate
Port-Barcarès
Maury
St-Paul-
de-Fenouillet
Rivesaltes
Salses
D83
Estagel
Baixas
Millas
D617
PERPIGNAN
Canet-Plage
N116
D612
Thuir
A9
E15
22
St-Cyprien-Plage
98
Prades
Vinca
40
N9
N114
Elne
Argeles-Plage
D618
Vernet-les-Bains
Céret
Argelès
Collioure
Port-Vendres
Le Boulou
54
Cap Béar
2784
PIC DU CANIGOU
Amélie-les-Bains
Arles
D115
Banyuls
Cap l'Abeille
Cerbère
Le Perthus
N II
Cap Cerbère
Prats-de-Mollo
La
Jonquera
Portbou
Col d'Ares
1513
34
Llançà
El Port de la Selva
e Freser
A7
Cabo Creus
Campodrón
Castelló
d'Empúries
Cadaqués
Joan
Castellfollit
de la Roca
C260
C252
16
Roses
Cabo Norfeu
es
asses
Figueres
Empúriabrava
Sant Pere Pescador
C150
C150
C260
Bahia
de Roses
Collado
de Coubet
1010
Besalú
Fluvià
Olot
C152
A7
Empúries
38
Viladamar
L'Escala
Banyoles
C150
C252
64
L'Estartit
Sant Quirze
de Besora
Torroella de Montgri
Embalse
de Susqueda
Girona
(Gerona)
44
C255
Begur
Embalse
de Sau
N141
La Bisbal
Aiguablava
Vic
Anglés
N II
C250
Cassà
de la Selva
Palafrugell
Llafranc
Calella de Palafrugell
Santa Coloma
de Farners
20
35
Palamós
Sant Hilari
Sacalm
A7
Llagostera
Santa
Cristina
d'Aro
La Platja d'Aro
Macanet
de la Selva
Sils
S'Agaró
Sant Feliú
de Guixols
SIERRA DE MONTSENY
28
1712
Tossa de Mar
Montseny
Hostalrich
47
Sant
Celoni
Tordera
Lloret de Mar
68
Blanes
Santa Susanna
M152
C251
53
Pineda de Mar
Cardedeu
A7
27
Calella de la Costa
Sant Pol de Mar
Granollers
N II
Canet de Mar
Arenys de Mar
La Roca
del Vallés
Caldes d'Estrac
Mellet
Mataró
A17
A19
Vilassar de Mar
Premiá de Mar
25
El Masnou
Montgat
Badalona

BARCELONA

COSTA BRAVA

Côte vermeille

ÑANYA

DORADA

V
MAÓ
(MENORCA)

V
IBIZA PALMA

E
2

3

4

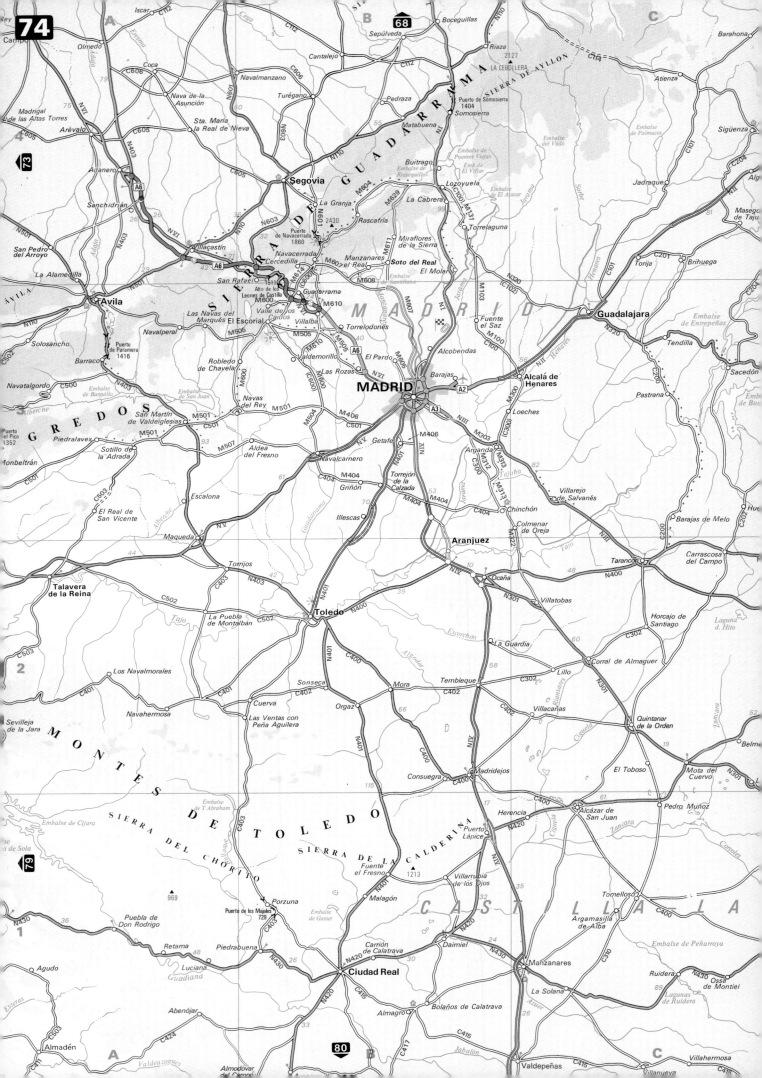

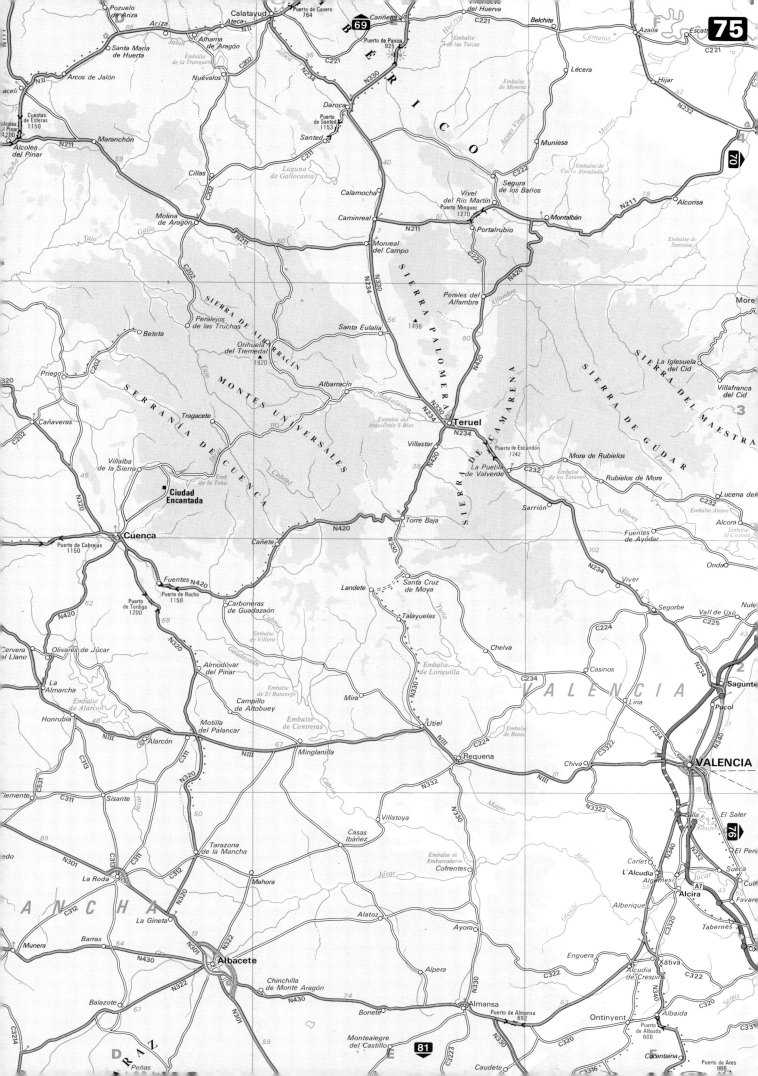

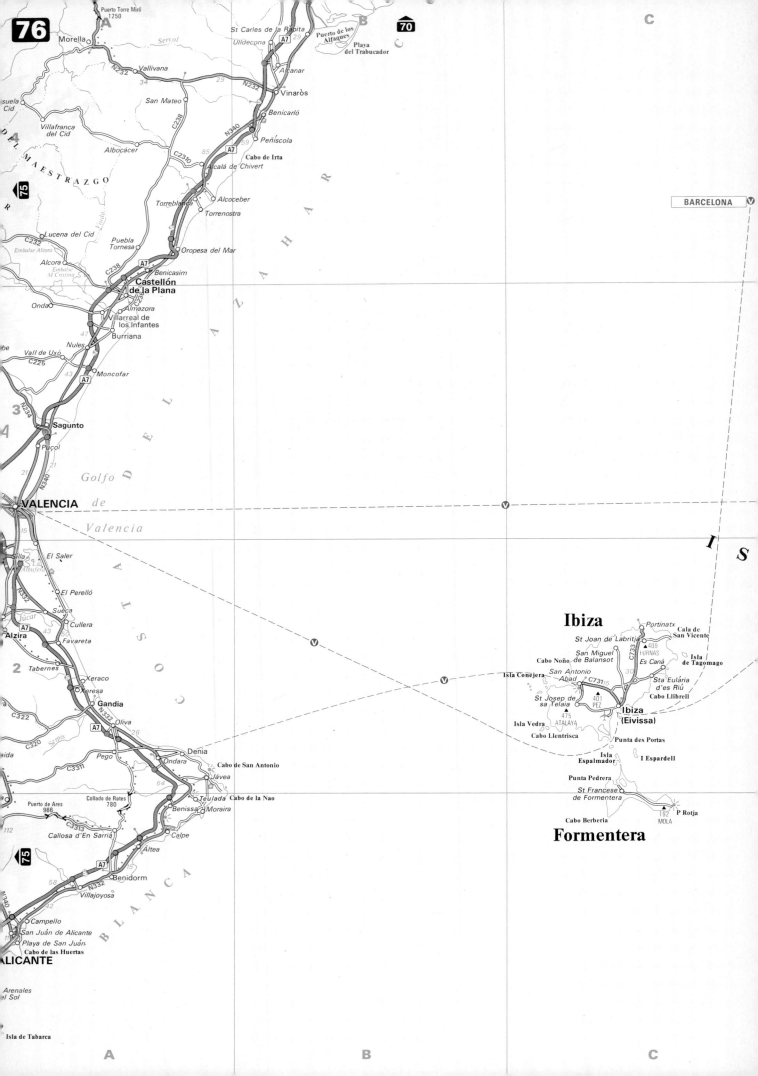

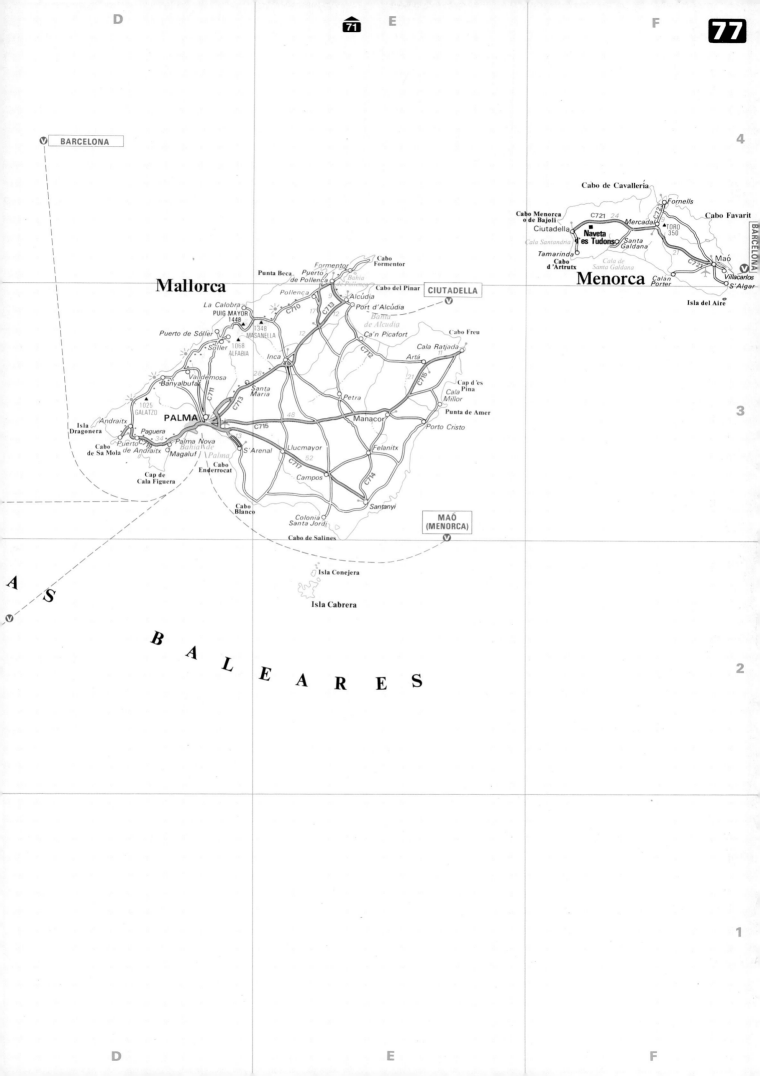

4

BARCELONA

Cabo de Cavallería

Cabo Menorca
o de Bajoli
Ciutadella

C721 24

Mercadal

C723 Fornells

Cabo Favarit

BARCELONA

**Naveta
d'es Tudons**

TORO
350

Cala Santandria
Tamarinda

Santa
Galdana

Maó

**Cabo
d'Artrutx**

Cala de
Santa Galdana

C721

Villacarlos

Menorca

Calan
Porter

S'Algar

Isla del Aire

Cabo
Formentor

Formentor

Punta Beca

Puerto
de Pollença

Bahía
de Pollença

Cabo del Pinar

CIUTADELLA

Mallorca

Pollença

C710

17

C713

9

Alcúdia

Port d'Alcúdia

La Calobra

PUIG MAYOR
1448

1348
MASANELLA

12

Bahía
de Alcudia

Ca'n Picafort

Cabo Freu

Puerto de Sóller

Sóller

1068
ALFABIA

Inca

C712

Cala Ratjada

Artá

C715

71

Valldemosa

Banyalbufar

C711

Santa
María

28

Petra

Cap d'es
Pina
Cala
Millor

1025
GALATZO

PALMA

C713

C715

48

Manacor

21

Punta de Amer

Isla
Dragonera

Andraitx

Paguera

34

Palma Nova

Porto Cristo

Cabo
de Sa Mola

Puerto
de Andraitx

C719

Magaluf

Bahía de
Palma

S'Arenal

Llucmayor

Felanitx

Cabo
Enderrocat

C715

C717

52

Campos

C714

Cap de
Cala Figuera

Cabo
Blanco

Santanyí

MAÓ
(MENORCA)

Colonia
Santa Jordi

Cabo de Salines

3

Isla Conejera

2

Isla Cabrera

A

S

B **A** **L** **E** **A** **R** **E** **S**

1

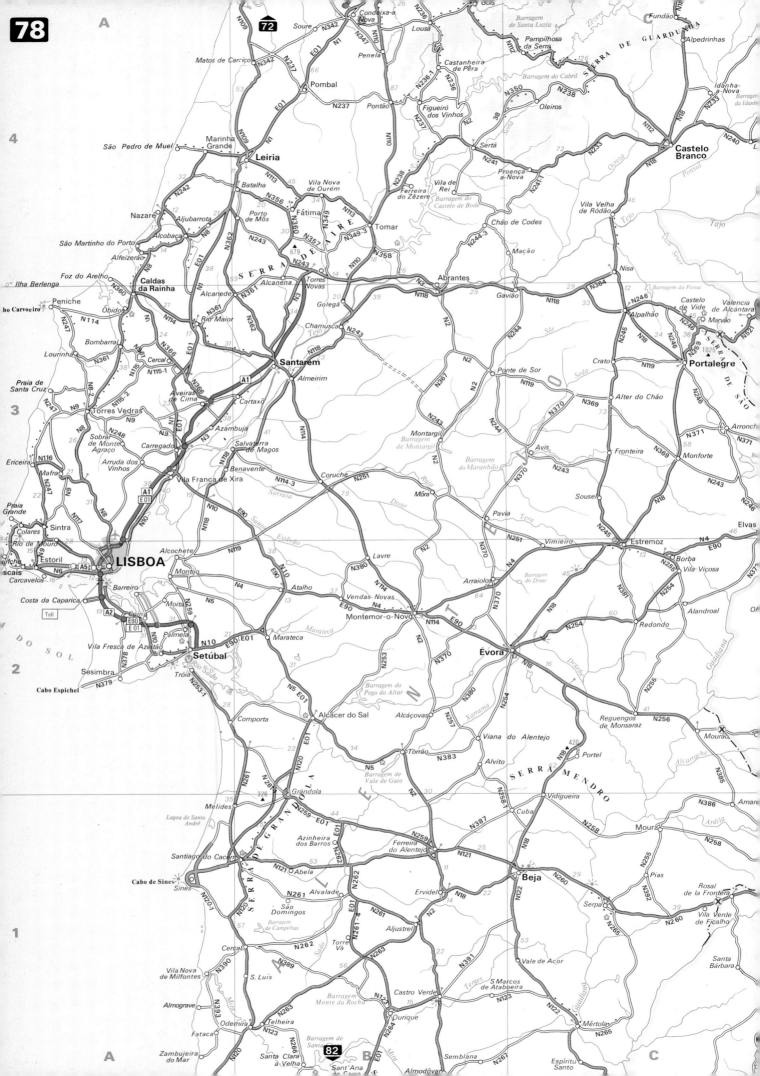

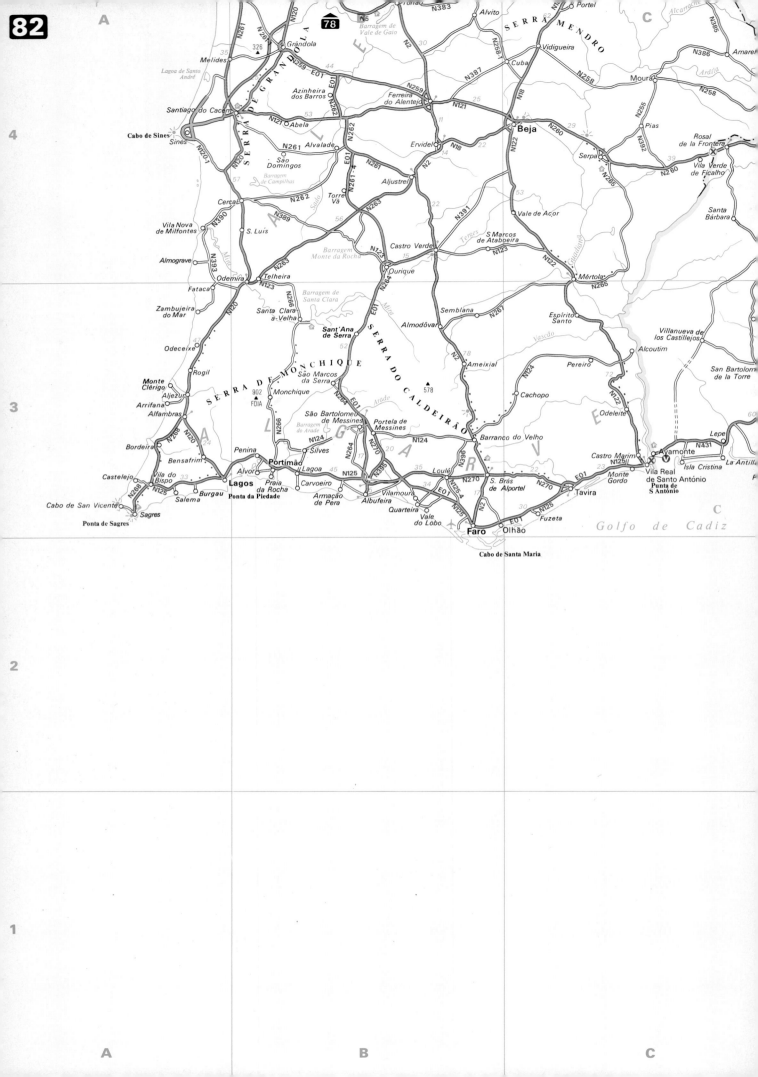

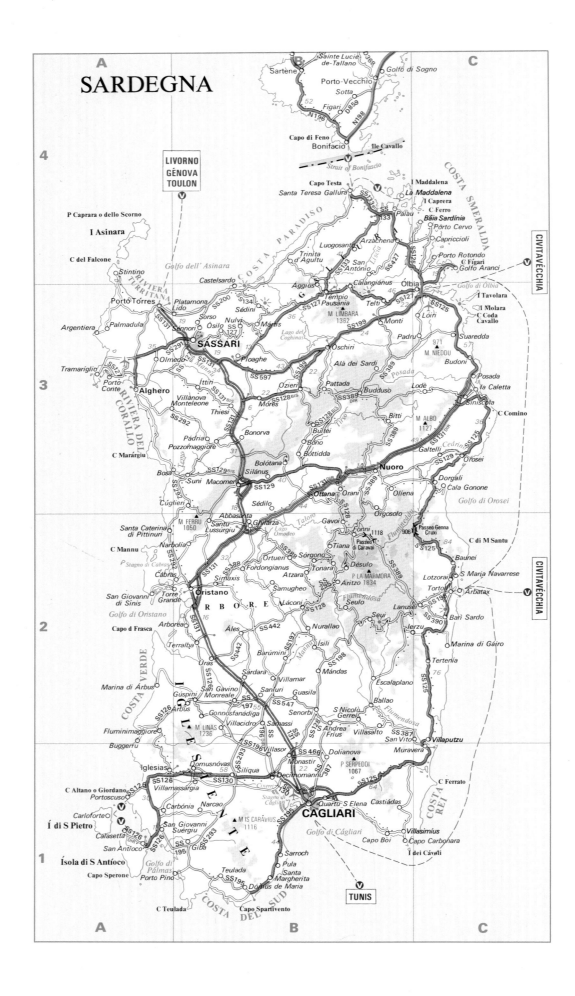

96

SARDEGNA

Castiglioncello
Rosignano-Marittimo
Volterra
Solvay
SS1
SS68
Saline di Volterra
SS68
Siena
Monte San
Savino
Castiglion Fiorentino
Cécina
Cécina
SS68
41
SS73
21
42
37
E35
Foiano di
Chiana
Cortona

Pomarance
SS73
SS2
SS326
Sinalunga
A1
Lago
Magi
Trasime

C O L L I N E   M E T A L L I F E R E
Larderello
28
SS326
Torrita di Siena
20
41

Marina di Castagneto-Donorático
T O S C A N A
1060
SS441
Monticiano
Buonconvento
Ombrone
Pienza
43
SS146
Montepulciano
SS454
Castiglione del
Lago

San Vincenzo
Massa Maríttima
Montalcino
San Quírico
d'Órcia
Chianciano Terme
Chiusi
SS599

SS439
Roccastrada
73
SS146
4

Populónia
SS323
Órcia
Citta di Pieve

Piombino
Follónica
SS1
Córnia
SS73
SS223
1738
MT AMIATA
Arcidosso
58
83
86

Capo Vita
I Palmaiola
Golfo di
Follónica
33
65
Ficulle

Portoferráio
Cavo
SS1
SS322
E80
Röccalbegna
SS321
SS2
SS71

Marciana Marina
Ísola d'Elba
Punta Ala
Grosseto
SS74
26

Marina di Campo
Lacona
Porto Azzurro
Castiglione della Pescáia
SS322
Acquapendente

Punta di Fetováia
Capolíveri
Marina di Grosseto
SS322
San Lorenzo Nuovo
Orvieto

Punta dei Ripalti
SS323
Scansano
Albegna
Paglia
Bolsena

Punta d Marchese
Magliano in
Toscána
SS1
Manciano
Pitigliano
Lago
di Bolsena
SS71
45

Punte Libéccio
Isola Pianosa
33
SS74
Valentano
SS74
Montefiasco

Punta Brigantini
SS323
Farnese
Marta

Í di Montecristo
0
Canino
Tuscánia
Viterbo

Orbetello
Fiora
Arrone
3

Porto San Stéfano
SS40
Ansedónia
65
SS312
Maro
Vetralla
SS2

Punta di Fenáio
Monte
Argentário
E80
SS1
Montalto di Castro
SS1bis
SS493

Gíglio Porto
Í del Gíglio
Port' Ércole
Tarquínia
3
Veiano

Punta d Capel Rosso
Tolfa
Lago d
Bracciar

Í di Giannutri
Civitavécchia
A12

Santa Marinella
E80
Cervete

Capo
Linaro
S Sevéra
87

Ladíspoli

ÓLBIA

Fregene

LEONARDO VI
Fium

CAGLIARI
Lido
Lido

1

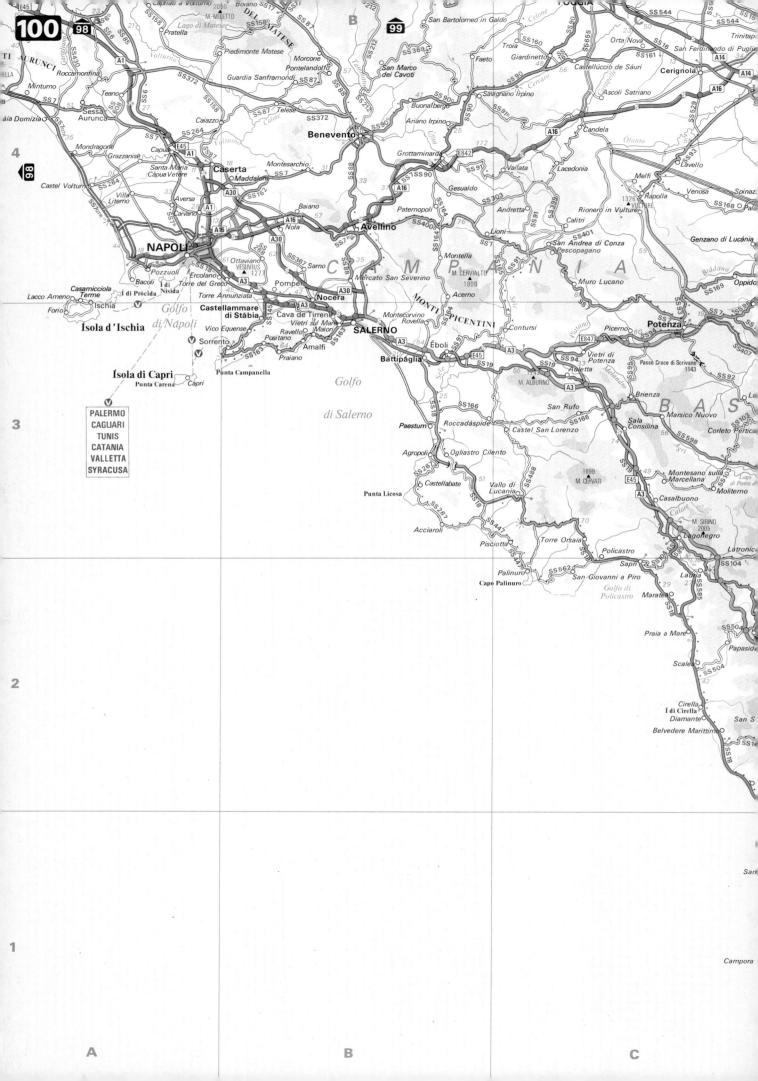

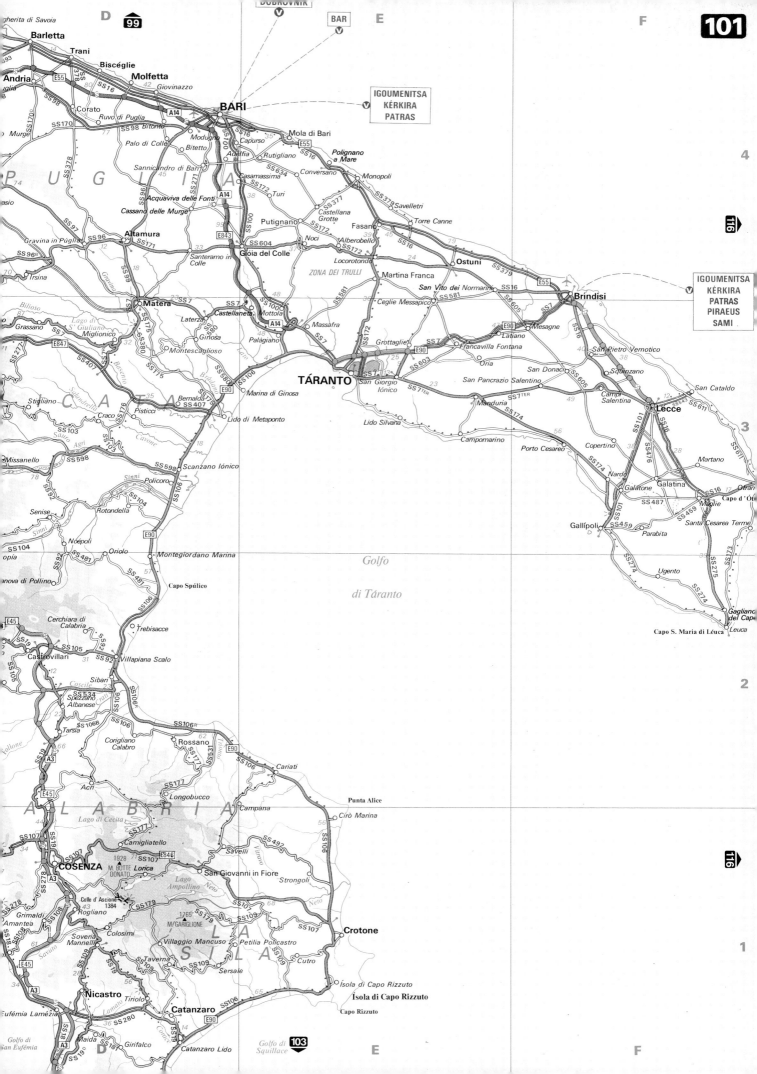

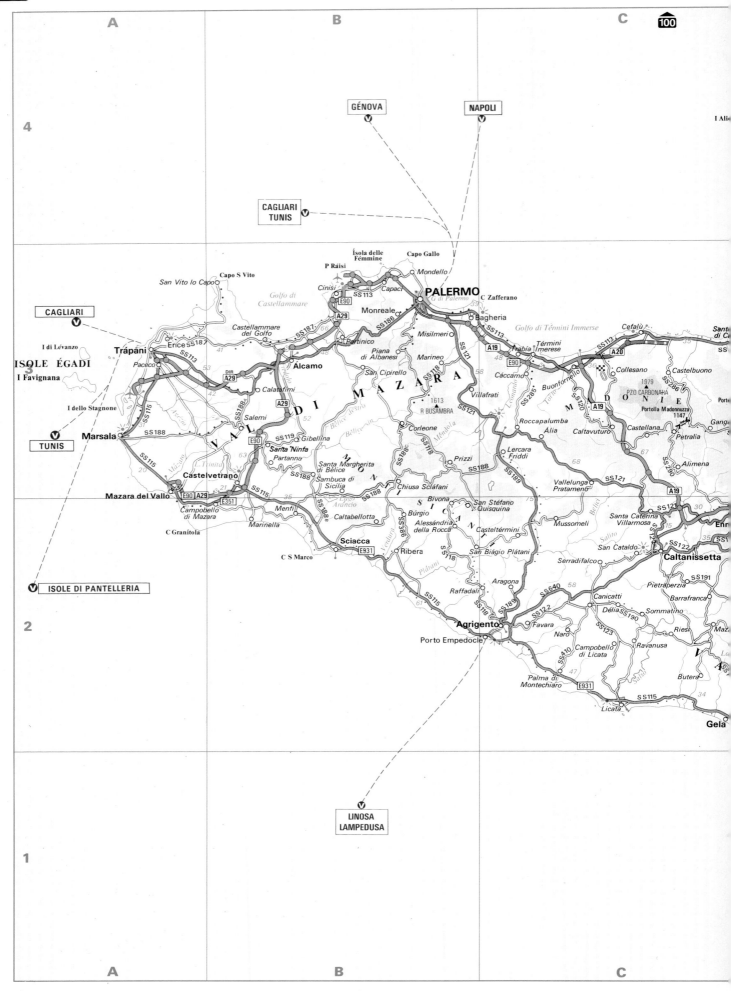

100

4

GÉNOVA

NAPOLI

I Alic

CAGLIARI
TUNIS

Ísola delle
Fémmine · Capo Gallo

P Ráisi · Mondello

Capo S Vito

San Vito lo Capo

Cínisi · Capaci

Golfo di
Castellammare

SS 113 · **PALERMO** · C Zafferano

CAGLIARI

Monreale · G di Palermo

Bagheria

Golfo di Términi Immerse · Cefalù · Sant
di Ce

I di Lévanzo

Trápani · Erice · SS 187

Castellammare
del Golfo

SS 187 · 66

SS 113

Misilmeri · SS 113 · A20

SS 286

Términi
Imerese · SS 113

ISOLE ÉGADI

I Favignana

Paceco

SS 113 · 53

41

Partinico

Piana
di Albanesi

SS 186

Marineo

A19

Trabia
Imerese · 48 · E90

Buonfornello · MADONIE

Collesano · Castelbuono

I dello Stagnone

DIR
A29

Alcamo

San Cipirello

SS 121 · 58

Cáccamo

SS 285 · Tortomanna · 1979
PZO CARBONARA

SS 121 · 42

Calatafimi

V A L DI M A Z A R A

1613
R BUSAMBRA

Villafrati

Roccapalumba
Ália

Portella Madonnuzza
1147

Gang

Petralia

TUNIS · Marsala

SS 188

Salemi

SS 119 · Gibellina · Bélice sin

Corleone

SS 121

Caltavuturo

Castellana

Alimena

SS 115

Santa Ninfa

SS 188 · Partanna

Santa Margherita
di Bélice

Prizzi

Lercara
Friddi

68

Vallelunga
Pratameno

SS 121

SS 290

A19

Castelvetrano

E90

63

Sambuca di
Sicília

Chiusa Scláfani

San Stéfano
Quisquina

SS 188

SS 122 · 30

Mazara del Vallo

E90 A29

21

SS 115 · 36

Campobello
di Mazara

Menfi

Caltabellotta

Búrgio

Alessándria
della Rócca

Bivona

Casteltérmini

Mussomeli

Santa Caterina
Villarmosa · 15 · Enn

San Cataldo · SS 122 · SS1

Enn

C Granítola

Marinella

SS 386

SS 118 · Ribera

San Biágio Plátani

Serradifalco

Caltanissetta

C S Marco

Sciacca

E931

Plátani

Aragona

Raffadali

SS 115 · 61

SS 118

SS 189

SS 640 · 58

SS 122 · Canicattì

SS 191 · Pietraperzia

Barrafranca

Délia · SS 190 · Sommatino

Riesi · Maz

ISOLE DI PANTELLERIA

2

Agrigento

Porto Empedocle

Favara

Naro

SS 123 · Ravanusa

SS 410 · Campobello
di Licata

Palma di
Montechiaro · 47

E931

Butera

Licata

SS 115 · 34

Gela

LINOSA
LAMPEDUSA

1

A · B · C

SICILIA

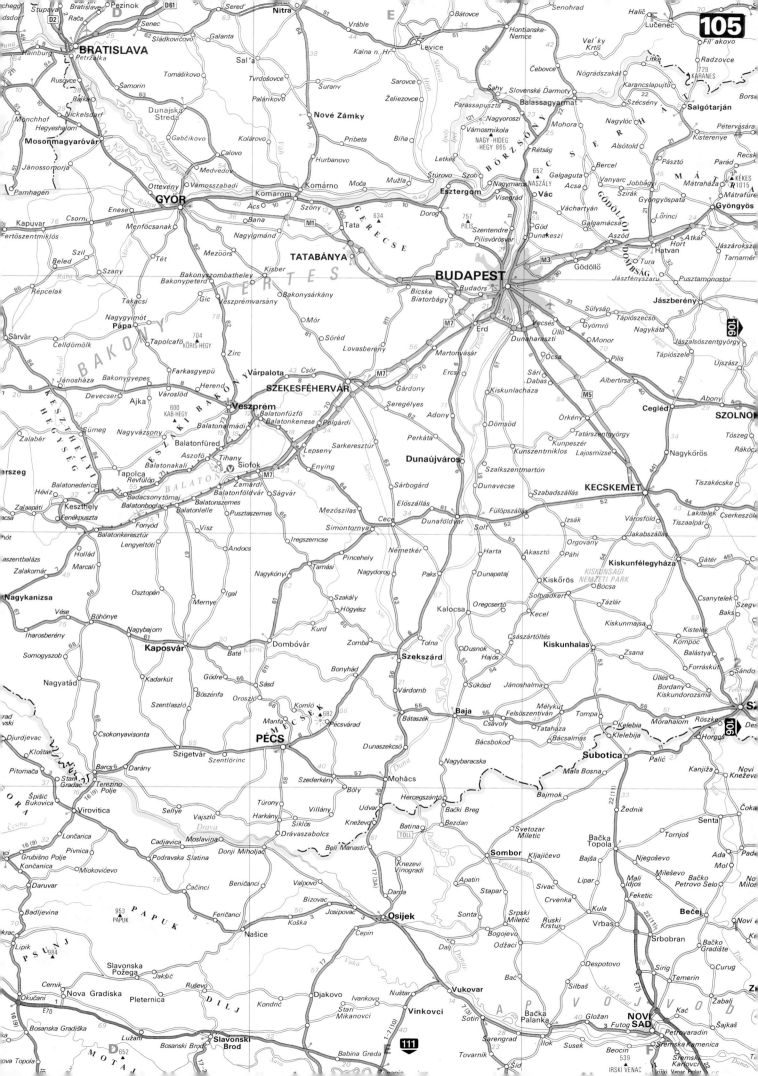

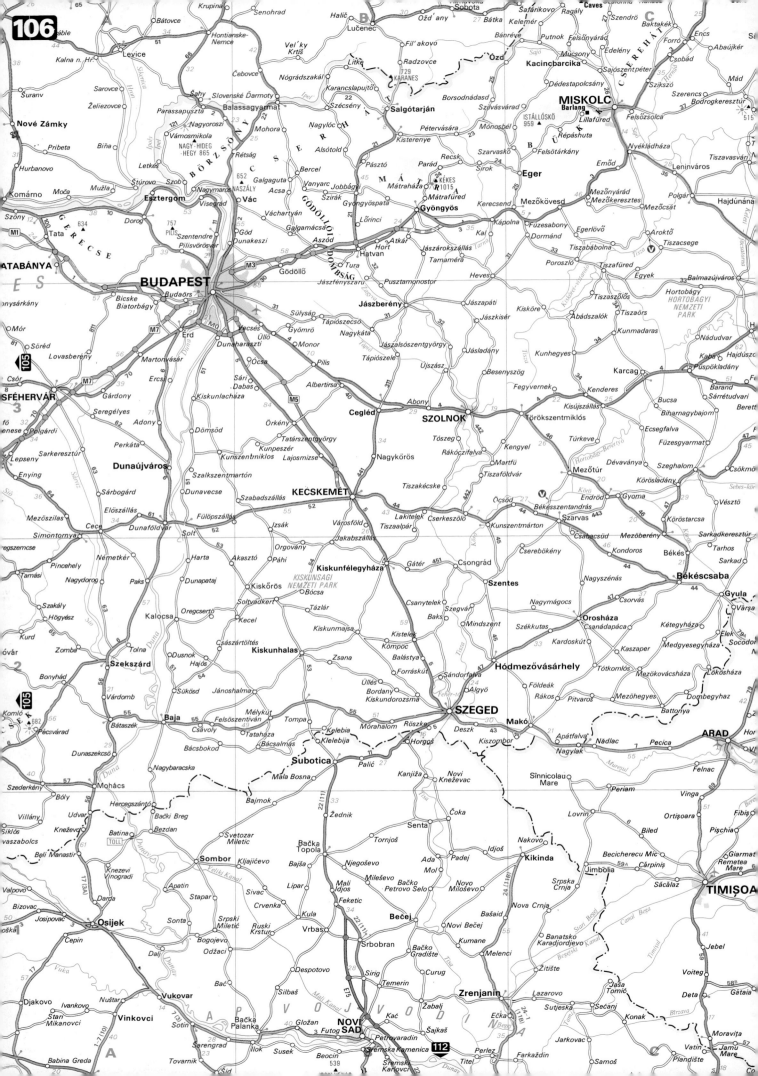

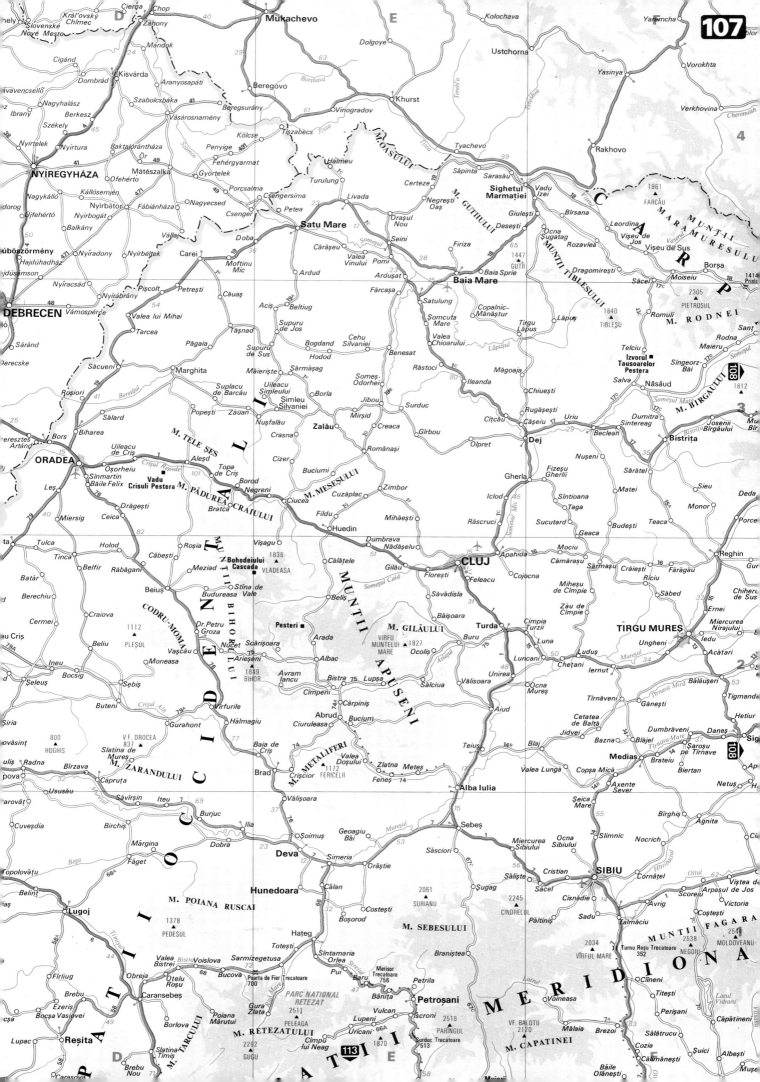

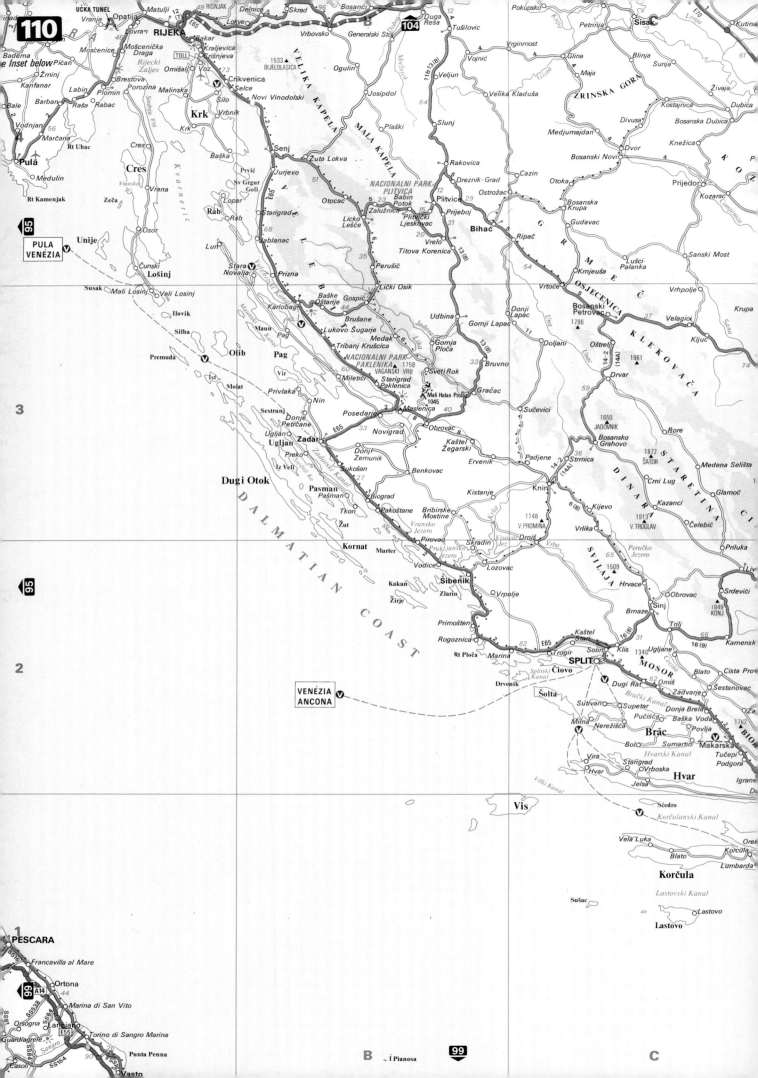

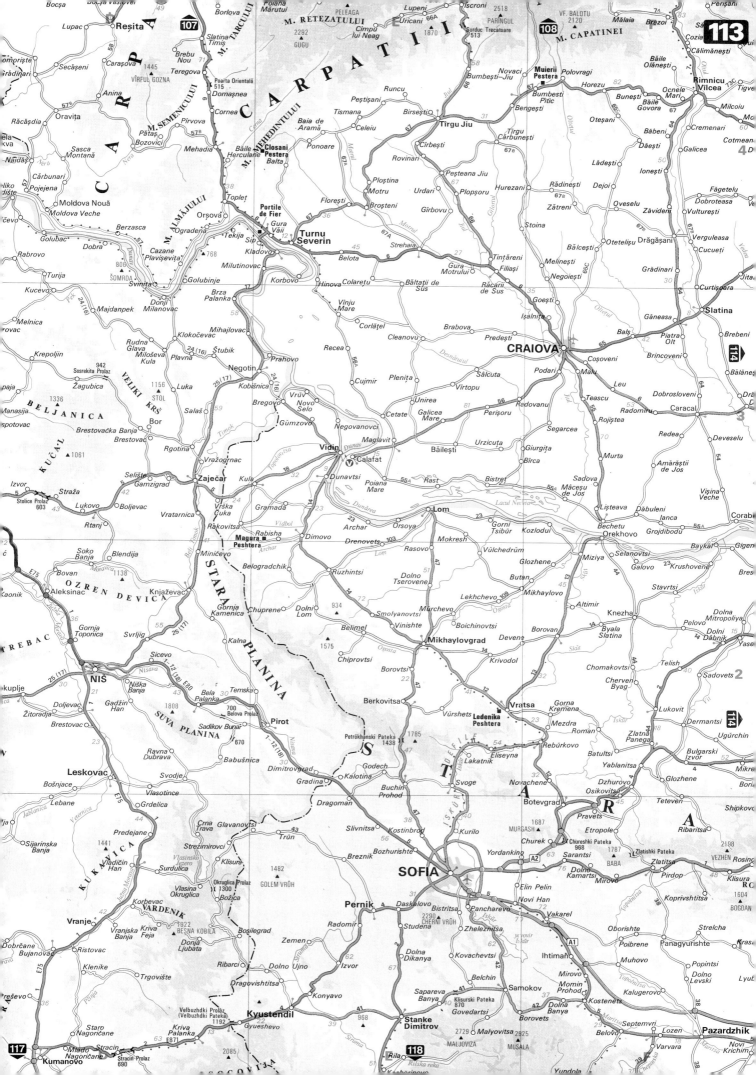

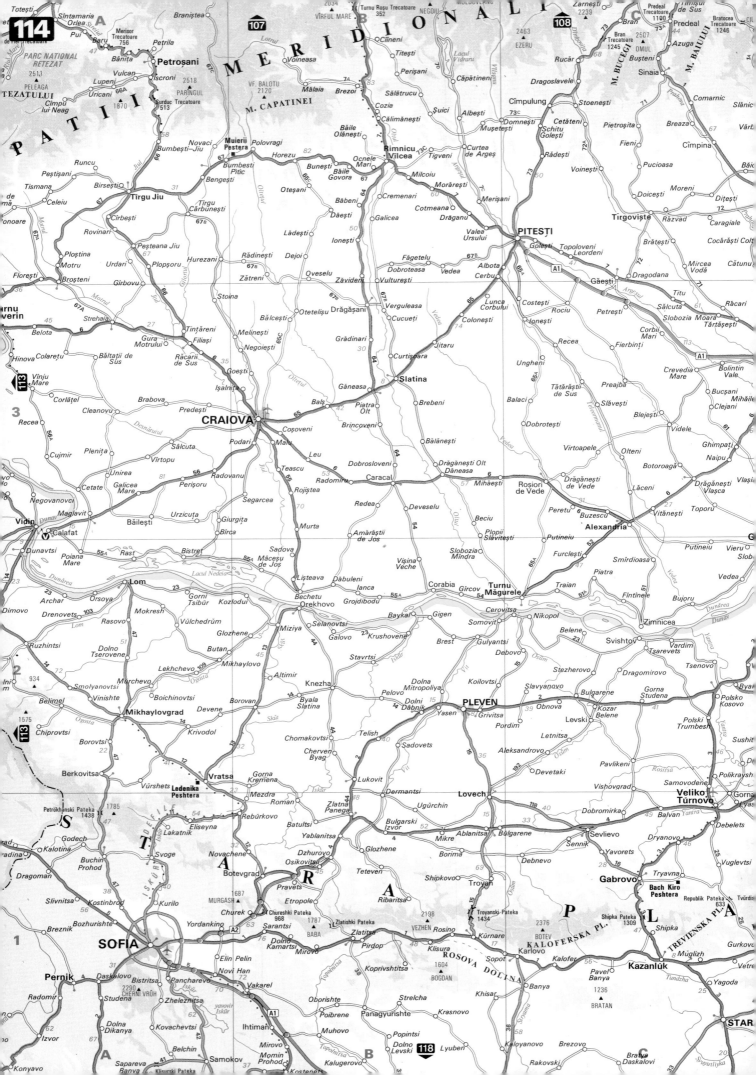

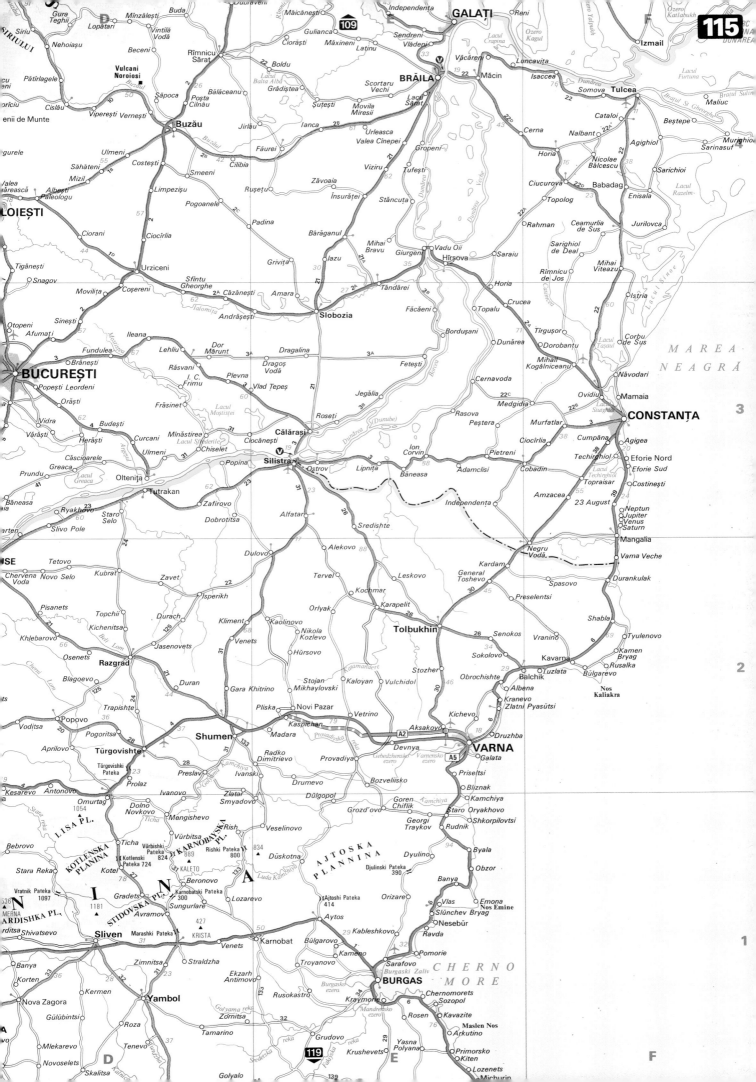

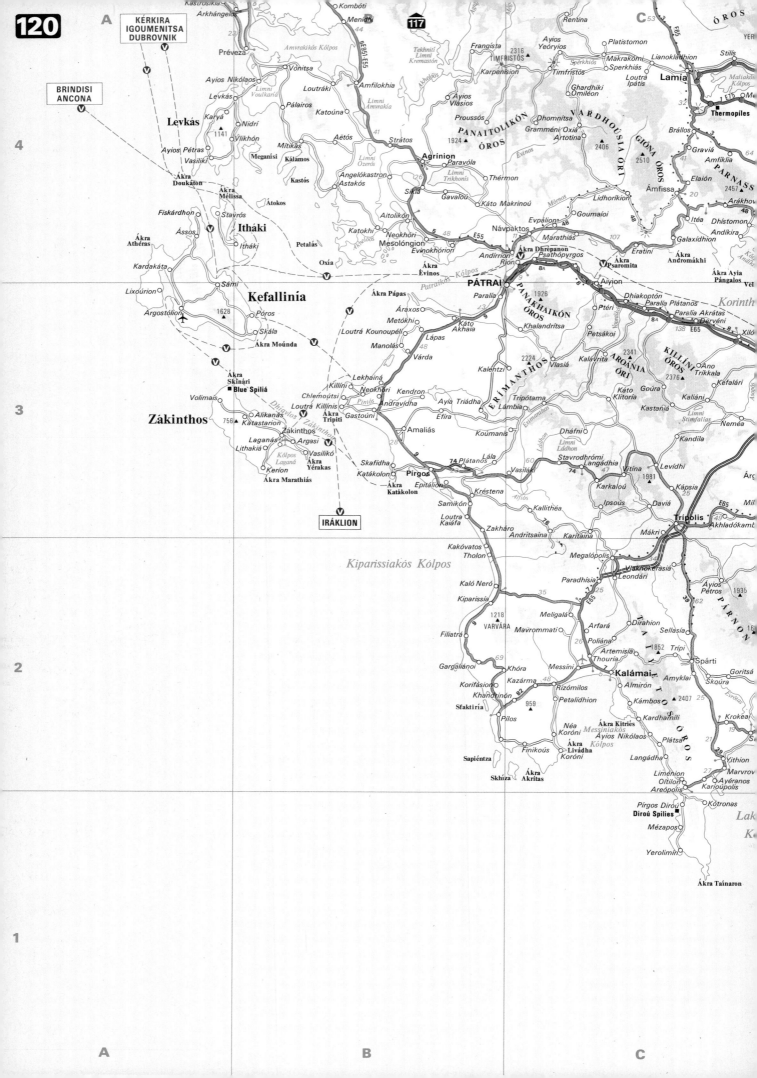

Skópelos

Skíros

Ákra
Kártsino

Skíros

Skiropoúla

Valaxa   Linariá

Ákra Lithári

Sarakinón

D

E

F

Psará

Andípsara   Psará

4

D

Agnondas

ΒΟΡΕΙΟΣ   ΣΠΟΡΑΔΕΣ

Glifa
Artemision
Agriovótanon
Ayiókambos   Istiaía   Vasiliká
Oreoí
Loutrá
Aidhipsoú   Ayia Ánna
na Voúrla   Strofiliá
Ákra   Arkítsa   Mandoúdhion
Arkitsa   Limni   Prokópion   Ákra
Sarakíniken
Skála
Atalánti   Malesina
Lárimna   Psakhná
E75   Martínon
57   Kástron
Akraífnion
airónia   Orkhomenós   Néa Artáki   Stení
Ákra
Gáidharos   **Khalkís**
3   Aliáras   Vasilikón

Évvoia

DHÍRFIS ÓROS

1743

Ákra
Kímis
Kími
Paralía
Kímis
Okhthoniá
Avlonárion

Ákra Kafirévs

**KHÍOS
LÉSVOS**

Alíartos   Vathí   Alivérion   Lépoura
Váyia   Limni   Erétria   Amárinthos   Kriezá
Thespiaí   Illiki   151   Káravos   Zárakes
Thísvi   Lévktra   **Thívai**   18   Skála   Kálamos   Almiropótamos
E962   Oropoú
Plataiaí   Erithraí   40   Avlón   Néa
Aigosthena   49   Kapandrítion   Stíra   Stíra
Villía   Oinói   Ag. Marina
PÁRNIS   Marathón
Kato   **ÓROS**   1413
Alepokhórí   E75   Ekáli   Néa Mákri
Mándra   Akharnaí   Kifisiá   Marmári
Perakhóra   1351   30   Rafína
YERÁNIA ÓROS   Mégara   **ATHÍNAI**   Stavrós   Petalioí
Dióriga   Loutráki   E94   Pallíni   Loútsa
rinthou   Ayioi Theodhoroi   **PIRAIÉVS**   Spáta   Pórto Ráfti
Ísthmia   Salamís   Glifádha   Paianía   Markópoulon
Loutrón Elénis   Voúla   Koropí   Keratéa
Sofikón   Várkiza   Thorikón
ÓNIA   **Aíyina**   Vouliagméni   Lagonísi
ÓRI   Lagonísi   Anávissos
1139   Ayía   Legrena   Soúnion
Angístrion   Marína   Patróklou   Ákra
Néa Epídhavros   Pérdhika   Soúnion
Ligoúrion   Palaiá
Epídhavros   Fanári   Méthana
Trakheiá   Kallóni
Platia   **Póros**
Paralía   1113   Póros
Irión   Dhídhimoi   Galatás
Ermióni   Ákra Spathí
Kranídhion   Thermísia
Portokhéli   Idhra
Ákra Kórax   Dhokós   **Ídhra**
Kósta   Spétsai
Spétsai
Ákra Savátaki
Leonídhion

1398   **ÓKHI**
Káristos

Ákra
Kambanós

Ándros

Gávrion   Batsí
994
Apoíkia
Palaiópolis   Andros
Ormos
Kórthion

Tínos
Pánormos   Ákra Livádha
Istérnia   Falatádos
650
Kiónia
Tínos   **Míkonos**

Kéa
Vourkári
Korisía
(Livádhi)   Kéa
Ákra
Tamélos

Yioúra

Síros
Galissás   Ermoúpolis
Posidhonía   Vári   Ríniá
Dhílos
Dílos

Míkonos
Míkonos

**IKARIA SÁMOS
PÁTMOS KÁLIMNOS
KOS RÓDHOS**

Ákra
Stavrós
Apóllon
Koronís
Mouts
Apíranth
Filóti
1001
Pirgakía   **Náxo**
Ko

Páros
Náoussa
Páros
(Parikiá)   Náxos
Sangrí
Marpissa
Ándiparos   Dhriós
Ándiparos   Alikí
Ákra
Petalida
Skhoinoússa
Iráklia
Iráklia

**IRÁKLION
ALEXANDRIA
HAIFA**

Loutrá
Kíthnos
Mérikhas
Dhriopís
Kíthnos
Ákra Áyia
Dhimítrios

Sérifos
585   Sérifos
Livádhi
Ákra Kíklops

Ákra Fílippos
Kamáres
Artemón
Apollonía
675   Platis
Yialós
Sifnos

Kímolos
Kímolos
Pollónia
Milos
(Plaka)   Políaigos
Adhámas
Zefiría
761
Ákra
Psális   **Mílos**

Ákra Kéfalos

Ákra Trimesón

Stenón Thermion

2

Íos
Síkinos   Ormos Iou
553   713
Síkinos   **Íos**
Folégandros
Folégandros   Ákra
Karavostásis   Achládi

**Thíra
(Santorini)**
Ákra
Mavrópetra   Oía
Thíra (Firá)
Pirgos
566
Akrotíri   Emboreíon

Khristianá

1

**IRÁKLION
ÁYIOS NIKÓLAOS**

Ákra
Tourkovíglia
1125
Sikéa
Papadhiánika
Monemvasía
Elaía
Neápolis
Ákra Iérax
Ákra Maléa
Ákra
Spathi
Karavás
Potamós   Aylia Pelayía
Kithira
506   Avlémonas
Kíthhira   Kapsáli

Andikíthira

KRITIKÓN   ΠΕΛΑΓΟΣ

P

D   E   F

1

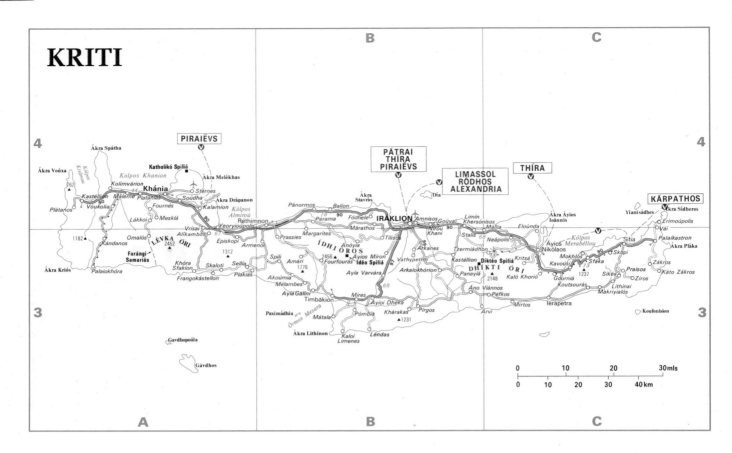

KRITI

PIRAIÉVS

Ákra Spátha
Ákra Voúxa
Katholikó Spiliá
Ákra Melékhas
Ákra Drápanon
Ákra Stavrós
PÁTRAI THÍRA PIRAIÉVS
LIMASSOL RÓDHOS ALEXANDRIA
THÍRA
KÁRPATHOS
Kolimvárion
Khánia
Kastéllion Máleme Plataniás
Soúdha
Kalamíon
Pánormos
Balion
Fódhele
Amnisos
Limín
Ákra Sidheros
Plátanos
Voukoliá
Lákkoi Mesklá
Fournés
Vrísai
Alíkambos
Yeoryioúpolis
Réthimnon
Prassies
Pérama
Márathos
Márathos
Tilisós
IRÁKLION
Goúval
Nírou
Khani
Khersónisos
Mália
Eloúnda
Vái
Erimoúpolis
Ákra Plaka
1182
Kándanos
Omalós
LÉVKA ÓRI 2452
Episkopi
Armenoí
Margarites
Anóyia
ÍDHI ÓROS
Ayios Míron
Árkanes
Kastéllion
Tzermiádhon
Diktéo Spiliá
Ákra Ávios Ioánnis
Neápolis
Nikólaos
Mokhlós
Sitia
Palaikastron
Farángi Samariás
Khóra Sfakion
Skaloti
Sellia
1312
Spili
Amári 1776
2456
Fourfourás
Idéo Spiliá
Vathypetro
Arkalokhórion
Panayiá
DHÍKTI ÓRI 2148
Kaló Khorió
Kavoúsi
Sfáka 73
Skopi
Praisos
Záktos
Ákra Kriós
Palaiokhóra
Frangokástellon
Plakiás
Akoúmia
Mélambes
Ayía Galíni
Timbákion
Mires
Ayía Varvára
Ayioi Dhéka
Áno Viánnos
Péfkos
Gourniá
1237
Sikéa
Lithinai
Makriyialós
Ierápetra
Paximádhia
Mátala
Pómbia
Léndas
Pirgos
Khárakas 1231
Arvi
Mirtos
Koutsourás
Ákra Lithinon
Kaloi Limenes
Koufonision
Gavdhopoúla
Gávdhos

0   10   20   30mls
0   10   20   30   40km

A   B   C

KYPROS/KIBRIS

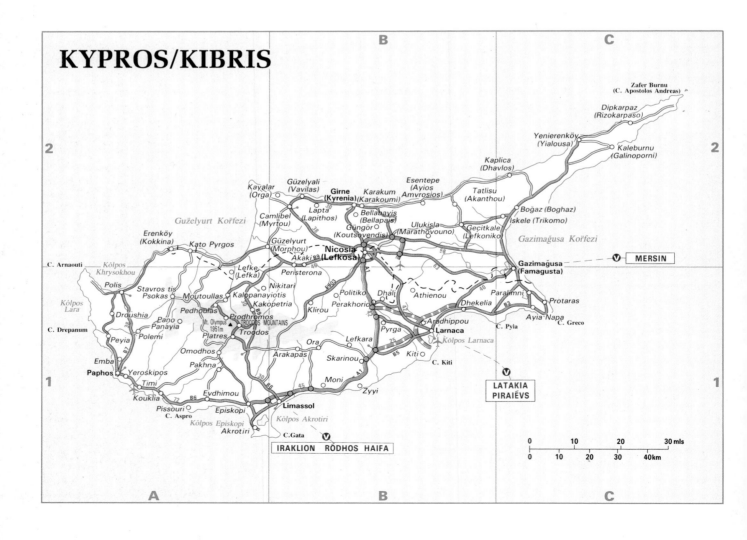

Zafer Burnu
(C. Apostolos Andreas)
Dipkarpaz
(Rizokarpaso)
Yenierenköy
(Yialousa)
Kaleburnu
(Galinoporni)
Kayalar
(Orga)
Güzelyali
(Vavilas)
Girne (Kyrenia)
Karakum
(Karakoumi)
Esentepe
(Ayios Amvrosios)
Kaplica
(Dhavlos)
Tatlisu
(Akanthou)
Lapta
(Lapithos)
Bellabayis
(Bellapais)
Camlibel
(Myrtou)
Güngör
(Koutsovendis)
Ulukisla
(Marathovouno)
Boğaz (Boghaz)
Iskele (Trikomo)
Erenköy
(Kokkina)
Káto Pyrgos
Güzelyurt
(Morphou)
Nicosia (Lefkosa)
Akaki
Gecitkale
(Lefkoniko)
Gazimağusa Körfezi
MERSIN
Güzelyurt Körfezi
C. Arnaouti
Kólpos Khrysokhou
Lefke
(Lefka)
Peristerona
Nikitari
Politiko
Dháli
Athienou
Gazimağusa (Famagusta)
Polis
Stavros tis Psokas
Kalopanayiotis
Kakópetria
Klirou
Perakhorio
Paralimni
Protaras
Kólpos Lára
Moutoullas
Pedhoulas
Prodhromos
Pyrga
Dhekelia
Ayia Napa
C. Greco
Drousha
Pano
Panayia
Mt. Olympus 1951m
TROODOS MOUNTAINS
Troodos
Ora
Lefkara
Aradhippou
Larnaca
C. Pyla
C. Drepanum
Peyia
Polemi
Platres
Omodhos
Arakapas
Skarinou
Pyrga
Kiti
C. Kiti
Kólpos Larnaca
Emba
Paphos
Yeroskipos
Pakhna
Moni
Zyyi
Timi
Kouklia
Evdhimou
Pissouri
Episkopi
Limassol
LATAKIA PIRAIÉVS
C. Aspro
Kólpos Episkopi
Akrotiri
Kólpos Akrotiri
C.Gata
IRAKLION RÓDHOS HAIFA

0   10   20   30 mls
0   10   20   30   40km

A   B   C

INDEX TO PLACE NAMES

To locate a place in the atlas first look up the name in the alphabetical index. The required page number is indicated in bold type. The letter and figure in light type related to the grid square containing the place on the atlas page. The placename is then found between the bottom of the lines linking the letters (running top and bottom of the page) and the numbers (at the left/right hand-side of the page).

A Caniza ... **66** ... B2
A Estrada ... **66** ... B3
A Garda ... **66** ... B2
A Gudiña ... **67** ... D2
A Rúa ... **67** ... D2
Aachen ... **40** ... A3
Aalborg ... **12** ... B3
Aalburg ... **29** ... D2
Aalen ... **45** ... E3
Aalsmeer ... **29** ... D2
Aalst (Alost) ... **30** ... C3
Aalten ... **29** ... F2
Aalter ... **30** ... C4
Äänekoski ... **5** ... E1
Aarau ... **84** ... B3
Aarberg ... **84** ... B3
Aarburg ... **84** ... B3
Aarschot ... **31** ... D3
Abádszalók ... **106** ... C3
Abaiykér ... **106** ... C4
Abano Terme ... **90** ... C2
Abbasanta ... **96** ... B2
Abbekås ... **13** ... D1
Abberffraw ... **22** ... B3
Abbeville ... **50** ... A3
Abbey Town ... **20** ... C2
Abbeydorney ... **16** ... B2
Abbeyfeale ... **16** ... B2
Abbeyleix ... **17** ... D3
Abbiategrasso ... **88** ... C2
Abborrträsk ... **4** ... B4
Abbots Bromley ... **23** ... D2
Abbotsbury ... **27** ... E2
Abejar ... **68** ... C2
Abela ... **78** ... B1
Abelvaer ... **3** ... D3
Abenberg ... **46** ... B4
Abeñojar ... **74** ... A1
Åbenrå ... **12** ... B1
Abensberg ... **46** ... C3
Aberaeron ... **22** ... B1
Aberchirder ... **19** ... E3
Aberchirder ... **19** ... E3
Aberdare ... **27** ... D3
Aberdaron ... **22** ... B2
Aberdeen ... **19** ... E2
Aberdovey ... **22** ... B2
Aberfeldy ... **19** ... D1
Aberfoyle ... **18** ... C1
Abergavenny ... **27** ... D4
Abergele ... **22** ... C3
Aberlady ... **21** ... D4
Aberlour ... **19** ... D3
Abermule ... **22** ... C2
Abernethy ... **19** ... D1
Aberporth ... **26** ... C4
Abersoch ... **22** ... B2
Abersychan ... **27** ... D3
Abertillery ... **27** ... D3
Aberystwyth ... **22** ... B1
Abetone ... **94** ... B3
Abingdon ... **27** ... F3
Abington ... **20** ... C3
Abla ... **80** ... C2
Ablanitsa ... **114** ... B1
Ablis ... **54** ... C3
Åbo (Turku) ... **3** ... E2
Abondance ... **61** ... E3
Abony ... **106** ... B3
Aboréa ... **96** ... B3
Aboyne ... **19** ... E2
Abrantes ... **78** ... B3
Abraure ... **4** ... B4
Abreschviller ... **56** ... C4
Abries ... **61** ... E1
Abrud ... **107** ... E2
Abtenau ... **86** ... B2
Abtshagen ... **35** ... D3
Åby ... **10** ... B1
Åbybro ... **12** ... B3
Åbyn ... **4** ... C3
Acatari ... **108** ... B2
Acate ... **103** ... D2
Acceglio ... **92** ... A3
Accettura ... **101** ... D3
Acciaroli ... **100** ... B3
Accous ... **62** ... B2
Acerno ... **100** ... B4
Acharacle ... **18** ... B1
Achenkirch ... **85** ... F3
Achern ... **44** ... C3
Acheux ... **30** ... B2
Achiltibuie ... **18** ... C3
Achim ... **33** ... D1
Achnasheen ... **18** ... C3

Aci Castello ... **103** ... D2
Aci Trezza ... **103** ... E2
Acireale ... **103** ... E3
Acis ... **107** ... E3
Acle ... **25** ... F4
Acqualagna ... **95** ... D2
Acquapendente ... **98** ... A3
Acquasanta Terme ... **98** ... C4
Acquasparta ... **98** ... B3
Acquaviva delle Fonti ... **101** ... D4
Acqui Terme ... **92** ... C4
Acri ... **101** ... D2
Ács ... **105** ... E4
Acsa ... **106** ... B4
Acton Turville ... **27** ... E3
Ada ... **106** ... B1
Adalsvollen ... **3** ... D2
Adámas ... **121** ... E2
Adamclisi ... **115** ... E3
Adamstown ... **17** ... D2
Adanero ... **74** ... A4
Adare ... **16** ... C2
Adaševci ... **112** ... B4
Addingham ... **23** ... D1
Adelboden ... **84** ... B2
Adelebsen ... **37** ... D2
Adelfia ... **101** ... D4
Adelsheim ... **41** ... D1
Adelsried ... **46** ... B2
Adenau ... **40** ... A3
Adjud ... **109** ... D2
Admont ... **86** ... C2
Ádneram ... **8** ... B2
Adony ... **105** ... E3
Adorf ... **42** ... C3
Adorno Micca ... **88** ... B2
Adra ... **80** ... C1
Adrano ... **103** ... D3
Adria ... **91** ... D1
Adrigole ... **16** ... B1
Adunaţii Copăceni ... **115** ... D3
Aérinón ... **117** ... F1
Aerzen ... **37** ... D3
Aetós ... **120** ... B4
Áfarnes ... **2** ... B1
Áfissos ... **118** ... A1
Áfitos ... **118** ... A2
Aflenz ... **87** ... D2
Afumaţi ... **115** ... D3
Ag Marina ... **121** ... E3
Agapia ... **109** ... D3
Agás ... **109** ... D2
Agay ... **65** ... E2
Agde ... **64** ... B2
Agen ... **63** ... D3
Agger ... **12** ... A3
Aggersund ... **12** ... B3
Ággius ... **96** ... B3
Aggsbach-Dorf ... **87** ... D3
Aggsbach-Markt ... **87** ... D3
Agigea ... **115** ... F3
Agighiol ... **115** ... F4
Agira ... **103** ... D3
Aglen ... **3** ... D3
Agnanderon ... **117** ... E1
Agnanta ... **117** ... D1
Agnita ... **108** ... B1
Agnónda ... **118** ... B1
Agnone ... **99** ... D3
Agoncillo ... **69** ... D3
Agordo ... **91** ... D3
Ágras ... **117** ... E3
Agreda ... **69** ... D2
Agriá ... **117** ... F1
Agrigento ... **102** ... C2
Agrinion ... **120** ... B4
Agriovótanon ... **121** ... D4
Agrópoli ... **100** ... B3
Aguda ... **72** ... B3
Agudo ... **79** ... F3
Águeda ... **72** ... B2
Aguiar da Beira ... **72** ... C3
Aguilar ... **80** ... A2
Aguilar de Campoo ... **68** ... B3
Águilas ... **81** ... E2
Ahascragh ... **16** ... C3
Ahaus ... **36** ... B3
Åheim ... **2** ... A1
Ahlainen ... **6** ... B2
Ahlbeck ... **35** ... D4
Ahlen ... **36** ... C2
Ahlhorn ... **32** ... C1
Ahmovaara ... **7** ... E4
Ahoghill ... **15** ... D2
Ahokylä ... **5** ... E3

Ahrensbök ... **33** ... E3
Ahrensburg ... **33** ... E3
Ahrweiler ... **40** ... B3
Ähtäri ... **5** ... D1
Ähtävä (Esse) ... **7** ... D7
Ahun ... **59** ... E3
Åhus ... **13** ... D2
Ahvensalmi ... **7** ... E3
Aicha ... **47** ... E3
Aichach ... **46** ... B3
Aidenbach ... **47** ... D3
Aidone ... **103** ... D2
Aigen ... **86** ... C4
Aigle ... **84** ... A2
Aiglsbach ... **46** ... C3
Aignay-le-Duc ... **55** ... F2
Aigosthena ... **121** ... D3
Aigre ... **58** ... C3
Aigrefeuille ... **58** ... B3
Aigrefeuille-Sur-Maine ... **53** ... D1
Aiguablava ... **71** ... E3
Aiguebelle ... **65** ... E2
Aiguebelle ... **61** ... E2
Aigueperse ... **60** ... A3
Aigues-Mortes ... **64** ... B2
Aiguillon ... **62** ... C4
Aigurande ... **59** ... E4
Äiiälä ... **61** ... E1
Ailefroide ... **61** ... E1
Aillant ... **55** ... D2
Aime ... **61** ... E2
Ainhoa ... **62** ... A2
Ainsa ... **70** ... A4
Airaines ... **50** ... A3
Airdrie ... **50** ... B4
Aire ... **50** ... B4
Aire-Sur-l'Adour ... **62** ... C3
Airolo ... **84** ... C2
Airvault ... **53** ... E1
Aisey-sur-Seine ... **55** ... E2
Aisy-sur-Armançon ... **55** ... E2
Aita Mare ... **108** ... C2
Aiterhofen ... **47** ... D3
Aitolikón ... **120** ... B4
Aitrach ... **45** ... E2
Aittojärvi ... **5** ... E2
Aittojärvi ... **5** ... E4
Aiud ... **107** ... E2
Aix-en-Othe ... **55** ... E3
Aix-en-Provence ... **65** ... D2
Aix-les-Bains ... **61** ... D2
Aixe ... **59** ... D3
Aíyina ... **121** ... D3
Aiyínion ... **117** ... E2
Aiyion ... **120** ... C3
Aizenay ... **58** ... A4
Ajaccio ... **57** ... E2
Ajaureforsen ... **3** ... F4
Ajdovščina ... **104** ... A2
Ajka ... **105** ... D3
Ajos ... **5** ... D4
Akalan ... **119** ... F3
Akasztó ... **106** ... B2
Akçay ... **119** ... E1
Aken ... **38** ... C2
Åker ... **10** ... C1
Åkersberga ... **10** ... C2
Akharnai ... **121** ... D3
Akhisar ... **119** ... F1
Akhládókambos ... **120** ... C3
Akhtopol ... **119** ... E4
Akiki ... **122** ... B2
Akirkeby ... **13** ... E1
Akland ... **8** ... C1
Akonpohja ... **7** ... E3
Akoúmia ... **122** ... B3
Akraifnion ... **121** ... D4
Åkrehamn ... **8** ... A2
Akrotíri ... **121** ... F1
Akrotíri ... **122** ... A1
Aksakal ... **119** ... F2
Aksakovo ... **115** ... E2
Ål ... **8** ... C3
Ala ... **90** ... B2
Alà dei Sardi ... **96** ... B3
Ala di Stura ... **88** ... A2
Ala-Honkajoki ... **6** ... B2
Ala-Paakkola ... **5** ... D4
Alaejos ... **73** ... F3
Alagna Valsesia ... **88** ... B2
Alagón ... **69** ... E1
Alahärmä ... **5** ... D2
Alandroal ... **78** ... C2

Ålandsbro ... **4** ... B1
Alange ... **79** ... E2
Alaniemi ... **5** ... E4
Alanis ... **79** ... E1
Alapitkä ... **7** ... D7
Alaraz ... **73** ... F2
Alarcón ... **75** ... D2
Alassio ... **92** ... B3
Alastaro ... **6** ... B2
Alatoz ... **75** ... E1
Alatri ... **98** ... C2
Alavattnet (Nedervetil) ... **6** ... B4
Alavieska ... **5** ... D3
Alavus ... **5** ... D1
Alba ... **92** ... B4
Alba Adriatica ... **98** ... C4
Alba de Tormes ... **73** ... F3
Alba Lulia ... **107** ... E2
Albac ... **107** ... E2
Albacete ... **75** ... D1
Ålbæk ... **12** ... B4
Albaida ... **81** ... F4
Alban ... **63** ... F3
Albano Laziale ... **98** ... B2
Albarella ... **89** ... D1
Albarracín ... **75** ... E3
Albatera ... **115** ... E2
Albenga ... **92** ... B3
Albens ... **61** ... D3
Alberga ... **10** ... B1
Albergaria a Velha ... **72** ... B3
Alberique ... **75** ... F1
Albernoa ... **78** ... A4
Albersdorf ... **33** ... D3
Albert ... **50** ... B3
Albertirsa ... **106** ... B3
Albertville ... **61** ... E2
Albeşti ... **114** ... B4
Albeşti ... **109** ... D4
Albeşti Paleologu ... **115** ... D4
Albi ... **63** ... E3
Albisola Marina ... **92** ... C3
Albita ... **109** ... E3
Albocácer ... **76** ... A4
Albota ... **114** ... C4
Albrighton ... **22** ... C2
Albufeira ... **82** ... B3
Albuñol ... **80** ... C1
Alburquerque ... **79** ... D3
Albury ... **25** ... D1
Alby ... **13** ... F2
Alcácer do Sal ... **78** ... B2
Alcáçovas ... **78** ... B2
Alcalá de Chivert ... **76** ... A4
Alcalá de Guadaira ... **83** ... E3
Alcalá de Henares ... **74** ... C3
Alcalá de los Gazules ... **83** ... E2
Alcalá del Río ... **83** ... E3
Alcalá la Real ... **80** ... B2
Álcamo ... **102** ... B3
Alcanar ... **76** ... A4
Alcanede ... **78** ... B3
Alcanena ... **78** ... B4
Alcañices ... **67** ... E1
Alcañiz ... **70** ... A1
Alcántara ... **79** ... D4
Alcantarilla ... **81** ... E3
Alcaracejos ... **79** ... F2
Alcaraz ... **81** ... D4
Alcarràs ... **70** ... B2
Alcaudete ... **80** ... B2
Alcázar de San Juan ... **74** ... C1
Alcobendas ... **74** ... B3
Alcoceber ... **76** ... A4
Alcochete ... **78** ... A2
Alcolea del Pinar ... **75** ... D4
Alconbury ... **23** ... F1
Alcora ... **76** ... A4
Alcorisa ... **75** ... F4
Alcoutim ... **82** ... C3
Alcover ... **70** ... B2
Alcoy ... **81** ... F4
Alcubierre ... **69** ... F2
Alcúdia ... **77** ... E3
Alcudia de Crespins ... **75** ... F1
Aldbourne ... **27** ... E3
Aldbrough ... **23** ... F4
Aldea del Cano ... **79** ... D3
Aldea del Fresno ... **74** ... B3
Aldeburgh ... **25** ... F3
Alderley Edge ... **23** ... D3
Aldermaston ... **27** ... F3
Aldershot ... **25** ... D1
Alekovo ... **115** ... E2

Aleksandrovac ... **112** ... C3
Aleksandrovo ... **114** ... C2
Aleksinac ... **113** ... D2
Ålem ... **13** ... F3
Ålen ... **3** ... D1
Alençon ... **53** ... F3
Aléria ... **57** ... F2
Alès ... **64** ... B3
Åles ... **96** ... B2
Aleşd ... **107** ... D3
Alessándria della Rocca ... **102** ... B2
Ålestrup ... **12** ... B3
Ålesund ... **2** ... B1
Alexandria ... **20** ... B4
Alexándria ... **117** ... E2
Alexandria ... **114** ... C3
Alexandroúpolis ... **119** ... D3
Alf ... **40** ... B2
Alfambras ... **82** ... A3
Alfajarín ... **69** ... F1
Alfaro ... **69** ... D2
Alfarrás ... **70** ... B3
Alfatar ... **115** ... E3
Alfedena ... **99** ... D2
Alfeizerão ... **78** ... A4
Alfeld ... **37** ... D3
Alfeld ... **42** ... C1
Alfonsine ... **95** ... D3
Alford ... **19** ... E2
Ålfoten ... **2** ... A1
Alfreton ... **23** ... E2
Alfta ... **10** ... B4
Álgarås ... **9** ... F1
Ålgård ... **8** ... A1
Algeciras ... **83** ... E1
Algemisí ... **75** ... F1
Ålgered ... **10** ... B4
Alghero ... **96** ... A3
Alghult ... **13** ... E3
Algodonales ... **83** ... E2
Algora ... **74** ... C4
Algoz ... **82** ... B3
Algsjö ... **4** ... A3
Algyő ... **106** ... B2
Alhama de Aragón ... **69** ... D1
Alhama de Granada ... **80** ... B1
Alhama de Murcia ... **81** ... E3
Alhaurín el Grande ... **80** ... A1
Alí Terme ... **103** ... E3
Ália ... **102** ... D3
Alibunar ... **112** ... C4
Alicante ... **81** ... F4
Alicartos ... **121** ... D4
Alijó ... **72** ... C3
Alikanás ... **120** ... B3
Aliki ... **118** ... C3
Aliki ... **121** ... F2
Alimena ... **102** ... C3
Alingsås ... **13** ... D4
Alistráti ... **118** ... B3
Alivérion ... **121** ... E3
Aljezur ... **82** ... A3
Aljubarrota ... **78** ... A4
Aljucén ... **79** ... D3
Aljustrel ... **82** ... B4
Alkhoven ... **86** ... B3
Alkmaar ... **29** ... D1
All ... **87** ... D2
Allaines ... **54** ... C3
Allainville ... **54** ... C3
Allanche ... **60** ... A4
Alland ... **87** ... E3
Allariz ... **66** ... C2
Alle ... **43** ... D3
Álleghe ... **91** ... D3
Allemond ... **61** ... D2
Allendale ... **21** ... D2
Allenheads ... **21** ... D2
Allensbach ... **45** ... D1
Allersberg ... **46** ... B4
Allershaus эn ... **46** ... C2
Allessandrá ... **92** ... C4
Allevard ... **61** ... D1
Allhallows-on-Sea ... **25** ... D2
Allihies ... **16** ... A1
Allingåbro ... **12** ... B3
Allinge ... **13** ... E1
Alloa ... **20** ... C4
Allones ... **53** ... F1
Allos ... **64** ... E3
Alloway ... **20** ... B3
Allstedt ... **38** ... B2
Almacelles ... **70** ... B2
Almadén ... **80** ... A4

Almagro ... **74** ... B1
Almansa ... **75** ... E1
Almargen ... **83** ... F2
Almazán ... **69** ... D1
Almazora ... **76** ... A3
Almeida ... **73** ... D2
Almeirim ... **78** ... B3
Almelo ... **39** ... F3
Almenar de Soria ... **69** ... D1
Almendral ... **79** ... D2
Almendralejo ... **79** ... D2
Almere ... **29** ... D3
Almeria ... **81** ... D1
Älmhult ... **13** ... D2
Almíron ... **120** ... C2
Almiropótamos ... **121** ... E3
Almirós ... **117** ... F1
Almodóvar ... **82** ... B3
Almodóvar del Campo ... **80** ... B4
Almodóvar del Pinar ... **41** ... D2
Almodóvar del Río ... **83** ... F4
Almogarve ... **82** ... A4
Almonaster la Real ... **83** ... D4
Almonte ... **83** ... D3
Älmsta ... **10** ... C2
Almuñécar ... **80** ... B1
Almunge ... **10** ... C2
Almvik ... **13** ... F4
Alness ... **19** ... E3
Alnmouth ... **21** ... E3
Alnwick ... **21** ... E3
Alocobaça ... **78** ... A4
Alónnisos ... **118** ... B1
Alora ... **80** ... A1
Alosno ... **82** ... C3
Alost (Aalst) ... **30** ... C3
Alp ... **70** ... C4
Alpalhão ... **78** ... C3
Alpbach ... **86** ... A2
Alpedrinhas ... **72** ... C1
Alpen ... **36** ... A2
Alpera ... **75** ... E1
Alphen-ann-de-Rijn ... **29** ... D2
Alpirsbach ... **44** ... C2
Alpua ... **5** ... E3
Alpullu ... **119** ... E3
Alquézar ... **70** ... A3
Alresford ... **27** ... F2
Alreswas ... **23** ... D2
Als ... **12** ... B3
Als ... **12** ... B1
Alsager ... **23** ... D2
Alsasua ... **69** ... D3
Alsfield ... **41** ... D3
Alsleben ... **38** ... C2
Alsop-en-le-Dale ... **23** ... D2
Alsótold ... **106** ... B4
Alstahaug ... **3** ... E4
Alstätte ... **36** ... B3
Alston ... **21** ... D2
Alt Schadow ... **39** ... E3
Altafulla ... **70** ... C2
Altamura ... **101** ... D4
Altaussee ... **86** ... C2
Altdorf ... **42** ... C1
Altdorf ... **84** ... C2
Altea ... **76** ... A1
Altedo ... **94** ... C3
Altena ... **36** ... B2
Altenahr ... **40** ... B3
Altenau ... **37** ... E2
Altenberg ... **43** ... E3
Altenberge ... **36** ... B3
Altenburg ... **43** ... D4
Altenhundem ... **36** ... C1
Altenkirchen ... **40** ... B3
Altenkirchen ... **35** ... D4
Altenlglan ... **40** ... B1
Altenmarkt ... **47** ... D2
Altenmarkt ... **104** ... B4
Altenmarkt ... **104** ... B4
Altenmarkt im Pongau ... **86** ... B2
Altenstadt ... **45** ... E2
Altensteig ... **44** ... C2
Altentreptow ... **35** ... D3
Altenwalde ... **32** ... C3
Alter do Chão ... **78** ... C3
Althausen ... **45** ... D2
Altheim ... **86** ... B3
Althorpe ... **23** ... E3
Altimir ... **114** ... B2
Altinoluk ... **119** ... D1
Altinova ... **119** ... E1
Altkirch ... **56** ... C2
Altmünster ... **86** ... C3

Altnaharra ...... 18 ... C4
Alton ...... 27 ... F3
Altötting ...... 47 ... D2
Altrincham ...... 23 ... D3
Altruppin ...... 35 ... D1
Altstätten ...... 85 ... D3
Alunda ...... 10 ... C2
Alva ...... 20 ... C4
Alvajärvi ...... 5 ... E2
Álvakarleby ...... 10 ... C3
Alvalade ...... 78 ... B1
Älvängen ...... 12 ... C4
Alvdal ...... 3 ... D1
Älvdalen ...... 9 ... F3
Alversund ...... 8 ... A3
Alvesta ...... 13 ... E3
Alvignac ...... 59 ... E1
Alvik ...... 8 ... B3
Alvik ...... 8 ... B3
Alvito ...... 78 ... B2
Alvor ...... 82 ... B3
Ålvros ...... 9 ... E4
Álvros ...... 10 ... A4
Älvsbyn ...... 4 ... C4
Ålvundeid ...... 2 ... C1
Alyth ...... 19 ... D1
Alzey ...... 40 ... C2
Alzira ...... 75 ... F1
Alzon ...... 64 ... B3
Alzonne ...... 63 ... E2
Åmål ...... 9 ... E1
Amalfi ...... 100 ... B3
Amaliápolis ...... 117 ... F1
Amaliás ...... 120 ... B3
Amance ...... 56 ... B2
Amancey ...... 56 ... B1
Amandola ...... 98 ... C4
Amantea ...... 101 ... D1
Amara ...... 115 ... E3
Amarante ...... 72 ... C3
Âmârâştü de Jos ...... 114 ... B3
Amareleja ...... 78 ... C1
Amárinthos ...... 121 ... F1
Amatrice ...... 98 ... C3
Amaxádhes ...... 118 ... C3
Amay ...... 31 ... E3
Ambarès ...... 58 ... B1
Ambasmestas ...... 67 ... D3
Ambazac ...... 59 ... D3
Ambelákia ...... 117 ... E1
Amberg ...... 42 ... C1
Ambergate ...... 23 ... D2
Ambérieu-en-Bugey ...... 61 ... D3
Ambert ...... 60 ... B2
Ambjörby ...... 9 ... E3
Amble ...... 21 ... E3
Ambleside ...... 20 ... C2
Amboise ...... 54 ... B2
Ambri-Piotta ...... 84 ... C2
Ambrières ...... 53 ... E3
Ameixial ...... 82 ... B3
Amélia ...... 98 ... B3
Amélie-les-Bains ...... 63 ... F1
Amelinghausen ...... 33 ... E2
Amerongen ...... 29 ... E2
Amersfoort ...... 29 ... D2
Amersham ...... 25 ... D2
Amesbury ...... 27 ... E3
Amfíklia ...... 120 ... C4
Amfilokhía ...... 120 ... B4
Ámfissa ...... 120 ... C4
Amiens ...... 50 ... B2
Amíndaion ...... 117 ... E3
Åmli ...... 8 ... C1
Amlwch ...... 22 ... B3
Ammanford ...... 26 ... C4
Ämmänsaari ...... 5 ... F4
Ammarnäs ...... 4 ... A4
Ammeberg ...... 10 ... A1
Amnisos ...... 122 ... B4
Amorbach ...... 41 ... D2
Åmot ...... 8 ... C2
Åmot ...... 9 ... D2
Åmot ...... 10 ... B3
Åmotfors ...... 9 ... E2
Amou ...... 62 ... B2
Ampezzo ...... 91 ... D2
Ampfing ...... 47 ... D2
Amphion ...... 61 ... E4
Amplepuis ...... 60 ... C3
Amposta ...... 70 ... B1
Ampthill ...... 25 ... D3
Amriswil ...... 85 ... D3
Amroth ...... 26 ... C4
Amrulree ...... 19 ... D1
Åmsele ...... 4 ... B3
Amsteg ...... 84 ... C2
Amsterdam ...... 29 ... D3
Amstetten ...... 87 ... D3
Amtervik ...... 9 ... E2
Amurrio ...... 68 ... C3
Amyklai ...... 120 ... C2
Amzacea ...... 115 ... F3
An Charraig (Carrick) ...... 14 ... B2
An Daingean (Dingle) ...... 16 ... A2
An Fhairche (Clanbur) ...... 14 ... B1
An Rinn (Ring) ...... 17 ... D1
An Spidéal (Spiddal) ...... 16 ... B3
Ána-Sira ...... 8 ... B1
Anadia ...... 72 ... B2
Anagni ...... 98 ... C2
Anascaul ...... 16 ... A2
Anäset ...... 4 ... C3
Anatolikón ...... 117 ... E2
Anávissos ...... 121 ... E3
Ancaster ...... 23 ... E2
Ancenis ...... 53 ... D2
Ancerville ...... 55 ... F4
Ancona ...... 95 ... E2
Ancy-le-Franc ...... 55 ... E2
Anda ...... 8 ... B4
Andalo ...... 90 ... B3

Ándalsnes ...... 2 ... B1
Andau ...... 87 ... F3
Anddírrion ...... 120 ... C4
Andelot ...... 56 ... A3
Andenne ...... 31 ... D3
Andermatt ...... 84 ... C2
Andernach ...... 40 ... B3
Andernos ...... 58 ... B1
Anderstorp ...... 13 ... D3
Andijk ...... 29 ... D3
Andíkira ...... 120 ... C4
Andipáros ...... 121 ... F2
Ándissa ...... 119 ... D1
Andocs ...... 105 ... D2
Andolsheim ...... 56 ... C3
Andorra la Vella ...... 70 ... C3
Andover ...... 27 ... F3
Andoversford ...... 27 ... E4
Andraitx ...... 77 ... D3
Andrăşeşti ...... 115 ... E3
Andravídha ...... 120 ... B3
Andreas ...... 20 ... B2
Andretta ...... 100 ... C4
Andrézieux-Bouthéon ...... 60 ... B2
Ándria ...... 99 ... F1
Andrijevica ...... 112 ... B1
Andritsaina ...... 120 ... C3
Ándros ...... 121 ... F3
Andújar ...... 80 ... B3
Anduze ...... 64 ... B3
Aneby ...... 13 ... E4
Ånes ...... 2 ... C2
Ånes ...... 9 ... E3
Anet ...... 54 ... B4
Ånge ...... 3 ... F1
Angeja ...... 72 ... B3
Ängelholm ...... 13 ... D2
Angelókastron ...... 120 ... B4
Anger ...... 87 ... E2
Angern ...... 87 ... F4
Angers ...... 53 ... E2
Angerville ...... 54 ... C3
Angle ...... 26 ... B3
Anglés ...... 71 ... D3
Anglet ...... 62 ... A2
Anglure ...... 55 ... E3
Angmering-on-Sea ...... 25 ... D1
Angoulême ...... 58 ... C2
Angües ...... 70 ... A3
Angvik ...... 2 ... C1
Aniane ...... 64 ... B3
Aniche ...... 50 ... C3
Anina ...... 113 ... D4
Anjala ...... 7 ... D2
Anjalankoski ...... 7 ... D2
Anjum ...... 29 ... E4
Ankaran ...... 104 ... A1
Ankarede ...... 3 ... F3
Ankarsrum ...... 13 ... F4
Ankarvattnet ...... 3 ... F3
Anklam ...... 35 ... D3
Ankum ...... 36 ... C3
Ånn ...... 3 ... E2
Anna Paulowna ...... 29 ... D3
Annaberg ...... 86 ... B2
Annaberg ...... 87 ... D3
Annaberg-Buchholz ...... 43 ... D3
Annalong ...... 15 ... E1
Annan ...... 20 ... C3
Anndalsvågen ...... 3 ... D4
Annecy ...... 61 ... D3
Annelund ...... 13 ... D4
Annemasse ...... 61 ... E3
Annenheim ...... 86 ... C1
Annestown ...... 17 ... D1
Annonay ...... 60 ... C2
Annot ...... 65 ... E3
Annweiler ...... 44 ... C4
Åno Trikkala ...... 120 ... C3
Áno Viánnos ...... 122 ... B3
Andýia ...... 122 ... B3
Ans ...... 12 ... B2
Ansbach ...... 46 ... B4
Anse ...... 60 ... C3
Ansedónia ...... 97 ... E3
Anseremme ...... 31 ... D2
Anstey ...... 23 ... E2
Anstruther ...... 19 ... E1
Antegnate ...... 89 ... D2
Antequera ...... 80 ... A1
Anterselva-Antholz ...... 91 ... D4
Anthéor ...... 65 ... E2
Antibes ...... 65 ... F3
Antifer ...... 49 ... E2
Antnäs ...... 4 ... C4
Antonovo ...... 115 ... D2
Antraigues ...... 60 ... C1
Antrain ...... 53 ... D3
Antrim ...... 15 ... E2
Antrodoco ...... 98 ... B3
Anttila ...... 5 ... F3
Anttola ...... 7 ... E3
Antwerpen (Anvers) ...... 31 ... D4
Anvers (Antwerpen) ...... 31 ... D4
Anzio ...... 98 ... B3
Aoiz ...... 69 ... E3
Aosta ...... 88 ... B2
Apahida ...... 107 ... C2
Apátfalva ...... 106 ... C2
Apatin ...... 105 ... E1
Apécchio ...... 95 ... D2
Apeldoorn ...... 29 ... E2
Apen ...... 32 ... C2
Apensen ...... 33 ... D2
Apiranthos ...... 121 ... F3
Apóikia ...... 121 ... F3
Apold ...... 108 ... B2
Apolda ...... 42 ... C4
Apóllona ...... 121 ... F2
Apollonía ...... 121 ... E2
Apollonia ...... 118 ... A2

Äppelbo ...... 9 ... F3
Appelhülsen ...... 36 ... B2
Appenweier ...... 44 ... C3
Appenzell ...... 85 ... D3
Appiano-Eppan ...... 90 ... C3
Appingedam ...... 29 ... F4
Appleby-in-Westmorland ...... 21 ... D2
Applecross ...... 18 ... B3
Appledore ...... 26 ... C2
Aprica ...... 89 ... E3
Apricena ...... 99 ... E2
Aprilia ...... 98 ... B2
Aprilovo ...... 115 ... D2
Apsalos ...... 117 ... E3
Apt ...... 65 ... D3
Aquileia ...... 91 ... E2
Aracena ...... 83 ... D4
Arachon ...... 58 ... B1
Arad ...... 106 ... C2
Arada ...... 107 ... E2
Aradhippou ...... 122 ... B1
Aragona ...... 102 ... C2
Arakapas ...... 122 ... B1
Arákhova ...... 120 ... C4
Aramits ...... 62 ... B2
Aranda de Duero ...... 68 ... B1
Arandjelovac ...... 112 ... C3
Aranjuez ...... 74 ... B3
Aranyosapáti ...... 107 ... D4
Áratos ...... 118 ... C3
Áraxos ...... 120 ... B3
Arbatax ...... 96 ... C2
Arbeca ...... 90 ... C2
Arbesbach ...... 87 ... D4
Arbois ...... 56 ... B1
Arbon ...... 85 ... D3
Arbore ...... 108 ... C4
Arbrå ...... 10 ... B4
Arbroath ...... 19 ... E1
Árbus ...... 96 ... B2
Arc-en-Barrois ...... 55 ... F2
Arce ...... 98 ... C2
Arcen ...... 29 ... E1
Arcévia ...... 95 ... E2
Archar ...... 113 ... E3
Archena ...... 81 ... E3
Arches ...... 56 ... B3
Archiac ...... 58 ... C2
Archidona ...... 80 ... A2
Arcidosso ...... 97 ... F4
Arcis-sur-Aube ...... 55 ... E3
Arco ...... 90 ... B2
Arcos de Jalón ...... 75 ... D4
Arcos de la Frontera ...... 83 ... D4
Arcos de Valdevez ...... 66 ... B1
Ardagh ...... 16 ... B2
Årdalsosen ...... 8 ... B2
Ardalstangen ...... 8 ... C4
Ardara ...... 14 ... C2
Ardbeg ...... 15 ... E4
Ardcath ...... 17 ... E4
Ardee ...... 17 ... E4
Arden ...... 12 ... B3
Ardentes ...... 59 ... E4
Ardentinny ...... 20 ... B4
Ardez ...... 85 ... E2
Ardfert ...... 16 ... B2
Ardfinnan ...... 16 ... C2
Ardgay ...... 18 ... C3
Ardglass ...... 15 ... E1
Ardgour ...... 18 ... C1
Ardgroom ...... 16 ... A1
Ardhéa ...... 117 ... E3
Ardino ...... 118 ... C4
Ardleigh ...... 25 ... E3
Ardlui ...... 18 ... C1
Ardlussa ...... 15 ... E4
Ardnave ...... 15 ... E4
Ardres ...... 50 ... C3
Ardrishaig ...... 15 ... E4
Ardrossan ...... 20 ... B4
Ardud ...... 107 ... E4
Ardusat ...... 107 ... E4
Ardvasar ...... 18 ... B2
Åre ...... 3 ... E2
Arenas ...... 68 ... A4
Arenas de San Pedro ...... 73 ... F2
Arendal ...... 8 ... C1
Arendonk ...... 31 ... D4
Arendsee ...... 34 ... C1
Arenys de Mar ...... 71 ... D2
Aréopolis ...... 120 ... C2
Arès ...... 58 ... B1
Ares ...... 66 ... C4
Arévalo ...... 74 ... A4
Arezzo ...... 94 ... C2
Arfará ...... 120 ... C2
Argalastí ...... 118 ... A1
Argamasilla de Alba ...... 74 ... C1
Argamasilla de Calatrava ...... 80 ... B4
Argancy ...... 51 ... F1
Arganda ...... 74 ... B3
Arganil ...... 72 ... B2
Argasi ...... 120 ... B3
Argegno ...... 89 ... D2
Argelès ...... 64 ... A1
Argelès-Gazost ...... 62 ... C2
Argelès-Plage ...... 64 ... A1
Argelès-sur-Mer ...... 64 ... A1
Argent ...... 54 ... C3
Argenta ...... 94 ... C3
Argentan ...... 53 ... F4
Argentat ...... 59 ... E2
Argentera ...... 96 ... A3
Argentière ...... 61 ... E3
Argenton-Château ...... 53 ... E1
Argenton-sur-Creuse ...... 59 ... E4
Argentré ...... 53 ... E3
Árgos ...... 120 ... C2
Árgos Orestikón ...... 117 ... D2
Argostólion ...... 120 ... B3
Arguedas ...... 69 ... E2

Arguis ...... 69 ... F2
Århus ...... 12 ... B2
Ariano Irpino ...... 99 ... E1
Ariano nel Polésine ...... 95 ... D4
Arieşeni ...... 107 ... E2
Arilje ...... 112 ... B3
Arinagour ...... 18 ... B1
Arinthod ...... 61 ... D4
Arisaig ...... 18 ... B2
Aritzo ...... 96 ... B2
Ariza ...... 69 ... D1
Ärjäng ...... 9 ... E2
Arjeplog ...... 85 ... D4
Arkalokhórion ...... 122 ... B3
Arkanes ...... 122 ... B3
Arkása ...... 120 ... A2
Arkhángelos ...... 117 ... D1
Arkitsa ...... 121 ... D4
Arklow ...... 17 ... E3
Arkösund ...... 13 ... F4
Arkutino ...... 115 ... E1
Arlanc ...... 60 ... B2
Arles ...... 64 ... C3
Arles ...... 63 ... F1
Arless ...... 17 ... D3
Arlon ...... 31 ... E1
Armação de Pera ...... 82 ... B3
Armadale ...... 20 ... C4
Armadale Pier ...... 18 ... B2
Armagh ...... 15 ... D2
Armenión ...... 117 ... E1
Arménoi ...... 122 ... B3
Armentières ...... 50 ... B4
Armiñón ...... 68 ... C3
Armoy ...... 15 ... E3
Armutova ...... 119 ... E1
Arna ...... 8 ... A3
Arnage ...... 53 ... F2
Arnaía ...... 118 ... B2
Arnay -le-Duc ...... 55 ... E1
Arncliffe ...... 21 ... D1
Arneburg ...... 38 ... C4
Arnedillo ...... 69 ... D2
Arnedo ...... 69 ... D2
Árnes ...... 3 ... D2
Árnes ...... 9 ... D2
Árnes ...... 29 ... E2
Arnhem ...... 29 ... E2
Arnissa ...... 117 ... E3
Arnold ...... 23 ... E2
Arnoldstein ...... 86 ... C1
Arnprior ...... 20 ... B4
Arnsberg ...... 36 ... C2
Arnschwang ...... 47 ... D4
Arnstadt ...... 42 ... B3
Arnstein ...... 41 ... E2
Aroktö ...... 106 ... C4
Arolla ...... 84 ... B1
Arolsen ...... 37 ... D2
Arona ...... 88 ... C2
Aronkylä ...... 5 ... D1
Arosa ...... 85 ... D2
Ærøskøbing ...... 12 ... B1
Årøsund ...... 12 ... B1
Arpajon ...... 54 ... C3
Arpasul de Jos ...... 108 ... B1
Arpela ...... 5 ... D4
Arquata del Tronto ...... 98 ... C4
Arquillos ...... 80 ... B3
Arraba ...... 90 ... C3
Arrabal (Oia) ...... 66 ... B2
Arracourt ...... 56 ... B4
Arrain ...... 118 ... A2
Arraiolos ...... 78 ... B2
Arrakoski ...... 6 ... C2
Arras ...... 50 ... B3
Arreau ...... 62 ... C1
Arrens ...... 62 ... C1
Arrifana ...... 82 ... A3
Arriendas ...... 67 ... F4
Arriondas ...... 67 ... F4
Arrochar ...... 20 ... C4
Arromanches ...... 49 ... D2
Arronches ...... 78 ... C3
Arroyo de la Luz ...... 79 ... D3
Arruda dos Vinhos ...... 78 ... A3
Ars ...... 51 ... F1
Års ...... 12 ... B3
Ars-en-Ré ...... 58 ... A3
Årsandøy ...... 3 ... E3
Arsie ...... 90 ... C2
Arsiero ...... 90 ... C2
Árslev ...... 12 ... B1
Årsunda ...... 10 ... B3
Arsy ...... 50 ... B2
Artá ...... 77 ... E3
Arta ...... 117 ... D1
Artärvi ...... 7 ... D2
Artemare ...... 61 ... D3
Artemisía ...... 120 ... C2
Artemisión ...... 121 ... D4
Artemón ...... 121 ... E2
Artena ...... 54 ... C3
Artern ...... 38 ... C2
Artesa de Segre ...... 70 ... B3
Arth ...... 46 ... C3
Arth ...... 84 ... C3
Arthurstown ...... 17 ... D2
Artíés ...... 70 ... B4
Artix ...... 62 ... B2
Artotína ...... 120 ... C4
Årup ...... 12 ... B1
Arundel ...... 25 ... D1
Årup ...... 12 ... B1
Arvagh ...... 14 ... C1
Arvi ...... 122 ... C3
Arvidsjaur ...... 4 ... B4
Arvieux ...... 61 ... E1
Árvik ...... 2 ... A1
Ărup ...... 9 ... D4
Arvika ...... 9 ... E2

Arzachena ...... 96 ... B4
Arzacq-Arraziguet ...... 62 ... B2
Arzberg ...... 42 ... C2
Arzignano ...... 90 ... C2
Arzl ...... 85 ... E3
Arzúa ...... 66 ... C3
As ...... 31 ... E3
Ås ...... 9 ... D2
Ås ...... 3 ... D1
Aš ...... 42 ... C2
Åsa ...... 12 ... C3
Åsa ...... 86 ... C4
Asach ...... 4 ... A1
Åsang ...... 3 ... F1
Åsarna ...... 13 ... E2
Åsarum ...... 10 ... A2
Åsbro ...... 62 ... A2
Ascain ...... 47 ... D3
Ascha ...... 47 ... D1
Aschach ...... 86 ... C4
Aschaffenburg ...... 41 ... D2
Aschau ...... 47 ... D1
Aschbach Markt ...... 104 ... B4
Ascheberg ...... 33 ... E3
Ascheberg ...... 36 ... B2
Aschendorf ...... 32 ... B2
Aschersleben ...... 38 ... C2
Asco ...... 57 ... E3
Ascó ...... 20 ... B4
Ascoli Piceno ...... 98 ... C4
Ascoli Satriano ...... 99 ... E1
Ascona ...... 84 ... C1
Ascot ...... 25 ... D2
Åseda ...... 13 ... E3
Åsele ...... 4 ... A2
Åsen ...... 3 ... D2
Åsen ...... 9 ... F4
Asendorf ...... 37 ... D4
Asenovgrad ...... 118 ... C4
Åsensbruk ...... 9 ... E1
Åseral ...... 8 ... B1
Asfáka ...... 117 ... D1
Asfeld ...... 51 ... D2
Åsgardstrand ...... 9 ... D2
Ashbourne ...... 23 ... D2
Ashbourne ...... 17 ... E4
Ashburton ...... 26 ... C1
Ashbury ...... 23 ... E2
Ashby-de-la-Zouch ...... 23 ... E2
Åsheim ...... 9 ... D4
Ashford ...... 25 ... E1
Ashford ...... 17 ... E3
Ashington ...... 21 ... E3
Ashton-under-Lyme ...... 23 ... D3
Ashurst ...... 27 ... F2
Asiago ...... 90 ... C2
Asikkala ...... 7 ... D2
Asini ...... 121 ... D3
Ask ...... 8 ... A3
Askainen ...... 6 ... B1
Askeaton ...... 16 ... B2
Asker ...... 9 ... D2
Askersund ...... 10 ... A1
Askim ...... 9 ... D2
Askim ...... 9 ... D2
Askin ...... 9 ... D2
Asköping ...... 10 ... B1
Askvoll ...... 8 ... A4
Åsljunga ...... 13 ... D2
Asmunti ...... 5 ... E4
Asola ...... 89 ... E1
Asopós ...... 121 ... D2
Aspang Markt ...... 87 ... E2
Aspatria ...... 20 ... C3
Aspe ...... 84 ... B2
Aspele ...... 4 ... B2
Aspet ...... 63 ... D2
Aspres-sur-Buëch ...... 65 ... D4
Asprópirgos ...... 118 ... B3
Ásprovalta ...... 118 ... B3
Assen ...... 29 ... F4
Assens ...... 12 ... B1
Assens ...... 12 ... B3
Ássiros ...... 117 ... F3
Assisi ...... 98 ... B4
Assling ...... 46 ... C2
Assmannshausen ...... 40 ... C2
Assos ...... 120 ... A4
Astaffort ...... 63 ... D3
Astakós ...... 120 ... B4
Asten ...... 31 ... E4
Asten ...... 86 ... C3
Asti ...... 92 ... B4
Aston Clinton ...... 25 ... D2
Astorga ...... 67 ... E2
Åstorp ...... 13 ... D2
Ástros ...... 120 ... C2
Astudillo ...... 68 ... B2
Aszód ...... 106 ... B4
Aszófő ...... 105 ... D3
Atalho ...... 78 ... B2
Ateca ...... 69 ... D1
Athboy ...... 17 ... D4
Athea ...... 16 ... B2
Atheleague ...... 16 ... C4
Athenry ...... 16 ... C3
Atherstone ...... 23 ... D2
Athienou ...... 122 ... B1
Athína ...... 121 ... D3
Athlone ...... 16 ... C3
Athy ...... 17 ... D3
Atienza ...... 74 ... C4
Atina ...... 98 ... C2
Atkár ...... 106 ... B4
Atlánti ...... 121 ... D4
Atn ...... 30 ... C3
Atnbrua ...... 9 ... D4
Atostugan ...... 3 ... F4
Åtran ...... 13 ... D3
Attel ...... 46 ... C2
Attendorn ...... 36 ... C3
Attersee ...... 86 ... C3
Attigny ...... 51 ... D2

Attleborough ...... 25 ... E3
Attlebridge ...... 25 ... F4
Attnang ...... 86 ... C3
Åtvidaberg ...... 13 ... F4
Atzara ...... 96 ... B2
Atzendorf ...... 38 ... C2
Aubagne ...... 65 ... D2
Aubange ...... 31 ... E1
Aubenas ...... 64 ... C4
Auberive ...... 55 ... F2
Aubeterre-sur-Dronne ...... 58 ... C2
Aubigny ...... 54 ... C2
Auboué ...... 51 ... E1
Aubusson ...... 59 ... E3
Auch ...... 62 ... C3
Auchinblae ...... 19 ... E2
Auchinleck ...... 20 ... B3
Auchterarder ...... 19 ... D1
Auchtermuchty ...... 19 ... D1
Auchtertyre ...... 18 ... B2
Auderville ...... 48 ... C2
Audeux ...... 56 ... B1
Audierne ...... 52 ... A3
Audincourt ...... 56 ... C2
Audlem ...... 23 ... D2
Audressein ...... 63 ... D1
Audun-le-Roman ...... 51 ... E2
Auerbach ...... 42 ... C2
Auerbach ...... 42 ... C2
Auffach ...... 86 ... A2
Augenge ...... 58 ... B1
Augher ...... 15 ... D2
Aughnacloy ...... 15 ... D2
Aughrim ...... 17 ... E3
Augsburg ...... 46 ... B2
Augusta ...... 103 ... E2
Augustenborg ...... 12 ... B1
Augustusburg ...... 43 ... D3
Auktsjaur ...... 4 ... A3
Auldearn ...... 19 ... D3
Auletta ...... 100 ... C3
Aulla ...... 93 ... D3
Aullène ...... 57 ... F2
Aulnay ...... 58 ... C3
Ault ...... 50 ... A3
Aultbea ...... 18 ... B3
Aultguish ...... 18 ... C3
Aultnamein Inn ...... 19 ... D3
Aulus-les-Bains ...... 63 ... D1
Auma ...... 42 ... C3
Aumale ...... 50 ... A2
Aumetz ...... 51 ... E2
Aumont-Aubrac ...... 60 ... A1
Aunay-sur-Odon ...... 49 ... D1
Auneau ...... 54 ... B3
Auneuil ...... 50 ... A2
Auning ...... 12 ... B3
Aups ...... 65 ... E3
Aura ...... 6 ... B1
Aurach ...... 86 ... A2
Aurach ...... 86 ... A2
Auray ...... 52 ... B2
Aurdal ...... 8 ... C3
Aure ...... 8 ... C3
Aurejärvi ...... 6 ... B3
Aurich ...... 32 ... B2
Aurignac ...... 62 ... C2
Aurillac ...... 59 ... F1
Aurland ...... 8 ... B3
Auronzo di Cadore ...... 91 ... D3
Aursmoen ...... 9 ... D2
Aursnes ...... 2 ... B2
Ausa Corno ...... 91 ... E2
Aussernbrünst ...... 47 ... E3
Austmarka ...... 9 ... E2
Auterive ...... 63 ... D2
Authon ...... 54 ... B3
Auttoinen ...... 6 ... C2
Autun ...... 55 ... E1
Auvillers-les-Forges ...... 51 ... D2
Auxerre ...... 55 ... D2
Auxi-le-Château ...... 50 ... B3
Auxonne ...... 56 ... A1
Auzances ...... 59 ... F3
Auzon ...... 60 ... A2
Avå ...... 6 ... A1
Availles ...... 59 ... D3
Avallon ...... 55 ... E2
Åvas ...... 119 ... D3
Avdhira ...... 118 ... C2
Avebury ...... 27 ... E3
Aveiras de Cima ...... 78 ... A3
Aveiro ...... 72 ... B2
Avellino ...... 100 ... B4
Avenches ...... 84 ... A2
Aversa ...... 100 ... A4
Avesnes ...... 50 ... C3
Avesnes-le-Comte ...... 50 ... B3
Avesta ...... 10 ... B2
Aveton Gifford ...... 26 ... C1
Avezzano ...... 98 ... C2
Aviano ...... 91 ... D3
Aviemore ...... 19 ... D2
Avignon ...... 64 ... C3
Ávila ...... 74 ... A3
Avilés ...... 67 ... E4
Avis ...... 78 ... C3
Avlémonas ...... 121 ... D1
Avlíotes ...... 116 ... A1
Avlón ...... 121 ... D3
Avlonárion ...... 121 ... E3
Avlum ...... 12 ... A2
Avoca ...... 17 ... E3
Avoch ...... 19 ... D3
Avola ...... 103 ... D1
Avonmouth ...... 27 ... D3
Avoriaz ...... 61 ... E3
Avram Lancu ...... 107 ... C2
Avrămeni ...... 109 ... D4
Avramov ...... 115 ... D3
Avranches ...... 53 ... D4

Avrig

Bechhofen

Avrig 108 B1
Avtovac 111 E1
Ax-les-Thermes 63 E1
Axat 63 E1
Axbridge 27 D3
Axel 30 C4
Axente Sever 108 B2
Axminster 27 D2
Ayagalip 119 D2
Ayamonte 82 C3
Ayas 88 B2
Ayéranos 120 C2
Ayerbe 69 F2
Ayesbury 25 D2
Ayiá 117 F1
Ayia Ánna 121 D4
Ayía Galíni 122 B3
Ayia Marina 121 D3
Ayia Napa 122 C1
Ayía Paraskevi 119 D1
Ayía Triadha 120 B3
Ayía Triás 117 F2
Ayía Varvára 122 B3
Ayiássos 119 D1
Ayiófillos 117 D2
Ayioi Dhéka 122 B3
Ayioi Theodhoroi 121 D3
Ayiókambos 121 D4
Ayiókambos 117 F1
Ayiókambos 121 D4
Ayios Andreas 120 C2
Ayios Dhimítrios 117 E2
Ayios Evstratios 118 C1
Ayios Kharálambos 118 C3
Ayios Konstandínos 121 D4
Ayios Miron 122 B3
Ayios Nikólaos 120 B4
Ayios Nikólaos 118 A2
Ayios Nikólaos 122 C3
Ayios Pétras 120 A4
Ayios Petros 117 E3
Ayios Petros 120 C2
Ayios Prodomos 118 A2
Ayios Vlásos 120 B4
Ayios Yeóryios 120 C4
Aylia Pelayía 121 D1
Ayllón 68 C1
Aylsham 25 F4
Ayna 80 D4
Aynho 27 F4
Ayora 75 E1
Ayr 20 B3
Aysgarth 21 D1
Ayton 21 D4
Aytos 115 E1
Ayvacik 119 D1
Ayvalik 119 D1
Azaila 69 F1
Azambuja 78 A3
Azay-le-Rideau 54 A1
Azinheira dos Barros 78 B1
Azpeitia 69 D4
Azuaga 79 E1
Azuga 108 C1
Azzano Decimo 91 D2

B

Baad 85 E3
Baale Nassau 29 D1
Baale Nassau 29 D1
Baamonde 66 C3
Baamonde 66 C3
Baar 46 B3
Baarn 29 D2
Baarn 29 D2
Babadag 115 F4
Babebski 119 E4
Babenhausen 41 D2
Babenhausen 46 A2
Băbeni 114 B4
Babigoszcz 35 E3
Babin Potok 110 B4
Babina Greda 111 E4
Babušnica 113 D2
Bać 106 B1
Bacău 109 D2
Baccarat 56 C3
Baccarat 56 C3
Băcesti 109 D3
Bacharach 40 B2
Bacharach 40 B2
Bachkovo 118 C4
Bachuovo 118 C4
Bačka Palanka 106 B1
Bačka Topola 106 B1
Backaland 19 F1
Bäckebo 13 F3
Bäckefors 9 E1
Bäckhammar 9 F1
Bački Breg 105 E1
Backnang 45 D3
Bačko Gradište 106 B1
Bačko Petrovo Selo 106 B1
Bacoli 100 A3
Bacquerville-en-Caux 49 F2
Bácsalmas 106 B2
Bácsbokod 105 E2
Bacton 25 F4
Baczyna 35 F1
Bad Abbach 46 C2
Bad Aibling 46 C2
Bad Aussee 86 C2
Bad Bentheim 36 B3
Bad Bergzabern 44 C3
Bad Berka 42 B3
Bad Berleburg 40 C4
Bad Berneck 42 C2
Bad Bertrich 40 B2
Bad Bevensen 33 E2
Bad Bibra 38 C1
Bad Blankenburg 42 B3
Bad Bramstedt 33 D3
Bad Breisig 40 B3
Bad Brückenau 41 D3
Bad Buchau 45 D2
Bad Doberan 34 C3
Bad Driburg 37 D2
Bad Düben 39 D2
Bad Dürkheim 40 C1
Bad Durrenberg 38 C2
Bad Dürrheim 44 C2
Bad Elster 42 C3
Bad Ems 40 B3
Bad Essen 36 C3
Bad Frankenhausen 38 B2
Bad Freienwalde 35 E1
Bad Friedrichshall 45 D4
Bad Gandersheim 37 E2
Bad Gleichenberg 87 E1
Bad Godesberg 40 B3
Bad Goisern 86 C2
Bad Gottleuba 43 E4
Bad Grund 37 E2
Bad Hall 86 C3
Bad Harzburg 37 E2
Bad Herrenalb 44 C3
Bad Hersfeld 4 D3
Bad Hofgastein 86 B2
Bad Homburg 40 C2
Bad Honnef 40 B3
Bad Hönnigen 40 B3
Bad Iburg 36 C3
Bad Ischl 86 C3
Bad Kissingen 41 E2
Bad Kleinen 34 B3
Bad König 41 D2
Bad Königshofen 41 E3
Bad Kösen 38 C1
Bad Kreuznach 40 C2
Bad Krozingen 44 B2
Bad Langensalza 38 B1
Bad Lauchstädt 38 C2
Bad Lausick 39 D1
Bad Lauterberg 37 E2
Bad Leonfelden 86 C4
Bad Liebenstein 41 E3
Bad Liebenwerda 39 D2
Bad Liebenzell 44 C3
Bad Lippspringe 37 D2
Bad Marienberg 40 C3
Bad Meinberg 37 D2
Bad Mergentheim 41 D1
Bad Mitterndorf 86 C2
Bad Münder 37 D3
Bad Münster Ebernberg 40 C2
Bad Münstereifel 40 B3
Bad Muskau 390 F2
Bad Nenndorf 37 D3
Bad Neuenahr 40 B3
Bad Neustadt 41 E3
Bad Oeynhausen 37 D3
Bad Oldesloe 33 E3
Bad Orb 41 D2
Bad Peterstal 44 C2
Bad Pyrmont 37 D3
Bad Ragaz 85 D2
Bad Reichenhall 47 D1
Bad Rippoldsau 44 C2
Bad Rothenfelde 36 C3
Bad Saarow-Pieskow 39
Bad Sachsa 37 E2
Bad Salzdetfurth 37 E3
Bad Salzuflen 36 C3
Bad Salzungen 41 E3
Bad Schallerbach 86 C3
Bad Schandau 43 E4
Bad Schmiederberg 39 D2
Bad Schönau 87 E3
Bad Schönborn 44 C4
Bad Schussenried 45 D2
Bad Schwalbach 40 C2
Bad Schwartau 33 E3
Bad Segeberg 33 E3
Bad St Leonhard 87 D1
Bad Sülze 34 C3
Bad Tennstedt 34 C3
Bad Tölz 46 C1
Bad Urach 45 D3
Bad Voslau 87 E3
Bad Waldsee 45 D2
Bad Wiessee 46 C1
Bad Wildungen 37 D1
Bad Wilsnack 34 C1
Bad Wimpfen 45 D4
Bad Windsheim 41 E1
Bad Wörishofen 46 B2
Bad Wurzach 45 E2
Bad Zwischenahn 32 C2
Bad-Spoden-Allendorf 37 E1
Badacsonytömaj 105 D3
Badajoz 79 D3
Badalona 71 D2
Baden 84 C3
Baden 87 E3
Baden(Laufenburg) 44 C1
Baden(Rheinfelden) 44 B1
Baden-Baden 44 C3
Badenweiler 44 B1
Baderna 91 E1
Badgastein 86 B2
Badia Polésine 90 C1
Badia Tedalda 95 D2
Badljevina 105 D1
Badminton 27 E3
Badonviller 56 C3
Bækmarksbro 12 A3
Baena 80 A2
Baeza 80 B3
Bågede 3 F3
Bagenkop 12 B1
Bagheria 102 B3
Bagn 8 C3
Bagnacavallo 940 C3
Bagnara Calabra 103 E4
Bagnères-de-Bigorre 62 C2
Bagnères-de-Luchon 62 C1
Bagni di Lucca 93 E2
Bagni di Masino 89 D3
Bagno di Romagna 94 C2
Bagnoles-de-l'Orne 53 E3
Bagnolo Mella 89 E2
Bagnols-en-Forêt 69 E2
Bagnols-les-Bains 64 B4
Bagnols-sur-Cèze 64 C3
Bågø 12 B1
Bagodvitenyéd 104 C3
Bagolino 89 E2
Bagshot 25 D2
Báia Domízia 98 C1
Baia de Criş 107 E2
Baia Mare 107 E4
Báia Sardínia 96 C4
Baia Sprie 107 E4
Baiano 100 B4
Băicoi 114 C4
Baiersbronn 44 C3
Baigneux-les-Juifs 55 E2
Băile Felix 107 D3
Băile Govora 114 B4
Băile Herculane 113 D4
Băile Olănesti 114 B4
Baile Tuşnad 108 C2
Bailén 80 B3
Băileşti 113 E3
Bailieborough 15 D1
Bailivanish 18 A3
Bailleul 50 B4
Bain-de-Bretagne 53 D2
Bains-les-Bains 56 B3
Bainton 21 F1
Baio 66 B4
Bais 53 E3
Baişeşti 108 C3
Băişoara 107 E2
Baix 60 C1
Baixas 63 F1
Baja 105 E2
Bajánsenye 104 C3
Bajina Bašta 112 B3
Bajmok 106 B1
Bajša 106 B1
Bajzë 112 B1
Bak 104 C3
Bakar 104 A1
Bakewell 23 D3
Bakio 68 C4
Bakke 119 F3
Bakonygyepes 105 D3
Bakonypeterd 105 D3
Bakonysárkány 105 E3
Bakonyszombatheley 105 E3
Baks 106 B2
Baktalórántháza 107 D4
Baktaték 106 C4
Bala 22 C2
Bălăbăneşti 109 E2
Bălăceanu 109 D1
Balaci 114 C3
Balaguer 70 B3
Balallan 18 B4
Balanegra 80 C1
Bălăneşti 114 B3
Balassagyarmat 106 B4
Balástya 106 B2
Balatonakali 105 D3
Balatonalmádi 105 D3
Balatonboglar 105 D3
Balatonederics 105 D3
Balatonföldvár 105 D3
Balatonfüred 105 D3
Balatonfüzfö 105 E3
Balatonkenese 105 E3
Balatonkeres 105 D3
Balatonlelle 105 D3
Balatonszemes 105 D3
Bălăuşeri 108 B2
Balazote 75 D1
Balbeggie 19 D1
Balbigny 60 B3
Balbriggan 17 E4
Bălceşti 114 B3
Balchik 115 E2
Baldersby 21 E1
Balderschwang 45 E1
Baldock 25 D3
Bale 104 A1
Balestrand 8 B4
Balfour 19 F1
Balikesir 119 F1
Balikliçeşme 119 E2
Bälinge 13 D2
Balingen 45 D2
Balintore 19 D3
Balíon 122 B4
Balkány 107 D4
Balla 16 B4
Ballaban 116 C2
Ballachulish 18 C1
Ballacolla 17 D3
Ballaghaderreen 14 B1
Ballantrae 20 B3
Ballao 96 B2
Ballasalla 20 B1
Ballater 19 E2
Ballaugh 20 B1
Ballen 12 B1
Ballenstedt 38 B2
Balleroy 49 D1
Ballerup 12 C2
Balli 119 E3
Ballina 16 C3
Ballina 14 B1
Ballinafad 14 C1
Ballinagh 15 D1
Ballinakill 17 D3
Ballinalee 17 D4
Ballinamallard 14 C2
Ballinamore 16 C4
Ballinamore 14 C1
Ballinascarty 16 B1
Ballinasloe 16 C3
Ballindine 16 B4
Ballineen 16 B1
Ballingarry 16 B2
Ballingarry 17 D2
Ballingeary 16 B1
Ballinhassig 16 C1
Ballinlough 16 C4
Ballinluig 19 D1
Ballinrobe 16 B4
Ballinspittle 16 C1
Ballintober 16 C4
Ballivor 17 D4
Balllintra 14 C2
Ballobar 70 A2
Balloch 20 B4
Ballon 17 D2
Ballon 53 F3
Ballum 12 A1
Ballybaun 16 C3
Ballybay 15 D1
Ballybofey 14 C2
Ballybunion 16 B2
Ballycanew 17 E2
Ballycarry 15 E2
Ballycastle 15 E3
Ballycastle 14 B2
Ballyclare 15 E2
Ballyconneely 16 A4
Ballycotton 16 C1
Ballycumber 17 D3
Ballydehob 16 B1
Ballydesmond 16 B2
Ballyduff 16 C1
Ballyduff 16 B2
Ballyfarnan 14 C1
Ballygalley 15 E2
Ballygar 16 C4
Ballygawley 15 D2
Ballygowan 15 E2
Ballyhaise 15 D1
Ballyhale 17 D2
Ballyhaunis 16 C4
Ballyhean 16 B4
Ballyheige 16 B2
Ballyjamesduff 17 D4
Ballykeeran 16 C3
Ballylanders 16 C2
Ballylongford 16 B2
Ballylooby 16 C2
Ballylynan 17 D3
Ballymahon 17 D4
Ballymakeery 16 B1
Ballymaloe 16 C1
Ballymena 15 E2
Ballymoe 16 C4
Ballymoney 15 D3
Ballymore 17 D4
Ballymore Eustace 17 E3
Ballymote 14 C1
Ballynahinch 15 E2
Ballynure 15 E2
Ballyragget 17 D2
Ballyroan 17 D3
Ballyronan 15 D2
Ballysadare 14 C1
Ballyshannon 14 C2
Ballyvaughan 16 B3
Ballywalter 15 E2
Balmaseda 68 C4
Balmara 20 B4
Balmazújváros 106 C4
Balme 88 A2
Balmúccia 88 B2
Balneario de Panticosa 69 F3
Balquhidder 18 C1
Balrothery 17 E4
Balş 114 B3
Balş 109 D3
Balsareny 70 C3
Bålsta 10 C2
Balsthal 84 B3
Balta 109 F4
Baltanás 68 B2
Baltasound 19 F4
Băltăteşti 109 D3
Balţaţi 109 D3
Bălţaţii de Sus 113 E3
Baltimore 16 B1
Baltinglass 17 D3
Baltrum 32 B3
Balvan 114 C1
Balya 119 E1
Bamberg 42 B2
Bamburgh 21 E4
Bampton 27 D2
Bampton 24 C2
Bana 105 D4
Banagher 16 C3
Banarli 119 E3
Banatski Karlovac 112 C4
Banatsko Karadjordjevo 106 C1
Banatsko Novo Selo 112 C4
Banavie 18 C2
Banbridge 15 E2
Banbury 27 F4
Banchory 19 E2
Bande 66 C2
Bandholm 12 C1
Bandirma 119 F2
Bandol 65 D2
Bandon 16 C1
Băneasa 115 D3
Băneasa 115 E3
Banff 19 E3
Bangor 22 B3
Bangor 15 E2
Bangor 52 B2
Bangor Erris 14 A1
Bangor-on-Dee 22 C2
Bangsund 3 D3
Banham 25 E3
Banie 35 E2
Băniţa 107 E1
Banja 112 B2
Banja Koviljača 111 E3
Banja Luka 111 D4
Banjska 112 C2
Bankeryd 13 D4
Bannalec 52 B3
Banon 65 D3
Baños de la Encina 80 B3
Baños de Montemayor 73 E2
Banréve 106 C4
Bansha 16 C2
Bansin 35 E3
Bansko 118 A4
Banteer 16 B1
Bantry 16 B1
Banwell 27 D3
Banya 115 D1
Banya 114 C1
Banya 115 D1
Banya 115 E1
Banyalbufar 77 D3
Banyoles 71 D3
Bapaume 50 B3
Bar 116 B4
Bar-le-Duc 56 A4
Bar-sur-Aube 55 F3
Bar-sur-Seine 55 E3
Bărăgunal 115 E4
Barahona 68 C1
Barajas 74 B3
Barajas de Melo 74 C3
Barand 106 C3
Baraolt 108 C2
Baraqueville 63 F3
Barban 104 A1
Barbaros 19 E3
Barbaste 62 C3
Barbastro 70 A3
Barbate 83 E1
Barbezieux 58 C2
Barbing 46 C3
Barbizon 54 C3
Barbotan 62 C3
Barca de Alva 73 D3
Barcellona 103 E3
Barcelona 71 D2
Barcelonnette 65 E4
Barcelos 72 B4
Bárcena de Pie de Concha 68 B4
Barchfeld 41 E3
Bárcis 91 D3
Barco de Valdeorras 67 D2
Barcs 105 D2
Bardi 93 D3
Bardney 23 F3
Bardolino 90 B2
Bardowick 33 E2
Bareiro 78 A2
Barenburg 37 D4
Barentin 49 F2
Barenton 53 E4
Barfleur 48 C2
Barga 93 E3
Bargoed 27 D3
Bargteheide 33 E3
Bari 101 D4
Bari Sardo 96 B3
Barisciano 98 C3
Barjac 64 C4
Barjols 65 D2
Barkald 9 D4
Barlborough 23 E3
Barletta 99 F1
Barley 25 E3
Barlinek 35 F2
Barmby-on-the-Moor 21 E1
Barmouth 22 B2
Barmstedt 33 D3
Barnard Castle 21 D2
Bärnau 43 D2
Barneberg 38 B3
Barneveld 29 E2
Barneville-Carteret 48 C2
Barnewitz 39 D4
Barnoldswick 21 D1
Barnsley 23 D3
Barnstaple 26 C2
Barnstorf 36 C4
Barnton 20 C4
Barntrup 37 D3
Barr 20 B3
Barr 56 C3
Barraco 74 A3
Barrafranca 102 C2
Barranco do Velho 82 B3
Barrancos 79 D1
Barrax 75 D1
Barre-des-Cévennes 64 B3
Barrea 98 C2
Barrême 65 E3
Barrhill 20 B3
Barrow in Furness 20 C1
Barrow-on-Soar 23 E2
Barry 27 D3
Barryporeen 16 C2
Barssel 32 C2
Barth 35 D4
Barton Mills 25 E3
Barton-on-Humber 23 E3
Baru 107 E1
Barúmini 96 B2
Baruth 39 D3
Barvas 18 B3
Barver 36 C4
Barzio 89 D2
Bašaid 106 C1
Basdahl 33 D2
Basel 84 B3
Basildon 25 E2
Basingstoke 27 F3
Baška 110 A4
Baška Oštarije 110 B3
Baška Voda 110 C2
Bassano del Grappa 90 C2
Bassella 70 C3
Bassenthwaite 20 C2
Bassum 32 C1
Båstad 13 D2
Bastelica 57 F2
Bastia 57 F3
Bastogne 31 E2
Baston 23 F2
Bastuträsk 4 B3
Batajnica 112 C4
Batak 118 B4
Batalha 78 B4
Batăr 107 D2
Bátaszék 105 E2
Baté 105 D2
Bath 27 E3
Bathgate 20 C4
Batina 105 E1
Bátka 106 B4
Batnfjordsøra 2 B1
Batočina 112 C3
Bátovce 105 E4
Batsí 121 E3
Battenberg 40 C4
Battice 31 E3
Battipáglia 100 B3
Battle 25 E1
Batultsi 114 B1
Batz 52 C2
Baud 52 B3
Baugé 53 F2
Baugy 54 C1
Baúlhe 72 C4
Baume-les-Dames 56 B2
Baumholder 40 B1
Baunei 96 C2
Bautzen 39 E2
Bavanište 112 C4
Bavay 50 C3
Baveno 88 C2
Bavorov 47 E4
Bawdeswell 25 E4
Bawdsey 25 F3
Bawtry 23 E3
Baycliffe 20 C1
Bayerisch Eisenstein 47 D4
Bayeux 49 D2
Baykal 114 B2
Bayon 56 B3
Bayonne 62 A2
Bayramiç 119 D1
Bayreuth 42 C2
Bayrischzell 46 C1
Baza 80 C2
Bazas 62 C4
Bazna 108 B2
Bazoches-sur-Hoëne 54 A3
Bazzano 94 B3
Beaconsfield 25 D2
Beadnell 21 E3
Beal 21 D4
Béal Átha an Ghaorfthaidh (Ballingeary) 16 B1
Béal an Mhuirhead (Belmullet) 14 A2
Beaminster 27 D2
Beasain 69 D4
Beattock 20 C3
Beaucaire 64 C3
Beaufort 16 B1
Beaufort 61 E3
Beaufort-en-Vallée 53 E2
Beaugency 54 B2
Beaulieu 27 F2
Beaulieu 65 F3
Beaulieu-sur-Dordogne 59 E1
Beauly 18 C3
Beaumaris 22 B3
Beaumes-de-Venise 64 C3
Beaumesnil 49 E1
Beaumetz 14 B3
Beaumont 59 D1
Beaumont 48 C2
Beaumont 30 C2
Beaumont le Roger 49 E1
Beaumont-de-Lomagne 63 D3
Beaumont-sur-Sarthe 53 F3
Beaune 55 F1
Beaune-la-Rolande 54 C3
Beaupréau 53 D1
Beauraing 31 D2
Beaurepaire 60 C2
Beaurepaire-en-Bresse 61 D4
Beauvais 50 A2
Beauvallon 65 E2
Beauvezer 65 E3
Beauvoir 52 C1
Beauvoir-sur-Niort 58 B3
Bebington 22 C3
Bebra 41 D4
Bebrovo 115 D1
Beccles 25 F3
Bečej 106 B1
Beceni 109 D1
Becerreá 67 D3
Bécherel 53 D3
Bechetu 114 B2
Bechhofen 46 B4

Becicherecu Mic

Borgosesia

Becicherecu Mic 106 C1
Becilla de Valderaduey 67 F2
Beciu 114 B3
Beckenried 84 C2
Beckhampton 27 E3
Beckington 27 E3
Beckum 36 C2
Beckum 36 C2
Beclean 108 B3
Becov nad Tepbu 43 D2
Becsehely 104 C2
Bedale 21 E1
Bédarieux 64 A2
Beddgelert 22 B2
Beddingestrand 13 D1
Bédée 53 D3
Bederkesa 33 D2
Bedford 23 E1
Bedlington 21 E3
Bedonia 93 D3
Bedous 62 B2
Bedsted 12 A3
Bedworth 23 E1
Bedzino 35 F4
Beeford 21 F1
Beek 31 E3
Beek en Donk 29 E1
Beelitz 39 D3
Beer 27 D2
Beerfelden 41 D1
Beeskow 39 E3
Beesten 36 B3
Beetham 21 D1
Beg-Meil 52 A3
Bégard 52 B4
Begndalen 9 D3
Beguildy 22 C1
Begunitsy 7 F1
Begur 71 E3
Béhobie 62 A2
Behramkale 119 D1
Behringersmühle 42 C2
Beilen 29 F3
Beilngries 46 C3
Beith 20 B4
Beitostølen 8 C4
Beiuş 107 D2
Beja 78 C1
Béjar 73 E2
Békés 106 C2
Békéscsaba 106 C2
Békésszentandrás 106 C3
Bela Crkya 113 D4
Bela Palanka 113 D2
Bělá pod Bezdězem 43 F3
Bélâbre 59 D4
Belalcázar 79 F2
Belcaire 63 E1
Belchin 113 E1
Belchite 69 F1
Belcoo 14 C2
Belecké 36 C2
Beled 105 D4
Belene 114 C2
Belfast 15 E2
Belfir 107 D2
Belford 21 D3
Belfort 56 C2
Belgern 39 D2
Belgirate 88 C2
Belgodère 57
Belgooly 16 C1
Beli Manastir 105 E1
Belimel 113 E2
Belin-Béliet 62 B4
Belintę 107 D1
Beliş 107 E2
Belitsa 118 A4
Beliu 107 D2
Beljina 112 C4
Bellabayis (Bellapais) 122 B2
Bellac 59 D3
Bellaghy 15 D2
Bellagio 89 D3
Bellano 89 D3
Bellária 95 D3
Belle-Isle-en-Terre 52 B4
Belleek 14 C2
Bellegarde 54 C2
Bellegarde 61 D3
Bellegarde-en-Marche 59 E3
Bellême 54 A3
Bellencombre 49 F2
Belleville 60 C3
Belleville-sur-Vie 58 A4
Belley 61 D3
Bellinge 12 B1
Bellingham 21 D3
Bellinzona 84 C1
Bellmullet (Béal an Mhuirhead) 14 A2
Bellochantuy 15 E3
Bellpuig 70 B2
Belluno 91 D3
Bellver de Cerdanya 70 C4
Belmont-sur-Rance 63 F3
Belmonte 74 C2
Belmonte 67 E4
Belmonte 72 C2
Belœil 30 C3
Belogradchik 113 E2
Belojin 112 C2
Belorado 68 C2
Belota 113 E4
Belova 118 B4
Belpasso 103 D2
Belper 23 D2
Belsay 21 D3
Belsen (Hohne) 37 E4
Beltinci 104 C2
Beltiug 107 E3
Beltsy 109 E4
Belturbet 15 D1
Belvedere Marittima 100 C2
Belvès 59 D1
Belz 52 B3
Belzig 39 D3
Bembibre 67 E2
Bembridge 27 F2
Bemposta 73 D3
Benabarre 70 B3
Benalmádena 80 A1
Benalmádena Costa 80 A1
Benasque 70 B4
Benátky nad Jizera 43 F3
Benavente 67 E1
Benavente 78 A3
Benburb 15 D2
Bendery 109 F3
Benediktbeuern 46 C1
Benesat 107 E3
Benešov 43 F2
Benešov nad Ploučnici 43 E3
Bénévent l'Abbaye 59 E3
Benevento 99 D1
Benfeld 57 D3
Bengeşti 113 E4
Bengtsfors 9 E1
Beničanci 105 E1
Benicarló 76 B4
Benicasím 76 A4
Benidorm 76 A1
Benissa 76 A1
Benitses 116 C1
Benkovac 110 B3
Benllech Bay 22 B3
Benneckenstein 38 B2
Bennetsbridge 17 D2
Bennstedt 38 C2
Bénodet 52 A3
Bensafrim 82 A3
Bensberg 40 B4
Bensersiel 32 B2
Bensheim 40 C2
Benson 27 F3
Bentley 25 D1
Benwick 23 F2
Beocin 112 B4
Beograd 112 C4
Beragh 15 D2
Berat 116 C3
Berberana 68 B4
Bercedo 68 B4
Bercel 106 B4
Berceto 93 D3
Berching 46 C4
Berchtesgaden 47 D1
Berck-Plage 50 A3
Bere Ferrers 26 C1
Bere Regis 27 E2
Berechiu 107 D2
Beregomet 108 C4
Beregovo 107 D4
Beregsurány 107 D4
Bereni 108 C2
Berettyóújfalu 107 D3
Berezeni 109 E2
Berg 46 C2
Berg 87 F3
Berg 3 E4
Berg 9 E3
Berga 70 C3
Berga 13 F3
Berga 38 B2
Bergama 119 E1
Bergamo 89 D2
Bergara 69 D4
Bergby 10 B3
Berge-Neustadt 40 B4
Bergedorf 33 E2
Bergeforsen 4 A1
Bergen 31 D3
Bergen 33 E1
Bergen 34 B1
Bergen 8 A3
Bergen 35 D4
Bergen (Mons) 30 C3
Bergen aan Zee 29 D3
Bergen op Zoom 29 C1
Berger 9 D2
Bergerac 58 C1
Bergheim 40 A4
Bergisch Gladbach 40 B4
Bergkvara 13 F2
Berglern 46 C2
Bergnäset 4 C4
Bergö 4 C1
Bergshamra 10 C2
Bergsjö 10 C4
Bergstrøm 9 D2
Bergsviken 4 C4
Bergues 50 B4
Bergum 29 E4
Bergün 84 D2
Bergvik 10 B3
Beringen 31 E4
Berja 80 C1
Berkåk 2 C1
Berkeley 27 E3
Berkenthin 33 E3
Berkesz 107 D4
Berkhamsted 25 D2
Berkheim 45 E2
Berkhof 37 D4
Berkovići 111 D1
Berkovitsa 113 E2
Berlanga 79 E2
Berlin Ost 39 D4
Berlin West 39 D4
Berlingen 84 C3
Bermeo 68 C4
Bermillo de Sayago 79 E3
Bern 84 B3
Bernalda 101 D3
Bernatice 43 F1
Bernau 47 D2
Bernau 39 D4
Bernaville 50 B3
Bernay 49 E1
Bernburg 38 C2
Berndorf 87 E3
Berne 32 C2
Bernhardsthal 87 F4
Bernisdale 18 B3
Bernkastel-Kues 40 B2
Bernsdorf 39 E2
Bernstein 87 E2
Beromünster 84 C3
Beronovo 115 D1
Beroun 43 E2
Berovo 117 F4
Berres 65 D2
Berriew 22 C2
Bersenbrück 36 C4
Bertinoro 95 D3
Bertrix 31 D2
Berwang 85 E3
Berwick- upon-Tweed 21 D4
Berzasca 113 D4
Berzovia 107 D1
Besalú 71 D3
Besançon 56 B1
Besande 68 A3
Besenyszög 106 B3
Besigheim 45 D3
Bessan 64 B2
Besse-en-Chandesse 60 A2
Besse-sur-Issole 65 E2
Bessheim 8 C4
Bessines-sur-Gartempe 59 D3
Beştepe 115 F4
Bestida 72 B3
Betanzos 66 C4
Betelu 69 D3
Beteta 75 D3
Bethersden 25 E1
Bethesda 22 B2
Betna 2 C2
Béthune 50 B3
Bettna 10 B1
Bettola 93 D4
Bettyhill 19 D4
Betws-y-Coed 22 B2
Betz 50 B1
Betzdorf 40 C3
Beuel 40 B3
Beuil 65 F3
Beulah 27 D4
Beuron 45 D2
Beuzeville 49 E2
Bevagna 98 B4
Beveren-Waas 31 D4
Beverley 23 E4
Beverstedt 33 D2
Beverungen 37 D2
Beverwijk 29 D3
Bewdley 23 D1
Bex 84 A1
Bexhill 25 E1
Beynac-et-Cazenac 59 D1
Beynat 59 E2
Bezau 85 D3
Bezdan 105 E1
Béziers 64 A2
Béznar 80 B1
Bianco 103 F3
Biarritz 62 A2
Bias 62 A1
Biasca 84 C1
Biatorbágy 105 E3
Bibbiena 94 C2
Biberach 44 C2
Biberach an der Riss 45 E2
Bibione 91 E2
Biborţeni 108 C2
Bibury 27 E3
Bicaj 116 C4
Bicaz 109 D3
Bicester 27 F4
Bichl 46 C1
Bickleigh 27 D2
Bicske 105 E3
Bidache 62 B2
Bidart 62 A2
Biddenden 25 E1
Biddulph 23 D2
Bideford 26 C2
Bidford-on-Avon 23 D1
Bieber 41 D2
Biebersdorf 39 E3
Biedenkopf 40 C4
Biel (Bienne) 84 B3
Bielefeld 36 C3
Biella 88 B2
Bielsa 70 A4
Bienenbüttel 33 E2
Bienne (Biel) 84 B3
Bienvenida 79 E2
Bierre-Lès-Semur 55 E2
Biertan 108 D2
Bierzwnik 35 F2
Biescas 69 F3
Biesenthal 35 E1
Bietigheim 45 D3
Biga 119 E2
Bigadiç 119 F1
Bigbury-on-Sea 26 C1
Biggar 20 C1
Biggar 21 C4
Biggleswade 25 D3
Bignasco 84 C1
Bihać 110 B4
Biharea 107 D3
Biharkeresztes 107 D3
Biharnagybajom 106 C3
Bijeljani 111 D1
Bijeljina 111 E3
Bijelo Polje 112 B2
Bilbao (Bilbo) 68 C4
Bilbo (Bilbao) 68 C4
Bilbster 19 D4
Bileća 111 E1
Biled 106 C1
Bilina 43 E3
Bilisht 117 D2
Biljanovac 112 C2
Billerbeck 36 B3
Billericay 25 E2
Billingham 21 E2
Billinghay 23 F2
Billingsfors 9 E1
Billingshurst 25 D1
Billom 60 A1
Billund 12 A2
Biña 105 E4
Binas 54 B2
Binasco 88 C2
Binche 30 C2
Binéfar 70 A3
Bingen 40 C2
Bingley 23 D4
Binic 32 C4
Binz 35 D4
Bioce 111 E1
Biograd 110 B3
Bioska 112 B3
Birca 113 E3
Birchington 25 F2
Birchiş 107 D1
Birdlip 27 E4
Birgham 21 D4
Bîrghiş 108 B1
Biri 9 D3
Birkeland 8 B1
Birkenfeld 40 B1
Birkenhead 22 C3
Birkenwerder 39 D4
Birkerød 12 C2
Birksdal 8 B4
Bîrlad 109 E2
Birmingham 23 D1
Birnam 19 D1
Birnau 45 D1
Birr 16 C3
Bîrsana 108 B4
Bîrseşti 113 E4
Birtley 21 E2
Bîrzava 107 D2
Biscarrosse 62 B4
Biscarrosse-Plage 62 A4
Bisceglie 99 F1
Bischofsgrün 42 C2
Bischofsheim 41 E3
Bischofswerda 39 E1
Bishop Auckland 21 E2
Bishop's Castle 22 C1
Bishop's Cleeve 27 E4
Bishop's Lydeard 27 D2
Bishop's Stortford 25 E2
Bishop's Waltham 27 F2
Bishopton 20 B4
Bismark 38 C4
Bismo 8 C4
Bispfors 4 A1
Bispgården 4 A1
Bispingen 33 E2
Bistra 107 E2
Bistret 113 E3
Bistrica 112 B2
Bistriţa 108 B3
Bistritsa 113 E1
Bitburg 40 A2
Bitche 56 C4
Bitetto 101 D4
Bitola 117 D3
Bitonto 101 D4
Bitterfeld 38 C2
Bitti 96 B3
Bivolari 109 E3
Bivona 102 B2
Bizovac 105 E1
Bjåen 8 B2
Bjärnum 13 D2
Bjästa 4 B1
Bjelovar 104 C2
Bjerkreim 8 A1
Bjerringbro 12 B2
Bjølstad 8 C4
Bjørbo 10 A3
Bjørkelangen 9 D2
Bjørkfläta 8 C3
Björkfors 3 F4
Björkling 10 C2
Björkö 11 D3
Björköby 4 C2
Björksele 4 B3
Bjørn 3 E4
Björna 4 B2
Björneborg 9 F1
Björnlunda 10 C1
Björnsholm 13 F4
Bjorvsvik 8 A3
Bjuråker 10 B4
Bjurberget 9 E3
Bjurholm 4 B2
Bjursås 10 B3
Bjuv 13 D2
Blace 112 C2
Blackburn 23 D3
Blackford 19 D1
Blacklion 14 C1
Blackmoor Gate 26 C2
Blackpool 22 C4
Blackstad 13 F4
Blackwater 17 E2
Blackwaterfoot 15 E3
Bladon 27 F4
Blaenau Ffestiniog 22 B2
Blaenavon 27 D3
Blaengarw 27 D3
Blagaj 111 D2
Blagdon 27 D3
Blagoevgrad 117 F4
Blagoevo 115 D2
Blaiken 4 A4
Blain 53 D2
Blair Atholl 19 D1
Blairgowrie 19 D1
Blaj 108 B2
Blâjel 108 B2
Blakeney 27 E3
Blakeney 25 E4
Blakstad 8 C1
Blâmont 56 C4
Blanchland 21 D2
Blandford Forum 27 E2
Blanefield 20 B4
Blanes 71 D3
Blangy 50 A3
Blankenberge 28 B1
Blankenburg 38 B2
Blankenfelde 39 D3
Blankenhain 42 B3
Blankenheim 40 A3
Blanzac 58 C2
Blarney 16 C1
Blatnà 43 E1
Blato 110 C1
Blato 110 C2
Blattnicksele 4 A4
Blaubeuren 45 E2
Blaufelden 45 E4
Blaustein 45 E2
Blåvand 12 A2
Blaye 58 B2
Bleckede 34 B2
Bled 104 A2
Bleddfa 22 C1
Bleiburg 87 D1
Bleicherode 38 B2
Blejeşti 114 C3
Blendija 113 D2
Bléneau 55 D2
Blérancourt 50 C2
Bléré 54 B1
Blériot-Plage 50 A4
Blessington 17 E3
Bletchley 25 D3
Bletterans 61 D4
Blewbury 27 F3
Blexen 32 C2
Bliekastel 44 B4
Bligny 55 F1
Blîndeşti 109 D4
Blinisht 116 C4
Blinja 104 C1
Blisworth 23 E1
Bliznak 115 E2
Blois 54 B2
Blokhus 12 B3
Blokzijl 29 E2
Blomberg 37 D3
Blomstermåla 13 F3
Bloška Polica 104 A2
Bloxham 27 F4
Blubberhouses 21 E1
Bludenz 85 D3
Blumberg 44 C1
Blyth 21 E3
Blythe Bridge 23 D2
Blyton 23 E3
Bø 8 C2
Boal 67 D4
Boário Terme 89 E2
Boat of Garten 19 D2
Bobbio 93 D4
Bobingen 46 B2
Bobitz 34 B3
Böblingen 45 D3
Bobrowice 39 F3
Bobuleşti 109 D4
Boceguillas 68 B1
Bocholt 36 A2
Bochum 36 B2
Bochum-Hövel 36 C2
Bockenem 37 E3
Böckstein 86 B2
Bocognano 57 F2
Bócsa 106 B2
Bocşa 107 D1
Bocşa Vasiovei 107 D1
Bocsig 107 D2
Bøda 13 F3
Boda 10 B3
Bodafors 13 E3
Boddam 19 F3
Bodegraven 29 D2
Boden 4 C4
Bodenmais 47 D4
Bodenteich 33 E1
Bodenwerder 37 D3
Bodenwöhr 47 D4
Bodesti 109 D3
Bodman 45 D1
Bodmin 26 C1
Bodon 3 D2
Bodrogkeresztúr 106 C4
Bodträskfors 4 C4
Boëge 61 E3
Boën 60 B3
Bogatic 112 B4
Bogatynia 43 F4
Boğaz (Boghaz) 122 C2
Bogdand 107 E3
Bogdâneşti 109 D2
Bogdaniec 35 F1
Bogen 47 D3
Bogense 12 B2
Bogetići 111 E1
Bognor Regis 25 D1
Bogø 12 C1
Bogojevo 105 E1
Bogorodica 117 E3
Bograngen 9 E3
Bogutovac 112 C2
Bohain-en-Vermandois 50 C3
Boherbue 16 B2
Bohinjska Bistrica 104 A2
Böhmenkirch 45 E3
Bohmte 36 C3
Boholm 13 E4
Böhönye 105 D2
Boiano 99 D2
Boichinovtsi 113 E2
Boitzenburg 35 D2
Boizenburg 34 B2
Bøjden 12 B1
Bol 110 C2
Bolayir 119 D2
Bolbec 49 E2
Boldon 21 E3
Boldu 109 E1
Bolemin 35 F1
Boleszkowice 35 E1
Boliden 4 C3
Bolintin Vale 114 C3
Boljanići 111 E2
Boljevac 113 D3
Bolkesjø 8 C2
Bollebygd 13 D4
Bollène 64 C4
Bollington 23 D3
Bollnäs 10 B4
Bollstabruk 4 A1
Bolney 25 D1
Bologna 94 C3
Bologne 56 A3
Bolótana 96 B3
Boloteşti 109 D1
Bolsena 98 A3
Bolsover 23 E3
Bolsward 29 E4
Boltaña 70 A4
Boltenhagen 34 B3
Boltigen 84 B2
Bolton 23 D3
Bolton Abbey 21 D1
Bolton Bridge 21 D1
Bolton-le-Sands 21 D1
Bóly 105 E1
Bolyarovo 119 D4
Bolzano-Bozen 90 C3
Bomarsund 11 D2
Bombarrel 78 A3
Bonaduz 85 D2
Boñar 67 F3
Bonar Bridge 18 C3
Bonassola 93 D3
Bonchester Bridge 21 D3
Bondal 8 C2
Bondeno 94 C4
Bonefro 99 E2
Bonete 75 E1
Bonifacio 57 F1
Bonlieu 61 D4
Bonn 40 B3
Bonnat 59 E3
Bonndorf 44 C1
Bønnerup Strand 12 C3
Bonnétable 54 A3
Bonneval 61 E2
Bonneval 54 B3
Bonneville 61 E3
Bonnières 50 A1
Bonnieux 65 D3
Bonny-sur-Loire 55 D2
Bonnyrigg 20 C4
Bono 96 B3
Bonorva 96 B3
Bont Newydd 22 B2
Bonyhád 105 E2
Boom 31 D3
Boos 49 F2
Boot 20 C2
Booth of Toft 19 F4
Bootle 20 C1
Bootle 22 C3
Bopfingen 45 E3
Boppard 40 B2
Bor 113 D3
Bor 43 D2
Borås 13 D4
Borba 78 C2
Borbona 98 B3
Borca 108 C3
Borchen 36 C2
Borculo 29 F2
Bordany 106 B2
Bordeaux 58 B1
Bordeira 82 A3
Bordères 62 C1
Bordesholm 33 E3
Bordighera 92 B2
Borduşani 115 E3
Borensberg 10 B1
Borgå (Porvoo) 7 D1
Borgafjäll 3 F3
Borgentreich 37 D2
Borger 29 F3
Börger 32 B1
Borggård 10 B1
Borghamn 13 E4
Borgholm 13 F3
Borgholzhausen 36 C3
Borghorst 36 B3
Borgo San Dalmazzo 92 B3
Borgo San Lorenzo 94 C2
Borgo Val di Taro 93 D3
Borgo Valsugana 90 C3
Borgomanero 88 C2
Borgonova Val Tidone 89 D1
Borgorose 98 C3
Borgosesia 88 C2

Borgue	19	D4	Bovallstrand	9	D1	Brčko	111	E4
Borgund	8	C4	Bovan	113	D2	Brdjani	112	C3
Borgvik	9	E2	Bovec	91	E3	Breakish	18	B2
Borima	114	B1	Bøverdal	8	C4	Brean Sands	27	D3
Borja	69	E2	Bovey Tracey	26	C2	Breasclete	18	B3
Börjelslandet	4	C4	Bovolone	90	C1	Breaza	114	C4
Borken	36	B2	Bovrup	12	B1	Brebeni	114	B3
Børkop	12	B2	Bowes	21	D2	Brebu	107	D1
Borla	107	E3	Bowmore	15	E4	Brebu Nou	113	D4
Borlänge	10	B3	Bowness	20	C2	Brécey	53	D4
Borlaug	8	C4	Bowness-on-Windermere	21	D2	Brechfa	26	C4
Borlova	107	D1	Boxberg	41	D1	Brechin	19	E1
Bormes-les-Mimosas	65	E2	Boxmeer	29	E1	Brecht	31	D4
Bórmio	89	E3	Boxtel	29	D1	Brecon	27	D4
Borna	39	D1	Boyalik	119	F3	Breda	29	D1
Bornhöved	33	E3	Boyle	14	C1	Bredaryd	4	B2
Bornos	83	E2	Božaj	112	B1	Bredbyn	4	B2
Boroaia	109	D3	Bozel	61	E2	Bredebro	12	A1
Borod	107	D3	Bozhurishte	113	E1	Bredelar	36	C2
Borodinskoye	7	E2	Božica	113	D1	Bredene	30	B4
Boroughbridge	21	E1	Bozienii de Sus	109	D3	Bredsel	4	C4
Borovan	114	B2	Bozovici	113	D4	Bredstedt	33	D4
Borovany	47	F3	Bozveliisko	115	E2	Bredwardine	27	D4
Borovets	118	A4	Bozzolo	89	E1	Bree	31	E4
Borovtsi	113	E2	Bra	92	B4	Bregenz	85	D3
Borrby	13	D1	Braås	13	E3	Bregovo	113	D1
Borris	17	D2	Brabova	113	E3	Bréhal	48	C1
Borris-in-Ossory	17	D3	Bracadale	18	B2	Brehna	38	C2
Borrisokane	16	C3	Bracciano	98	A2	Breifonn	8	B2
Borrisoleigh	16	C2	Bracieux	54	B2	Breil-sur-Roya	65	F2
Borrowdale	20	C2	Bräcke	3	F1	Breisach	44	B2
Bors	107	D3	Brackenheim	45	D3	Breisen	39	D4
Børsa	3	D2	Bracklesham Bay	25	D1	Breistein	8	A3
Borşa	108	B4	Brackley	27	F4	Breitengüssbach	42	B2
Borsec	108	C3	Bracknagh	17	D3	Brekke	8	A4
Borsh	116	C2	Bracknell	25	D2	Brekken	3	D1
Borsodnádasd	106	B4	Brackwede	36	C3	Brekkvasselv	3	C3
Bort-les-Orgues	59	F2	Braco	19	D1	Brekstad	2	C2
Borth	22	B1	Brad	107	E2	Bremen	32	C2
Börtnan	3	E1	Bradford	23	D4	Bremervörde	32	C2
Borzonţ	108	C2	Bradford-on-Avon	27	E3	Bremervörde	33	D2
Bosa	96	A3	Bradina	111	D2	Bremsnes	2	B2
Bosanci	104	B1	Brading	27	F2	Breno	89	E2
Bosanska Dubica	104	C1	Bradwell-on-Sea	25	E2	Brentwood	25	E2
Bosanska Gradiška	105	D1	Bradworthy	26	C2	Brenzett	25	E1
Bosanska Krupa	110	C4	Brae	19	F4	Bréscia	89	E2
Bosanska Rača	112	B4	Braedstrup	12	B2	Breskens	28	C1
Bosanski Brod	111	D4	Braemar	19	D2	Bressanone-Brixen	90	C4
Bosanski Novi	110	C4	Braemore Junction	18	C3	Bressuire	53	E1
Bosanski Petrovac	110	C3	Brăeşti	109	D4	Brest	52	A3
Bosanski Šamac	111	E4	Braeswick	19	F1	Brest	114	B2
Bosansko Grahovo	110	C3	Braga	72	B4	Brestova	104	A1
Boscastle	26	C2	Bragança	67	D1	Brestovac	113	D2
Bosco Chiesanuova	90	B2	Brăila	109	E1	Brestovac	113	D3
Boscombe	27	E2	Braine	50	C2	Brestovačka Banja	113	D3
Bosherston	26	B3	Braine-le-Comte	30	C3	Breţcu	109	D2
Bosilegrad	113	D1	Braintree	25	E2	Bretenoux	59	E1
Boskoop	29	D2	Braithwaite	20	C2	Breteuil	54	B4
Bösnjace	113	D2	Brake	32	C2	Breteuil-sur-Noye	50	B2
Bošnjace	111	E4	Brakel	30	C3	Brettabister	19	F4
Boşorod	107	E1	Brakel	37	D2	Bretten	44	C3
Bossbøen	8	C2	Bräkne-Hoby	13	E2	Breuil-Cervínia	88	B3
Bossòst	70	B4	Brålanda	9	E1	Brevik	8	C1
Boston	23	F2	Brållos	120	C4	Brevik	10	C1
Boston Spa	21	E1	Bramhope	23	D4	Breza	111	E3
Bostrak	8	C1	Bramley	25	D1	Brežice	104	B2
Böszénfa	105	D2	Bramming	12	A2	Breznica	104	C2
Botevgrad	114	B1	Brampton	21	D2	Breznice	43	E2
Bothel	20	C2	Brampton	23	F1	Breznik	113	E1
Botngård	2	C2	Bramsche	36	C3	Brezoi	108	B1
Botoroagă	114	C2	Bran	108	C1	Brezolles	54	B4
Botoşani	109	D4	Brancaleone	103	F3	Brezovica	112	C1
Botsmark	4	C3	Brancaster	25	E4	Brezovo	114	C1
Bottesford	23	E2	Brancion	60	C4	Brezovo Polje	111	E4
Bóttida	96	B3	Brand	85	D3	Briançon	61	E1
Bottrop	36	B2	Brand-Erbisdorf	43	D3	Briare	54	C2
Botun	117	D3	Brandal	2	B1	Bribirske Mostine	110	B3
Bouaye	53	D1	Brandbu	9	D3	Brichany	109	D4
Boudry	84	A3	Brande	12	B2	Bricquebec	48	C2
Bouillon	31	D2	Brandenberg	86	A2	Bride	20	B2
Bouilly	55	E3	Brandenburg	39	D3	Bridestowe	26	C2
Boulay-Moselle	51	F1	Brandis	39	D3	Bridge of Alford	19	E2
Boulogne-sur-Gesse	63	D2	Brändö	6	A1	Bridge of Allan	20	C4
Boulogne-sur-Mer	50	A4	Brandon	21	E2	Bridge of Balgie	18	C1
Bouloire	54	A2	Brandon	25	E3	Bridge of Cally	19	D1
Bourbon Lancy	60	B4	Brandval	9	E3	Bridge of Don	19	E2
Bourbon-l'Archambault	60	A4	Brandys nad Labem	43	F3	Bridge of Earn	19	D1
Bourbonne-les-Bains	56	B2	Brandýsek	43	E3	Bridge of Orchy	18	C1
Bourbourg	50	B4	Brânești	115	D3	Bridge of Weir	20	B4
Bourbriac	52	B3	Braničevo	113	D4	Bridgend	15	E4
Bourdeaux	64	C4	Braniștea	107	E1	Bridgend	27	D3
Bourg	58	B1	Branne	58	C1	Bridgetown	17	E2
Bourg-Achard	49	E2	Brannenburg	46	C1	Bridgnorth	23	D2
Bourg-Argental	60	C2	Branscombe	27	D2	Bridgwater	27	D2
Bourg-de-Péage	60	C1	Branston	23	D2	Bridlington	21	F1
Bourg-en-Bresse	60	C3	Brantôme	59	D2	Bridport	27	D2
Bourg-Lastic	59	F2	Branzi	89	D3	Brie-Comte-Robert	54	C4
Bourg-Madame	63	E1	Braskereidfoss	9	E3	Briec	52	A3
Bourg-St-Andéol	64	C4	Braşov	108	C1	Brielle	28	C2
Bourg-St-Maurice	61	E2	Brassac	63	F2	Brienne-le-Château	55	E3
Bourganeuf	59	E3	Brasschaat	31	D4	Brienz	84	B2
Bourges	54	C1	Brastad	9	D1	Brienza	100	C3
Bourgneuf-en-Retz	52	C1	Brataj	116	C2	Brieskow-Finkenheerd	39	E3
Bourgogne	51	D2	Bratca	107	D3	Briey	51	E2
Bourgoin-Jallieu	61	D2	Brateiu	108	B2	Brig	84	B1
Bourgtheroulde	49	F2	Brates	109	D1	Brighouse	23	E3
Bourgueil	53	F1	Brătești	114	C4	Brightlingsea	25	E2
Bourmont	56	B3	Bratton	27	E3	Brighton	25	D1
Bourne	23	F2	Brattvåg	2	B1	Brignogan	52	A4
Bourne End	24	D2	Bratunac	112	B3	Brignoles	65	E2
Bournemouth	27	E2	Bratya Daskalovi	114	C1	Brignound	61	D2
Bourneville	49	E2	Braubach	40	B2	Brihuega	74	C4
Bourton on the Water	27	E4	Braunau	86	B3	Brilon	36	C2
Boussac	59	E4	Braunfels	40	C3	Brimmes	8	B3
Boussens	63	D2	Braunlage	37	E2	Brincoveni	114	B3
Bouvignes	31	D2	Braunschweig	37	E3	Brindisi	101	F4
Bouvron	53	D2	Braunton	26	C2	Brinklow	23	E1
Bouxwiller	56	C4	Bray	17	E3	Brinkum	32	C1
Bouzonville	51	F2	Bray	50	B3	Brinyan	19	F1
Bova Marina	103	E3	Bray-sur-Seine	55	D3	Briones	68	C3
Bovalino Marina	103	F3	Brazatortas	80	A4	Brionne	49	E1

Brioude	60	A2	Bubry	52	B3	Burgkunstadt	42	B2
Brioux	58	C2	Buccheri	103	C2	Burglengenfeld	46	C4
Briouze	53	E4	Bucchianico	99	D3	Burgos	68	B2
Brisighella	94	C3	Bucecea	109	D4	Burgsinn	41	D2
Brissac-Quincé	53	E2	Buchen	41	D1	Burgsteinfurt	36	B3
Brissago	84	C1	Büchen	33	E2	Burgsvik	11	E1
Bristol	27	E3	Buchenwald	42	B4	Burguete	69	E3
Brittas	17	E3	Buchholz	33	E2	Burhaniye	119	E1
Brive-la-Gaillarde	59	E2	Buchin Prohhod	113	E2	Burie	58	B3
Briviesca	68	C3	Büchloe	46	B2	Burjuc	107	D1
Brixham	27	D1	Buchlyvie	20	B4	Burladingen	45	D2
Brixlegg	86	A2	Buchs	85	D3	Burley	27	E2
Brixworth	23	E1	Buchy	49	F2	Burley-in-Wharfedale	21	E1
Broad Chalke	27	E2	Búcine	94	C2	Burnham Market	25	E4
Broad Hinton	27	E3	Bucium	107	E2	Burnham-on-Crouch	25	E2
Broadford	18	B2	Buciumi	107	E3	Burnham-on-Sea	27	D3
Broadford	16	B2	Buckden	21	D1	Burnley	23	D3
Broadford	16	C3	Bückeburg	37	D3	Burnsall	21	D1
Broadhaven	26	B3	Bücken	37	D4	Burntisland	20	C4
Broadstairs	25	F2	Buckfastleigh	26	C1	Burravoe	19	F4
Broadway	27	E4	Buckhaven	20	C4	Burrel	116	C4
Broby	13	D2	Buckie	19	E2	Burriana	76	A3
Brockdish	25	F3	Buckingham	27	F4	Burry Port	26	C4
Bröckel	37	E3	Buckow	39	E4	Burslem	23	D2
Brockenhurst	27	F2	Bucksburn	19	E2	Bürstadt	40	C1
Brockworth	27	E4	Bucova	107	D1	Burton Agnes	21	F1
Brod	111	E2	Bucquoy	50	B3	Burton Latimer	23	E1
Brod na Kupi	104	B1	Bucşani	114	C2	Burton upon Trent	23	D2
Brodarevo	112	B2	Bucureşti	115	D3	Burton-in-Kendal	21	D1
Brodenbach	40	B2	Bud	2	B2	Burträsk	4	C3
Brodick	20	B3	Buda	109	D1	Buru	107	E2
Brody	39	F3	Buda	109	D2	Burwell	25	E3
Broglie	49	E1	Budaörs	105	E3	Bury	23	D3
Brohl	40	B3	Budapest	105	E3	Bury St. Edmunds	25	E3
Brolo	103	D3	Budduso	96	B3	Busalla	92	B3
Bromarv	6	B1	Bude	26	C2	Busana	93	E3
Brome	38	B4	Budești	108	B3	Busca	92	B3
Bromfield	22	C1	Budești	115	D3	Busdorf	33	D4
Bromma	8	C3	Büdingen	41	D2	Bushat	116	C4
Bromölla	13	E2	Budleigh Salterton	27	D2	Bushmills	15	D3
Bromsgrove	23	D1	Budoni	96	C3	Busovača	111	D3
Bromyard	23	D1	Budureasa	107	D2	Bussang	56	C2
Brønderslev	12	B3	Budva	112	A1	Busseto	93	D4
Broni	89	D1	Budyně nad Ohří	43	E3	Bussum	29	D2
Bronllys	27	D4	Buftea	115	D3	Bușteni	108	C1
Bronte	27	E2	Buğdayli	119	E1	Busto Arsízio	88	C2
Brook	27	E2	Bugeat	59	E2	Büsum	33	D4
Brooke	25	F4	Buggerru	96	A2	Butan	113	F3
Broons	52	C3	Bugle	26	B1	Buteni	107	D2
Brora	19	D3	Bugojno	111	D3	Butera	102	C2
Brørup	12	A2	Bühl	44	C3	Butler's Bridge	15	D1
Brösarp	13	D2	Buhuşi	109	D2	Butrint	116	C1
Brossac	58	C2	Builth Wells	27	D4	Buttelstedt	42	B4
Broșteni	108	C3	Buis-les-Baronnies	65	D3	Buttermere	20	C2
Broșteni	113	E4	Buitenpost	29	E4	Buttevant	16	C2
Brestrud	8	C3	Buitrago	74	B4	Buttstädt	38	C4
Broto	70	A4	Bujalance	80	A3	Butzbach	40	C3
Brottby	10	C2	Bujanovac	113	D1	Bützow	34	C3
Bröttem	3	D2	Bujaraloz	70	A2	Buvik	2	C2
Brou	54	B3	Buje	91	E2	Buvika	9	E4
Brough	21	D2	Bujoru	114	C2	Buxted	25	E1
Broughshane	15	D2	Bukovi	112	B3	Buxtehude	33	D2
Broughton	20	C4	Bülach	84	C3	Buxton	23	D3
Broughton	25	D3	Bulford	27	E3	Buxy	60	C4
Broughton in Furness	20	C1	Bülgarene	114	B1	Büyükçekmece	119	F3
Broughty Ferry	19	E1	Bŭlgarevo	115	F2	Büyükkaristiran	119	E3
Brouvelieures	56	C3	Bŭlgarovo	115	E2	Buzançais	54	B1
Brouwershaven	28	C2	Bŭlgarski Izvor	114	B1	Buzau	51	D2
Brovst	12	B3	Bulgnéville	56	B3	Buzău	115	D4
Brownhills	23	D2	Bulken	8	B3	Buzescu	114	C3
Broxburn	20	C4	Bullas	81	E3	Buzet	104	A1
Brozas	79	D4	Bulle	84	A2	Buziaş	107	D1
Bruchhausen-Vilsen	33	D1	Bultei	96	B3	Buziaş	118	C4
Bruchsal	44	C4	Bulwick	23	E1	Byal Izvor	114	C2
Bruck	47	D4	Bumbesti Pitic	113	E4	Byala	115	E1
Brück	39	D3	Bumbești-Jui	113	E4	Byala Slatina	114	B2
Bruck an der Grossglocknerstrasse	86	B2	Buna	111	D2	Byerum	13	F3
Bruck an der Mur	87	D2	Bunclody	17	E2	Byfield	23	E1
Bruck-an-der-Leitha	87	F3	Buncrana	15	D3	Bygdeå	4	C2
Brückl	87	D1	Bunde	32	B2	Bygdin	8	C4
Brüel	34	C2	Bünde	36	B2	Bygdsiljum	4	C3
Bruff	16	C2	Bundoran	14	C1	Bygland	8	B1
Brugg	84	C2	Bunessan	18	B1	Byglandsfjord	8	B4
Brugge	30	C4	Bunești	114	B4	Bygstad	8	B4
Bruhagen	2	B2	Bungay	25	F3	Bykle	8	B1
Brühl	40	B3	Bunkris	9	E4	Bykovets	109	E2
Brûlon	53	E3	Bunmahon	17	D2	Bylchau	22	C2
Brumath	57	D4	Bunnyconnellan	14	B1	Byrkjedal	8	B1
Brummen	29	E2	Buntingford	25	D3	Byrkjelo	8	B4
Brumunddal	9	D3	Buonalbergo	99	E1	Byrness	21	D3
Brunau	38	B4	Buonconvento	94	C2	Byrum	12	C3
Brunflo	3	F1	Buonfornello	102	C3	Byske	4	C3
Brunico-Bruneck	90	C4	Burbach	40	C3	Bystřice	43	F2
Bruniquel	63	E3	Burbage	27	E3	Byxelkrok	13	F3
Brunkeberg	8	C2	Bureå	4	C2			
Brunnen	84	C2	Burelo de Cabo	67	D4			
Brunsbüttel	33	D3	Büren	36	C2			
Brunssum	31	D3	Büren	84	B3			
Bruravik	8	B3	Burg	25	D1			
Bruree	16	C2	Burg	34	B4	C		
Brus	113	D3	Burg	38	C3			
Brušane	110	B3	Burg	39	E2	Ca'n Picafort	77	E3
Brussel (Bruxelles)	31	D3	Burg Stagard	35	D2	Caatelnau-de-Montmiral	63	E3
Brüssow	35	E3	Burgau	82	A3	Cabañaquinta	67	E3
Brusturi	109	D3	Burgau	45	E3	Cabañas	66	C4
Bruton	27	E2	Burgbernheim	41	E4	Cabanes	66	C4
Bruvno	110	B3	Burgdorf	37	E3	Căbești	107	D2
Bruvoll	9	E3	Burgdorf	84	B2	Cabeza del Buey	79	F4
Bruxelles (Brussel)	31	D3	Burgebrach	42	A2	Cabezas Rubias	82	C4
Bryn-Crug	22	B2	Burgel	42	B2	Cabezuela del Valle	73	E2
Brynamman	26	C4	Burgh-Haamstede	28	C2	Cabo de Palos	81	F2
Bryne	8	A1	Burgh-le-Marsh	25	E4	Cabo de San Vicente	82	A3
Brynmawr	27	D4	Burghausen	47	D2	Cabourg	49	E2
Brza Palanka	113	D3	Burghead	19	D2	Cabra	80	A2
Brzeće	112	C2	Burgjoss	41	D2	Cabras	96	B4
Bua	9	D1	Búrgio	102	C3	Cabreiros	66	C4
Buavåg	8	A2	Búrgio	102	C3	Cabrerets	63	E4
						Cabuérniga	68	B4
						Čačak	112	C3
						Cáccamo	102	C3
						Cáceres	79	D3

Cachopo .... 82 ... C3
Čačinci .... 105 ... D1
Cadamstown .... 17 ... D3
Cadaqués .... 71 ... E4
Cadelbosco di Sopra .... 94 ... B4
Cadenabbia .... 89 ... D3
Cadenberge .... 33 ... D3
Cadenet .... 65 ... D3
Cadgwith .... 26 ... B1
Cadillac .... 62 ... C4
Cádiz .... 83 ... D2
Cadjavica .... 105 ... D1
Cadnam .... 27 ... F2
Caen .... 49 ... D1
Caerelon .... 27 ... D3
Caergwrle .... 22 ... C2
Caernarfon .... 22 ... B2
Caerphilly .... 27 ... D3
Caersws .... 22 ... C1
Cáfasan .... 117 ... D3
Çağis .... 119 ... F1
Cagli .... 95 ... D2
Cagliari .... 96 ... B1
Cagnano Varano .... 99 ... F2
Cagnes .... 65 ... F3
Caherconlish .... 16 ... C2
Caherdaniel .... 16 ... A1
Cahir .... 16 ... C2
Cahirciveen .... 16 ... A1
Cahors .... 63 ... D4
Caiazzo .... 99 ... D1
Cairndow .... 18 ... C1
Cairnryan .... 20 ... B3
Caister .... 23 ... F3
Caister-on-Sea .... 25 ... F4
Căiuti .... 109 ... D2
Caivano .... 100 ... A4
Cajarc .... 63 ... E4
Čajetina .... 112 ... B3
Čajniče .... 111 ... E2
Cakovec .... 104 ... C2
Cala Gonone .... 96 ... C3
Cala Millor .... 77 ... E3
Cala Moral .... 80 ... A1
Cala Ratjada .... 77 ... E3
Calabor .... 67 ... D1
Calacuccia .... 57 ... E3
Calaf .... 70 ... C3
Calafat .... 113 ... E3
Calafell .... 70 ... C2
Calahonda .... 80 ... A1
Calahonda .... 80 ... B1
Calahorra .... 69 ... D2
Calais .... 50 ... A4
Čalan .... 107 ... E1
Calán Porter .... 77 ... F4
Calangiánus .... 96 ... B3
Călăraşi .... 115 ... E3
Calasetta .... 96 ... A1
Calasparra .... 81 ... E3
Calatafimi .... 102 ... B3
Calatañazor .... 68 ... C1
Calatayud .... 69 ... E1
Călăţele .... 107 ... E2
Calau .... 39 ... C2
Calbe .... 38 ... C3
Caldarola .... 95 ... E1
Caldas da Rainha .... 78 ... A3
Caldas de Reis .... 66 ... B3
Caldas de Vizela .... 72 ... B4
Caldercruix .... 20 ... C4
Caldes d'Estrac .... 71 ... D2
Caldes de Montbui .... 71 ... D3
Caldicot .... 27 ... D3
Caldirola .... 92 ... C4
Caledon .... 15 ... D2
Calella de la Costa .... 71 ... D3
Calella de Palafrugell .... 71 ... E3
Calenzana .... 57 ... E3
Calfsound .... 19 ... F1
Calgary .... 18 ... B1
Calignac .... 62 ... C3
Călimăneşti .... 114 ... B4
Calitri .... 100 ... C4
Callac .... 52 ... B3
Callan .... 17 ... D2
Callander .... 19 ... D1
Callington .... 26 ... C1
Callosa d'En Sarriá .... 76 ... A1
Calmbach .... 44 ... C3
Calne .... 27 ... E3
Calovo .... 105 ... D4
Calpe .... 76 ... A1
Caltabellotta .... 102 ... B2
Caltagirone .... 103 ... D2
Caltanissetta .... 102 ... C2
Caltavuturo .... 102 ... C3
Caltra .... 16 ... C3
Călugăreni .... 115 ... D3
Caluso .... 88 ... C2
Calver .... 23 ... D3
Calvörde .... 38 ... C3
Calw .... 44 ... C3
Calzadilla de la Cueza .... 68 ... A2
Camaiore .... 93 ... D2
Cămăraşu .... 108 ... B2
Camarès .... 63 ... F3
Camaret .... 52 ... A3
Camariñas .... 66 ... A3
Camarzana .... 67 ... E2
Cambados .... 66 ... B2
Cambeo .... 66 ... C2
Camber .... 25 ... E1
Camberg .... 40 ... C2
Camberley .... 25 ... D2
Cambo-les-Bains .... 62 ... A2
Cambourne .... 26 ... B1
Cambrai .... 50 ... C3
Cambre .... 66 ... B4
Cambremer .... 49 ... E1
Cambridge .... 27 ... E3

Cambridge .... 25 ... E3
Cambrils de Mar .... 70 ... B2
Camburg .... 42 ... C4
Camelford .... 26 ... C2
Camerino .... 95 ... E1
Camigliatello .... 101 ... D1
Caminha .... 66 ... B1
Caminomorisco .... 73 ... E2
Caminreal .... 75 ... E4
Camlibel (Myrtou) .... 122 ... B2
Camogli .... 92 ... C3
Camolin .... 17 ... E2
Camp .... 16 ... A2
Camp Tûres-Sand in Taufers .... 90 ... C4
Campan .... 62 ... C2
Campana .... 101 ... D2
Campanario .... 79 ... E3
Campello .... 81 ... F4
Campi Salentina .... 101 ... F3
Campillo de Arenas .... 80 ... C2
Campillos .... 83 ... F2
Campillo de Altobuey .... 75 ... D2
Campillo de Altobuey .... 75 ... D2
Campocologno .... 85 ... E1
Campodrón .... 71 ... D4
Campomanes .... 67 ... E3
Campomarino .... 99 ... E2
Campomarino .... 101 ... E3
Campora San Giovanni .... 101 ... D1
Campos .... 79 ... E3
Camposampiero .... 90 ... C2
Çan .... 119 ... E2
Çanakkale .... 119 ... E2
Canas de Senhorim .... 72 ... C2
Cañaveras .... 75 ... D3
Canazei .... 90 ... C3
Cancale .... 53 ... D4
Cancon .... 63 ... D4
Candanchú .... 69 ... F3
Çandarli .... 119 ... E1
Candas .... 67 ... E4
Candasnos .... 70 ... A2
Candé .... 53 ... D2
Candela .... 99 ... E1
Candeleda .... 73 ... F2
Canelli .... 92 ... C4
Canero .... 67 ... E4
Canet de Mar .... 71 ... D2
Canet-Plage .... 64 ... A1
Cañete .... 75 ... E2
Canford Cliffs .... 27 ... E2
Canfranc .... 69 ... F3
Cangas .... 66 ... B2
Cangas de Narcea .... 67 ... D3
Cangas de Onis .... 67 ... F4
Canicada .... 66 ... B1
Canicatti .... 102 ... C2
Canicattini Bagni .... 103 ... D2
Caniles .... 80 ... C2
Canino .... 97 ... F3
Cañizal .... 73 ... F3
Canjáyar .... 80 ... C1
Cannero Riviera .... 88 ... C3
Cannes .... 65 ... F2
Canneto-San-Óglio .... 89 ... E1
Cannich .... 18 ... C2
Cannóbio .... 88 ... C3
Cannock .... 23 ... D2
Canonbie .... 20 ... C3
Canosa di Puglia .... 99 ... F1
Cantalejo .... 68 ... B1
Cantanhede .... 72 ... B2
Canterbury .... 25 ... F2
Cantoral .... 68 ... A3
Cantoria .... 81 ... D2
Cantù .... 88 ... C2
Canvey Island .... 25 ... E2
Cany-Barville .... 49 ... E2
Cáorle .... 91 ... D2
Cap Ferret .... 58 ... A1
Cap Gris Nez .... 50 ... A4
Cap-d'Ail .... 65 ... F3
Capaci .... 102 ... B3
Caparde .... 111 ... E3
Căpăţîneni .... 108 ... B1
Capbreton .... 62 ... A3
Capel .... 25 ... D1
Capel Bangor .... 22 ... B1
Capel Curig .... 22 ... C1
Capestang .... 64 ... A2
Capistrello .... 98 ... C2
Capljina .... 111 ... D1
Capo Carbonara .... 96 ... B1
Capo d'Orlando .... 103 ... D3
Capo di Ponte .... 89 ... E3
Capolíveri .... 97 ... D4
Cappagh White .... 16 ... C2
Cappamore .... 16 ... C2
Cappoquin .... 16 ... C1
Capri .... 100 ... A3
Capriati a Volturno .... 99 ... D1
Capríccioli .... 96 ... C4
Căpruţa .... 107 ... D2
Captieux .... 62 ... C4
Capua .... 100 ... A4
Capurso .... 101 ... D4
Caracal .... 114 ... B3
Caragiale .... 114 ... C4
Caraman .... 63 ... E2
Caramulo .... 72 ... B2
Caranga .... 67 ... E3
Caransebes .... 107 ... D1
Carantec .... 52 ... B4
Cărăşeu .... 107 ... E4
Caraşova .... 113 ... D4
Caravaca .... 81 ... D3

Carballiño .... 66 ... D2
Carballo .... 66 ... B4
Carbis Bay .... 26 ... B1
Carbon-Blanc .... 58 ... B1
Carboneras .... 81 ... D1
Carboneras de Guadazón .... 75 ... D2
Carbónia .... 96 ... A1
Carbonin-Schludersbach .... 91 ... D1
Carbonne .... 63 ... D2
Carbost .... 18 ... B2
Cărbunari .... 113 ... D4
Carcans .... 58 ... B2
Carcans Plage .... 58 ... B2
Carcare .... 92 ... B3
Carcassonne .... 63 ... E2
Carcastillo .... 69 ... E2
Carcavelos .... 78 ... A2
Carcès .... 65 ... E2
Çardak .... 119 ... D2
Cardedeu .... 71 ... D2
Cardiff .... 27 ... D3
Cardigan .... 26 ... C4
Cardona .... 70 ... C3
Cardross .... 20 ... B4
Caregal do Sal .... 72 ... C2
Carei .... 107 ... D4
Carennac .... 59 ... E1
Carentan .... 48 ... C2
Carev Dvor .... 117 ... D3
Carew .... 26 ... B3
Cargèse .... 57 ... E2
Carhaix-Plouguer .... 52 ... B3
Cariati .... 101 ... E2
Carignan .... 51 ... E2
Carignano .... 92 ... B4
Cariñena .... 69 ... E1
Carisbrooke .... 27 ... F2
Cark .... 20 ... C1
Carlanstown .... 17 ... D4
Carlet .... 75 ... F1
Carling .... 51 ... F1
Carlingford .... 15 ... D2
Carlisle .... 21 ... D2
Carloforte .... 96 ... A1
Carlops .... 20 ... C4
Carlow .... 17 ... D2
Carlow .... 34 ... B3
Carlton .... 23 ... E3
Carluke .... 20 ... C4
Carmagnol .... 92 ... B4
Carmarthen .... 26 ... C3
Carmaux .... 63 ... E3
Carmona .... 83 ... E3
Carnac .... 52 ... B2
Carndonagh .... 15 ... D3
Carnew .... 17 ... E2
Carnforth .... 21 ... D1
Carnia .... 91 ... E3
Carnlough .... 15 ... E3
Carno .... 22 ... C2
Carnota .... 66 ... B3
Carnoustie .... 19 ... E1
Carnwath .... 20 ... C4
Carolinensiel .... 32 ... C3
Carpaneto Piacentino .... 93 ... D4
Carpenedolo .... 89 ... E2
Carpentras .... 64 ... C3
Carpi .... 94 ... B4
Carpineto Romano .... 98 ... B2
Cărpiniş .... 107 ... E2
Cărpiniş .... 106 ... C1
Carpione .... 99 ... D2
Carquefou .... 53 ... D1
Carqueiranne .... 65 ... E2
Carracastle .... 14 ... B1
Carradale .... 15 ... E3
Carrara .... 93 ... D3
Carrascosa del Campo .... 74 ... C2
Carrazeda de Ansiaês .... 72 ... C3
Carrbridge .... 19 ... D2
Carregado .... 78 ... A3
Carrick (An Charraig) .... 14 ... C2
Carrick-on-Shannon .... 14 ... C1
Carrick-on-Suir .... 17 ... D2
Carrickfergus .... 15 ... E3
Carrickmacross .... 15 ... D1
Carrickmore .... 15 ... D2
Carrigahorig .... 16 ... C1
Carrigaline .... 16 ... C1
Carrigallen .... 14 ... C1
Carriganimmy .... 16 ... B1
Carrigans .... 15 ... D3
Carrigtohill .... 16 ... C1
Carrión de Calatrava .... 74 ... B1
Carrión de los Condes .... 68 ... A2
Carro .... 64 ... C2
Carronbridge .... 20 ... C3
Carrouges .... 55 ... F3
Carrowkeel .... 15 ... D3
Carry-le-Rouet .... 64 ... C2
Carryduff .... 15 ... E2
Carsoli .... 98 ... B2
Carsphairn .... 20 ... B3
Carstairs .... 20 ... C4
Cartagena .... 81 ... E2
Cartaxo .... 78 ... B3
Carter Bar .... 21 ... D3
Carteret .... 48 ... C2
Carvin .... 50 ... B3
Carvoeiro .... 82 ... B3
Casacalenda .... 99 ... D2
Casalarreina .... 68 ... C3
Casalbuono .... 100 ... C4
Casale Monferrato .... 88 ... C1
Casalecchio di Reno .... 94 ... B4
Casalmaggiore .... 93 ... E4
Casalpusterlengo .... 89 ... D1
Casamassima .... 101 ... D4
Casamicciola Terme .... 100 ... A4
Casamozza .... 57 ... F3
Casas Ibañez .... 75 ... E1
Cascais .... 78 ... A2

Cascia .... 98 ... B3
Casciana Terme .... 93 ... E2
Cáscina .... 93 ... E2
Căscioarele .... 115 ... D3
Căşeiu .... 108 ... B3
Casekow .... 35 ... E2
Caselle .... 88 ... B1
Caserta .... 100 ... A4
Cashel .... 16 ... C2
Caşin Mănăstirea .... 109 ... D2
Casina .... 93 ... E3
Casinos .... 41 ... F2
Casoli .... 99 ... D3
Caspe .... 70 ... A2
Cassá de la Selva .... 71 ... D3
Cassagnes-Bégonhès .... 63 ... F3
Cassano delle Murge .... 101 ... D4
Cassel .... 50 ... B4
Cassine .... 98 ... C2
Cassino .... 65 ... D2
Cassis .... 65 ... D2
Cassonay .... 84 ... A2
Castanheira de Pêra .... 72 ... B1
Casteau .... 30 ... C2
Casteggio .... 88 ... C1
Castejón de Monegros .... 69 ... F1
Castejón de Sos .... 70 ... B4
Castel di Sangro .... 99 ... D2
Castel San Giovanni .... 89 ... D1
Castel San Lorenzo .... 100 ... C3
Castel San Pietro Terme .... 94 ... C3
Castel Volturno .... 100 ... A4
Castel-l'Arquato Lugagnano .... 93 ... D4
Castelbuono .... 102 ... C3
Casteldelfino .... 92 ... A4
Castelejo .... 82 ... A3
Castelfiorentino .... 94 ... B2
Castelfranco Emilia .... 94 ... B3
Castelfranco Véneto .... 90 ... C2
Casteljaloux .... 62 ... C4
Castell de Ferro .... 80 ... C1
Castellabate .... 100 ... B3
Castellammare del Golfo .... 102 ... B3
Castellammare di Stábia .... 100 ... B2
Castellamonte .... 88 ... B2
Castellana .... 102 ... C3
Castellana Grotte .... 101 ... E4
Castellane .... 65 ... E3
Castellaneta .... 101 ... E3
Castellar de la Frontera .... 83 ... E1
Castellar de Santisteban .... 80 ... C3
Castellazzo Bormida .... 92 ... C4
Castelldefels .... 70 ... C2
Castelleone .... 89 ... D1
Castellfollit de la Roca .... 71 ... D3
Castellina in Chianti .... 94 ... C2
Castelló d'Empuries .... 71 ... E4
Castellón de la Plana .... 76 ... A4
Castellúccio de Sáuri .... 99 ... E1
Castelmassa .... 94 ... C4
Castelmauro .... 99 ... D2
Castelmoron .... 62 ... C4
Castelnau-de-Médoc .... 58 ... B1
Castelnau-Magnoac .... 62 ... C2
Castelnaudary .... 63 ... E2
Castelnuovo di Daunia .... 99 ... E2
Castelnuovo di Garfagnana .... 93 ... E3
Castelnuovo di Porto .... 98 ... B2
Castelnuovo Scrivia .... 88 ... C1
Castelo Branco .... 72 ... C1
Castelo de Paiva (Sobrada) .... 72 ... B3
Castelo de Vide .... 78 ... C3
Castelraimondo .... 95 ... E1
Castelsardo .... 96 ... B3
Castelsarrasin .... 63 ... D3
Casteltérmini .... 102 ... C2
Castelvecchio Subequo .... 98 ... C2
Castelvetrano .... 102 ... B3
Casterton .... 21 ... D1
Castets .... 62 ... B3
Castiádas .... 96 ... B1
Castiglion Fiorentino .... 94 ... C1
Castiglioncello .... 93 ... E1
Castiglione del Lago .... 95 ... D1
Castiglione del Pepoli .... 94 ... C3
Castiglione delle Prescáia .... 97 ... E4
Castiglione di Stiviere .... 89 ... E2
Castiglione Messer Marino .... 99 ... D2
Castillon-la-Bataille .... 58 ... C1
Castillonnès .... 63 ... D4
Castle Acre .... 25 ... E4
Castle Carrock .... 21 ... D2
Castle Cary .... 27 ... D2
Castle Coombe .... 27 ... E3
Castle Cove .... 16 ... A1
Castle Douglas .... 20 ... C2
Castle Hedingham .... 25 ... E4
Castle Rising .... 25 ... E4
Castlebar .... 14 ... B1
Castlebay .... 18 ... A2
Castlebellingham .... 17 ... E4
Castleblayney .... 15 ... D1
Castlebridge .... 17 ... E2
Castlecomer .... 17 ... D2
Castledermot .... 17 ... D2
Castlederg .... 14 ... C2
Castleisland .... 16 ... B1
Castlemaine .... 16 ... B1
Castlemartyr .... 16 ... C1
Castleplunkett .... 14 ... C1
Castlepollard .... 17 ... D4
Castlerea .... 14 ... C1
Castlerock .... 15 ... D3
Castleshane .... 15 ... D1
Castleside .... 21 ... D2
Castletown .... 20 ... B1
Castletown .... 19 ... D3
Castletown .... 17 ... D3
Castletownroche .... 16 ... A1
Castletownshend .... 16 ... B1
Castlewellan .... 15 ... E1
Castres .... 63 ... E2

Castricum .... 29 ... D3
Castries .... 64 ... B3
Castro Caldelas .... 66 ... C3
Castro Daire .... 72 ... C3
Castro del Río .... 80 ... A3
Castro Marim .... 82 ... C3
Castro Urdiales .... 68 ... C4
Castro Verde .... 82 ... B4
Castrocaro Terme .... 94 ... C3
Castrocontrigo .... 67 ... E2
Castrojeriz .... 68 ... B2
Castromonte .... 67 ... F1
Castrop-Rauxel .... 36 ... B2
Castropol .... 67 ... D4
Castroreale .... 103 ... E3
Castroreale Terme .... 103 ... D3
Castrovede of Cerrato .... 68 ... B1
Castrovillari .... 101 ... D2
Castuera .... 79 ... E2
Çatalca .... 119 ... F3
Cataloi .... 115 ... F4
Catánia .... 103 ... D2
Catanzaro .... 101 ... D1
Catanzaro Lido .... 101 ... D1
Catenanuova .... 103 ... D2
Caterham .... 25 ... E1
Caton .... 21 ... D1
Catterick .... 21 ... E2
Cattólica .... 95 ... D3
Cătun .... 114 ... C4
Catus .... 63 ... D4
Čáuas .... 107 ... D3
Caudebec .... 49 ... E2
Caudete .... 81 ... E4
Caudry .... 50 ... C3
Caumont .... 49 ... D1
Caunes .... 63 ... F2
Cauro .... 57 ... E2
Causeway .... 16 ... B2
Caussade .... 63 ... D3
Cauterets .... 62 ... C1
Cauville .... 49 ... E2
Cava de Tirreni .... 100 ... B3
Cavaglia .... 88 ... B2
Cavaillon .... 64 ... C3
Cavalaire-sur-Mer .... 65 ... E2
Cavalese .... 90 ... C3
Cavalière .... 65 ... E2
Cavan .... 15 ... D1
Cavárzere .... 91 ... D1
Cavendish .... 25 ... E3
Caversham .... 27 ... F3
Cavo .... 97 ... D4
Cavour .... 92 ... B4
Cavtat .... 111 ... D1
Cawdor .... 19 ... D3
Cawsand .... 26 ... C1
Cawston .... 25 ... F4
Caylus .... 63 ... E3
Cayton Bay .... 21 ... F1
Cazals .... 63 ... D4
Cazalla de la Sierra .... 83 ... E4
Cazane Plaviševiţa .... 113 ... D4
Căzăneşti .... 115 ... D3
Cazères .... 63 ... D2
Cazin .... 110 ... C4
Cazma .... 104 ... C1
Cazoria .... 80 ... C3
Ceamurlia de Sus .... 115 ... F4
Ceanannus Mor .... 17 ... D4
Cebovce .... 106 ... B4
Cebreiro .... 67 ... D3
Ceccano .... 98 ... C2
Cece .... 105 ... E3
Cechtice .... 43 ... F2
Cécina .... 93 ... E1
Cedeira .... 66 ... C4
Cedynia .... 35 ... E1
Cee .... 66 ... B3
Cefalù .... 102 ... C3
Ceglèd .... 106 ... B2
Ceglie Messápico .... 101 ... E3
Cehegin .... 81 ... D3
Cehu Silvaniei .... 107 ... E4
Ceica .... 107 ... D3
Čelákovice .... 43 ... F3
Celano .... 98 ... C2
Celanova .... 66 ... C2
Celbridge .... 17 ... E3
Čelebić .... 110 ... C3
Celeiu .... 113 ... E4
Celerina .... 81 ... E2
Čelić .... 111 ... E3
Celje .... 104 ... B2
Celldömölk .... 105 ... D3
Celle .... 37 ... E4
Celle Ligure .... 92 ... C3
Celopeci .... 117 ... D4
Celorico da Beira .... 72 ... C2
Celorico de Basto .... 72 ... C4
Cemaes Bay .... 22 ... B3
Cemerno .... 111 ... E2
Cemmaes Road .... 22 ... B2
Ceninghe .... 90 ... C3
Cenicero .... 68 ... C3
Čenta .... 112 ... C4
Cento .... 94 ... C4
Centúri .... 57 ... F2
Centúripe .... 103 ... D3
Čepin .... 105 ... E1
Ceprano .... 98 ... C2
Cerami .... 103 ... D3
Cerbère .... 64 ... A1
Cerbu .... 114 ... B4
Cercal .... 78 ... A3
Cercal .... 82 ... B4
Cercedilla .... 68 ... B1
Cerchiara di Calabria .... 101 ... D2
Cerea .... 90 ... C1
Ceresole Reale .... 88 ... A2
Céret .... 63 ... F1
Cerignola .... 99 ... F1
Cerilly .... 59 ... F4

Cerisiers .... 55 ... D3
Cerizay .... 53 ... E1
Cerkezköy .... 119 ... F3
Cerknica .... 104 ... A2
Cermei .... 107 ... D2
Černá .... 47 ... E3
Cerna .... 115 ... E4
Cernavoda .... 115 ... E3
Cernay .... 56 ... C2
Cerne Abbas .... 27 ... E2
Cernégula .... 68 ... B3
Cernik .... 105 ... D1
Černobbio .... 88 ... C2
Černošin .... 43 ... D2
Černovice .... 43 ... F1
Cerovitsa .... 114 ... C2
Cerrigydrudion .... 22 ... C2
Cérrik .... 116 ... C3
Certaldo .... 94 ... B2
Certeze .... 107 ... E4
Cervera .... 70 ... C2
Cervera de Pisuerga .... 68 ... A3
Cervera del Llano .... 75 ... D2
Cervera del Río Alhama .... 69 ... D2
Cerveteri .... 98 ... A2
Cérvia .... 95 ... D3
Cervignano .... 91 ... E2
Cervione .... 57 ... F3
Cervo .... 67 ... D4
Cesarò .... 103 ... D3
Cesena .... 95 ... D3
Cesenático .... 95 ... D3
Česká Kamenice .... 43 ... E4
Česka Lipa .... 43 ... F3
České Budějovice .... 47 ... F3
Česke Velenice .... 47 ... F3
Český Brod .... 43 ... F3
Český Krumlov .... 47 ... F3
Cetate .... 113 ... E3
Cetatea de Baltă .... 108 ... B2
Cetăţeni .... 114 ... C4
Cetinje .... 111 ... E1
Cetraro .... 100 ... C2
Ceva .... 92 ... B3
Ceyzériat .... 61 ... D3
Chabanais .... 59 ... D3
Chabeuil .... 60 ... C1
Chablis .... 55 ... E2
Chabris .... 54 ... B1
Chagford .... 26 ... C2
Chagny .... 55 ... F3
Chaillé-les-Marais .... 58 ... B4
Chalabre .... 63 ... E1
Chalais .... 58 ... C2
Chalamont .... 60 ... C3
Chalampé .... 57 ... D2
Chale .... 27 ... F2
Challans .... 52 ... C1
Challes-les-Eaux .... 61 ... D2
Challock .... 25 ... E1
Chalon-sur-Saône .... 60 ... C4
Chalonnes .... 53 ... E2
Châlons-sur-Marne .... 51 ... D1
Chálus .... 59 ... D2
Cham .... 47 ... D4
Cham .... 84 ... C3
Chambéry .... 61 ... D2
Chambley .... 51 ... F3
Chambon-sur-Lac .... 60 ... A2
Chambon-sur-Voueize .... 59 ... F3
Chambord .... 54 ... B2
Chamonix .... 61 ... E2
Champagne-Mouton .... 58 ... C3
Champagnole .... 61 ... D4
Champaubert .... 55 ... E4
Champdeniers .... 58 ... C3
Champeix .... 60 ... A2
Champéry .... 84 ... A1
Champex .... 84 ... A1
Champier .... 61 ... D2
Champigné .... 53 ... E2
Champillon .... 55 ... D1
Champion .... 31 ... E2
Champlitte .... 56 ... B2
Champoluc .... 88 ... B2
Champtoceaux .... 53 ... D2
Chamusca .... 78 ... B3
Chanas .... 60 ... C2
Chanion .... 118 ... A2
Chantada .... 66 ... C3
Chantelle .... 60 ... A3
Chantemerle .... 61 ... E1
Chantilly .... 50 ... B1
Chantonnay .... 58 ... B4
Chão de Codes .... 78 ... B4
Chaource .... 54 ... E3
Chapelle-Royale .... 54 ... B3
Charavines .... 61 ... D2
Chard .... 27 ... D2
Charenton-sur-Cher .... 59 ... F4
Charing .... 25 ... E1
Charlbury .... 27 ... F1
Charleroi .... 31 ... D1
Charlestown .... 14 ... B1
Charleville (Rath Luire) .... 16 ... C2
Charleville-Mézières .... 51 ... D2
Charlieu .... 60 ... B3
Charly .... 50 ... C1
Charmes .... 56 ... B3
Charn .... 55 ... D2
Charolles .... 60 ... B3
Charost .... 54 ... C1
Charroux .... 58 ... C3
Chartres .... 55 ... D3
Chartwell .... 25 ... E1
Chasetown .... 23 ... D2
Chassigny .... 56 ... A2
Chatburn .... 23 ... D4
Château-Arnoux .... 65 ... D2
Château-Chinon .... 55 ... E1
Château-du-Loir .... 54 ... A2
Château-Gontier .... 53 ... E2

Château-la-Vallière ...53... F2
Château-Porcien ...51... D2
Château-Queyras ...61... C3
Château-Renault ...54... B2
Château-Salins ...56... B4
Château-Thierry ...50... C1
Châteaubourg ...53... D3
Châteaubriant ...53... D2
Châteaudun ...54... B3
Châteaugiron ...53... D3
Châteaulin ...52... A3
Châteaumeillant ...59... E4
Châteauneuf ...58... C2
Châteauneuf-de-Faou ...52... B3
Châteauneuf-de-Randon ...64... B4
Châteauneuf-du-Pape ...64... C3
Châteauneuf-en-Thymerais ...54... B3
Châteauneuf-sur-Cher ...54... C1
Châteauneuf-sur-Loire ...54... C1
Châteauneuf-sur-Sarthe ...53... E2
Châteauponsac ...59... D3
Châteaurenard ...55... D2
Châteauroux ...59... E4
Châteauvillain ...55... F3
Château d'Oex ...84... A2
Chatel ...61... C3
Châtel-St.Denis ...84... A2
Châtelaillon-Plage ...58... B2
Châtelet ...31... D2
Châtelguyon ...60... A3
Châtellerault ...59... D4
Châtelus-Malvaleix ...59... E3
Châtenois ...56... B3
Chatham ...25... E2
Châtillon ...88... B2
Châtillon-Coligny ...55... D2
Châtillon-en-Bazois ...55... D1
Châtillon-en-Diois ...61... D1
Châtillon-sur-Chalaronne ...60... C3
Châtillon-sur-Indre ...54... B1
Châtillon-sur-Loire ...55... D2
Châtillon-sur-Marne ...50... C1
Châtillon-sur-Seine ...55... E2
Chatteris ...23... F1
Chatton ...21... D3
Chaudes-Aigues ...60... A1
Chauffailles ...60... B3
Chaufor ...49... F1
Chaumergy ...56... B1
Chaumont ...56... A3
Chaumont ...54... B2
Chaunay ...58... C3
Chauny ...50... C2
Chaussin ...56... A1
Chauvigny ...59... D4
Chazelles ...60... C2
Cheadle ...23... D2
Cheadle Hulme ...23... D3
Cheb ...43... D2
Cheddar ...27... D3
Chef-Boutonne ...58... C3
Cheia ...108... C1
Chelmsford ...25... E2
Cheltenham ...27... E4
Chelterma ...11... F1
Chelva ...75... E2
Chemillé ...53... E1
Chemin ...56... A1
Chemnitz ...43... D3
Chénérailles ...59... E3
Chenonceaux ...54... B1
Chepelare ...118... B4
Chepstow ...27... D3
Chernomorets ...115... C1
Chernovtsy ...108... C4
Chéroy ...55... D3
Cherven Byag ...114... B2
Chervena Voda ...115... D2
Chesham ...25... D2
Chester ...22... C3
Chester-le-Street ...21... E2
Chesterfield ...24... C4
Chetani ...108... B2
Chevagnes ...60... B4
Chevanceaux ...58... C2
Chevreuse ...54... C4
Chewton Mendip ...27... E3
Chianciano Terme ...98... A4
Chiaravalle ...103... F4
Chiari ...89... D2
Chiasso ...84... C1
Chiavari ...93... D3
Chiavenna ...89... D3
Chichester ...25... D1
Chichis ...108... C1
Chicklade ...27... E2
Chiclana de la Frontera ...83... E2
Chiddingfold ...25... D1
Chideock ...27... D2
Chieming ...47... D2
Chieri ...88... B2
Chiesa in Valmalenco ...89... D3
Chieti ...99... D3
Chigwell ...25... E2
Chiheru de Sus ...108... C2
Chilcompton ...27... E3
Chilham ...25... E1
Chimay ...31... D2
Chinchón ...74... B3
Chincilla de Monte Aragón ...75... E1
Chinon ...53... F1
Chióggia ...91... D1
Chipiona ...83... D2
Chippenham ...27... E3
Chipping Campden ...27... E4
Chipping Norton ...27... E4
Chipping Sodbury ...27... E3
Chiprovtsi ...113... E2
Chirbury ...22... C2
Chiril ...108... C3
Chirk ...22... C2

Chirnside ...21... D4
Chirpan ...118... C4
Chiseldon ...27... E3
Chiselet ...115... D3
Chișineu Criș ...107... D2
Chiuești ...108... B3
Chiusa di Pesio ...92... B3
Chiusa Sclàfani ...102... B3
Chiusa-Klausen ...90... C4
Chiusaforte ...91... E3
Chiusi ...98... A4
Chiva ...75... F2
Chivasso ...88... B1
Chlebowo ...39... F3
Chlemoútsi ...120... B3
Chobham ...25... D2
Chociwel ...35... F2
Chodová Planá ...43... D2
Chojna ...35... E2
Cholet ...53... E1
Chollerford ...21... D3
Chomakovtsi ...114... B2
Chomutov ...43... E3
Chop ...107... D4
Chorges ...65... E4
Chorley ...22... C3
Choszczno ...35... F2
Choye ...56... B2
Chrastava ...43... F4
Christchurch ...27... E2
Christiansfeld ...12... B1
Chulmleigh ...26... C2
Chuprene ...113... E2
Chur ...85... D2
Church Stoke ...22... C2
Church Stretton ...22... C2
Churchill ...27... D3
Churek ...114... B1
Churston Ferrers ...27... D1
Churt ...25... D1
Chynava ...43... E2
Chynov ...43... F1
Ciboure ...62... A2
Cićevac ...113... D2
Cidones ...68... C2
Cierp ...62... C1
Cieza ...81... E3
Cifuentes ...74... C4
Cigánd ...107... D4
Cigliano ...88... B2
Ciineni ...108... B1
Cilibia ...115... D4
Cilipi ...111... D1
Cillas ...75... D4
Cîmpeni ...107... E2
Cimpia Turzii ...108... B2
Cîmpina ...114... C4
Cîmpu lui Neag ...107... E1
Cîmpulung ...108... C1
Cîmpulung Moldovenesc ...108... C3
Cînarli ...119... D2
Cincu ...108... B1
Cinderford ...27... E4
Ciney ...31... D2
Cinfães ...720... C3
Cingoli ...95... E1
Cínisi ...102... B3
Cinovec ...43... E3
Cintegabelle ...63... E2
Cintruénigo ...69... D2
Ciocănești ...108... C3
Ciocănești ...115... D3
Ciocîrlia ...115... F3
Ciorani ...115... D4
Ciorăști ...109... E1
Ciorcîrlia ...115... D4
Ciorogirla ...114... C3
Cîrbești ...113... E4
Cirella ...100... C2
Cirencester ...27... E3
Cirey ...56... C4
Ciriè ...88... B1
Cîrlibaba ...108... C3
Cirò Marina ...101... E1
Cislău ...109... D1
Cisnădie ...108... B1
Cista Provo ...110... C2
Cisterna di Latina ...98... B2
Cistierna ...67... F3
Cîtcău ...107... E3
Città di Castello ...95... D2
Città di Pieve ...98... A4
Città San Angelo ...98... C3
Cittadella ...90... C2
Cittaducale ...98... B3
Cittanova ...103... F4
Ciucea ...107... E3
Ciucurova ...115... F4
Ciudad Real ...74... B1
Ciudad Rodrigo ...73... D2
Ciumeghiu ...107... D2
Ciurulease ...107... E2
Ciutadella ...77... F4
Cividale di Friuli ...91... E3
Civita Castellana ...98... B3
Civitanova ...95... E1
Civitavécchia ...97... F2
Civitella Rovebo ...98... C2
Civray ...58... C3
Civrieux-d'A. ...60... C3
Cizer ...107... E3
Clabhach ...18... B1
Clachan ...15... E4
Clackmannan ...20... C4
Clacton-on-Sea ...25... F2
Cladich ...18... C1
Clady ...14... C2
Clairvaux-les-Lacs ...61... D4
Clamecy ...55... D2
Clane ...17... E3
Claonaig ...15... E4

Clapham ...21... D1
Clapham ...23... E1
Clara ...17... D3
Clare ...25... E3
Clarecastle ...16... B3
Claremorris ...16... B4
Clarinbridge ...16... C3
Clashmore ...19... D3
Clashmore ...16... C1
Clashnessie ...18... C4
Claudy ...15... D2
Clausthal-Zellerfeld ...37... E2
Clavière ...61... E1
Clay Cross ...23... E3
Cleanovu ...113... E3
Cleat ...19... F1
Cleator Moor ...20... C1
Clécy ...49... D1
Cleethorpes ...23... F3
Cleeve ...27... D3
Clefmont ...56... A3
Clejani ...114... C3
Clelles ...61... D1
Cléon ...50... B2
Clermont ...50... B2
Clermont-en-Argonne ...51... D1
Clermont-Ferrand ...60... A3
Clermont-l'Hérault ...64... B2
Clerval ...56... C2
Clervaux ...31... E2
Cléry ...54... B2
Cles ...90... B3
Clevedon ...27... D3
Cley-next-the-Sea ...25... E4
Clifden ...16... B4
Cliffe ...25... E2
Cliffony ...14... C2
Cliftonville ...25... E2
Clisson ...53... D1
Clitheroe ...23... D4
Cliveden ...25... D2
Clogan ...16... C3
Clogh ...17... D3
Clogheen ...16... C2
Clogher ...15... D2
Clohamon ...17... E2
Clonakilty ...16... B1
Clonard ...17... D3
Clonaslee ...17... D3
Clonbulloge ...17... D3
Clonbur ...16... B4
Clondalkin ...17... E3
Clones ...15... D1
Clonkeen ...16... B1
Clonmany ...15... D3
Clonmel ...17... D2
Clonmellon ...17... D4
Clonmore ...16... C3
Clonony ...16... C3
Clonoulty ...16... C2
Clonroche ...17... D2
Clontibret ...15... D1
Cloomdara ...16... C4
Cloonbannin ...16... B1
Cloonlara ...16... C2
Clophill ...25... D3
Cloppenburg ...32... C1
Clough ...19... D1
Cloughjordan ...16... C3
Clova ...19... D2
Clovelly ...26... C2
Clovenfords ...21... D4
Clows Top ...23... D1
Cloyes ...54... B3
Cloyne ...16... C1
Cluain ...18... C2
Cluj ...107... E2
Clun ...22... C1
Cluny ...60... C4
Cluses ...61... E2
Clusone ...89... D2
Clydach ...26... C4
Clydebank ...20... B4
Clynnogfawr ...22... B2
Clyro ...27... D4
Clyst Honiton ...27... D2
Čmpuri ...109... D2
Coachford ...16... B1
Coagh ...15... D2
Coalisland ...15... D2
Coalville ...23... E2
Cobadin ...115... F3
Cobh ...16... C1
Coburg ...42... B2
Coca ...74... A4
Cocârăști Colt ...114... C4
Cocentaina ...81... F4
Cochem ...40... B2
Cock Bridge ...19... D2
Cockburnspath ...21... D4
Cockermouth ...20... C2
Coddenham ...25... F3
Codicote ...25... D2
Codigoro ...95... D4
Codlea ...108... C1
Codogno ...89... D1
Codróipo ...91... E2
Coedpoeth ...22... C2
Coesfeld ...36... B3
Coevorden ...29... F3
Cofrentes ...75... E1
Coggeshall ...25... E2
Cognac ...58... C3
Cogolin ...65... E2
Coimbra ...72... B2
Coín ...80... A1
Coina ...78... A2
Cojocna ...108... B2
Coka ...106... C4
Colares ...78... A3

Colarețu ...113... E4
Cölbe ...40... C3
Colbitz ...36... C3
Colchester ...25... E2
Coldingham ...21... D4
Coldstream ...21... D4
Colditz ...39... D1
Coleford ...27... D3
Coleraine ...15... D3
Coleshill ...23... D1
Colfiorito ...98... B4
Colico ...89... D3
Coligny ...61... D4
Colintraive ...20... B4
Coll de Nargó ...70... C3
Colle di Vald'Elsa ...94... B1
Colle Isarco-Gossensass ...90... C4
Colleccnio ...93... E4
Colleferro ...98... B2
Collesalvetti ...93... E2
Collesano ...102... C3
Collin ...20... C3
Collinée ...52... C3
Collinstown ...17... D4
Collio ...89... C2
Collioure ...64... A1
Collodi ...94... B2
Collon ...17... A4
Collonges ...61... D3
Collooney ...14... C1
Colmar ...56... C3
Colmars ...65... E3
Colmenar ...80... A1
Colmenar de Oreja ...74... C3
Colmonell ...20... B3
Colne ...23... D4
Cologna Véneta ...90... C1
Cologne ...63... D3
Colombey-les-Belles ...56... B3
Colombey-les-deux-Églises ...55... F3
Colonești ...114... B3
Colorno ...93... E4
Colonia Santa Jordi ...77... E3
Colosimi ...101... D1
Colsterworth ...23... E2
Coltishall ...25... F4
Colunga ...67... F4
Colwall ...27... E4
Colwyn Bay ...22... B3
Colyton ...27... D2
Coma-ruga ...70... C2
Comácchio ...95... D3
Comana ...108... C1
Comănești ...109... D2
Comarnic ...108... C1
Combe Martin ...26... C3
Combeaufontaine ...56... B2
Comber ...15... E2
Combourg ...53... D3
Combronde ...60... A3
Comillas ...68... B4
Cómiso ...103... D1
Commentry ...59... F3
Commercy ...56... B4
Como ...88... C2
Comoriște ...113... D4
Compiègne ...50... B2
Comporta ...78... A2
Comps-sur-Artuby ...65... E3
Comrie ...19... D1
Concarneau ...52... A3
Conches ...49... F1
Concurbión ...66... A3
Condat ...59... F2
Condé-en-Brie ...50... C1
Condé-sur-Noireau ...53... E4
Condeixa-a-Nova ...72... B2
Condom ...62... C3
Condrieu ...60... C2
Conegliano ...91... D2
Conflans ...51... E1
Confolens ...59... D3
Congleton ...23... D3
Congresbury ...27... D3
Conil de la Frontera ...83... E1
Coningsby ...23... F3
Coniston ...20... C2
Conlie ...53... F3
Conna ...16... C1
Connah's Quay ...22... C3
Connel ...18... C1
Connerré ...54... A3
Conon Bridge ...18... C3
Conques ...63... F4
Conselice ...94... C3
Conselve ...90... C1
Consett ...21... D2
Constanța ...115... F3
Constantina ...83... E4
Constantine ...26... B1
Consuegra ...74... B2
Consuma ...94... C2
Contarina ...95... D4
Contay ...50... B3
Contigliano ...98... B3
Contin ...18... C3
Contres ...54... B2
Contrexéville ...56... B3
Conty ...50... B2
Conwil Elvet ...26... C4
Conwy ...22... B3
Cookstown ...15... D2
Coole ...17... D4
Coombe Bissett ...27... E3
Coombe Hill ...27... E4
Cootehill ...15... D1
Copalnic-Mănăștur ...107... D2
Copertino ...101... F3
Cöpköy ...119... D3

Copparo ...94... C4
Coppenbrügge ...37... D3
Copplestone ...26... C2
Copșa Mică ...108... B2
Corabia ...114... B2
Coray ...52... B3
Corbie ...50... B3
Corbigny ...55... D1
Corbii Mari ...114... C3
Corbridge ...21... D3
Corbu de Sus ...115... F3
Corby ...23... E1
Corby Glen ...23... E2
Corcieux ...56... C3
Corconte ...68... B3
Cordes ...63... E3
Córdoba ...80... A3
Cordun ...109... D3
Corella ...69... D2
Corfe Castle ...27... E2
Corfe Mullen ...27... E2
Coria ...73... D1
Corigliano Calabro ...101... D2
Corinaldo ...95... E2
Cork ...16... C1
Corlátel ...113... E3
Corlay ...52... B3
Corleone ...102... B3
Corleto Perticara ...100... C3
Çorlu ...119... E3
Cormainville ...54... B3
Cormeilles ...49... E2
Cormery ...54... A1
Cornamona ...16... B4
Cornățel ...108... B1
Cornea ...113... D4
Cornellana ...67... E4
Cornhill-on-Tweed ...21... D4
Corníglio ...93... D3
Cornimont ...56... C3
Cornuda la Valle ...91... D2
Corofin ...16... B3
Coropceni ...109... E3
Corovodë ...116... C2
Corpach ...18... C2
Corps ...61... D1
Corral de Almaguer ...74... C2
Corréggio ...94... B4
Corrie ...20... B4
Corris ...22... B2
Corsham ...27... E3
Corsock ...20... C3
Corstorphine ...20... C4
Cortachy ...19... E1
Corte ...57... F3
Cortegana ...83... D4
Cortemaggiore ...89... D1
Cortemilia ...92... B3
Cortes ...69... E2
Cortina d'Ampezzo ...91... D3
Corton ...25... F4
Cortona ...94... C1
Coruche ...78... B3
Corund ...108... C2
Corvara in Badia-Kurfar ...90... C3
Corwen ...22... C2
Coryton ...101... D1
Cosenza ...101... D2
Cosereni ...115... D3
Coshieville ...19... D1
Cosne ...55... D2
Cosne d'Allier ...59... F4
Cosoveni ...114... B3
Cossato ...88... B2
Cossé-le-Vivien ...53... E3
Costa da Caparica ...78... A2
Costa Nova ...72... B2
Costache Negri ...109... E1
Costești ...107... E1
Costești ...108... B1
Costești ...114... C3
Costești ...115... F3
Costinești ...115... F3
Costuleni ...109... E3
Coswig ...38... C3
Cotignac ...65... E2
Cotmeana ...114... B4
Cottbus ...39... E2
Cottesmore ...23... E2
Cottingham ...23... E4
Couches ...55... F1
Coucy ...50... C2
Couhé ...58... C3
Couilly ...55... D4
Couiza ...63... E1
Coulommiers ...55... D4
Coulon ...58... B4
Coulonges ...58... B4
Coulport ...20... B4
Coupar Angus ...19... D1
Couptrain ...53... E3
Cour-Cheverny ...54... B2
Courcheval ...61... E1
Courçon ...58... B3
Courmayeur ...88... A2
Courpière ...60... B3
Courseulles-sur-Mer ...49... D2
Courson-les-Carrières ...55... D2
Courteilles ...49... E1
Courtenay ...55... D3
Courtmacsherry ...16... C1
Courtomer ...53... F4
Courtown Harbour ...17... E2
Courtrai (Kortrijk) ...30... C3
Courville ...54... B3
Coutainville ...48... C1
Coutances ...48... C1
Couterne ...53... E3
Coutevroult ...55... D4

Coutras ...58... C1
Couvet ...84... A3
Couvin ...31... D2
Covadonga ...67... F3
Covaleda ...68... C2
Covarrubias ...68... B2
Covăsînt ...107... D2
Covasna ...109... D1
Cove ...18... B3
Coventry ...23... D1
Coverack ...26... B1
Covilhã ...72... C2
Cowbridge ...27... D3
Cowdenbeath ...20... C4
Cowes ...27... F2
Cowfold ...25... D1
Coylton ...20... B3
Coylumbridge ...19... D2
Cozes ...58... B2
Cozia ...114... B4
Crackington Haven ...26... C2
Craco ...101... D3
Craiești ...109... E1
Craiești ...108... B2
Craigavon ...15... D2
Craigellachie ...19... D3
Craighouse ...15... E4
Craigneish ...18... B1
Craignure ...18... B1
Crail ...19... E1
Crailsheim ...45... E4
Craiova ...107... D2
Craiova ...114... B3
Cranbourne ...27... E2
Cranbrook ...25... E1
Cranleigh ...25... D1
Crans ...84... B1
Cranwell ...23... E2
Craon ...53... E2
Craponne-sur-Arzon ...60... B2
Crarae ...18... C1
Crasna ...107... E3
Crasna ...109... E2
Crasna ...109... D1
Craster ...21... E3
Crato ...78... C3
Craughwell ...16... C3
Craven Arms ...22... C1
Crawford ...20... C3
Crawfordjohn ...20... C3
Crawley ...25... D1
Creaca ...107... E3
Creches-sur-Saône ...60... C3
Crécy ...55... D4
Crécy-en-Ponthieu ...50... A3
Crécy-sur-Serre ...50... C2
Credenhill ...27... D4
Crediton ...27... D2
Creetown ...20... B2
Creggs ...16... C4
Creglingen ...45... E4
Creil ...50... B1
Crema ...89... D2
Cremenari ...114... B4
Cremona ...89... D1
Créon ...58... C1
Crepaja ...112... C4
Crépy-en-Valois ...50... B2
Cres ...110... A4
Crescentino ...88... B1
Crespin ...50... C3
Crespino ...94... C4
Cressage ...22... C2
Cressensac ...59... E1
Cresslough ...14... C3
Crest ...60... C1
Cresta ...85... D2
Crețești ...109... E2
Creussen ...42... C2
Creutzwald ...51... F1
Crevalcore ...94... D4
Crèvecœur ...50... A2
Crevedia Mare ...114... C3
Crevillente ...81... E3
Crewe ...23... D3
Crewkerne ...27... D2
Crianlarich ...18... C1
Criccieth ...22... B2
Crich ...23... E3
Crick ...23... E1
Crickhowell ...27... D4
Cricklade ...27... E3
Crieff ...19... D1
Crikvenica ...104... A1
Crimmitschau ...42... C3
Crinan ...15... E4
Crișcior ...107... E2
Crișnjeva ...104... A1
Crissolo ...92... A4
Cristian ...108... B1
Cristuru Secuiesc ...108... C2
Crit ...108... C2
Crivitz ...34... C2
Crna ...104... B2
Crna Trava ...113... D1
Crnča ...112... B3
Crni Lug ...110... B3
Crnomelj ...104... B1
Croagh ...16... B2
Crocketford ...20... C3
Crocq ...59... E3
Crookedwood ...17... D4
Cromarty ...19... D3
Cromer ...25... F4
Cromford ...23... D2
Crook ...21... D2
Crookhaven ...16... B1
Crooklands ...21... D1
Crookstown ...16... B1
Croom ...16... C2

Crosby ... 20 ... B1
Cross Barry ... 16 ... C1
Cross Foxes ... 22 ... B2
Cross Hands ... 26 ... C4
Cross-in-Hand ... 25 ... E1
Crossgates ... 22 ... C1
Crosshaven ... 16 ... C1
Crosshill ... 20 ... B3
Crossmaglen ... 15 ... D1
Crossmichael ... 20 ... C3
Crossmolina ... 14 ... B1
Crosssakeel ... 17 ... D4
Crotone ... 101 ... E1
Crowborough ... 25 ... E1
Crowland ... 23 ... F2
Croy ... 19 ... D3
Croyde ... 26 ... C2
Croydon ... 25 ... D2
Crozon ... 52 ... A3
Crucea ... 115 ... E3
Cruden Bay ... 19 ... E3
Crumlin ... 15 ... E2
Cruseilles ... 61 ... D3
Crusheen ... 16 ... B3
Cruzy ... 64 ... A2
Crvenka ... 106 ... B1
Csabacsüd ... 106 ... C3
Csanádpáca ... 106 ... C2
Csanytelek ... 106 ... B2
Császártöltés ... 105 ... E2
Csávoly ... 105 ... E2
Csenger ... 107 ... D4
Csengersima ... 107 ... E4
Cserebökény ... 106 ... C2
Cserkeszölö ... 106 ... B3
Csobád ... 106 ... C4
Csökmö ... 106 ... C3
Csokonyavisonta ... 105 ... D2
Csongrád ... 106 ... B2
Csór ... 105 ... E3
Csorna ... 105 ... D4
Csorvás ... 106 ... C2
Cuba ... 78 ... C1
Cuckfield ... 25 ... D1
Cuckney ... 23 ... E3
Cucueti ... 114 ... B3
Cudalbi ... 109 ... E1
Cudillero ... 67 ... E4
Cuéllar ... 68 ... A1
Cuenca ... 75 ... D2
Cuers ... 65 ... E2
Cuerva ... 74 ... B2
Cueva de la Pileta ... 83 ... F2
Cuevas del Almanzora ... 81 ... D2
Cuevas del Becarro ... 83 ... F2
Cúglieri ... 96 ... B3
Cuijk ... 29 ... E2
Cuiseaux ... 61 ... D4
Cuisery ... 60 ... C4
Cujmir ... 113 ... E3
Culan ... 59 ... E4
Culdaff ... 15 ... D3
Culemborg ... 29 ... D2
Cúllar de Baza ... 81 ... D2
Cullen ... 19 ... E3
Cullera ... 76 ... A2
Culleybackey ... 15 ... E2
Cullompton ... 27 ... D2
Culoz ... 61 ... D3
Culross ... 20 ... C4
Cults ... 19 ... E2
Cumbernauld ... 20 ... C4
Cummertrees ... 20 ... C3
Cumnock ... 20 ... B3
Cumpăna ... 115 ... F3
Cúneo ... 92 ... B3
Čunski ... 110 ... A4
Cuntis ... 66 ... B3
Cuorgnè ... 88 ... B2
Cupar ... 19 ... E1
Cupello ... 99 ... D2
Čuprija ... 112 ... C3
Curcani ... 115 ... D3
Curia ... 72 ... B2
Curracloe ... 17 ... E2
Curraghboy ... 16 ... C4
Curry ... 14 ... B1
Curry Rivel ... 27 ... D2
Curtea de Argeş ... 114 ... B4
Curtişoara ... 114 ... B3
Curug ... 106 ... B1
Cusset ... 60 ... B3
Cutro ... 101 ... E1
Cuvesdia ... 107 ... D1
Cuvilly ... 50 ... B2
Cuxhaven ... 32 ... C3
Cuzăplac ... 107 ... E3
Cvikov ... 43 ... F3
Cwmbran ... 27 ... D3
Cwmystwyth ... 22 ... B1
Cybinka ... 39 ... F3
Cymmer ... 27 ... D3

D

Dabas ... 106 ... B3
Dabie ... 35 ... E3
Dabilja ... 117 ... F4
Dabo ... 56 ... C4
Dăbuleni ... 114 ... B2
Dachau ... 46 ... C2
Dăeşti ... 114 ... B4
Dagali ... 8 ... C3
Dagebüll ... 32 ... C4
Dahlen ... 39 ... D2
Dahlenburg ... 34 ... B2
Dahme ... 33 ... F3

Dahme ... 39 ... D3
Dahmen ... 34 ... C3
Dahn ... 44 ... B4
Daia ... 115 ... D3
Diamante ... 100 ... C2
Daimiel ... 74 ... B1
Daingean ... 17 ... D3
Dairsie ... 19 ... E1
Dajkanvik ... 4 ... A4
Dal ... 9 ... D3
Dala-Järna ... 10 ... A3
Dalarö ... 10 ... C1
Dalbeattie ... 20 ... C2
Dalby ... 13 ... D2
Dale ... 26 ... B3
Dale ... 8 ... B3
Dale ... 8 ... B4
Dalen ... 8 ... C2
Daliburgh ... 18 ... A2
Dalj ... 105 ... E1
Dalkeith ... 20 ... C4
Dallas ... 19 ... D3
Dalmally ... 18 ... C1
Dalmellington ... 20 ... B3
Dalnaspidal ... 19 ... D2
Dalry ... 20 ... B4
Dalry ... 20 ... B3
Dalrymple ... 20 ... B3
Dals Högen ... 9 ... D1
Dals Långed ... 9 ... E1
Dalsbruk (Taalintehdas) ... 6 ... B1
Dalskog ... 9 ... E1
Dalston ... 20 ... C3
Dalwhinnie ... 19 ... D2
Dammartin-en-Goële ... 50 ... B1
Damp 2000 ... 33 ... E4
Dampierre ... 56 ... B1
Dampierre-sur-Boutonne ... 58 ... C3
Dampierre-sur-Salon ... 56 ... B2
Damville ... 54 ... B4
Damvillers ... 51 ... E2
Danbury ... 25 ... E2
Dăneasa ... 114 ... B3
Daneş ... 108 ... B3
Dangé-St-Romain ... 54 ... A1
Danilovgrad ... 111 ... E1
Danişment ... 119 ... E2
Dannemarie ... 56 ... C2
Dannenberg ... 34 ... B2
Daoulas ... 52 ... A3
Daphni ... 118 ... B2
Darabani ... 109 ... D4
Darány ... 105 ... D2
Darda ... 105 ... E1
Dardesheim ... 38 ... B3
Dargun ... 35 ... D3
Därlingen ... 84 ... B2
Darlington ... 21 ... E2
Dărmăneşti ... 109 ... D2
Darmstadt ... 40 ... C2
Darney ... 56 ... B3
Daroca ... 25 ... E2
Dartford ... 25 ... E2
Dartington ... 26 ... C1
Dartmouth ... 27 ... D1
Daruvar ... 105 ... D1
Darvel ... 20 ... B3
Darwen ... 23 ... D3
Dasing ... 46 ... B2
Daskalovo ... 113 ... E1
Dassel ... 37 ... D2
Dassow ... 34 ... B3
Dasswang ... 46 ... C4
Datteln ... 36 ... B2
Daun ... 40 ... B2
Dava ... 19 ... D3
Dăvăneşti ... 105 ... D3
Daventry ... 23 ... E1
Daviá ... 120 ... C3
Daviot ... 19 ... D3
Davle ... 43 ... F2
Davos ... 85 ... D2
Dawley ... 23 ... D2
Dawlish ... 27 ... D2
Dawlish Warren ... 27 ... D2
Dax ... 62 ... B3
De Cocksdorp ... 29 ... D4
De Haan ... 30 ... B4
De Koog ... 29 ... D4
De Panne ... 30 ... B4
Deal ... 25 ... F1
Deauville ... 49 ... E2
Deba ... 116 ... C4
Debelets ... 114 ... C1
Debenham ... 25 ... E4
Debnevo ... 114 ... C1
Debno ... 35 ... F1
Debovo ... 114 ... C2
Debrc ... 112 ... B4
Debrecen ... 107 ... D3
Debŭr ... 118 ... C4
Decazeville ... 63 ... E4
Decimomannu ... 96 ... B3
Decin ... 43 ... E3
Decize ... 60 ... B4
Deda ... 108 ... B3
Deddington ... 27 ... F4
Dedemsvaart ... 29 ... F3
Dédestapolcsány ... 106 ... C4
Dedham ... 25 ... E3
Degerby ... 6 ... A1
Degerby ... 6 ... C1
Degerfors ... 9 ... F1
Degerhamn ... 13 ... F2
Degerndorf ... 46 ... C1
Degernes ... 9 ... D2
Deggendorf ... 47 ... D3
Dehesa de Campoamor ... 81 ... F3
Deidesheim ... 40 ... C1
Deinze ... 30 ... C3
Dej ... 108 ... B3
Deje ... 9 ... E2

Dejoi ... 114 ... B4
Delbrück ... 36 ... C2
Delčevo ... 117 ... F4
Delden ... 29 ... F2
Délémont ... 84 ... B3
Delft ... 28 ... C2
Delfzijl ... 29 ... F4
Délia ... 102 ... C2
Delianuova ... 103 ... E4
Delitzsch ... 38 ... C2
Delle ... 56 ... C2
Delme ... 56 ... B4
Delmenhorst ... 32 ... C1
Delnice ... 104 ... B1
Delphi ... 120 ... C4
Delsbo ... 10 ... B4
Delvin ... 17 ... D4
Delvina ... 116 ... C2
Demir Kapija ... 117 ... E3
Demirci ... 119 ... F1
Demirköy ... 119 ... E4
Demmin ... 35 ... D3
Den Burg ... 29 ... D4
Den Haag ... 28 ... C2
Den Helder ... 29 ... D3
Den Oever ... 29 ... D3
Denain ... 50 ... C3
Denbigh ... 22 ... C3
Dendermonde ... 30 ... C3
Denekamp ... 29 ... F3
Denholme ... 21 ... D3
Denia ... 76 ... A2
Denizkent ... 119 ... E2
Denkendorf ... 46 ... C3
Dennington ... 25 ... E3
Denny ... 20 ... C4
Dent ... 21 ... D1
Denton ... 23 ... D3
Derby ... 23 ... D2
Derecske ... 107 ... D3
Dereham ... 25 ... E4
Dereköy ... 119 ... E4
Dermantsi ... 114 ... B1
Dermbach ... 41 ... E3
Derneburg ... 37 ... E3
Derrygonnelly ... 14 ... C2
Derrylin ... 14 ... C1
Dersingham ... 25 ... E4
Deruta ... 98 ... B4
Dervaig ... 18 ... B1
Derval ... 53 ... D2
Dervéni ... 120 ... C3
Derventa ... 111 ... D4
Dervock ... 15 ... D3
Desborough ... 23 ... E1
Descartes ... 54 ... A1
Desenzano ... 89 ... E2
Deseşti ... 108 ... B4
Desimirevac ... 112 ... C3
Despotovac ... 113 ... D3
Despotovo ... 106 ... B1
Dessau ... 38 ... C2
Désulo ... 96 ... B2
Desvres ... 50 ... A4
Deszk ... 106 ... B2
Deta ... 106 ... C1
Detmold ... 37 ... D3
Dettelbach ... 41 ... E2
Deurne ... 29 ... E1
Deutsch-Wagram ... 87 ... F4
Deutschkreutz ... 87 ... F3
Deutschlandsberg ... 87 ... D1
Deva ... 69 ... D4
Deva ... 107 ... E1
Dévaványa ... 106 ... C3
Devecser ... 105 ... D3
Devene ... 113 ... E2
Deventer ... 29 ... E2
Deveselu ... 114 ... B3
Devetaki ... 114 ... C2
Devils Bridge ... 22 ... B1
Devin ... 118 ... B4
Devizes ... 27 ... E3
Devnya ... 115 ... E2
Dewsbury ... 23 ... D3
Dháfni ... 120 ... C3
Dhaimoniá ... 121 ... D1
Dhali ... 122 ... B1
Dhamási ... 117 ... E1
Dhekelia ... 122 ... B1
Dhérmi ... 116 ... C2
Dheskáti ... 117 ... E2
Dhiakoptón ... 120 ... C3
Dhídhimoi ... 121 ... D2
Dhidhimótikhon ... 119 ... D3
Dhispilión ... 117 ... D2
Dhístomon ... 120 ... C4
Dhodhóni ... 117 ... D1
Dhoménikon ... 117 ... E1
Dhomnítsa ... 120 ... C4
Dhomokós ... 117 ... E1
Dhoxáton ... 118 ... B3
Dhriópis ... 121 ... D2
Dhrosiá ... 121 ... D2
Dhroushia ... 122 ... A1
Diabaig ... 18 ... B3
Diano Marina ... 92 ... B2
Diavatá ... 117 ... F3
Dicomano ... 94 ... C2
Didcot ... 27 ... F3
Die ... 61 ... D1
Dieburg ... 41 ... D2
Diekirch ... 31 ... E1
Diemelstadt ... 37 ... D2
Dienten ... 86 ... B2
Diepholz ... 36 ... C4
Dieppe ... 49 ... F3
Dierdorf ... 40 ... B3
Dieren ... 29 ... E2
Diesdorf ... 38 ... B4
Diessen ... 46 ... B2
Diest ... 31 ... D3

Dietenheim ... 45 ... E2
Dietfurt ... 46 ... C3
Dietikon ... 84 ... C3
Dietmannsried ... 45 ... E1
Dieulefit ... 64 ... C4
Dieulouard ... 56 ... B4
Dieuze ... 56 ... C4
Diever ... 29 ... E3
Diez ... 40 ... C3
Differdange ... 31 ... E1
Dignano ... 91 ... E3
Digne ... 65 ... E3
Digoin ... 60 ... B4
Dijon ... 55 ... F1
Dikanäs ... 4 ... A4
Dikili ... 119 ... E1
Diksmuide ... 30 ... B4
Dillenberg ... 45 ... C3
Dillingen ... 45 ... E3
Dillingen ... 45 ... A4
Dilwyn ... 22 ... C1
Dimaro ... 90 ... B3
Dimitrovgrad ... 118 ... C4
Dimitrovgrad ... 113 ... E2
Dimovo ... 113 ... E3
Dinan ... 52 ... C3
Dinant ... 31 ... D2
Dinard ... 53 ... D4
Dingelstädt ... 37 ... E2
Dîngeni ... 109 ... D4
Dingle (An Daingean) ... 16 ... A2
Dingolfing ... 47 ... D3
Dingwall ... 18 ... C3
Dinkelsbühl ... 45 ... E3
Dinklage ... 36 ... C4
Dinnet ... 19 ... E2
Dinoze ... 56 ... C3
Dinslaken ... 36 ... B2
Dipkarpaz (Rizokarpaso) ... 122 ... C2
Dippoldiswalde ... 43 ... E4
Dirahion ... 120 ... C2
Dirleton ... 21 ... D4
Disentis-Muster ... 84 ... C2
Dishforth ... 21 ... E1
Diss ... 25 ... F3
Dissen ... 36 ... C3
Distington ... 20 ... C2
Ditchling ... 25 ... D1
Diţeşti ... 114 ... C4
Ditrău ... 108 ... C2
Ditzingen ... 45 ... D3
Dives-sur-Mer ... 49 ... E2
Divonne ... 61 ... D4
Divusa ... 104 ... C1
Djakovica ... 112 ... C1
Djakovo ... 105 ... E1
Djurakovac ... 112 ... C1
Djurås ... 10 ... B3
Djurdjevac ... 105 ... D2
Djurdjevica Tara ... 111 ... E1
Doagh ... 15 ... E2
Doba ... 107 ... E4
Dobanovci ... 112 ... B4
Dobbiaco-Toblach ... 91 ... D4
Dobel ... 44 ... C3
Döbeln ... 39 ... D1
Doberlug Kirchhain ... 39 ... E2
Döbern ... 39 ... F2
Dobersberg ... 87 ... D4
Doboj ... 111 ... D3
Dobra ... 114 ... D4
Dobra ... 107 ... D1
Dobra ... 35 ... F2
Dobřčane ... 113 ... D1
Dobreni ... 109 ... D3
Döbriach ... 86 ... C1
Dobřichovice ... 43 ... E2
Dobrinishte ... 118 ... A4
Dobříš ... 43 ... E2
Dobro Polje ... 111 ... E2
Dobromani ... 111 ... D1
Dobromirka ... 114 ... C1
Dobromirtsi ... 118 ... C3
Dobrosloveni ... 114 ... B3
Dobroteasa ... 114 ... B4
Dobroteşti ... 115 ... D3
Dobrotitsa ... 115 ... D3
Dobrun ... 112 ... B3
Dobrzany ... 35 ... F2
Dobwalls ... 26 ... C1
Docking ... 25 ... E4
Doddington ... 23 ... F2
Doesburg ... 29 ... E2
Doetinchem ... 29 ... E2
Doganović ... 112 ... C1
Dogliani ... 92 ... B3
Doicesti ... 114 ... C4
Dokka ... 9 ... D3
Dokkum ... 29 ... E4
Doksy ... 43 ... F3
Dol-de-Bretagne ... 53 ... D4
Dole ... 56 ... B1
Dølemo ... 8 ... C1
Dolenci ... 117 ... D3
Dolenja Vas ... 104 ... B1
Dolga Vas ... 104 ... C2
Dolgellau ... 22 ... B2
Dolgoye ... 107 ... D3
Dolhasca ... 109 ... D3
Dolíanova ... 96 ... B1
Dolice ... 61 ... D4
Doljani ... 110 ... C3
Doljevac ... 113 ... D2
Döllach ... 86 ... B1
Dollar ... 20 ... C4
Döllbach ... 41 ... D3
Dolle ... 38 ... C4
Döllstädt ... 42 ... B4
Dolna Banya ... 118 ... B4
Dolna Dikanya ... 113 ... E1
Dolna Mitropoliya ... 114 ... B2
Dolni Dâbnik ... 114 ... B2

Dolni Dvořiště ... 47 ... F3
Dolni Lom ... 113 ... E2
Dolno Kamartsi ... 114 ... B1
Dolno Kosovrasti ... 117 ... D4
Dolno Levski ... 114 ... B1
Dolno Novkovo ... 115 ... D1
Dolno Osenovo ... 118 ... A4
Dolno Tserovene ... 113 ... E2
Dolno Ujno ... 113 ... E1
Dolo ... 91 ... D2
Dolores ... 81 ... F3
Dolphington ... 20 ... C4
Dolwyddelan ... 22 ... B2
Domanovići ... 111 ... D1
Domaşnea ... 113 ... D4
Domazle ... 104 ... A2
Domažlice ... 47 ... D4
Dombås ... 2 ... C1
Dombasle ... 56 ... B4
Dombegyhaz ... 106 ... C2
Dombóvár ... 105 ... E2
Dombrot-le-Sec ... 56 ... B3
Domburg ... 28 ... C1
Domèvre-en-Haye ... 56 ... B4
Domfront ... 53 ... E4
Dömitz ... 34 ... B2
Dommitzsch ... 39 ... D2
Domnesti ... 114 ... C4
Domodossola ... 88 ... C3
Dompaire ... 56 ... B3
Dompierre ... 60 ... B4
Domrémy-la-Pucelle ... 56 ... B3
Dómus de Maria ... 96 ... B1
Dömsöd ... 105 ... E3
Don Benito ... 79 ... E3
Doña Mencía ... 80 ... A2
Donaghadee ... 15 ... E2
Donaghmore ... 17 ... D3
Donaueschingen ... 44 ... C2
Donaustauf ... 46 ... B3
Donauwörth ... 46 ... B3
Doncaster ... 23 ... E3
Donegal ... 14 ... C2
Doneraile ... 16 ... C2
Donington ... 23 ... F2
Donja Brela ... 110 ... C2
Donja Brezna ... 111 ... E1
Donja Bukovica ... 111 ... E1
Donja Kamenica ... 112 ... B3
Donja Ljubata ... 113 ... D1
Donja Ljupče ... 112 ... C1
Donja Šatornja ... 112 ... C3
Donje Petrčane ... 110 ... B3
Donji Lapac ... 105 ... B3
Donji Miholjac ... 105 ... E1
Donji Milanovac ... 113 ... D3
Donji Vakuf ... 111 ... D3
Donji Zemunik ... 110 ... B3
Donnersbach ... 86 ... C2
Donnington ... 23 ... D2
Donostia (San Sebastián) ... 69 ... D4
Dontilly ... 55 ... D3
Donzenac ... 59 ... E2
Donzère ... 64 ... C4
Donzy ... 55 ... D1
Doonbeg ... 16 ... B2
Doorn ... 29 ... D2
Doornik (Tournai) ... 30 ... C3
Dor Mărunt ... 115 ... D3
Dorchester ... 27 ... E2
Dorchester ... 27 ... F3
Dordives ... 55 ... D3
Dordrecht ... 29 ... D2
Dores ... 18 ... C2
Dorfen ... 46 ... C2
Dorfmark ... 33 ... D1
Dorgali ... 96 ... C3
Dorking ... 25 ... D1
Dormagen ... 36 ... B1
Dormánd ... 106 ... C4
Dormans ... 50 ... C1
Dornauberg ... 86 ... A1
Dornbirn ... 85 ... D3
Dornburg ... 42 ... C4
Dorndorf ... 41 ... E3
Dornes ... 60 ... A4
Dornie ... 18 ... B2
Dornoch ... 18 ... C3
Dornstetten ... 44 ... C2
Dornum ... 32 ... B2
Dorobanţu ... 115 ... F3
Dorog ... 105 ... E4
Dorohoi ... 109 ... D4
Dorotea ... 4 ... A3
Dörpen ... 32 ... B1
Dörpstedt ... 33 ... D4
Dorrington ... 22 ... C2
Dorsten ... 36 ... B2
Dortan ... 61 ... D3
Dortmund ... 36 ... B2
Dorum ... 32 ... C2
Dörverden ... 33 ... D1
Dörzbach ... 45 ... E3
Dos Hermanas ... 83 ... E3
Dospat ... 118 ... A4
Douai ... 50 ... C3
Douarnenez ... 52 ... A3
Douchy ... 55 ... D2
Doucier ... 61 ... D4
Doudeville ... 49 ... E3
Doué-la-Fontaine ... 53 ... E1
Douglas ... 20 ... B1
Douglas ... 20 ... C4
Douglas ... 16 ... C1
Doulaincourt ... 56 ... A3
Doulevant-le-Château ... 55 ... F3
Doullens ... 50 ... B3
Doúnby ... 19 ... F1
Doune ... 20 ... B4
Dourdan ... 54 ... C3

Douvaine ... 61 ... E4
Douzy ... 51 ... D2
Dovedale ... 23 ... D2
Dover ... 25 ... F1
Dovercourt ... 25 ... F3
Dovre ... 8 ... C4
Downend ... 27 ... E3
Downham Market ... 25 ... E4
Downpatrick ... 15 ... E1
Downton ... 27 ... E2
Dowra ... 14 ... C1
Dozulé ... 49 ... E1
Dr Petru Groza ... 107 ... D2
Drachselried ... 47 ... D4
Drachten ... 29 ... E4
Dragalina ... 115 ... E3
Drăgăneşti ... 109 ... E1
Drăgăneşti de Vede ... 114 ... C3
Drăgăneşti Olt ... 114 ... B3
Drăgăneşti Vlaşca ... 114 ... C3
Drăganu ... 114 ... B4
Drăgăşani ... 114 ... B3
Drăgeşti ... 107 ... D3
Draginje ... 112 ... B4
Dragocvet ... 112 ... C3
Dragodana ... 114 ... C4
Dragoman ... 113 ... E1
Dragomireşti ... 109 ... E2
Dragomireşti ... 108 ... B4
Dragomirovo ... 114 ... C2
Dragomirovo ... 114 ... C2
Drager ... 13 ... D1
Dragos Vodă ... 115 ... E3
Dragoslavele ... 108 ... C1
Dragovishtitsa ... 113 ... E1
Dragsfjärd ... 6 ... B1
Dragsvik ... 8 ... B4
Draguignan ... 65 ... E2
Dragusení ... 109 ... D3
Dráma ... 118 ... B3
Drammen ... 9 ... D2
Drangedal ... 8 ... C1
Dransfeld ... 37 ... D2
Dranske ... 35 ... D4
Draperstown ... 15 ... D2
Drasenhofen ... 87 ... F4
Dravaszabolcs ... 105 ... E1
Draviskos ... 118 ... B3
Dravograd ... 104 ... B3
Drawno ... 35 ... F2
Drawsko Pomorski ... 35 ... F3
Draženov ... 43 ... D1
Drebakau ... 39 ... E2
Dreghorn ... 20 ... B3
Drenovets ... 113 ... E3
Drensteinfurt ... 36 ... B2
Dresden ... 39 ... E1
Dreux ... 54 ... B4
Drevsjø ... 9 ... D3
Drewitz ... 39 ... D3
Drewitz ... 38 ... C3
Dreznik-Grad ... 110 ... B4
Driebergen ... 29 ... D2
Drimnin ... 18 ... B1
Drimoleague ... 16 ... B1
Drimós ... 117 ... E3
Drînceni ... 109 ... E3
Drinjača ... 111 ... E3
Drinovci ... 111 ... D2
Dripsey ... 16 ... C1
Drivstua ... 2 ... C1
Drlače ... 112 ... B3
Drniš ... 110 ... C2
Drøbak ... 9 ... D2
Drochtersen ... 33 ... D3
Drogheda ... 17 ... E4
Droichead Nua (Newbridge) ... 17 ... D3
Droitwich ... 23 ... D1
Dromahair ... 14 ... C1
Dromcolliher ... 16 ... B2
Dromore ... 15 ... D2
Dromore ... 15 ... E2
Dromore West ... 14 ... B1
Dronero ... 92 ... A3
Dronfield ... 23 ... E3
Dronninglund ... 12 ... B3
Dronten ... 29 ... E3
Drosendorf Stadt ... 87 ... E4
Droxford ... 27 ... F2
Drum ... 15 ... D1
Drumberg ... 18 ... C2
Drumconrath ... 17 ... E4
Drumkeeran ... 14 ... C1
Drumlish ... 17 ... D4
Drummore ... 20 ... B2
Drumnadrochit ... 18 ... C2
Drumod ... 16 ... C4
Drumquin ... 14 ... C2
Drumsna ... 14 ... C1
Drusenheim ... 57 ... D4
Drvar ... 110 ... C3
Drvenik ... 110 ... C2
Dryanovo ... 114 ... C1
Drymen ... 20 ... B4
Drynoch ... 18 ... B2
Duagh ... 16 ... B2
Dubá ... 43 ... F3
Duben ... 39 ... E3
Dubica ... 104 ... C1
Dublin Airport ... 17 ... E3
Dubna ... 118 ... B4
Dubossary ... 109 ... E3
Dubovac ... 112 ... C4
Dubrăveni ... 109 ... D1
Dubrovnik ... 111 ... D1
Ducey ... 53 ... D4
Ducherow ... 35 ... E3
Duclair ... 49 ... F2

Name	Page	Grid
Duddon Bridge	20	C1
Dudelange	31	E1
Duderstadt	37	D2
Düdingen	84	B2
Dudley	23	D1
Dueñas	68	A2
Duesund	8	A4
Duffield	23	D2
Dufftown	19	D3
Duga Poljana	112	B2
Duga Resa	104	B4
Dugi Rat	110	C2
Dugo Selo	104	C1
Dübök Izvor	118	C4
Duingt	61	E3
Duino	91	E2
Duisberg	36	A2
Dukat	116	C2
Duleek	17	E4
Dülgopol	115	E1
Dülken	36	A1
Dülmen	36	B2
Dulnain Bridge	19	D2
Dulovo	115	E2
Dulverton	27	D2
Dumaca	112	B4
Dumbarton	20	B4
Dumbrava	107	E2
Dumbrăveni	108	B2
Dumbrăveni	109	D4
Dumfries	20	C3
Dumitra	108	B3
Dun	51	E2
Dun Laoghaire	17	E3
Dun-le-Palestel	59	E3
Dun-sur-Auron	54	C1
Dunaföldvár	105	E3
Dunaharaszti	105	E3
Dunajska Streda	105	D4
Dunakeszi	106	B4
Dunapataj	105	E2
Dunărea	115	E3
Dunaszekcsö	105	E2
Dunaújáros	105	E3
Dunavecse	105	E2
Dunbar	21	D4
Dunbeath	19	D4
Dunblane	20	C4
Dunboyne	17	E3
Dunchurch	23	E1
Duncormick	17	D2
Dundalk	15	D1
Dundee	19	E1
Dunderrow	16	C1
Dundonnell	18	C3
Dundrennan	20	C2
Dundrum	15	E1
Dunfanaghy	14	C3
Dunfermline	20	C4
Dungannon	15	D2
Dungarvan	17	D1
Dungarvan	17	D2
Dungiven	15	D2
Dungloe	14	C3
Dungourney	16	C1
Dunkeld	19	D1
Dunkerque	50	B4
Dunkerque Ouest	50	B4
Dunkineely	14	C2
Dunlavin	17	D3
Dunleer	17	E4
Dunlop	20	B4
Dunloy	15	D3
Dunmanway	16	B1
Dunmore	16	C4
Dunmore East	17	D1
Dunmurry	15	E2
Dunnet	19	D1
Dunning	19	D1
Dunoon	20	B4
Duns	21	D4
Dunscore	20	C3
Dunsford	26	C2
Dunshaughlin	17	E4
Dunstable	25	D2
Dunster	27	D3
Duntulm	18	B3
Dunure	20	B3
Dunvegan	18	B3
Dunwich	25	F3
Durach	115	D2
Durak	119	F1
Duran	115	D2
Durango	68	C4
Durankulak	115	F2
Duras	58	C1
Durban-Corbières	63	F1
Dúrcal	80	B1
Düren	40	A3
Durham	21	E2
Durness	18	C4
Dürnstein	87	E4
Durrës	116	B3
Durrow	17	D3
Durrus	16	B1
Dursley	23	E1
Dursunbey	119	F1
Durtal	53	E2
Düsketna	105	E1
Dusnok	105	E2
Dusseldorf	36	B1
Duved	3	E2
Düvertepe	119	F1
Duvno	111	D2
Dve Mogili	114	C2
Dvor	110	C4
Dwingeloo	29	E3
Dyce	19	E2
Dyffryn Ardudwy	22	B2
Dymchurch	25	F1
Dymock	27	E4
Dyrnesvågen	2	C2
Dyulino	115	E1
Dzhurovo	114	B1
Dziwnow	35	E3
Džumajlija	117	E4

E

Name	Page	Grid
Eaglescliffe	21	E2
Eaglesham	20	B4
Ealing	25	D2
Eáni	117	E2
Eardisley	27	D4
Earith	23	F1
Earl Shilton	23	E2
Earl's Colne	25	E3
Earlston	21	D4
Earsham	25	F3
Easdale	18	B1
Easington	21	E2
Easingwold	21	E1
Easky	14	B2
East Ayton	21	F1
East Bergolt	25	E3
East Cowes	27	F2
East Grinstead	25	E1
East Harling	25	E3
East Kilbride	20	B4
East Knoyle	27	E2
East Linton	21	D4
East Portlemouth	26	C1
East Retford	23	E3
Eastbourne	25	E1
Eastleigh	27	F2
Eastriggs	20	C2
Eastwood	23	E2
Eaton Socon	23	F1
Eaux-Bonnes	62	B1
Eaux-Chaudes	62	B1
Eauze	62	C3
Ebbo (Epoo)	7	D1
Ebbw Vale	27	D3
Ebchester	21	D2
Ebelsbach	42	B2
Ebeltoft	12	B2
Ebeltoft Ferry	12	B2
Eben	86	B2
Ebenfurth	87	F3
Ebensee	86	C3
Eberbach	41	D1
Ebermannstadt	42	B2
Ebern	42	B2
Ebersbach	39	F1
Ebersberg	46	C2
Eberschwang	86	C3
Ebersdorf	33	D2
Eberstein	87	D1
Eberswalde	35	E1
Ebingen	45	D2
Éboli	100	B3
Ebrach	41	E2
Ebreichsdorf	87	E3
Ebreuil	60	A3
Eccles	21	D4
Eccleshall	23	D2
Eceabat	119	D2
Echallens	84	A2
Echallon	61	D3
Echarri-Aranaz	69	D3
Echte	19	E2
Echte	37	E2
Écija	83	F3
Ečka	106	C1
Eckartsberga	38	C1
Eckernförde	33	D4
Eckerö	11	D2
Eckington	23	D3
Ecommoy	53	F2
Ecouis	49	F2
Ecsegfalva	106	C3
Ecueillé	54	B1
Ecury	55	E4
Ed	9	D1
Eda glasbruk	9	E4
Edam	29	D3
Edane	9	E2
Edderton	19	D3
Eddleston	20	C4
Ede	29	E2
Edebäck	9	E2
Edefors	3	F2
Edelény	106	C4
Edenbridge	25	E1
Edenderry	17	D3
Edenkoben	44	C4
Edersee	37	D1
Edewecht	32	C2
Edgeworthstown	17	D4
Edhessa	117	E3
Edinbain	18	B3
Edinburgh	20	C4
Edirne	119	D4
Edland	8	B2
Édolo	89	E3
Edremit	119	E1
Edsbro	10	C2
Edsbruck	13	F4
Edsbyn	10	B4
Edsele	4	A2
Edsleskog	9	E1
Edsvalla	9	E2
Edzell	19	E2
Eelde-Paterswolde	29	F4
Eferding	86	C4
Efira	120	B3
Efkarpia	117	F3
Eforie Nord	115	F3
Eforie Sud	115	F3
Egein	38	C3
Egense	12	B3
Eger	106	C4
Egerlövö	106	C4
Egernsund	12	B1
Egersund	8	A1
Egervár	104	C3
Egestorf	33	E2
Egg	85	D3
Eggedal	8	C3
Eggenburg	87	E4
Eggelfelden	47	D2
Eggesford	26	C2
Eggesin	35	E3
Egglestone	21	D2
Eghezée	31	D3
Egletons	59	E2
Eglingham	21	D3
Eglinton	15	D3
Egmond aan Zee	29	D3
Egremont	20	C2
Egtved	12	B2
Eguzon	59	E4
Egwyswrw	22	A1
Egyek	106	C4
Ehingen	45	D2
Ehnen	31	F1
Ehra-Lessien	38	B4
Ehrwald	85	E3
Eibar	69	D4
Eibenstock	43	D3
Eibergen	29	F2
Eibiswald	87	D1
Eichendorf	47	D3
Eichstätt	46	B3
Eide	8	A1
Eide	2	B2
Eidefoss	9	D2
Eidfjord	8	B3
Eidsburgarden	8	C4
Eidsdal	2	C1
Eidsøra	2	C1
Eidsvåg	2	C1
Eidsvoll	9	D3
Eikelandsosen	8	A3
Eikenes	8	A4
Eiksund	2	A1
Eilenburg	39	D2
Eilsleben	38	B3
Einavoll	9	D3
Einbeck	37	E2
Eindhoven	29	E1
Einsiedeln	84	C3
Eisenach	41	E4
Eisenberg	42	C4
Eisenerz	87	D2
Eisenhüttenstadt	39	F3
Eisenkappel	87	D1
Eisenstadt	87	F3
Eisfeld	42	B3
Eisleben	38	C2
Eislingen	45	D3
Eitorf	40	B3
Eivissa (Ibiza)	76	C2
Ejea de los Caballeros	69	E2
Ejstrup	12	B2
Ekáli	121	E3
Ekenäs (Tammisaari)	6	C1
Ekenässjön	13	E3
Ekhinos	118	C3
Ekshärad	9	E2
Eksjö	13	E4
Ekzarh Antimovo	115	D1
El Arahal	83	E4
El Barco de Avila	73	E2
El Barco de Valdeorras	67	D2
El Berrón	67	E4
El Bodón	73	D2
El Bonillo	75	D1
El Bosque	83	E1
El Burgo	83	F2
El Burgo de Ebro	69	F1
El Burgo de Osma	68	C1
El Cabaco	73	E2
El Cubo de Tierra del Vino	73	E3
El Escorial	74	B3
El Grado	70	A3
El Masnou	71	D2
El Molar	74	B4
El Pardo	74	B3
El Pedroso	83	E4
El Perelló	70	B1
El Perelló	76	A2
El Plade de María	70	C2
El Pont de Suert	70	B4
El Port de la Selva	71	E4
El Portil	82	C3
El Puente del Arzobispo	79	F4
El Puerto de Santa Maria	83	D2
El Real de San Vicente	74	A3
El Rocío	83	D3
El Ronquillo	83	E4
El Saler	75	F1
El Saucejo	83	F3
El Serrat	70	C4
El Toboso	74	C2
El Vendrell	70	C2
El Villar de Arnedo	69	D2
Elaia	121	D1
Elaiokhória	117	F2
Elaión	120	C4
Elämäjärvi	5	E2
Elan	22	C1
Elantxobe	68	C4
Elassón	117	E4
Elátia	120	C4
Elbasan	116	C3
Elbeuf	49	F2
Elbigenalp	85	E3
Elbingerode	38	B2
Elburg	29	E3
Elche	81	D4
Elche de la Sierra	81	D4
Elda	81	F4
Eldalsosen	8	B4
Eldena	34	B2
Eleftherokhóri	117	D2
Eleftheroúpolis	118	B3
Elek	106	C2
Elena	115	D1
Elevthérion	117	E1
Elgå	9	E4
Elgg	84	C3
Elgin	19	D3
Elgóiba	69	D4
Elgol	18	B2
Elie	19	E1
Elika	121	D2
Elimäki	7	D2
Elin Pelin	113	E1
Eliseyna	113	E2
Elizondo	69	E4
Elkhovo	119	D4
Ellenberg	45	E3
Ellesmere	22	C2
Elligen	46	B3
Ellinko	121	D3
Ellon	19	E2
Ellös	12	C4
Ellwangen	45	E2
Elmpt	36	A1
Elmshorn	33	D3
Elne	64	A1
Elnesvågen	2	B1
Elöszállás	105	E3
Eloúnda	122	C4
Elphin	16	C4
Elsdon	21	D3
Elsfleth	32	C2
Elst	29	E2
Elstead	25	D1
Elster	39	D2
Elsterberg	42	C3
Elsterwerda	39	E2
Elten	36	A2
Eltmann	42	B2
Eltville	40	C2
Elvas	78	C3
Elvbruna	9	E4
Elvedon	25	E3
Elverum	9	D3
Elvestad	9	D2
Elvsis	121	D3
Elzach	44	C2
Elze	37	D3
Emba	122	A1
Embleton	21	E3
Emboreion	121	F1
Embrun	65	E4
Emden	32	B2
Emlichheim	36	B4
Emmaboda	13	E2
Emmaste	11	E1
Emmeloord	29	E3
Emmen	29	F3
Emmendingen	44	C2
Emmerich	36	A2
Emöd	106	C4
Emona	115	E1
Empoli	94	B2
Empúriabrava	71	E4
Emsdetten	36	B3
Emskirchen	42	B1
Emstek	32	C1
Emsworth	25	D2
Emyvale	15	D2
Enåger	10	B4
Encamp	70	C4
Encinasola	79	D1
Encio	68	C3
Enden	9	D4
Endicik	119	E2
Endorf	47	D2
Endröd	106	C3
Enebakk	9	D2
Enese	105	D4
Enfesta (Pontecesures)	66	B3
Enfield	17	D3
Engelberg	84	C2
Engelhartszell	86	C4
Engelia	9	D3
Engelskirchen	40	B4
Engen	45	D2
Enger	36	C3
Engerdal	9	D3
Engerneset	9	E3
Enghien	30	C3
Engjan	2	C2
Englefontaine	50	C3
Enguera	75	F1
Enisala	115	F4
Enkhuizen	29	D3
Enklinge	11	D3
Enköping	10	C2
Enna	102	C2
Ennerdale	20	C2
Ennis	16	B3
Enniscorthy	17	D2
Enniscrone	14	B1
Enniskean	16	B1
Enniskillen	14	C2
Ennistymon	16	B3
Enns	87	D3
Eno	7	F4
Enonkoski	7	E3
Enschede	29	F2
Ensisheim	56	C2
Enstingen	45	D3
Enstone	27	F4
Entlebuch	84	B2
Entraygues-sur-Truyère	63	F4
Entrevaux	65	E3
Entrèves	88	C2
Enviken	10	B3
Enying	105	E3
Epanomí	117	F2
Epannes	58	B3
Epe	29	E3
Epe	36	B3
Épernay	50	C1
Épernon	54	B3
Épila	69	E1
Épinal	56	B3
Episcopía	101	D2
Episkopi	122	A3
Episkopi	122	A1
Epitálion	120	B3
Epône	54	C4
Epoo (Ebbo)	7	D1
Eppingen	45	D4
Epsom	25	D2
Eptakhórion	117	D2
Epureni	109	E2
Ervy-le-Châtel	55	E3
Eraclea	91	D2
Eräjärvi	6	C2
Eratini	120	C4
Erba	89	D2
Erbach	41	D1
Erbalunga	57	F3
Erbendorf	42	C2
Ercolano	100	A3
Ercsi	105	E3
Érd	105	E3
Erdek	119	E2
Erding	46	C2
Eremitu	108	C2
Erenköy (Kokkina)	122	A3
Eressós	119	D1
Erétria	121	D4
Érévent	50	B3
Erfde	33	D3
Ergama	119	E1
Ergoldsbach	46	C3
Erice	102	A3
Ericeira	78	A3
Eriksberg	4	A3
Erikslund	3	F1
Eriksmåla	13	E3
Erimoúpolis	122	C4
Erithrai	121	D3
Erkelenz	40	A4
Erlangen	42	B1
Erlsbach	86	A1
Ermenonville	50	B1
Ermióni	121	D2
Ermoúpolis	121	F3
Ermsleben	38	B2
Erndtebrück	40	C4
Erneé	53	E3
Ernei	108	B2
Ernstbrunn	87	E4
Erquy	52	C4
Errazu	69	E4
Erro	18	C2
Errol	19	D1
Ersekë	117	D2
Erstein	57	D3
Ertuğrul	119	E1
Ervenik	110	B3
Ervidel	78	B1
Erwitte	36	C4
Erwood	27	D4
Erxleben	38	B3
Esbjerg	12	A2
Esbo (Espoo)	6	C1
Escalaplano	96	B2
Escalona	74	A3
Escaroz	69	E3
Escatrón	69	F1
Esch	31	E2
Esch-sur-Alzette	31	E1
Eschede	37	E4
Eschenbach	42	C2
Eschenburg-Eibelshausen	40	C3
Eschenlohe	46	B1
Eschershausen	37	D2
Eschwege	37	E1
Eschweiler	40	A3
Escombreras	81	F2
Esens	32	B3
Esentepe (Ayios Amvrosios)	122	B2
Esími	119	D3
Eskdale	20	C2
Eskilstuna	10	B1
Eslohe	36	C1
Eslöv	13	D2
Esneux	31	D2
Espalion	63	F4
Espedale	8	A2
Espejo	80	A3
Espelette	62	A2
Espeli	8	B1
Espelkamp	36	C3
Espiel	79	F1
Espinama	68	A4
Espinosa de los Monteros	68	B4
Espírito Santo	82	C3
Espoo (Esbo)	6	C1
Espot	70	B4
Esse (Ähtävä)	5	D2
Essen	36	C4
Essen	36	B2
Essenbach	46	C3
Esslingen	45	D3
Estagel	63	F1
Estaires	50	B4
Estarreja	72	B3
Estavayer-le-Lac	84	A2
Este	90	C1
Estella	69	D3
Estepa	83	F3
Estepona	83	F1
Esternay	55	D4
Esterri de Anéu	70	B4
Esterwegen	32	B1
Estissac	55	E3
Estoril	78	A2
Estrées-St-Denis	50	B2
Estremoz	78	C2
Esztergom	105	E4
Étables-sur-Mer	52	C4
Etain	51	E1
Etalle	31	E1
Étampes	54	C3
Etaples	50	A3
Eteläinen	6	C2
Etensjøen	8	A2
Etili	119	E2
Etretat	49	E2
Etropole	114	B1
Ettelbruck	31	E1
Ettenheim	44	C2
Ettington	27	E4
Ettlingen	44	C3
Eu	49	F3
Eupen	51	E3
Eura	6	B2
Eurajoki	6	B2
Eurooport	28	C2
Euskirchen	40	A3
Eutin	33	E3
Eutzsch	39	D2
Evanger	8	B3
Evanton	18	C3
Evaux-les-Bains	59	F3
Evdhimou	122	A1
Evendorf	33	E2
Evesham	27	E4
Evian	61	E4
Evijärvi	5	D2
Evinokhórion	120	B4
Evisa	57	E3
Evje	8	B1
Evolène	84	B1
Évora	78	C2
Evpálion	120	C4
Evran	53	D3
Evreux	49	F1
Evron	53	E3
Evry	54	C4
Evzoni	117	E3
Excideuil	59	D2
Exertal	37	D3
Exeter	27	D2
Exford	27	D2
Exmes	53	F4
Exmouth	27	D2
Exokhi	118	B3
Eye	23	F2
Eye	25	E3
Eyemouth	21	D4
Eyguières	64	C3
Eygurande	59	F2
Eymet	58	C1
Eymoutiers	59	E3
Eyrecourt	16	C3
Ezcaray	68	C2
Ezeriş	107	D1
Ezine	119	D1

F

Name	Page	Grid
Faak	86	C1
Fåberg	9	D4
Fábiánháza	107	D4
Fåborg	12	B1
Fabriano	95	D1
Făcăeni	115	E3
Facture	58	B1
Faenza	94	C3
Faeto	99	E1
Fågáraş	108	C1
Fågelsjö	10	A4
Fågelsundet	10	C3
Fagernes	9	E2
Fagerhult	13	E3
Fagernes	9	E2
Fagersta	10	B2
Fagerstrand	9	D2
Fåget	107	D1
Fågetelu	114	B4
Faido	84	C2
Fairford	27	E3
Fairlie	20	B4
Fakenham	25	E4
Fakse	12	C1
Fakse Ladeplads	12	C1
Falaise	53	E4
Falatados	121	F3
Falcade	90	C3
Fălciu	109	E2
Falconara Marittima	95	E2
Falcone	103	D3
Faleshty	109	E4
Falkenberg	13	D3
Falkenberg	39	D2
Falkenstein	43	D3
Falkirk	20	C4
Falkland	19	D1
Falköping	13	D4
Fallersleben	38	B3
Fällfors	4	C4

Fallingbostel ....33....D1
Falmouth ....26....B1
Falset ....70....B2
Falsterbo ....13....D1
Falstone ....21....D3
Fălticeni ....109....D3
Falun ....10....B3
Fanári ....121....D3
Fanárion ....117....E1
Fanárion ....118....C3
Fangersanna ....9....F1
Fanjeaux ....67....E2
Fano ....95....E2
Fărăgău ....108....B2
Fårbo ....13....F3
Fărcașa ....107....E3
Farebersviller ....51....F1
Fareham ....27....F2
Färgelanda ....9....E1
Färila ....10....B4
Faringdon ....27....E3
Färjestaden ....13....F2
Farkadhon ....117....E1
Farkasgyepü ....105....D3
Farkaždin ....112....C4
Färna ....10....B2
Farnaght ....17....D4
Färnäs ....10....A3
Farnborough ....25....D1
Farnese ....97....F3
Farnham ....25....D1
Faro ....82....B3
Fårösund ....11....F2
Farranfore ....16....B2
Fársala ....117....E1
Far Sawrey ....20....C2
Farsø ....12....B3
Farstad ....2....B2
Farsund ....8....B1
Farum ....12....C2
Fasano ....101....E4
Fataca ....82....A3
Fátima ....78....B4
Fättjaur ....3....F4
Faucogney ....56....C2
Fauldhouse ....20....C4
Faulensee ....84....B2
Faulquemont ....51....F1
Făurei ....109....D1
Fauville ....49....E2
Fåvang ....9....D4
Favara ....102....C2
Favareta ....76....A2
Faverges ....59....E3
Faverney ....56....B2
Faversham ....25....E2
Fawley ....27....F2
Fayence ....65....E3
Fayl-Billot ....56....B2
Feakle ....16....C3
Fearnan ....19....D1
Fécamp ....49....E2
Feces de Abajo ....66....C1
Feda ....8....B1
Fegen ....13....D3
Feggeklit ....12....B3
Fegyvernek ....106....C2
Fehérgyarmat ....107....D4
Fehrbellin ....35....D1
Fehring ....87....E1
Feiring ....9....D3
Feketic ....106....B1
Felanitx ....77....E3
Feld ....86....C1
Feldafing ....46....C2
Feldbach ....87....E1
Feldberg ....44....C2
Feldberg ....35....D2
Feldioara ....108....C1
Feldkirch ....85....D3
Feldkirchen ....46....C2
Feldkirchen ....86....C1
Feleacu ....107....C2
Felgueiras ....72....B4
Felixstowe ....25....F3
Fellbach ....45....D3
Felletin ....59....E3
Felnac ....106....C2
Felsönyárád ....106....C4
Felsösolca ....106....C4
Felsöszentiván ....105....C2
Felsötárkány ....106....C4
Felton ....21....E3
Feltre ....90....C4
Femundsenden ....9....E4
Fenagh ....17....C1
Fene ....66....C4
Fenékpuszta ....105....D3
Fener ....90....C2
Fenes ....107....E2
Fenestrelle ....88....A1
Fénétrange ....56....C4
Fenwick ....20....B4
Feolin Ferry ....15....E4
Ferangen ....3....D1
Ferdinandshof ....35....E3
Fère-Champenoise ....55....E4
Fère-en-Tardenois ....50....C1
Ferentino ....98....C2
Feria ....79....C2
Feričanci ....105....D1
Ferleiten ....86....B2
Fermo ....95....E1
Fermoselle ....73....E3
Fermoy ....16....C1
Ferness ....19....D3
Ferns ....17....E2
Ferrara ....94....C4
Ferreira do Alentejo ....78....B1
Ferreira do Zêzere ....78....B4
Ferrette ....56....C2
Ferriere ....93....D3

Ferrières ....55....D3
Ferring ....12....A3
Ferrol ....66....C4
Ferryhill ....21....E2
Ferryside ....26....C4
Fertöszentmiklós ....105....D4
Festøy ....2....B1
Fetești ....115....E3
Fethard ....17....D1
Fethard ....17....D2
Fetsund ....9....D2
Fettercairn ....19....E2
Feucht ....42....B1
Feuchtwangen ....45....E4
Feurs ....60....B3
Fevåg ....2....C2
Fevik ....8....C1
Ffestiniog ....22....B2
Fiamignano ....98....C3
Fibis ....106....C1
Ficulle ....98....A4
Fidenza ....93....D4
Fieberbrunn ....86....B2
Fieni ....114....C4
Fier ....116....C3
Fiera di Primiero ....90....C3
Fierbinți ....114....C3
Fiesch ....84....B2
Fiésde ....94....C2
Figari ....37....F1
Figeac ....63....E4
Figeholm ....13....F3
Figueira da Foz ....72....B2
Figueira de Castelo Rodrigo ....73....D3
Figueiro dos Vinhos ....72....B1
Figueres ....71....D4
Filákion ....119....D4
Fil'akovo ....106....B4
Filey ....25....F4
Fildu ....107....E3
Filevo ....118....C4
Filey ....21....F1
Filia ....119....D1
Filiași ....113....E4
Filiátes ....116....C1
Filitrá ....120....B2
Filipești ....109....D2
Filipstad ....9....F2
Fillan ....2....C2
Filóti ....121....F2
Filottrano ....95....E1
Finale Emília ....94....C4
Finale Ligure ....92....C3
Finby (Särkisalo) ....6....B1
Findhorn ....19....D3
Findon ....25....D1
Finedon ....23....E1
Finikoús ....120....C2
Finja ....13....D2
Finnea ....17....D4
Finnentrop ....36....C1
Finow ....35....E1
Finsand ....9....D3
Finspång ....10....B1
Finsterwalde ....39....E2
Finstown ....19....F1
Finström ....11....D2
Fintinele ....114....C2
Fintona ....15....D2
Fionnphort ....18....B1
Fiorenzuola d'Arda ....93....D4
Firanli ....119....D1
Firenze ....94....C2
Firenzuola ....94....C3
Firiza ....107....E4
Firliug ....107....D1
Firminy ....60....B2
Fischamend ....87....F3
Fischbeck ....38....C4
Fischen ....45....E1
Fishbach ....44....B3
Fishbourne ....27....F2
Fishguard ....26....B4
Fishnish ....18....B1
Fiskårdho ....120....A4
Fiskebäckskil ....12....C4
Fiskö ....11....D3
Fismes ....50....C2
Fisterra ....66....A3
Fitero ....69....D2
Fitjar ....8....A3
Fittleworth ....25....D1
Fiumefreddo ....103....E3
Fiumicino ....98....A2
Five Oaks ....22....C3
Fivemiletown ....15....D2
Fivizzano ....93....E3
Fizeșcu Gherlii ....108....B3
Fjæra ....8....B2
Fjälklinge ....13....D2
Fjällbacka ....9....D1
Fjällnäs ....3....D1
Fjand Gårde ....12....A3
Fjärdhundra ....10....B2
Fjellerup ....12....B3
Fjellsrud ....9....D2
Fjerritslev ....12....B3
Fjugesta ....10....A1
Flå ....8....C3
Fladdabista ....19....F3
Flaine ....61....E3
Flak ....3....D2
Flåm ....8....B3
Flamborough ....21....F1
Flatabø ....8....B3
Flateby ....9....D2
Flateland ....8....B2
Flatmark ....2....C2
Flatråker ....8....A3
Flatval ....2....C1
Flavigny-sur-Moselle ....56....B3
Fleet ....25....D1

Fleetwood ....22....C4
Flekke ....8....A4
Flen ....10....B1
Flensburg ....33....D4
Flers ....53....E4
Flesberg ....8....C2
Fleurance ....63....D3
Fleuré ....59....D4
Fleurier ....84....A2
Fleurus ....31....D3
Fleury ....49....F2
Flims Waldhaus ....85....D2
Flins ....50....A1
Flint ....22....C3
Flisa ....9....E3
Flix ....70....B2
Flize ....51....D2
Floda ....13....D4
Flogny-la-Chapelle ....55....E2
Flöha ....43....D4
Florac ....64....B4
Florennes ....31....D2
Florenville ....31....D2
Floreshty ....109....E4
Florești ....113....E4
Florești ....107....E2
Florídia ....103....E2
Flórina ....117....D3
Florø ....8....A4
Flötningen ....9....E4
Fluberg ....9....D3
Flüelen ....84....C2
Flumet ....61....E3
Fluminimaggiore ....96....A2
Flums ....85....D3
Foča ....111....E2
Fochabers ....19....D3
Fockbek ....33....D3
Focșani ....109....E1
Fodele ....122....B4
Fódhele ....122....B4
Foggia ....99....E2
Föglö ....11....D2
Fohnsdorf ....87....D2
Foiano di Chiana ....94....C1
Foix ....63....E1
Fojnica ....111....E2
Földeák ....106....C2
Foldereid ....3....E3
Földes ....106....C3
Folégandros ....121....F1
Folgaria ....90....C2
Foligno ....98....B4
Folkestad ....2....A1
Folkestone ....25....F1
Follafoss ....3....D2
Folldal ....2....C1
Föllinge ....3....F2
Follónica ....97....E4
Folmava ....43....D1
Foltești ....109....E1
Fondi ....98....C1
Fondo ....90....C3
Fonni ....96....B2
Fonsagrada ....67....D3
Fontainebleau ....54....C3
Fontaine-Française ....56....A2
Fontaine-le-Dun ....49....F2
Fontecha ....68....C3
Fontenay-le-Comte ....58....B4
Fontenay-Trésigny ....55....D4
Font-Romeu ....63....E1
Fontstown ....17....D3
Fonyód ....105....D3
Fonzaso ....90....C3
Foppolo ....89....D3
Forbach ....51....F1
Forbach ....44....C3
Forcalquier ....65....D3
Forchheim ....42....B2
Ford ....15....E4
Førde ....8....A2
Førde ....8....B4
Fordingbridge ....27....E2
Fordongianus ....96....B2
Forest Row ....25....D1
Forfar ....19....E1
Forges-les-Eaux ....50....A2
Forio ....100....A3
Forli ....95....D3
Forli di Sannio ....99....D2
Forlimpopoli ....95....D3
Formazza ....88....C3
Formby ....22....C3
Formentor ....77....E4
Formerie ....50....A2
Formia ....98....C1
Formigine ....94....C3
Formofoss ....3....E3
Fornaci di Barga ....93....E3
Fornells ....77....F4
Forni di Sopra ....91....D3
Forno di Zoldo ....91....D3
Fornos de Algodres ....72....C2
Fornovo di Taro ....94....A4
Forráskút ....106....B2
Forres ....19....D3
Forró ....106....C4
Fors ....10....B2
Forsbacka ....10....B3
Forsby (Koskendylä) ....7....D1
Forserum ....13....E4
Forshaga ....9....F2
Forsheda ....13....D4
Forsinard ....19....D4
Forsmark ....4....A4
Forsmo ....4....A1
Forsnes ....2....C2
Forssa ....6....C2
Forst ....39....F2
Fort Augustus ....18....C2
Forte dei Marmi ....93....E2

Forth ....42....B1
Forton ....21....D1
Fortrose ....19....D3
Fortun ....8....C4
Fortuna ....81....E3
Fort William ....18....C2
Forvik ....3....E4
Fos ....63....D1
Fossano ....92....B3
Fosses ....31....D2
Fossombrone ....95....D2
Fos-sur-Mer ....64....C2
Foucarmont ....50....A2
Fouesnant ....52....A3
Fougères ....53....D3
Fougerolles ....56....B2
Foulain ....56....A3
Foulkesmills ....17....D2
Fouras ....58....B3
Fourcès ....62....C3
Fourfourás ....122....B3
Four Marks ....27....F2
Fourmies ....50....C1
Fournels ....60....A3
Fournés ....122....A4
Fours ....60....B4
Fowey ....26....C1
Fownhope ....27....D4
Foxdale ....20....B1
Foxford ....14....B1
Foyers ....18....C2
Foynes ....16....B2
Foz ....67....D2
Foz do Arelho ....78....A4
Frabosa Soprano ....92....B3
Fraddon ....26....B1
Fraga ....70....A2
Fraize ....56....C3
Framlev ....12....B2
Framlingham ....25....F3
Frammersbach ....41....D2
Francardo ....57....F3
Francavilla al Mare ....99....D3
Francavilla Fontana ....101....E4
Francavilla di Sicilia ....103....D3
Francofonte ....103....D2
Franeker ....29....E4
Frangista ....120....B4
Frangkástellon ....122....A3
Frangy ....61....D3
Frankenberg ....40....C4
Frankenberg ....104....A4
Frankenburg ....86....B3
Frankenmarkt ....86....B3
Frankenthal ....40....C1
Frankfurt-am-Main ....40....C2
Frankfurt-an-der-Oder ....39....E4
Fränsta ....4....A1
Frant ....25....E1
Františkovy Lázné ....43....D1
Franzburg ....35....D3
Franz Jospehs-Hohe ....86....B1
Frascati ....98....B2
Frasdorf ....47....D2
Fraserburgh ....19....E3
Frashër ....116....C2
Frasin ....108....C3
Fräsned ....115....D3
Fråsvik ....47....D3
Frauenau ....47....D3
Frauenfeld ....84....C3
Frauenstein ....43....E3
Frayssinet ....63....D3
Frechen ....40....B3
Freckenhorst ....36....C2
Fredensborg ....12....C2
Fredenstenborg ....12....C2
Fredericia ....12....B3
Frederikshavn ....12....B3
Frederikssund ....12....C2
Frederiksvårk ....12....C2
Fredrika ....4....B2
Fredriksberg ....9....F2
Fredrikstad ....9....D1
Freemount ....16....B2
Fregenal de la Sierra ....79....D1
Fregene ....98....A2
Freiberg ....43....D4
Freiburg ....33....D3
Freiburg ....44....C2
Freihung ....42....C1
Freilassing ....47....D2
Freising ....46....C3
Freistadt ....47....F3
Freital ....43....E4
Freixo de Espada á Cinta ....73....D2
Fréjus ....65....E2
Frenchpark ....14....C1
Frensham ....25....D1
Freren ....36....B3
Freshford ....17....D2
Freshwater ....27....F2
Fresnay-sur-Sarthe ....53....F3
Fresnes ....51....D3
Fresnes ....56....B2
Fresnes-en-Woëvre ....51....E1
Fréteval ....54....B2
Fretigney ....56....B2
Fretzdorf ....34....C1
Freudenberg ....41....D2
Freudenberg ....40....C4
Freudenstadt ....44....C2
Freyenstein ....34....C2
Freyming Merlebach ....51....F1
Freystadt ....46....C4
Freyung ....47....E3
Fribourg ....84....A2
Frick ....84....B3
Fridaythorpe ....21....F1
Fridingen ....45....D2
Friedberg ....40....C3
Friedberg ....46....B2
Friedberg ....87....D3
Friedeburg ....32....C2

Friedersdorf ....39....E3
Friedland ....37....E2
Friedland ....35....D3
Friedland ....39....E3
Friedrichroda ....41....E3
Friedrichshafen ....45....D1
Friedrichskoog ....33....D3
Friedrichsladt ....33....D4
Friedrichsort ....33....E4
Friesach ....86....C1
Friesack ....39....D4
Friesoythe ....32....C1
Friggesund ....10....B4
Frilford ....27....F3
Frillesås ....12....C3
Frimley ....25....D1
Frinton-on-Sea ....25....F2
Friockheim ....19....E1
Fristad ....13....D4
Fritsla ....13....D4
Fritton ....25....F4
Fritzlar ....37....D1
Frizington ....20....C2
Frodsham ....22....C3
Frohburg ....39....D1
Frohnleiten ....87....D2
Froissy ....50....B2
Frome ....27....E3
Fromentel ....53....E4
Frómista ....68....A2
Fronsac ....63....D1
Frontenhausen ....47....D3
Frontignan ....64....B2
Frosinone ....98....C2
Frövi ....10....B2
Fruges ....50....B3
Frumoasa ....108....C2
Frumosu ....108....C4
Frumușica ....109....D3
Frutigen ....84....B2
Frýdlant ....43....F4
Fucécchio ....94....B2
Fuencaliente ....80....A4
Fuendejalon ....69....E1
Fuengirola ....80....A1
Fuenmayor ....64....C3
Fuente de Cantos ....79....D1
Fuente el Fresno ....74....B1
Fuente el Saz ....74....B3
Fuente-Obejuna ....79....F1
Fuentes ....75....D2
Fuentesaúco ....79....F3
Fuentes de Ayódar ....75....F3
Fuentes de Ebro ....69....F1
Fuentes de Oñoro ....73....D2
Fuerty ....16....C4
Fügen ....86....A2
Fuglebjerg ....12....C1
Fuhrberg ....37....E4
Fulda ....41....D3
Fülöpszállás ....105....E3
Fulpmes ....85....F3
Fulunäs ....9....E4
Fumay ....51....D3
Fumel ....63....D4
Funäsdalen ....3....E1
Fundão ....72....C2
Fundulea ....115....D3
Furadouro Praia ....72....B3
Furculești ....114....C2
Furnace ....20....B4
Furnès (Veurne) ....30....B3
Fürstenau ....36....B3
Fürstenberg ....32....C2
Fürstenberg ....34....C2
Fürstenfeld ....87....E2
Fürstenfeldbruck ....46....C2
Fürstenwalde ....39....E4
Fürstenwerder ....35....D2
Fürstenzell ....47....E3
Furta ....106....C3
Fürth ....42....B1
Furth im Wald ....47....D4
Furtwangen ....44....C2
Furudal ....10....B3
Furuvik ....10....B3
Fusa ....8....A3
Fusch ....86....B2
Fusché Arrëz ....116....C4
Fusché Muhurr ....116....C4
Fuschl ....86....B3
Füssen ....46....B1
Futog ....106....B1
Füzesabony ....106....C4
Füzesgyarmat ....106....C3
Fuzeta ....82....C3
Fyield ....27....F3
Fynshav ....12....B1
Fyresdal ....8....C2
Fyvie ....19....E3″

G

Gabarret ....62....C3
Gabčíkovo ....105....D4
Gabicce Mare ....95....D2
Gabrovo ....114....C1
Gacé ....53....F4
Gacko ....111....E1
Gäddede ....3....F3
Gadebusch ....34....B3
Gadžin Han ....113....D2
Găești ....114....C4
Găgești ....109....E3
Gaggenau ....44....C3
Gagliano del Capo ....101....F2

Gagnef ....10....B3
Gaildorf ....45....D3
Gailey ....23....D2
Gaillac ....63....E3
Gaillon ....49....F1
Gainsborough ....23....E3
Gåio ....116....C1
Gairloch ....18....B3
Gairlochy ....18....C2
Gaj ....112....C4
Galanta ....105....D4
Galashiels ....21....D4
Galata ....115....E2
Galatás ....121....D3
Galați ....109....E1
Galati Marina ....103....E3
Galatina ....101....F3
Galatone ....101....F3
Gålåutas ....108....C3
Galaxidhion ....120....C4
Galbally ....16....C2
Galeata ....94....C2
Galgaguta ....106....B4
Galgamácsa ....106....B4
Galicea ....114....B4
Galicea Mare ....113....E3
Galissas ....121....F3
Galizano ....68....B4
Gallarate ....88....C2
Gallargues ....64....B3
Galliate ....88....C2
Gallípoli ....101....F3
Gallneukirchen ....86....C4
Gällö ....3....F1
Gallur ....69....E2
Galovo ....114....B2
Galston ....20....B3
Galtelli ....96....C3
Galten ....9....E4
Galtür ....85....E2
Galway ....16....B3
Gamaches ....50....A3
Gambárie ....103....E3
Gaming ....87....D3
Gamleby ....13....F4
Gamlingay ....23....F1
Gammel Skagen ....12....C4
Gammelstad ....4....C4
Gammertingen ....45....D2
Gams ....85....D3
Gamzigrad ....113....D3
Gan ....62....B2
Ganacker ....47....D3
Gand (Gent) ....30....C3
Ganderkesee ....32....C1
Gandesa ....70....B1
Gandia ....76....A2
Gandino ....89....D2
Gandria ....84....C1
Gănești ....108....B2
Gănești ....109....C2
Ganges ....64....B3
Gangi ....102....C3
Gangkofen ....47....D3
Ganllwyd ....22....B2
Gannat ....60....A3
Gänserndorf ....87....F4
Gap ....65....D4
Gara Khitrino ....115....D2
Garboldisham ....25....F3
Garching ....47....D2
Garda ....90....B2
Gardanne ....65....D2
Gårdby ....13....F2
Gardelegen ....38....B3
Garding ....32....C4
Gardone Riviera ....90....B2
Gardone Val Trompia ....89....E2
Gárdony ....105....E3
Gårdskär ....10....C3
Gärdslösa ....13....F3
Gardstad ....3....D3
Garelochhead ....20....B4
Garen ....8....B3
Gareśnica ....104....C1
Garessio ....92....B3
Garfenau ....87....E3
Gargaliánoi ....120....B2
Gargellen ....85....D2
Gargnano ....90....B2
Gargnäs ....4....B4
Gargrave ....21....D1
Garlasco ....88....C1
Garlieston ....20....B2
Garlstorf ....33....E2
Garmisch Partenkirchen ....46....B1
Garraf ....70....C2
Garray ....69....D2
Garrel ....32....C1
Garrison ....14....C2
Garristown ....17....E4
Garrovillas ....79....D4
Garrucha ....81....D2
Gars am Kamp ....87....E3
Garthmyl ....22....C2
Gartow ....34....B1
Gartz ....35....E2
Garvagh ....15....D3
Garvald ....21....D4
Garve ....18....C3
Garz ....35....D4
Gaschurn ....85....E2
Gasteiz (Vitoria) ....68....C3
Gastoúni ....120....B3
Gasztony ....104....C3
Gátaia ....106....C1
Gatchina ....7....F1
Gatehouse of Fleet ....20....B2
Gáter ....106....B2
Gateshead ....21....E3
Gattinara ....88....C2
Gatwick ....25....D1

Gaucín...83...F2
Gaupne...8...B4
Gavaloú...120...B4
Gavardo...89...E2
Gavarnie...62...C1
Gávavencselló...107...D4
Gavi...92...C4
Gavião...78...C3
Gävle...10...C3
Gavoi...96...B2
Gavray...48...C1
Gávrion...121...E3
Gávunda...9...F3
Gäxasjö...3...F2
Gaydon...23...E1
Gazimağusa (Famagusta)...122...C1
Geaca...108...B3
Geashill...17...D3
Gebesee...38...B1
Gedem...41...D3
Gedinne...31...D2
Gedney Drove End...25...E4
Gedser...12...C1
Gedsted...12...B3
Geel...31...D4
Geertruidenberg...29...D2
Geesthacht...33...E2
Gefell...42...C3
Gefrees...42...C2
Gehren...42...B3
Geilenkirchen...40...A4
Geilo...8...C3
Geiranger...2...B1
Geiselhöring...47...D3
Geisenfeld...46...C3
Geisenhausen...47...D3
Geisingen...44...C2
Geislingen...45...C3
Geisnes...3...D3
Geithain...39...D1
Geithus...8...C3
Gela...102...C2
Geldern...36...A2
Geldrop...29...E1
Geleen...31...E3
Gelembe...119...F1
Gelibolu...119...D2
Gelida...70...C2
Gelnhausen...41...D2
Gelsenkirchen...36...B2
Gelting...33...D4
Gembloux...31...D3
Gémenos...65...D2
Gemert...29...E1
Gemona di Friuli...91...E3
Gémozac...58...B2
Gemünd...40...A3
Gemünden...41...D4
Gemünden...41...D2
Gemünden...40...B2
Genappe...31...D3
Gençay...58...C4
Gençitkale (Lefkoniko)...122...B2
Génelard...60...B4
General Toshevo...115...E2
Generalski Stol...104...B1
Genève...61...E3
Genk...31...E3
Genlis...56...A1
Gennep...29...E2
Gennes...53...E2
Génolhac...64...B4
Génova...92...C3
Gent (Gand)...30...C3
Genthin...38...C4
Gentioux...59...E3
Genzano di Lucánia...100...C4
Genzano di Roma...98...B2
Geoagiu Băi...107...E1
Georgi Traykov...115...E1
Georgshiel...32...B2
Gera...42...C3
Geraardsbergen...30...C3
Gerabronn...45...E4
Gerace...103...F4
Gérardmer...56...C3
Geras...87...E4
Gerbéviller...56...B3
Gerbstedt...38...C2
Geretsried...46...C2
Gérgal...81...D2
Gerlos...86...A2
Germay...56...A3
Germersheim...44...C4
Gernika-Lumo...68...C4
Gernrode...38...B2
Gernsbach...44...C3
Gernsheim...40...C2
Gerolstein...40...A2
Gerolzhofen...41...E2
Gerona (Girona)...71...D3
Gerovo...104...A1
Gerrards Cross...25...D2
Gersfeld...41...E3
Gersthofen...46...B2
Gescher...36...B3
Geseke...36...C2
Gesualdo...100...B4
Gesunda...10...A3
Geta...11...D3
Getafe...74...B3
Getxo-Algorta...68...C4
Gevgelija...117...E3
Gevrey-Chambertin...55...F1
Gex...61...D4
Geyikli...119...D3
Gföhl...85...D4
Ghalipsós...118...B3
Ghardhiki Ömiléon...120...C4
Ghávros...117...D2
Ghedi...89...E2

Gheorghe Gheorghiu-Dej...109...D2
Gheorgheni...108...C2
Gherla...108...B3
Ghilarza...96...B2
Ghimpați...114...C3
Ghindari...108...C2
Ghisonaccia...57...F2
Ghisoni...57...F2
Giardinetto...99...E1
Giardini...103...E3
Giarmata...106...C1
Giarrantana...103...D2
Giarre...103...E3
Giba...96...B1
Gibellina...102...B3
Gibraleón...83...D3
Gibraltar...83...F1
Gic...105...D3
Gieboldehausen...37...E2
Gien...54...C2
Giengen...45...E3
Giens...65...E2
Gieselwerder...37...D2
Giessbach...84...B2
Giessen...40...C3
Gieten...29...F4
Giethoorn...29...E3
Gifford...21...D4
Gifhorn...37...E3
Gigen...114...B2
Giglio Porto...97...E3
Gignac...64...B2
Gijón...67...E4
Gílău...107...E2
Gilford...15...D2
Gilleleje...12...C2
Gillingham...27...E2
Gillingham...25...E2
Gilwern...27...D4
Gimo...10...C2
Gimont...63...D2
Ginosa...101...D3
Gióia del Colle...101...E4
Gióia Táuro...103...E4
Gioiosa Marea...103...D3
Giornico...84...C2
Giovinazzo...101...D4
Girbou...107...E3
Gîrbou...113...E4
Gírcov...114...B2
Girifalco...101...D1
Girna (Kyrenia)...122...B2
Giromagny...56...C2
Girona (Gerona)...71...D3
Gironella...70...C2
Girov...109...D3
Girvan...20...B3
Gisburn...21...D1
Gislaved...13...D3
Gisors...50...A2
Gistel...30...B4
Gistrup...12...B3
Giuleşti...108...B4
Giulianova...98...C4
Giurgeni...115...E4
Giurgita...113...E3
Giurgiu...115...D2
Give...12...B2
Givet...51...D3
Givors...60...C2
Givry...60...C4
Givry...30...C2
Givry-en-Argonne...51...D1
Gizeux...53...F2
Gjemnes...2...B2
Gjerde...8...B4
Gjermundshamn...8...B3
Gjerrild...12...C3
Gjersvik...3...E3
Gjirokastër...116...C2
Gjø vik...9...D3
Gjølme...2...C2
Gjøra...2...C1
Glachau...43...D3
Gladbeck...36...B2
Gladenbach...40...C3
Glamis...19...E1
Glamoč...110...C3
Glâmos...3...D1
Glamsbjerg...12...B1
Glandore...16...B1
Glanmire...16...C1
Glanworth...16...C1
Glarus...84...C3
Glasgow...20...B4
Glashütte...43...E4
Glaslough...15...D2
Glassan...16...C4
Glastonbury...27...D2
Glava...9...E2
Glavan...119...D4
Glavanovtsi...113...E3
Glavičice...112...A2
Glavnik...112...C1
Gleann Cholm Cille (Glencolumb-kille)...14...B2
Gleisdorf...87...E2
Glenamaddy...16...C4
Glenavy...15...E2
Glenbeigh...16...A1
Glenborrodale...18...B1
Glenbrittle...18...B2
Glencaple...20...C3
Glencarm...15...E3
Glencoe...18...C1
Glencolumbkille (Gleann Cholm Cille)...14...B2
Glendalough...17...E3
Glendaruel...20...B4
Gleneagles...19...D1
Glenealy...17...E3

Glenelg...18...B2
Glenfarne...14...C1
Glenfinnan...18...C2
Glengarriff...16...B1
Glénic...59...E3
Glenluce...20...B2
Glenmore...17...D2
Glenrothes...20...C4
Glenties...14...C2
Glenville...16...C1
Glewitz...35...D3
Glifa...121...D4
Glifádha...121...D3
Gliki...117...D1
Glimåkra...13...D2
Glin...16...B2
Glina...104...C1
Glinsk (Glinsce)...16...B3
Glissjöberg...9...F4
Gloduri...109...D2
Gloggnitz...87...E3
Glommersträsk...4...B4
Glömminge...13...F3
Glóssa...118...B1
Glossop...23...D3
Gloucester...27...E4
Glowe...35...D4
Glöwen...34...C1
Gložan...106...B1
Glozhene...114...B1
Glozhene...113...F2
Glücksburg...33...D4
Glückstadt...33...D3
Gluobinje...113...D4
Glušci...112...B4
Glyn Ceiriog...22...C2
Glyn Neath...27...D3
Glyncorrwg...27...D3
Glyndebourne...25...E1
Glyngøre...12...A3
Gmund...46...C1
Gmünd...86...B1
Gmünd...87...D4
Gmunden...86...C3
Gnarp...10...C4
Gnarrenburg...33...D2
Gnesta...10...C1
Gnisvärd...11...E1
Gnjilane...113...D1
Gnoien...35...D3
Gnosall...23...D2
Gnosjö...13...D3
Goathland...21...E2
Göbel...119...F2
Gobowen...22...C2
Goch...36...A2
Godalming...25...D1
Godby...11...D2
Godech...113...E2
Godelheim...37...D2
Goderville...49...E2
Godmanchester...23...F1
Gödöllő...106...B4
Godovič...104...A2
Gödre...105...D2
Godshill...27...F2
Goes...28...C1
Goeşti...114...B3
Göhren...35...D4
Goirle...29...D1
Góis...72...B2
Goito...90...B1
Gokels...33...D3
Gol...8...C3
Golå...4...D4
Golada...66...C3
Golchen...350...D3
Golczewo...35...F3
Goldbach...41...D2
Goldberg...34...C2
Goldelund...33...D4
Golden...16...C2
Goldenstedt...36...C4
Goleen...16...B1
Golegã...78...B3
Goleniów...35...F3
Goleşti...114...C4
Golfe Juan...65...F2
Golfo Aranci...96...C4
Golfo di Sogno...57...F1
Golfo di Sogno...57...F1
Gollhofen...41...E1
Golling...86...B2
Golpejas...73...E3
Golspie...19...D3
Golssen...39...E3
Golubac...113...D4
Golubovci...112...A1
Golyalo Krushevo...119...D4
Golzow...39...D3
Gómara...69...D1
Gommern...38...C3
Gomshall...25...D1
Gönc...106...C4
Goncelin...61...D2
Gondrecourt...56...A3
Gondrin...62...C1
Gönen...119...E2
Gonnosfanádiga...96...B2
Goodwick...26...B4
Goodwood...25...D1
Goole...23...E3
Goor...29...F2
Goppenstein...84...B2
Göppingen...45...D3
Goražde...112...A2
Gördes...65...D3
Gordes...119...F1

Gordon...21...D4
Gorebridge...20...C4
Goren Chiflik...115...E1
Gorenja Vas...104...A2
Goresbridge...17...D2
Gorey...17...E2
Gorgonzola...89...D2
Goričan...104...C2
Gorinchem...29...D2
Goring...27...F3
Goring-by-Sea...25...D1
Goritsá...120...C2
Göritz...35...E2
Gorizia...91...E2
Gorleston...25...F4
Gorlev...12...C1
Görlitz...39...F2
Gorna Kremana...113...F2
Gorna Oryakhovitsa...114...C1
Gorna Studena...114...C2
Gorni Tsibŭr...113...E3
Gornja Grabovica...111...D2
Gornja Kamenica...113...D2
Gornja Klina...112...C1
Gornja Ploča...110...B3
Gornja Sabanta...112...C3
Gornja Toponica...113...D2
Gornja Tuzla...111...E3
Gornji Lapac...110...C3
Gornji Milanovac...112...C3
Gornji Podgradci...111...D4
Gornji Vakuf...111...D2
Gorran Haven...26...B1
Gorredijk...29...E4
Gorron...53...E3
Gort...16...C3
Gortin...15...D2
Görzke...38...C3
Gorzów Wielkopolski...35...F1
Górzyca...39...F4
Gosau...86...B2
Göschenen...84...C2
Góscino...35...F3
Gosforth...20...C2
Goslar...37...E2
Gospić...110...B3
Gosport...27...F2
Gossau...85...D3
Gössl...86...C2
Gössweinstein...42...C2
Gösting...87...D3
Gostivar...117...D4
Goszczanowo...35...F1
Göteborg...12...C4
Götene...9...E1
Gotha...42...B4
Gotse Delchev...118...B4
Göttingen...37...E2
Götzis...85...D3
Gouarec...52...B3
Gouda...29...D2
Goudhurst...25...E1
Goumáoi...120...C4
Gouménissa...117...E3
Goumois...84...A4
Goúra...120...C3
Gourdon...59...D1
Gourin...52...B3
Gournay-en-Brae...50...A2
Gourniá...122...C3
Gourock...20...B4
Goúvai...122...B4
Gouviá...116...C1
Gouzon...59...E3
Govedartsi...118...A4
Govedjari...111...D1
Gowran...17...D2
Gozdnica...39...F2
Graal-Müritz...34...C3
Grabow...34...C2
Gračac...110...B3
Gračanica...112...B3
Gračanica...112...C1
Graçay...54...C1
Grächen...84...B1
Gradac...111...D3
Gradačac...111...E4
Graddo...11...D2
Gradets...115...D1
Gradevo...118...A4
Gradina...113...E2
Grădinari...113...B3
Grădinari...113...D4
Gradisca...91...E2
Grădiştea...109...E1
Grado...67...E4
Grado...91...E2
Gradsko...117...E4
Grafath...46...B2
Grafenau...47...E2
Gräfenberg...72...B2
Gräfenhainichen...38...C2
Gräfenwöhr...42...C2
Grafing...46...C2
Gräfsnäs...13...D4
Grahovo...111...E1
Graiguenamanagh...17...D2
Grallagh...14...C1
Gram...12...A1
Gramada...113...D3
Gramat...59...E1
Gramatikovo...119...E4
Grametten...87...D4
Gramkow...34...B3
Gramméni Oxiá...120...C4
Grammichele...103...D2
Grampound...26...B1
Gramsh...116...C3
Gramzow...35...E2
Granada...80...B2
Granard...17...D4
Grancey...55...F2

Grand-Champ...52...C2
Grandas de Salime...67...D3
Grandcamp...49...D2
Grande Fougeray...53...D2
Grândola...78...B1
Grandpré...51...D2
Grandrieu...60...B1
Grandtully...19...D1
Grandvilliers...50...E2
Grangärde...10...A2
Grange...14...C2
Grange-Over-Sands...21...D1
Granges-sur-Vologne...56...C3
Grängesberg...10...A2
Grăniceşti...108...C4
Granja...72...B3
Grankulla (Kauniainen)...6...C1
Grankullavik...13...F3
Gränna...13...E4
Granollers...71...D2
Granön...4...B3
Gransee...35...D2
Gransherad...8...C2
Grantham...23...E2
Grantown-on-Spey...19...D2
Grantshouse...21...D4
Granville...53...D4
Granvin...8...B3
Grasmere...20...C2
Grassano...101...D3
Grassau...47...D1
Grasse...65...E3
Grästorp...13...D4
Gratkorn...87...D2
Graulhet...63...E3
Graus...70...A3
Grave...29...E2
Gravedona...89...D3
Gravelines...50...B4
Gravellona-Toce...88...C3
Gravesend...25...E2
Graviá...120...C4
Gravina di Puglia...101...D4
Gravouna...118...B3
Gray...56...B2
Grays...25...E2
Graz...87...E2
Grazalema...83...F2
Grazzanise...100...A4
Grčak...112...C2
Grdelica...113...D1
Greaca...115...D3
Great Ayton...21...E2
Great Bookham...25...D1
Great Crosby...22...C3
Great Dalby...23...E2
Great Driffield...21...F1
Great Dunmow...25...E2
Great Glen...23...E2
Great Malvern...27...E4
Great Missenden...25...D2
Great Offley...25...D2
Great Shefford...27...F3
Great Shelford...23...F2
Great Smeaton...21...E2
Great Staughton...23...F1
Great Witley...23...D3
Great Yarmouth...25...F4
Great Yeldham...25...E2
Greatstone-on-Sea...25...F1
Grebbestad...9...D1
Grebenstein...37...D2
Greding...46...C3
Green Hammerton...21...E1
Greencastle...15...D1
Greenhead...21...D3
Greenlaw...21...D4
Greenock...20...B4
Greenodd...20...C1
Greetsiel...32...B2
Greifenburg...86...B1
Greiffenberg...35...E2
Greifswald...35...D3
Grein...87...D3
Greiz...42...C3
Grenå...12...C3
Grenade...63...D2
Grenade...62...C2
Grenchen...84...B3
Grenoble...61...D2
Gréoux-les-Bains...65...D2
Gresford...22...C2
Gressoney-la-Trinité...88...B2
Gressoney-St-Jean...88...B2
Gresten...87...D3
Greta Bridge...21...D2
Gretna Green...20...C3
Greussen...38...B1
Greve...94...C2
Greven...36...B3
Grevená...117...D2
Grevenbroich...40...A4
Grevenbrück...36...C1
Grevenmacher...31...F1
Grevesmühlen...34...B3
Greyabbey...15...E2
Greystones...17...E3
Grez-en-Bouère...53...E2
Gries-am-Brenner...85...D3
Gries-in-Sellrain...85...D3
Griesbach...47...E3
Grieskirchen...86...C3
Griffen...87...D1
Grignan...64...C4
Grignols...62...C4
Grigoriopol...109...F3
Grillby...10...C1
Grimaldi...101...D1
Grimaud...64...E2
Grimma...39...D1
Grimmen...35...D3

Grimsbu...2...C1
Grimsby...23...F3
Grimstad...8...C1
Grindaheim...8...C4
Grinde...8...A2
Grindelwald...84...B2
Grindleford Bridge...23...D3
Griñón...74...B3
Grinsted...12...A2
Gripenberg...13...E4
Grisignano di Zocco...90...C2
Grisolles...63...D3
Grisslehamn...10...C2
Grivița...115...E4
Grivitsa...114...B2
Gröbers...38...C2
Gröbming...86...C2
Grocka...112...C4
Gröditz...39...D2
Groenlo...29...F2
Grogport...15...E4
Gröhögen...13...F2
Grojdibodu...114...B2
Grömitz...34...B3
Gronau...36...B3
Grong...3...E3
Groningen...29...F4
Groningen...38...B3
Grønnes...2...B1
Grönskåra...13...E3
Gropeni...115...E4
Gropnița...109...D3
Grósio...89...E3
Gross Desingen...37...E4
Gross Räschen...39...E2
Gross Schönebeck...35...D1
Gross-Gerau...40...C2
Gross-Umstadt...41...D2
Grossarl...86...B2
Grossbeeren...39...D3
Grossbreitenbach...42...B3
Grossburgwedel...37...E3
Grosselies...31...D3
Grossenbrode...34...B4
Grossenhain...39...E2
Grossenkneten...32...C1
Grossenzersdorf...87...E3
Grosseto...97...E4
Grossgerungs...87...D3
Grosshabersdorf...42...B1
Grosshöchstetten...84...B2
Grossiegharts...87...D4
Grosspetersdorf...87...E2
Grossraming...87...D3
Grostenquin...51...F1
Grosuplje...104...C2
Grötli...2...B1
Grottáglie...101...E4
Grottaminarda...100...B4
Grottammare...98...C4
Grova...8...C2
Grozd'ovo...115...E1
Grua...9...D3
Grubišno Polje...105...D1
Gruda...111...E1
Grudovo...115...E1
Grums...9...E2
Grünau...86...C2
Grünberg...41...D3
Grünburg...86...C3
Grundfors...3...E4
Grundforsen...9...E4
Grundlsee...86...C2
Grundsel...4...C4
Grundsund...12...C4
Grünenplan...37...D3
Grünheide...39...E4
Grünstadt...40...C1
Grupčin...117...D4
Grüsch...85...D3
Gruyères...84...A2
Gruža...112...C3
Grycksbo...10...B3
Gryfice...35...F3
Gryfino...35...E2
Gryfów Śląski...69...F1
Gryt...13...F4
Grythyttan...10...A2
Gschnitz...85...D3
Gschwend...45...D3
Gstaad...84...B2
Gstadt...47...D2
Gsteig...84...B2
Guadahortuna...80...C2
Guadalajara...74...C3
Guadalcanal...79...E1
Guadalmina...83...F2
Guadalupe...79...F3
Guadarrama...74...B3
Guadix...80...C2
Gualdo Tadino...95...D1
Guarcino...99...D1
Guard Bridge...19...E1
Guarda...72...C2
Guardamar del Segura...81...D2
Guardia Sanframondi...99...D1
Guardiagrele...99...D3
Guardo...68...A3
Guareña...79...E2
Guarromán...80...B3
Guastalla...94...B4
Gubbio...95...D1
Guberevac...112...C3
Gubin...39...F3
Gudavac...110...C4
Gudhjem...13...E1
Gudow...34...B3
Gudvangen...8...B3
Guebwiller...56...C2

Guémené....52....B3
Guémené-Penfao....53....D2
Guer....52....C3
Guérande....52....C2
Guéret....59....E3
Guérigny....55....D1
Guethary....62....A2
Gueugnon....60....B4
Güglingen....45....D3
Guglionesi....99....E2
Guichen....53....D3
Guignes....55....D4
Guijuelo....73....E2
Guildford....25....D1
Guillaumes....65....E3
Guillestre....61....E1
Guilvinec....52....A2
Guimarães....72....B4
Guincho....78....A2
Guînes....50....A4
Guingamp....52....B4
Guipry....53....D2
Guisamo....66....C4
Guisborough....21....E2
Guise....50....C2
Guisnje....112....B1
Guist....25....E4
Guitiriz....66....C3
Guitres....58....C1
Gujan-Mestras....58....B1
Gulianca....109....E1
Gulladuff....15....D2
Gullane....21....D4
Gullspang....9....F1
Gullstein....2....C2
Gülpinar....119....D1
Gulsele....4....A2
Gulsvik....8....C3
Gülubintsi....115....D1
Gülübovo....119....D4
Gulyantsi....114....B2
Gumiel de Hizán....68....B1
Gummersbach....40....B4
Gumpoldskirchen....87....E3
Gumtow....34....C1
Gümzovo....113....E3
Gundelfingen....45....E3
Gundelsheim....45....D4
Güngör (Koutsovendis)....122....B2
Güngörmez....119....E1
Gunnarn....4....A3
Gunnebo....13....F4
Gunnislake....26....C1
Gunten....84....B2
Günthersberge....38....B2
Guntin de Pallares....66....C3
Günzburg....45....E2
Gunzenhausen....46....B4
Gura Humorului....108....C3
Gura Montrului....113....E4
Gura Teghii....109....D1
Gura Văii....113....E4
Gura Zlata....107....E1
Gurahont....107....D2
Güreci....119....E2
Gurghiu....108....B2
Gurk....86....C1
Gurkovo....114....C1
Gurtnellen....84....C2
Gúspini....96....B2
Güssing....87....E2
Gustavsberg....10....C1
Gustavsfors....9....E1
Gustrow....34....C3
Gusum....13....F4
Gutcher....19....F4
Gutenstein....87....E3
Gütersloh....36....C2
Guttannen....84....C2
Gützkow....35....D3
Guyhirn....23....F2
Güzelyah (Vavilas)....122....B2
Güzelyurt (Morphou)....122....B2
Gvarv....8....C2
Gvozd....111....E1
Gwatt....84....B2
Gwbert-on-Sea....26....C4
Gweek....26....B1
Gwithian....26....B1
Gwyddelwern....22....C2
Gy....56....B2
Gylling....12....B2
Gyoma....106....C3
Gyömrö....106....B3
Gyöngyös....106....B4
Gyöngyöspata....106....B4
Györ....105....D4
Györtelek....107....D4
Gysinge....10....B2
Gyttorp....10....A2
Gyueshovo....113....D1
Gyula....106....C2

H

Haag....46....C2
Haag....87....D3
Haag am Hausruck....86....C3
Haaksbergen....29....F2
Haapamäki....5....E1
Haapamäki....5....E2
Haapasaari....7....E1
Haapavesi....5....E3
Haapajärvi....5....E2
Haar....46....C2
Haaren....36....C2
Haarlem....29....D3

Habartice....39....F1
Habay....31....E1
Habo....13....D4
Hachenburg....40....C3
Hachmühlen....37....D3
Hackås....3....F1
Hacketstown....17....E3
Hackland....19....F1
Hadamar....40....C3
Haddenham....25....E3
Haddington....21....D4
Haddiscoe....25....F3
Haderslev....12....B1
Haderup....12....A2
Hadleigh....25....E2
Hadleigh....25....E3
Hadlow....25....E1
Hadmersleben....38....B3
Hadsten....12....B2
Hadsund....12....B3
Hadžići....111....B3
Hægeland....8....B1
Hagby....13....F2
Hagen....36....B2
Hagenow....34....B2
Hagetmau....62....B3
Hagfors....9....E2
Häggenäs....3....F2
Häggsjömon....4....B2
Haglebu....8....C3
Hagnau....45....D1
Hagondange....51....F2
Haguenau....57....D4
Hahnbach....42....C1
Hahót....105....D2
Haigerloch....44....C2
Hailsham....25....E1
Hailuoto....5....E4
Hainburg....87....F3
Hainfeld....87....E3
Hainichen....43....D4
Hajdúböszörmény....107....D4
Hajdúdorog....107....D4
Hajdúhadház....107....D4
Hajdúnánás....106....D4
Hajdúsámson....107....D4
Hajdúszovát....106....C3
Hajós....105....E2
Hakkenpää....6....B1
Halámky....47....F3
Hălăucești....109....D3
Halberstadt....38....B2
Halberton....27....D2
Halden....9....D1
Haldensee....85....E3
Haldensleben....38....B3
Halesowen....23....D1
Halesworth....25....F3
Halhjem....8....A3
Halič....106....B4
Halifax....23....D3
Halikko....6....B1
Halk....12....B1
Halkirk....19....D4
Hall in Tirol....85....F3
Halland....25....E1
Halle....31....D3
Halle....36....C3
Halle....38....C2
Hällefors....10....A2
Hallein....86....B2
Hallen....3....E1
Hallenberg....36....C1
Hällevadsholm....9....D1
Hälleviksstrand....12....C4
Hallingby....9....D3
Hällnäs....4....B3
Hallsands....27....D1
Hallsberg....10....A1
Hallstahammar....10....B2
Hallstatt....86....C2
Hallstavik....10....C2
Hallworthy....26....C2
Hålmagiu....107....D2
Halmeu....107....E4
Halmstad....13....D3
Hals....12....B3
Halsanaustan....2....C2
Halsskov....12....C1
Halstead....25....E3
Halsteren....28....C1
Halsua....5....D2
Halsworthy....26....C2
Haltdalen....3....D1
Haltern....36....B2
Haltwhistle....21....D3
Haluna....7....D4
Halver....36....B1
Halwill....26....C2
Ham....50....B2
Ham Street....25....E1
Hamalagraosen....8....B3
Hamar....9....D3
Hambergen....33....D2
Hambleton....22....C4
Hamburg....33....E2
Hamburgsund....9....D1
Hamdorf....33....D3
Hämeenkyrö....6....B2
Hämeenlinna....6....C2
Hameln....37....D3
Hamersleben....38....B3
Hamidiye....119....D3
Hamilton....20....C4
Hamina....7....D2
Hamm....36....C2
Hammarland....11....D2
Hammarstrand....4....A1
Hammaslahti....7....E4
Hammel....12....B2
Hammelburg....41....E2
Hammer....3....E2

Hammer....10....A1
Hammerdal....3....F2
Hamminkeln....36....A2
Hamoir....31....E2
Hamra....10....B4
Hamrångefjärden....10....C3
Hamula....5....F2
Hån....9....D2
Han i Hotit....112....B1
Han Pijesak....111....E3
Hanau....41....D2
Handcross....25....D1
Handegg....84....C2
Handen....10....C1
Handley....22....C2
Handöl....3....E2
Hanerau-Hademarschen....33....D3
Hanestad....9....D4
Hăneşti....109....D4
Hango (Hanko)....6....B1
Hangu....108....C3
Hankamäki....7....E4
Hankasalmi....5....F1
Hankensbüttel....37....E4
Hanko (Hango)....6....B1
Hann-Münden....37....D3
Hannover....37....D3
Hannut....31....D3
Hans-sur-Lesse....31....D2
Hanstedt....33....E2
Hanstholm....12....A3
Hanya....119....F1
Haparanda....5....D4
Häppälä....5....F1
Happisburgh....25....F4
Harads....4....C4
Harboøre....12....A3
Harburg....33....E2
Harburg....46....B3
Hårby....12....B1
Hardegg....87....E4
Hardegsen....37....E2
Hardelot-Plage....50....A4
Hardenberg....29....F3
Harderwijk....29....E3
Hardeshøj....12....B1
Hardheim....41....D1
Hardwicke....27....E4
Hareid....2....B1
Haren....29....F4
Haren....36....B4
Harestua....9....D3
Harewood....23....D4
Harfleur....49....E2
Hargshamn....10....C2
Harjavalta....6....B2
Harjunmaa....7....D3
Harjunsalmi....6....C3
Harkány....105....E1
Harlech....22....B2
Harleston....25....F3
Hårlev....12....C1
Harlingen....29....E4
Harlösa....13....D2
Harlow....25....E2
Härman....108....C1
Harmånger....10....C4
Härmänmäki....5....F3
Härnösänd....4....B1
Haro....68....C3
Haroldswick....19....F4
Haroué....56....B3
Harpefoss....9....D4
Harpenden....25....D2
Harpstedt....32....C1
Harran....3....E1
Harrogate....21....E1
Harrow....25....D2
Harsefeld....33....D2
Harsewinkel....36....C3
Harta....105....E2
Hartberg....87....E2
Hartha....39....D1
Hartington....23....D2
Hartland....26....C2
Hartlepool....21....E2
Hartley Wintney....25....D1
Hartmannshain....41....D3
Hartola....7....D2
Harvik....3....D3
Harwich....25....F2
Harzgerode....38....B2
Haselund....33....D4
Haselünne....36....B4
Hasköy....119....D4
Haslach....44....C2
Haslach....86....C4
Hasle....13....E1
Haslemere....25....D1
Haslev....12....C1
Hasparren....62....A2
Hassel....37....D4
Hassela....10....B4
Hasselfelde....38....B2
Hasselt....31....E3
Hasselt....31....E3
Hassfurt....41....E2
Hasslach....42....B3
Hassleben....35....C2
Hässleholm....13....D2
Hästholmen....13....E4
Hastings....25....E1
Hästveda....13....D2
Hatch Beauchamp....27....D2
Hateg....107....E1
Hatfield....25....D2
Hatherleigh....26....C2
Hathersage....23....D3
Hattem....29....E3
Hatten....3....E4
Hattfjelldal....3....F1
Hattingen....36....B2

Hattstedt....33....D4
Hattula....6....C2
Hattuvaara....7....F4
Hatvan....106....B4
Hatvik....8....A3
Haugastøl....8....C2
Hauge....8....A1
Haugesund....8....A2
Hauggrend....8....C2
Haugsdorf....87....E4
Haugster....8....C4
Hauho....6....C2
Haukå....8....A4
Haukeligrend....8....B2
Haukelister....8....B2
Haukipudas....5....E4
Haukivuori....7....D3
Haunersdorf....47....D3
Hausach....44....C2
Häusern....44....C1
Hausham....46....C1
Hausjärvi....6....C2
Haut-Asco....57....E3
Haute-Nendaz....84....B1
Hauteville Plage....48....C1
Havant....25....D1
Havelange....31....D2
Havelberg....34....C1
Haverfordwest....26....B3
Haverhill....25....E3
Havneby....12....A1
Havnsø....12....C2
Havran....119....E1
Havsa....119....D4
Havstenssund....9....D1
Hawarden....22....C3
Hawes....21....D1
Hawick....21....D3
Hawkhurst....25....E1
Hawkinge....25....F1
Hay-on-Wye....27....D4
Hayange....51....E2
Haydon Bridge....21....D3
Hayle....26....B1
Hayling Island....27....F2
Hayrabolu....119....E2
Haywards Heath....25....E1
Hazebrouck....50....B4
Hazel Grove....23....D3
Hazlov....42....C2
Headcorn....25....E1
Headford....16....B4
Headford....23....E2
Heanor....23....E2
Heathfield....25....E1
Heby....10....B2
Hechingen....45....D2
Hechtel....31....E4
Heckington....23....F2
Heddal....8....C2
Hédé....53....D3
Hedemora....10....B2
Hedensted....12....B2
Hedesunda....10....B3
Hedeviken....3....E1
Hedon....23....F3
Hee....12....A2
Heek....36....B3
Heemstede....29....D3
Heerde....29....E3
Heerenveen....29....E3
Heerlen....31....E3
Heeze....31....E4
Heggenes....8....C4
Heglibister....19....F4
Hegra....3....D2
Hegyeshalom....105....D4
Hegyhátsál....104....C3
Heidelberg....40....C1
Heiden....36....B2
Heidenau....43....E4
Heidenheim....45....E3
Heidenreichstein....87....D4
Heikendorf....33....E4
Heilbronn....45....D4
Heiligenberg....45....D1
Heiligenblut....86....B1
Heiligenhafen....34....B4
Heiligenstadt....37....E2
Heilligenkreuz....87....E1
Heilsbronn....45....E3
Heimdal....3....D2
Heimertingen....45....E2
Heinävaara....7....F4
Heinävesi....7....E4
Heino....29....E3
Heinola....7....D2
Heinsberg....40....A4
Heist....28....B1
Heiterwang....85....E3
Heituinlahti....7....D2
Hejlsminde....12....B1
Heldrungen....38....B2
Helensburgh....20....B4
Helford Passage....26....B1
Helgum....4....A1
Hell....8....C4
Hella....8....B4
Hella....8....A1
Helleland....8....A1
Hellendoorn....29....F3
Hellesylt....8....B1
Hellevik....8....A4
Hellevoetsluis....28....C2
Hellin....81....E4
Hellsö....8....A1
Helmond....29....E1
Helmsdale....19....D4
Helmsley....21....E1
Helmstedt....38....B3
Helsa....37....D1
Helsby....22....C3
Helsingborg....13....D2

Helsinge....12....C2
Helsingfors (Helsinki)....6....C1
Helsinger....13....D2
Helsinki (Helsingfors)....6....C1
Helston....26....B1
Hemau....46....C3
Hemel Hempstead....25....D2
Hemer....36....C2
Hèming....56....C4
Hemling....4....B2
Hemmoor....33....D3
Hemsby....25....F4
Hemse....11....F1
Hemsedal....8....C3
Hemslingen....33....D2
Hemyock....27....D2
Henån....12....C4
Hendaye....62....A2
Hendorf....108....B2
Henfield....25....D1
Hengelo....29....F2
Hengersberg....47....D3
Hénin Beaumont....50....B3
Henley in Arden....23....D1
Henley-on-Thames....25....D2
Henlow....25....D3
Hennan....10....B4
Henne Strand....12....A2
Henneberg....41....E3
Hennebont....52....B2
Hennef....40....B3
Henrichement....54....C1
Henriksfjäll....3....F4
Henstedt-Ulzburg....33....E3
Henstridge....27....E2
Heppenheim....40....C1
Heradsbygd....9....E3
Herăşti....115....D3
Herbault....54....B2
Herbertingen....45....D2
Herbertstown....16....C2
Herbestnal....31....E3
Herbeumont....31....D1
Herborn....40....C3
Herbrechtingen....45....E3
Hercegnovi....111....E1
Hercegov Goleša....112....B2
Hercegovac....105....D1
Hercegszántó....105....E1
Herdla....8....A3
Hereford....27....D4
Herencia....74....C1
Herend....105....D3
Herentals....31....D4
Herford....36....C3
Hergiswil....84....C2
Héricourt....56....C2
Heringsdorf....35....E3
Herisau....85....D3
Hérisson....59....F4
Herleshausen....41....E4
Hermagor....86....B1
Hermannsburg....33....E1
Hermansverk....8....B4
Herment....59....F3
Hermeskeil....40....B1
Herne....36....B2
Herne Bay....25....F2
Herning....12....A2
Heroldsberg....42....B1
Herre....8....C1
Herrenberg....45....D3
Herrera de Duque....79....F3
Herrera de Pisuerga....68....A3
Herreruela....79....D3
Herrljunga....13....D4
Herrnburg....34....B3
Herrnhut....39....F1
Herrsching....46....B2
Herrskog....4....B1
Hersbruck....42....C1
Herselt....31....D3
Herstmonceux....25....E1
Hertford....25....D2
Herzberg....37....E2
Herzberg....39....D2
Herzfelde....39....E4
Herzlake....36....B4
Herzogenaurach....42....B1
Herzogenburg....87....E3
Herzsprung....34....C1
Hesdin....50....A3
Hesel....32....B2
Hesnæs....12....C1
Hess Oldendorf....37....D3
Hessisch-Lichtenau....37....D1
Hestenesøyri....8....B4
Hestra....13....D3
Hestwall....19....E1
Hetiur....108....B2
Hettange....51....F2
Hettstedt....38....C2
Heustreu....41....E3
Heves....106....B4
Héviz....105....D3
Hewsall....22....C3
Hexham....21....D3
Heyrieux....60....C2
Heysham....21....D1
Heytesbury....27....E2
Hidra....8....B1
Hiede....33....D3
Hieflau....87....D2
Hiersac....58....C2
Hietanen....7....D3
High Hesket....21....D2
High Wycombe....25....D2
Higham Ferrers....23....E1
Highbridge....27....D2
Highclere....27....F3
Highcliffe-on-Sea....27....E2

Highworth....27....E3
Hiirola....7....D3
Hijar....75....F4
Hilchenbach....40....C4
Hildal....8....B3
Hildburghausen....42....B3
Hilden....36....B1
Hildesheim....37....E3
Hill of Fearn....19....D3
Hillegom....29....D3
Hillerød....12....C2
Hillerstorp....13....D3
Hillsborough....15....E2
Hillswick....19....F4
Hilltown....15....E1
Hilmo....3....D1
Hilpolstein....46....B4
Hilterfingen....84....B2
Hilton....23....D2
Hilvarenbeek....29....D1
Hilversum....29....D2
Himanka....5....D2
Himarë....116....C2
Himmelpforten....33....D2
Hinckley....23....D2
Hindås....13....D4
Hindelang....45....E1
Hindhead....25....D1
Hingham....25....E4
Hinnerjoki....6....B2
Hinojosa del Duque....79....F2
Hinova....113....E4
Hinterrhein....85....D2
Hintersee....35....E3
Hinterstoder....86....C2
Hinterthal....86....B2
Hintertux....85....F3
Hinterweidenthal....44....B4
Hinterzarten....44....C2
Hîrja....109....D2
Hîrlău....109....D3
Hirschaid....42....B2
Hirschau....42....C1
Hirschberg....42....C3
Hirschegg....85....E3
Hirsilä....6....C2
Hirsingue....56....C2
Hirson....50....C3
Hîrsova....115....E4
Hirtshals....12....B4
Hirvaskoski....5....F4
Hirvensalmi....7....D3
Hirwaun....27....D3
Hitcham....25....E3
Hitchin....25....D3
Hitias....107....D1
Hitis (Hiitinen)....6....B1
Hittarp....13....D2
Hitterdal....3....D1
Hitzacker....34....B2
Hiukkajoki....7....E3
Hjallerup....12....B3
Hjelle....8....B4
Hjelle....2....A1
Hjellstad....8....A3
Hjelmeland....8....B2
Hjerkinn....2....C1
Hjerpsted....12....A1
Hjerting....12....A1
Hjo....13....E4
Hjullund....12....B2
Hjørring....12....B4
Hjorte....12....B1
Hjortkvarn....10....B1
Hobro....12....B3
Höchberg....41....D2
Hochdonn....33....D3
Hochdorf....84....C3
Höchenschwand....44....C1
Hochfelden....57....D4
Hochspeyer....44....C1
Höchst....41....D2
Höchstadt....42....B2
Höchstädt....45....E2
Hockenheim....44....C4
Hockham....25....E3
Hockliffe....25....D2
Hodalen....3....D1
Hodde....12....A2
Hoddesden....25....E2
Hodenhagen....37....D4
Hodkovice nad Mohelkou....43....F3
Hódmezővásárhely....106....B2
Hodnet....22....C2
Hodod....107....E3
Hodošan....104....C2
Hoedekenskerke....28....C1
Hoek van Holland....28....C1
Hof....84....C3
Hoffstad....3....D3
Hofgeismar....37....D2
Hofheim....41....E2
Høfjellshotel....8....C2
Hofles....3....D3
Hofors....10....B3
Hog`s Back....25....D1
Höganäs....13....D2
Högfors....10....A2
Hoghiz....108....C2
Högsäter....9....E1
Högsby....13....E3
Høgset....2....B2
Högyész....105....E2
Hohenberg....87....E3
Hohenbrunn....46....C2
Hohenems....85....D3
Höhenkirchen....46....C2
Hohenlimburg....36....B2
Hohenlinden....46....C2
Hohenlockstedt....33....D3
Hohenpeissenberg....46....B1
Hohenschwangau....46....B1

Hohentauern...87....D2
Hohenwestedt...33....D3
Hohne (Belsen)...37....E4
Hohwacht...33....E4
Hoisko...5....D1
Højer...12....A1
Højslev Stby...12....B3
Hok...13....E3
Hokksund...9....D2
Hol...8....C3
Holand...3....E3
Holbæk...12....C2
Holbeach...23....F2
Holdorf...36....C4
Holeby...12....C1
Holford...27....D2
Höljes...9....E9
Holkham...25....E4
Hollabrunn...87....E4
Hollád...105....D2
Holland-on-Sea...25....F2
Hollenstedt...33....D2
Hollfeld...42....B2
Hollingsholm...2....B1
Hollola...7....F4
Hollum...29....E4
Holm...9....D1
Holm...3....E4
Holm...5....D2
Holme-upon-Spalding Moor...23....E4
Holmec...104....B2
Holmes Chapel...23....D3
Holmestrand...9....D2
Holmfirth...23....D3
Holmrook...20....C2
Holmsund...4....C2
Holmsveden...10....B3
Holod...107....D2
Holøydal...3....D1
Holstebro...12....A2
Holsted...12....A2
Holt...25....E4
Holt...22....C2
Holt Heath...23....D1
Holten...29....E2
Holten Heath...27....E2
Holtet...9....D1
Holtet...9....E3
Holwerd...29....E4
Holycross...16....C2
Holyhead...22....B3
Holywell...27....E2
Holywell...22....C3
Holywell Bay...26....B1
Holywood...15....E2
Holzdorf...39....D2
Holzgau...85....E3
Holzkirchen...46....C2
Holzminden...37....D2
Homberg...41....D3
Homburg...44....B4
Hommelsta...3....E4
Hommelvik...3....D2
Hommersåk...8....A2
Homoríciu...109....D1
Homorod...108....C2
Homps...63....F2
Hondarribia...69....D4
Hønefoss...9....D3
Honfleur...49....E2
Høng...12....C1
Honiton...27....D2
Honkajoki...6....B3
Honkakoski...6....B2
Honningsvåg...2....A1
Honrubia...75....D2
Hontianske-Nemce...105....E4
Hontoria del Pinar...68....C2
Hoogerheide...28....C1
Hoogeveen...29....F3
Hoogezand...29....F4
Hoogkarspel...29....D3
Hoogstraten...29....D1
Hook...27....F3
Hooksiel...32....C2
Höör...13....D2
Hoorn...29....D3
Hope Cove...26....C1
Hope-under-Dinmore...22....C1
Hopeman...19....D3
Hopen...2....C2
Hopfgarten...86....A2
Hoplandsjøen...8....A4
Hopsten...36....B3
Hopton-on-Sea...25....F4
Hoptrup...12....B1
Hora-Sv.-Sebestiána...43....D3
Horaźd'ovice...43....E1
Horb...44....C2
Horbelev...12....C1
Hörby...13....D2
Horcajo de Santiago...74....C2
Hordain...50....C3
Horezu...114....B4
Horgen...84....C3
Horgoš...106....C2
Horia...106....C2
Horia...115....E3
Horia...115....F4
Horitschon...87....F3
Horn...87....E4
Horn...45....D1
Horn...87....E4
Horn...9....D3
Horn...3....E4
Horn...13....E4
Hornberg...44....C2
Hornburg...37....E3
Hornby...21....D1
Horncastle...23....E3
Horndal...10....B2
Horndean...27....F2

Horneburg...33....D2
Hornefors...4....B2
Horní Planá...47....E3
Horní Vltavice...47....E3
Hornindal...2....B1
Horning...25....F4
Hørning...12....B2
Hornnes...8....B1
Hornos...80....C3
Hornoy...50....A2
Hornsea...21....F1
Hörnum...32....C4
Hornum...12....B3
Hořovice...43....E2
Horred...13....D3
Horsens...12....B2
Horsforth...23....D4
Horsham...25....D1
Hørsholm...12....C2
Horšovský Týn...43....D1
Horst...29....E1
Horst...33....E2
Hörstel...36....B3
Horstmar...36....B3
Hort...106....B4
Horten...9....D2
Hortezuela...68....C1
Hortigüela...68....B2
Hortobágy...106....C3
Horton...27....D2
Horton-in-Ribblesdale...21....D1
Hørve...12....C2
Horw...84....C3
Hospental...84....C2
Hospital...16....C2
Hossegor...62....A3
Hostalrich...71....D3
Hostens...62....B4
Hostomice...43....E2
Hotagen...3....E2
Hoting...3....A2
Hoton...23....E2
Hotton...31....E2
Hou...12....B3
Houdain...50....B3
Houdan...54....B4
Houdelaincourt...56....A3
Houeillès...62....C3
Houffalize...31....E2
Houghton le Spring...21....E2
Hougne...61....E4
Houlgate...49....E2
Hourtin...58....B2
Hourtin Plage...58....B2
Houton...19....F1
Houtsala...6....B1
Houtskär (Houtskari)...6....B1
Houtskari (Houtskär)...6....B1
Hov...12....B2
Hov...9....D3
Hova...9....F1
Hovda...8....C3
Hovden...8....B2
Hove...25....D1
Høve...12....C2
Hövelhof...36....C2
Hoven...12....A2
Hovet...8....C3
Hovin...8....C2
Hovingham...21....E1
Hovland...8....B3
Hovmantorp...13....E3
Howgate...20....C4
Howtn...17....E3
Höxter...37....D2
Hoya...37....D2
Høyanger...8....B4
Hoyerswerda...39....E2
Hoylake...22....C3
Høylandet...3....E3
Hoyos...39....D2
Hradek nad Nisou...43....F4
Hřensko...43....E4
Hrob...43....E3
Hrtkovci...112....B4
Hrvace...110....C2
Huben...86....B1
Hucknall...23....E2
Hucqueliers...50....A4
Huddersfield...23....D3
Huddinge...10....C1
Hudiksvall...10....C4
Huedin...107....E3
Huelgoat...52....B2
Huelma...80....B2
Huelva...83....D3
Huércal-Overa...81....D2
Huesca...69....F2
Huescar...81....D3
Huete...74....C3
Hüfingen...44....C2
Huhdasjärvi...7....D2
Huhus...7....F4
Huittinen...6....B2
Huizen...29....D3
Hull...23....E3
Hullsjön...4....A1
Hult...13....E4
Hultanäs...13....E3
Hultsfred...13....E3
Humble...12....B1
Humlebæk...12....C3
Humlum...12....A3
Humor...108....C3
Humppi...5....E1
Humppila...6....B2
Hundested...12....C2
Hundorp...9....D4
Hunedoara...107....E1
Hünfeld...41....D3
Hungen...41....D3

Hungerford...27....F3
Hunnebostrand...9....D1
Hunstanton...25....E4
Hunstanworth...21....D2
Huntingdon...23....F1
Huntley...27....E4
Huntly...19....E3
Huopanankoski...5....E1
Hurbanovo...105....E4
Hurdal...9....D3
Hurdugi...109....E2
Hurezani...113....E4
Huriel...59....F2
Hurissalo...7....E3
Hurliness...19....F1
Hurn...27....E2
Hursley...27....F2
Hürsovo...115....E2
Hurst Green...25....E1
Hurstbourne Tarrant...27....F3
Hurstpierpoint...25....D1
Hurup...12....A3
Hurva...13....D2
Husbands Bosworth...23....E1
Hushinish...18....A3
Huşi...109....E2
Husinec...47....E4
Huskvarna...13....E4
Husnes...8....A3
Husum...33....D4
Husum...4....B2
Hüttinen (Hitis)...6....B1
Hüttschlag...86....B2
Huttwil...84....B3
Huy...31....D3
Hvar...110....C2
Hvide Sande...12....A2
Hvittingfoss...9....D2
Hyde...23....D3
Hyen...8....B4
Hyeres...65....E2
Hylestad...8....B2
Hyltebruk...13....D3
Hynneskleiv...8....C1
Hyrynsalmi...5....F3
Hythe...25....F1
Hytti...7....E2
Hyvinkää...6....C1

I

I.C.Frimu...115....D3
Iacobeni...108....C3
Ianca...114....B2
Ianca...115....E4
Iaşi...109....E3
Íasmos...118....C3
Iazu...115....E4
Ibăneşti...108....C2
Ibeas-de-Juarres...68....B2
Ibi...81....F4
Ibiza (Eivissa)...76....C2
Ibrany...107....D4
Ibstock...23....E2
Ichenhausen...45....E2
Iclod...107....E3
Idanha-a-Nova...72....C1
Idar-Oberstein...40....B2
Ídhra...121....D2
Idjoš...106....B1
Idre...9....E4
Idrija...104....A2
Idro...89....E2
Idstein...40....C2
Iedu...108....B2
Ielsi...99....D2
Ieper (Ypres)...30....B3
Ierissós...118....B2
Iernut...108....B2
Ierzo...96....C2
Igal...105....D2
Igea...111....E1
Igea Marina...95....D3
Igelfors...10....B1
Iggesund...10....C4
Iglesias...96....A1
Igls...85....F3
Iğneada...119....E4
Igoumenítsa...116....C1
Igrane...110....C2
Igualada...70....C2
Iharosberény...105....D2
Ihtiman...114....B1
Ii...5....E4
Iimenau...42....B3
Iisalmi...5....F2
Iisenburg...38....B2
Iitti...7....D2
Ijmuiden...29....D3
Ikaalinen...6....B1
Ikast...12....B2
Ilanz...85....D2
Ilchester...27....D2
Ile Rousse...57....E3
Ileana...115....D3
Ileanda...107....E3
Ilfracombe...26....C3
Ilia...107....D1
Ilidža...111....E2
Ilijirska Bistrica...104....A1
Iliişeşti...107....C3
Ilkeston...23....E2
Ilkley...21....E1
Illano...67....D4
Illar...80....C1
Illby (Ilola)...7....D1

Illertissen...45....E2
Illescas...74....B3
Illiers...54....B3
Illingen...45....D3
Illmitz...87....F3
Illo...6....B2
Ilmajoki...5....D1
Ilminster...27....D2
Ilok...112....B4
Ilola (Illby)...7....D1
Ilomantsi...7....F4
Ilowa...39....F2
Ilshofen...45....E4
Ilvesjoki...5....D1
Imatra...7....E2
Immenstadt...45....D1
Immenstadt...45....E1
Immingham...23....F3
Imola...94....C3
Imotski...111....D2
Imperia...92....B2
Imphy...55....D1
Imst...85....E3
Inca...77....E3
Inch...16....A2
Inchigeelagh...16....B1
Inchnadamph...18....C4
Incisa in Val d'Arno...94....C2
Indal...4....A1
Independenta...109....E1
Independenta...115....E3
Indian Queens...26....B1
Indjija...112....B4
Inece...119....E4
Inecik...119....E3
Ineu...107....D2
Infiesto...67....F4
Ingå (Inkoo)...6....C1
Ingatestone...25....E2
Ingelmunster...30....C3
Ingelstad...13....E3
Ingleton...21....D1
Ingoldmells...25....E4
Ingolstadt...46....C3
Ingwiller...56....C4
Iniö...6....B1
Inishannon...16....C1
Inkee...5....F4
Inkoo (Ingå)...6....C1
Innbygda...9....E4
Innellan...20....B4
Innerleithan...20....C4
Innertkirchen...84....C2
Innfjorden...2....B1
Inning...46....B2
Innsbruck...85....F3
Ins...84....A3
Insch...19....E2
Insh...19....D2
Insjön...10....B3
Instow...26....C2
Însurăţei...115....E4
Intepe...119....D2
Interlaken...84....B2
Întorsura Buzăului...109....D1
Intra...88....C3
Inveraray...18....C1
Inverbervie...19....E2
Inverey...19....D2
Invergarry...18....C2
Invergordon...19....D3
Inverkeilor...19....E1
Inverkirkaig...18....C4
Invermoriston...18....C2
Inverness...19....D3
Invershin...18....C3
Inversnaid...18....C1
Inverurie...19....E2
Inzell...47....D1
Ioánnina...117....D1
Iolanda di Savóia...94....C4
Ion Corvin...115....E3
Ioneşti...114....B4
Ioneşti...114....C3
Íos...121....F2
Iphofen...41....E2
Ipsala...119....D3
Ipsos...116....C1
Ipsoús...120....C3
Ipswich...25....F3
Irákleia...118....A3
Iráklia...122....B4
Irdning...85....D2
Irgszemcse...105....E2
Irig...112....B4
Ironbridge...23....D2
Irsina...101....D4
Irthlingborough...23....E1
Irun...69....D4
Irunea (Pamplona)...69....E3
Irurita...69....E4
Irurzun...69....D3
Irvine...20....B3
Irvinestown...14....C2
Is-sur-Tille...56....A2
Isaba...69....E3
Isaccea...109....F1
Işalniţa...114....F3
Isane...2....A1
Isbister...19....F4
Iscar...68....A1
Ischgl...85....E2
Ischia...100....A3
Iscroni...107....E1
Isdes...54....C2
Iselle...88....C3
Iselsberg...86....B1
Iseo...89....D2
Iserlohn...36....B2
Isfjorden...2....B1
Isigny...49....E2
Ísili...96....B2

Iskele (Trikomo)...122....C2
Isla Cristina...82....C3
Isle Ornsay...18....B2
Isle of Whithorn...20....B2
Ismaning...46....C2
Isnäs...7....D1
Isny...45....E1
Iso-Äiniö...6....C2
Iso-Evo...6....C2
Isojoki...6....B3
Isola...65....F3
Isola 2000...65....F3
Isola del Liri...98....C2
Isola della Scala...90....B1
Ísola dí Capo Rizzuto...101....E1
Isona...70....B3
Isperikh...115....D2
Íspica...103....D1
Isselburg...36....A2
Issernia...99....D2
Issoire...60....A2
Issoudun...54....C1
Istiaía...121....D4
Istanbul...119....F3
Istarske Toplice...104....A1
Isthmía...121....D3
Istibanja...117....E4
Istna...37....D2
Istranca...119....F4
Istres...64....C2
Istria...115....F3
Istrnia...121....F3
Istunmäki...5....F1
Itäkylä...5....D2
Itéa...120....C4
Iteu...107....D1
Itháki...120....B4
Itri...98....C1
Íttiri...96....B3
Itxassou...62....A2
Itzehoe...33....D3
Ivančići...111....E3
Ivangrad...112....B1
Ivanić Grad...104....C1
Ivanjica...112....B2
Ivanjska...111....D4
Ivankovo...105....E1
Ivanovo...115....D1
Ivanski...115....D2
Ivaylovgrad...119....D4
Iveşti...109....E1
Iveşti...109....E2
Ivréa...88....B2
Ivrindi...119....E1
Ivry-la-Bataille...54....B4
Ivybridge...26....C1
Ixworth...25....E3
Izeda...73....D4
Izegem...30....C3
Izenore...61....D3
Izgrev...119....E4
Izmail...109....F1
Iznájar...80....A2
Iznalloz...80....B2
Izola...91....E2
Izsák...106....B3
Izvor...117....E4
Izvor...113....D3
Izvor...117....D4
Izvor...113....E1

J

Jaakonvaara...7....F4
Jaala...7....D2
Jaalanka...5....F3
Jablanac...110....B4
Jablanica...111....D2
Jablonec nad Nisou...43....F3
Jablonné v Podještědí...43....F3
Jabuka...111....E2
Jabuka...112....B2
Jabuka...112....C4
Jaca...69....F3
Jáchymov...43....D3
Jade...32....C2
Jadraque...74....C4
Jægerspris...12....C2
Jaén...80....B2
Jaenovac...104....C1
Jagel...33....D4
Jagsthausen...45....D4
Jajce...111....D3
Jakabszállás...106....B2
Jakobstad (Pietarsaari)...5....D2
Jakokoski...7....E4
Jakšić...105....D1
Jakuszyce...43....E4
Jalasjärvi...5....D1
Jaligny-sur-Besbre...60....B4
Jämijärvi...6....B3
Jäminkipohja...6....C3
Jämjö...13....E2
Jammerdal...9....E4
Jamnička Kiselica...104....C1
Jámu Mare...112....B4
Janakkala...6....C2
Janetztown...19....D4
Janja...112....B4
Janja...111....D1
Jánoshalma...106....B2
Jánosháza...105....D3
Jánossomorja...105....D2
Janovice nad Úhlava...43....D1

Janville...54....C3
Janzé...53....D3
Jäppilä...7....D3
Jaracó...76....A2
Jaraicejo...79....E4
Jarandilla...73....E1
Järbo...10....B3
Jard-sur-Mer...58....A4
Jaren...9....D3
Jargeau...54....C2
Jarkovac...106....C1
Järkvissle...4....A1
Jarlåsa...10....C2
Jarmen...35....D3
Jarnac...58....C3
Jarnages...59....E3
Jarny...51....E1
Järpen...3....E2
Jarrow...21....E3
Järvelä...6....C2
Järvenpää...6....C1
Järvsö...10....B4
Jaša Tomić...106....C1
Jasenovets...115....D2
Jasenovo...112....B1
Jasień...39....F2
Jásladány...106....B3
Jastrebarsko...104....B1
Jászalsószentgyörgy...106....B3
Jászapáti...106....B3
Jászárokszállás...106....B4
Jászberény...106....B3
Jászfénysaru...106....B4
Jászkisér...106....B3
Jaun...84....B2
Jausiers...65....E4
Jávall...9....D2
Jávea...76....A2
Jävenitz...38....C2
Jävre...53....D3
Javron...53....E3
Jebel...106....C1
Jedburgh...21....D3
Jegália...115....E3
Jektevik...8....A3
Jelah...111....D3
Jelling...12....B2
Jels...12....A1
Jelsa...8....A2
Jelsa...110....C2
Jena...42....C4
Jenbach...82....C2
Jeneč...43....E2
Jennersdorf...87....E1
Jeppo (Jepua)...5....D2
Jepua (Jeppo)...5....D2
Jerez de la Frontera...83....E2
Jerez de los Caballeros...79....D2
Jergucati...116....C2
Jerichow...38....C4
Jerxheim...38....B3
Jesenice...104....A2
Jesenice...43....E2
Jesi...95....E2
Jésolo...91....D2
Jessen...9....D2
Jessheim...9....D2
Jeumont...51....D3
Jevenstedt...33....D3
Jever...32....C2
Jevnaker...9....D3
Jezero...111....D3
Jezersko...104....D2
Jibou...107....E3
Jičín...43....F3
Jidvei...108....B2
Jijona...81....F4
Jilava...115....D3
Jílové u Prahy...43....F2
Jiltjer...4....A4
Jimbolia...106....C1
Jimena...80....B3
Jimena de la Frontera...83....E2
Jince...43....E2
Jindřichův Hradec...47....F4
Jirkov...43....E3
Jirlău...115....E4
Jitaru...114....B3
Joachimsthal...35....E2
Jobbágyi...106....B4
Jódar...80....C3
Jodoigne...31....D3
Joensuu...7....F3
Joesjö...3....F4
Johanngeorgenstadt...43....D3
Johannisholm...9....F3
John O'Groats...19....D4
Johnstone...20....B4
Johnstown...17....D2
Joigny...55....D2
Joinville...56....A3
Jokijärvi...5....F2
Jokikylä...5....E2
Jokikylä...5....E2
Jokioinen...6....C2
Jokiperä...5....D1
Jokipii...5....D1
Joloskylä...5....F3
Jomala...11....D2
Jonåker...10....B1
Jondal...8....A3
Jönköping...10....D4
Jonzac...58....B2
Jördenstorf...34....C3
Jordet...9....E4
Jörlanda...12....C4
Jormvattnet...3....F3
Jörn...4....B3
Joroinen...7....E3

Jørpeland....8....A2
Jošanička Banja....112....C2
Joseni....108....C2
Josenii Bîrgăului....108....B3
Josipdol....104....B1
Josipovac....105....E1
Jössefors....9....C2
Josselin....52....C3
Jostedal....8....B4
Joten....9....E4
Jougne....61....E4
Joukokylä....5....F4
Joure....29....E4
Journaankylä....7....D1
Joutsa....7....D3
Joutseno....7....E2
Joyeuse....64....B4
Józsa....107....D4
Juan-les-Pins....65....F2
Juankoski....7....E4
Judenburg....87....D2
Judinsalo....7....D3
Juelsminde....12....B2
Jugon....52....C3
Juillac....59....D2
Juist....32....B3
Jule....3....E3
Jülich....40....A4
Jullouville....53....D4
Jumeaux....60....A2
Jumièges....49....F2
Jumilla....81....E4
Jungueira....73....D3
Juniville....51....D2
Junsele....4....A2
Juojärvi....7....E4
Juokslahti....6....C3
Juorkuna....5....F4
Jupiter....115....F3
Jur pri Bratislave....105....D4
Jurilovca....115....F4
Jurjevo....110....B4
Jurmala....7....A1
Jurmo....6....B1
Jurmu....5....F4
Jurva....4....C1
Jurvala....7....E2
Jussey....56....B2
Jüterbog....39....D3
Juuka....7....E4
Juupajoki....6....C3
Juva....7....E3
Juvigny-le-Tertre....53....E4
Juvola....7....E3
Juzennecourt....55....F3
Jyderup....12....C2
Jyllinge....12....C2
Jyllinkoski....6....B3
Jyväskylä....5....E1

K

Kaanaa....6....C3
Kaarssen....34....B2
Kaatsheuvel....29....D2
Kaavi....7....E4
Kaba....106....C3
Kabakca....119....F3
Kabböle....7....D1
Kåbdalis....4....B4
Kableshkovo....115....E1
Kać....106....B1
Kaćanik....112....C1
Kacikol....112....C1
Kacincbarcika....106....C4
Kácov....43....F2
Kadan....43....D3
Kadarkút....105....D2
Kadiköy....119....E3
Kadrifakovo....117....E4
Kåge....4....C3
Kågeröd....13....D2
Kagul....109....E1
Kahla....42....C2
Kainasto....5....D1
Kaindorf....87....E2
Kainu....5....D2
Kaipiainen....7....D2
Kaisersesch....40....B2
Kaiserslautern....40....B1
Kaisheim....46....B3
Kaivanto....5....F3
Kajaani....5....F3
Kakanj....111....D3
Kakavi....116....C2
Käkilahti....5....F3
Kakopetria....122....A1
Kakóvatos....120....B3
Kal....106....B4
Kälä....7....D3
Kalá Nerá....117....F1
Kalabáka....117....E1
Kalaja....5....E2
Kalajoki....5....D1
Kalakoski....5....D1
Kalámai....120....C2
Kalamákion....117....F1
Kalamion....122....A4
Kálamos....121....E3
Kálandra....118....A2
Kalanti....6....B1
Kalarash....109....E5
Kälarne....4....A1
Kalávrita....120....C2
Kalbe....38....B4
Kalce....104....A2
Kaleburnu (Galinoporni)....122....C2

Kaleköy....119....D2
Kaléntzi....117....D1
Kaléntzi....120....C3
Kalesija....111....E3
Kaliáni....120....C3
Kalinovik....111....E2
Kalix....5....D4
Kalkar....36....A2
Kall....3....E2
Kallbäck....7....D1
Kallinge....13....E2
Kallislahti....7....E3
Kallithéa....120....C3
Kallithéa....118....A2
Kallithéa Olímbou....117....E2
Kallmünz....46....C4
Kalloni....119....D1
Kalloni....121....D3
Kállósemjén....107....D4
Kallsedet....3....E2
Kalmar....13....F2
Kalmari....5....E1
Kalna....113....D2
Kalna nad Hradec....105....E4
Kaló Khorió....122....C3
Kaló Neró....120....B2
Kalocsa....107....C4
Kalofer....114....C1
Kaloí Limènes....122....B3
Kalokhóri....117....D2
Kalonéri....117....D2
Kalopanayiotis....122....A1
Kalotina....113....C2
Kaloyan....115....E2
Kaloyanovo....114....B1
Kalpáki....117....D2
Kals....86....B1
Kalsdorf....87....E1
Kaltenkirchen....33....E3
Kaltennordheim....41....E3
Kalugerovo....114....B1
Kalundborg....12....C2
Kalvåg....2....A1
Kälviä....5....D2
Kalvitsa....7....D3
Kalvola....6....C2
Kalwang....87....D2
Kám....105....D3
Kamarina....117....D1
Kamariótissa....118....C2
Kamáros....121....E2
Kámbos....120....C2
Kamchiya....115....E1
Kamen....36....B2
Kamen Bryag....115....F2
Kámena Voúrla....121....D4
Kamenari....111....E1
Kamenica....117....E4
Kamenica nad Lipou....43....F1
Kamenka....109....F4
Kamenka....7....E2
Kamennogorsk....7....E2
Kameno....115....E1
Kamensko....110....C2
Kamenz....39....E2
Kamień Pomorski....35....E3
Kamnik....104....A2
Kamp Lintfort....36....A2
Kampen....29....E3
Kamula....5....E3
Kanala....5....E2
Kanália....117....F1
Kándanos....122....A3
Kandel....44....C3
Kandern....44....B1
Kandersteg....84....B2
Kandersterne....12....B4
Kandila....120....C3
Kanfanar....104....A1
Kangasaho....5....E1
Kangasala....6....C2
Kangaskylä....5....E2
Kangaslampi....7....E3
Kangasniemi....7....D3
Kanjiža....106....B2
Kankaanpää....6....B3
Kannonkoski....5....E1
Kannus....5....D2
Kantala....7....D3
Kantti....6....B3
Kanturk....16....B2
Kaolinovo....115....E2
Kaonik....111....D3
Kapandrition....121....E3
Kapfenberg....87....D2
Kapitan Andreevo....119....D4
Kaplica (Dharlos)....122....C2
Kaplice....47....F3
Kápolna....106....B4
Kaposvár....105....D2
Kapp....9....D3
Kappeln....33....E4
Kappelshamn....11....E2
Kappelskär....11....D2
Kaprun....86....B2
Kapsáli....121....D1
Kápsia....120....C3
Kapuvar....105....D4
Karabiga....119....E2
Karacabey....119....F2
Karacaköy....119....F4
Karacalar....119....E1
Karacaoğlan....119....E4
Karakum (Karakoumi)....122....B2
Karancslapujtó....106....B4
Karapelit....115....E2
Karavás....121....D1
Karavostásis....121....F1
Karcag....106....C3

Kardakáta....120....A4
Kardam....115....E2
Kardašova-Řečice....77....F4
Kardeljevo....111....D1
Kardhamili....120....C2
Kardhítsa....117....E1
Kardoskút....106....C2
Karhula....7....D1
Kariaí....118....B2
Karijoki....4....C1
Karinkanta....5....E3
Kariótissa....117....E3
Karioúpolis....120....C2
Karis (Karjaa)....6....C1
Káristos....121....E3
Karítaina....120....C3
Karjaa (Karis)....6....C1
Karjala....6....B1
Karkaloú....120....C3
Karkkila....6....C1
Karkku....6....B2
Kärkölä....6....C2
Karlby....11....D2
Karleby (Kokkola)....5....D2
Karlholmsbruk....10....C3
Karlino....35....F3
Karlobag....110....B3
Karlovac....104....B1
Karlovo....114....C1
Karlovy Vary....43....D2
Karlsborg....5....D4
Karlsborg....9....F1
Karlshafen....37....D2
Karlsham....13....E2
Karlskoga....10....A1
Karlskrona....13....E2
Karlslunde Strand....12....C1
Karlsruhe....44....C3
Karlstad....9....E2
Karlstadt....41....D2
Karlstift....87....D4
Karnobat....115....E1
Karousádhes....116....C1
Karow....34....C2
Karpenísion....120....C4
Karrebæksminde....12....C1
Kärsämä....5....E3
Kärsämäki....5....E2
Karsikas....5....E2
Karstadt....34....C2
Karstula....5....E1
Karttula....5....F1
Karungi....5....D4
Karunki....5....D4
Karup....5....B2
Karvala....5....D1
Kärväskylä....5....E2
Karvia....6....B3
Karvio....7....E4
Karyá....120....A4
Kås....12....B3
Kasejovice....43....E1
Kaskii....7....E3
Kaskinen (Kaskö)....4....C1
Kašperské Hory....77....E4
Kaspichan....115....E2
Kassandreia....118....A2
Kassel....37....D2
Kassiópi....116....C1
Kastaména....117....E1
Kastanéai....119....D4
Kastaniá....117....E2
Kastaniá....120....C3
Kaštel Stari....110....C2
Kaštel Žegarski....110....B3
Kastellaun....40....B2
Kastéllion....122....A4
Kastéllion....122....B3
Kasterlee....31....D4
Kastl....41....C1
Kastlösa....13....F2
Kastorf....33....E3
Kastoría....117....D2
Kástron....121....D4
Kastrosikiá....117....D1
Kastrup....7....C2
Kaszaper....106....C2
Katákolon....120....B3
Katastárion....120....B3
Katerbow....35....D1
Kateríni....117....E2
Katlanovo....117....E4
Katlenburg-Duhm....37....E2
Káto Akhaía....120....B3
Kato Alepokhóri....121....D3
Káto Klitoría....120....C3
Káto Makrinoú....120....B4
Káto Nevrokópion....118....B3
Kato Pyrgos....122....A2
Káto Zákros....122....C3
Katokhi....120....B4
Katoúna....120....B4
Katovice....77....E4
Katrineholm....10....B1
Katthammarsvik....11....F1
Kattisavan....4....B3
Katuntsi....118....A3
Katwijk aan Zee....29....D2
Kaub....40....B2
Kaufbeuren....46....B2
Kaufering....46....B2
Kaufungen....37....D1
Kauhajoki....5....D1
Kauhajärvi....7....D2
Kaukalampi....7....D2
Kaulinranta....6....C1
Kauniainen (Grankulla)....6....C1
Kauns....85....E3
Kaupanger....8....B4
Kausala....7....D2

Kaushany....109....F2
Kaustinen....5....D2
Kauttua....6....B2
Kavacik....119....F1
Kavadarci....117....E4
Kavajë....116....C3
Kavak....119....E2
Kaválla....118....B3
Kavarna....115....F2
Kavazite....115....E1
Kåvlinge....13....D2
Kávos....116....C1
Kavoúsi....122....C3
Kaxholmen....13....E4
Kayalar (Orga)....122....B2
Kaysersberg....56....C3
Kazanci....110....C3
Kažani....117....D3
Kazanlŭk....114....C1
Kazárma....120....C2
Kdyně....43....D1
Kéa....121....E3
Keadue....14....C1
Keady....15....D1
Kecel....106....B2
Kecskemét....106....B3
Kédhros....117....E1
Keel....14....A1
Keenagh....16....C4
Kefalári....120....C3
Kefaloz....119....D2
Kefmarket....87....D4
Kegworth....23....E2
Kehl....44....C3
Keighley....23....D4
Keikyä....6....B2
Keitele....5....E2
Keith....19....E3
Kelberg....40....B2
Kelbra....38....B2
Kélcyrë....116....C2
Kelebia....106....B2
Kelemér....106....C4
Kelheim....46....C3
Kellinghausen....34....B3
Kélli....117....E3
Kellinghusen....33....D3
Kello....5....E4
Kells....15....E2
Kells (Ceanannus Mor)....17....D4
Kelsall....22....C3
Kelso....21....D3
Kemberg....39....D2
Kemble....27....E3
Kemer....119....E2
Kemi....5....D4
Kemio (Kimito)....6....B1
Kemitz....35....D3
Kemnath....42....C2
Kemnay....19....E2
Kempele....5....E3
Kempen....33....A2
Kempsey....27....E4
Kempston....25....D3
Kempten....45....E1
Kendal....21....D1
Kenderes....106....C3
Kendron....120....B3
Kenilworth....23....D1
Kenmare....16....B1
Kenmore....19....D1
Kennacraig....15....E4
Kenninghall....25....E2
Kentford....25....E3
Kentrikón....117....F3
Kenzingen....44....B2
Kepez....119....D2
Kepsut....119....F1
Keramoti....118....C3
Kerasson....117....D1
Keratéa....121....E3
Kerava....6....C1
Kerecsend....106....C4
Keri....120....B3
Kerimäki....7....E3
Kerken....36....A2
Kérkira....116....C1
Kerkrade....31....E4
Kerma....7....E4
Kermen....115....D1
Kernovo....7....E1
Kerpen....40....A3
Kerry....22....C1
Kerteminde....12....B1
Kerzers....84....B3
Kesälahti....7....F3
Keşan....119....D3
Kesarevo....115....D2
Kesh....14....C2
Keskikylä....5....F3
Kessingland....25....F3
Kestilä....5....E3
Keswick....20....C2
Keszthely....105....D3
Kétegyháza....106....C2
Kettering....23....E1
Kettletoft....19....F1
Ketton....23....E2
Kettwig....36....B2
Ketzin....39....D3
Keula....37....E2
Keuruu....5....E1
Kevelaer....36....A2
Keynsham....27....E3
Khairónia....121....D4
Khalandritsa....120....C3
Khálka....117....E1
Khalkiádhes....117....E1
Khalkís....121....D4
Khandrinón....120....C2

Khánia....122....A4
Khárakas....122....B3
Kharmanli....119....D4
Khaskovo....115....C4
Khiitola....7....F2
Khilmódhion....111....D3
Khisar....114....B1
Khlebarovo....115....D2
Khóra....120....C2
Khóra Sfakíon....122....A3
Khorevto....117....F1
Khoristí....118....B3
Khoumnikón....118....A3
Khrisokhóri....118....C3
Khrisoúpolis....118....C3
Khrojna....118....B4
Khurst....107....E4
Kiaton....120....C3
Kibæk....12....A2
Kičevo....117....D4
Kichenitsa....115....D2
Kichevo....115....D2
Kidderminster....23....D1
Kidlington....27....F4
Kidsgrove....23....D2
Kidwelly....26....C4
Kiel....33....E4
Kielder....21....D3
Kiental....84....B2
Kiesilä....7....D2
Kifisiá....121....E3
Kihelkonna....11....E1
Kihniö....6....B2
Kiihtelysvaara....7....F4
Kiikka....6....B2
Kiikala....6....C1
Kiikoinen....6....B2
Kiiminki....5....E4
Kiiskilä....5....E2
Kijevo....110....C3
Kijevo....112....C1
Kikinda....106....C1
Kil....8....C1
Kil....9....E2
Kilafors....10....B3
Kilbeggan....17....D3
Kilberry....15....E4
Kilberry....17....E4
Kilbirnie....20....B4
Kilbride....18....A2
Kilbrittain....16....C1
Kilcar (Cill Charthaigh)....14....C2
Kilchattan....20....B4
Kilchenzie....15....E3
Kilchiaran....15....D4
Kilchoan....18....B1
Kilchoman....15....D4
Kilcock....17....E3
Kilcogan....16....C3
Kilconnell....16....C3
Kilconnell....16....C3
Kilcoole....17....E3
Kilcormac....17....D3
Kilcullen....17....D3
Kilcurry....15....D1
Kildare....17....D3
Kildavin....17....D2
Kildonan....19....D4
Kildorrery....16....C2
Kildress....15....D2
Kilfenora....16....B3
Kilfinnane....16....C2
Kilgarvan....16....B1
Kilkee....16....B2
Kilkeel....15....E1
Kilkelly....14....B1
Kilkenny....17....D2
Kilkhampton....26....C2
Kilkieran (Cill Ciaráin)....16....B3
Kilkinlea....16....B2
Kilkís....117....F3
Kill....17....D1
Killadysert....16....B2
Killala....14....B1
Killaloe....16....C3
Killarney....16....B1
Killashandra....14....C1
Killashee....16....C4
Killeagh....16....C1
Killearn....20....B4
Killeigh....17....D3
Killenaule....16....C2
Killiecrankie....19....D1
Killimer....16....B2
Killimor....16....C3
Killin....18....C1
Killiney....19....E2
Killini....120....B3
Killinick....17....E2
Killinkoski....5....D1
Killorglin....16....B1
Killough....15....E1
Killucan....17....D4
Killybegs....14....C2
Killyleagh....15....E2
Kilmacanoge....17....E3
Kilmacolm....20....B4
Kilmacrenan....14....C3
Kilmacthomas....16....C2
Kilmaganny....16....C2
Kilmaine....16....B4
Kilmallock....16....C2
Kilmaluaig....18....B2
Kilmanagh....16....C2
Kilmarnock....20....B3
Kilmartin....15....E4
Kilmaurs....20....B4
Kilmeadan....16....C2
Kilmeage....17....D3
Kilmeedy....16....B2
Kilmelford....18....B1

Kilmichael....16....B1
Kilmore Quay....17....E1
Kilmory....15....E4
Kilmory....20....B3
Kilnaleck....17....D4
Kilninver....18....B1
Kilpua....5....E3
Kilrea....15....D2
Kilrush....16....B2
Kilsheelan....17....D2
Kilsyth....20....B4
Kiltealy....17....D2
Kiltegan....17....E3
Kiltimagh....14....B1
Kiltoom....16....C4
Kilvakkala....6....B3
Kilwinning....20....B4
Kimbolton....23....F1
Kími....121....E3
Kiminki....5....E1
Kimito (Kemio)....6....B1
Kimméria....118....C3
Kimolos....121....E2
Kinbrace....19....D4
Kincardine....18....C3
Kincardine....20....C4
Kincardine O'Neil....19....E2
Kincraig....19....D2
Kindberg....87....E2
Kindelbrück....38....B1
Kinéta....121....E3
King's Lynn....25....E4
King's Somborne....27....F2
Kinghorn....20....C4
Kingisepp....11....E1
Kingsbridge....26....C1
Kingsclere....27....F3
Kingscourt....15....D1
Kingsdown....25....F1
Kingston....19....D3
Kingswear....27....D1
Kington....22....C1
Kingussie....19....D2
Kinik....119....E1
Kinloch Hourn....18....C2
Kinloch Rannoch....19....D1
Kinlochbervie....18....C4
Kinlochcheil....18....C2
Kinlochewe....18....C3
Kinlochleven....18....C1
Kinlochmoidart....18....B2
Kinloss....19....D3
Kinlough....14....C2
Kinna....13....D3
Kinnarp....13....D4
Kinnegad....17....D3
Kinnitty....17....D3
Kinnula....5....E2
Kinross....19....D1
Kinsale....16....C1
Kinsarvik....8....B3
Kintaus....5....E1
Kintore....19....E2
Kinvarra....16....B3
Kionia....121....F3
Kiparissía....120....B2
Kipinä....5....E3
Kippen....19....B4
Kirazli....119....D2
Kirby in Furness....20....C1
Kirby-in-Ashfield....23....E2
Kircasilih....119....D3
Kirchbach....87....E1
Kirchberg....45....E4
Kirchberg....40....B2
Kirchberg....86....A2
Kirchberg-an-der-Pielach....87....D3
Kirchdorf....86....C3
Kircheim-unter-Teck....45....D3
Kirchenlamitz....42....C2
Kirchenthumbach....42....C2
Kirchhain....41....D4
Kirchheim....41....D3
Kirchheimbolanden....40....C1
Kirchhundem....40....C4
Kirchlintein....33....D1
Kirchschlag....87....E2
Kircubbin....15....E2
Kireç....119....F1
Kirk Michael....20....B1
Kirkabister....19....F3
Kirkağaç....119....E1
Kirkbean....20....C2
Kirkbride....20....C2
Kirkby Lonsdale....21....D1
Kirkby Moorside....21....E1
Kirkby Stephen....21....D2
Kirkcaldy....20....C4
Kirkcolm....20....B2
Kirkconnel....20....B2
Kirkcowan....20....B2
Kirkcudbright....20....C2
Kirkenær....9....E3
Kirkham....20....C3
Kirkinner....20....B2
Kirkkonummi (Kyrkslätt)....6....C1
Kirklareli....119....E4
Kirkmichael....19....D1
Kirkmuirhill....20....C4
Kirknewton....21....D3
Kirkoswald....20....C3
Kirkpatrick Fleming....20....C3
Kirkwall....19....F2
Kirkwhelpington....21....D3
Kirn....40....B2
Kirpoşa (Karpas)....122....C2
Kirriemuir....19....E1
Kirton....19....E3
Kirton-in-Lindsey....23....E2
Kirtorf....41....D3
Kisa....13....E4
Kisber....105....E3

Kiseljak .... 111 .... D2
Kishinev .... 109 .... F3
Kishorn .... 18 .... B2
Kisko .... 6 .... C1
Kisköre .... 106 .... C3
Kiskörös .... 106 .... B2
Kiskundorozsma .... 106 .... B2
Kiskunfélegyháza .... 106 .... B2
Kiskunhalas .... 106 .... B2
Kiskunlacháza .... 105 .... E3
Kiskunmajsa .... 106 .... B2
Kisslegg .... 45 .... E1
Kistanje .... 110 .... B3
Kistelek .... 106 .... B2
Kisterenye .... 106 .... B4
Kisújszállás .... 106 .... C3
Kisvárda .... 107 .... D4
Kiszombor .... 106 .... C2
Kitajaur .... 4 .... B4
Kitee .... 7 .... F3
Kiten .... 115 .... E1
Kithira .... 121 .... D1
Kithnos .... 121 .... E3
Kiti .... 122 .... B1
Kitros .... 117 .... E2
Kitsi .... 7 .... F4
Kittelfjall .... 3 .... F4
Kittsee .... 87 .... F3
Kitula .... 6 .... C1
Kitzbühel .... 86 .... A2
Kitzingen .... 41 .... E2
Kiuruvesi .... 5 .... F2
Kivéri .... 120 .... C3
Kivesjärvi .... 5 .... F3
Kiviapaja .... 7 .... E3
Kivijärvi .... 5 .... E2
Kivilahti .... 7 .... F4
Kivotós .... 117 .... D2
Kiyiköy .... 119 .... F4
Kjellerup .... 12 .... B2
Kjerret .... 9 .... E2
Kjerringvåg .... 2 .... C2
Kjerringvik .... 3 .... D2
Kladanj .... 111 .... E3
Kladno .... 43 .... E2
Kladovo .... 113 .... E4
Klagenfurt .... 86 .... C1
Klamila .... 7 .... E1
Klanxbüll .... 32 .... C4
Klarup .... 12 .... B3
Klašnice .... 111 .... D4
Klässbol .... 9 .... E2
Klaštere nad Ohre .... 43 .... D3
Klatovy .... 43 .... E1
Klaukkala .... 6 .... C1
Klaus an der Pyhrnbahn .... 86 .... C3
Klausdorf .... 39 .... D3
Klazienaveen .... 29 .... F3
Kleinhaugsdorf .... 87 .... E4
Kleisoúra .... 117 .... D1
Klelebija .... 106 .... B2
Klenike .... 8 .... A1
Kleppe .... 8 .... A3
Kleppestø .... 8 .... C2
Klevar .... 36 .... A2
Kleve .... 39 .... F2
Kliczków .... 38 .... C4
Klietz .... 117 .... D1
Klimatiá .... 115 .... D2
Kliment .... 3 .... F3
Klimpfjall .... 112 .... C1
Klina .... 104 .... B1
Klinča Selo .... 87 .... F3
Klingenbach .... 43 .... D3
Klingenthal .... 35 .... D2
Klink .... 11 .... E1
Klintehamn .... 13 .... D2
Klippan .... 112 .... B1
Klirou .... 110 .... C2
Klis .... 113 .... D1
Klisura .... 114 .... B1
Klitmøller .... 12 .... A3
Kljajićevo .... 106 .... B1
Ključ .... 110 .... C3
Klodawa .... 35 .... F1
Klodočevac .... 113 .... D3
Kløfta .... 9 .... D2
Klokkarvik .... 8 .... A3
Klos .... 116 .... C4
Kloštar .... 105 .... D2
Klösterle .... 84 .... E3
Klosterneuburg .... 87 .... E4
Klosters .... 85 .... D2
Kloten .... 10 .... B2
Klötze .... 38 .... B4
Klupe .... 111 .... D3
Klütz .... 34 .... B3
Knäred .... 13 .... D2
Knaresborough .... 21 .... E1
Knarvik .... 8 .... A3
Knazhevo .... 119 .... D4
Knebel .... 12 .... B2
Knezevi Vinogradi .... 105 .... E1
Kneževo .... 105 .... E1
Knezha .... 114 .... B2
Knežica .... 104 .... C1
Knić .... 112 .... C3
Kniebis .... 44 .... C2
Knighton .... 22 .... C1
Knin .... 110 .... C3
Knislinge .... 13 .... D2
Knittelfeld .... 87 .... D2
Knivsta .... 10 .... C2
Knjaževac .... 113 .... D2
Knock .... 16 .... C4
Knockan .... 18 .... C4
Knockcroghery .... 16 .... C4
Knocklofty .... 16 .... C4
Knockmahon .... 17 .... D1
Knocktopher .... 17 .... D2
Knokke-Heist .... 28 .... B1

Knottingley .... 23 .... E3
Knowle .... 27 .... D2
Knudshoved .... 12 .... B1
Knutsford .... 23 .... D3
Křivoklát .... 43 .... E2
Kobarid .... 104 .... A2
København .... 12 .... C2
Kobilyane .... 118 .... C4
Kobišnica .... 113 .... E3
Koblenz .... 40 .... B3
Kočani .... 117 .... E4
Koceljevo .... 112 .... B3
Kočerin .... 111 .... D2
Kočevje .... 104 .... B1
Kochel .... 46 .... C1
Kocherinovo .... 117 .... F4
Kochmar .... 115 .... E2
Kofçaz .... 119 .... E4
Köflach .... 87 .... D2
Køge .... 12 .... C1
Koilovtsi .... 114 .... B2
Koirakoski .... 5 .... F2
Koivulahti (Kvevlax) .... 6 .... B4
Koivumäki .... 7 .... E4
Kokar .... 11 .... D2
Kokemäki .... 6 .... B2
Kokin Brod .... 112 .... B2
Kokkokylä .... 5 .... E4
Kokkola (Karleby) .... 5 .... D2
Koklé .... 116 .... C3
Kokonvaara .... 7 .... E4
Koksijde-Bad .... 30 .... B4
Kolari .... 112 .... C4
Kolárovo .... 105 .... E4
Kolašin .... 112 .... B1
Kolbäck .... 10 .... B2
Kolbaskowo .... 35 .... E2
Kolbermoor .... 74 .... C2
Kolby Kås .... 12 .... B1
Kölcse .... 107 .... E4
Kolczewo .... 35 .... E3
Kolding .... 12 .... B2
Koli .... 5 .... E1
Koli .... 7 .... E4
Kolimvárion .... 122 .... A4
Kolín .... 43 .... F2
Kölleda .... 38 .... B1
Kolmården .... 10 .... B1
Köln .... 40 .... B4
Kolobrzeg .... 35 .... F4
Kolochava .... 107 .... E4
Koloveč .... 43 .... D1
Kolpino .... 7 .... F1
Kölsillre .... 3 .... F1
Kolsva .... 10 .... B2
Kolvereid .... 3 .... D3
Komádi .... 106 .... C3
Komárno .... 105 .... E4
Komarom .... 105 .... E4
Kombóti .... 117 .... D1
Komló .... 105 .... E2
Komorane .... 112 .... C1
Komotini .... 118 .... C3
Kömpöc .... 106 .... B2
Komuniga .... 118 .... C4
Konak .... 106 .... C1
Končanica .... 105 .... D1
Kondiá .... 118 .... C1
Kondokáli .... 116 .... C1
Kondolovo .... 119 .... E4
Kondopoúlion .... 118 .... C2
Kondoros .... 106 .... C2
Kondrić .... 105 .... E1
Kongerslev .... 12 .... B3
Konginkangas .... 5 .... E1
Kongsberg .... 8 .... C2
Kongsvinger .... 9 .... E2
Königs-Wusterhausen .... 39 .... E3
Königsbrück .... 39 .... E2
Königsbrunn .... 46 .... B2
Königsee .... 42 .... B3
Königsfeld .... 44 .... C2
Königshofen .... 41 .... D1
Königslutter .... 38 .... B3
Königssee .... 47 .... D1
Königstein .... 40 .... C2
Königstein .... 43 .... E4
Königswiesen .... 87 .... D4
Königswinter .... 40 .... B3
Konispol .... 116 .... C1
Kónitsa .... 117 .... D2
Konjic .... 111 .... D2
Könnern .... 38 .... C2
Konnevsi .... 5 .... F1
Konotop .... 35 .... F2
Konstanz .... 45 .... D1
Kontinjoki .... 5 .... F3
Kontiolahti .... 7 .... E4
Kontiomäki .... 5 .... F3
Kontkala .... 7 .... E4
Konush .... 118 .... C4
Konyavo .... 113 .... E1
Konz .... 40 .... A1
Koparnes .... 2 .... A1
Koper .... 104 .... A1
Köpernitz .... 35 .... D2
Kopervik .... 8 .... A2
Kopidlno .... 43 .... F3
Köping .... 10 .... B2
Koplik .... 112 .... B1
Köpmanholmen .... 4 .... B1
Köpmannebro .... 9 .... E1
Kopparberg .... 10 .... A2
Koppang .... 3 .... D2
Kopparby .... 33 .... E4
Kopperby .... 9 .... E2
Koprivets .... 114 .... C2
Koprivnica .... 104 .... C1
Koprivshtitsa .... 114 .... B1

Korbach .... 37 .... D1
Korbevac .... 113 .... D1
Korbovo .... 113 .... E4
Korçë .... 117 .... D2
Korçula .... 110 .... C1
Korczyców .... 39 .... F3
Korentovaara .... 7 .... F4
Korgen .... 3 .... E4
Koria .... 7 .... D2
Korifásion .... 120 .... B2
Kórinthos .... 121 .... D1
Korisia (Livádhi) .... 121 .... E3
Korissós .... 117 .... D2
Korita .... 111 .... D1
Kormend .... 104 .... C3
Korneshty .... 109 .... E1
Korneuburg .... 87 .... E4
Kornsjö .... 9 .... D1
Kornwestheim .... 45 .... D3
Koróni .... 120 .... C2
Koronís .... 121 .... F2
Koropi .... 121 .... E3
Körösladány .... 106 .... C3
Köröstarcsa .... 106 .... C3
Korpavar .... 105 .... D2
Korpilahti .... 6 .... C3
Korpo (Korppoo) .... 6 .... B1
Korpoström .... 6 .... B1
Korppoo (Korpo) .... 6 .... B1
Korskrogen .... 10 .... B4
Korsmo .... 9 .... D3
Korsnäs .... 4 .... C1
Korsør .... 12 .... C1
Korsveien .... 3 .... D2
Korten .... 115 .... D1
Kortesjärvi .... 5 .... D1
Korthion .... 121 .... F3
Kortrijk (Courtrai) .... 30 .... C3
Korvaluoma .... 6 .... B3
Korvovo .... 113 .... E4
Korydhalós .... 117 .... D1
Kosanica .... 111 .... E1
Kosel .... 117 .... D3
Koserow .... 35 .... E3
Košetice .... 43 .... F2
Kosjerić .... 112 .... B3
Koška .... 105 .... E1
Koskenkorva .... 5 .... D1
Koskenkylä (Forsby) .... 7 .... D1
Koskenpää .... 5 .... E1
Koski .... 6 .... B1
Koski .... 6 .... C2
Koskimäki .... 4 .... C1
Koskue .... 6 .... B3
Kosmás .... 120 .... C2
Kosov .... 108 .... C4
Kosovo Polje .... 112 .... C1
Kosta .... 13 .... E3
Kösta .... 121 .... D2
Kostajnica .... 104 .... C1
Kostelec nad Čer.-Lesy .... 43 .... F2
Kostelec nad Labem .... 43 .... F3
Kostenets .... 118 .... B4
Kostinbrod .... 113 .... E1
Kostolac .... 112 .... C4
Kostrzyn .... 39 .... E4
Kosturino .... 117 .... E3
Koszeg .... 104 .... C3
Kotala .... 6 .... C3
Kotel .... 115 .... D1
Köthen .... 38 .... C2
Kotka .... 7 .... D1
Kotor .... 111 .... E1
Kotor Varoš .... 111 .... D3
Kotorsko .... 111 .... D4
Kotovsk .... 109 .... F3
Kótronas .... 120 .... C1
Kötschach-Mauthen .... 86 .... B1
Kotten .... 29 .... F2
Kötzting .... 47 .... D4
Koufália .... 117 .... E3
Koufós .... 118 .... B2
Kouklia .... 122 .... A1
Koukounaries .... 118 .... A1
Koúmanis .... 120 .... C3
Koutsókheron .... 117 .... E1
Koutsourás .... 122 .... C3
Kouvola .... 7 .... D2
Kovachevtsi .... 113 .... E1
Kovačica .... 112 .... C4
Kovero .... 7 .... F4
Kovin .... 112 .... C4
Kovland .... 4 .... A1
Köylio .... 6 .... B2
Kozáni .... 117 .... E2
Kozar Belene .... 114 .... C2
Kozarac .... 110 .... C4
Kozica .... 110 .... C2
Kozina .... 104 .... A1
Kozlodui .... 113 .... F3
Kozluk .... 111 .... E3
Kozolupy .... 43 .... D2
Kräckelbäcken .... 9 .... F4
Kragenæs .... 12 .... C1
Kragerø .... 8 .... C1
Kragujevac .... 112 .... C3
Krajn .... 116 .... C4
Krajnik Dolny .... 35 .... E2
Krakhella .... 8 .... A4
Krakow am See .... 34 .... C3
Kräklingbo .... 112 .... B1
Kraljevica .... 104 .... A1
Kraljevo .... 112 .... C3
Kralovice .... 43 .... E2
Kralupy nad Vltava .... 43 .... E3
Kramfors .... 4 .... B1
Kranenburg .... 36 .... A2
Kranevo .... 115 .... E2
Kranichfeld .... 42 .... B3
Kranídhion .... 121 .... D2
Kranj .... 104 .... A2

Kranjska Gora .... 104 .... A3
Krapina .... 104 .... C2
Kraslice .... 43 .... D3
Krasná Lipa .... 43 .... E4
Krasnovo .... 114 .... B1
Krasnoye Selo .... 7 .... F1
Krasnye Okny .... 109 .... F4
Krátigos .... 119 .... D1
Kratovo .... 117 .... E4
Kratovska Stena .... 112 .... B3
Krauchenwies .... 45 .... D2
Kraymorie .... 115 .... E1
Krefeld .... 36 .... A2
Kremen .... 35 .... D1
Kremna .... 112 .... B3
Krems .... 87 .... E4
Kremsmünster .... 86 .... C3
Krepoljin .... 113 .... D3
Kresna .... 118 .... A4
Kréstena .... 120 .... B3
Kreuth .... 46 .... C1
Kreuzlingen .... 85 .... D3
Kreuztal .... 40 .... C4
Krichim .... 118 .... B4
Krieglach .... 87 .... E2
Kriezá .... 121 .... E3
Krimml .... 86 .... A2
Krimpen .... 29 .... D2
Kristdala .... 13 .... F3
Kristianopel .... 13 .... E2
Kristiansand .... 8 .... B1
Kristianstad .... 13 .... D2
Kristiansund .... 2 .... B2
Kristiinankaupunki (Kristinestad) .... 4 .... C1
Kristinehamn .... 9 .... F1
Kristinehov .... 13 .... D2
Kristinestad (Kristiinankaupunki) .... 4 .... C1
Kristóni .... 117 .... F3
Kritsá .... 122 .... C3
Kriva Feja .... 113 .... D1
Kriva Palanka .... 117 .... D1
Krivodol .... 113 .... C2
Krivogaštani .... 117 .... D3
Križevci .... 104 .... C2
Krjstá .... 122 .... C3
Krk .... 104 .... A1
Krnjaca .... 112 .... C4
Krnjeuša .... 110 .... C4
Krøderen .... 9 .... D2
Krogsbølle .... 12 .... B2
Krokeaí .... 120 .... C2
Krokedol .... 9 .... D2
Kroken .... 3 .... F4
Krokom .... 3 .... F2
Krokstadøra .... 3 .... D2
Kronach .... 42 .... B2
Kronoby (Kruunupyy) .... 5 .... D2
Kronshtadt .... 7 .... F1
Kröpelin .... 34 .... C3
Kropenstedt .... 38 .... B3
Kropp .... 33 .... D4
Kropstadt .... 39 .... D3
Krosno Ordrzánskie .... 39 .... F3
Krossbu .... 8 .... C4
Krško .... 104 .... B2
Kruiningen .... 28 .... C1
Krujë .... 116 .... C4
Krumbach .... 45 .... E2
Krumovgrad .... 118 .... C4
Krumpendorf .... 86 .... C1
Krün .... 46 .... C1
Krunnupyy (Kronoby) .... 5 .... D2
Krupá .... 43 .... E2
Krupa na Vrbasu .... 111 .... D3
Krupac .... 113 .... E2
Krupaja .... 113 .... D3
Krupanj .... 112 .... B3
Krupište .... 117 .... E4
Krusá .... 12 .... B1
Kruševac .... 112 .... C2
Kruševo .... 117 .... D3
Krushevets .... 115 .... E1
Krushovene .... 114 .... B2
Krutvatn .... 3 .... F4
Krzęcin .... 35 .... F2
Krzeszyce .... 39 .... F4
Kubbe .... 35 .... E2
Küblis .... 85 .... D2
Kubrat .... 115 .... D2
Kuç .... 116 .... C2
Kucevo .... 113 .... D3
Kuchl .... 86 .... B2
Kuçiste .... 112 .... B1
Küçükcekmece .... 119 .... E4
Küçükkuyu .... 119 .... D1
Kufstein .... 86 .... A2
Kuha .... 5 .... E4
Kuhmoinen .... 6 .... C3
Kuhstedt .... 33 .... D2
Kühtai .... 85 .... F3
Kuivaniemi .... 5 .... D1
Kuivasjärvi .... 6 .... B3
Kükës .... 116 .... C4
Kukko .... 5 .... D1
Kukuyevci .... 112 .... B4
Kula .... 118 .... A3
Kula .... 106 .... B1
Kulata .... 118 .... A3
Kuleli .... 119 .... E4
Kulennoinen .... 7 .... E3
Kulhuse .... 12 .... C1
Kullaa .... 6 .... B2
Kulmbach .... 42 .... B2
Kulungsborn .... 34 .... C3
Kumane .... 106 .... B1
Kumanovo .... 117 .... D4
Kumbağ .... 119 .... E3
Kumkale .... 119 .... D1
Kumla .... 10 .... B1
Kumlinge .... 11 .... D1
Kumrovec .... 104 .... C2
Kungälv .... 12 .... C4

Kungsängen .... 10 .... C2
Kungsbacka .... 12 .... C3
Kungshamn .... 12 .... C4
Kungsör .... 10 .... B2
Kunhegyes .... 106 .... C3
Kunmadaras .... 106 .... C3
Kunpeszér .... 106 .... B3
Kunrau .... 48 .... B4
Kunszentmárton .... 106 .... B3
Kunszentmiklos .... 105 .... E3
Künzelsau .... 45 .... D4
Kuona .... 5 .... E2
Kuopio .... 7 .... D4
Kuortane .... 5 .... D1
Kupferberg .... 42 .... C2
Kupferzell .... 45 .... D4
Kupres .... 111 .... D3
Kurd .... 105 .... E2
Kŭrdzhali .... 118 .... C4
Kurejoki .... 5 .... D1
Kurikka .... 5 .... D1
Kurilo .... 113 .... E1
Kurkijoki .... 7 .... F2
Kürnare .... 114 .... B1
Kuršumlija .... 112 .... C2
Kursumlijska Banja .... 112 .... C2
Kuru .... 6 .... C3
Kusel .... 40 .... B1
Küssnacht .... 84 .... C3
Kustavi .... 6 .... B1
Kutemajärvi .... 5 .... F1
Kutina .... 104 .... C1
Kutná Hora .... 43 .... F2
Kuty .... 108 .... C2
Kuusa .... 5 .... E2
Kuusamo .... 5 .... F4
Kuusankoski .... 7 .... D2
Kuusjärvi .... 7 .... E4
Kuzmin .... 112 .... B4
Kvaerndrup .... 12 .... B1
Kvaløyseter .... 3 .... D3
Kvalvåg .... 2 .... B2
Kvam .... 3 .... D4
Kvanndal .... 8 .... B3
Kvanne .... 2 .... C1
Kvarnberg .... 10 .... A4
Kvelde .... 8 .... C1
Kvevlax (Koivulahti) .... 4 .... C1
Kvicksund .... 10 .... B2
Kvikne .... 3 .... D1
Kvillsfors .... 13 .... E3
Kvinesdal .... 8 .... B1
Kvissleby .... 4 .... A1
Kvisvik .... 2 .... C2
Kviteseid .... 8 .... C2
Kvitnes .... 2 .... C2
Kyläinpää .... 5 .... D1
Kyle of Lochalsh .... 18 .... B2
Kyleakin .... 18 .... B2
Kylerhea .... 18 .... B2
Kylestrome .... 18 .... C4
Kyllburg .... 40 .... A2
Kylmäkoski .... 5 .... E2
Kymönkoski .... 5 .... E2
Kyritz .... 34 .... C1
Kyrksæterøra .... 2 .... C2
Kyrkslätt (Kirkonummi) .... 6 .... C1
Kyrö .... 6 .... C1
Kyrönlahti .... 6 .... B2
Kyröskoski .... 6 .... B2
Kyšice .... 43 .... E2
Kytömäki .... 5 .... F4
Kyustendil .... 113 .... E1
Kyyjärvi .... 5 .... E1

L

L'Aber-Wrac'h .... 52 .... A4
L'Aigle .... 54 .... A4
L'Aiguillon .... 58 .... B4
L'Albi .... 70 .... B2
L'Alcudia .... 75 .... F1
L'Aldea .... 70 .... B1
L'Alpe-d'Huez .... 61 .... D2
L'Ametlla de Mar .... 70 .... B1
L'Ampolla .... 70 .... B1
L'Aquila .... 98 .... C3
L'Arbresle .... 60 .... C2
L'Argentière-la-Bessée .... 61 .... E1
L'Echalp .... 61 .... E1
L'Escala .... 71 .... E3
L'Escarène .... 65 .... F3
L'Espluga de Francoli .... 70 .... B2
L'Estartit .... 71 .... E3
L'Hospitalet de l'Infant .... 70 .... B1
L'Isle-Adam .... 50 .... B1
L'Isle-de-Noé .... 62 .... C2
L'Isle-en-Dodon .... 63 .... D2
L'Isle-Jourdain .... 59 .... D3
L'Isle-Jourdain .... 63 .... D2
L'Isle-sur-la-Sorgue .... 64 .... C3
L'Isle-sur-le-Doubs .... 56 .... C2
L'Ile-Bouchard .... 53 .... F1
La Rousse .... 57 .... L3
La Alamedilla .... 74 .... A4
La Alberca .... 73 .... E4
La Albuera .... 79 .... D2
La Almarcha .... 69 .... D1
La Almolda .... 69 .... E1
La Almunia de Doña Godina .... 69 .... E1
La Bañeza .... 67 .... D4
La Barrela .... 66 .... C2
La Barrosa .... 83 .... E1
La Bassée .... 50 .... B4

La Bastide-Puylaurent .... 64 .... B4
La Bastode de-Sérou .... 63 .... D1
La Bâtie-Neuve .... 65 .... E4
La Baule .... 52 .... C2
La Bazouche-Gouét .... 54 .... B3
La Belle Etoile .... 55 .... E3
La Bérarde .... 61 .... E1
La Bisbal .... 71 .... E3
La Bourboule .... 59 .... F2
La Bóvdeda de Toro .... 73 .... F3
La Bresse .... 56 .... C3
La Brillane .... 65 .... D3
La Cabrera .... 74 .... B4
La Caletta .... 96 .... C3
La Colobra .... 77 .... D3
La Calzada de Calatrava .... 80 .... B4
La Canourgue .... 64 .... A4
La Capelle .... 50 .... C3
La Capte .... 65 .... E2
La Carlota .... 83 .... F3
La Carolina .... 80 .... B3
La Cava .... 70 .... B1
La Cavalerie .... 64 .... A3
La Celle-Dunoise .... 59 .... E3
La Chambre .... 61 .... E2
La Chapelle .... 60 .... C3
La Chapelle-d'Angillon .... 54 .... B4
La Chapelle-en-Vercors .... 61 .... D1
La Chapelle-Glain .... 53 .... D2
La Charité .... 55 .... D1
La Charte .... 54 .... A2
La Châtaigneraie .... 58 .... B4
La Châtre .... 59 .... E4
La Chaux-de-Fonds .... 84 .... A3
La Ciotat .... 65 .... D2
La Clayette .... 60 .... B3
La Clusaz .... 61 .... E3
La Cluse .... 61 .... D3
La Cluse-et-Mijoux .... 56 .... B1
La Coquille .... 59 .... D2
La Coruña (A Coruña) .... 66 .... B4
La Côte-St-Andre .... 61 .... D2
La Courtine .... 59 .... E2
La Croisère .... 59 .... D3
La Croix-Valmer .... 65 .... E2
La Croixille .... 53 .... D3
La Cure .... 61 .... D4
La Espina .... 67 .... E4
La Estrada .... 66 .... B3
La Fère .... 50 .... C2
La Ferté Gaucher .... 55 .... D4
La Ferté Macé .... 53 .... E4
La Ferté-Bernard .... 54 .... A3
La Ferté-Milon .... 50 .... C1
La Ferté-St-Aubin .... 54 .... C2
La Ferté-sous-Jouarre .... 55 .... D4
La Ferté-Vidame .... 54 .... B3
La Flèche .... 53 .... F2
La Flotte .... 58 .... B3
La Gacilly .... 52 .... C2
La Garde-Freinet .... 65 .... E2
La Gineta .... 75 .... D1
La Granadella .... 70 .... B2
La Grand-Combe .... 64 .... B3
La Grande-Motte .... 64 .... B2
La Granja .... 74 .... B4
La Grave .... 61 .... E2
La Guardia .... 74 .... B2
La Guerche .... 55 .... D1
La Guerche-de-Bretagne .... 53 .... D3
La Haye-du-Puits .... 48 .... C2
La Hermida .... 68 .... A4
La Hutte .... 53 .... F3
La Iglesuela del Cid .... 75 .... F3
La Isla .... 67 .... F4
La Javie .... 65 .... E3
La Jonquera .... 71 .... D4
La Lima .... 94 .... B3
La Linea de la Concepción .... 83 .... F1
La Loupe .... 54 .... B3
La Louvière .... 30 .... C3
La Machine .... 55 .... D1
La Maddalena .... 96 .... B4
La Magdalena .... 67 .... E3
La Malène .... 64 .... A4
La Manga del Mar Menor .... 81 .... F3
La Maucarrière .... 53 .... E1
La Molina .... 70 .... C4
La Mongie .... 70 .... A4
La Mothe-Achard .... 58 .... A4
La Motte-Chalancon .... 65 .... D4
La Mudarra .... 67 .... F1
La Muela .... 69 .... E1
La Mure .... 61 .... D1
La Napoule-Plage .... 65 .... E2
La Nava de Ricomálilló .... 79 .... F4
La Neuve-Lyre .... 54 .... A4
La Neuveville .... 84 .... A3
La Paca .... 81 .... D3
La Pacaudière .... 60 .... B3
La Pallice .... 58 .... B3
La Palma del Condado .... 83 .... D3
La Palmyre .... 58 .... B3
La Palud-sur-Verdon .... 65 .... E3
La Petite-Pierre .... 56 .... C4
La Plagne .... 61 .... E2
La Platja d'Aro .... 71 .... E3
La Pobla de Segur .... 70 .... B3
La Pola de Gordon .... 67 .... E3
La Puebla de Cazalla .... 83 .... F3
La Puebla de Montalban .... 74 .... A2
La Puebla de Valverde .... 75 .... E3
La Punt .... 85 .... D2
La Rambla .... 80 .... A2
La Réole .... 62 .... C4
La Robla .... 67 .... D3
La Roca de la Sierra .... 79 .... D3
La Roca del Vallés .... 71 .... D2
La Roche-Bernard .... 52 .... C2
La Roche-Chalais .... 58 .... C2
La Roche-en-Ardenne .... 31 .... E2
La Roche-Posay .... 59 .... D4

137

La Roche-sur-Yon

Leuna

La Roche-sur-Yon 58 A41
La Rochefoucauld 58 C3
La Rochelle 58 B3
La Rochette 61 D2
La Roda 75 D1
La Roque-Gageac 59 D1
La Roquebrussanne 65 D2
La Salvetat 63 E3
La Salvetat-sur-Agout 63 F3
La Seu d'Urgell 70 C4
La Seyne 65 D2
La Solana 74 C1
La Souterraine 59 E3
La Spézia 93 D3
La Suze 53 F2
La Thuile 88 A2
La Tour-du-Pin 61 D2
La Tranche-sur-Mer 58 A4
La Tremblade 58 B3
La Trimouille 59 D4
La Trinité 52 B2
La Trinité-Porhoët 52 C3
La Turbie 63 F3
La Unión 81 F2
La Vecilla 67 F3
La Voulte 60 C1
La Wantezenau 57 D4
La-Roches-sur-Foron 61 E3
Laa an der Thaya 87 E4
Laage 34 C3
Laajoki 6 B2
Laarbruch 36 A2
Laakajärvi 5 F2
Laasphe 40 C4
Labastide-d'Armagnac 62 C3
Labastide-Murat 63 E4
Labedzie 35 F3
Labenne 62 A3
Labin 104 A1
Labinot Fushë 116 C3
Laboe 33 E4
Labouheyre 62 B3
Labrède 58 B1
Labrit 62 B3
Laç 116 C4
Lacalahorra 80 C2
Lacanau 58 B1
Lacanau-Océan 58 B1
Lacapelle-Marival 59 E1
Laćarak 112 B4
Lacaune 63 F3
Lacco Ameno 100 A4
Laceby 23 F3
Lacedonia 100 C4
Lăceni 114 C3
Lacona 97 D4
Láconi 96 B2
Lacq 62 B2
Lacu Roşu 108 C2
Lacu Sărat 109 E1
Ladbergen 36 B3
Lădeşti 114 B4
Ládhi 119 D4
Ladispoli 98 A2
Ladoeiro 72 C1
Ladon 54 C2
Ladybank 19 D1
Lærdalsøyri 8 B4
Laferté 56 B2
Laffrey 61 D1
Laforsen 10 B4
Lafrançaise 63 D3
Lagan 13 D3
Laganás 120 B3
Lage 37 D3
Lagg 15 E4
Laggan Bridge 18 C2
Lagniueu 61 D3
Lagny 54 C4
Lagoa 82 B3
Lagonegro 100 C3
Lagonísi 121 E3
Lagos 82 A3
Lagów 39 F3
Lagrasse 63 F2
Laguardia 68 C3
Laguépie 63 E3
Laguiole 59 F1
Lahinch 16 B3
Lahnstein 40 B3
Laholm 13 D2
Lahr 44 C2
Lahti 7 D2
Laichingen 45 D2
Laide 18 B3
Laignes 55 E2
Laigueglia 92 B3
Laihia 4 C1
Laikko 7 E2
Laimbach 87 D3
Lairg 18 C3
Laissac 63 F4
Laisvall 4 A4
Laitikkala 6 C2
Laitila 6 B2
Lajkovac 112 B3
Lajosmizse 106 B3
Lakatnik 113 E2
Lakavica 117 E4
Lake Side 20 C1
Lakhanás 118 A3
Lakhdenpok'ya 7 F3
Lakitelek 106 B3
Lakka 116 C1
Lákkoi 122 A4
Lákkoma 118 C2
Lakolk 12 A1
Laktasi 111 D4
Lála 120 B3
Lalapasa 119 D4
Lalin 66 C3
Lalinde 59 D1
Lalm 8 C4
Lalouvesc 60 C2
Lam 47 D4
Lama di Peligni 99 D2
Lamalou-les-Bains 64 A2
Lamarche 56 B3
Lamarque 58 B2
Lamastre 60 C1
Lambach 86 C3
Lamballe 52 C3
Lamberhurst 25 E1
Lambesc 65 D3
Lámbia 120 C3
Lambourne 27 F3
Lambrecht 44 C4
Lamego 72 C3
Lamía 120 C4
Lamlash 20 B3
Lammhult 13 E3
Lammi 6 C2
Lamorna Cove 26 B1
Lamotte-Beuvron 54 C2
Lampaanjärvi 5 F2
Lampaul-Plourzel 52 A4
Lampeland 8 C2
Lampeter 26 C4
Lamprechtshausen 86 B3
Lamsfeld 39 E3
Lamstedt 33 D2
Lamure 60 D3
Lana 90 C3
Lanark 20 C4
Lancaster 21 D1
Lanchester 21 E2
Lanciano 99 D3
Lancing 25 D1
Land's End 26 B1
Landau 44 D4
Landeck 85 E3
Landerneau 52 A4
Landesbergen 37 D3
Landete 75 E2
Landévennec 52 A3
Landivisiau 52 A4
Landivy 53 E3
Landkirchen 34 B4
Landön 3 F2
Landquart 85 D2
Landrecies 50 C3
Landsberg 46 B2
Landsberg 38 C2
Landsbro 13 E3
Landshut 46 C3
Landskrona 13 D2
Landstuhl 40 B1
Lanesborough 16 C4
Langå 12 B2
Långå 3 E1
Langádha 120 C2
Langadhás 117 F3
Langádhia 120 C3
Langadhikia 118 A2
Långåminne 4 C1
Langangen 8 C1
Langballig 33 D4
Långban 9 F2
Langdale 20 C2
Langeac 60 B2
Langeais 53 F1
Langefni 22 B3
Längelmäki 6 C3
Langelsheim 37 E3
Langen 32 C2
Langen 84 E3
Langenargen 45 D1
Langenburg 45 E4
Langenfeld 36 B1
Längenfeld 85 F3
Langenhahn 40 C3
Langenisarhofen 47 D3
Langenlois 87 E4
Langennaundorf 39 D2
Langenselbold 41 D2
Langenthal 84 B3
Langentière 64 B4
Langenwang 87 E2
Langenzenn 42 B1
Langeoog 32 B3
Langeskov 12 B1
Langesund 8 C1
Langevåg 8 A2
Langevåg 2 B1
Langewiese 36 C1
Långflon 9 E3
Langhirano 93 E3
Langholm 20 C3
Langland Bay 26 C4
Långlöt 13 F3
Långnäs 11 D2
Langnau-im-Emmental 84 B2
Langø 12 B1
Langogne 60 B1
Langoiran 58 B1
Langon 62 C4
Langport 27 D2
Langquaid 46 C3
Langres 56 A2
Långsele 4 A1
Långshyttan 10 B3
Långträsk 4 C4
Langula 37 E1
Langwarden 32 C2
Langwathby 21 D2
Langwedel 33 D1
Langweid 46 B3
Lanjarón 80 B1
Länkipohja 6 C3
Lanmeur 52 B4
Lannabruk 10 A1
Lannemezan 62 C2
Lannevesi 5 E1
Lannilis 52 A4
Lannion 52 B4
Lanouaille 59 D2
Lanreath 26 C1
Lanslebourg 61 E2
Lantosque 65 F3
Lanusei 96 C3
Lanvollon 52 C4
Lanzo Torinese 88 B2
Laon 50 C2
Lapalisse 60 B3
Lápas 120 B3
Lapinjärvi (Lappträsk) 7 D1
Lapinlahti 7 D4
Laplume 62 C3
Lapoutroie 56 C3
Lapovo 112 C3
Lappajärvi 5 D2
Läppe 10 B1
Lappeenranta 7 E2
Lappfjärd (Lapväärtti) 4 C1
Lappfors 5 D2
Lappi 6 B2
Lappo 6 A1
Lappohja (Lappvik) 6 C1
Lappträsk (Lapinjärvi) 7 D1
Lappvattnet 4 C3
Lappvik (Lappohja) 6 C1
Lapseki 119 D2
Lapta (Lapithos) 122 B2
Lapua 5 D1
Lăpuş 108 B3
Lăpuşna 108 C2
Lapväärtti (Lappfjärd) 4 C1
Laragh 17 E3
Laragne-Montéglin 65 D4
Lärbo 11 F1
Larche 59 D2
Larche 65 E4
Lårdal 8 C2
Larderello 94 B1
Laredo 68 C4
Largo 19 E1
Largs 20 B4
Lárimna 121 D4
Larino 99 E2
Lárisa 117 E1
Larkhall 20 C4
Larkollen 9 D2
Larmor 52 B2
Larnaca 122 B1
Larne 15 E2
Larochette 31 E1
Laroque-des-Arcs 63 D4
Laroquebrou 59 E1
Larrau 62 B2
Larsmo (Luoto) 5 D2
Larsnes 2 A1
Laruns 62 B2
Larvik 9 D1
Las Cabezas de San Juan 83 E2
Las Caldas de Besaya 68 B4
Las Campanas 69 E3
Las Navas del Marqués 74 A3
Las Negras 81 D1
Las Pedroñeras 74 C2
Las Rozas 74 B3
Las Ventas con Peña Aguilera 74 B2
Läsänkoski 7 D3
Laško 104 B2
Lasko 29 F2
Lassan 35 E3
Lassay 53 E3
Lassigny 50 B2
Lastovo 110 C1
Lastra a Signa 94 B2
Lastrup 36 C4
Lastva 111 E1
Lašva 111 D3
Latchingdon 25 E2
Laterza 101 D3
Lathen 31 B1
Latheron 19 D4
Latiano 101 E3
Latikberg 4 A3
Latina 98 B1
Latinu 109 E1
Latisana 91 E2
Latronico 100 C3
Laubrièrs 53 D2
Laucha 38 C1
Lauchhammer 39 E2
Lauder 21 D4
Laudio 68 C4
Lauenau 37 D3
Lauenburg 33 E2
Lauenstein 43 E3
Lauf 42 B1
Laufen 47 D2
Laufen 84 B3
Laufenburg 84 C3
Laufenburg (Baden) 80 C4
Lauffen 45 D3
Laugharne 26 C4
Lauingen 45 E3
Laujar de Andarax 80 C1
Laukaa 5 E1
Laukka 5 E3
Launceston 26 C2
Laupen 84 B2
Laupheim 45 E2
Lauragh 16 B1
Laurencekirk 19 E2
Laurencetown 16 C3
Laurenzana 100 C3
Lauria 100 C2
Laurière 59 E3
Laurieston 20 C2
Lausanne 84 A2
Lauterbach 41 D3
Lauterbrunnen 84 B2
Lauterecken 40 B1
Lauterhofen 42 C1
Lautiosaari 5 D4
Lautrec 63 E3
Lauvsnes 3 D3
Lauvstad 2 A1
Lauvvik 8 A1
Lauwersoog 29 E4
Lauzerte 63 D3
Lauzun 62 C4
Lavagna 93 D3
Laval 53 E3
Lavamund 87 D1
Lávara 119 D3
Lavardac 62 C3
Lavarone 90 C2
Lavaur 63 E3
Lavelanet 63 E1
Lavello 100 C4
Lavelsloh 36 C3
Lavenham 25 E3
Lavia 6 B2
Lavik 8 B4
Lavinio-Lido di Enea 98 B2
Lavoûte-Chilhac 60 B2
Lavoûte-sur-Loire 60 B2
Lavre 78 B2
Lávrion 121 E3
Lawers 19 D1
Laxå 10 A1
Laxe 66 B4
Laxey 20 B1
Laxford Bridge 18 C4
Laxo 19 F4
Laxsjö 3 F2
Laxtjärn 9 F2
Laxviken 3 F2
Läyliäinen 6 C1
Lazarevac 112 B3
Lazarovo 106 C1
Lazise 90 B2
Lázne Kynžvart 43 D2
Lazonby 21 D2
Le Bar 65 F3
Le Barp 58 B1
Le Beausset 65 D2
Le Blanc 59 D4
Le Boulou 63 F1
Le Bourg d'Oisans 61 D2
Le Bourget 61 D2
Le Bugue 59 D1
Le Cap d'Agde 64 B2
Le Catelet 50 C3
Le Caylar 64 A3
Le Chateau-d'Oléron 58 B3
Le Châtelard 61 D2
Le Châtelet 59 E4
Le Chesne 51 D2
Le Cheylard 60 C1
Le Conquet 52 A3
Le Creusot 60 C4
Le Croisic 52 C2
Le Crotoy 50 A3
Le Donjon 60 B4
Le Dorat 59 D3
Le Faou 52 A3
Le Faouët 52 B3
Le Fossat 63 D2
Le Grand Bourg 59 E3
Le Grand-Lucé 54 A2
Le Grand-Pressigny 54 A1
Le Grau-du-Rii 64 B2
Le Havre 49 E2
Le Hohwald 56 C3
Le Lauzet-Ubaye 65 E4
Le Lavandou 65 E2
Le Lion-D'Angers 53 E2
Le Locle 84 A3
Le Logis-du-Pin 65 E3
Le Loroux Bottereau 53 D1
Le Louroux 53 E2
Le Luc 65 E2
Le Lude 53 F2
Le Mans 53 F3
Le Markstein 56 C2
Le Mas-d'Azil 63 D2
Le Mayet 60 B3
Le Merlerault 53 F4
Le Monastier 60 B1
Le Monêtier 61 E1
Le Mont-Dore 59 F2
Le Mont-St Michel 53 D4
Le Montet 60 A4
Le Muret 62 B4
Le Muy 65 E2
Le Neubourg 49 F1
Le Nouvion-en-Thierache 50 C3
Le Palais 52 B2
Le Péage-de-Rousillon 60 C2
Le Perthus 63 F1
Le Pin-au-Haras 53 F4
Le Poiré-sur-Vie 58 A4
Le Pont-de-Beauvoision 61 D2
Le Pont-de-Claix 61 D2
Le Pontet d'Eyrans 58 B2
Le Portel 50 A4
Le Pouldu 52 B2
Le Pouzin 60 C1
Le Puy 60 B1
Le Quesnoy 50 C3
Le Rabot 54 C2
Le Rozier 64 A3
Le Russey 56 C1
Le Teil 64 C4
Le Teilleul 53 E3
Le Thillot 56 C2
Le Touquet 50 A4
Le Touvet 61 D2
Le Trayas 65 E2
Le Tréport 49 F3
Le Val-André 52 C4
Le Vaudreuil 49 F1
Le Vernet 65 E4
Le Vigan 64 B3
Leadburn 20 C4
Leaden Roding 25 E2
Leadenham 23 E2
Leadhills 20 C3
Leamington Spa 23 D1
Leap 16 B1
Leatherhead 25 D2
Leba 13 F1
Lebach 40 B1
Lebane 113 D1
Lebrija 83 E2
Lebus 39 E4
Lecce 101 F3
Lecco 89 D2
Lécera 75 F4
Lech 84 E3
Lechlade 27 E3
Leck 33 D4
Lectoure 63 D3
Leczyca 35 F2
Ledbury 27 E4
Ledesma 73 E3
Lédignan 64 B3
Ledigos 68 A2
Ledmore Junction 18 C4
Leeds 23 D4
Leek 23 D2
Leek 29 E1
Leeming Bar 23 D4
Leenene 16 B4
Leer 32 B2
Leerdam 29 D2
Leese 37 D3
Leeuwarden 29 E4
Lefkara 122 B1
Lefke (Lefka) 122 A1
Legden 36 B3
Legé 53 D1
Legnago 90 C1
Legnano 88 C2
Legrena 121 E3
Léguevin 63 D2
Legutiano 68 C3
Lehliu 115 D3
Lehnin 39 D3
Lehrberg 45 E4
Lehre 38 B3
Lehrte 37 E3
Lehtimäki 5 D1
Leibnitz 87 E1
Leicester 23 E2
Leiden 29 D2
Leighlinbridge 17 D2
Leighton Buzzard 25 D2
Leikanger 2 A1
Leikanger 8 B4
Leinefeide 38 A2
Leinesodden 3 E4
Leintwardine 22 C1
Leipheim 45 E2
Leipzig 38 C2
Leira 8 C3
Leiria 72 B1
Leirosen 3 E4
Leirvik 8 A2
Leirvik 8 A4
Leisnig 39 D1
Leissigen 84 B2
Leiston 25 F3
Leitrim 14 C1
Leitza 69 D4
Leitzkau 38 C3
Leivonmäki 7 D3
Leixlip 17 E3
Lekáni 118 B3
Lekeitio 69 D4
Lekenik 104 C1
Lekhainá 120 B3
Lekhchevo 113 E2
Lékhovon 117 D2
Leknes 2 B1
Leknica 39 F2
Leksand 10 A3
Leksvik 3 D2
Lekumberri 69 D3
Lelystad 29 E3
Lem 12 A2
Lembach 57 D4
Lembeye 62 C2
Lemförde 36 C3
Lemgo 37 D3
Lemke 37 D4
Lemland 11 D2
Lemmer 29 E3
Lemnia 109 D2
Lempäälä 6 C2
Lempdes 60 A2
Lemreway 18 B3
Lemvig 12 A3
Lemybrien 17 D1
Lena 9 D3
Lenart 104 C2
Lencloître 58 C4
Lend 86 B2
Léndas 122 B3
Lendava 104 C2
Lendinara 90 C1
Lengerich 36 C3
Lenggries 46 C1
Lengyeltóti 105 D2
Lenhovda 13 E3
Leningrad 7 F1
Leninváros 106 C4
Lenk 84 B2
Lenna 89 D2
Lenningen 9 D4
Lenno 89 D3
Lennoxtown 20 B4
Lens 50 B3
Lensahn 34 B3
Lensvik 2 C2
Lentföhrden 33 D3
Lenti 104 C2
Lenting 46 C3
Lentini 102 D2
Lenzburg 84 C3
Lenzen 34 B2
Lenzerheide 85 D2
Lenzkirch 44 C2
Leoben 87 D2
Leogang 86 B2
Leominster 22 C1
Léon 62 A3
León 67 F2
Leonberg 45 D3
Leondári 120 C2
Leonforte 103 D3
Leonídhion 121 D2
Leopoldsburg 31 E4
Leopoldsdorf 87 F3
Leordeni 114 C4
Leordina 108 B4
Lepe 82 C3
Lepetane 111 E1
Lepoglava 104 C2
Leposavić 112 C2
Lépoura 121 E3
Leppälahti 7 E4
Leppävesi 5 E1
Leppävirta 7 D4
Leppiniemi 5 E3
Lepşa 109 D1
Lepseny 105 E3
Lercara Friddi 102 C3
Lerici 93 D3
Lerma 68 B2
Lermoos 85 E3
Lerum 12 C4
Lerwick 19 F4
Lés 70 B4
Leş 107 D3
Les Abrets 61 D2
Les Adrets 65 E2
Les Aix 18 C1
Les Andelys 49 F1
Les Arcs 65 E2
Les Arcs 61 E2
Les Baux 64 C3
Les Borges Blanques 70 B2
Les Cabannes 70 C4
Les Contamines 61 E3
Les Deux-Alpes 61 D1
Les Diablerets 84 A2
Les Echarmeaux 60 C3
Les Echelles 61 D2
Les Epesses 53 E1
Les Escaldes 70 C4
Les Essarts 58 B4
Les Eyzies 59 D1
Les Gets 61 E3
Les Halles 60 C3
Les Haudères 84 B1
Les Hayons 49 F2
Les Herbiers 53 D1
Les Houches 61 E3
Les Issambres 65 E2
Les Laumes 55 E2
Les Lecques 65 D2
Les Menuires 61 E2
Les Pieux 48 C2
Les Planches 61 D4
Les Ponts-de Ce 53 E2
Les Riceys 55 E2
Les Rosiers 53 E2
Les Rousses 61 D4
Les Sables-d'Olonne 58 A4
Les Trois-Epis 56 C3
Les Trois-Moutiers 53 F1
Les Vans 64 B4
Les Verrières 84 A3
Lesa 88 C2
Lešak 112 C2
Lesbury 21 E3
Lescar 62 B2
Lesina 99 E2
Lesja 2 C1
Lesjaskog 2 C1
Lesjaverk 2 C1
Lesjöfors 9 F2
Leskelä 5 E3
Leskovac 113 D2
Leskovik 117 D2
Leskovo 115 E2
Leslie 19 D1
Lesmahagow 20 C4
Lésna 39 F1
Lesneven 52 A4
Lešnica 112 B4
Lésniów Wielki 39 F3
Lesogorskiy 7 E2
Lesparre-Médoc 58 B2
Lespezi 109 D3
Lessay 48 C2
Lessebo 13 E3
Lessines 30 C3
Lestelle Bétharram 62 C2
Lestijärvi 5 E2
Lesum 32 C2
Letchworth 25 D3
Letenye 104 C2
Letkés 105 E4
Letmathe 36 B2
Letnitsa 114 C2
Letschin 39 E4
Letterfrack 16 B4
Letterkenny 14 C3
Leu 114 B3
Leuca 101 F2
Leucate 64 A1
Leuchars 19 E1
Leuglay 55 F2
Leuk 84 B1
Leukerbad 84 B2
Leuna 38 C2

Leusheny 109 E3
Leutasch 85 F3
Leutenberg 42 C3
Leutkirch 45 E1
Leutschach 87 E1
Leuven (Louvain) 31 D3
Leuze 30 C3
Levádhia 121 D4
Levan 116 B3
Levanger 3 D2
Levanto 93 D3
Levanto 7 D2
Leven 20 C4
Levens 21 D1
Levens 65 F3
Leverkusen 40 B4
Levet 54 C1
Levice 105 E4
Levico Terme 90 C3
Levídhi 120 C3
Levie 57 F2
Levier 56 B1
Levisham 21 E2
Levkádhia 117 E3
Levkás 120 B4
Levkímmi 116 C1
Lévktra 121 D4
Levroux 54 B1
Levski 114 C2
Lewes 25 E1
Leyburn 21 E1
Leyre 69 E3
Leysdown 25 E2
Leysin 84 A2
Lezay 58 C3
Lezhë 116 C4
Lézignan-Corbières 63 F2
Lezoux 60 A3
Lianokládhion 120 C4
Liapádhes 116 C1
Libáň 43 F3
Liberec 43 F3
Libochovice 43 E3
Libourne 58 C1
Libramont 31 E2
Librazhd 116 C3
Licata 102 C2
Lich 41 D3
Lichfield 23 D2
Lichtenau 37 D2
Lichtenberg 42 C3
Lichtenfels 42 B3
Lichtenstein 43 D3
Lichtenvoorde 29 F2
Lički Osik 110 B3
Licko Lešće 110 B4
Liden 4 A1
Lidhorikion 120 C4
Lidingö 10 C2
Lidköping 9 E1
Lido di Camiore 93 E2
Lido di Castel Fusano 98 B2
Lido di Estensi 95 D3
Lido di Jésolo 91 D2
Lido di Latina 98 B1
Lido di Metaponto 101 D3
Lido di Nazioni 95 D4
Lido di Óstia 98 A2
Lido di Pomposa 95 D4
Lido di Spina 95 D3
Lido di Torre Mileto 99 E2
Lido di Venézia 91 D2
Lido Silvana 101 E3
Lidsjöberg 3 F3
Liebenau 37 D4
Liebenwalde 35 D1
Lieberose 39 E3
Liedenpohja 5 D1
Liege (Luik) 31 E3
Lieksa 7 E4
Lienz 86 B1
Lier 31 D4
Liernais 55 E1
Liesjärvi 5 E1
Liestal 84 B3
Liesti 109 E1
Lieto 6 B1
Lieurey 49 E1
Lievestuore 5 F1
Lievikoski 6 B2
Liezen 86 C2
Lifford 15 D2
Liffré 53 D3
Ligneuville 31 E2
Lignano Pineta 91 E2
Lignano Sabbiadoro 91 E2
Lignières 59 E4
Ligny-en-Barrois 56 A4
Ligourión 121 D3
Liguiel 54 A1
Lihme 12 A3
Lijeva Rijeka 112 B1
Likenäs 9 E3
Lild Strand 12 B3
Lilienfeld 87 E3
Liljendal 7 D1
Lilla Edet 12 C4
Lillafüred 106 C4
Lille 50 B4
Lillebonne 49 E2
Lillehammer 9 D3
Lillerød 12 C4
Lillers 50 B4
Lillesand 8 C1
Lillestrøm 9 D2
Lillhärdal 9 F4
Lillholmsjö 3 F3
Lillo 74 C2
Lillögda 4 A3
Limassol 122 B1
Limavady 15 D3
Limburg 40 C3

Limedsforsen 9 E3
Limenaria 118 B2
Liménion 120 C2
Limerick 16 C2
Limhamn 13 D1
Liminka 5 E4
Limin Khersónisos 122 B4
Liminpuro 5 F3
Limmared 13 D3
Limnária 121 D1
Limni 121 D4
Limoges 59 D3
Limogne 63 E4
Limone 90 B2
Limone Piemonte 92 B3
Limonest 60 C3
Limours 54 C4
Limoux 63 E2
Limpezişu 115 D4
Limpley Stoke 27 E3
Linares 80 B3
Linares de Riofrio 73 E2
Linariá 121 E3
Lincoln 23 E3
Lind 12 A2
Lindås 13 E2
Lindau 45 D1
Lindau 38 C3
Linde 12 A3
Lindbryde 19 D3
Lindenberg 45 E1
Lindenfels 40 C2
Linderhof 46 B1
Lindern 32 C1
Lindesberg 10 B2
Lindome 12 C4
Lindoso 66 B1
Lindow 35 D1
Linë 43 D2
Lingbo 10 B3
Linge 2 B1
Lingen 36 B3
Lingfield 25 E1
Linghed 10 B3
Linguaglossa 103 D3
Linköping 13 E4
Linlithgow 20 C4
Linneryd 13 E3
Linsdal 13 E3
Linseu 5 F4
Linthal 84 C2
Linton 25 E3
Lintzel 33 E1
Linz 40 B3
Linz 86 C3
Lioni 100 B4
Lion of Dee 19 D2
Lipar 106 B1
Liperi 7 E4
Liphook 25 D1
Lipiany 35 F2
Lipica 104 A1
Lipik 105 D1
Lipinki Luzyckie 39 F2
Lipkany 112 C1
Lipljan 112 C1
Lipnita 115 E3
Lipno 47 F3
Lipova 107 D2
Lippstadt 36 C2
Liria 75 F2
Lisbellaw 14 C2
Lisboa 78 A2
Lisburn 15 E2
Liscarroll 16 B2
Lisdoonvarna 16 B3
Liseleje 12 C2
Lisieux 49 E1
Liskeard 26 C1
Lisle 63 E3
Lismore 16 C1
Lisna 109 D4
Lisnaskea 15 D1
Lišnja 111 D4
Lišov 47 F4
Lisryan 17 D4
Liss 25 D2
Lisskogsåsen 9 E3
List 12 A1
Listeava 114 B2
Lištica 111 D2
Listowel 16 B2
Lit 3 F2
Lit-en-Mixe 62 A3
Lithakiá 120 B3
Lithinai Makriyialós 122 C3
Líti 117 E3
Litija 104 B2
Litke 106 B4
Litókhoron 117 E2
Litoměřice 43 E3
Little Clacton 25 F2
Little Walsingham 25 E4
Littlehampton 25 D1
Littleport 25 E3
Littlestone 25 F1
Litvinov 43 E4
Livada 107 E4
Livádhi 91 E1
Livádhi 121 D1
Livádhi (Korisía) 121 E3
Livarot 49 E1
Livernon 27 E4
Liverpool 22 C3
Livigno 90 B3
Livingston 20 C4
Livno 110 C2
Livron 60 C1
Lixoúrion 120 A3
Lizard 26 B1
Lizy 50 B1
Ljig 112 B3

Ljubanista 117 D3
Ljubelj 104 A2
Ljubinje 111 D1
Ljubljana 104 A2
Ljubno 104 A1
Ljuboviia 112 B3
Ljubuški 111 D2
Ljugarn 11 F1
Ljungby 13 D3
Ljungbyhed 13 D3
Ljungbyholm 13 F2
Ljungdalen 3 E1
Ljungsbro 10 B1
Ljungskile 12 C4
Ljusdal 10 B4
Ljusfallshammar 10 B1
Ljusne 10 C3
Ljutići 112 B2
Ljutomer 104 C2
Llafranch 71 E3
Llagostera 71 E3
Llanaelhaearn 22 B2
Llanarmon Dyffryn Ceiriog 22 C2
Llanarth 22 B1
Llanbedr 22 B2
Llanbedrog 22 B2
Llanberis 22 B2
Llanbister 22 C1
Llanbrynmair 22 C2
Llançà 71 E4
Llanddarog 26 C4
Llandeilo 26 C4
Llandiloes 22 C1
Llandinam 22 C1
Llandissilio 26 B4
Llandovery 26 C4
Llandrillo 22 C2
Llandrindod Wells 22 C1
Llandrinio 22 C2
Llandudno 22 B3
Llandyssul 26 C4
Llanelli 26 C4
Llanerchymedd 22 B3
Llanerfyl 22 C2
Llanes 68 A4
Llanfair Caereinion 22 C2
Llanfair P.G. 22 B3
Llanfair Talhaiarn 22 C3
Llanfairfechan 22 B3
Llanfarian 22 B1
Llanfihangel Crucorney 27 D4
Llanfyllin 22 C2
Llangadog 26 C4
Llangefni 22 B3
Llangennith 26 C4
Llangernyw 22 B3
Llangollen 22 C2
Llangranog 26 C4
Llangurig 22 C1
Llanguynog 22 C2
Llanhaedr 22 C2
Llanrhidian 26 C4
Llanrhystud 22 B1
Llanrwst 22 B2
Llansantffraed 27 D3
Llansantffraid-ym-Mechain 22 C2
Llanstephan 26 C4
Llanthony 27 D4
Llantrisant 27 D3
Llanuwchyllyn 22 B2
Llanwit Major 27 D3
Llanwrda 26 C4
Llanwrtyd Wells 27 D4
Llanwyddyn 22 C2
Llanybydder 26 C4
Llanymynech 22 C2
Llanystumdwy 22 B2
Llavorsi 70 B4
Lleida (Lérida) 70 B4
Llerena 79 E1
Lles 70 C4
Lloret de Mar 71 D3
Llucmajor 77 E3
Llwyngwril 22 B2
Llynclys 22 C2
Llyswen 27 D4
Loanhead 20 C4
Loano 92 B3
Löbau 39 F1
Lobenstein 42 C3
Lönsboda 13 D2
Loburg 38 C3
Locarno 84 C1
Loccum 37 D3
Lochailort 18 B2
Lochaline 18 B2
Lochanza 15 E4
Locharbriggs 20 C3
Lochboisdale 18 A2
Lochbuie 18 B1
Lochcarron 18 B2
Lochdonhead 18 B1
Lochearnhead 18 C1
Lochem 29 E2
Loches 54 A1
Lochgair 15 E4
Lochgilphead 15 E4
Lochgoilhead 20 B4
Lochinver 18 C2
Lochmaddy 18 A3
Lochwinnoch 20 B4
Lockenhaus 87 F2
Lockerbie 20 C3
Locknitz 35 E2
Locmaria 52 B2
Locmariaquer 52 C3
Locminé 52 C3
Locorotondo 101 E2
Locquirec 52 B2
Locri 103 F4
Locronan 52 A3

Loctudy 52 A3
Loddon 25 F4
Lodè 96 C3
Lodève 89 D1
Lodi 89 D1
Lodosa 69 D3
Lödöse 12 C4
Loeches 74 C3
Loen 8 B4
Løfallstrand 8 B3
Lofer 86 B3
Lofsdalen 9 E4
Loftus 21 E2
Loga 32 B2
Logatec 104 A2
Lögdeå 4 B2
Loghill 16 B2
Logroño 69 D3
Logrosán 79 E3
Løgstein 3 D2
Løgstør 12 B3
Løgumkloster 12 A1
Lohals 12 B1
Lohberg 47 D4
Lohéac 53 D2
Lohikoski 7 E3
Lohja 6 C1
Löhne 36 C3
Lohne 36 C4
Lohnsfeld 40 C1
Lohr 41 D2
Lohtaja 5 D2
Loiano 94 C3
Loimaa 6 B2
Lóiri 96 C3
Loitz 35 D3
Loja 80 B2
Lokakylä 5 E2
Lokalahti 6 B1
Løken 9 D2
Lokeren 30 C4
Løkken 117 F3
Lököshaza 106 C2
Lokve 112 C4
Lokve 104 B1
Lom 8 C4
Lom 113 E3
Lombez 63 D2
Lomello 88 C1
Lomen 8 C4
Lomma 13 D2
Lomme 50 B4
Lommel 31 E4
Lomnice nad Lužnicí 47 F4
Lomonosov 7 F1
Lonato 89 E4
Lončari 111 E4
Lončarica 105 D1
Londinières 49 F2
London 25 D2
Londonderry 15 D3
Long Bennington 23 E2
Long Compton 27 E4
Long Eaton 23 E2
Long Melford 25 E3
Long Preston 21 D1
Long Stratton 25 F3
Long Sutton 23 F2
Longarone 91 D3
Longbridge Deverill 27 E3
Longeau 56 A2
Longford 17 D4
Longframlington 21 D3
Longhorsley 21 E3
Longhoughton 21 E3
Longleat 27 E3
Longnor 23 D3
Longny 54 A3
Longobucco 101 D2
Longridge 22 C2
Longtown 20 C3
Longué 53 E2
Longuyon 51 E2
Longville 22 C1
Longwy 51 E2
Lonigo 90 C2
Löningen 36 C4
Lono 8 B2
Lons-le-Saunier 55 D4
Lönsboda 13 D2
Lønset 2 C1
Lønset 8 B1
Lønstrup 12 B4
Looe 26 C1
Loosdorf 87 D3
Loose 25 E1
Lopar 110 A4
Lopare 111 E3
Lopătari 109 D1
Lopatica 117 D3
Lopera 80 B3
Loppi 6 C1
Lopud 111 D1
Lora del Río 83 E3
Lorca 81 D3
Lorcé 31 E2
Lorch 54 B1
Lorch 40 C2
Lorentzen 56 C4
Loreo 91 D1
Loreto 95 E1
Loreto Aprutino 98 C1
Lorgues 65 D4
Lorica 99 D2
Lorient 52 B2
Lőrinci 106 B4
Loriol-sur-Drôme 60 C1
Lormes 55 E1
Lormont 59 E1
Lörrach 44 B1
Lorris 54 C2

Lorup 32 B1
Los 10 B4
Los Alcázares 81 F3
Los Arcos 69 D3
Los Arenales del Sol 81 F3
Los Barrios 83 E1
Los Navalmorales 74 A2
Los Palacios y Villafranca 83 E3
Los Urrutias 81 F3
Losar de la Vera 73 E1
Losenstein 86 C3
Losheim 40 A1
Losheim 40 A2
Lossburg 44 C2
Lossiemouth 19 D3
Lostwithiel 26 C1
Lote 2 A1
Lotorp 10 B1
Lotte 36 C3
Lotzorai 96 B3
Loudéac 52 C3
Loudes 60 B1
Loudun 53 F1
Loué 53 E3
Loughborough 23 E2
Loughbrickland 15 E1
Loughgall 15 D2
Loughglinn 16 C4
Loughrea 16 C3
Louhans 60 C4
Louisburgh 16 B4
Loukusa 5 F4
Loulay 58 B3
Loulé 82 B3
Louny 43 E3
Lourdes 62 C2
Louredo 66 B1
Lourinha 78 A3
Loúros 117 D1
Lousã 72 B2
Lousada 72 B3
Louth 23 F3
Loutrá 117 F3
Loutrá 121 E3
Loutrá 119 D1
Loutrá Aidhipsoú 121 D4
Loutrá Eleftherón 118 B3
Loutrá Ipátis 120 C4
Loutrá Kaiáfa 120 B3
Loutrá Killínis 120 B3
Loutrá Kounoúpeli 120 B3
Loutrá Smokóvou 117 E1
Loutrá Términs 119 D1
Loutrá Vólvis 118 A2
Loutráki 121 D3
Loutráki 120 B4
Loutrón Elénis 121 D3
Loutrós 119 D3
Loútsa 121 E3
Louvain (Leuven) 31 D3
Louviers 49 F1
Lövånger 4 C3
Lovasberény 105 E3
Lövberga 3 F2
Lovech 114 B1
Lovère 89 E2
Loviisa (Lovisa) 7 D1
Lovios 66 C1
Lovisa (Loviisa) 7 D1
Lövö 105 D4
Lovosice 43 E3
Lovran 104 A1
Lovrin 106 C1
Lövstabruk 10 C3
Lowdham 23 E2
Löwenberg 35 D1
Lowestoft 25 F3
Loweswater 20 C2
Lowick 21 D4
Loz 104 A1
Lozarevo 115 D1
Lozen 118 B4
Lozenets 119 E4
Loznica 111 E3
Lozovac 110 B2
Lozoyuela 74 B4
Lozzo di Cadore 91 D3

Ludgershall 27 E3
Lüdinghausen 36 B2
Ludlow 22 C1
Ludus 108 B2
Ludvika 10 B2
Ludwigsburg 45 D3
Ludwigshafen 40 C1
Ludwigshafen 45 D3
Ludwigslust 34 B2
Lugano 84 C1
Lügde 37 D3
Lugo 66 C2
Lugo 94 C3
Lugoj 107 D1
Lugones 67 E3
Luhalahti 6 B3
Luhanka 7 F4
Luhtapohja 7 F4
Luhtikylä 7 D2
Luib 18 C1
Luigny 54 B3
Luino 88 C2
Luik (Liege) 31 E3
Luikon Lahti 7 F4
Luka 113 D3
Lukavac 111 E3
Lüki 118 C4
Lukovica 104 B2
Lukovit 114 B2
Lukovo 113 D3
Lukovo 117 D3
Lukovo Šugarje 110 B3
Luleå 4 C4
Lüleburgaz 119 E3
Lumbarda 110 C1
Lumbier 69 E3
Lumbrales 73 D3
Lumbres 50 B4
Lumijoki 5 E3
Lumparland 11 D2
Lumphanan 19 E2
Lumsås 12 C2
Lumsden 19 E2
Lun 57 F4
Luna 108 B2
Lunas 64 A3
Lunca Corbului 114 B3
Lunca de Jos 108 C2
Lunca de Sus 108 C2
Luncani 108 B2
Lunci 109 D2
Luncavita 109 E1
Lund 13 D2
Lunda 10 C2
Lunde 8 B4
Lunde 8 B1
Lunde 4 B1
Lundeborg 12 B1
Lunden 33 D4
Lüneburg 33 E2
Lunel 64 B3
Lünen 36 B2
Lunéville 56 B4
Lungern 84 C2
Lungro 101 D2
Lungvik 4 B1
Lünne 36 B3
Lunz 87 D3
Luogosanto 96 B4
Luopioinen 6 C2
Luoto (Larsmo) 5 D2
Lupac 107 D1
Lupeni 107 E1
Lupeni 108 C2
Lupoglav 104 C1
Lupşa 107 E2
Lurcy-Lévis 60 A4
Lure 56 C2
Lureuil 59 D4
Lurgan 15 E2
Luri 57 F4
Lus-la-Croix-Haute 65 D4
Lušci Palanka 110 C3
Lushnjë 116 C3
Lusi 7 D2
Lusignan 58 C4
Lusigny 55 E3
Lusk 17 E4
Luso 72 B2
Luss 20 B4
Lussac-les-Châteaux 59 D4
Lussan 64 C3
Lustenau 85 D3
Luster 8 C4
Lutherstadt Wittenberg 39 D3
Lütjenburg 33 E3
Lutnes 9 E3
Lutol Suchy 39 F3
Luton 25 D2
Lutterworth 23 E1
Lutry 38 C2
Lutzmannsburg 87 F2
Lützow 34 B2
Luumäki 7 E2
Luvia 6 B2
Luxembourg 31 E1
Luxeuil-les-Bains 56 B2
Luz-St-Sauveur 62 C1
Lužani 105 D1
Lzarches 50 B1
Luzern 84 C3
Luzy 56 A4
Luzzara 94 B4
Lyaskelya 7 F3
Lyaskovets 114 C2
Lybster 19 D1
Lychen 35 D2
Lycksele 4 B3
Lydbury North 22 C1
Lydd 25 E1
Lydford 26 C2

Lydford on Fosse ... 27 ... E2
Lydham ... 22 ... C1
Lydney ... 27 ... E3
Lyme Regis ... 27 ... D2
Lymington ... 25 ... F1
Lympne ... 25 ... F1
Lyndhurst ... 27 ... E2
Lyneham ... 27 ... E3
Lyness ... 19 ... F1
Lyngdal ... 8 ... B1
Lynmouth ... 26 ... C3
Lynton ... 26 ... C3
Lyon ... 60 ... C3
Lyons-la-Forêt ... 50 ... A2
Lysá nad Labem ... 43 ... F3
Lysekil ... 12 ... C4
Lysøysund ... 3 ... D2
Lyss ... 84 ... B3
Lysvik ... 9 ... E2
Lytham St. Annes ... 22 ... C3
Lythe ... 21 ... E2
Lyuben ... 114 ... B1
Lyubimets ... 119 ... D4
l'Ile Rousse ... 57 ... E3

M

Maalahti (Malax) ... 4 ... C1
Maaninka ... 7 ... D4
Maanselkä ... 5 ... F3
Maarianhamina (Mereihamn) ... 11 ... D2
Maarianvaara ... 7 ... E4
Maaseik ... 31 ... E3
Maasmechelen ... 31 ... E3
Maassluis ... 28 ... C2
Maastricht ... 31 ... E3
Mablethorpe ... 23 ... F3
Maçanet de la Selva ... 71 ... D3
Mação ... 78 ... C4
Macclesfield ... 23 ... D3
Macduff ... 19 ... E3
Macedo de Cavaleiros ... 73 ... D4
Macerata ... 95 ... E1
Macerata Féltria ... 95 ... D2
Mãceşu de Jos ... 114 ... B2
Machault ... 51 ... D2
Machecoul ... 53 ... D1
Máchin ... 109 ... E1
Machrie ... 15 ... E3
Machrihanish ... 15 ... E3
Machynlleth ... 22 ... B2
Mackenrode ... 37 ... E2
Măcin ... 109 ... E1
Macomer ... 96 ... B3
Mâcon ... 60 ... C3
Macroom ... 16 ... B1
Macugnaga ... 88 ... B3
Mád ... 106 ... C4
Madan ... 118 ... C4
Madângsholm ... 13 ... D4
Madara ... 115 ... E2
Maddaloni ... 100 ... B4
Made ... 29 ... D2
Madekoski ... 5 ... E4
Madésimo ... 89 ... D3
Mãdirjac ... 109 ... D3
Madonna di Campiglio ... 90 ... B3
Madrid ... 74 ... B3
Madridejos ... 74 ... B2
Madrigal de las Atal Torres ... 73 ... F3
Maella ... 70 ... A2
Mære ... 3 ... D2
Mærus ... 108 ... C1
Mafra ... 78 ... A3
Magallón ... 69 ... E2
Magaluf ... 77 ... D3
Magaz ... 68 ... A2
Magdeburg ... 38 ... C3
Magellarë ... 116 ... C4
Magenta ... 88 ... C2
Magerholm ... 2 ... B1
Magescq ... 62 ... A3
Maghera ... 15 ... D2
Maghera ... 109 ... D4
Magherafelt ... 15 ... D2
Magione ... 95 ... D1
Mãgiresti ... 109 ... D2
Maglaj ... 111 ... D3
Maglavit ... 113 ... E3
Maglehem ... 13 ... D2
Maglehej Strand ... 12 ... C1
Magliano di Marsi ... 98 ... C2
Magliano di Toscana ... 97 ... E3
Magliano Sabina ... 98 ... B3
Maglić ... 112 ... C2
Maglie ... 101 ... F3
Magnac-Laval ... 59 ... D2
Magnor ... 9 ... E2
Magny-en-Vexin ... 50 ... A1
Mãgoaja ... 108 ... B3
Maguiresbridge ... 15 ... D1
Mãgurele ... 115 ... D4
Mahllu ... 5 ... E1
Mahora ... 75 ... E1
Maials ... 70 ... B2
Mãicãnesti ... 109 ... E1
Maîche ... 56 ... C1
Maida ... 101 ... D1
Maiden Bradley ... 27 ... E2
Maiden Newton ... 27 ... D1
Maidencombe ... 27 ... D1
Maidenhead ... 25 ... D2
Maidstone ... 25 ... E1
Maienfeld ... 85 ... D2
Mãieriste ... 107 ... E1
Maieru ... 108 ... B3
Mailly-le-Camp ... 55 ... E4

Mainburg ... 46 ... C3
Maintenon ... 54 ... B3
Mainua ... 5 ... F3
Mainz ... 40 ... C2
Maiori ... 100 ... B3
Maisach ... 46 ... C2
Maissau ... 87 ... E4
Maja ... 104 ... C1
Majaniemi ... 5 ... D4
Majavatn ... 3 ... E4
Majdanpek ... 113 ... D3
Makarska ... 110 ... C2
Makedonski Brod ... 117 ... D4
Makkola ... 7 ... E3
Makó ... 106 ... C2
Makrakómi ... 120 ... C4
Mákri ... 120 ... C3
Mákri ... 118 ... C3
Makri Ammos ... 118 ... C3
Maksamaa (Maxmo) ... 4 ... C2
Malå ... 4 ... B4
Mala Bosna ... 106 ... B2
Mala Krsna ... 112 ... C4
Málaga ... 80 ... A1
Malagón ... 74 ... B1
Malahide ... 17 ... E3
Málaia ... 108 ... B1
Malaucène ... 64 ... C3
Malax (Maalahti) ... 4 ... C1
Malbuisson ... 61 ... E4
Malchin ... 39 ... D3
Malchow ... 34 ... C2
Maldegem ... 30 ... C4
Maldon ... 25 ... E2
Malé ... 90 ... B3
Máleme ... 122 ... A4
Malente-Gremsmühlen ... 33 ... E3
Malesherbes ... 54 ... C3
Malesina ... 121 ... D4
Malestroit ... 52 ... C2
Malham ... 21 ... D1
Mali Idjos ... 106 ... B1
Mali Losinj ... 110 ... A3
Malicorne ... 53 ... F2
Malilla ... 13 ... E3
Malin ... 15 ... D3
Malin More ... 14 ... B2
Malines (Mechelen) ... 31 ... D3
Malinska ... 104 ... A1
Maliq ... 117 ... D3
Mališevo ... 112 ... C1
Maliskylä ... 5 ... E2
Maliuc ... 109 ... F1
Malkara ... 119 ... E3
Malko Gradishte ... 119 ... D4
Malko Turnovo ... 119 ... E4
Mallaig ... 18 ... B2
Mallersdorf ... 47 ... D3
Malles Venosta-Mals ... 90 ... B4
Mállia ... 122 ... C4
Malling ... 12 ... B2
Mallnitz ... 86 ... B1
Mallow ... 16 ... C1
Mallwyd ... 22 ... B2
Malm ... 3 ... D2
Malmbäck ... 13 ... D1
Malmédy ... 31 ... E2
Malmesbury ... 27 ... E3
Malmköping ... 10 ... B1
Malmö ... 13 ... D1
Malnas ... 108 ... C2
Malo ... 90 ... C2
Malo-les-Bains ... 50 ... B4
Maloja ... 85 ... D1
Måløy ... 2 ... A1
Malpartida de Cáceres ... 79 ... D3
Malpas ... 22 ... C2
Malpica ... 66 ... B4
Malšice ... 43 ... F1
Maltby ... 23 ... E3
Malton ... 21 ... E1
Malu ... 114 ... B3
Malung ... 9 ... F1
Malungen ... 9 ... D3
Malvik ... 3 ... D2
Malyovitsa ... 118 ... A4
Mamaia ... 115 ... F3
Mamers ... 53 ... F3
Mammola ... 103 ... F4
Manacor ... 77 ... D3
Manamansalo ... 5 ... F3
Manasija ... 112 ... C4
Mãnãstirea Neamt ... 109 ... D3
Mancha Real ... 80 ... B3
Manchester ... 23 ... D3
Manching ... 46 ... C2
Manciano ... 97 ... F3
Mandal ... 8 ... B1
Måndalen ... 2 ... B1
Mándamádhos ... 119 ... D1
Mándas ... 96 ... B2
Mandelieu ... 65 ... E2
Manderscheid ... 40 ... B2
Mándok ... 107 ... D4
Mandoúdhion ... 121 ... D3
Mándra ... 121 ... D3
Mándra ... 119 ... D3
Manduria ... 101 ... E3
Mãnecu Ungureni ... 108 ... C1
Manerbio ... 86 ... B2
Manétin ... 43 ... D2
Manfa ... 105 ... E2
Manfredónia ... 99 ... F2
Mangalia ... 115 ... F3
Manger ... 8 ... A3
Mangualde ... 72 ... C2
Maniago ... 91 ... D3
Manikainen ... 5 ... F3
Manisa ... 119 ... D1
Mank ... 87 ... D3
Mânkarbo ... 10 ... C2
Mannheim ... 40 ... C1
Manningtree ... 25 ... F3

Manolás ... 120 ... B3
Manoleasa ... 109 ... D4
Manorbier ... 26 ... B3
Manorhamilton ... 14 ... C2
Manosque ... 65 ... D3
Manresa ... 70 ... C3
Mansfeld ... 38 ... C2
Mansfield ... 23 ... E3
Mansfield Woodhouse ... 23 ... E3
Mansilla de las Mulas ... 67 ... F2
Mansle ... 58 ... C3
Mansoniemi ... 6 ... B3
Manteigas ... 72 ... C2
Mantes ... 50 ... A1
Mántorp ... 13 ... E4
Mantova ... 90 ... B1
Mäntsälä ... 7 ... D1
Mänttä ... 6 ... C3
Mántyharju ... 7 ... D2
Mäntylahti ... 7 ... D4
Mäntyluoto ... 6 ... B2
Manyas ... 119 ... F2
Manzanares ... 74 ... C1
Manzanares el Real ... 74 ... B4
Manzat ... 60 ... A3
Maó ... 77 ... F4
Maqueda ... 74 ... A3
Maranchón ... 75 ... D4
Maranello ... 94 ... C3
Marano ... 91 ... E2
Marans ... 58 ... B4
Mãrãsesti ... 109 ... E1
Marateca ... 78 ... B2
Marateca ... 100 ... C2
Marathiás ... 120 ... C4
Marathón ... 121 ... E3
Márathos ... 122 ... B4
Marazion ... 26 ... B1
Marbach ... 45 ... D3
Marbella ... 83 ... F2
Marboz ... 60 ... C4
Marburg ... 40 ... C3
Marcali ... 105 ... D2
Marčana ... 104 ... A1
March ... 23 ... F2
Marchaux ... 56 ... B1
Marche-en-Famenne ... 31 ... E2
Marchegg ... 87 ... F4
Marchena ... 83 ... F3
Marcheprime ... 58 ... B1
Marchwiel ... 22 ... C2
Marciac ... 62 ... C2
Marciana Marina ... 97 ... D4
Marcigny ... 60 ... B3
Marcilla ... 69 ... D2
Marcillac-Vallon ... 63 ... F4
Marcillat ... 59 ... F3
Marcilly-le-Hayer ... 55 ... D3
Marckolsheim ... 57 ... D3
Marden ... 25 ... E1
Mareham-le-Fen ... 23 ... F3
Marennes ... 58 ... B3
Mareuil ... 58 ... B4
Mareuil ... 58 ... C2
Margarites ... 122 ... B3
Margarítion ... 116 ... C1
Margate ... 25 ... F2
Margherita di Savoia ... 99 ... F1
Marghita ... 107 ... D3
Márgina ... 107 ... D3
Marginea ... 108 ... C4
Maria Laach ... 40 ... B3
Maria Taferl ... 87 ... D3
Maria Wörth ... 104 ... A3
Mariager ... 12 ... B3
Mariannelund ... 13 ... E4
Mariánské Lázně ... 43 ... D2
Mariazell ... 87 ... D3
Maribo ... 12 ... C1
Maribor ... 104 ... B2
Mariefred ... 10 ... C1
Mariehamn (Maarianhamina) ... 11 ... D2
Marieholm ... 13 ... D2
Marielyst ... 12 ... C1
Marienberg ... 43 ... D3
Marienborn ... 38 ... C3
Marienstad ... 9 ... E1
Marifjøra ... 8 ... B4
Marignane ... 65 ... D2
Marigny-le-Châtel ... 55 ... D3
Marikostinovo ... 118 ... A3
Marín ... 52 ... B3
Marina ... 110 ... B2
Marina ... 117 ... D3
Marina di Árbus ... 96 ... B3
Marina di Badolato ... 103 ... F4
Marina di Campo ... 97 ... D4
Marina di Caronia ... 103 ... D3
Marina di Carrara ... 93 ... D2
Marina di Castagneto-Donorático ... 93 ... E1
Marina di Chiéuti ... 99 ... E2
Marina di Gáiro ... 96 ... C2
Marina di Ginosa ... 101 ... E3
Marina di Gioiosa Jónica ... 103 ... F4
Marina di Grosseto ... 97 ... E3
Marina di Pietrasanta ... 93 ... D2
Marina di Pisa ... 93 ... D2
Marina di Ragusa ... 103 ... D1
Marina di Ravenna ... 95 ... D3
Marina di San Vito ... 99 ... D3
Marina Romea ... 95 ... D3
Marinella ... 102 ... B2
Marineo ... 102 ... B2
Marines ... 60 ... A3
Maringues ... 60 ... A3
Marinha Grande ... 72 ... A1
Marinkainen ... 5 ... E3
Maritsa ... 119 ... D4
Marjaniemi ... 5 ... D4
Marjovaara ... 7 ... F2
Mark Cross ... 25 ... E1

Markaryd ... 13 ... D2
Markdorf ... 45 ... D1
Market Deeping ... 23 ... F2
Market Drayton ... 23 ... D2
Market Harborough ... 23 ... E1
Market Rasen ... 23 ... F3
Market Warsop ... 23 ... E3
Market Weighton ... 23 ... E4
Markethill ... 15 ... D1
Markeugast ... 42 ... C2
Markfield ... 23 ... E1
Markham Moor ... 23 ... E3
Märkisch Buchholz ... 39 ... E3
Markneukirchen ... 42 ... C3
Markópoulon ... 121 ... E3
Markovac ... 112 ... C3
Markranstädt ... 38 ... C2
Marks Tey ... 25 ... E2
Marksbury ... 27 ... E3
Markt Bibart ... 41 ... E1
Markt Erlbach ... 42 ... B1
Markt St. Florian ... 86 ... C3
Markt St. Martin ... 87 ... F3
Markt-Indersdorf ... 46 ... C2
Marktheidenfeld ... 41 ... D2
Marktl ... 47 ... D2
Marktoberdorf ... 46 ... B1
Marktredwitz ... 42 ... C2
Marktzeuln ... 42 ... B2
Marl ... 36 ... B2
Marlborough ... 27 ... E3
Marle ... 50 ... C2
Marlenheim ... 57 ... D4
Marlow ... 100 ... C2
Marlow ... 25 ... D2
Marma ... 10 ... C3
Marmande ... 62 ... C4
Marmarereğlisi ... 119 ... F3
Marmári ... 121 ... E3
Marmoutier ... 56 ... C4
Marnay ... 56 ... B1
Marne ... 33 ... D3
Marnitz ... 34 ... C2
Maróneia ... 118 ... C3
Maróstica ... 90 ... C2
Marotta ... 95 ... E2
Marpissa ... 121 ... F2
Marquartstein ... 47 ... D1
Marquion ... 50 ... B3
Marquise ... 50 ... A4
Marradi ... 94 ... C3
Marsala ... 102 ... A3
Marsberg ... 37 ... D2
Marsciano ... 98 ... B4
Marseillan ... 64 ... B2
Marseillan-Plage ... 64 ... B2
Marseille ... 65 ... D2
Marseille-en-Beauvaisis ... 50 ... A2
Marshfield ... 27 ... E3
Marsico Nuovo ... 100 ... C3
Märsta ... 10 ... C2
Marstal ... 12 ... B1
Marstrand ... 12 ... C4
Marta ... 98 ... A3
Martano ... 101 ... F3
Martel ... 59 ... E1
Martelange ... 115 ... D3
Martfü ... 106 ... B3
Martigné-Ferchard ... 53 ... D2
Martigny ... 84 ... A1
Martigues ... 64 ... C2
Martin de Yeltes ... 73 ... E3
Martina Franca ... 101 ... E4
Martina-Martinsbruck ... 85 ... E2
Martinniemi ... 5 ... E4
Martínon ... 121 ... D4
Mártis ... 96 ... B3
Martock ... 27 ... D2
Martofte ... 12 ... B2
Martonvaara ... 7 ... E4
Martonvásár ... 105 ... E3
Martorell ... 70 ... C2
Martos ... 80 ... B3
Marvão ... 78 ... C3
Marvejols ... 64 ... A4
Marvrovoúni ... 120 ... C2
Marxwalde ... 39 ... E4
Marykirk ... 19 ... E2
Maryport ... 20 ... C2
Marzabotto ... 39 ... D3
Marzahna ... 39 ... D4
Maschen ... 33 ... E2
Masegoso de Tajuña ... 74 ... C4
Masevaux ... 56 ... C2
Masham ... 21 ... E1
Masku ... 6 ... B1
Maslenica ... 110 ... B3
Maslovare ... 111 ... D3
Massa ... 93 ... D3
Massa Marittima ... 71 ... D3
Massafra ... 101 ... E3
Massat ... 63 ... D1
Masseube ... 62 ... C2
Massay ... 54 ... C1
Massiac ... 60 ... A2
Mässlingen ... 3 ... E1
Maszewo ... 35 ... F2
Matabuena ... 74 ... B4
Matalebreras ... 69 ... D2
Matallana ... 67 ... F2
Mataró ... 71 ... D2
Mataruška Banja ... 112 ... C2
Matei ... 108 ... B3
Matelica ... 95 ... E1
Matera ... 101 ... D3
Mateševo ... 112 ... D1
Mátészalka ... 107 ... D4
Matfors ... 4 ... A1

Matha ... 58 ... C3
Mathay ... 56 ... C2
Matignon ... 52 ... C4
Matka ... 117 ... D4
Matlock ... 23 ... D2
Matlock Bath ... 23 ... D2
Matos de Carrico ... 72 ... B1
Matosinhos ... 72 ... B3
Matour ... 60 ... C3
Mátrafüred ... 106 ... B4
Mátraháza ... 106 ... B1
Matrei in Osttirol ... 86 ... A1
Matrei-am-Brenner ... 85 ... F3
Mattersburg ... 87 ... E3
Mattinata ... 99 ... F2
Mattinghofen ... 86 ... B3
Mattsee ... 86 ... B3
Matulji ... 104 ... A1
Maubeuge ... 50 ... C3
Maubourguet ... 62 ... C2
Mauchline ... 20 ... B3
Mauerkirchen ... 86 ... B3
Maughold ... 20 ... B1
Maulbronn ... 44 ... D3
Mauléon ... 53 ... E1
Mauléon-Licharre ... 62 ... B2
Maulévrier ... 53 ... E1
Maupertus ... 48 ... C2
Maura ... 9 ... D3
Maure ... 52 ... C2
Mauriac ... 59 ... E2
Mauron ... 52 ... C3
Maurs ... 59 ... E1
Maurstad ... 2 ... A1
Maury ... 63 ... F1
Mautern ... 84 ... C2
Mauterndorf ... 86 ... C2
Mauth ... 47 ... E3
Mauthausen ... 87 ... D3
Mauvezin ... 63 ... D3
Mauvoisin ... 84 ... B1
Mauze ... 58 ... B3
Mavrommati ... 118 ... B3
Mavrothálassa ... 118 ... B3
Mavrovi Hanovi ... 117 ... D4
Mavrovo ... 117 ... D4
Mawgan Porth ... 26 ... B1
Mawnan Smith ... 26 ... B1
Maybole ... 20 ... B3
Mayen ... 40 ... B3
Mayenne ... 53 ... E3
Mayet ... 53 ... F2
Mayfield ... 23 ... D2
Mayfield ... 25 ... E1
Maynooth ... 17 ... E3
Mayorga ... 67 ... F2
Mayrhofen ... 86 ... A2
Mäyry ... 5 ... D1
Mazagón ... 83 ... D3
Mazamet ... 63 ... E2
Mazara del Vallo ... 102 ... A3
Mazarron ... 81 ... E2
Maze ... 15 ... E2
Mazères ... 63 ... D2
Mázia ... 117 ... D1
Mazzarino ... 103 ... D2
Mazzaró ... 103 ... E3
Mealhada ... 72 ... B2
Measham ... 23 ... D2
Meaux ... 50 ... B1
Mechelen (Malines) ... 31 ... D3
Mechernich ... 40 ... A3
Meckenbeuren ... 45 ... D1
Medak ... 110 ... B3
Mede ... 88 ... C1
Medebach ... 36 ... C2
Medellín ... 79 ... E3
Medemblik ... 29 ... D3
Medena Selišta ... 110 ... C3
Medevi ... 10 ... A1
Medgidia ... 115 ... F3
Medgyesegyháza ... 106 ... C2
Medias ... 108 ... B2
Medicina ... 94 ... C3
Medina de Rioseco ... 67 ... F1
Medina del Campo ... 73 ... F3
Medina-Sidonia ... 83 ... E2
Medinaceli ... 75 ... D4
Medjumajdan ... 104 ... C1
Medle ... 4 ... C3
Medskogen ... 9 ... E3
Medstugan ... 3 ... E2
Medulin ... 110 ... A4
Medvedja ... 113 ... D1
Medvedov ... 105 ... D4
Medvode ... 104 ... A2
Medžitlija ... 117 ... D3
Meerane ... 43 ... D3
Meersburg ... 45 ... D1
Meeth ... 26 ... C2
Megáli Vólvi ... 118 ... A2
Megalo Khorió ... 117 ... E1
Megalópolis ... 120 ... C2
Mégara ... 121 ... D3
Megève ... 61 ... E3
Mehadia ... 113 ... D4
Mehov Krš ... 112 ... C2
Mehun ... 54 ... C1
Meifod ... 22 ... C2
Meigle ... 19 ... D1
Meijel ... 31 ... E3
Meilen ... 84 ... C3
Meina ... 37 ... D3
Meinerzhagen ... 36 ... B2
Meiningen ... 41 ... E3
Meira ... 67 ... D3
Meiringen ... 84 ... C3
Meisenheim ... 40 ... B2
Meissen ... 39 ... E1

Meitingen ... 46 ... B3
Mel ... 91 ... D3
Mélambes ... 122 ... B3
Melbeck ... 33 ... E2
Melbourn ... 25 ... E3
Melbourne ... 23 ... E2
Meldal ... 2 ... C1
Meldola ... 95 ... D3
Meldorf ... 33 ... D3
Melegano ... 89 ... D2
Melenci ... 106 ... B1
Melfi ... 100 ... C4
Melgaço ... 66 ... B2
Melhus ... 3 ... D2
Melide ... 66 ... C3
Melides ... 78 ... B1
Meligalá ... 120 ... C2
Meliki ... 117 ... E2
Melilli ... 103 ... D2
Melinesti ... 113 ... F1
Mélisey ... 56 ... C2
Melissi ... 117 ... D2
Melito di Porto Salvo ... 103 ... E3
Melk ... 87 ... D3
Melksham ... 27 ... E3
Mellansel ... 4 ... B2
Melle ... 36 ... C3
Mellendorf ... 37 ... D3
Mellerud ... 9 ... E1
Mellilä ... 6 ... B1
Mellin ... 38 ... B4
Mellrichstadt ... 41 ... E3
Melmerby ... 21 ... D2
Melnica ... 113 ... D3
Mélník ... 43 ... F3
Mělník ... 118 ... A4
Melnikovo ... 7 ... F2
Melrose ... 21 ... D3
Melsungen ... 37 ... D1
Melton Constable ... 25 ... E3
Melton Mowbray ... 23 ... E2
Melun ... 54 ... C3
Melvaig ... 18 ... B3
Melvich ... 19 ... D4
Mélykút ... 106 ... B2
Memmingen ... 45 ... E2
Menaggio ... 89 ... D3
Menan ... 30 ... B3
Menat ... 60 ... A3
Mendavia ... 69 ... D3
Mende ... 64 ... B4
Menden ... 36 ... C2
Menfi ... 102 ... B2
Menfőcsanak ... 105 ... D4
Mengen ... 45 ... D2
Mengeš ... 104 ... B2
Mengibar ... 80 ... B3
Mengishevo ... 115 ... D1
Menidhi ... 120 ... B4
Mens ... 61 ... D1
Menthon ... 61 ... E3
Menton ... 65 ... F3
Meppel ... 29 ... E3
Meppen ... 36 ... B4
Mequinenza ... 70 ... A2
Mer ... 54 ... B2
Meråker ... 3 ... D2
Merano-Meran ... 90 ... C4
Mercadal ... 77 ... F4
Mercatale ... 95 ... D1
Mercatino Conca ... 95 ... D2
Mercato San Severino ... 100 ... B3
Mercato Saraceno ... 95 ... D2
Merdrignac ... 52 ... C3
Mere ... 27 ... E2
Méréville ... 54 ... C3
Méribel ... 61 ... E2
Merichleri ... 118 ... C4
Mérida ... 79 ... D3
Merijärvi ... 5 ... D3
Merikarvia ... 6 ... B3
Mérikhas ... 121 ... E2
Merimasku ... 6 ... B1
Mering ... 46 ... B2
Merisani ... 114 ... B4
Merkendorf ... 46 ... B1
Merklingen ... 45 ... D3
Merligen ... 84 ... B2
Mernye ... 105 ... D2
Mersch ... 31 ... E2
Merseburg ... 38 ... C2
Merthyr Tydfil ... 27 ... D3
Mertola ... 82 ... C4
Merton ... 26 ... C2
Méru ... 50 ... B1
Meru ... 66 ... C4
Mervans ... 60 ... C4
Méry ... 55 ... E3
Merzig ... 40 ... A1
Mesagne ... 101 ... F3
Mesão Frio ... 72 ... C3
Meschede ... 36 ... C2
Meschers-sur-Gironde ... 58 ... B2
Mešeišta ... 117 ... D3
Mesenikólas ... 117 ... E1
Meslá ... 122 ... A4
Meslay ... 53 ... E2
Mesnalien ... 9 ... D3
Mesnil-Val ... 49 ... F3
Mesocco ... 85 ... D1
Mesokhóra ... 117 ... D1
Mesolóngion ... 120 ... B4
Mesón de Vento ... 66 ... B3
Mesopótamo ... 116 ... C1
Mespelbrunn ... 41 ... D2
Messdorf ... 38 ... C4
Messina ... 103 ... E3
Messingham ... 23 ... E3
Messíni ... 120 ... C2
Messkirch ... 45 ... D2

Messonghi ... 116 ... C1
Messtetten ... 45 ... D2
Mésti ... 118 ... C3
Mestlín ... 34 ... C2
Mestre ... 91 ... D2
Mesvres ... 55 ... E1
Metabief ... 61 ... E4
Metaljka ... 111 ... E2
Metamórfossis ... 118 ... A2
Metaxás ... 117 ... C2
Méteren ... 50 ... B4
Metes ... 107 ... E2
Méthana ... 121 ... D3
Metheringham ... 23 ... E3
Methil ... 20 ... C4
Methlick ... 19 ... E3
Methóni ... 120 ... B2
Methóni ... 117 ... E2
Methven ... 19 ... D1
Methwold ... 25 ... E3
Metković ... 111 ... D1
Metlika ... 104 ... B1
Metnitz ... 86 ... C1
Metókhi ... 120 ... B3
Metsäkylä ... 5 ... F4
Metsäkylä ... 7 ... D2
Metsälä (Ömossa) ... 6 ... B3
Métsovon ... 117 ... D1
Metten ... 47 ... D3
Mettet ... 31 ... D2
Mettingen ... 36 ... C3
Mettlach ... 40 ... A1
Mettmaan ... 36 ... B1
Metz ... 51 ... F1
Metzervisse ... 51 ... F2
Metzingen ... 45 ... D3
Meulan ... 50 ... A1
Meung ... 54 ... B2
Meuselwitz ... 42 ... C4
Mevagissy ... 26 ... B1
Meximieux ... 60 ... C3
Meyenburg ... 34 ... C2
Meymac ... 59 ... E2
Meyrargues ... 65 ... D3
Meyrueis ... 64 ... B3
Meyzieu ... 60 ... C3
Mézapos ... 120 ... C1
Mezdra ... 113 ... F2
Mèze ... 64 ... B2
Mézel ... 65 ... E3
Meziad ... 107 ... D2
Mézières ... 59 ... D3
Mézières-en-Brenne ... 59 ... D4
Mézilhac ... 60 ... C1
Mézin ... 62 ... C3
Mezöberény ... 106 ... C3
Mezöcsát ... 106 ... C4
Mezöhegyes ... 106 ... C2
Mezökeresztes ... 106 ... C4
Mezökovácsháza ... 106 ... C2
Mezökövesd ... 106 ... C4
Mezönyárád ... 106 ... C4
Mezöörs ... 105 ... D4
Mezöszilas ... 106 ... E3
Mezötúr ... 106 ... C3
Mezzolombardo ... 90 ... C3
Miajadas ... 79 ... E3
Miami Platja ... 70 ... B1
Miavaig ... 18 ... A4
Micfalău ... 108 ... C3
Micheldorf ... 86 ... C3
Michelstadt ... 41 ... D2
Michurin ... 119 ... E4
Mickleover ... 23 ... D2
Mid Yell ... 19 ... F4
Midbea ... 19 ... F1
Middelkerke-Bad ... 30 ... B4
Middle Rasen ... 23 ... E3
Middle Wallop ... 27 ... E2
Middleburg ... 28 ... C1
Middlefart ... 12 ... B2
Middleham ... 21 ... E1
Middleharnis ... 28 ... C2
Middlesbrough ... 21 ... E2
Middleton ... 25 ... D1
Middleton Cheney ... 27 ... F4
Middleton in Teesdale ... 21 ... D2
Middleton-on-the-Wolds ... 21 ... F1
Middletown ... 15 ... D1
Middlewich ... 23 ... D3
Midhurst ... 25 ... D1
Midleton ... 16 ... C1
Midlum ... 32 ... C3
Midsland ... 29 ... E4
Midstkogberget ... 9 ... E3
Midtgulen ... 8 ... A4
Mieders ... 85 ... F3
Międzyrzecz ... 39 ... F4
Miedzywodzie ... 35 ... E3
Miedzyzdroje ... 35 ... E3
Miehikkälä ... 7 ... E2
Miélan ... 62 ... C2
Mieluskylä ... 5 ... E3
Miercurea Ciuc ... 108 ... C2
Miercurea Nirajului ... 108 ... B2
Miercurea Sibiului ... 108 ... B1
Mieres ... 67 ... E3
Miersig ... 107 ... D3
Miesbach ... 46 ... C1
Mieste ... 38 ... B3
Miesterhorst ... 38 ... B3
Mieszkowice ... 35 ... E1
Mietoinen ... 6 ... B1
Mifol ... 116 ... B2
Migennes ... 55 ... D2
Migliarino ... 95 ... D4
Miglionico ... 101 ... D3
Mihăești ... 114 ... B3
Mihăești ... 115 ... D1
Mihai Bravu ... 115 ... E4
Mihai Viteazu ... 115 ... F4
Mihail Kogălniceanu ... 115 ... F3

Mihăileni ... 108 ... C4
Mihăilești ... 114 ... C3
Mihajlovac ... 113 ... D3
Mihesu de Cîmpie ... 108 ... B2
Mihla ... 41 ... E4
Mijas ... 80 ... A1
Mijoux ... 61 ... D4
Mikhalovo ... 113 ... B4
Mikhaylovgrad ... 113 ... E2
Mikhaylovo ... 113 ... E2
Mikkeli ... 7 ... D3
Mikonos ... 121 ... F3
Mikre ... 114 ... B1
Mikrón Dhérion ... 119 ... D3
Mikrothívai ... 117 ... F1
Miland ... 8 ... C2
Milano ... 89 ... D2
Milano Marittima ... 95 ... D3
Milazzo ... 103 ... E3
Milborne Port ... 27 ... E2
Milcoiu ... 114 ... B4
Mildenhall ... 25 ... E3
Mileševo ... 112 ... B2
Mileševo ... 112 ... B1
Miletići ... 110 ... B3
Mileto ... 103 ... F4
Milevsko ... 43 ... F1
Milford ... 25 ... D1
Milford ... 14 ... C3
Milford Haven ... 26 ... B3
Milford-on-Sea ... 27 ... F2
Milići ... 111 ... E3
Milín ... 43 ... E2
Milina ... 118 ... A1
Millas ... 63 ... F1
Millau ... 64 ... A3
Millom ... 20 ... C1
Millport ... 20 ... B4
Millstatt ... 86 ... C1
Millstreet ... 16 ... B1
Milltown ... 16 ... B1
Milltown Malbay ... 16 ... B3
Milly ... 54 ... C2
Milmersdorf ... 35 ... D2
Milna ... 110 ... C2
Milnathort ... 19 ... D1
Milnthorpe ... 21 ... D1
Miločer ... 112 ... A1
Miloi ... 120 ... C3
Milos (Plaka) ... 121 ... E2
Miloševa Kula ... 113 ... D3
Milovaig ... 18 ... A3
Milow ... 34 ... C2
Miltach ... 47 ... D4
Miltenberg ... 41 ... D2
Milton Keynes ... 25 ... D3
Milutinovac ... 113 ... E4
Mimizan ... 62 ... A3
Mimizan-Plage ... 62 ... A4
Mimoň ... 43 ... F3
Mînăstirea ... 115 ... D3
Mindelheim ... 45 ... E2
Minden ... 37 ... D3
Mindszent ... 106 ... B2
Mindin ... 52 ... C1
Minehead ... 27 ... D3
Minervino Murge ... 99 ... F1
Minglanilla ... 75 ... E2
Minićevo ... 113 ... D2
Minnesund ... 9 ... D3
Minsen ... 32 ... C3
Minster-in-Sheppey ... 25 ... E2
Minsterley ... 22 ... C2
Mintlaw ... 19 ... E3
Minturno ... 98 ... C1
Mînzălești ... 109 ... D1
Miokovićevo ... 105 ... D1
Mionica ... 112 ... B3
Mira ... 75 ... E2
Mira ... 72 ... B2
Mira ... 91 ... D2
Miraflores de la Sierra ... 74 ... B4
Miramar ... 65 ... E2
Miramar ... 72 ... B3
Miramare ... 95 ... D2
Miramas ... 64 ... C2
Mirambeau ... 58 ... B2
Miramont-de-Guyenne ... 62 ... C4
Miranda de Ebro ... 68 ... C3
Miranda do Douro ... 73 ... E4
Mirande ... 62 ... C2
Mirandela ... 73 ... D4
Mirándola ... 94 ... B4
Mirantes ... 67 ... E3
Miravet ... 70 ... B1
Mircea Vodă ... 114 ... C4
Mirebeau ... 56 ... A2
Mirebeau ... 58 ... C4
Mirecourt ... 56 ... B3
Mirepoix ... 63 ... E2
Mires ... 122 ... B3
Mirina ... 118 ... C1
Miroslăvești ... 109 ... D3
Mirošov ... 43 ... E2
Mirovice ... 43 ... E1
Mirovo ... 114 ... B1
Mirovo ... 114 ... B1
Mirow ... 35 ... D2
Mirşid ... 107 ... E3
Mirsk ... 39 ... F1
Mirtos ... 122 ... C4
Misilmeri ... 102 ... B3
Missanello ... 101 ... D3
Missegná ... 119 ... D1
Mistelbach ... 87 ... E4
Misterbianco ... 103 ... D2
Misterton ... 23 ... E3
Mistrás ... 120 ... C2
Mistretta ... 103 ... E3
Misurina ... 91 ... D3
Mitcheldean ... 27 ... E4

Mitchelstown ... 16 ... C2
Mithimna ... 119 ... D1
Mitikas ... 120 ... A4
Mitilíni ... 119 ... D1
Mitrašinci ... 117 ... F4
Mitrópolis ... 117 ... E1
Mittådalen ... 3 ... E1
Mittelberg ... 45 ... E1
Mittelberg ... 85 ... E2
Mittenwald ... 46 ... C1
Mittenwalde ... 35 ... C2
Mittenwalde ... 39 ... D3
Mittersill ... 86 ... A2
Mitterteich ... 42 ... C2
Mittweida ... 43 ... D4
Mitwitz ... 42 ... B2
Mizil ... 115 ... D4
Miziya ... 114 ... B2
Mjölby ... 13 ... E4
Mjølrund ... 9 ... D3
Mladá Boleslav ... 43 ... F3
Mladá-Vožice ... 43 ... F2
Mladenovac ... 112 ... C3
Mlado Nagoričane ... 117 ... E4
Mlekarevo ... 115 ... D1
Mlini ... 111 ... D1
Mnichovo Hradiště ... 43 ... F3
Mníšek pod Brdy ... 43 ... E2
Mo ... 9 ... D3
Moaña ... 66 ... B2
Moate ... 17 ... D3
Moča ... 105 ... E4
Mociu ... 108 ... B2
Möckern ... 38 ... C3
Mockfjärd ... 10 ... A3
Mockmühl ... 45 ... D4
Modane ... 61 ... E2
Modave ... 31 ... E2
Modbury ... 26 ... C1
Modena ... 94 ... C3
Módica ... 103 ... D1
Modigliana ... 94 ... C3
Modra ... 87 ... E3
Modrica ... 111 ... E4
Modugno ... 101 ... D4
Moelv ... 9 ... D3
Moena ... 3 ... E2
Moena ... 90 ... C3
Moers ... 36 ... A2
Moesgärd ... 12 ... B2
Moffat ... 20 ... C3
Moftinu Mic ... 107 ... D4
Mogadouro ... 73 ... D3
Móglia ... 94 ... B4
Moglicë ... 116 ... C3
Mogón ... 80 ... C3
Moguer ... 83 ... D3
Mohács ... 105 ... E2
Moheda ... 13 ... E3
Mohill ... 14 ... C1
Moholm ... 9 ... F1
Mohora ... 106 ... B4
Moi ... 8 ... B1
Moià ... 70 ... C3
Moikipää (Molpe) ... 4 ... C1
Moimenta da Beira ... 72 ... C3
Moinești ... 109 ... D2
Moira ... 61 ... D2
Moirans ... 61 ... D2
Moirans-en-Montagne ... 61 ... D4
Moissac ... 63 ... D3
Moisseiu ... 108 ... B4
Moita ... 79 ... A2
Mójácar ... 81 ... D2
Mojkovac ... 112 ... B2
Mokhlos ... 122 ... C3
Mokra Gora ... 112 ... B3
Mokresh ... 113 ... E3
Mokrós ... 118 ... B3
Möksy ... 5 ... E1
Mol ... 31 ... D4
Mol ... 106 ... B1
Mola di Bari ... 101 ... E4
Molái ... 121 ... D2
Molare ... 92 ... C3
Molde ... 2 ... B1
Moldova Nouă ... 113 ... D4
Moldova Veche ... 113 ... D4
Moledo ... 66 ... B1
Molfetta ... 101 ... D4
Moliden ... 4 ... B2
Molina de Aragón ... 75 ... D4
Molinella ... 94 ... C3
Molins de Rei ... 70 ... C2
Moliterno ... 100 ... C3
Molkom ... 9 ... E2
Möllbrucke ... 86 ... B1
Mölle ... 12 ... C2
Möllenbeck ... 35 ... D2
Mollerussa ... 70 ... B2
Mollet ... 71 ... D2
Mollina ... 33 ... E2
Mollösund ... 12 ... C4
Molls Gap ... 16 ... B1
Molltorp ... 9 ... F1
Mölndal ... 12 ... C4
Mölnlycke ... 12 ... C4
Mólos ... 120 ... C4
Moloy ... 55 ... F2
Molpe (Moikipää) ... 4 ... C1
Molsheim ... 57 ... D3
Molveno ... 90 ... B3
Momčilgrad ... 118 ... C4
Momin Prohod ... 114 ... B3
Mommark ... 12 ... B1
Monachil ... 80 ... B2
Monaco ... 65 ... F3
Monaghan ... 15 ... D1
Monasterace Marina ... 103 ... F4
Monasterevin ... 17 ... D3
Monastir ... 96 ... B1

Monbeltrán ... 73 ... F2
Moncalieri ... 88 ... B1
Moncao ... 66 ... B2
Monchdorf ... 87 ... D4
Monchengladbach ... 36 ... A1
Monchique ... 82 ... B3
Mönchof ... 87 ... F3
Moncófar ... 76 ... A3
Moncontour ... 52 ... C3
Mondariz Balneario ... 66 ... B2
Mondello ... 102 ... B3
Mondim de Basto ... 72 ... C4
Mondolfo ... 95 ... E2
Mondonedo ... 67 ... D4
Mondorf-les-Bains ... 51 ... F2
Mondovi ... 92 ... B3
Mondragón ... 69 ... D2
Mondragone ... 100 ... A4
Mondsee ... 86 ... B3
Moneasa ... 107 ... D2
Monéglia ... 93 ... D3
Monemor-o-Novo ... 78 ... B2
Monemvasia ... 121 ... D2
Monesterio ... 79 ... D1
Monestier-de-Clermont ... 61 ... D1
Moneygall ... 16 ... C3
Moneymore ... 15 ... D2
Monfalcone ... 91 ... E2
Monflanquin ... 63 ... D4
Monforte ... 78 ... C3
Monforte de Lemos ... 66 ... C2
Mongstad ... 8 ... A4
Monguelfo-Welsberg ... 91 ... D4
Monheim ... 46 ... B3
Moni ... 122 ... B1
Moniaive ... 20 ... C3
Mönichkirchen ... 87 ... E2
Monifieth ... 19 ... E1
Monistrol-d'Allier ... 60 ... B1
Monistrol-sur-Loire ... 60 ... B2
Monivea ... 16 ... C3
Monmouth ... 27 ... D4
Monnickendam ... 29 ... D3
Monninkylä ... 7 ... D1
Monopoli ... 101 ... E4
Monor ... 106 ... B3
Monor ... 108 ... B3
Mónosbél ... 106 ... C4
Monóvar ... 81 ... F4
Monpazier ... 59 ... D1
Monplaisir ... 54 ... B2
Monreal ... 69 ... E3
Monreal del Campo ... 75 ... E4
Monreale ... 102 ... B3
Monroyo ... 70 ... A1
Mons (Bergen) ... 30 ... C3
Monschau ... 40 ... A3
Monségur ... 62 ... C4
Monselice ... 90 ... C1
Monsheim ... 40 ... C1
Mønsted ... 12 ... B3
Mönsterås ... 13 ... F3
Monsummano Terme ... 94 ... B2
Mont-de-Marsan ... 62 ... B3
Mont-Louis ... 63 ... E1
Mont-sous-Vaudrey ... 56 ... B1
Mont-sur-Guesnes ... 53 ... F1
Montabaur ... 40 ... C3
Montagnac ... 64 ... B2
Montagnana ... 90 ... C1
Montaigu ... 53 ... D1
Montaigu-de-Quercy ... 63 ... D4
Montaigut ... 59 ... F3
Montalbán ... 75 ... F4
Montalcino ... 97 ... C4
Montalivet ... 58 ... B2
Montalto del Marche ... 98 ... C4
Montalto di Castro ... 97 ... F3
Montamarta ... 73 ... E3
Montana ... 84 ... B1
Montañana ... 69 ... F1
Montánchez ... 79 ... E3
Montaren ... 64 ... C3
Montargil ... 78 ... B3
Montargis ... 54 ... C2
Montastruc-la-Conseillère ... 63 ... E3
Montauban ... 63 ... D3
Montbard ... 55 ... E2
Montbazens ... 63 ... E2
Montbazon ... 54 ... A1
Montbéliard ... 56 ... C2
Montbenoît ... 56 ... C1
Montblanc ... 70 ... B2
Montbonnot ... 61 ... D2
Montbron ... 59 ... D2
Montbrun-les-Bains ... 65 ... D3
Montceau-les-Mines ... 60 ... C4
Montcornet ... 50 ... C2
Montcoutant ... 58 ... B4
Montcuq ... 63 ... D4
Montdidier ... 50 ... C1
Montdoubleau ... 54 ... A2
Monte Clérigo ... 82 ... A3
Monte Gordo ... 82 ... C3
Monte San Angelo ... 99 ... F2
Monte San Savino ... 94 ... C1
Monte-Carlo ... 65 ... F3
Monteagudo del Castillo ... 81 ... E4
Montebelluna ... 91 ... D2
Montebourg ... 49 ... D2
Montecchio ... 95 ... D2
Montecchio Moggiore ... 90 ... C2
Montecorvino Rovella ... 100 ... B3
Montefalco ... 98 ... B4
Montefiascone ... 98 ... A3
Montefiorino ... 94 ... B3
Montefrío ... 80 ... B2
Montegiordano Marina ... 101 ... D2
Montegrotto Terme ... 90 ... C1
Montehermoso ... 73 ... D1
Montélimar ... 64 ... C4

Montella ... 100 ... B4
Montemor-o-Novo ... 78 ... B2
Montemor-o-Velho ... 72 ... B2
Montendre ... 58 ... B2
Montenero di Bisaccia ... 99 ... D2
Montepulciano ... 97 ... F4
Montereale ... 98 ... C3
Montereau ... 55 ... D3
Monterotondo ... 98 ... B2
Monterroso ... 66 ... C3
Montesano sulla Marcellana ... 100 ... C3
Montesarchio ... 100 ... B4
Montescaglioso ... 101 ... D3
Montesilvano Marina ... 99 ... D3
Montesquieu-Volvestre ... 63 ... D2
Montesquiou ... 62 ... C2
Montevarchi ... 94 ... C2
Montfaucon-en-Velay ... 60 ... C2
Montfort ... 62 ... B3
Montfort ... 54 ... C4
Montgat ... 71 ... D2
Montgenèvre ... 61 ... E1
Montgiscard ... 63 ... E2
Montgomery ... 22 ... C2
Montguyon ... 58 ... C2
Montherme ... 51 ... D3
Monthey ... 84 ... A1
Monthois ... 51 ... D2
Monthureaux ... 56 ... B3
Monti ... 96 ... B3
Montichiari ... 89 ... E2
Monticiano ... 94 ... C1
Montier-en-Der ... 55 ... F3
Montignac ... 59 ... D1
Montigny-le-Roi ... 56 ... A3
Montigny-sur-Aube ... 55 ... F2
Montijo ... 79 ... D3
Montijo ... 44 ... A2
Montilla ... 80 ... A2
Montivilliers ... 49 ... E2
Montlieu ... 58 ... C2
Montluçon ... 59 ... F3
Montluel ... 60 ... C3
Montmarault ... 60 ... A3
Montmédy ... 51 ... E2
Montmélian ... 61 ... D2
Montmirail ... 55 ... D4
Montmirail ... 54 ... A3
Montmirey ... 56 ... B1
Montmoreau ... 58 ... C2
Montmorillon ... 59 ... D4
Montmort ... 55 ... D4
Montoire ... 54 ... B2
Montorio ... 68 ... B3
Montorio al Vomano ... 98 ... C3
Montoro ... 80 ... A3
Montpellier ... 64 ... C3
Montpezat ... 63 ... D3
Montpon-Ménestérol ... 58 ... C1
Montréal ... 63 ... E2
Montréal ... 62 ... C3
Montréjeau ... 62 ... C2
Montrésor ... 54 ... B1
Montret ... 60 ... C4
Montreuil ... 50 ... A3
Montreuil-aux-Lions ... 50 ... C1
Montreuil-Bellay ... 53 ... E1
Montreux ... 84 ... A2
Montrevel ... 60 ... C3
Montrichard ... 54 ... B1
Montrond-les-Bains ... 60 ... B2
Montrose ... 19 ... E1
Montsalvy ... 59 ... F1
Montsauche ... 53 ... E1
Montsoreau ... 53 ... F1
Montsûrs ... 53 ... E3
Monza ... 89 ... D2
Monzón ... 70 ... A2
Mooncoin ... 17 ... D2
Moordorf ... 32 ... B2
Moorfields ... 15 ... D2
Moosburg ... 46 ... C2
Moosinning ... 46 ... C2
Mór ... 105 ... E3
Móra ... 74 ... B2
Móra ... 78 ... B3
Mora ... 10 ... A3
Mora d'Ebre ... 70 ... B1
Mora de Rubielos ... 75 ... F4
Mora la Nova ... 70 ... B2
Morača ... 112 ... B1
Mórahalom ... 106 ... B2
Moraitika ... 116 ... C2
Morano Cálabro ... 101 ... D2
Morar ... 18 ... B2
Morasverdes ... 73 ... D2
Moratalla ... 81 ... D3
Moravita ... 106 ... C1
Morbach ... 40 ... B2
Morbegno ... 89 ... D3
Mörbisch ... 87 ... F3
Mörbylånda ... 13 ... F2
Morcenx ... 62 ... B3
Morciano di Romagna ... 95 ... D2
Morcone ... 99 ... D3
Morcote ... 84 ... C1
Mordelles ... 53 ... D3
Morebattle ... 21 ... D3
Morecambe ... 21 ... D1
Moreda ... 80 ... B2
Morella ... 70 ... A1
Morella ... 114 ... C4
Móres ... 96 ... B3
Morestel ... 61 ... D2
Moreton in Marsh ... 27 ... E4
Moretonhampstead ... 26 ... C2
Moretta ... 92 ... B4

Moreuil ... 50 ... B2
Morez ... 61 ... D4
Morfa Nefyn ... 22 ... B2
Morfelden ... 40 ... C2
Mórfion ... 116 ... C3
Morgat ... 52 ... A3
Morgedal ... 8 ... C2
Morges ... 84 ... A2
Morgex ... 88 ... A2
Morgins ... 84 ... A1
Morgongåva ... 10 ... B2
Morhange ... 51 ... F1
Mori ... 90 ... B2
Morjärv ... 5 ... D4
Mørke ... 12 ... B2
Mørkov ... 12 ... B2
Morlaàs ... 62 ... C2
Morlaix ... 52 ... B4
Mörlunda ... 13 ... E3
Mormanno ... 100 ... C2
Mormant ... 55 ... D3
Morón de Almazán ... 69 ... D1
Morón de la Frontera ... 83 ... E3
Morón de la Frontera ... 83 ... E3
Morosaglia ... 57 ... F3
Morović ... 111 ... E4
Morpeth ... 21 ... E3
Mörrum ... 13 ... E2
Mörrum ... 13 ... E2
Mörsil ... 3 ... E2
Mörskom (Myrskylä) ... 7 ... D2
Mortagne-au-Perche ... 54 ... A3
Mortagne-sur-Sèvre ... 53 ... D1
Mortara ... 53 ... E4
Morteau ... 88 ... C2
Mortehoe ... 56 ... C1
Mortimer's Cross ... 26 ... C2
Mortizburg ... 22 ... C1
Mortrée ... 39 ... E1
Mortrée ... 53 ... F4
Morutca ... 23 ... D2
Morwenstow ... 26 ... C2
Moryń ... 35 ... E1
Morzine ... 61 ... E3
Morzyczyn ... 35 ... F2
Mosbach ... 45 ... D4
Mosby ... 8 ... B1
Mošcenice ... 104 ... A1
Mošcenička Draga ... 104 ... A1
Moschendorf ... 87 ... F2
Mosjøen ... 3 ... E4
Moskog ... 8 ... B4
Moskosel ... 4 ... B4
Moslavina ... 105 ... D1
Mosonmagyaróvár ... 105 ... D4
Moss ... 9 ... D2
Mössingen ... 45 ... D2
Most ... 43 ... E3
Mostar ... 111 ... D2
Mosterhamn ... 8 ... A2
Mostyn ... 22 ... C3
Mota del Cuervo ... 74 ... C2
Mota del Marques ... 73 ... F4
Motala ... 10 ... A1
Motca ... 109 ... D3
Motherwell ... 20 ... C4
Motilla del Palancar ... 75 ... D2
Motoşeni ... 109 ... E2
Motovun ... 104 ... A1
Motril ... 80 ... B1
Motru ... 113 ... E4
Motta di Livenza ... 91 ... D2
Mottola ... 101 ... E3
Möttönen ... 5 ... E2
Mouchard ... 56 ... B1
Moúdhros ... 118 ... C1
Moudon ... 84 ... A2
Mougins ... 65 ... F3
Mouhijärvi ... 6 ... B2
Mouliherne ... 53 ... F2
Moulins ... 60 ... A4
Moulins-Engilbert ... 55 ... E1
Moulins-la-Marche ... 54 ... A4
Mound Station ... 19 ... D3
Mount Bellew ... 16 ... C4
Mount Charles ... 14 ... C2
Mountain Ash ... 27 ... D3
Mountmellick ... 17 ... D3
Mountrath ... 17 ... D3
Mountshannon ... 16 ... C3
Moura ... 78 ... C1
Mourão ... 78 ... C1
Mourne Abbey ... 16 ... C1
Mousehole ... 26 ... B1
Moustiers-Ste-Marie ... 65 ... E3
Mouthe ... 61 ... D4
Mouthier ... 56 ... B1
Mouthoumet ... 63 ... F1
Moutier ... 84 ... B3
Moutiers ... 58 ... A4
Moûtiers ... 61 ... E2
Moutoullas ... 122 ... A1
Moutsoúna ... 121 ... F2
Mouy ... 50 ... B2
Mouzáki ... 117 ... E1
Mouzon ... 51 ... D2
Movila Miresii ... 109 ... E1
Movilita ... 115 ... D3
Moville ... 15 ... D3
Moy ... 15 ... D2
Moylett ... 15 ... D1
Moynalty ... 17 ... D4
Mrčajevci ... 112 ... C3
Mrkonjić-Grad ... 110 ... C3
Mrzeżyno ... 35 ... F3
Mšeno ... 43 ... F3
Muccia ... 98 ... B4
Much ... 40 ... B3
Much Marcle ... 27 ... E4
Much Wenlock ... 23 ... D2
Mücheln ... 38 ... C2

Muckross ... 16 ... B1
Múcsony ... 106 ... C4
Mudau ... 41 ... D1
Mudeford ... 27 ... E2
Müden ... 33 ... E1
Müdrets ... 119 ... D4
Muelas del Pan ... 73 ... E4
Muff ... 15 ... D3
Mügeln ... 39 ... D2
Mugeni ... 108 ... C2
Muggenddorf ... 42 ... B2
Múggia ... 91 ... E1
Múglizh ... 114 ... C1
Mugron ... 62 ... B3
Mühlacker ... 45 ... D3
Mühlbach ... 86 ... B2
Mühlberg ... 39 ... D2
Mühldorf ... 47 ... D2
Mühlhausen ... 38 ... E2
Muhola ... 5 ... E2
Muhos ... 5 ... E3
Muhovo ... 114 ... B1
Muine Bheag ... 17 ... D2
Muir of Ord ... 18 ... C3
Muirhead ... 19 ... D1
Muirkirk ... 20 ... B3
Mukachevo ... 107 ... E4
Mühlhausen ... 45 ... D3
Mula ... 81 ... E3
Mülheim ... 36 ... B2
Mülheim ... 40 ... B2
Mulhouse ... 56 ... C2
Mullabohy ... 15 ... D1
Mullagh ... 17 ... E3
Müllheim ... 44 ... B1
Mullinavat ... 17 ... D2
Mullingar ... 17 ... D4
Müllrose ... 39 ... E3
Mullsjö ... 13 ... D4
Multia ... 5 ... E1
Mumbles ... 26 ... C4
Muncelu ... 109 ... D1
Münchberg ... 42 ... C2
Münchberg ... 39 ... E4
München ... 46 ... C2
Münchhausen ... 40 ... C4
Münchhausen ... 39 ... E2
Mundesley ... 25 ... F4
Mundford ... 25 ... E3
Mundheim ... 8 ... B3
Munera ... 75 ... D1
Mungia ... 68 ... C4
Muñico ... 73 ... F2
Muniesa ... 75 ... F4
Munka-Ljunby ... 13 ... D2
Munkebo ... 12 ... B1
Munkedal ... 9 ... D1
Munkfors ... 9 ... E2
Munlochy ... 19 ... D3
Münnerstadt ... 41 ... E2
Munsala ... 5 ... D2
Münsingen ... 45 ... D2
Münsingen ... 84 ... B2
Munster ... 56 ... C3
Münster ... 36 ... B3
Münster ... 84 ... C2
Munster-Lager ... 33 ... E1
Münstertal ... 44 ... B2
Munteni ... 109 ... E1
Münzkirchen ... 86 ... C4
Mur-de-Barrez ... 59 ... F1
Mur-de-Bretagne ... 52 ... B3
Murano ... 91 ... D2
Murat ... 59 ... F2
Murat-sur-Vebre ... 63 ... F3
Muratli ... 119 ... E3
Murato ... 57 ... F3
Murau ... 86 ... C2
Muravera ... 96 ... C1
Murça ... 72 ... C2
Mürchevo ... 113 ... E2
Murchin ... 35 ... E3
Murcia ... 81 ... E3
Mureck ... 87 ... E1
Mürefte ... 119 ... E3
Mureşenii Bîrgăului ... 108 ... B3
Muret ... 63 ... D2
Murfatlar ... 115 ... F3
Murgaševo ... 117 ... D3
Murgeni ... 109 ... E2
Murguia ... 68 ... C3
Muri ... 84 ... C3
Murighiol ... 115 ... F4
Murino ... 112 ... B1
Murnau ... 46 ... B1
Muro ... 57 ... C3
Muro Lucano ... 100 ... C3
Muros ... 66 ... B3
Mürren ... 84 ... B2
Murrhardt ... 45 ... D3
Murska Sobota ... 104 ... C3
Mursko Središče ... 104 ... C2
Murta ... 114 ... B3
Murten ... 84 ... A2
Murtosa ... 72 ... B3
Mürzsteg ... 87 ... E3
Mürzzuschlag ... 87 ... E2
Muşeteşti ... 114 ... B4
Muskiz ... 68 ... C4
Mussalo ... 7 ... D1
Musselburgh ... 20 ... C4
Musselkanaal ... 29 ... F3
Mussidan ... 58 ... C1
Mussomeli ... 102 ... C2
Mustafa Kemalpasa ... 119 ... F2
Müstair ... 85 ... E2
Mutalahti ... 7 ... F4
Mutrico ... 69 ... D4
Mutterstadt ... 40 ... C1
Muurame ... 5 ... E1
Muurasjärvi ... 5 ... E1
Muurikkala ... 7 ... E2

Muurla ... 6 ... C1
Muurola ... 7 ... E2
Muzillac ... 52 ... C2
Mužla ... 105 ... E4
Myllykoski ... 7 ... D2
Myllymäki ... 5 ... E1
Mynämäki ... 6 ... B1
Myrdal ... 8 ... B3
Myrskylä (Mörskom) ... 7 ... D2
Myrtos ... 122 ... C3
Mysen ... 9 ... D2
Myshall ... 17 ... D2
Mysliborz ... 35 ... F2
Mýto ... 43 ... E2

N

Nå ... 8 ... B3
Naantali ... 6 ... B1
Naarden ... 29 ... D3
Naarva ... 7 ... F4
Naas ... 17 ... E3
Nabburg ... 42 ... C1
Nacka ... 10 ... C1
Nad ... 16 ... B1
Nådab ... 106 ... C2
Nådäselu ... 107 ... E2
Nadela ... 66 ... C3
Nådlac ... 106 ... C2
Nadrin ... 31 ... E2
Nådudvar ... 106 ... C3
Naestved ... 12 ... C1
Näfels ... 84 ... C3
Nagold ... 44 ... C3
Nagu (Nauvo) ... 6 ... B1
Nagyatád ... 105 ... D2
Nagybajom ... 105 ... D2
Nagybaracska ... 105 ... E2
Nagycenk ... 104 ... C4
Nagycserkesz ... 107 ... D4
Nagydorog ... 105 ... D2
Nagyecsed ... 107 ... D4
Nagygyimót ... 105 ... D3
Nagyhalász ... 107 ... D4
Nagyigmánd ... 105 ... E4
Nagykálló ... 107 ... D4
Nagykanizsa ... 105 ... D2
Nagykáta ... 106 ... B3
Nagykónyi ... 105 ... E2
Nagykörös ... 106 ... B3
Nagylak ... 106 ... C2
Nagylóc ... 106 ... B4
Nagymágocs ... 106 ... C2
Nagymaros ... 105 ... E4
Nagyoroszi ... 105 ... E4
Nagyszénás ... 106 ... C2
Nagyvázsony ... 105 ... D3
Nahe ... 33 ... E3
Naidaş ... 113 ... D4
Naila ... 42 ... C3
Nailloux ... 63 ... E2
Nailsea ... 27 ... D3
Nailsworth ... 27 ... E3
Naipu ... 114 ... C3
Nairn ... 19 ... D3
Najac ... 63 ... E3
Nájera ... 68 ... C2
Nakkila ... 6 ... B2
Nakovo ... 106 ... C1
Nalbant ... 115 ... F4
Nålden ... 3 ... E2
Näljänkä ... 5 ... F4
Nalzen ... 63 ... E1
Namdalsheid ... 3 ... D3
Namsos ... 3 ... D3
Namsskogen ... 3 ... E3
Namur ... 31 ... D2
Nanclares de Oca ... 68 ... C3
Nancy ... 56 ... B4
Nănești ... 109 ... E1
Nangis ... 55 ... D3
Nannestad ... 9 ... D3
Nans-les-Pins ... 65 ... D2
Nant ... 64 ... A3
Nantes ... 53 ... D1
Nanteuil-le-Haudouin ... 50 ... B1
Nantiat ... 59 ... D3
Nantua ... 61 ... D3
Nantwich ... 23 ... D2
Náousa ... 117 ... E2
Náoussa ... 121 ... F2
Napoli ... 100 ... A4
Narberth ... 26 ... B3
Narbolia ... 96 ... B2
Narbonne ... 64 ... A2
Narborough ... 25 ... E4
Narbuvoll ... 3 ... D1
Narcao ... 96 ... B1
Narechenski Bani ... 118 ... C4
Narila ... 7 ... D3
Narni ... 98 ... B3
Naro ... 102 ... C2
Nérac ... 62 ... C3
Neratovice ... 43 ... F3
Neresheim ... 45 ... E3
Nereto ... 98 ... C2 (*see note*)
Néris-les-Bains ... 59 ... F3
Nerja ... 80 ... B1
Nérondes ... 55 ... D1
Nersingen ... 45 ... E2
Nerskogen ... 2 ... C1
Nervi ... 92 ... C3
Nes ... 29 ... E4
Nes ... 8 ... B4
Nes ... 9 ... D3
Nesbyen ... 8 ... C3

Näsviken ... 10 ... B4
Natalinci ... 112 ... C3
Nättraby ... 13 ... E2
Naturno-Naturns ... 90 ... B4
Nauders ... 85 ... E2
Nauen ... 39 ... D4
Naul ... 17 ... E4
Naumburg ... 38 ... C1
Naunhof ... 43 ... D4
Naustbukta ... 3 ... D3
Naustdal ... 8 ... B4
Nauste ... 2 ... C1
Nauvo (Nagu) ... 6 ... B1
Nava ... 67 ... F4
Nava de la Asunción ... 74 ... A4
Nava del Rey ... 73 ... F3
Navacerrada ... 74 ... B4
Navahermosa ... 74 ... A2
Navalcarnero ... 74 ... B3
Navalmanzano ... 74 ... B4
Navalmoral de la Mata ... 73 ... E1
Navalperal ... 74 ... A3
Navan ... 17 ... E4
Navarrenx ... 62 ... B2
Navarrete ... 68 ... C3
Navas de San Juan ... 80 ... C3
Navas del Rey ... 74 ... B3
Navatalgordo ... 74 ... A3
Navelli ... 98 ... C3
Navenby ... 23 ... E2
Naverstad ... 9 ... D1
Navia ... 67 ... D4
Navilly ... 56 ... A1
Návodari ... 115 ... F3
Návpaktos ... 120 ... C4
Návplion ... 121 ... D3
Náxos ... 121 ... F2
Nayland ... 25 ... E3
Nazare ... 78 ... A4
Néa Ankhíalos ... 117 ... F1
Néa Artáki ... 121 ... D4
Néa Epidhavros ... 121 ... D3
Néa Filippiás ... 117 ... D1
Néa Fókaia ... 118 ... A2
Néa Kallikráteia ... 117 ... F2
Néa Karváli ... 118 ... B3
Néa Kerdhíllia ... 118 ... B3
Néa Khalkidhón ... 117 ... E3
Néa Koróni ... 120 ... C2
Néa Mádhitos ... 118 ... A2
Néa Mákri ... 121 ... E3
Néa Mikhanióna ... 117 ... F2
Néa Moudhaniá ... 118 ... A2
Néa Péramos ... 118 ... B3
Néa Potídhaia ... 118 ... A2
Néa Ródha ... 118 ... B2
Néa Skióni ... 118 ... A2
Néa Stira ... 121 ... E3
Néa Tríglia ... 118 ... A2
Néa Zíkhna ... 118 ... A3
Neale ... 16 ... B4
Neapolis ... 122 ... C3
Neápolis ... 121 ... D1
Neápolis ... 117 ... D2
Neath ... 26 ... C4
Nebra ... 38 ... C1
Neckarelz ... 45 ... D4
Neckargemünd ... 40 ... C1
Neckargerach ... 41 ... D1
Neckarsteinach ... 41 ... D1
Neckarsulm ... 45 ... D1
Neda ... 66 ... C4
Nedelišče ... 104 ... C2
Nedervetil (Alaveteli) ... 5 ... D2
Nedstrand ... 8 ... A2
Neede ... 29 ... F2
Needham Market ... 25 ... E3
Neermoor ... 32 ... B2
Nefyn ... 22 ... B2
Negoiești ... 113 ... F4
Negorci ... 117 ... E3
Negotin ... 113 ... E3
Negotino ... 117 ... E4
Negovanovci ... 113 ... E3
Negreni ... 107 ... E3
Negresti ... 109 ... E3
Negrești Oaş ... 107 ... E4
Negru Vodă ... 115 ... F2
Neheim-Hüsten ... 36 ... C2
Nehoiaşu ... 109 ... D1
Nejdek ... 43 ... D3
Neksø ... 13 ... E1
Nelas ... 72 ... C2
Nelson ... 23 ... D1
Neméa ... 120 ... C3
Németker ... 105 ... E2
Nemours ... 54 ... C3
Nenagh ... 16 ... C3
Nendeln ... 85 ... D3
Nenthead ... 21 ... D2
Neokhóri ... 120 ... B3
Neokhórion ... 111 ... E1
Néon Monastírion ... 117 ... E1
Néon Petrítsi ... 118 ... A3
Néos Marmarás ... 118 ... B2
Nepi ... 98 ... B3
Nepomuk ... 43 ... E1
Neptun ... 115 ... F3
Nérac ... 62 ... C3
Neratovice ... 43 ... F3
Neresheim ... 45 ... E3
Nerežišča ... 110 ... C2
Néris-les-Bains ... 59 ... F3
Nerja ... 80 ... B1
Nérondes ... 55 ... D1
Nersingen ... 45 ... E2
Nerskogen ... 2 ... C1
Nervi ... 92 ... C3
Nes ... 29 ... E4
Nes ... 8 ... B4
Nes ... 9 ... D3
Nesbyen ... 8 ... C3

Nesebŭr ... 115 ... E1
Nesflaten ... 8 ... B2
Nesle ... 50 ... B2
Nesoddtangen ... 9 ... D2
Nesscliffe ... 22 ... C2
Nesselwang ... 46 ... B1
Neston ... 22 ... C3
Nestórion ... 117 ... D2
Nesttun ... 8 ... A3
Nethy Bridge ... 19 ... D2
Netolice ... 47 ... E4
Netretic ... 104 ... B1
Nettancourt ... 55 ... F4
Nettetal ... 36 ... A2
Nettuno ... 98 ... B1
Netuş ... 108 ... B2
Neu Darchau ... 34 ... B2
Neu Moresnet ... 31 ... E3
Neu Mukran ... 35 ... D4
Neu-Isenburg ... 40 ... C2
Neubeckum ... 36 ... C2
Neubrandenburg ... 35 ... D2
Neubukow ... 34 ... C3
Neuburg ... 46 ... B3
Neuchâtel (Neuenburg) ... 84 ... A3
Neudorf ... 44 ... C4
Neudorf-Platendorf ... 37 ... E3
Neuenbürg ... 44 ... C3
Neuenburg ... 32 ... C2
Neuenburg ... 44 ... B1
Neuenhaus ... 36 ... B3
Neuenkirchen ... 33 ... D1
Neuenwalde ... 32 ... C2
Neuf-Brisach ... 57 ... D3
Neufahrn ... 46 ... C3
Neufchâteau ... 56 ... B3
Neufchâteau ... 31 ... E2
Neufchâtel ... 50 ... C2
Neufchâtel-en-Bray ... 49 ... F2
Neufelden ... 86 ... C4
Neuhaus ... 33 ... D3
Neuhaus ... 47 ... E3
Neuhaus ... 37 ... D2
Neuhaus ... 42 ... C1
Neuhaus ... 34 ... B2
Neuhaus ... 42 ... B3
Neuhausen ... 84 ... C4
Neuhof ... 39 ... D3
Neuhofen an der Krems ... 86 ... C3
Neuillé Pont-Pierre ... 54 ... A2
Neuilly-l'Evêque ... 56 ... A2
Neuilly-St-Front ... 50 ... C1
Neukalen ... 35 ... D3
Neukirch ... 39 ... E1
Neukirchen ... 86 ... A4
Neukloster ... 34 ... C3
Neulengbach ... 87 ... E3
Neum ... 111 ... D1
Neumarkt ... 47 ... E2
Neumarkt ... 46 ... C4
Neumarkt ... 86 ... B3
Neumarkt-St. Veit ... 47 ... D2
Neumünster ... 33 ... E3
Neunagelberg ... 87 ... D4
Neunburg ... 43 ... D1
Neung ... 54 ... B2
Neunkirchen ... 44 ... B4
Neunkirchen ... 87 ... E3
Neuötting ... 47 ... D2
Neupölla ... 87 ... D4
Neuruppin ... 35 ... D1
Neusiedl am See ... 87 ... F3
Neuss ... 36 ... A1
Neustadt ... 41 ... D3
Neustadt ... 44 ... C2
Neustadt ... 42 ... B3
Neustadt ... 34 ... B3
Neustadt ... 46 ... C3
Neustadt ... 42 ... C3
Neustadt ... 39 ... E1
Neustadt am Rübenberge ... 37 ... D3
Neustadt an der Dosse ... 34 ... C1
Neustadt an der Waldnaab ... 42 ... C2
Neustadt-an-der-Aisch ... 42 ... B1
Neustadt-an-der-Weinstrasse ... 44 ... C4
Neustadt-Glewe ... 34 ... C2
Neustift ... 85 ... D2
Neustrelitz ... 35 ... D2
Neuves-Maisons ... 56 ... B4
Neuvic ... 59 ... E2
Neuvic ... 58 ... C2
Neuville ... 60 ... C3
Neuville ... 58 ... C4
Neuville-aux-Bois ... 54 ... C3
Neuvy ... 59 ... E4
Neuvy-sur-Barangeon ... 54 ... C2
Neuwied ... 40 ... B3
Nevern ... 26 ... B4
Nevers ... 55 ... D1
Nevesinje ... 111 ... D2
Nevlunghavn ... 8 ... C1
New Abbey ... 20 ... C3
New Aberdour ... 19 ... E3
New Cumnock ... 20 ... B3
New Galloway ... 20 ... B3
New Holland ... 23 ... E2
New Luce ... 20 ... B2
New Pitsligo ... 19 ... E3
New Quay ... 22 ... B1
New Radnor ... 22 ... C1
New Romney ... 17 ... E2
New Ross ... 17 ... D2
New Scone ... 19 ... F1
Newark ... 19 ... D1
Newark-on-Trent ... 55 ... D1 (*see note*)
Newbiggin-by-the-Sea ... 21 ... E3
Newbliss ... 15 ... D1
Newbold-upon-Stour ... 27 ... E4
Newborough ... 22 ... B2
Newbridge ... 20 ... C3
Newbridge (Droichead Nua) ... 17 ... D2
Newbridge-on-Wye ... 22 ... C1

Newburgh ... 19 ... D1
Newburgh ... 19 ... E2
Newburn ... 21 ... E3
Newbury ... 27 ... F3
Newby Bridge ... 20 ... C1
Newbyth ... 19 ... E3
Newcasdtle upon Tyne ... 21 ... E3
Newcastle ... 15 ... E1
Newcastle Emlyn ... 26 ... C4
Newcastle West ... 16 ... B2
Newcastle-under-Lyme ... 23 ... D2
Newcastleton ... 21 ... D3
Newent ... 27 ... E4
Newgale ... 26 ... B4
Newhaven ... 25 ... E1
Newinn ... 16 ... C2
Newlyn ... 26 ... B1
Newmains ... 20 ... C4
Newmarket ... 25 ... E3
Newmarket ... 16 ... B2
Newmarket-on-Fergus ... 16 ... B2
Newnham ... 27 ... E3
Newnham ... 23 ... D1
Newport ... 26 ... B4
Newport ... 23 ... D2
Newport ... 27 ... D3
Newport ... 27 ... F2
Newport ... 25 ... E3
Newport ... 23 ... E3
Newport ... 16 ... C2
Newport ... 14 ... B1
Newport Pagnell ... 25 ... D3
Newport-on-Tay ... 19 ... E1
Newquay ... 26 ... B1
Newry ... 15 ... E1
Newton Abbot ... 27 ... D1
Newton Ferrers ... 26 ... C1
Newton Forbes ... 16 ... C4
Newton St. Cyres ... 27 ... D2
Newton Stewart ... 20 ... B2
Newton-on-Trent ... 23 ... E3
Newtownabbey ... 15 ... E2
Newtownferry ... 18 ... A3
Newtonhamilton ... 15 ... D1
Newtonmore ... 19 ... D2
Newtonstewart ... 15 ... D2
Newtown ... 22 ... C1
Newtown ... 27 ... E4
Newtown ... 17 ... D3
Newtown Butler ... 15 ... D1
Newtown Mount Kennedy ... 17 ... E3
Newtownards ... 15 ... E2
Nexon ... 59 ... D2
Neyland ... 26 ... B3
Nibe ... 12 ... B3
Nicastro ... 101 ... D1
Nice ... 65 ... F3
Nickelsdorf ... 87 ... F3
Nicolae Bălcescu ... 109 ... D2
Nicolae Bălcescu ... 109 ... D3
Nicolae Bălcescu ... 115 ... F4
Nicolosi ... 103 ... D1
Nicosia ... 103 ... D3
Nicosia (Lefkoşa) ... 122 ... B2
Nidderau ... 41 ... D2
Nidri ... 120 ... B4
Niebla ... 83 ... D1
Nieby ... 33 ... E4
Niechorze ... 35 ... F3
Nieder Stotzingen ... 45 ... E3
Nieder Winkling ... 47 ... D3
Nieder-Wöllstadt ... 40 ... C2
Niederalteich ... 47 ... D3
Niederau ... 86 ... A2
Niederaula ... 41 ... D3
Niederkrüchten ... 36 ... A1
Niemegk ... 39 ... D3
Niemisel ... 4 ... C4
Niemisjärvi ... 5 ... F1
Nienburg ... 37 ... D4
Nienhagen ... 34 ... C3
Nieppe ... 50 ... B4
Nierderbronn ... 57 ... D4
Nierstein ... 40 ... C2
Niesky ... 39 ... F2
Nieul ... 58 ... C3
Nieuweschans ... 29 ... F4
Nieuwpoort ... 30 ... B4
Nigg ... 19 ... D3
Nigrita ... 118 ... A3
Niinimäki ... 7 ... E3
Niinisalo ... 6 ... B3
Niinivesi ... 5 ... F1
Nijar ... 81 ... D1
Nijkerk ... 29 ... E2
Nijmegen ... 29 ... E2
Nijverdal ... 29 ... E2
Nikaia ... 117 ... E1
Niki ... 117 ... D3
Nikiforos ... 118 ... B3
Nikitari ... 122 ... A1
Nikitas ... 118 ... B2
Nikkaroinen ... 7 ... D2
Nikola Kozlevo ... 115 ... E2
Nikopol ... 114 ... C2
Nikšić ... 111 ... D2
Nilsiä ... 7 ... D4
Nîmes ... 64 ... C3
Nin ... 110 ... B3
Ninfield ... 25 ... E1
Ninove ... 30 ... C3
Niort ... 58 ... B4
Nirou Khani ... 122 ... B4
Niš ... 113 ... D2
Nisa ... 78 ... C4
Niška Banja ... 113 ... D2
Nisákion ... 116 ... C1
Nissilä ... 5 ... F3
Niton ... 27 ... F2
Nitra ... 105 ... E4
Nitry ... 55 ... E2
Nittedal ... 9 ... D2

Nittenau ... 47 ... D3
Nittendorf ... 46 ... C3
Nivå ... 12 ... C2
Nivelles ... 31 ... D3
Nizza Monferrato ... 92 ... C4
Njegoševo ... 106 ... B1
Njurunda ... 10 ... C4
Noailles ... 50 ... B2
Noain ... 69 ... E3
Nobber ... 17 ... D4
Nocera ... 100 ... B3
Nocera Umbra ... 95 ... D1
Noceto ... 93 ... E4
Noci ... 101 ... E4
Nocrich ... 108 ... B1
Noépoli ... 101 ... D3
Nœux ... 50 ... B3
Nogara ... 90 ... B1
Nogaro ... 62 ... C3
Nogent ... 56 ... B3
Nogent-le-Roi ... 54 ... B4
Nogent-le-Rotrou ... 54 ... B3
Nogent-sur-Seine ... 55 ... D3
Nógrádszakál ... 106 ... B4
Nohfelden ... 40 ... B1
Noia ... 66 ... B3
Noirétable ... 60 ... B3
Noirmoutier ... 52 ... C1
Nokia ... 6 ... C2
Nola ... 100 ... B4
Nolay ... 55 ... F1
Noli ... 92 ... C3
Nomeny ... 56 ... B4
Nomexy ... 56 ... B3
Nonancourt ... 54 ... B4
Nonant-le-Pin ... 53 ... F4
Nonnenhorn ... 45 ... D1
Nontron ... 59 ... D2
Nonza ... 57 ... F3
Noordwijk aan Zee ... 29 ... D2
Noormarkku ... 6 ... B2
Nora ... 10 ... A2
Norager ... 12 ... B3
Norberg ... 9 ... D2
Norbonne-Plage ... 64 ... A2
Norcia ... 98 ... B4
Nordausques ... 50 ... A4
Nordberg ... 8 ... C4
Nordborg ... 12 ... B1
Nordby ... 12 ... B2
Norddeich ... 32 ... B2
Nordre Osen ... 9 ... E4
Nordeide ... 8 ... B4
Norden ... 32 ... B2
Nordenham ... 32 ... C2
Norderney ... 32 ... B3
Norderstedt ... 33 ... E2
Nordfjordeid ... 2 ... A1
Nordhalben ... 42 ... C3
Nordhausen ... 38 ... B2
Nordhorn ... 36 ... B3
Nordli ... 3 ... E3
Nördlingen ... 45 ... E3
Nordmaling ... 4 ... B2
Nordmark ... 9 ... F2
Nordskov ... 12 ... B2
Noresund ... 8 ... C3
Norg ... 29 ... E3
Norheimsund ... 8 ... B3
Norman Cross ... 23 ... F2
Norra Hede ... 3 ... E1
Norrahammar ... 13 ... D4
Norra Tresund ... 3 ... D3
Norrboda ... 10 ... C3
Nørre Åby ... 12 ... B1
Nørre Aslev ... 12 ... B1
Nørre Broby ... 12 ... B1
Nørre Lyndelse ... 12 ... B1
Nørre Nebel ... 12 ... A2
Nørre Snede ... 12 ... B2
Nørre Vorupør ... 12 ... A3
Nørresundby ... 12 ... B3
Norrhult ... 13 ... E3
Norrköping ... 10 ... B1
Nornäs ... 4 ... C1
Norrsundet ... 10 ... C3
Norrtälje ... 10 ... C2
Norsholm ... 10 ... B1
Norsjö ... 4 ... B3
Norsjøvallen ... 4 ... B3
Nort ... 53 ... D2
Nörten-Hardenberg ... 37 ... E2
North Ballachulish ... 18 ... C1
North Berwick ... 21 ... D4
North Cave ... 23 ... E4
North Collingham ... 23 ... E3
North Elmham ... 25 ... F4
North Erradale ... 18 ... B3
North Ferriby ... 23 ... E4
North Grimston ... 23 ... F1
North Kessock ... 19 ... D3
North Kilworth ... 23 ... E1
North Shields ... 21 ... E3
North Tawton ... 26 ... C2
North Tolsta ... 18 ... B3
North Walsham ... 25 ... F4
Northallerton ... 21 ... E2
Northam ... 23 ... E1
Northampton ... 23 ... E1
Northeim ... 37 ... E2
Northfleet ... 25 ... E2
Northleach ... 27 ... E4
Northpunds ... 19 ... F3
Northop ... 22 ... C3
Northwich ... 23 ... D3
Northwold ... 25 ... E4
Norton ... 21 ... E1
Norton Fitzwarren ... 27 ... D3
Norton St. Phillip ... 27 ... E3
Nortorf ... 33 ... D3

Norwich ... 25 ... F4
Nossen ... 39 ... D1
Note-of-the-Gate ... 21 ... D3
Noto ... 103 ... D1
Nötö ... 6 ... B1
Notodden ... 8 ... C2
Nottingham ... 23 ... E2
Nottuln ... 36 ... B3
Nouan-le-Fuzelier ... 54 ... C2
Nouans-les-Fontaines ... 54 ... B1
Nouvion ... 50 ... A3
Nova ... 104 ... C3
Nova Bystrice ... 47 ... F4
Nova Crnja ... 106 ... C1
Nova Gorica ... 104 ... A2
Nova Gradiska ... 105 ... D1
Nova Kassaba ... 111 ... E3
Nova Levante-Welschnofen ... 90 ... C3
Nova Pazova ... 112 ... B4
Nova Topola ... 111 ... D4
Nova Varoš ... 112 ... B2
Nova Zagora ... 115 ... D1
Novachene ... 113 ... F2
Novaci ... 113 ... E4
Novaféltria ... 95 ... D2
Novara ... 88 ... C2
Novara di Sicilia ... 103 ... D3
Nové Hrady ... 47 ... F3
Nové Strašecí ... 43 ... E2
Nové Zámky ... 105 ... E4
Novella ... 81 ... F4
Novellara ... 94 ... B4
Novento Vicentina ... 90 ... C1
Noves ... 64 ... C3
Novi Bečej ... 106 ... B1
Novi Dojran ... 117 ... F3
Novi di Módena ... 94 ... B4
Novi Han ... 113 ... E1
Novi Kneževac ... 106 ... B2
Novi Krichim ... 118 ... B4
Novi Ligure ... 92 ... C4
Novi Marof ... 104 ... C2
Novi Pazar ... 112 ... C2
Novi Pazar ... 115 ... E2
Novi Sad ... 106 ... B1
Novi Vinodolski ... 104 ... B1
Novigrad ... 110 ... B3
Novigrad ... 91 ... E1
Novigrad Podravski ... 105 ... D2
Novion-Porcien ... 51 ... D2
Novo Mesto ... 104 ... B2
Novo Miloševo ... 106 ... B1
Novo Selo ... 117 ... F4
Novo Selo ... 113 ... E3
Novo Selo ... 115 ... D2
Novoselė ... 116 ... B3
Novoselets ... 115 ... D1
Novoselitsa ... 109 ... D4
Novska ... 104 ... C1
Nový Bor ... 43 ... F3
Nový Knín ... 43 ... E2
Nowe Warpno ... 35 ... E3
Nowogard ... 35 ... F3
Nowogród Bobrzański ... 39 ... F3
Nowogrodziec ... 39 ... F2
Noyant ... 53 ... F2
Noyers ... 55 ... E2
Noyers-sur-Jabron ... 65 ... D3
Noyon ... 50 ... B2
Nozay ... 53 ... D2
Nozeroy ... 61 ... D4
Nucet ... 107 ... C2
Nuévalos ... 75 ... D4
Nuijamaa ... 7 ... E2
Nuits-St-Georges ... 55 ... F1
Nules ... 76 ... A3
Nulvi ... 96 ... B3
Numana ... 95 ... E2
Nummela ... 6 ... C1
Nummi ... 6 ... C1
Nummijärvi ... 5 ... D1
Nummikoski ... 5 ... D1
Nuneaton ... 23 ... E2
Nunnanlahti ... 7 ... E4
Nunney ... 27 ... D2
Nunsdorf ... 39 ... D3
Nunspeet ... 29 ... E3
Nuojua ... 5 ... E3
Nuoro ... 96 ... B3
Nurallao ... 96 ... B2
Nürburg ... 40 ... B3
Nurmaa ... 7 ... D2
Nurmijärvi ... 6 ... C1
Nurmo ... 5 ... D1
Nürnberg ... 42 ... B1
Nürtingen ... 45 ... D3
Nuşeni ... 108 ... B3
Nuşfalău ... 117 ... E3
Nuštar ... 105 ... E1
Nutheim ... 8 ... C2
Nuttlar ... 36 ... C2
Nyåker ... 4 ... B2
Nybergsund ... 9 ... E4
Nyborg ... 12 ... B1
Nybro ... 13 ... E3
Nyékládháza ... 106 ... C4
Nyhammar ... 10 ... A2
Nyírábrány ... 107 ... D3
Nyíracsád ... 107 ... D3
Nyíradony ... 107 ... D4
Nyírbátor ... 107 ... D4
Nyírbéltek ... 107 ... D4
Nyírbogát ... 107 ... D4
Nyíregyháza ... 107 ... D4
Nyírtelek ... 107 ... D4
Nyírtura ... 107 ... D4
Nykarleby (Uusikaarlepyy) ... 5 ... D2
Nykøbing ... 12 ... A3
Nykøbing ... 12 ... C2
Nyköping ... 12 ... C1
Nyköping ... 10 ... C1
Nykrogen ... 10 ... B2

Nykroppa ... 9 ... F2
Nyland ... 4 ... A1
Nymburk ... 43 ... F3
Nymindegab ... 12 ... A2
Nynäshamn ... 10 ... C1
Nyon ... 61 ... E3
Nyons ... 64 ... C4
Nýrsko ... 43 ... D1
Nysäter ... 9 ... E1
Nyskolla ... 9 ... D1
Nysted ... 12 ... C1
Nystova ... 8 ... C4
Nythem ... 3 ... F1

O Cadabo (Baleira) ... 67 ... D3
O Grove ... 66 ... B2
Oakley ... 27 ... F4
Oancea ... 109 ... E1
Oanes ... 8 ... A2
Oban ... 18 ... C1
Ober-Roden ... 41 ... D2
Oberammergau ... 46 ... B1
Oberau ... 46 ... B1
Oberaudorf ... 46 ... C1
Oberdrauburg ... 86 ... B1
Obergrafendorf ... 87 ... E3
Obergünzburg ... 45 ... E2
Obergurgl ... 85 ... F2
Oberhausen ... 36 ... B2
Oberhof ... 42 ... B3
Oberhofen ... 84 ... B2
Oberjoch ... 45 ... E1
Oberkirch ... 44 ... C3
Oberkochen ... 45 ... E3
Obernai ... 57 ... D3
Obernberg ... 86 ... B3
Oberndorf ... 41 ... D2
Oberndorf ... 44 ... C2
Oberndorf ... 86 ... B3
Obernzell ... 47 ... E3
Oberpullendorf ... 87 ... F2
Oberriet ... 85 ... D3
Obersickte ... 38 ... B3
Obersontheim ... 45 ... E3
Oberstaufen ... 45 ... E1
Oberstdorf ... 45 ... E1
Obertauern ... 86 ... C2
Obertraubling ... 46 ... C3
Obertraun ... 86 ... C2
Obertraun ... 104 ... A4
Obervellach ... 86 ... B1
Oberviechtach ... 43 ... D1
Oberwald ... 84 ... C2
Oberwart ... 87 ... F2
Oberwesel ... 40 ... B2
Oberwiesenthal ... 43 ... D3
Oberwölz ... 86 ... C2
Oberzeiring ... 86 ... C2
Óbidos ... 78 ... A3
Obing ... 47 ... D2
Öblarn ... 86 ... C2
Oborniki ... 36 ... C2
Oborishte ... 114 ... B1
Obrenovac ... 112 ... B4
Obrochishte ... 115 ... E2
Obrovac ... 110 ... C2
Obrovac ... 110 ... B3
Obsteig ... 85 ... E3
Obzor ... 115 ... E1
Ocaña ... 74 ... B2
Occhiobello ... 94 ... C4
Ochagavia ... 69 ... E3
Ochiltree ... 20 ... B3
Ochsenfurt ... 41 ... E1
Ochsenhausen ... 45 ... E2
Ochtrup ... 36 ... B3
Ockelbo ... 10 ... B3
Ockley ... 25 ... D1
Ocland ... 108 ... C2
Ocna Mureş ... 108 ... B2
Ocna Sibiului ... 108 ... B1
Ocna Sugatag ... 108 ... B4
Ocrkavlje ... 111 ... E2
Ócsa ... 106 ... B3
Öcsöd ... 106 ... C3
Odda ... 8 ... B3
Odeceixe ... 82 ... A3
Odeleite ... 82 ... C3
Odelzhausen ... 46 ... B2
Odemira ... 82 ... B4
Odense ... 12 ... B1
Oderberg ... 39 ... E1
Oderzo ... 91 ... D2
Ödeshög ... 13 ... E4
Odiham ... 25 ... D1
Odobeşti ... 109 ... D1
Odorheiu Secuiesc ... 108 ... C2
Ødsted ... 12 ... B2
Ødum ... 12 ... B2
Odžaci ... 106 ... B1
Odžak ... 112 ... B2
Oebisdfelde ... 38 ... B3
Oederan ... 43 ... D4
Oeding ... 36 ... B3
Oelde ... 36 ... C2
Oelsnitz ... 42 ... C3
Oettingen ... 46 ... B3
Oetz ... 85 ... E3
Ofehérto ... 107 ... D4
Offenbach ... 40 ... C2
Offenburg ... 44 ... C3
Ofir ... 72 ... B4
Ofte ... 8 ... C2
Ogbourne-St-George ... 27 ... E3

Ogenbargen ... 32 ... B2
Ogliastro Cilento ... 100 ... B3
Ogmore-by-Sea ... 27 ... D3
Ogradena ... 113 ... D4
Ogulin ... 104 ... B1
Ohrdruf ... 42 ... B3
Ohrid ... 117 ... D3
Öhringen ... 45 ... D4
Ohtaja ... 5 ... D2
Oía ... 121 ... F1
Oijarvi ... 5 ... E4
Oilgate ... 17 ... E2
Oinói ... 121 ... D3
Oirschot ... 29 ... D1
Oisement ... 50 ... A3
Oissel ... 49 ... F2
Oisterwijk ... 29 ... D1
Oitilon ... 120 ... C2
Oitti ... 6 ... C2
Ojakylä ... 5 ... E3
Ojdula ... 109 ... D1
Ojén ... 83 ... F2
Okehampton ... 26 ... C2
Økendalsøra ... 2 ... C1
Oker ... 37 ... D2
Okhthoniá ... 121 ... E3
Oksakoski ... 5 ... E2
Oksböl ... 12 ... A2
Oksdøl ... 3 ... D3
Okučani ... 105 ... D1
Olargues ... 64 ... A2
Olazagutiá ... 69 ... D3
Olbernhau ... 43 ... D3
Ólbia ... 96 ... C3
Old Leake ... 23 ... F2
Old Warden ... 25 ... D3
Oldcastle ... 17 ... D4
Oldeide ... 2 ... A1
Olden ... 8 ... B4
Oldenburg ... 32 ... C2
Oldenburg ... 34 ... B3
Oldenzaal ... 29 ... F2
Oldham ... 23 ... D3
Oldmeldrum ... 19 ... E2
Oléggio ... 88 ... C2
Oleiros ... 66 ... B3
Oleiros ... 72 ... C1
Ølenjøen ... 8 ... A2
Oletta ... 57 ... F3
Olette ... 63 ... E1
Ølgod ... 12 ... A2
Olgopol ... 109 ... F4
Olhao ... 82 ... B3
Olhava ... 5 ... E4
Olíena ... 96 ... B3
Olite ... 69 ... E3
Olivares de Júcar ... 75 ... D2
Olivares de Azeméis ... 72 ... B3
Oliveira de Frades ... 72 ... B3
Oliveira do Bairro ... 72 ... B2
Oliveira do Hospital ... 72 ... C2
Olivenza ... 79 ... D2
Olivet ... 54 ... C2
Olivone ... 84 ... C2
Ollaberry ... 19 ... F4
Ollerton ... 23 ... E3
Ollerup ... 12 ... B1
Olliergues ... 60 ... B2
Ollölä ... 7 ... F4
Olmedillo de Roa ... 68 ... B1
Olmedo ... 68 ... A1
Olmedo ... 96 ... A3
Olmeto ... 57 ... E2
Olmillos de Sasamón ... 68 ... B2
Olney ... 23 ... E1
Olofstrøm ... 13 ... E2
Olonzac ... 63 ... F2
Oloron-Ste-Marie ... 62 ... B2
Olot ... 71 ... D3
Olovo ... 111 ... E3
Olpe ... 40 ... C4
Olpret ... 107 ... E3
Øls ... 12 ... B3
Olsberg ... 36 ... C2
Olshammar ... 10 ... A1
Olst ... 29 ... E3
Olszyna ... 39 ... F1
Oltedal ... 8 ... A1
Olten ... 84 ... B3
Olteni ... 114 ... C3
Olteniţa ... 115 ... D3
Olvega ... 69 ... D1
Olvera ... 83 ... F2
Olympia ... 120 ... B3
Olympiás ... 118 ... B2
Omagh ... 15 ... D2
Omalós ... 122 ... A3
Ombersley ... 23 ... D1
Omeath ... 15 ... E1
Omegna ... 88 ... C2
Ömerköy ... 119 ... F2
Omiš ... 110 ... C2
Omišalj ... 104 ... A1
Omma ... 13 ... D2
Ommen ... 29 ... F3
Omodhos ... 122 ... A1
Omossa (Metsälä) ... 6 ... B3
Omurtag ... 115 ... D1
Oña ... 68 ... C2
Onchan ... 20 ... B1
Onda ... 76 ... A3
Ondara ... 76 ... A2
Onguyon ... 51 ... E2
Onich ... 18 ... C1
Onkamo ... 7 ... F4
Onnaing ... 50 ... C3
Onsaker ... 9 ... D3
Onsala ... 12 ... C3
Ontinyent ... 81 ... F4
Ontur ... 81 ... E4
Oola ... 16 ... C2

Oostburg ... 28 ... C1
Oostehout ... 29 ... D1
Oostende ... 30 ... B4
Oosterbeek ... 29 ... E2
Oosterend ... 29 ... E4
Oosterwolde ... 29 ... E4
Oostmalle ... 30 ... D4
Ootmarsum ... 29 ... F3
Opatija ... 104 ... A1
Opicina ... 91 ... E2
Opladen ... 40 ... B4
Opovo ... 112 ... C4
Oppach ... 39 ... F1
Oppenau ... 44 ... C2
Oppeneheim ... 40 ... C2
Opphaug ... 2 ... C2
Oppheim ... 8 ... B3
Oppido Lucano ... 100 ... C3
Oppido Mamertina ... 103 ... E4
Opuzen ... 111 ... D1
Ör ... 107 ... D4
Ora ... 122 ... B1
Ora-Auer ... 90 ... C3
Oradea ... 107 ... D3
Orahovac ... 112 ... C1
Oraison ... 65 ... D3
Orange ... 64 ... C3
Orani ... 96 ... B3
Oranienbaum ... 38 ... C2
Oranienburg ... 35 ... D1
Oranmore ... 16 ... B3
Orašje ... 111 ... E4
Orăşti ... 115 ... D3
Orăştie ... 107 ... E1
Oraşul Nou ... 107 ... E4
Oravainen (Oravais) ... 5 ... D2
Oravi ... 7 ... E3
Oravikoski ... 7 ... D4
Oravisalo ... 7 ... F4
Oraviţa ... 113 ... D4
Ørbæk ... 12 ... B1
Orbassano ... 88 ... B1
Orbe ... 84 ... A2
Orbec ... 49 ... E1
Orbetello ... 97 ... E3
Orbey ... 56 ... C3
Orcera ... 80 ... C3
Orchies ... 50 ... C3
Orcières ... 61 ... E1
Ord ... 18 ... B2
Ordes ... 66 ... B3
Ordino ... 70 ... C4
Orduña ... 68 ... C3
Ore ... 25 ... E1
Orebic ... 110 ... C1
Örebro ... 10 ... B1
Oregçsertö ... 105 ... E2
Øregrund ... 10 ... C2
Øren ... 119 ... E1
Orense (Ourense) ... 66 ... C2
Oreoi ... 121 ... D4
Orestias ... 119 ... D4
Orford ... 25 ... F3
Orgaz ... 74 ... B2
Orgelet ... 61 ... D4
Orgeval ... 54 ... C4
Orgeyev ... 109 ... F3
Orgil ... 19 ... F1
Orgiva ... 84 ... A2
Orgon ... 64 ... C3
Orgosolo ... 96 ... B3
Orgovány ... 106 ... B2
Orhanlar ... 119 ... E2
Oria ... 101 ... E3
Orihuela del Tremedal ... 75 ... E3
Orihuela ... 81 ... F3
Orimattila ... 7 ... D2
Oriolo ... 101 ... D2
Oripää ... 6 ... B2
Oristano ... 96 ... B2
Örisztpéter ... 104 ... C3
Orivesi ... 6 ... C2
Orizare ... 115 ... E1
Ørjarvik ... 2 ... B2
Ørje ... 9 ... D2
Örjiva ... 80 ... B1
Orkanger ... 2 ... C2
Örkelljunga ... 13 ... D2
Örkény ... 106 ... B2
Orkhomenós ... 121 ... D4
Orléans ... 54 ... C2
Orly ... 54 ... C4
Orlyak ... 115 ... E2
Ormanli ... 119 ... F4
Ormea ... 92 ... B3
Ormemyr ... 8 ... C2
Ormos ... 121 ... F3
Ormos Iou ... 121 ... D4
Ormós Panayias ... 118 ... B2
Órmos Prínou ... 118 ... C3
Ormož ... 104 ... C2
Ormsjø ... 4 ... A3
Ormskirk ... 22 ... C3
Ornans ... 56 ... B1
Ornes ... 3 ... E3
Örnsköldsvik ... 4 ... B2
Orol ... 66 ... C4
Oron-la-Ville ... 84 ... A2
Oropesa ... 73 ... F1
Oropesa del Mar ... 76 ... A4
Orosei ... 96 ... C3
Orosháza ... 106 ... C2
Oroszló ... 105 ... E2
Orovais (Oravainen) ... 5 ... D2
Orpington ... 25 ... E2
Orrefors ... 13 ... E3
Orsa ... 10 ... A3
Orsières ... 84 ... A1
Örsjö ... 13 ... E3
Orsogna ... 99 ... D3
Orşova ... 113 ... D4

Orsoya ... 113 ... E3
Ørsta ... 2 ... B1
Ørsted ... 12 ... B3
Ørsundbro ... 10 ... C2
Ort ... 86 ... B3
Orta Nova ... 99 ... E1
Orta San Giulio ... 88 ... C2
Ortaca ... 119 ... D2
Orte ... 98 ... B3
Ortenburg ... 86 ... B4
Orth ... 87 ... F3
Orthez ... 62 ... B2
Orthovoúni ... 117 ... D1
Ortigueira ... 66 ... C4
Ortisei-St Ulrich ... 90 ... C3
Ortişoara ... 106 ... C1
Ortkrug ... 34 ... B2
Orton ... 21 ... D2
Ortona ... 99 ... D3
Ortrand ... 39 ... E2
Örträsk ... 4 ... B2
Ortueri ... 96 ... B2
Ørum ... 12 ... B3
Örvella ... 8 ... C2
Orvieto ... 98 ... A3
Orvinio ... 98 ... B3
Orzinuovi ... 89 ... D2
Os ... 3 ... D1
Osby ... 13 ... D2
Oschatz ... 39 ... D2
Oschersleben ... 38 ... B3
Öschiri ... 96 ... B3
Ose ... 8 ... B1
Osečina ... 112 ... B3
Oseja de Sajambre ... 67 ... F3
Osen ... 3 ... D3
Osenets ... 115 ... D2
Osera ... 69 ... F1
Osijek ... 105 ... E1
Osikovitsa ... 114 ... B1
Ósilo ... 96 ... B3
Osimo ... 95 ... E2
Ósios Loukás ... 120 ... C4
Osipaonica ... 112 ... C4
Osječenica ... 111 ... E1
Oskarshamn ... 13 ... F3
Oskarström ... 13 ... D3
Oslany ... 9 ... D2
Oslo ... 9 ... D2
Osmington ... 27 ... C2
Osnabrück ... 36 ... C3
Osoi ... 109 ... E3
Osor ... 110 ... A4
Osorheiu ... 107 ... D3
Osorno ... 68 ... A2
Osova ... 8 ... A3
Ospedaletti ... 92 ... B2
Oss ... 29 ... E2
Ossa de Montiel ... 74 ... C1
Ossiach ... 86 ... C1
Óssa ... 118 ... B3
Ostanvik ... 10 ... B3
Östavall ... 3 ... F1
Ostbevern ... 36 ... C3
Østbirk ... 12 ... B2
Østby ... 9 ... E4
Østed ... 12 ... C1
Øster Hurup ... 57 ... F3
Øster Vrå ... 12 ... B3
Østerbo ... 8 ... C4
Østerburg ... 34 ... C1
Østerburken ... 41 ... D1
Østerby Havn ... 12 ... C3
Østerbybruk ... 10 ... C2
Østerbymo ... 13 ... E4
Österfärnebo ... 10 ... B2
Österhofen ... 47 ... D3
Osterholz-Scharmbeck ... 32 ... D2
Østerild ... 12 ... A3
Österkorsberga ... 13 ... E3
Osterode ... 37 ... E2
Östersund ... 3 ... F1
Östersundom ... 6 ... C1
Østervåla ... 10 ... C2
Östhammar ... 10 ... C2
Ostiglia ... 90 ... C1
Ostiz ... 69 ... E3
Ostra ... 95 ... E2
Ostrach ... 45 ... D2
Östrelj ... 110 ... C3
Østreljp ... 39 ... F1
Ostrov ... 43 ... D3
Ostrov ... 115 ... E3
Ostrožac ... 111 ... D2
Ostrožac ... 110 ... B4
Ostuni ... 101 ... E3
Osuna ... 83 ... F2
Oswaldkirk ... 21 ... E1
Oswestry ... 22 ... C2
Osztopán ... 105 ... D2
Otalampi ... 6 ... C1
Otanmäki ... 5 ... F3
Otava ... 7 ... D3
Oţelu Roşu ... 107 ... D1
Oterma ... 5 ... F3
Otero de Bodas ... 67 ... E1
Oteşani ... 114 ... B3
Oteševo ... 117 ... D3
Otetelişu ... 114 ... B3
Othery ... 27 ... D2
Otley ... 23 ... D2
Otnes ... 9 ... D4
Otocec ... 110 ... B4
Otok ... 110 ... C2
Otopeni ... 115 ... D3
Otranto ... 101 ... F3
Otta ... 9 ... D4
Ottana ... 96 ... B3
Ottaviano ... 100 ... B4
Ottenschlag ... 87 ... D4

Ottensheim ... 86 ... C3
Otter Ferry ... 15 ... F4
Otterburn ... 21 ... D3
Otterlo ... 29 ... E2
Otterndorf ... 33 ... D3
Ottersberg ... 33 ... D2
Ottersøy ... 3 ... D3
Otterup ... 12 ... B1
Ottevény ... 105 ... D4
Ottobeuren ... 45 ... E2
Ottone ... 93 ... D3
Ottsjö ... 3 ... E2
Ottweiler ... 40 ... B1
Oucques ... 54 ... B2
Oud Beijerland ... 29 ... D2
Ouddorp ... 28 ... C2
Oude-Pekela ... 29 ... F4
Oudenaarde ... 30 ... C3
Oughterard ... 16 ... B4
Ouistreham ... 49 ... D2
Oulainen ... 5 ... E3
Oulujoki ... 5 ... E4
Oulton Broad ... 25 ... F3
Oulu ... 5 ... E4
Oulunsalo ... 5 ... E4
Oulx ... 88 ... A1
Oundle ... 23 ... E2
Ouranópolis ... 118 ... B2
Ourique ... 82 ... B4
Oust ... 63 ... D1
Outokumpu ... 7 ... E4
Outwell ... 25 ... E4
Ouzouer-le-Marche ... 54 ... B2
Ovada ... 92 ... C4
Ovar ... 72 ... B3
Ovčar Banja ... 112 ... B3
Ovelgönne ... 33 ... D2
Ovens ... 16 ... C1
Ovenstädt ... 37 ... D3
Over Jerstal ... 12 ... B1
Överåneset ... 2 ... B1
Overath ... 40 ... B4
Overhalla ... 3 ... E3
Överlida ... 13 ... D3
Övermark (Ylimarkku) ... 4 ... C1
Överö ... 11 ... D2
Overscaig ... 18 ... C4
Overstrand ... 25 ... F4
Övertänger ... 10 ... B3
Overton ... 27 ... F3
Overton-on-Dee ... 22 ... C2
Överturingen ... 3 ... F1
Øverum ... 13 ... F4
Oveselu ... 114 ... B4
Ovidiu ... 115 ... F3
Oviedo ... 67 ... E4
Ovindoli ... 98 ... C3
Øvre Årdal ... 8 ... C4
Øvre Rendal ... 9 ... D4
Øvrestøl ... 2 ... B1
Ower ... 27 ... F2
Oxberg ... 9 ... F3
Oxelösund ... 10 ... C1
Oxford ... 27 ... F3
Oxwich ... 26 ... C4
Øyer ... 9 ... D4
Øyermoen ... 9 ... E3
Oykell Bridge ... 18 ... C3
Øystese ... 8 ... B3
Oyten ... 33 ... D2
Ozalj ... 104 ... B1
Ožbalt ... 104 ... B3
Ozd ... 106 ... B4
Ožd'any ... 106 ... B4
Ozieri ... 96 ... B3
Ozun ... 108 ... C1

Pääjarvi ... 5 ... E1
Paakkila ... 7 ... E4
Paatinen ... 6 ... B1
Paavola ... 5 ... E3
Paceco ... 102 ... A3
Pachino ... 103 ... D1
Pacov ... 43 ... F1
Pacsa ... 105 ... D2
Pacy-sur-Eure ... 49 ... F1
Padasjoki ... 6 ... C2
Padej ... 106 ... B1
Paderborn ... 36 ... C2
Padiham ... 23 ... D4
Padina ... 112 ... C4
Padina ... 115 ... D4
Padjene ... 110 ... C3
Padova ... 90 ... C2
Pádria ... 96 ... B3
Padron ... 66 ... B3
Padru ... 96 ... C3
Padstow ... 26 ... B1
Padul ... 80 ... B1
Paesana ... 92 ... A4
Paestum ... 100 ... B3
Pag ... 107 ... D3
Págaia ... 121 ... D1
Pagham ... 25 ... D1
Pagny ... 56 ... B1
Págue ... 77 ... D3
Páhi ... 106 ... B3
Paianía ... 121 ... E3
Paignton ... 27 ... D1
Paijärvi ... 7 ... D2
Pailton ... 23 ... E1
Paimbœuf ... 52 ... C2
Paimpol ... 52 ... B4
Painswick ... 27 ... E3
Paisley ... 20 ... B4

Pakhna ...122... A1
Pakoštane ...110... B3
Pakrac ...105... D1
Paks ...105... D2
Palacios de Sanabria ...67... D2
Palacios del Sil ...67... E3
Paladru ...61... D2
Palafrugell ...71... E3
Palagiano ...101... E3
Palagonia ...103... D2
Palaiá Epídhavros ...121... D3
Palaiókastron ...122... C3
Palaiokastritsa ...116... C1
Palaiokhóra ...122... A3
Palaiokhórion ...118... B2
Palaiópolis ...118... C2
Palaiópolis ...121... F3
Pálairos ...120... B4
Palamás ...117... E1
Palamós ...71... E3
Palanca ...109... D2
Palárikovo ...105... E4
Palas de Rei ...66... C3
Palatítsia ...117... E2
Palau ...96... B4
Palavas ...64... B2
Palazzo San Gervasio ...100... C4
Palazzolo ...89... D2
Palazzolo Acréide ...103... D2
Pale ...111... E2
Palena ...99... D2
Palencia ...68... A2
Palermo ...102... B3
Palestrina ...98... B2
Palheiros de Mira ...72... B2
Palheiros de Quiaios ...72... A2
Palheiros de Tocha ...72... B2
Palić ...106... B2
Palinuro ...100... C2
Paliomonastíri ...117... E1
Palioúrion ...118... B2
Paliseul ...31... D2
Pälkäne ...6... C2
Pallasgreen ...16... C2
Pallíni ...121... E3
Palma ...77... D3
Palma del Rio ...83... F4
Palma di Montechiaro ...102... C2
Palma Nova ...77... D3
Palmadula ...96... A3
Palmanova ...91... E2
Palmela ...78... A2
Palmi ...103... E4
Palnackie ...20... C2
Palo di Colle ...101... D4
Palokastër ...116... C2
Palokki ...7... E4
Palomäki ...7... E4
Palomares ...81... D2
Palombara Sabina ...98... B2
Pålsboda ...10... B1
Paltamo ...5... F3
Paltaniemi ...5... F3
Păltiniş ...108... B1
Păltinoasa ...108... C3
Paluzza ...91... E2
Pamiers ...63... E2
Pampilhosa da Serra ...72... C1
Pamplona (Irunea) ...69... E3
Pamporovo ...118... B4
Panagyurishte ...114... B1
Panajë ...116... B2
Panassac ...62... C2
Panayiá ...122... B3
Panayiá ...118... C3
Pančevo ...112... C4
Pancharevo ...113... E1
Panciu ...109... D1
Pancorvo ...68... C3
Pandánassa ...121... D1
Pandino ...89... D2
Pandrup ...12... B3
Panes ...68... A4
Pangbourne ...27... F3
Pano Panayia ...122... A1
Panórmitis ...122... B4
Pánormos ...121... F3
Pántene ...5... D1
Pantanna ...102... B3
Panxon ...66... B2
Paola ...101... D1
Pápa ...105... D2
Papadhiánika ...121... D2
Papasídero ...100... C2
Papenburg ...32... B2
Paphos ...122... A1
Pappenheim ...46... B3
Par ...26... C1
Parabita ...101... E3
Paraćin ...113... D3
Parád ...106... B4
Paradhisia ...120... C2
Parainen (Pargas) ...6... B1
Paralía ...121... E3
Paralía ...120... B3
Paralía ...117... E2
Paralía Akrátas ...120... C3
Paralía Iríon ...121... D3
Paralía Kímis ...121... E3
Paralía Piátanos ...120... C3
Paralímni ...122... C1
Parálion Ástrous ...120... C2
Paramithiá ...116... C1
Paranéstion ...118... B3
Parantala ...5... E1
Parapótamos ...116... C1
Parassapuszta ...105... E4
Paravóla ...120... B4
Paray-le-Monial ...60... B4
Parchim ...34... C2
Paredes ...72... B3
Paredes de Nava ...68... A2

Parentis-en-Born ...62... B4
Parey ...38... C3
Párga ...116... C1
Pargas (Parainen) ...6... B1
Pargolovo ...7... F1
Parikia (Páros) ...121... F2
Parikkala ...7... E3
Paris ...54... C4
Parkano ...6... B3
Parkeston Quay ...25... F3
Parkkila ...5... E2
Parkkima ...5... E2
Parknasilla ...16... A1
Parkumäki ...7... E3
Parlówko ...35... E3
Parma ...93... E4
Páros (Parikia) ...121... F2
Parpan ...85... D2
Parsberg ...46... C4
Partakoski ...7... E2
Partenen ...85... E2
Parthenay ...58... C4
Partille ...12... C4
Partinello ...57... E3
Partinico ...102... B3
Partizani ...112... C3
Partizanske Vode ...112... B3
Partry ...16... B4
Påryd ...13... E2
Pas de la Casa ...63... E1
Pas-en-Artois ...50... B3
Pasaia ...69... D4
Pasçani ...109... D3
Pasewalk ...35... E2
Påskallavik ...13... F3
Pašman ...110... B3
Passage East ...17... D2
Passage West ...16... C1
Passau ...47... E3
Passignano sul Trasimeno ...95... D1
Pastrana ...74... C3
Pásztó ...106... B4
Pàtas ...113... D4
Patay ...54... B3
Pateley Bridge ...21... E1
Patergassen ...86... C1
Paternion ...86... C1
Paternò ...103... D2
Paternopoli ...100... B4
Patersdorf ...47... D3
Pătîrlagele ...109... D1
Patitíri ...118... B1
Pátrai ...120... C3
Patrickswell ...16... C2
Patrington ...23... F3
Patsch ...85... F3
Pattada ...96... B3
Pattensen ...37... D3
Patterdale ...20... C2
Pattijoki ...5... E3
Pau ...62... B2
Pauillac ...58... B2
Paulhaguet ...60... B2
Páuliş ...107... D2
Paulstown ...17... D2
Pavel Banya ...114... C1
Pavia ...78... B3
Pavia ...89... D1
Pavilly ...49... F2
Pavlíkeni ...114... C2
Pavullo nel Frignano ...94... C3
Payerne ...84... A2
Payrac ...59... D1
Pazardzhik ...118... B4
Pazin ...104... A1
Pchelarovo ...118... C4
Peal dè Becerro ...80... C3
Péaule ...52... C2
Peć ...112... B1
Pechea ...109... E1
Pecica ...106... C2
Peckelsheim ...37... D2
Pécs ...105... E2
Pécsvárad ...105... E2
Pedhoulas ...122... A1
Pedráces-Pedratsches ...90... C3
Pedras Salgadas ...72... C4
Pedraza ...74... B4
Pedro Muñoz ...74... C1
Peebles ...20... C4
Peel ...20... B1
Peenemünde ...35... D3
Pegau ...38... C1
Peggau ...87... D2
Pegli ...92... C3
Pegnitz ...42... C2
Pego ...76... A2
Peine ...37... E3
Peira-Cava ...65... F3
Peiss ...46... C2
Peissenberg ...46... B1
Peiting ...46... B1
Peitz ...39... E3
Pelasyía ...121... D4
Pelczyce ...35... F2
Pélekas ...116... C1
Pella ...117... E3
Pellegrino Parmense ...93... D4
Pellegrue ...58... C1
Pellinge (Pellinki) ...7... D1
Pellinki (Pellinge) ...7... D1
Pellosniemi ...7... D2
Pelovo ...114... B2
Peltosalmi ...7... D4
Pelynt ...26... C1
Pembridge ...22... C1
Pembroke ...26... B3
Pembury ...25... E1
Pen-y-groes ...22... B2
Pen-y-gwryd ...22... B2
Penácova ...72... B2

Peñafiel ...68... B1
Penafiel ...72... B3
Penally ...26... B3
Penamacor ...73... D2
Penaranda ...68... B1
Peñaranda de Bracamonte ...73... F3
Peñárroya-Pueblonuevo ...79... F2
Penarth ...27... D3
Peñas de San Pedro ...81... D4
Pencaitland ...20... C4
Pendálofon ...117... D2
Pendine ...26... C4
Pendoggett ...26... B4
Penela ...72... B1
Peniche ...78... A3
Penicuik ...20... C4
Penina ...82... B3
Peñíscola ...76... B4
Penkridge ...23... D2
Penkum ...35... E2
Penmaenmawr ...22... B3
Pennabilli ...95... D2
Pennal ...22... B2
Penne ...98... C3
Penrhyndeudraeth ...22... B2
Penrith ...21... D2
Penryn ...26... B1
Pensford ...27... E3
Penshurst ...25... E1
Pentewan ...26... B1
Pentraeth ...22... B3
Pentrefoelas ...22... B2
Pentrez-Plage ...52... A3
Penybont ...22... C1
Penybontfawr ...22... C2
Penyige ...107... D4
Penzance ...26... B1
Penzberg ...46... C1
Péoi ...90... B3
Peqin ...116... C3
Peraía ...117... F2
Perakhóra ...121... D3
Perakhorio ...122... B1
Peralta ...4... C1
Peralejos de las Truchas ...75... D3
Perales del Alfambra ...75... E3
Peralta ...69... D2
Pérama ...117... D1
Peranka ...5... F4
Peräseinäjoki ...5... D1
Perast ...111... E1
Perchtoldsdorf ...87... E3
Percy ...48... C1
Pérdhika ...121... D3
Pérdhika ...116... C1
Pereiro ...82... C3
Peretu ...114... C3
Perg ...87... D3
Pérgine Valsugana ...90... C3
Pergola ...95... D2
Perho ...6... C2
Periam ...106... C2
Périers ...48... C2
Périgueux ...59... D2
Perişani ...108... B1
Perişoru ...113... E3
Peristerona ...122... B2
Perkáta ...105... E3
Perkpolder ...28... C1
Perleberg ...34... C1
Perlez ...112... C4
Përmet ...116... C2
Pernå ...7... D1
Pernes ...64... C3
Pernik ...113... E1
Perniö ...6... B1
Pernitz ...87... E3
Péronne ...50... B3
Pérouges ...60... C3
Perpignan ...64... A1
Perranporth ...26... B1
Perros-Guirec ...48... B2
Persani ...108... C1
Persberg ...9... F2
Persenbeug ...87... D3
Pershore ...27... E4
Perstorp ...13... D2
Perth ...19... D1
Pertisau ...85... F3
Pertteli ...6... B1
Pertuis ...65... D3
Pertunmaa ...7... D2
Perúgia ...95... D1
Perušić ...110... B4
Péruwelz ...30... C3
Pervomaisk ...7... F1
Pésaro ...95... D2
Pescara ...99... D3
Pescasseroli ...98... C2
Peschici ...99... F2
Peschiera di Garda ...94... B2
Péscia ...98... C2
Pescina ...98... C2
Pescocostanzo ...99... D2
Pescolanciano ...99... D2
Pescopagano ...100... C4
Peshkëpija ...116... C2
Peshkopi ...116... C4
Peshtera ...118... B4
Pesiökylä ...5... F4
Pesmes ...56... B1
Pesocani ...117... D3
Pessin ...39... D4
Peštani ...116... C4
Pesteana Jiu ...113... E4
Pestera ...115... E3
Peştişani ...113... E4
Pešurići ...111... E2
Péta ...117... D1
Petäjävesi ...5... E1
Petalidhion ...120... C2
Petange ...31... D3

Petea ...107... E4
Peterborough ...23... F2
Peterchurch ...27... D4
Peterculter ...19... E2
Peterhead ...19... F3
Peterlee ...21... E2
Petersdorf ...34... B4
Petersdorf ...34... C3
Petersfield ...25... D1
Petershagen ...37... D3
Pétervására ...106... B4
Petília Policastro ...101... D1
Petkus ...39... D3
Petlovača ...112... B4
Petra ...77... E3
Pétra ...117... E2
Pétra ...119... D1
Petralia-San Lucia ...102... C3
Petraná ...117... E2
Petrella Tifernina ...99... D2
Petreşti ...107... D4
Petreşti ...114... C3
Petreto-Bicchisano ...57... E2
Petrich ...118... A3
Petrila ...107... E1
Petrinja ...104... C1
Petrodvorets ...7... F1
Petroşani ...107... E1
Petroúli ...117... D1
Petroúsa ...118... B3
Petrovac ...112... A1
Petrovac ...113... D3
Petrovaradin ...106... B1
Petrovice ...43... F2
Petržalka ...105... D4
Petsákoi ...120... C3
Pettenbach ...86... C3
Pettigo ...14... C2
Petworth ...25... D1
Peuerbach ...86... C4
Pevensey ...25... E1
Pevensey Bay ...25... E1
Pewsey ...27... E3
Peyia ...122... A1
Peyrat-le-Chateau ...59... E3
Peyrehorade ...62... B2
Peyrolles ...65... D3
Peyruis ...65... D3
Pézenas ...64... B2
Pfaffenhausen ...45... E2
Pfaffenhofen ...46... C3
Pfäffikon ...84... C3
Pfafflar ...85... E3
Pfarrkirchen ...47... D3
Pfatter ...47... D3
Pfeffenhausen ...46... C3
Pfreimd ...42... C1
Pforzheim ...44... C3
Pfronten ...46... B1
Pfullendorf ...45... D2
Pfullingen ...45... D2
Pfunds ...85... E2
Pfungstadt ...40... C2
Phalsbourg ...56... C4
Philippeville ...31... D2
Philippsreut ...47... E3
Phyäntaka ...7... D2
Phyásalmi ...5... E2
Piacenza ...89... D1
Piadena ...89... E1
Piana ...57... E3
Piana Crixia ...92... B3
Piana di Albanesi ...102... B3
Pianora ...94... C3
Pías ...78... C1
Piatra ...114... C2
Piatra Neamţ ...109... D3
Piatra Olt ...114... B3
Piazza Armerina ...103... D2
Piazza al Serchio ...93... C3
Picacho de Veleta ...80... C1
Pićan ...104... A1
Picerno ...100... C3
Pickering ...21... E1
Pico ...98... C1
Picquigny ...50... B3
Piedicroce ...57... F3
Piediluco ...98... B3
Piedimonte Matese ...99... D3
Piedrabuena ...74... B1
Piedrafita de Babia ...67... E3
Piedrahita ...73... F2
Piedralaves ...74... A3
Piekszämäki ...7... D3
Pielavesi ...7... F2
Pienza ...97... F4
Piercebridge ...21... E2
Pierowall ...19... F1
Pierre-Buffiere ...59... D2
Pierre-de-Bresse ...56... A1
Pierrefitte ...56... A4
Pierrefitte-Nestalos ...62... C1
Pierrefonds ...50... B2
Pierrefort ...59... F1
Pierrelatte ...64... C2
Pierroton ...58... B1
Pieski ...39... F4
Pietarsaari (Jakobstad) ...5... D2
Pietra Ligure ...92... B3
Pietraperzia ...102... C2
Pietrasanta ...93... E2
Pietreni ...115... E2
Pietroşita ...114... C3
Pieve di Cadore ...91... D3
Pieve di Teco ...92... B3
Pieve San Stéfano ...95... D2
Pievepelago ...94... B3
Pihkala ...5... E2
Pihlajalahti ...7... E3
Pihlajavaara ...7... F4
Pihlava ...6... B2

Pihtipudas ...5... E2
Piikkiö ...6... B1
Piipola ...5... E3
Piispajärvi ...5... F4
Pilat-Plage ...62... B4
Pilgrimstad ...3... F1
Pilis ...106... B3
Pilisvörösvar ...105... E4
Pilos ...120... B2
Pina de Ebro ...69... F1
Pinarhisar ...119... E4
Pincehely ...105... E2
Pinchbeck ...23... F2
Pineda de Mar ...71... D3
Pinerolo ...92... A4
Pineto ...99... D3
Piney ...55... E3
Pinheiro ...72... B4
Pinhel ...73... D3
Pinkafeld ...87... E2
Pinneberg ...33... D2
Pino ...57... F4
Pinols ...60... B1
Pinos Puente ...80... B2
Pinoso ...81... E4
Pintamo ...5... F4
Pinwherry ...20... B3
Pinzolo ...90... B3
Pióbbico ...95... D2
Piombino ...97... E4
Pionsat ...59... F3
Piove di Sacco ...90... C1
Piovene-Rocchette ...90... C2
Pipriac ...53... D2
Piqeras ...116... C2
Piraiévs ...121... D3
Piran ...91... E2
Pirdop ...114... B1
Pirgos ...117... F2
Pirgos ...121... F1
Pirgos ...120... B3
Pirgos Diroú ...120... C1
Piriac ...52... C2
Pirin ...118... A4
Pirmasens ...44... B4
Pirna ...43... E4
Pirnmill ...15... E4
Pirot ...113... E2
Pirou-Plage ...48... C2
Pirovac ...110... B2
Pîrvova ...113... D4
Pisa ...93... E2
Pisanets ...115... D2
Pischia ...106... C1
Pisciotta ...100... C3
Piscolt ...107... D3
Pisek ...43... E1
Pisodhèrion ...117... D3
Pisogne ...89... E2
Pissos ...62... B4
Pissouri ...122... A1
Pistiána ...117... D1
Pisticci ...101... D3
Pistóia ...94... B2
Piteå ...4... C1
Piteşti ...114... C4
Pithiviers ...54... C3
Pitigliano ...97... F3
Pitkäjärvi ...6... B1
Pitkälahti ...7... D4
Pitlochry ...19... D1
Pitmedden ...19... E2
Pitomača ...105... D2
Pitvaros ...106... C2
Pivka ...104... A1
Pivnika ...105... D1
Piysóyiani ...117... D2
Pizzo ...103... F4
Pizzoli ...98... C3
Plabennec ...52... A4
Plaisance ...62... C2
Pláka ...118... C2
Plaka (Milos) ...121... E2
Plakiás ...122... A3
Plana ...111... E1
Plana ...43... D2
Plana nad Lužnicí ...43... F1
Plancoët ...52... C4
Plandište ...112... C4
Plánice ...43... E1
Planina ...104... A2
Plansee ...85... E3
Plasencia ...73... E1
Plaški ...104... B1
Plasy ...43... E2
Plataiaí ...121... D3
Platamón ...117... E2
Platamón ...118... B3
Platamona Lido ...96... B3
Platania ...118... A1
Platanias ...122... A4
Plátanos ...120... C4
Plataria ...116... C1
Plati ...103... F4
Platikambos ...117... E1
Platis Yialós ...121... E2
Platistomon ...120... C4
Plátres ...122... A1
Plátsa ...120... C2
Plattling ...47... D3
Plau ...34... C2
Plaue ...38... C4
Plauen ...42... B1
Playa de San Juán ...81... F4
Pleasley ...23... E3
Pleaux ...59... E2
Pleinfeld ...46... B4
Plélan-le-Grand ...52... C3
Plémet ...52... C3
Pleniţa ...113... E3

Plentzia ...68... C4
Plestin ...52... B4
Pleternica ...105... D1
Plettenberg ...36... C1
Pleumartin ...59... D4
Pleven ...114... B2
Plevna ...115... D3
Pleyben ...52... A3
Pliska ...115... E2
Plitra ...121... D2
Plitvice ...110... B4
Plitvički Ljeskovac ...110... B4
Pljevlja ...112... B2
Ploaghe ...96... B3
Plochingen ...45... D3
Plockton ...18... B2
Ploërmel ...52... C3
Ploieşti ...115... D4
Plomárion ...119... D1
Plombières ...56... B3
Plön ...33... D2
Plonéour Lanvern ...52... A3
Plopana ...109... D2
Plopii Slăviteşti ...114... B3
Plopşoru ...113... E4
Ploştina ...113... E4
Ploty ...35... F3
Plouay ...52... B3
Ploubalay ...52... C4
Ploudalmezeau ...52... A4
Plouescat ...52... A4
Plougasnou ...52... B4
Plouguenast ...52... C3
Plouha ...52... C4
Plouigneau ...52... B4
Plouray ...52... B3
Plouvet ...52... B4
Plovdiv ...118... C4
Plozévet ...52... A3
Plumbridge ...15... D2
Pluton ...108... C3
Pluvigner ...52... B2
Plužine ...111... E1
Plymouth ...26... C1
Plympton ...26... C1
Plzeň ...43... E2
Pobes ...68... C3
Pobierowo ...35... F3
Pöchlarn ...87... D4
Počitelj ...111... D1
Pocking ...47... E3
Pocklington ...21... E1
Pocuta ...112... B3
Podari ...114... B3
Podbořany ...43... E3
Podčetrtek ...104... C1
Podersac ...58... B1
Podersdorf am See ...87... F3
Podgarić ...104... C1
Podgora ...110... C2
Podgrad ...104... A1
Podgradec ...117... D3
Podhokhórion ...104... B3
Podkoren ...104... A3
Podkova ...118... C3
Podkrepa ...118... C4
Podnovlje ...111... D4
Podoleni ...109... D2
Podravska Slatina ...105... D2
Podromanija ...111... E2
Podslon ...115... D1
Podu Turcului ...109... E2
Podujevo ...113... D2
Podul Iloaiei ...109... D3
Podunavci ...104... A1
Poeldijk ...28... C2
Pogana ...109... E2
Poggendorf ...35... D3
Poggibonsi ...94... C2
Póggio Rusco ...94... C4
Pogoanele ...115... D4
Pogoritsa ...115... D2
Pohja ...6... C2
Pohja (Pojo) ...6... C1
Pohja-Lankila ...7... E3
Pohjoislahti ...5... E1
Poiana Mare ...113... E3
Poiana Mărutui ...107... D3
Poiana Stampei ...108... C3
Poiana Teiului ...108... C3
Poibrene ...114... B1
Pointe de Grave ...58... B2
Pointe de Penmarch ...52... A3
Pointe du Raz ...52... A3
Poirino ...92... B4
Poissons ...56... A3
Poitiers ...58... C4
Poix ...50... A2
Poix-Terron ...51... D2
Pojate ...113... D3
Pojejena ...113... D4
Pojo (Pohja) ...6... C1
Pojorîta ...108... C3
Pokupsko ...104... C1
Pola de Allande ...67... D4
Pola de Laviana ...67... F3
Pola de Lena ...67... E4
Pola de Siero ...67... E4
Pola de Somiedo ...67... D2
Pola de Trives ...67... D2
Polbathic ...26... C1
Polegate ...25... E1
Polemi ...122... A1
Polesella ...94... C4
Polgár ...105... F4
Polgárdi ...105... E2
Poliána ...120... C2
Policastro ...100... C3
Police ...35... E2
Policoro ...101... D3
Polignano a Mare ...101... E4

Poligny...56...B1
Polikastron...117...E3
Polikhnitos...119...D1
Polikrayshte...114...C2
Polis...122...A1
Polistena...103...F4
Politiko...122...B1
Políyiros...118...A2
Poljana...112...C4
Pölläkkä...7...E3
Polle...37...D2
Pollença...77...E3
Pollfoss...2...B1
Pollónia...121...E2
Polovragi...114...B4
Polperro...26...C1
Polruan...26...C1
Polski Gradets...119...D4
Polski Trumbesh...114...C2
Polsko Kosovo...114...C2
Polvela...7...E4
Polvijärvi...7...E4
Polyany...7...F1
Polzeath...26...C1
Pomarance...94...C1
Pomarkku...6...D2
Pombal...72...B1
Pomellen...35...E2
Pomeroy...15...D2
Pomezí nad Ohří...42...C2
Pomézia...98...B2
Pomi...107...E4
Pommersfelden...42...B2
Pomorie...115...E1
Pompaples...84...A4
Pompei...100...B3
Pompey...56...B4
Pomposa...95...D4
Poncin...61...D3
Ponferrada...67...D2
Ponoare...113...E4
Pons...58...B2
Ponsa...6...C2
Ponsacco...93...E2
Pont Aberglaslyn...22...B2
Pont de Salars...63...F3
Pont Scorff...52...B2
Pont-Audemer...49...E2
Pont-Aven...52...B3
Pont-à-Mousson...56...B4
Pont-Croix...52...A3
Pont-d'Ain...61...D3
Pont-de-Vaux...60...C4
Pont-de-Briques...50...A4
Pont-de-Dore...60...B3
Pont-de-Roide...56...C2
Pont-en-Royans...61...D1
Pont-l'Abbe...52...A3
Pont-l'Evêque...49...E2
Pont-Réan...53...D3
Pont-St-Esprit...64...C3
Pont-St-Martin...88...B2
Pont-St-Vincent...56...B4
Pont-sur-Yonne...55...D3
Pontacq...62...C2
Pontailler...56...A1
Pontão...72...B1
Pontardawe...26...C4
Pontardulais...26...C4
Pontarion...59...E3
Pontarlier...56...B1
Pontassieve...94...C2
Pontaubault...53...D4
Pontaumur...59...F3
Pontcharra...61...D2
Pontchartrain...54...C4
Pontchâteau...52...C2
Ponte Barxas...66...C2
Ponte da Barca...66...B1
Ponte de Lima...66...B1
Ponte de Sor...78...B3
Ponte di Arche...90...B3
Ponte di Legno...89...E3
Ponte di Piave...91...D2
Ponte nelle Alpi...91...D3
Ponte Tresa...84...C1
Ponte Venturina...94...B3
Ponte-Caldelas...66...B2
Ponte-Leccia...57...F3
Ponteareas...66...B2
Pontebba...91...E3
Pontedecimo...92...C3
Pontedera...94...B2
Pontedeume...52...C4
Pontefract...23...E3
Ponteland...21...E3
Pontelandolfo...99...D1
Pontelongo...91...D1
Ponterwyd...22...B1
Pontevedra...66...B2
Pontevico...89...E1
Pontgibaud...59...F3
Pontigny...55...D2
Pontisménon...118...A3
Pontivy...52...B3
Pontlevoy...54...B2
Pontllanfraith...27...D3
Pontoise...50...A1
Pontokómi...117...E2
Pontorson...53...D4
Pontremoli...93...D3
Pontresina...85...D2
Pontrhydfendigaid...22...B1
Pontrieux...52...B4
Pontrilas...27...D4
Ponts...70...B3
Pontvallain...53...F2
Pontypool...27...D3
Pontypridd...27...D3
Pool-in-Wharfedale...21...E1
Poolewe...18...B3

Pooley Bridge...21...D2
Popeni...109...E2
Poperinge...30...B3
Popeşti...107...D3
Popeşti...109...D1
Popeşti Leordeni...115...D3
Popina...115...D3
Popintsi...114...B1
Popoli...98...C3
Popovaca...104...C1
Popovitsa...118...C4
Popovo...115...D2
Poppenhausen...41...E2
Poppi...94...C2
Popsko...119...D4
Populónia...97...D4
Porcești...108...B3
Porcsalma...107...D4
Porcuna...80...B3
Pordenone...91...D2
Pordim...114...C2
Poreč...91...E1
Pori...6...B2
Porlock...27...D3
Porlock Weir...27...D3
Pörnbach...46...C3
Pornic...52...C1
Pornichet...52...C1
Póros...121...D3
Póros...120...B3
Poroszló...106...C4
Porozina...104...A1
Porquerolles...65...E2
Porrentruy...84...A3
Porretta Terme...94...B3
Porriño...66...B2
Porsgrunn...8...C1
Port Askaig...15...E4
Port Bannatyne...20...B4
Port Camargue...64...C2
Port Charlotte...15...E4
Port d'Alcúdia...77...E3
Port Dinorwic...22...B3
Port Ellen...15...E4
Port Erin...20...B1
Port Eynon...26...C4
Port Grimaud...65...E2
Port Henderson...18...B3
Port Isaac...26...B2
Port Laoise...17...D3
Port Logan...20...B2
Port of Ness...18...B3
Port Talbot...26...C4
Port William...20...B2
Port-Barcarès...64...A1
Port-Cros...65...E2
Port-de-Bouc...64...C2
Port-en-Bessin...49...D2
Port-Leucate...64...A1
Port-Louis...52...B2
Port-la-Nouvelle...64...A1
Port-Manech...52...B2
Port-Navalo...52...B2
Port-St-Louis-du-Rhône...64...C2
Port-Ste Marie...62...C3
Port-sur-Saône...56...B2
Port-Vendres...64...A1
Portadown...15...D2
Portaferry...15...E2
Portalegre...78...B3
Portalrubio...75...E4
Portarià...117...F1
Portarlington...17...D3
Portavogie...15...E2
Portbail...48...C2
Portbou...71...A4
Portel...78...C2
Portela de Messines...82...B3
Portela do Homen...66...C1
Portelo...67...D1
Portglenone...15...D2
Porth...27...D3
Porthcawl...26...C4
Porthcurno...26...B1
Porthleven...26...B1
Porthmadog...22...B2
Porthtowan...26...B1
Porticcio...57...E2
Portishead...27...D3
Portland...26...B1
Portloe...26...B1
Portmahomack...19...D3
Portmarnock...17...E3
Portmeirion...22...B2
Portnacroish...18...C1
Portnahaven...15...D4
Portnockie...19...E3
Porto...57...E3
Porto Azzurro...97...D4
Porto Carras...118...B2
Porto Cervo...96...C4
Porto Cesareo...101...F3
Porto Conte...96...A3
Porto Corsini...95...D2
Porto Cristo...77...E3
Porto d'Àscoli...98...C4
Porto de Mós...78...B4
Porto do Son...66...B3
Porto Empedocle...102...C2
Porto Garibaldi...95...D3
Pórto Lágo...118...C3
Porto Plno...96...B1
Pórto Ráfti...121...E3
Porto Recanati...95...E1
Porto Rotondo...96...C4
Porto San Giorgio...95...E1
Porto San Stéfano...97...E3
Porto Tolle...95...D4
Porto Tórres...96...A3
Porto-Vecchio...57...F1
Portoferráio...97...D4

Portofino...92...C3
Portogruaro...91...D2
Portokhéli...121...D2
Pörtom (Pirttikylä)...4...C1
Portomaggiore...94...C4
Portomarín...66...C3
Portomouro...66...B3
Portorož...91...E2
Portoscuso...96...A1
Portovenere...93...D3
Portpatrick...20...B2
Portrane...17...E4
Portreath...26...B1
Portree...18...B3
Portroe...16...C3
Portrush...15...D3
Portscatho...26...B1
Pörtschach...86...C1
Portsmouth...27...F2
Portsonachan...18...C1
Portsoy...19...E3
Portstewart...15...D3
Portumna...16...C3
Porubne...108...C4
Porumbeni...108...C2
Porvoo (Borgå)...7...D1
Porzuna...74...B1
Posada...96...C3
Posadas...83...F4
Poschiavo...85...D1
Posedarje...110...B3
Poshnjë...116...C3
Posidhonia...121...F2
Posta...98...B3
Poşta Cîlnău...109...D1
Postbridge...26...C1
Postojna...104...A2
Postoloprty...43...E3
Posušje...111...D2
Potamiá...118...C3
Potamoí...118...B3
Potamós...121...D1
Potenza...100...C3
Potes...68...A4
Potoci...111...D2
Potok...104...C1
Potsdam...39...D3
Pottenstein...42...C2
Pottenstein...87...E3
Potter Heigham...25...F4
Potterne...27...E3
Potters Bar...25...D2
Pöttmes...46...B3
Potton...23...F1
Pouancé...53...D2
Pougues-les-Eaux...55...D1
Pouilly...55...D1
Pouilly-en-Auxois...55...E1
Poulton-le-Fylde...22...C4
Pouyastruc...62...C2
Pouzauges...58...B4
Povlja...110...C2
Póvoa de Varzim...72...B4
Powburn...21...D3
Powick...27...E4
Poyntzpass...15...D1
Poyrali...119...E4
Poysdorf...87...E4
Požarevac...112...C2
Požega...112...B3
Pozeranje...112...C1
Pozo Alcón...80...C3
Pozoblanco...79...F2
Pózrzadło...39...F3
Pozuelo de Ariza...69...D1
Pozuelo de Zarzón...73...D2
Pozzallo...103...D1
Pozzo di Gotto...103...E3
Pozzomaggiore...96...B3
Pozzuoli...100...A3
Prača...111...E2
Prachatice...47...E4
Pradelles...60...B1
Prades...63...F1
Pradillo...68...C2
Præstø...12...C1
Prägraten...86...A1
Praha...43...F2
Prahecq...58...C3
Prahovo...113...E3
Praia a Mare...100...C2
Praia da Rocha...82...B3
Praia de Santa Cruz...78...A3
Praia Grande...78...A3
Praiano...100...B3
Praid...108...C2
Praisós...122...C3
Pralognan...61...E2
Prámanta...117...D1
Prassies...122...B3
Pratella...99...D1
Prato...94...B2
Prats de Llucanès...70...C3
Prats-de-Mollo...63...F1
Prauthoy...56...A2
Pravia...114...B1
Pravets...67...E4
Pré St-Didier...88...A2
Pré-en-Pail...53...E3
Preajba...114...C3
Précy-sous-Thil...55...E2
Predappio...94...C3
Predazzo...90...C3
Preddvor...104...A2
Predeal...108...C1
Predejane...113...D1
Predel...104...A2
Predești...113...E3
Predlitz...86...C1

Predoi-Prettau...91...D4
Preesall...22...C4
Preetz...33...E3
Pregarten...87...D4
Prejmer...108...C1
Preko...110...B3
Prémery...55...D1
Premnitz...38...C2
Prenjas...116...C3
Prenzlau...35...E2
Prenzlin...35...E2
Prerow...34...C4
Preselentsi...115...E2
Preševo...113...D1
Preslav...115...D2
Pressac...59...D3
Pressath...42...C2
Pressbaum...87...E3
Prestatyn...22...C3
Presteigne...22...C1
Prestfoss...8...C2
Přeštice...43...E1
Preston...22...C3
Preston Candover...27...F3
Prestonpans...20...C4
Prestwick...20...B3
Prettin...39...D2
Pretzsch...39...D2
Preuilly-sur-Claise...54...B1
Preuţteşti...109...D3
Préveza...120...B4
Pribeta...105...E4
Priboj...75...D3
Priboj...112...B2
Příbram...43...E2
Prichsenstadt...41...E2
Priego...75...D3
Priego de Córdoba...80...B2
Prien...47...D2
Prijeboj...110...B4
Prijedor...110...C4
Prijepolje...112...B2
Prilep...117...D3
Prilike...112...B2
Priluka...110...C2
Primel-Trégastel...52...B4
Primiá de Mar...71...D3
Primolano...90...C2
Primorsk...7...E1
Primorsko...115...E1
Primošten...110...B2
Primstal...40...B1
Princes Risborough...25...D2
Princetown...26...C1
Priozersk...7...F2
Priseltsi...115...E2
Priština...112...C1
Pritzerbe...38...C4
Pritzier...34...C2
Pritzwalk...34...C2
Privas...60...C1
Priverno...98...C1
Privlaka...110...B3
Prizren...112...C1
Prizzi...102...B3
Prnjavor...111...D4
Prnjavor...112...B4
Probištip...117...E4
Probstzella...42...C3
Prodhromos...122...A1
Pródromos...121...D4
Proença-a-Nova...78...C4
Profitis...118...A2
Profondeville...31...D2
Progled...118...B4
Prokhoma...117...E3
Prokópion...121...D4
Prokuplje...113...D2
Prolaz...115...D2
Promakhón...118...A3
Pronsfeld...40...A2
Propriano...57...E2
Prosotsáni...118...B3
Protaras...122...C1
Protivín...47...E4
Prötzel...39...E4
Proussós...120...B4
Provadiya...115...E2
Provins...55...D3
Prozor...111...D2
Prudhoe...21...D3
Prüm...40...A2
Prundu...115...D3
Prunete-Cervione...57...F3
Prunn...46...C3
Przybiernów...35...E3
Przytoczna...39...F4
Psakhná...121...D4
Psará...121...F4
Psathópyrgos...120...C4
Ptéri...117...E2
Ptolemais...117...E2
Ptuj...104...C2
Puchberg...87...E3
Puchenii Mari...115...D4
Pucioasa...114...C4
Pučišća...110...C2
Puckeridge...25...E2
Pucol...75...F2
Pudasjärvi...5...D3
Puddletown...27...E2
Puebla de Alcocer...79...F3
Puebla de Don Fadrique...81...D3
Puebla de Don Rodrigo...74...A1
Puebla de Lillo...67...D3
Puebla de Obando...79...D3
Puebla de Sanabria...67...D2
Puebla Tornesa...76...A4
Puente la Reina...74...C2
Puente Viesgo...68...B4
Puente-Genil...80...A2
Puentecesures...66...B3

Puentelarra...68...C3
Puerto Banús...83...F2
Puerto Castilla...73...C2
Puerto de Andraitx...77...D3
Puerto de Mazarrón...81...E2
Puerto de Pollença...77...E3
Puerto de San Vicente...79...F3
Puerto de Sóller...77...D3
Puerto Lápice...74...B1
Puerto Lastres...67...F4
Puerto Real...83...E2
Puerto-Lumbreras...81...D2
Puertollano...80...B4
Puffendorf...40...A4
Puget-sur-Argens...65...E2
Puget-Théniers...65...E3
Puget-Ville...65...E2
Puhos...5...F4
Puhos...7...F3
Pui...107...E1
Puieşti...109...E2
Puiseaux...54...C3
Puivert...63...E1
Pukavik...13...E2
Pukë...116...C4
Pula...96...B1
Pula...110...A4
Pulborough...25...D1
Pulkau...87...E4
Pulkkila...5...E3
Pulsnitz...39...E1
Pumpsaint...26...C4
Pungeşti...109...E2
Punkalaidun...6...B2
Punta Ala...97...E4
Punta Umbría...83...D3
Puokio...5...F3
Puolanka...5...F4
Purbach...87...F3
Purchena...81...D2
Purgstall...87...D3
Purkersdorf...87...D3
Purmerend...29...D3
Purton...27...E2
Pürvomay...118...C4
Pushkin...7...F1
Püspökladány...106...C3
Pusula...6...C1
Pusztamonostor...106...B3
Pusztaszemes...105...D3
Putaja...6...B2
Putanges...53...E4
Putbus...35...D1
Putignano...101...E4
Putikko...7...E3
Putila...108...C4
Putinci...112...B4
Putineiu...114...C2
Putlitz...34...C2
Putna...108...C3
Putnok...106...C3
Puttelange...51...F1
Putten...29...E2
Puttgarden...34...B4
Puumala...7...E2
Puy de Dôme...60...A3
Puy-Guillaume...60...B3
Puy-l'Evêque...63...D2
Puylaurens...63...E2
Pwllheli...22...B2
Pyecombe...25...D1
Pyhäjärvi...5...E2
Pyhäjoki...5...D3
Pyhäkylä...5...F4
Pyhältö...7...D2
Pyhämaa...5...E3
Pyhäntä...5...E3
Pyhäranta...5...E3
Pyhäsalmi...5...E2
Pyhäselkä...7...E2
Pyhtää (Pyttis)...7...D1
Pyla-sur-Mer...58...B1
Pyli...117...D1
Pylkönmäki...5...E1
Pyntäinen...6...B3
Pyrga...122...B1
Pyrgoi...117...E3
Pyrzyce...35...F2
Pyšely...43...F2
Pyttis (Pyhtää)...7...D1

Q

Quakenbrück...36...C4
Quarré-le-Tombes...55...E2
Quartu Sant'Elene...96...B1
Quateira...82...B3
Quedlinburg...38...B2
Quendon...25...E3
Querfurt...38...C2
Quesada...80...C3
Questembert...52...B2
Quettehou...48...C2
Quiberon...52...B2
Quickborn...33...E3
Quillan...63...E1
Quimper...52...A3
Quimperlé...52...B3
Quinéville...48...C2
Quingey...56...B1
Quintana de la Serena...79...E2
Quintana del Puente...68...B3
Quintanaortuño...68...B3
Quintanar de la Orden...74...C2
Quintanar de la Sierra...68...C2
Quintanilha...67...D1
Quintanilla-Escalada...68...B3

Quintin...52...C3
Quinto...69...F1
Quiroga...67...D2
Quissac...64...B3
Qyteti Stalin...116...C3

R

Raab...86...C4
Raabs-an-der-Thaya...87...D4
Raahe...5...D3
Rääkkylä...7...E4
Raalte...29...E3
Rab...110...A4
Rabac...104...A1
Rabade...66...D3
Rábafüzes...104...C3
Răbăgani...107...D2
Rabastens...63...E3
Rabastens-de-Bigorre...62...C2
Rabisha...113...E3
Rabrovo...113...D4
Rača...112...C3
Rača...105...D4
Răcăiuni...109...D2
Răcari...114...C3
Răcarii de Sus...113...E4
Răcăşdia...113...D4
Racconigi...92...B4
Răchitoasa...109...E2
Rackwick...19...E1
Racu...108...C2
Råda...9...E3
Rădăuţi...108...C4
Rădăuţi Prut...109...D4
Radcliffe-on-Trent...23...E2
Rade...33...D2
Råde...8...D2
Radeberg...39...E1
Radebeul...39...E1
Radeburg...39...E1
Radeče...104...B2
Radegast...38...C2
Radenci...104...C3
Radenthein...86...C1
Rădeşti...114...C4
Radevormwald...36...B1
Radimlje...111...D1
Rădineşti...113...F4
Radiumbad Brambach...42...C2
Radkersburg...87...E2
Radko Dimitrievo...115...E2
Radlje ob Dravi...104...B3
Radmirje...104...B2
Radna...107...D3
Radnevo...115...D1
Radnica...39...F3
Radnice...43...E2
Radolfzell...45...D1
Radomir...113...E1
Radomiru...114...B3
Radotin...43...F2
Radovanu...115...D4
Radovets...119...D4
Radoviš...117...E4
Radovljica...104...A2
Radstadt...86...B2
Radstock...27...E3
Răducăneni...109...E3
Radzovce...106...B4
Raesfeld...36...B2
Raffadali...102...C2
Rafina...121...E3
Ragály...106...C4
Ragaška Slatina...104...B2
Rågeleje...12...C2
Raglan...27...D3
Ragusa...103...D1
Raharney...17...D4
Rahden...36...C3
Rahman...115...F4
Rain...46...B3
Rainham...25...E2
Raippaluoto (Replot)...4...C2
Raisio...6...B1
Raivala...6...B2
Rajamäki...6...C1
Rajka...105...D4
Rakaca...106...C4
Rakamaz...106...C4
Rákhes...121...D4
Rakhovo...108...B4
Rakitovo...118...B4
Rakkestad...9...D2
Rákóczifalva...106...B3
Rákos...106...C2
Rakovica...110...C3
Rakovitsa...113...D3
Rakovník...43...E2
Rakovski...118...C4
Ralja...112...C4
Ramacastañas...73...F2
Ramacca...103...D2
Ramales de la Victoria...68...B4
Rambervillers...56...C3
Rambin...35...D4
Rambouillet...54...C4
Rampside...20...C1
Ramsau...86...C2
Ramsele...4...A2
Ramsey...20...B1
Ramsey...25...D3
Ramsgate...25...F2
Rämshyttan...10...B2

Ramsjö ... **10** ... B4	Recklinghausen ... **36** ... B2	Révigny ... **55** ... F4	Riomar ... **70** ... B1	Rohrbach ... **86** ... C4	Rothenburg ob der Tauber ... **45** ... E4
Ramstein ... **40** ... B1	Recoaro Terme ... **90** ... C2	Revin ... **51** ... D3	Rion ... **120** ... C4	Rohrberg ... **38** ... B4	Rothéneuf ... **53** ... D4
Ramvik ... **4** ... B1	Recologne ... **56** ... B1	Revničov ... **43** ... C2	Rionero in Vulture ... **100** ... C4	Roisel ... **50** ... B3	Rotherham ... **23** ... E3
Ranalt ... **85** ... F2	Recsk ... **106** ... B4	Revonlahti ... **5** ... E3	Riopar ... **81** ... D4	Rojiştea ... **114** ... B3	Rothes ... **19** ... D3
Randaberg ... **8** ... A2	Recz ... **35** ... F2	Revsnes ... **8** ... B4	Riotinto ... **83** ... D4	Rökkum ... **2** ... C1	Rothesay ... **20** ... B4
Randalstown ... **15** ... E2	Red Wharf Bay ... **22** ... B3	Revsnes ... **3** ... D3	Rioz ... **56** ... B2	Roknäs ... **4** ... C4	Rothwell ... **23** ... E1
Randan ... **60** ... A3	Redalen ... **9** ... D3	Rewal ... **35** ... F3	Ripač ... **110** ... C4	Rokua ... **5** ... E3	Rotondella ... **101** ... D3
Randazzo ... **103** ... D3	Redbrook ... **27** ... D3	Rezina ... **109** ... F4	Ripatransone ... **98** ... C4	Rokycany ... **43** ... E2	Rott ... **46** ... B2
Randen ... **8** ... C4	Redcar ... **21** ... E2	Rezovo ... **119** ... F4	Ripley ... **23** ... E2	Røldal ... **8** ... B2	Rott ... **46** ... C2
Randers ... **12** ... B3	Redditch ... **23** ... D1	Rgotina ... **113** ... D3	Ripley ... **21** ... E1	Rolle ... **80** ... A2	Rottach-Egern ... **46** ... C1
Randsverk ... **8** ... C4	Redea ... **114** ... B3	Rhayader ... **22** ... C1	Ripoll ... **71** ... D3	Rollesby ... **25** ... F4	Rottenbach ... **42** ... B3
Råneå ... **4** ... C4	Redefin ... **34** ... B2	Rheda ... **36** ... C2	Ripon ... **21** ... E1	Rolvenden ... **25** ... E1	Rottenburg ... **45** ... D2
Rånes ... **53** ... E4	Redhill ... **25** ... D1	Rhede ... **36** ... A2	Riposto ... **103** ... E3	Roma ... **11** ... F1	Rottenburg ... **46** ... C3
Rankweil ... **85** ... D3	Redland ... **19** ... F1	Rhede ... **32** ... B2	Ripponden ... **23** ... D3	Roma ... **98** ... B2	Rottenmann ... **86** ... C2
Rantasalmi ... **7** ... E3	Redon ... **52** ... C2	Rheinau ... **44** ... B2	Riquewihr ... **56** ... C3	Romagnano Sésia ... **88** ... C2	Rotterdam ... **29** ... D2
Rantsila ... **5** ... E3	Redondela ... **66** ... B2	Rheinbach ... **40** ... B3	Risan ... **111** ... E1	Roman ... **109** ... D3	Rotthalmünster ... **47** ... E3
Ranua ... **5** ... E4	Redondo ... **78** ... C2	Rheinberg ... **36** ... A2	Risbäck ... **3** ... F3	Roman ... **114** ... B1	Rottingdean ... **25** ... E1
Ranum ... **12** ... B3	Redruth ... **26** ... B1	Rheinböllen ... **40** ... B2	Risca ... **27** ... D3	Românaşi ... **107** ... E3	Röttingen ... **41** ... E1
Raon-l'Etape ... **56** ... C3	Reedham ... **25** ... F4	Rheindahlen ... **36** ... A1	Riscle ... **62** ... C3	Romania ... **111** ... E2	Rottneros ... **9** ... E2
Rapallo ... **93** ... D3	Rees ... **36** ... A2	Rheine ... **36** ... B3	Rish ... **115** ... D1	Romanija ... **111** ... E2	Rottweil ... **44** ... C2
Rapness ... **19** ... F1	Reftele ... **21** ... D2	Rheinfelden ... **84** ... B3	Risnes ... **8** ... A4	Romanno Bridge ... **20** ... C4	Rötz ... **43** ... D1
Rapolla ... **100** ... C4	Regalbuto ... **103** ... D3	Rheinfelden (Baden) ... **44** ... B1	Rîşnov ... **108** ... C1	Romans-sur-Isère ... **60** ... C1	Roubaix ... **50** ... C4
Rapperswil ... **84** ... C3	Regen ... **47** ... D3	Rheinsberg ... **35** ... D2	Risør ... **8** ... C1	Romanshorn ... **84** ... D3	Roudnice nad Labem ... **43** ... E3
Rapsáni ... **117** ... E2	Regensburg ... **46** ... B3	Rheinzabern ... **44** ... C4	Ristiina ... **7** ... D3	Rombas ... **51** ... F1	Rouen ... **49** ... F2
Raron ... **84** ... B1	Regenstauf ... **46** ... C4	Rhenen ... **29** ... E2	Ristijärvi ... **5** ... F3	Romford ... **25** ... E2	Rouffach ... **56** ... C3
Raša ... **104** ... A1	Reggello ... **94** ... C2	Rhens ... **40** ... B2	Ristinge ... **12** ... B1	Romilly-sur-Seine ... **55** ... D3	Rouge ... **53** ... D2
Rascafría ... **74** ... B4	Réggio di Calàbria ... **103** ... E3	Rheydt ... **36** ... A1	Ristovac ... **113** ... D1	Romont ... **84** ... A2	Rougemont ... **56** ... B2
Răscruci ... **107** ... E3	Réggio Nell'Emilia ... **94** ... B4	Rhiconich ... **18** ... C4	Risum-Lindholm ... **33** ... D4	Romorantin-Lanthenay ... **54** ... B1	Rougemont ... **56** ... C2
Rasharkin ... **15** ... D2	Reggiolo ... **94** ... B4	Rhinow ... **38** ... C4	Rittmanshausen ... **41** ... E4	Romppala ... **7** ... E4	Rough Close ... **23** ... D2
Rasivaara ... **7** ... E3	Reghin ... **108** ... B2	Rho ... **88** ... C2	Riva ... **90** ... B2	Romsey ... **27** ... F2	Roughton ... **25** ... F4
Raška ... **112** ... C2	Regua ... **72** ... C3	Rhoose ... **27** ... D3	Riva-Bella ... **49** ... D2	Romuli ... **108** ... B3	Rouillac ... **58** ... C3
Rasova ... **115** ... E3	Reguengos de Monsaraz ... **78** ... C2	Rhosneigr ... **22** ... B3	Rivarolo Canavese ... **88** ... B2	Roncal ... **69** ... E3	Roujan ... **64** ... A2
Rasovo ... **113** ... E2	Rehau ... **42** ... C2	Rhossili ... **26** ... C4	Rive-de-Gier ... **60** ... C2	Roncegno ... **90** ... C3	Roulers (Roeselare) ... **30** ... B3
Rast ... **113** ... E3	Rehden ... **36** ... C4	Rhu ... **20** ... B4	Riverstown ... **16** ... C3	Roncesvalles ... **69** ... E3	Roundstone ... **16** ... B4
Rastatt ... **44** ... C3	Rehna ... **34** ... B2	Rhuddlan ... **22** ... C3	Rivesaltes ... **71** ... D4	Ronchamp ... **56** ... C2	Roundwood ... **17** ... E3
Råsted ... **12** ... B3	Reichenau ... **87** ... E3	Rhyd-ddu ... **22** ... B3	Rivoli ... **88** ... B1	Ronchi ... **91** ... E2	Roussillon ... **65** ... D3
Rastede ... **36** ... C2	Reichenbach ... **42** ... C3	Rhyl ... **22** ... C3	Rizárion ... **117** ... E3	Ronciglione ... **98** ... A3	Rouvres-en-Xaintois ... **56** ... B3
Rastenfeld ... **87** ... D4	Reichenbach ... **39** ... F1	Rhymney ... **27** ... D3	Rizómilos ... **120** ... C2	Ronda ... **83** ... F2	Rovato ... **89** ... D2
Răstoaca ... **109** ... E1	Reichertshausen ... **46** ... C3	Rhynern ... **36** ... C2	Rizómilos ... **117** ... F1	Rønde ... **12** ... B2	Roveredo ... **90** ... B2
Răstoci ... **107** ... E3	Reichertshofen ... **46** ... C3	Rhynie ... **19** ... E2	Rjånes ... **2** ... A1	Ronehamn ... **11** ... F1	Rövershagen ... **34** ... C3
Răstolnita ... **108** ... C3	Reigate ... **25** ... D1	Riaillé ... **53** ... D2	Rjukan ... **8** ... C2	Rönnäng ... **12** ... C4	Roverud ... **9** ... E3
Råsvani ... **115** ... D3	Reighton ... **21** ... F1	Riaño ... **67** ... F3	Roa ... **68** ... B1	Rönninge ... **13** ... E1	Rovigo ... **90** ... C1
Rätansbyn ... **3** ... F1	Reignier ... **61** ... E3	Rians ... **65** ... D2	Roa ... **9** ... D3	Ronneburg ... **42** ... C3	Rovinari ... **113** ... E4
Ratece ... **91** ... E3	Reila ... **6** ... B2	Riaza ... **68** ... B1	Roade ... **23** ... E1	Ronneby ... **13** ... E2	Rovinj ... **91** ... E1
Rath Luirc (Charleville) ... **16** ... C2	Reims ... **50** ... C1	Riba de Ave ... **72** ... B4	Roanne ... **60** ... B3	Ronnede ... **12** ... C1	Rovišće ... **104** ... C2
Rathangen ... **17** ... D3	Reinach ... **84** ... C3	Ribadavia ... **66** ... C2	Röbel ... **34** ... C2	Ronse (Renaix) ... **30** ... C3	Rów ... **35** ... F2
Rathcoole ... **17** ... E3	Reinach ... **84** ... B3	Ribadelago ... **67** ... D2	Robertsbridge ... **25** ... E1	Roodeschool ... **29** ... F4	Rowlands Gill ... **21** ... E2
Rathcormack ... **16** ... C1	Reinberg ... **35** ... D3	Ribadeo ... **67** ... D2	Robertsfors ... **4** ... C3	Roosendaal ... **29** ... D1	Rowsley ... **23** ... D3
Rathdowney ... **17** ... D3	Reinfeld ... **33** ... E3	Ribadesella ... **67** ... F4	Robin Hood's Bay ... **21** ... F2	Roosky ... **16** ... C4	Roy Bridge ... **18** ... C2
Rathdrum ... **17** ... E3	Reinhardshagen ... **37** ... D2	Ribarci ... **113** ... D1	Robledo de Chavela ... **74** ... B3	Ropeid ... **8** ... B2	Royan ... **58** ... B2
Rathenow ... **38** ... C4	Reinheim ... **41** ... D2	Ribarice ... **112** ... C2	Roborough ... **26** ... C1	Ropotovo ... **117** ... D4	Royat ... **60** ... A3
Rathfriland ... **15** ... E1	Reinosa ... **68** ... B3	Ribaritsa ... **114** ... B1	Rocach ... **42** ... B3	Roquebilliere ... **65** ... F3	Roybon ... **61** ... D2
Rathkeale ... **16** ... B2	Reinsfeld ... **40** ... B2	Ribe ... **12** ... A1	Rocamadour ... **59** ... E1	Roquebrune-Cap-Martin ... **65** ... F3	Roye ... **50** ... B2
Rathmelton ... **14** ... C3	Reinsvoll ... **9** ... D3	Ribeauville ... **56** ... C3	Rocca di Mezzo ... **98** ... C3	Roquefort ... **62** ... B3	Royère ... **59** ... E3
Rathmolyon ... **17** ... D4	Reisbach ... **47** ... D3	Ribécourt ... **50** ... B2	Rocca San Casciano ... **94** ... C3	Roquefort-sur-Soulzon ... **64** ... A3	Røykenvik ... **9** ... D3
Rathmore ... **16** ... B1	Reischach ... **47** ... D2	Ribeira ... **66** ... B3	Roccadáspide ... **100** ... B3	Roquetas de Mar ... **80** ... C1	Røyrvik ... **3** ... E2
Rathmullan ... **14** ... C3	Reischenhart ... **46** ... C1	Ribemont ... **50** ... C2	Roccalbegna ... **97** ... C4	Rore ... **110** ... C3	Røysheim ... **8** ... C4
Rathnew ... **17** ... E3	Reisjärvi ... **5** ... E2	Ribera ... **102** ... B2	Roccalumera ... **103** ... E3	Røros ... **3** ... D1	Royston ... **25** ... D3
Rathowen ... **17** ... D4	Reiss ... **19** ... D4	Ribérac ... **58** ... C2	Roccamonfina ... **98** ... C1	Rorschach ... **85** ... D3	Röyttä ... **5** ... D4
Rathvilty ... **17** ... D3	Reit im Winkl ... **47** ... D2	Ribes de Freser ... **71** ... C4	Roccapalumbra ... **102** ... C3	Rørvig ... **12** ... C2	Roza ... **115** ... D1
Ratingen ... **36** ... B2	Reitzehain ... **43** ... D1	Ribnica ... **104** ... B1	Roccaraso ... **99** ... D2	Rørvik ... **3** ... D2	Rožaj ... **112** ... B1
Ratoath ... **17** ... E4	Rejmyre ... **10** ... B1	Ribnitz-Damgarten ... **34** ... C3	Roccastrada ... **97** ... C4	Rosal de la Frontera ... **78** ... C1	Rózanki ... **35** ... F3
Ratten ... **87** ... E2	Reken ... **36** ... B2	Říčany ... **43** ... F2	Rocella Jónica ... **103** ... F4	Rosala ... **6** ... B1	Rozavlea ... **108** ... B4
Rattenberg ... **86** ... A2	Remagen ... **40** ... B3	Riccia ... **99** ... D2	Rocester ... **23** ... D2	Rosans ... **65** ... D4	Rozay-en-Brie ... **55** ... D3
Rattersdorf ... **87** ... F2	Rémalard ... **54** ... A3	Riccione ... **95** ... D2	Rochdale ... **23** ... D3	Rosapenna ... **14** ... C3	Rozhnov ... **108** ... C4
Rattray ... **19** ... D1	Remels ... **32** ... C2	Richelieu ... **53** ... F1	Roche ... **26** ... B1	Rosarno ... **103** ... E4	Rožmitál pod Tremšínen ... **43** ... E2
Rättvik ... **10** ... B3	Remeskylä ... **5** ... E2	Richmond ... **21** ... E2	Rochechouart ... **59** ... D3	Rosche ... **34** ... B1	Roznov ... **109** ... D1
Ratzeburg ... **34** ... B3	Remetea Mare ... **114** ... B1	Richtenberg ... **35** ... D3	Rochefort ... **58** ... B3	Roscoff ... **52** ... B4	Rozoy ... **51** ... D2
Raubling ... **46** ... C1	Remich ... **31** ... F2	Říčiu ... **108** ... B2	Rochefort ... **31** ... D2	Roscommon ... **16** ... C4	Rozvadov ... **43** ... D2
Raudaskylä ... **5** ... E2	Remiremont ... **56** ... C3	Rickling ... **33** ... E3	Rochefort-en-Terre ... **52** ... C2	Roscrea ... **16** ... C3	Rtanj ... **113** ... D3
Raudeberg ... **2** ... A1	Remnes ... **3** ... E4	Riddarhyttan ... **9** ... E4	Rochefort-sur-Nenon ... **56** ... B1	Rosedale Abbey ... **21** ... E2	Ruabon ... **22** ... C2
Raufoss ... **9** ... D3	Remouchamps ... **31** ... E2	Riding Mill ... **21** ... E2	Rochehaut ... **31** ... D2	Rosegg ... **86** ... C1	Rubbestadneset ... **8** ... A3
Rauhaniemi ... **7** ... E3	Remoulins ... **64** ... B3	Ried ... **85** ... E2	Rochemaure ... **64** ... C4	Rosehall ... **18** ... C3	Rubena ... **68** ... B2
Rauland Høyfjellshotel ... **8** ... C2	Remscheid ... **36** ... B1	Ried ... **86** ... B3	Rocheservière ... **53** ... D1	Rosehearty ... **19** ... E3	Rubeži ... **111** ... E1
Rauma ... **6** ... B2	Rémuzat ... **65** ... D4	Riedenburg ... **46** ... C3	Rochester ... **25** ... E2	Rosemarkie ... **19** ... D3	Rubielos de Mora ... **75** ... D3
Rauris ... **86** ... B2	Rena ... **9** ... D3	Riedlingen ... **45** ... D2	Rochlitz ... **43** ... D4	Rosen ... **115** ... E1	Rubiera ... **94** ... C3
Räuseni ... **109** ... D3	Renaison ... **60** ... B3	Riegel ... **44** ... B2	Rociu ... **114** ... C3	Rosendal ... **8** ... B3	Rucăr ... **108** ... C1
Rautajärvi ... **6** ... C2	Renaix (Ronse) ... **30** ... B1	Riegersburg ... **87** ... E1	Rock ... **26** ... B1	Rosenheim ... **46** ... C2	Rudare ... **112** ... C2
Rautalampi ... **5** ... F1	Renchen ... **44** ... C3	Riesa ... **39** ... D2	Rockcliffe ... **20** ... C2	Roses ... **71** ... E4	Rudawica ... **39** ... F2
Rautavaara ... **5** ... F2	Rendal ... **2** ... C2	Riesi ... **102** ... C2	Rockcorry ... **15** ... D1	Roseţi ... **115** ... E3	Rüdesheim ... **40** ... C2
Rautila ... **6** ... B1	Rendsburg ... **33** ... D3	Riestedt ... **38** ... B2	Rockenhausen ... **40** ... C1	Roseto degli Abruzzi ... **98** ... C3	Rudkøbing ... **12** ... B1
Rautjärvi ... **7** ... E2	Reni ... **109** ... E1	Rietberg ... **36** ... C2	Rockingham ... **23** ... E2	Rosia ... **107** ... D2	Rudna Glava ... **113** ... D3
Ravanusa ... **102** ... C2	Renko ... **6** ... C2	Rieti ... **98** ... B3	Rockley Sands ... **27** ... E2	Rosignano-Marittimo ... **93** ... C1	Rudnica ... **112** ... B2
Ravatn ... **3** ... E4	Renkum ... **29** ... E2	Rieumes ... **63** ... D2	Rockneby ... **13** ... F3	Rosino ... **101** ... B1	Rudnica ... **112** ... C2
Ravda ... **115** ... E1	Rennebu ... **2** ... C1	Rieupeyroux ... **63** ... E4	Rocroi ... **51** ... D3	Roşiori ... **107** ... D3	Rudnik ... **112** ... C1
Ravello ... **100** ... B3	Rennerod ... **40** ... C3	Rieux ... **63** ... D2	Rodach ... **42** ... B3	Roşiori de Vede ... **114** ... C3	Rudnik ... **115** ... E1
Rävemåla ... **13** ... E2	Rennes ... **53** ... D3	Riez ... **65** ... E3	Rødberg ... **8** ... C1	Roskilde ... **12** ... C2	Rudolphstein ... **42** ... C3
Ravenglass ... **20** ... C2	Rennweg ... **86** ... C1	Riezlern ... **85** ... E3	Rødbyhavn ... **12** ... C1	Roslev ... **12** ... B3	Rudolstadt ... **42** ... B3
Ravenna ... **95** ... D3	Rens ... **12** ... A1	Rignac ... **63** ... E4	Rødding ... **12** ... A1	Rosolina Mare ... **91** ... D1	Rudozem ... **118** ... C4
Ravensbrück ... **35** ... D2	Rentína ... **117** ... E1	Riihimäki ... **6** ... C2	Rødby ... **12** ... C2	Rosolini ... **103** ... D1	Ruds-Vedby ... **12** ... C1
Ravensburg ... **45** ... D1	Rentína ... **118** ... A2	Riihivalkama ... **6** ... C1	Rødekro ... **12** ... B1	Rosoman ... **117** ... E4	Rudston ... **21** ... F1
Ravenscar ... **21** ... F2	Répáshuta ... **106** ... C4	Riistavesi ... **7** ... E4	Rødel ... **18** ... A3	Rosporden ... **52** ... B3	Rue ... **50** ... A3
Ravenstonedale ... **21** ... D2	Répcelak ... **105** ... D3	Rijeka ... **104** ... A1	Roden ... **29** ... F4	Ross ... **27** ... E4	Ruelle ... **58** ... C2
Raversijde ... **30** ... B4	Repino ... **7** ... F1	Rijeka Crnojevića ... **111** ... E1	Rodenkirchen ... **32** ... C2	Ross Carbery ... **16** ... B1	Ruffec ... **59** ... C3
Ravna Dubrava ... **113** ... D2	Replot (Raippaluoto) ... **4** ... C2	Rijssen ... **29** ... E2	Rodewald ... **37** ... D4	Rossano ... **101** ... D2	Ruffieux ... **61** ... D2
Rawtenstall ... **23** ... D3	Reposaari ... **6** ... A2	Rila ... **114** ... F4	Rodewisch ... **43** ... D3	Rosscor ... **14** ... C2	Rufford ... **22** ... C3
Ray ... **14** ... C3	Requena ... **75** ... E2	Rillé ... **53** ... F2	Rodez ... **63** ... F4	Rosses Point ... **16** ... B1	Rugăşeşti ... **108** ... B3
Rayleigh ... **25** ... E2	Réquista ... **63** ... F3	Rillington ... **21** ... F1	Ródha ... **116** ... C1	Rosshaupten ... **46** ... B1	Rugby ... **23** ... E1
Rayol ... **65** ... E2	Rerik ... **34** ... C3	Rimbo ... **10** ... C2	Rodhópolis ... **117** ... F3	Rossla ... **38** ... B2	Rugeley ... **23** ... D2
Räyrinki ... **5** ... D2	Resana ... **90** ... C2	Rimforsa ... **13** ... E4	Rødhus ... **12** ... B3	Rosslare Harbour ... **17** ... E2	Ruginoasa ... **109** ... D3
Razbojna ... **112** ... C2	Resen ... **117** ... D3	Rimini ... **95** ... D2	Rodi Gargánico ... **99** ... F2	Rosslau ... **38** ... C3	Rugles ... **54** ... A4
Razdrto ... **91** ... F2	Reşita ... **107** ... D1	Rîmnicu de Jos ... **115** ... F4	Roding ... **47** ... D4	Rosslea ... **15** ... D1	Rühen ... **38** ... B3
Razgrad ... **115** ... D2	Resko ... **35** ... F3	Rîmnicu Sărat ... **109** ... D1	Rodna ... **108** ... B3	Rossnes ... **8** ... A3	Ruhland ... **39** ... E2
Razlog ... **118** ... A4	Ressons ... **50** ... B2	Rîmnicu Vîlcea ... **113** ... E4	Rodrigatos ... **67** ... E2	Rosson ... **4** ... A2	Ruhmannsfelden ... **47** ... D1
Răzvad ... **114** ... C4	Retama ... **74** ... A1	Rimske Toplice ... **104** ... B2	Rødvig ... **12** ... C1	Røssvassbukt ... **3** ... F4	Ruhpolding ... **47** ... D1
Reading ... **27** ... F3	Rethel ... **51** ... D2	Rincón de la Victoria ... **80** ... C1	Roermond ... **31** ... E4	Röstånga ... **13** ... D2	Ruidera ... **74** ... C1
Réalmont ... **63** ... E3	Rethem ... **37** ... D4	Rindal ... **2** ... C2	Roesbrugge ... **30** ... B3	Rostassac ... **63** ... D4	Rülzheim ... **44** ... C4
Realp ... **84** ... C2	Réthimnon ... **122** ... B4	Ring (An Rinn) ... **17** ... D1	Rogačica ... **112** ... B3	Rostock ... **34** ... C3	Rum ... **105** ... D3
Reay ... **19** ... D4	Retiers ... **53** ... D2	Ringaskiddy ... **16** ... C1	Rogart ... **19** ... D3	Rostrenen ... **52** ... B3	Ruma ... **112** ... B4
Rebais ... **55** ... D4	Retournac ... **60** ... B2	Ringe ... **12** ... B1	Rogatica ... **111** ... E2	Rostrevor ... **15** ... E1	Rumbling Bridge ... **17** ... F4
Rebordelo ... **67** ... D1	Rétság ... **106** ... B4	Ringebu ... **9** ... D4	Rogätz ... **38** ... C3	Rosvik ... **20** ... C4	Rumburk ... **43** ... F4
Rebūrkovo ... **113** ... F2	Rettendon ... **25** ... E2	Ringford ... **20** ... C2	Rogil ... **82** ... A3	Röszke ... **106** ... B2	Rumigny ... **51** ... D3
Reç ... **116** ... C4	Retz ... **87** ... E4	Ringsted ... **12** ... C1	Rogliano ... **101** ... D1	Rot ... **9** ... F4	Rumilly ... **61** ... D3
Recanati ... **95** ... E1	Reuilly ... **54** ... C1	Ringwood ... **27** ... E2	Rogna ... **83** ... D2	Rota ... **83** ... D2	Runcorn ... **22** ... C3
Recaş ... **106** ... C1	Reus ... **70** ... B2	Rinteln ... **37** ... D3	Rognac ... **65** ... D2	Rotenburg ... **33** ... D2	Runcu ... **113** ... E4
Recea ... **113** ... E3	Reusel ... **31** ... D4	Rînzeşti ... **109** ... E2	Rognes ... **3** ... D1	Rotenburg ... **41** ... D1	Rundfloen ... **9** ... E3
Recea ... **114** ... C3	Reuterstadt Stavenhagen ... **35** ... D3	Rio de Mouro ... **78** ... A3	Rogoznhë ... **116** ... C3	Roth ... **46** ... B4	Rundvik ... **4** ... B1
Recey-sur-Ource ... **55** ... F2	Reutlingen ... **45** ... D3	Rio Maior ... **78** ... A3	Rogoznica ... **110** ... B2	Rotha ... **38** ... C2	Runni ... **5** ... F2
Rechnitz ... **87** ... F2	Reutte ... **85** ... E3	Riom ... **60** ... A3	Rogoźno ... **52** ... C3	Rothbury ... **21** ... D3	Runswick ... **21** ... F2
Reci ... **108** ... C1	Revel ... **63** ... E2	Riom-ès-Montagnes ... **59** ... F2	Rogil ... **82** ... A3	Rothenburg ... **39** ... F2	Ruokolahti ... **7** ... E2
Recke ... **36** ... B3	Revfülöp ... **105** ... D3	Riomaggiore ... **93** ... D3	Rohrbach ... **56** ... C4		

Ruona 5 D1
Ruorasmäki 7 D3
Ruovesi 6 C3
Rupa 104 A1
Rupea 108 C2
Rupt 56 C2
Rusalka 115 F2
Ruse 115 D2
Ruşeţu 115 E4
Ruševo 105 D1
Rusfors 4 B3
Rush 17 E4
Rushden 23 E1
Ruski Krstur 106 B1
Ruskila 7 E4
Ruskington 23 F2
Rusksele 4 B3
Rusokastro 115 E1
Rusovce 105 D4
Russelsheim 40 C2
Russi 95 D3
Russkaya 108 C4
Rust 44 B2
Rust 87 F3
Rustad 9 D3
Rustington 25 D1
Ruswil 84 C3
Rutalahti 7 D3
Rute 80 A2
Rutenbrock 32 B1
Rüthen 36 C2
Ruthin 22 C2
Rüti 84 C3
Rutigliano 101 E4
Rutledal 8 A4
Ruurlo 29 F2
Ruutana 6 C2
Ruvo di Puglia 99 F1
Ruwer 40 A2
Ruyton of the Eleven Towns 22 C2
Ruzhintsi 113 E2
Ry 12 B2
Ryakhovo 115 D3
Rybnitsa 109 F4
Ryd 13 E2
Rydaholm 13 E3
Rydal 20 C2
Ryde 27 F2
Rye 25 E1
Ryhälä 7 E3
Rymań 35 F3
Rymättylä 6 B1
Rysum 32 B2
Rzepin 39 F3

S

Sääksjärvi 5 D2
Sääksmäki 6 C2
Saal 46 C3
Saalbach 86 B2
Saales 56 C3
Saalfeld 42 B3
Saalfelden 86 B2
Saanen 84 B2
Saarbrücken 44 B4
Saarburg 40 A1
Saarijärvi 5 E1
Saarlouis 44 A4
Saas-Fee 84 B1
Šabac 112 B4
Sabadell 70 C2
Săbăoani 109 D3
Sabaudia 98 B1
Sabbioneta 93 E4
Săbed 108 B2
Sabiñánigo 69 F3
Sables-d'Or 52 C4
Sablé-sur-Sarthe 53 E2
Sabres 62 B3
Sabrosa 72 C3
Sabugal 73 D2
Săcălaz 106 C1
Sacedón 74 C3
Săcel 108 B1
Săcel 108 B4
Sacile 91 D2
Săcueni 107 D3
Sadaba 69 E2
Sadanski 118 A4
Saddell 15 E3
Sadikov Bunar 113 D2
Sadova 114 B2
Sadovets 114 B2
Sadovo 118 C4
Sadów 39 F3
Sadská 43 F2
Sadu 108 B1
Sæbø 8 B3
Sæbø 2 B1
Sæby 12 B3
Sælvig 12 B2
Saerbeck 36 B3
Sætre 9 D2
Saeul 31 E1
Sævråsvåg 8 A3
Säffle 9 E1
Saffron Walden 25 E3
Sagard 35 D4
S'Agaró 71 E2
Sagone 57 E2
Sagres 82 A3
Sagunto 76 A3
Sagvåg 8 A2
Ságvár 105 E3
Sahagún 67 F2

Sahalahti 6 C2
Sähäteni 115 D4
Sahrajärvi 5 E1
Šahy 105 E4
Saignelégier 84 A3
Saillagouse 63 E1
Saillans 61 D1
Sains 50 C2
Sainte Anne-d'Auray 52 B2
Sainte Anne-la-Palud 52 A3
Sainte Croix-Volvestre 63 D2
Sainte Enimie 64 B4
Sainte Foy-la-Grande 58 C1
Sainte Gauburge-Sainte Colombe 54 A4
Sainte Hermine 58 B4
Sainte Marie-aux-Mines 56 C3
Sainte Marie-de-Campan 62 C1
Sainte Maries-de-la-Mer 64 C2
Sainte Maure-de-Touraine 54 A1
Sainte Maxime 65 E2
Sainte Menehould 51 D1
Sainte Mère-Église 48 C2
Saintes 58 B3
Sainte Sévère 59 E4
Sainte Suzanne 53 E3
Sainte Tulle 65 D3
Saintfield 15 E2
Saissac 63 E2
Šajkaš 106 B1
Sajószentpéter 106 C4
Sakskøbing 12 C1
Sákylä 6 D2
Sala 10 B2
Sal'a 105 E4
Sala Consilina 100 C3
Salahmi 5 F2
Salakovac 112 C4
Salamanca 73 E3
Salamea de la Serena 79 E2
Salamís 121 D3
Sálard 107 D3
Salardú 70 B4
Salas 67 E4
Salaš 113 D3
Salas de los Infantes 68 C2
Sălătrucu 108 B1
Salbohed 10 B2
Salbris 54 C2
Sálciua 107 E2
Salcombe 26 C1
Sălcuta 113 E3
Sălcuta 114 C3
Saldaña 68 A3
Sale 23 D3
Sale 88 C1
Salem 45 D1
Salema 82 A3
Salemi 102 B3
Salen 18 B1
Salen 18 B1
Sälen 9 E3
Salernes 65 E2
Salerno 100 B3
Salers 59 F2
Salford 23 D3
S'Algar 77 F4
Salgótarján 106 B4
Salies-de-Béarn 62 B2
Salies-du-Salat 63 D2
Salignac-Éyvignes 59 D1
Saline di Volterra 94 B1
Salins 6 C2
Salinas 6 B1
Salisbury 27 E2
Sáliste 108 B1
Sallanches 61 E3
Sallent de Gállego 69 F3
Salles 62 B4
Salles 63 E2
Salles-Curan 63 F3
Sallins 17 E3
Salo 6 B1
Salò 89 E2
Salobreña 80 B1
Saloinen 5 D3
Salon 55 E3
Salon-de-Provence 64 C3
Salonta 107 D2
Salou 70 B2
Salsbruket 3 E2
Salses 63 E2
Salsomaggiore Terme 93 D4
Saltash 26 C1
Saltbæk 12 C2
Saltburn 21 E2
Saltcoats 20 B4
Saltsjöbaden 10 C1
Saltvik 11 D2
Saluzzo 92 A4
Salva 108 B3
Salvatera de Magos 78 A3
Salvatierra 69 D3
Salviac 59 D1
Salzburg 86 B3
Salzgitter-Bad 37 E3
Salzgitter-Lebenstedt 37 E3
Salzhausen 33 E2
Salzkotten 36 C2
Salzwedel 34 B1
Salzweg 47 E3
Sama de Langreo 67 E4
Samadet 62 B3
Samassi 96 B2
Samatan 63 D2
Sambucca di Sicília 102 B3
Samedan 85 D2
Samer 50 A4
Sámi 120 A3
Samikón 120 B3
Samitier 70 A3
Samobor 104 B1
Samoëns 61 E3

Samokov 113 E1
Šamorin 105 D4
Samos 67 D3
Samoš 112 C4
Samothráki 118 C2
Samovodene 114 C2
Samtens 35 D4
Samugheo 96 B2
San Andrea di Conza 100 C4
San Ángelo in Vado 95 D2
San Antíoco 96 A1
San António 96 B4
San Bartolomé de la Torre 82 C3
San Bartolomeo in Galdo 99 E1
San Bendetto del Tronto 98 C4
San Bendetto in Alpe 94 C2
San Bendetto Po 90 B1
San Bernadino 85 D2
San Biágio Plátani 102 B2
San Bonifácio 90 C2
San Candido-Innichen 91 D4
San Casciano in Val di Pesa 94 C2
San Cataldo 102 C2
San Cataldo 101 F3
San Cipirello 102 B3
San Clemente 75 D1
San Cosme 67 D4
San Daniele del Friuli 91 E3
San Donaci 101 F3
San Emiliano 67 E3
San Esteban de Gormaz 68 C1
San Eufémia Lamézia 101 D1
San Felice Circeo 98 B1
San Felice San Panaro 94 C4
San Ferdinando di Puglia 99 F1
San Fernando 83 D2
San Fratello 103 D3
San Gavino Monreale 96 B2
San Germano 88 C2
San Gimignano 94 B2
San Giorgio di Nogaro 91 E2
San Giorgio Iónico 101 F3
San Giovanni a Piro 100 C2
San Giovanni di Sinis 96 A2
San Giovanni-in-Croce 89 E1
San Giovanni in Fiore 101 D1
San Giovanni in Persiceto 94 C3
San Giovanni Rotondo 99 E2
San Giovanni Valdarno 94 C2
San Giuliano Terme 93 E2
San Giustino 95 D2
San Javier 81 F3
San José 81 D1
San Juán de Alicante 81 F4
San Juan del Puerto 83 D3
San Leonardo de Yagüe 68 C2
San Leonardo in Passír-a-St Leonard in Pass 90 C4
San Lorenzo Nuovo 98 A3
San Lucido 101 D1
San Luis 82 B4
San Marcello Pistoiese 94 B3
San Marco dei Cavoti 99 E1
San Marco in Lamis 99 E2
San Marcos de Ataboeira 82 B4
San Marino 95 D2
San Martín del Pedrosc 67 D1
San Martín de Unx 69 E3
San Martín de Valdeiglesias 74 A3
San Martino di Castrozza 90 C3
San Mateo 76 A4
San Michele all'Adige 90 C3
San Miguel de Bernúy 68 B1
San Miguel de las Dueñas 67 D2
San Millán de Cogolla 68 C2
San Miniato 94 B2
San Nicolò Ferrara 94 C4
San Nicolò Gerrei 57 F4
San Pancrazio Salentino 101 F3
San Pedro de Alcántare 83 F2
San Pedro del Pinatar 81 F3
San Pedro do Sul 72 C3
San Pellegrino Terme 89 D2
San Piero a Sieve 94 C2
San Pietro in Casale 94 C3
San Pietro Vernotico 101 F3
San Polo d'Enza 93 E3
San Quírico d'Orcia 97 F4
San Raphael 74 B4
San Remo 92 B2
San Roque 83 E1
San Rufo 100 C3
San Sebastián (Donostia) 69 D4
San Severino Marche 95 E1
San Severo 99 E2
San Sofia 94 C2
San Sosti 101 D2
San Stéfano di Cadore 91 D3
San Stéfano Quisquina 102 B2
San Stino di Livenza 91 D2
San Valentino alla Muta-St Valentin an der Haide 90 B4
San Vigilio-St Vigil 90 C4
San Vincente de la Barquera 68 A4
San Vincenzo 93 E1
San Vito 96 C2
San Vito al Tagliamento 91 D2
San Vito dei Normanni 101 E4
San Vito di Cadore 91 D3
San Vito lo Capo 102 B3
Sanaigmore 15 E4
Sanary 65 D2
Sancergues 55 D1
Sancerre 55 D1
Sancoins 60 A4
Sancti-Spiritus 73 D2
Sand 9 D3
Sandane 8 B4
Sandared 13 D4
Sandarne 10 C3

Sandau 34 C1
Sandbach 23 D2
Sandbank 20 B4
Sandbanks 27 E2
Sande 32 C2
Sande 8 B4
Sande 9 D2
Sandefjord 9 D1
Sandeid 8 A2
Sanden 8 C2
Sandgate 25 F1
Sandhead 20 B2
Sandhurst 25 D2
Sandiway 22 C3
Sandl 87 D4
Sandnäset 4 A1
Sandnes 8 A1
Sandnessjøen 3 E4
Sandon 23 D2
Sándorfalva 106 B2
Sandown 27 F2
Sandrigo 90 C2
Sandringham 25 E4
Sandstad 2 C2
Sandstedt 32 C2
Sånduleni 109 D2
Sandvatn 8 B1
Sandvig 13 E1
Sandvik 13 F3
Sandvika 9 D2
Sandvika 3 E2
Sandvika 10 B3
Sandvikvåg 8 A3
Sandwich 25 F2
Sandwick 19 F3
Sandy 23 F1
Sangerhausen 38 B2
Sanginkylä 5 E3
Sangis 5 D4
Sangrí 121 D3
Sangüesa 69 E3
Sanguinet 62 B4
Sani 118 A2
Sanitz 34 C3
Sankt-Micaelisdonn 33 D3
Sanlúcar de Barrameda 83 D2
Sanlúcar la Mayor 83 E3
Sanluri 96 B2
Sannazzaro de Burgandi 88 C1
Sannicandro di Bari 101 D4
Sannicandro Garganico 99 E2
Sanquhar 20 C3
Sansepolcro 95 D2
Sanski Most 110 C4
Sant'Andrea Fríus 96 B2
Sant Celoni 71 D3
Sant Elia a Pianist 99 D2
Sant Feliu de Guixols 71 E3
Sant Hilari Sacalm 71 D3
Sant Julià de Lória 70 C4
Sant Pere Pescador 71 E3
Sant Pol de Mar 71 D2
Sant Quirze de Besora 71 D3
Sant Sadurni d'Anoiu 70 C2
Sant 108 B3
Santa Bárbara 82 C4
Santa Caterina di Pittinuri 96 A2
Santa Caterina Valfurva 89 E3
Santa Caterina Villarmosa 102 C2
Santa Cesarea Terme 101 F3
Santa Clara-a-Velha 48 B3
Santa Coloma de Farnés 71 D3
Santa Coloma de Queralt 70 C2
Santa Comba 66 B3
Santa Comba Dão 72 B2
Santa Cristina d'Aro 71 D3
Santa Cristina-St Christina 90 C3
Santa Croce di Magliano 99 E2
Santa Cruz de Moya 75 E2
Santa Donà di Piave 91 D2
Santa Elena 80 B4
Santa Eufemia 79 F2
Santa Eulalia 75 E3
Santa Eulária d'es Riú 76 C2
Santafé 80 B2
Santa Galdana 77 F4
Sant'Ágata di Militello 103 D3
Santa Joan de la Abadesses 71 D3
Santa Lucia del Mela 103 E3
Santa Margherita 96 B1
Santa Margherita di Belice 102 B3
Santa Margherita Ligure 92 C3
Santa María 77 D3
Santa María Cápua Vetere 100 A4
Santa María de Huerta 69 D1
Santa María del Campo 68 B4
Santa María del Páramo 67 E2
Santa María la Real de Nieva 74 A4
Santa María Maggiore 88 C3
Santa María Navarrese 96 C2
Santa Maria-Siche 57 E2
Santa Marinella 97 F2
Santa Marta 79 D2
Santa da Serra 82 B3
Santander 68 B4
Sant'Angelo Lodigiano 89 D1
Santa Ninfa 102 B3
Santanyí 77 D3
Santa Olalla del Cala 83 E4
Santa Pola 81 F3
Santarcangelo in Colle 101 D4
Santarcángelo di Romagna 95 D3
Santarém 78 B3
Santa Severa 57 F4
Santa Severa 98 A2
Santa Susanna 71 D3
Santa Teresa di Riva 103 E3
Santa Teresa Gallura 96 B4
Santed 75 E4
Santena 88 B1
Santesteban 69 D4
Santhià 88 B2

Santiago de Compostela 66 B3
Santiago de la Ribera 81 F3
Santiago do Cacém 78 B1
Santillana del Mar 68 B4
Santisteban del Puerto 80 C3
Santo Domingo de la Calzada 68 C3
Santo Domingo de Silos 68 B2
Santok 35 F1
Santon 20 B1
Santoña 68 B4
Santo Stefano di Comastra 103 D3
Santo Tirso 72 B4
Santuario d'Oropa 88 B2
Santu Lussúrgiu 96 B2
Santurtzi 68 C4
Sanxenxo 66 B2
São Bartolomeu de Messines 82 B3
São Brás de Alportel 82 B3
São Domingos 78 B1
São Gregório 66 B2
São João da Madeira 72 B3
São João de Pesqueira 72 C3
São Marcos da Serra 82 B3
São Martinho do Porto 78 A4
São Pedro de Muel 72 A1
Sápai 118 C3
Sapareva Banya 118 A4
Šapinta 107 E4
Sápoca 109 D1
Sappada 91 D3
Sappee 5 C2
Sappemeer 29 F4
Sapri 100 C2
Saqués 69 F3
Sarafovo 115 E1
Säräisniemi 5 F3
Saraiu 115 E4
Sarajevo 111 E4
Saramon 63 D2
Sáránd 107 D3
Saranda 116 C2
Sarantsi 114 B1
Sarasáu 105 B4
Sárátel 108 B3
Sărăteni 108 C2
Saray 119 E4
Sarbinowo 39 E4
Sarbinowo 35 F4
Sárbogárd 106 B2
Sárdara 96 B2
S'Arenal 77 D3
Sárengrad 112 B4
Sarentino-Sarntal 90 C4
Sárgans 85 D3
Sári 106 B3
Sarichioi 115 F4
Sarighiol de Deal 115 F4
Sariköy 119 E4
Sarinasuf 115 F4
Sariñena 70 A3
Sarkadkeresztúr 106 C3
Sarkeresztúr 70 C2
Šarkiärvi 5 F1
Šárkilahti 7 D2
Šárkilahti 7 E3
Sárkisalmi 7 E3
Sárkisalo (Finby) 6 B1
Šarköy 119 E3
Sarlat-la-Canéda 59 D1
Sármásag 107 E3
Sármasu 108 B2
Sarmizegetusa 107 E1
Sârna 9 E4
Sarnaheden 9 E4
Sarnaheden 9 E4
Sarnano 98 C4
Sarnen 84 C2
Sárnico 89 D2
Sarno 100 B3
Šaro 12 C3
Saronno 88 C2
Sárospatek 107 D4
Saroşu pe Tîrnave 108 B2
Sarovce 105 E4
Sarpsborg 9 D2
Sarracín 68 B2
Sarralbe 56 C4
Sarre 25 F2
Sarrebourg 56 C4
Sarreguemines 56 C4
Sárrétudvari 106 C3
Sarre-Union 56 C4
Sarria 66 C3
Sarrion 72 F3
Sarron 62 C2
Sarroch 96 B1
Sarron 62 C2
Sársina 95 D2
Sarstedt 37 E3
Sártène 57 E1
Sárti 118 B2
Sartilly 53 D4
Sárvár 105 D2
Sarvijoki 4 C1
Sarvikumpu 7 E4
Sarzana 93 D3
Sarzeau 52 C2
Sasca Montană 113 D4
Saschiz 108 B2
Săscìori 107 E1
Sascut 105 D2
Säsd 105 E2
Sasi Giovanni Suérgiu 96 B3
Sassari 96 B2
Sassenage 61 D2
Sassenberg 29 E4
Sassenheim 29 D3
Sassnitz 35 D4
Sassoferrato 95 D1
Sasso Marconi 93 F3

Sassuolo 94 C3
Satão 72 C3
Sätenäs 9 E1
Sater 10 B3
Sátoraljaújhely 107 D4
Satovcha 118 B4
Satow 34 C3
Satrup 33 D4
Satulung 107 E3
Satu Mare 107 E4
Saturn 115 F3
Saucats 58 B1
Sauda 8 B2
Sauerlach 46 C2
Saugues 60 B1
Saujon 58 B3
Saukkola 6 C1
Saukonkyla 5 D1
Sauland 8 C2
Saulgau 45 D2
Saulieu 55 E1
Sault 65 D3
Saulx 56 B2
Saulxures 56 C3
Saumur 53 F1
Saunby 23 E3
Saundersfoot 26 C4
Saunton 26 C2
Sauve 64 B3
Sauveterre-de-Béarn 62 B2
Sauveterre-de-Guyenne 58 C1
Sauvo 6 B1
Sauxillanges 60 A2
Sauze d'Oulx 88 A1
Sauzé-Vaussais 58 C3
Sauzon 52 B2
Sävar 4 C2
Savastepe 119 E1
Savelletri 101 E4
Savelli 101 D1
Säveni 52 C2
Săveni 109 D4
Saverdun 63 E2
Savernake 27 E3
Saverne 56 C4
Savigliano 92 B4
Savignac-les-Eglises 59 D2
Savignano Irpino 99 E1
Savignano sul Rubicone 95 D3
Savigny-sur-Braye 54 A2
Savines-le-Lac 65 E4
Săvîrşin 107 D1
Savitaipale 7 E2
Šavnik 111 E1
Savognin 85 D2
Savona 92 C3
Savonlinna 7 F3
Savonranta 7 F3
Sävsjö 13 E3
Savudrija 91 E2
Sawbridgeworth 25 E3
Sawston 25 E3
Saxilby 23 E3
Saxmundham 25 F3
Saxnäs 3 F3
Saxthorpe 25 F3
Säynätsalo 5 E4
Säyneinen 7 E1
Scaër 52 B3
Scafa 98 C3
Scalasaig 15 E4
Scalby 21 F2
Scalea 100 C2
Scalloway 19 F3
Scandiano 94 C3
Scanno 98 C2
Scansano 97 E3
Scanzano Iónico 101 D4
Scarborough 21 F2
Scardovari 95 D4
Scarinish 18 A1
Scărişoara 107 E2
Scarriff 16 C3
Scartaglen 14 B3
Scarva 15 D2
Ščepan Polje 111 E2
Schaan 85 D3
Schachendorf 87 F2
Schaffhausen 85 C4
Schafstädt 38 C2
Schaftlarn 46 C2
Schagen 29 D3
Scharbeutz 34 B3
Schärding 86 A1
Scharnitz 85 F3
Scharnstein 86 C3
Scharzfeld 42 C1
Scheer 45 D2
Scheessel 33 D2
Scheggia 95 D1
Scheibbs 87 D3
Scheifling 86 C2
Scheinfeld 41 E1
Schenefeld 33 D3
Scherfede 37 D2
Schermbeck 36 B2
Schesslitz 42 B2
Scheveningen 28 C2
Scheyern 46 C1
Schieder 37 D2
Schiermonnikoog 29 E4
Schiersee 46 C1
Schifferstadt 45 D2
Schilpario 89 D3
Schiltach 44 C2
Schio 90 C2
Schirnding 42 C2
Schitu Goleşti 114 C4
Schkeuditz 38 C2
Schladming 86 C2
Schlangenbad 40 C2

Schleching ....47....D1
Schleiden ....40....A3
Schleiz ....42....C3
Schleswig ....33....D4
Schleusingen ....42....B3
Schlieben ....39....D2
Schliersee ....46....C3
Schlitz ....41....D3
Schlotheim ....38....B1
Schluchsee ....44....C1
Schlüchtern ....41....D3
Schlüsselfeld ....42....B2
Schlutup ....34....B3
Schmalkalden ....41....E3
Schmallenberg ....36....C1
Schmidmühlen ....46....C4
Schmilka ....43....E4
Schmölln ....42....C4
Schmölln ....35....E2
Schnackenburg ....34....C2
Schnaittenbach ....42....C1
Schneeberg ....43....D3
Schneverdingen ....33....D2
Schöder ....86....C2
Schönau ....44....C1
Schönbeck ....35....D2
Schönberg ....33....E4
Schönberg ....47....E3
Schönberg ....85....F3
Schönberg ....33....E3
Schönberg ....42....C2
Schönberger-Strand ...33....E4
Schönebeck ....34....C2
Schönebeck ....38....C3
Schönecken ....40....A2
Schongau ....46....B1
Schönhagen ....33....E4
Schöningen ....38....B3
Schönthal ....43....D1
Schönwald ....44....C2
Schönwalde ....34....B3
Schönwalde ....39....D4
Schoondijke ....28....C1
Schoonebeek ....29....F3
Schoonhoven ....29....D2
Schoonoord ....29....F3
Schopfheim ....44....B1
Schöppenstedt ....38....B3
Schoppernau ....85....E3
Schorndorf ....45....D3
Schotten ....41....D3
Schramberg ....44....C2
Schrems ....87....D4
Schriesheim ....40....C1
Schrobenhausen ....46....C3
Schröken ....85....E3
Schruns ....85....D3
Schull ....16....B1
Schüpfheim ....84....B2
Schüttorf ....36....B3
Schwaan ....34....C3
Schwabach ....46....B4
Schwabhausen ....46....C2
Schwäbisch Gmünd ...45....E3
Schwäbisch Hall ....45....D4
Schwabmünchen ....46....B2
Schwaigern ....45....D4
Schwalenberg ....37....D2
Schwalmstadt-Ziegenhain ...41....D3
Schwanden ....85....D2
Schwandorf ....46....C4
Schwanebeck ....38....B3
Schwanenstadt ....86....C3
Schwanewede ....32....C2
Schwaney ....37....D2
Schwarmstedt ....36....D4
Schwarzach ....86....B2
Schwarzenbach ....42....C2
Schwarzenbek ....33....E2
Schwarzenberg ....43....D3
Schwarzsee ....84....B2
Schwaz ....85....F3
Schwechat ....87....F3
Schwedt ....35....E2
Schweich ....40....A2
Schweinfurt ....41....E2
Schwelm ....36....B1
Schwenningen ....44....C2
Schwerin ....34....B2
Schwerte ....36....B2
Schwetzingen ....44....C4
Schwyz ....84....C3
Sciacca ....102....B2
Scicli ....103....D1
Scilla ....103....E4
Scînteia ....109....E3
Scole ....25....F3
Sconser ....18....B2
Scopwick ....23....E2
Scoreiu ....108....B1
Scortaru Vechi ....109....E1
Scorțeni ....109....D2
Scorze ....91....D2
Scotch Corner ....21....E2
Scourie ....18....C4
Scrabster ....19....D4
Scramoge ....16....C4
Scribbagh ....14....C2
Scunthorpe ....23....E3
Scuol-Schuls ....85....E3
Seaford ....25....E1
Seaham Harbour ....21....E2
Sea Houses ....21....E3
Seamer ....21....F1
Sea Palling ....25....F4
Seascale ....20....C2
Seatoller ....20....C2
Seaton ....27....D2
Seaton Carew ....21....E2
Sebbersund ....12....B3
Sebečevo ....112....C2
Sebeș ....107....E1

Şebiş ....107....D2
Sebnitz ....43....E4
Sebrenica ....112....B3
Seč ....43....E1
Sečanj ....106....C1
Sečašeni ....113....D4
Seckau ....87....D2
Seclin ....50....B4
Secondigny ....58....C4
Secuieni ....109....D2
Sedan ....51....D2
Sedbergh ....21....D1
Seddülbahir ....119....D2
Séderon ....65....D3
Sedgefield ....21....E2
Sédico ....91....D3
Sédilo ....96....B3
Sédini ....96....B3
Sedlčany ....43....F2
Sedlice ....43....E1
Sedrun ....84....C2
Seeboden ....86....C1
Seebruck ....47....D2
Seefeld ....85....F3
Seehausen ....38....B3
Seehausen ....34....C1
Seehausen ....39....D3
Seelbach ....44....C2
Seelow ....39....E4
Seend ....27....E3
Seeon ....47....D2
Sées ....53....F4
Seesen ....37....D2
Seeshaupt ....46....C2
Seewalchen ....86....C3
Seewiesen ....87....D2
Segarcea ....113....F3
Segelstad bru ....9....D4
Segerstad ....13....F2
Seglinge ....11....D2
Segman ....9....E1
Segonzac ....58....C2
Segorbe ....75....F2
Segovia ....74....B4
Segré ....53....E2
Segura ....73....D1
Segura ....79....D1
Segura de León ....79....D1
Segura de los Baños ..75....E4
Sehnde ....37....E3
Seia ....72....C2
Seica Mare ....108....B1
Seiches ....53....E2
Seifhennersdorf ....43....F4
Seilhac ....59....E2
Seinäjoki ....5....D1
Seini ....107....E4
Seitenstetten ....87....D3
Sejs ....12....B2
Selanovtsi ....114....B2
Selb ....42....C2
Selbu ....3....D2
Selby ....23....E4
Selce ....104....A1
Selenicë ....116....C2
Selent ....33....E3
Sélestat ....57....D3
Seleuş ....107....D2
Selište ....113....D3
Selje ....2....A1
Seljestad ....8....B2
Seljord ....8....C2
Selkirk ....21....D3
Sellasí ....120....C2
Selles ....54....B1
Sellía ....122....A3
Sellières ....61....D4
Sellin ....35....D4
Sellye ....105....D1
Selmsdorf ....34....B3
Selnes ....3....C2
Selongey ....56....A2
Selsey ....25....D1
Selsingen ....33....D2
Seltz ....57....D4
Selva-Wolkenstein ....90....C3
Selvik ....8....A4
Selvino ....89....D2
Sem ....9....D2
Semblana ....82....B3
Semily ....43....F3
Semizovac ....111....E2
Semmering ....87....E2
Semur-en-Auxois .....55....E2
Sénas ....64....C3
Senden ....36....B2
Sendenhorst ....36....C2
Sendreni ....109....E1
Senec ....105....D4
Senftenberg ....39....E2
Senigállia ....95....E2
Senise ....101....D3
Senj ....110....B4
Senlis ....50....B1
Sennecey-le-Grand ...60....C4
Sennelager ....36....C2
Sennen ....26....B1
Sennestadt ....36....C3
Sennik ....114....C1
Sénnori ....96....B3
Sennybridge ....27....D4
Senokos ....115....E2
Senonches ....54....B3
Senones ....56....C3
Senorbi ....96....B3
Senožeče ....104....A1
Sens ....55....D3
Senta ....106....B1
Sentilj ....104....B3
Septemvri ....118....B4
Sept-Saulx ....51....D1
Sepúlveda ....68....B1

Sequeros ....73....E2
Seraing ....31....E3
Seravezza ....93....C2
Sercaia ....108....C1
Sered' ....105....D4
Seregélyes ....105....E3
Seregno ....89....D2
Serém ....72....B2
Sérent ....52....C2
Sérfaus ....85....E2
Seriate ....89....D2
Sérifos ....121....E2
Sermaize-les-Bains ...55....F4
Sermide ....94....C4
Serón ....81....D2
Seròs ....70....B2
Serpa ....78....C1
Serracapriola ....99....E2
Serradifalco ....102....C2
Sérrai ....118....A3
Serra San Bruno ....103....F4
Serres ....65....D4
Serrières ....60....C2
Sersale ....101....D1
Sertã ....72....B1
Sérvia ....117....E2
Serviana ....117....D1
Servigliano ....98....C4
Sesimbra ....78....A2
Seskinore ....15....D2
Sesklon ....117....F1
Sesma ....69....D3
Sessa Aurunca ....98....C1
Šestanovac ....110....C2
Sesto Calende ....88....C2
Sesto Fiorentino ......94....C2
Sestola ....94....C3
Sesto-Sexten ....91....D4
Sestriere ....88....A1
Sestri Levante ....93....C3
Sestroretsk ....7....F1
Sesvete ....104....C1
Setchey ....25....E4
Sète ....64....B2
Seter ....3....D1
Settebagni ....98....B2
Settimo Torinese ......88....B1
Settle ....21....D1
Setúbal ....78....A2
Seui ....96....B2
Seulo ....96....B2
Seurre ....56....A1
Sevaster ....116....C2
Sevenoaks ....25....E2
Sever ....72....B3
Sévérac-le-Château ...64....A4
Severin ....34....C2
Sevilla ....83....D3
Sevilla de la Jara ......79....F4
Sevnica ....104....B2
Sevojne ....112....B3
Sevrier ....61....D3
Seyches ....62....C4
Seyda ....39....D3
Seymen ....119....F3
Seyne ....65....E4
Seyssel ....61....D3
Sézanne ....55....D4
Sézze ....104....A1
Sfáka ....122....C3
Sfîntu Gheorghe ......115....D3
Sforzacosta ....95....E1
Shabla ....115....F2
Shaftesbury ....27....E2
Shaldon ....27....D1
Shanagolden ....16....B2
Shandon ....20....B4
Shanklin ....27....F2
Shannon Airport ......16....B2
Shannonbridge ....16....C3
Shap ....21....D2
Shardlow ....23....E2
Sharnevo ....114....C1
Shawbury ....22....C2
Sheerness ....25....E2
Sheffield ....23....D3
Shefford ....25....D3
Sheigra ....18....C4
Shëngjin ....116....C4
Shënmëri ....116....C4
Shepot ....108....C4
Shepshed ....23....E2
Shepton Mallet ....27....E3
Sherborne ....27....E2
Sherburn ....21....F1
Shercock ....15....D1
Sheriff Hutton ....21....E1
Sheringham ....25....F4
Shiel Bridge ....18....C2
Shieldaig ....18....B3
Shifnal ....23....D2
Shijak ....116....C3
Shildon ....21....E2
Shillelagh ....16....C3
Shinrone ....16....C3
Shipdham ....25....E4
Shipka ....114....C1
Shipkovo ....114....B1
Shipley ....23....D4
Shipston-on-Stour ...27....E4
Shiroka Lŭka ....118....B4
Shivatsevo ....115....D1
Shkodër ....104....A1
Shkorpilovtsi ....115....E1
Shoeburyness ....25....E2
Shoreham-by-Sea ....25....D1
Shotley ....25....F3
Shotts ....20....C4
Shrewsbury ....22....C2

Shrewton ....27....E3
Shrivenham ....27....E3
Shrule ....16....B4
Shugborough ....23....D2
Shumen ....115....D2
Siátista ....117....D2
Sibari ....101....D2
Sinnicolau Mare ....106....C2
Sibbo (Sipoo) ....7....D1
Šibenik ....110....B2
Siberstedt ....33....D4
Sibiu ....108....B1
Sibsey ....23....F2
Sícevci ....110....C3
Sicevo ....113....D2
Šid ....112....B4
Sidárion ....116....C1
Sideby (Siipyy) ....6....A3
Sidensjö ....4....B2
Siderno ....103....F4
Sidford ....27....D2
Sidmouth ....27....D2
Sidzburg ....40....B3
Siegen ....40....C4
Siegenburg ....46....C3
Sieggraben ....87....E3
Siegsdorf ....47....D2
Siekierki ....35....E1
Siena ....94....C1
Sieniawka ....43....F4
Sierck ....51....F2
Sierentz ....57....D2
Sierning ....86....C3
Sierre ....84....B1
Sieu ....108....B3
Sievi ....5....E2
Sigean ....64....A2
Siggjarvåg ....8....A2
Sighetul Marmației ..108....B4
Sighișoara ....108....B2
Sigmaringen ....45....D2
Signy-l'Abbaye ....51....D2
Sigri ....119....D1
Sigtuna ....10....C2
Sigüeiro ....66....B3
Sigüenza ....74....C4
Siikainen ....6....B3
Siikajoki ....5....E3
Siilinjärvi ....7....D4
Siipy (Sideby) ....6....A3
Siivikko ....5....F4
Sijarinska Banja ......113....D1
Sikéa ....121....D2
Sikéa ....118....B2
Sikéa ....122....C3
Sikeå ....4....C2
Sikiá ....120....B4
Sikiá ....118....B3
Sikinos ....121....F2
Siklós ....105....E1
Sikoúrion ....117....E1
Siksjön ....4....B4
Silandro-Schlanders ..90....B4
Silánus ....96....B3
Silba ....106....B1
Sileby ....23....E2
Silifke ....119....F3
Siligo ....96....B3
Silistra ....115....E3
Silivri ....119....F3
Siljan ....8....C2
Siljansnäs ....10....A3
Silkeborg ....12....B2
Silleda ....66....B3
Sillé-le-Guillaume ....53....F3
Sillian ....86....A1
Silloth ....20....C2
Šilo ....104....A1
Sils ....71....D3
Sils-Maria ....85....D2
Silvaplana ....85....D2
Silverdalen ....13....E3
Silvermines ....16....C2
Silverstone ....27....F4
Silves ....82....B3
Silvi Marina ....99....D3
Silz ....85....E3
Símancas ....68....A1
Șimand ....106....C2
Simaság ....105....D3
Simaxis ....96....B2
Simbach ....47....D3
Simbach ....47....D2
Simeria ....107....E1
Simitli ....117....F4
Șimleu Silvaniei ......107....E3
Simmerath ....40....A3
Simmerberg ....45....E1
Simmern ....40....B2
Simo ....5....E4
Simonsbath ....26....C2
Simontornya ....105....E3
Símpele ....7....E3
Simplon Dorf ....84....B1
Simrishamn ....13....D1
Sinaia ....108....C1
Sinalunga ....94....C1
Sinanaj ....116....C2
Sînca Nouă ....108....C1
Sînca Veche ....108....C1
Sindal ....12....B4
Sindelfingen ....45....D3
Sindirgi ....119....F1
Sindominic ....108....C2
Sinekçi ....119....E2
Sinekli ....119....F2
Sinemorets ....119....F1
Sines ....78....A1
Sineşti ....109....D3
Sineşti ....109....D2
Sîngeorgiu de Pădure ..108....B2
Sîngeorz-Băi ....108....B3

Singleton ....25....D1
Singsås ....3....D1
Siniscola ....96....C3
Sinj ....110....C2
Sînmartin ....107....D3
Sinnes ....8....B1
Sinnicolau Mare ....106....C2
Sinopoli ....103....E4
Sinsheim ....45....D4
Sînta Maria ....109....E4
Sîntamaria Orlea .....107....E1
Sintereag ....108....B3
Sîntioana ....108....B3
Sintra ....78....A3
Sinzig ....40....B3
Siófok ....105....E3
Sion ....84....B1
Sion Mills ....15....D2
Siorac-en-Périgord ..59....D1
Sip ....113....E4
Sipoo (Sibbo) ....7....D1
Şipote ....109....D3
Sira ....8....B1
Siracusa ....103....C2
Siret ....108....C4
Síria ....107....D2
Sirig ....106....B1
Siriu ....109....D1
Sirmione ....90....B2
Sirnach ....84....C3
Sirok ....106....B4
Sirolo ....95....E2
Sisak ....104....C1
Sisante ....75....D1
Sissach ....84....B3
Sistarovät ....107....D1
Sisteron ....65....D3
Sistiana ....91....E2
Sitges ....70....C2
Sitía ....122....C3
Sittard ....31....E3
Sittensen ....33....D2
Sittingbourne ....25....E2
Siurua ....5....E4
Siusi ....90....C3
Sivac ....106....B1
Sivakkavaara ....7....E4
Siverskiy ....7....F1
Siviri ....118....A2
Six-Fours ....65....D2
Six Hills ....23....E2
Six Mile Bottom ......25....E3
Sixmilebridge ....16....C2
Sizun ....52....A3
Sjaellands Odde ......12....C2
Sjenica ....112....B2
Sjoa ....9....D4
Sjøåsen ....3....D3
Sjöbo ....13....D1
Sjøholt ....3....B1
Sjørup ....12....B3
Sjötorp ....9....F1
Sjoutnäset ....3....F3
Sjuntorp ....12....C4
Sjusjøen ....9....D4
Skælskør ....12....C1
Skærbæk ....12....A1
Skafidhá ....120....B3
Skaftung ....6....A3
Skagen ....12....C4
Skála ....120....C2
Skála ....121....D4
Skála ....120....B3
Skála Eressou ....119....D1
Skála Leptokariá .....117....E2
Skála Litókhoran .....117....E2
Skálan ....3....E1
Skála Oropoú ....121....D2
Skalitsa ....115....D1
Skalmoldalen ....3....F4
Skaloti ....122....A3
Skaloti ....118....B3
Skals ....12....B3
Skålsjön ....10....B3
Skalstugan ....3....E2
Skandaborg ....12....B2
Skandháli ....118....C1
Skånevik ....8....A2
Skänninge ....13....E4
Skanör ....13....D1
Skanses ....3....D2
Skansholm ....4....A3
Skara ....13....D4
Skåre ....12....C4
Skärhamn ....12....C4
Skarinou ....122....C3
Skärplinge ....10....C3
Skårup ....12....B1
Skarvsjö ....4....A3
Skattungbyn ....10....A3
Skave ....12....B3
Skeabost Bridge .....18....B3
Skebobruk ....10....C2
Skedsmokorset ......10....C1
Skee ....12....B4
Skegness ....25....F2
Skei ....8....A1
Skei ....3....C1
Skei ....3....D1
Skeie ....112....B4
Skela ....112....B4
Skellefteå ....4....C3
Skellefthamn ....4....C3
Skelleftestrand ....4....C3
Skelmorlie ....20....B4
Skene ....13....D3
Skenfrith ....27....D4
Skerries ....17....E4
Ski ....9....D2
Skiathos ....118....A1
Skibbereen ....16....B1
Skibby ....12....C2

Skidra ....117....E3
Skien ....8....C2
Skillingaryd ....13....D3
Skillinge ....13....D1
Skinnskatteberg ......10....B2
Skipness ....15....E4
Skipsea ....21....F1
Skipton ....21....D1
Skiptvet ....9....D2
Skíros ....121....D3
Skive ....12....B3
Skivarne ....12....B4
Skivjane ....112....C1
Skjærhalden ....9....D1
Skjeberg ....9....D1
Skjelten ....2....B1
Skjern ....12....A2
Skjold ....8....A2
Skjolden ....8....C4
Skjønhaug ....9....D2
Skodje ....2....B1
Skødstrup ....12....B2
Škofja Loka ....104....A2
Škofljica ....104....A2
Skog ....10....B3
Skogn ....3....D2
Skogstorp ....10....B1
Sköldinge ....10....B1
Skollenberg ....8....C2
Sköllersta ....10....B1
Skomdal ....8....C1
Skópelos ....118....B1
Skopi ....122....C3
Skopje ....117....D4
Skorovatn ....3....E3
Skørping ....12....B3
Skotterud ....9....E2
Skoúra ....120....C2
Skoútari ....118....A3
Skovballe ....12....B1
Skövde ....13....D4
Skrad ....104....B1
Skradin ....110....B2
Skreia ....9....D3
Skudeneshavn ....8....A2
Skultorp ....13....D4
Skultuna ....10....B2
Skurup ....13....D1
Skutskär ....10....C3
Skwierzyna ....35....F1
Skyttmon ....3....F2
Sládkovičovo ....105....D4
Slagelse ....12....C1
Slagnäs ....4....B3
Slaidburn ....21....D1
Slane ....17....E4
Slánic ....114....C4
Slănic Moldova ....109....D2
Slano ....111....D1
Slaný ....43....E3
Slatina ....104....C2
Slatina ....112....C3
Slatina ....114....B3
Slatina de Mureș .....107....D2
Slatina Timiş ....113....D4
Slatina ....117....D4
Slåttevik ....8....A2
Slattum ....9....D2
Slavešti ....114....C3
Slavonska Požega ...105....D2
Slavonski Brod ....111....D4
Slavyanovo ....114....C2
Slawoborze ....35....F3
Sleaford ....23....E2
Sledmere ....21....F1
Sleights ....21....F2
Sliedrecht ....29....D2
Sligachan ....18....B2
Sligo ....14....C1
Slimbridge ....27....E3
Slimnic ....108....B1
Slite ....11....F1
Sliven ....115....D1
Slivnitsa ....113....E1
Slivo Pole ....115....D3
Slobozia ....114....C2
Slobozia Mîndra .....114....B2
Slobozia Moara ......114....C2
Słońsk ....35....F1
Sloten ....29....E3
Slough ....25....D2
Slovac ....112....B3
Slovenj Gradec ......104....B2
Slovenska Bistrica ...104....B2
Slovenské Ďarmoty ...106....A4
Slovenské Konjice ...104....B2
Slovenské Nové Mesto ...107....D4
Slubice ....39....E3
Sluderno-Schluderns ..90....B4
Sluis ....28....C1
Sluis ....28....C1
Slŭnchev Bryag ......115....E1
Slunj ....104....B1
Smålandsstenar ......13....D3
Smålasen ....3....D3
Směděc ....47....E3
Smederevo ....112....C4
Smederevska-Palanka ...112....C4
Smedjebacken ....10....B2
Smeeni ....115....D4
Smethwick ....29....E3
Smilde ....29....E3
Smirnitsa ....114....C2
Smîrdioasa ....114....C2
Smithborough ....15....D1
Smögen ....12....C4
Smolianovtsi ....113....E2
Smolyan ....118....B4
Smørhamn ....2....A1
Smyadovo ....115....D1
Smygehamn ....13....D1

Snagov
Ştefan cel Mare

Snagov 115 D4
Snainton 21 F1
Snape 25 F3
Snaptun 12 B2
Snåsa 3 E3
Snedsted 12 A3
Sneek 29 E4
Sneem 16 A1
Snettisham 25 E4
Snøde 12 B1
Snogebæk 13 E1
Soave 90 C2
Soběslav 43 F1
Sobotka 43 F3
Sobra 111 D1
Sobral de Mònte Agraço 78 A3
Søby 12 B1
Sočanica 112 C2
Socodor 106 C2
Socovos 81 D4
Söderåkra 13 F2
Söderbärke 10 B2
Söderfors 10 C3
Söderhamn 10 C4
Söderköping 13 F4
Södertälje 10 C1
Södra Vi 13 E4
Sodražica 104 A2
Sødring 12 B3
Soest 36 C2
Sœst 29 D2
Soestdijk 29 D2
Sofádhes 117 E1
Sofia 113 E1
Sofikón 121 D3
Sögel 32 B1
Sogge bru 2 B1
Sogndal 8 B4
Søgne 8 B1
Söğütalan 119 F2
Soham 25 E3
Soignies 30 C3
Şoimuş 107 E1
Soini 5 E1
Soissons 50 C2
Sokhós 118 A3
Sokna 9 D3
Sokndalstrand 8 A1
Soko Banja 113 D2
Sokolac 111 E2
Sokolov 43 D2
Sokolovo 115 E2
Sola 8 A2
Solares 68 B4
Solberg 4 A2
Solca 108 C4
Solda-Sulden 90 B3
Sölden 85 F2
Soldeu 70 C4
Solenzara 57 F2
Soleşti 109 E3
Solevåg 2 B1
Solf (Sulva) 4 C1
Solfonn 8 B2
Solheim 8 A4
Solihull 23 D1
Solin 110 C2
Solingen 36 B1
Söll 86 A2
Sollebrun 13 D4
Sollefteå 4 A1
Sollenau 87 E3
Sollentuna 10 C1
Sóller 77 D3
Sollerön 10 A3
Søllested 12 C1
Solliès-Pont 65 E2
Solosancho 73 F2
Solothurn 84 B3
Solrød Strand 12 C1
Sølsnes 2 B1
Solsona 70 C3
Solsvik 8 A3
Solt 105 E3
Soltau 33 D1
Soltvadkert 106 B2
Solund 8 A4
Solva 26 B4
Solvay 94 B1
Sölvesborg 13 E2
Solvorn 8 B4
Solynieve 80 B2
Soma 119 E1
Sombernon 55 F1
Sombor 105 E1
Şomcuta Mare 107 E3
Somerniemi 6 C1
Somero 6 C1
Somersham 23 F1
Somerton 27 D2
Someş-Odorhei 107 E3
Sommatino 102 C2
Sommen 13 E4
Sömmerda 38 B1
Sommesous 55 E4
Sommières 64 B3
Somogyszob 105 D2
Somosierra 74 B4
Somova 109 F1
Somovit 114 B2
Sonceboz 84 B3
Soncillo 68 B3
Soncino 89 D2
Sondalo 90 B3
Søndeled 8 C1
Sønderborg 12 B1
Sønderby 12 A2
Sønder Dråby 12 A3
Sønder Felding 12 A2
Sønderho 12 A1
Sønder Omme 12 A2
Sondershausen 38 B2
Søndersø 12 B1
Sønderup 12 B3
Søndervig 12 A2
Søndervika 3 D1
Sondrio 89 D3
Sonkajärvi 5 F2
Sonneberg 42 B3
Sonogno 84 C1
Sonsbeck 36 A2
Sonseca 74 B2
Sonta 105 E1
Sonthofen 45 E1
Sontra 41 E4
Sopeira 70 B3
Sopoćani 112 C2
Sopot 112 C4
Sopot 114 B1
Sopron 104 C4
Sora 98 C2
Soragna 93 E4
Söråker 4 A1
Sorbas 81 D2
Sorbie 20 B2
Sore 62 B4
Söréd 105 E3
Soresina 89 D1
Sórgono 96 B2
Sørgutvik 3 E4
Soria 69 D1
Soriano nel Cimino 98 A3
Sorisdale 18 B1
Sørli 3 E3
Sorø 12 C1
Soroki 109 E4
Sorrento 100 B3
Sorsele 4 A4
Sörsjön 9 E4
Sorso 96 B3
Sort 70 B4
Sortavala 7 F3
Sortillo de la Adradá 74 A3
Sortino 103 D2
Sørumsand 9 D2
Sörup 33 D4
Sörvattnet 9 E4
Soschiz 108 C2
Sösdala 13 D2
Sos del Rey Católico 69 E3
Soses 70 B2
Sosnovo 7 F2
Sospel 65 F3
Sotaseter 8 C4
Sotin 105 E1
Sotkamo 5 F3
Sotkuma 7 E4
Soto del Real 74 B4
Sotogrande 83 F1
Sotta 57 F1
Sottomarina 91 D1
Sottrum 33 D2
Sottunga 11 D2
Soúdha 122 A4
Souesmes 54 C2
Soufflenheim 57 D4
Souflíon 119 D3
Souillac 59 E1
Souilly 51 E1
Soulac 58 B2
Soulópoulon 117 D1
Soultz 57 D4
Soultz 56 C2
Soumoulou 62 C2
Soúnion 121 E3
Souppes 54 C3
Sourdeval 53 E4
Soure 72 B2
Soúrpi 117 F1
Sousceyrac 59 E1
Sousel 78 C3
Soustons 62 A3
Southam 23 E1
Southampton 27 F2
Southborough 25 E1
South Brent 26 C1
Southend 15 E3
Southend-on-Sea 25 E2
Southerndown 27 D3
Southery 25 E3
South Harting 25 D1
South Kilworth 23 E1
Southminster 25 E2
South Molton 26 C2
Southport 22 C3
South Queensferry 20 C4
Southsea 27 F2
South Shields 21 E3
Southwell 23 E2
Southwold 25 F3
Souvigny 60 A4
Søvassli 2 C2
Sovata 108 C2
Soveja 109 D1
Soverato 103 F4
Soveria Mannelli 101 D1
Sövestad 13 D1
Sovetskiy 7 E2
Søvik 2 B1
Søyland 8 A1
Sozopol 115 E1
Spa 31 E2
Spaichingen 44 C2
Spakenburg 29 D2
Spalding 23 F2
Spálene Poříče 43 E2
Spalt 46 B4
Spandau 39 D4
Spangenberg 37 D1
Sparkford 27 E2
Sparreholm 100 B1
Sparta 103 E4
Spárti 120 C2
Spasovo 115 F2
Spáta 121 E3
Spean Bridge 18 C2
Spello 98 B4
Spennymoor 21 E2
Sperkhiás 120 C4
Spetchley 23 D1
Spétsai 121 D2
Spettisbury 27 E2
Speyer 44 C4
Spezzano Albanese 101 D2
Spiddal (An Spidéal) 167 D3
Spiegelau 47 E3
Spiekeroog 32 C3
Spielfeld 87 E1
Spiez 84 B2
Spijkenisse 28 C2
Spili 122 B3
Spilimbergo 91 D3
Spilsby 23 F3
Spinazzola 101 D4
Spincourt 51 E2
Spionica Donja 111 E3
Špišić Bukovica 105 D1
Spital 86 C2
Spittal 86 B1
Spittal of Glenshee 19 D2
Spitz 87 D4
Spjald 12 A2
Spjelkavik 2 B1
Spjutsund 7 D1
Split 110 C2
Splügen 85 D2
Spodsbjerg 12 B1
Spoleto 98 B3
Sporthouse Cross Roads 17 D2
Spotorno 92 C3
Spøttrup 12 A3
Sprakensehl 37 E4
Spremberg 39 E2
Spresiano 91 D2
Springe 37 D3
Sprlonga 98 C1
Sproatley 23 F4
Squinzano 101 F3
Srbobran 106 B1
Srdevići 110 C2
Sredets 118 C4
Sredishte 115 E3
Srednogortsi 118 C4
Sredska 117 D4
Sremska Kamenica 112 B4
Sremska Mitrovica 112 B4
Sremska Rača 112 B4
Sremski Karlovci 112 B4
Šrengrad 112 B4
Sringholm 20 C3
Srpa 78 C1
Srpska Crnja 106 C1
Srpski Miletić 105 E1
St Abbs 21 D4
St Aegyd 87 E3
St Affrique 63 F3
St Agnant 58 B3
St Agnes 26 B1
St Agrève 60 C1
St Aignan 54 B1
St Alban 60 A1
St Albans 25 D2
St Amand-en-Puisaye 55 D2
St Amand-les-Eaux 50 C3
St Amand Longpré 54 B2
St Amans 64 B4
St Amant-Roche-Savine 60 B2
St Ambroix 64 B3
St Amé 56 C3
St Amour 61 D4
St Andrä 87 D1
St André 54 B4
St Andreasberg 37 E2
St André-du-Cubzac 58 B1
St André-les-Alpes 65 E3
St Andrews 19 E1
St Annaparochie 29 E4
St Anthème 60 B2
St Anton 85 E3
St Antonin-Noble-Val 63 E3
St Armand-Montrond 59 F4
St Asaph 22 C3
St Athan 27 D3
St Aubin-d'Aubigné 53 D3
St Aubin-du-Cormier 53 D3
St Aubin-sur-Mer 49 D2
St Aulaye 58 C2
St Austell 26 B1
St Avold 51 F1
St Aygulf 65 E2
St Bard Maison Rouge 59 F3
St Béat 63 D1
St Beauzély 64 A3
St Bees 20 C2
St Benin 55 D1
St Benoît 59 D4
St Benoit-sur-Loire 54 C2
St Bertrand-de-Comminges 62 C2
St Blasien 44 C1
St Blazey 26 C1
St Blin 56 A3
St Bonnet 61 D1
St Bonnet de Joux 60 C4
St Bonnet-le-Chateau 60 B2
St Boswells 21 D3
St Brévin 52 C1
St Briavel's 27 D3
St Brice-en-Coglès 53 D3
St Brieuc 52 C4
St Calais 54 A2
St Carles de la Ràpita 70 B1
St Cast 52 C4
St Céré 59 E1
St Cergue 61 D4
St Cernin 59 F1
St Chamas 64 C2
St Chamond 60 C2
St Chély-d'Apcher 60 A1
St Chely-d'Aubrac 64 A4
St Chinian 64 A2
St Christoph 84 E3
St Ciers 58 B2
St Clar 63 D3
St Claud 58 C3
St Claude 61 D4
St Clears 26 C4
St Cyprien 59 D1
St Cyprien-Plage 64 A1
St Cyrus 19 E2
St Davids 26 B4
St Denis 50 B1
St Denis d'Oléron 58 A3
St Denis d'Orques 53 E3
St Didier-en-Velay 60 B2
St Dié 56 C3
St Dizier 55 F4
St Donat-sur-l'Herbasse 60 C2
St Emilion 58 C1
St Englmar 47 D3
St Etienne 60 C2
St Etienne 65 D3
St Etienne-de-Baigory 62 A2
St Etienne-de-St-Geoirs 61 D2
St Etienne-de-Tinée 65 E4
St Fargeau 55 D2
St Fillans 19 D1
St Firmin 61 D1
St Florent 54 C1
St Florent 57 F3
St Florent 53 D2
St Florentin 55 E3
St Flour 60 A1
St Francese de Formentera 76 C2
St Fulgent 53 D1
St Gallen 85 D3
St Gallen 87 D2
St Gallenkirch 85 D2
St Galmier 60 C2
St Gaudens 63 D2
St Gaultier 59 D4
St Geniez-d'Olt 64 A4
St Genis-de-Saintonge 58 B2
St Genix 61 D2
St Georgen 44 C2
St Georgen 87 D2
St Georgen 86 B3
St Georges 53 E2
St Georges-de-Didonne 58 B2
St Germain 54 C4
St Germain 59 E2
St Germain-de-Joux 61 D3
St Germain-des-Vaux 48 C2
St Germain-du-Bois 60 C4
St Germain-du-Plain 60 C4
St Germain-Laval 60 B3
St Germain-Lembron 60 A2
St Germain-l'Herm 60 B2
St Germain -Plage 48 C2
St Gervais 64 A2
St Gervais 61 E3
St Gervais-d'Auvergne 59 F3
St Géry 63 E4
St Gildas-des-Bois 52 C2
St Gilgen 86 B3
St Gilles 64 C3
St Gilles-Croix-de-Vie 58 A4
St Gingolph 84 A2
St Giron-Plage 62 A3
St Girons 63 D1
St Goar 40 B2
St Goarshausen 40 B2
St Gorgan-Main 56 B1
St Guénolé 52 A3
St Helens 22 C3
St Helier 48 C2
St Hilaire-de-Villefranche 58 B3
St Hilaire-du-Harcouët 53 D4
St Hippolyte 56 C2
St Hippolyte-du-Fort 64 C3
St Honoré 55 E1
St Hubert 31 E2
St Imier 84 A3
St Ingbert 44 B4
St Ives 26 B1
St Ives 23 F1
St Jacut 52 C4
St Jakob im Rosental 86 C1
St James 53 D3
St Jean-Brévelay 52 C2
St Jean-Cap-Ferrat 65 F3
St Jean-d'Angély 58 B3
St Jean-de-Bournay 60 C2
St Jean-de-Losne 56 A1
St Jean-de-Luz 62 A2
St Jean-de-Maurienne 61 E2
St Jean-de-Monts 52 C1
St Jean du Bruel 64 A3
St Jean du Gard 64 B3
St Jean-le-Thomas 53 D4
St Jean-Pied-de-Port 62 A2
St Jeoire 61 E3
St Joan de Labritja 76 C2
St Johann-am-Tauern 87 D2
St Johann-im-Pongau 86 B2
St Johann in Tirol 86 A2
St Johnstown 15 D2
St Jorioz 61 D3
St Josep de sa Telaia 76 C2
St Jouan-de-l'Isle 52 C3
St Jude 20 B1
St Julian-en-Genevois 61 D3
St Julien-Chapteuil 60 B1
St Julien-de-Vouvantes 53 D2
St Julien-en-Beauchêne 65 D4
St Julien-l'Ars 59 D4
St Junien 59 D3
St Just 26 B1
St Just-en-Chaussée 50 B2
St Just-en-Chevalet 60 B3
St Kevene 26 B1
St Lambrecht 86 C2
St Lary-Soulan 62 C1
St Laurent 49 D2
St Laurent 59 D3
St Laurent-en-Grandvaux 61 D4
St Laurent-et-Benon 58 B2
St Leger 55 E1
St Léonard-de-Noblat 59 E3
St Leonards 27 E2
St Leonards-on-Sea 25 E1
St Leonhard 87 D3
St Lô 49 D1
St Lorenzen 86 B1
St Louis 57 D2
St Loup-sur-Semouse 56 B2
St Luc 84 B1
St Lunaire 52 C4
St Lys 63 D2
St Macaire 62 C4
St Maclou 49 E2
St Maixent-l'Ecole 58 C4
St Malo 53 D4
St Marcellin 61 D2
St Margaret's Bay 25 F1
St Margaret's Hope 19 F1
St Märgen 44 C2
St Mars-la-Jaille 53 D2
St Martin-d'Auxigny 56 C1
St Martin-de-Londres 64 B3
St Martin-de-Ré 58 A3
St Martin-Vésubie 65 F3
St Martory 63 D2
St Marys 19 F1
St Marys Bay 25 F1
St Mathieu 59 D2
St Maurice 84 A1
St Maurice-sur-Moselle 56 C2
St Mawes 26 B1
St Mawgan 26 B1
St Maximin-la-Sainte-Baume 65 D2
St Méen 52 C3
St Merryn 26 B1
St Michael 86 C2
St Michael 87 D2
St Michael 87 E2
St Michel-de-Maurienne 61 E2
St Michel-en-Greve 52 B4
St Michel-en-l'Herm 58 B4
St Mihiel 56 A4
St Mohan's 19 E1
St Mortiz 85 D2
St Nazaire 52 C2
St Nectaire 60 A2
St Neots 23 F1
St Nicholas-de-Port 56 B4
St Nicholas-du-Pélem 52 B3
St Niklaas 30 C4
St Niklaus 84 B1
St Nikolai 86 C2
St Oedenrode 29 E1
St Olof 13 D1
St Omer 50 B4
St Oswald 87 D4
St Palais 62 B2
St Palais-sur-Mer 58 B2
St Pardoux-la-Rivière 59 D2
St Paul 65 F3
St Paul 65 E4
St Paul 87 D1
St Paul-Cap-de-Joux 63 E2
St Paul-de-Fenouillet 63 F1
St Pauliene 60 B2
St Pé 62 C2
St Péray 60 C1
St Père-en-Retz 52 C1
St Peter-Ording 32 C3
St Peter Port 48 B2
St Philbert 53 D1
St Pierre-d'Albigny 61 D2
St Pierre-de-Chartreuse 61 D2
St Pierre-de-Chignac 59 D2
St Pierre-d'Oléron 58 B3
St Pierre-Église 48 C2
St Pierre-le-Moûtier 60 A4
St Pierre-Quiberon 52 B2
St Pierre-sur-Dives 49 E1
St Pois 53 D4
St Pol-de-Léon 52 A4
St Pol-sur-Ternoise 50 B3
St Pölten 87 E3
St Pons 63 F2
St Porchaire 58 B3
St Pourcain 60 A3
St Quay-Portrieux 52 C4
St Quentin 50 C2
St Rambert-d'Albon 60 C2
St Rambert-en-Bugey 61 D3
St Raphael 65 E2
St Rémy-de-Provence 64 C3
St Renan 52 A4
St Riquier 50 A3
St Rome-de-Tarn 64 A3
St Saëns 49 F2
St Satur 55 D1
St Saulge 55 D1
St Sauvant 58 C4
St Sauveur-en-Puisaye 55 D2
St Sauveur-le-Vicomte 48 C2
St Sauveur-sur-Tinée 65 F3
St Savin 58 B2
St Savin 59 D4
St Seine-l'Abbaye 55 F2
St Sernin-sur-Rance 63 F3
St Sever 53 E4
St Sever 62 B3
St Symphorien 62 B4
St Symphorien-de Lay 60 B3
St Symphorien-d'Ozon 60 C2
St Symphorien-sur-Coise 60 C2
St Thiébault 56 B3
St Trivier-de-Courtes 60 C4
St Tropez 65 E2
St Truiden 31 D3
St Vaast-la-Hougue 48 C2
St Valentin 87 D3
St Valery-en-Caux 49 E2
St Valery-sur-Somme 50 A3
St Vallier-de-Thiey 65 E3
St Vallier-sur-Rhône 60 C2
St Vaury 59 E3
St Veit 86 C1
St Véran 61 E1
St Vigilio-St Vigil 90 C4
St Vincent 88 B2
St Vincent-de-Tyrosse 62 A3
St Vith 31 E2
St Vivien-de-Médoc 58 B2
St Wendel 40 B1
St Wolfgang 86 B3
St Yrieix-la-Perche 59 D2
Staaken 39 D4
Stachy 47 E4
Stade 33 D2
Stadhampton 27 F3
Stadskanaal 29 F4
Stadt Allendorf 41 D3
Stadthagen 37 D3
Stadtilm 42 B3
Stadtkyll 40 A3
Stadtlauringen 41 E2
Stadtlohn 36 B3
Stadtoldendorf 37 D2
Stadtroda 42 C3
Stadtsteinach 42 C2
Staffelstein 42 B2
Staffin 18 B3
Stafford 23 D2
Stagshaw Bank 21 D3
Stahle 37 D2
Stai 9 D4
Stainach 86 C2
Staindrop 21 E2
Staines 25 D2
Stainforth 21 D1
Stainville 56 A4
Stainz 87 D1
Staithes 21 E2
Stalać 113 D2
Stalden 84 B1
Stalham 25 F4
Stalheim 8 B3
Stalis 122 B4
Stallarholmen 10 C1
Ställdalen 10 A2
Stalon 3 F3
Stamford 23 E2
Stamford Bridge 21 E1
Stams 85 F3
Stăncuţa 115 E4
Standon 25 E2
Stange 9 D3
Stanhope 21 D2
Stănileşti 109 E2
Stanke Dimitrov 113 E1
Staňkov 43 D1
Stanley 19 D1
Stanley 21 E2
Stans 84 C2
Stansstad 84 C2
Stansted 25 E2
Stapar 105 E1
Staple Fitzpaine 27 D2
Stapleford 23 E2
Staplehurst 25 E1
Stara Pazova 112 B4
Stara Reka 115 D1
Stara Zagora 114 C1
Starcross 27 D2
Stare Czarnowo 35 F2
Stargard-Szczeciński 35 F2
Stårheim 2 A1
Starigrad 110 B4
Starigrad 110 C2
Stari Gradac 105 D2
Starigrad Paklenica 110 B3
Stari Mikanovci 105 E1
Starnberg 46 C2
Starogard 35 F3
Staro Nagoričane 113 D1
Staro Oryakhovo 115 E1
Staro Selo 115 D3
Starup 12 A2
Stathelle 8 C1
Statland 3 D3
Stavang 8 A4
Stavanger 8 A2
Stavelot 31 E2
Staveley 23 E3
Stavenisse 28 C1
Staveren 29 E3
Stavern 9 D1
Staverton 23 E1
Stavrodhrómi 120 C3
Stavrós 120 A4
Stavrós 118 B2
Stavrós 121 E3
Stavros tis Psokas 122 A1
Stavroúpolis 118 B3
Stavrtsi 114 B2
Stavsjø 9 D3
Staxton 21 F1
Stáyeira 118 B2
Steane 8 C2
Stechelberg 84 B2
Štěchovice 43 F2
Steckborn 84 C4
Steeg 85 E3
Steenbergen 28 C1
Ste-Enimie 64 B4
Steenvoorde 50 B4
Steenwijk 29 E3
Ştefan cel Mare 109 E2

Ştefăneşti.....109....D4
Stefáni.....117....D1
Stege.....12....C1
Stegersbach.....87....E2
Stein.....18....B3
Stein.....84....C4
Steinach.....85....F3
Steinau.....41....D3
Steinberg.....33....D4
Steinestø.....8....A3
Steinfeld.....36....C4
Steinfeld.....86....B1
Steingaden.....46....B1
Steinhausen.....45....D2
Steinheim.....37....D2
Steinholt.....8....C2
Steinhorst.....37....E4
Steinkjer.....3....D2
Steinløysa.....2....B1
Stellendam.....28....C2
Stenay.....51....E2
Stenbjerg.....12....A3
Stendal.....38....C4
Steni.....121....E3
Stenlille.....12....C1
Stenness.....19....F1
Stensele.....4....A3
Stensjön.....13....E4
Stenstorp.....13....D4
Stenstrup.....12....B1
Stenungsund.....12....C4
Stepanci.....117....E4
Stepojevac.....112....C4
Sternberg.....34....C3
Stérnes.....122....A4
Štěti.....43....E3
Stevenage.....25....D2
Stewarton.....20....B4
Stewartstown.....15....D2
Steyning.....25....D1
Steyr.....86....C3
Steyrermühl.....86....C3
Stezherovo.....114....C2
St-Geours-de-Maremne.....62....A3
Stia.....94....C2
Stibb Cross.....26....C2
Stickney.....23....F2
Stiens.....29....E4
Stiffkey.....25....E4
Stigen.....9....E1
Stigliano.....101....D3
Stigtomta.....10....B1
Stiklestad.....3....D2
Stilis.....120....C4
Stilligarry.....18....A2
Stillington.....21....E1
Stilo.....103....F4
Stilton.....23....F2
Štimlje.....112....C1
Stína de Vale.....107....D2
Stînceni.....108....C3
Stintino.....96....A4
Štip.....117....E4
Stíra.....121....E3
Stirling.....20....C4
Stjärnsund.....10....B3
Stjørdal.....3....D2
St-Jory.....63....D3
Støa.....9....E4
Stobi.....117....E4
Stocka.....10....C4
Stockach.....45....D1
Stockaryd.....13....E3
Stockbridge.....27....F2
Stockelsdorf.....33....E3
Stockerau.....87....E4
Stockheim.....42....B3
Stockholm.....10....C1
Stockport.....23....D3
Stockton on Tees.....21....E2
Stod.....43....D2
Stode.....4....A1
Stoeneşti.....114....C4
Stoer.....18....C4
Stoina.....113....E4
Stojan Mikhaylovski.....115....E2
Stoke Canon.....27....D2
Stoke Ferry.....25....E4
Stoke Fleming.....27....D1
Stoke Mandeville.....25....D2
Stoke-on-Trent.....23....D2
Stokesley.....21....E2
Stokkemarke.....12....C1
Stolac.....111....D1
Stolberg.....40....A3
Stollberg.....43....D3
Stöllet.....9....E3
Stolzenau.....37....D3
Stómion.....117....F2
Ston.....111....D1
Stone.....23....D2
Stonebridge.....23....D1
Stonehaven.....19....E2
Stonehouse.....20....C4
Stongfjorden.....8....A4
Stonyford.....17....D2
Stony Stratford.....25....D3
Stopanja.....112....C2
Storå.....10....B2
Stora Blåsjön.....3....E3
Storås.....2....C2
Storbergvika.....3....E2
Storby.....11....D2
Stordal.....2....B1
Storebro.....13....E3
Storebru.....8....B4
Store Heddinge.....12....C1
Store Merløse.....12....C1
Støren.....3....D1
Storestølen.....8....C3
Storfjellsæter.....9....D4
Storfors.....9....F2

Storkow.....39....E3
Storli.....2....C1
Storlien.....3....D2
Stormi.....6....B2
Stormyren.....4....A4
Stornoway.....18....B3
Storo.....90....B2
Storoddan.....2....C2
Storozhinets.....108....C4
Storsätern.....9....E4
Storsjö.....3....E1
Storuman.....4....A3
Storveta.....10....C2
Storvik.....10....B3
Stotel.....32....C2
Stotfold.....25....D3
Stotternheim.....42....B4
Stouby.....12....B2
Stourbridge.....23....D1
Stourport-on-Severn.....23....D1
Støvring.....12....B3
Stow.....21....D4
Stowmarket.....25....E3
Stow on the Wold.....27....E4
Stozher.....115....E2
Strä.....91....D2
Straach.....39....D3
Strabane.....15....D2
Strachan.....19....E2
Strachur.....20....B4
Stracin.....117....E4
Stradbally.....17....D3
Stradbally.....17....D3
Stradbroke.....25....F3
Stradella.....89....D1
Stradishall.....25....E3
Stradone.....15....D1
Stradsett.....25....E4
Straelen.....36....A2
Straiton.....20....B3
Strakonice.....43....E1
Straldzha.....115....D1
Stralsund.....35....D4
Stranda.....2....B1
Strandby.....12....B4
Strande.....33....E4
Strandebarm.....8....A3
Strandhill.....14....C1
Strangford.....15....E2
Strängnäs.....10....B1
Strängsjö.....10....B1
Stranice.....104....B2
Stranorlar.....14....C2
Stranraer.....20....B2
Strasbourg.....57....D4
Strasburg.....35....E2
Strasheny.....109....F3
Strassburg.....86....C1
Strassfurt.....38....C2
Strasswalchen.....86....B3
Stratford.....17....E3
Stratford-upon-Avon.....23....D1
Strathaven.....20....C4
Strathblane.....20....B4
Strathcarron.....18....C3
Strathdon.....19....D2
Strathmiglo.....19....D2
Strathpeffer.....18....C3
Strathyre.....18....C1
Stratoníki.....118....A3
Stratónion.....118....B2
Strátos.....120....B4
Stratton-on-the-Fosse.....27....E3
Straubing.....47....D3
Straume.....8....B3
Straumen.....2....C2
Straupitz.....39....E3
Strausberg.....39....E4
Straussfurt.....38....B1
Straža.....113....D3
Straža.....112....C4
Strážný.....47....E3
Streatley.....27....F3
Street.....27....D2
Strehaia.....113....E4
Strehla.....39....D2
Streitberg.....42....B2
Strelcha.....114....B1
Strengberg.....87....D3
Strensall.....21....E1
Stresa.....88....C2
Stretford.....23....D3
Stretham.....25....E3
Stretton.....23....E2
Strezimirovci.....113....D1
Stříbro.....43....D2
Strichen.....19....E3
Strimasund.....3....F4
Strmica.....110....C3
Strmilov.....43....F1
Strobl.....86....B3
Strøby Egede.....12....C1
Strofiliá.....121....D4
Strokestown.....16....C4
Strömaker.....4....A3
Stromberg.....40....B2
Stromeferry.....18....B2
Strömfors.....4....C3
Strømmen.....2....D2
Strømmen.....3....D2
Strömnäs.....4....A3
Stromness.....19....E1
Strömsbruk.....10....C4
Strömsnäsbruk.....13....D2
Strömstad.....9....D1
Strömsund.....3....F2
Stronachlacher.....18....C1
Strone.....20....B4
Strongoli.....101....E1
Strontian.....18....B1
Stroud.....27....E3
Strücklingen.....32....B2

Struer.....12....A3
Struga.....117....D3
Strumica.....117....E4
Stryama.....118....C4
Stryn.....2....B1
Strzelce Krajeńskie.....35....F1
Stubbekøbing.....12....C1
Stuben.....84....E3
Štubik.....113....D3
Stubline.....112....B4
Stuckenborstel.....33....D2
Studena.....113....E1
Studená.....43....F1
Studenica.....112....C2
Studland.....27....E2
Studley.....23....D1
Stugudal.....3....D1
Stuguflåten.....2....B1
Stugun.....3....F1
Stühlingen.....44....C1
Stukenbrock.....36....C2
Stülpe.....39....D3
Stupava.....105....D4
Stupnik.....104....C1
Sturminster Newton.....27....E2
Štúrovo.....105....E4
Sturry.....25....F2
Stuttgart.....45....D3
Styri.....9....D3
Suances.....68....B4
Suaredda.....96....C3
Subbiano.....94....C2
Subiaco.....98....B2
Subotica.....106....B2
Suceava.....109....D4
Sučevici.....110....C3
Sučevita.....108....C4
Suchań.....35....F2
Suchdol nad Luž.....47....F3
Süchteln.....36....A2
Sućuraj.....110....C1
Sudbury.....23....D2
Sudbury.....25....E3
Suden.....33....D4
Suderbrarup.....33....D4
Sueca.....76....A2
Sugag.....107....E1
Suhl.....111....E3
Suho Polje.....111....E3
Šuica.....111....D2
Šuici.....114....B4
Suippes.....51....D1
Sukeva.....5....F2
Sukošan.....110....B3
Sükösd.....105....E2
Sul.....3....D2
Suldalsosen.....8....B2
Sulęcin.....39....F4
Sulesund.....2....B1
Suling.....36....C4
Sulita.....109....D4
Sulkava.....7....E3
Sulkavanjärvi.....5....E2
Sully.....54....C2
Sulmona.....98....C2
Süloğlu.....119....D4
Sultanköy.....119....F3
Sulva (Solf).....4....C1
Sulysáp.....106....B3
Sulz.....44....C2
Sulzbach.....45....D3
Sulzbach-Rosenberg.....42....C1
Sumartin.....110....C2
Šumburk.....43....F4
Sümeg.....105....D3
Sumiswald.....84....B3
Summa.....7....D1
Summerhill.....17....D4
Sund.....11....D2
Sundborn.....10....B3
Sundbron.....4....B1
Sundbyberg.....10....C1
Sunde.....109....D4
Sunde.....2....C2
Sunderland.....21....E2
Sünderlügum.....33....D4
Sundern.....36....C2
Sundhultsbrunn.....13....E4
Sunds.....12....A2
Sundsvall.....4....A1
Sundvollen.....9....D2
Sungurlare.....115....D1
Suni.....96....B3
Sunja.....104....C1
Sunnansjö.....10....A2
Sunndalsøra.....2....C1
Sunne.....9....E2
Sunnemo.....9....F2
Sunnersta.....10....C2
Suodenniemi.....6....B2
Suolahti.....5....E1
Suomenniemi.....7....E2
Suomijärvi.....6....B3
Suomusjärvi.....6....C1
Suonenjoki.....7....D4
Suopelto.....7....D2
Suovanlahti.....5....E1
Suovigny.....60....A4
Supetar.....110....C2
Suplacu de Barcău.....107....D3
Supuru de Jos.....107....D3
Supuru de Sus.....107....E3
Surahammar.....10....B2
Šurany.....105....E4
Šurčin.....112....C4
Surduc.....107....E3
Surdulica.....113....D1
Surgères.....58....B3
Súria.....70....C3
Surnitsa.....118....B4
Sursee.....84....C3

Surte.....12....C4
Survilliers.....50....B1
Susa.....88....A1
Susch.....85....E2
Susek.....112....B4
Sushitsa.....114....C2
Sušice.....47....E4
Süssen.....45....D3
Susurluk.....119....F2
Suţeşti.....109....E1
Sutivan.....110....C2
Sutjeska.....106....C1
Sutomore.....112....A1
Sutri.....98....A3
Sutterton.....23....F2
Sutton.....25....E4
Sutton Coldfield.....23....D2
Sutton-on-Sea.....23....F3
Sutton-on-the-Forest.....21....E1
Sutton Scotney.....27....F3
Suystamo.....7....F3
Suza Reka.....112....C1
Suzzara.....94....B4
Svaneke.....13....E1
Svanesund.....12....C4
Svärdsjö.....10....B3
Svarstad.....9....D2
Svartå.....10....A1
Svartå.....4....C4
Svedala.....13....D1
Sveg.....10....A4
Sveindal.....8....B1
Svelgen.....8....B4
Svellingen.....2....C2
Svendborg.....12....B1
Svenljunga.....13....D3
Svenstavik.....3....F1
Svenstrup.....12....B3
Svervlik.....9....D2
Svetla.....16....A1
Švermov.....43....E2
Sveti Naum.....117....D3
Sveti Nikole.....117....E4
Sveti Rok.....110....B3
Sveti Stefan.....112....A1
Svetogorsk.....7....E2
Svetozarevo.....112....C3
Svetozar Miletic.....105....E1
Švihov.....43....D1
Svilajnac.....112....C3
Svilengrad.....119....D4
Svinesund.....9....D1
Svingstad.....9....D3
Svingvoll.....9....D4
Svinița.....113....D3
Svinninge.....12....C2
Svishtov.....114....C2
Svodje.....113....D2
Svoge.....113....E2
Svorkmo.....2....C2
Svrljig.....113....D2
Svulrya.....9....E3
Swaffam.....25....E4
Swalmen.....31....E4
Swanage.....27....E2
Swanlinbar.....14....C1
Swansea.....26....C4
Swatragh.....15....D2
Sway.....27....E2
Świdnica.....39....F3
Świdwin.....35....F3
Świebodzin.....39....F3
Świecko.....39....E3
Świeradów-Zdrój.....43....F4
Świerzno.....35....F3
Swindon.....27....E3
Swineshead.....23....F2
Swinford.....23....E1
Swinford.....14....B1
Świnoujście.....35....E3
Swinton.....21....D4
Swords.....17....E3
Sykäräinen.....5....E2
Syke.....33....D1
Sykkylven.....2....B1
Sylling.....9....D2
Sylt Ost.....32....C4
Symbister.....19....F4
Symington.....20....C3
Symond`s Yat.....27....D4
Synod.....26....C4
Syre.....19....D4
Sysmä.....7....D2
Sysslebäck.....9....E3
Syston.....23....E2
Syvänniemi.....7....D4
Syvde.....2....A1
Syvsten.....12....B3
Syyspohja.....7....F3
Szabadszállás.....106....B3
Szabolcsbáka.....107....D4
Szakály.....105....E2
Szalkszentmárton.....105....E3
Szalonna.....106....C4
Szany.....105....D4
Szarvas.....106....C3
Szarvaskö.....106....C4
Szczecin.....35....E2
Szécsény.....106....B4
Szederkény.....105....E2
Szeged.....106....B2
Szeghalom.....106....C3
Szegvár.....106....B2
Székely.....107....D4
Székesfehérvár.....105....E2
Szekszárd.....105....E2
Szendrő.....106....C4
Szentendre.....105....E4
Szentes.....106....B2
Szentlászló.....105....E2
Szentlőrinc.....105....D2

Szerencs.....106....C4
Szigetvár.....105....D2
Szikszó.....106....C4
Szil.....105....D4
Szilvásvárad.....106....C4
Szirák.....106....B4
Szob.....105....E4
Szolnok.....106....B3
Szombathely.....104....C3
Szőny.....105....E4

T

Taalintehdas (Dalsbruk).....6....B1
Taavetti.....7....E2
Tábara.....67....E1
Tabarz.....42....B3
Tabernas.....81....D1
Tabernes.....76....A2
Taboada.....66....C3
Tabor.....43....F1
Tábua.....72....B2
Tabuaço.....72....C3
Täby.....10....C2
Tachov.....43....D2
Tadcaster.....23....E4
Tælavåg.....8....A3
Tafalla.....69....D3
Taga.....108....B3
Taggia.....92....B2
Taghmon.....17....E2
Tagliacozzo.....98....C2
Táglio di Po.....95....D4
Tagoat.....17....E2
Tahilla.....16....A1
Tai di Cadore.....91....D3
Tailfingen.....45....D2
Tain.....19....D3
Tain-l'Hermitage.....60....C2
Taipaleenkyla.....5....D1
Taipalsaari.....7....E2
Taivalkoski.....5....F4
Taivassalo.....6....B1
Takacsi.....105....D3
Talavera de la Reina.....74....A2
Talayuelas.....75....E2
Talgarth.....27....D4
Talladale.....18....C3
Tallaght.....17....E3
Tallard.....65....D4
Tällberg.....10....A3
Talley.....26....C4
Talloires.....61....E3
Tallow.....16....C1
Tallowbridge.....16....C1
Talmáciu.....108....B1
Talmont.....58....B2
Talmont-St-Hilaire.....58....A4
Talsarnau.....22....B2
Talybont.....22....B1
Tal-y-bont.....22....B2
Tal-y-Cafn.....22....B3
Tamames.....73....E2
Tamarinda.....77....F4
Tamarite de Litera.....70....B3
Tamási.....105....E2
Tammela.....6....C2
Tammijärvi.....7....D3
Tammisaari (Ekenäs).....6....C1
Tampere.....6....C2
Tamsweg.....86....C2
Tamworth.....23....D2
Tancarville.....49....E2
Tändärei.....115....E2
Tandragee.....15....D2
Tandsjöborg.....10....A4
Tang.....17....D4
Tangen.....9....D1
Tangen.....9....D3
Tangerhütte.....38....C4
Tangermünde.....38....C4
Taninges.....61....E3
Tann.....41....E3
Tannadice.....19....E1
Tännäs.....3....E1
Tanne.....38....B2
Tannheim.....85....E3
Tannila.....5....E4
Tanumshede.....9....D1
Tanveld.....43....F3
Tanygroes.....26....C4
Taormina.....103....E3
Tapolcafő.....105....D3
Tapia de Casariego.....67....D4
Tápiószecső.....106....B3
Tápiószele.....106....B3
Tapolca.....105....D3
Tarakliya.....109....F1
Tarancón.....74....C2
Táranto.....101....E3
Tarare.....60....C3
Tarashcha.....64....C3
Tarascon-sur-Ariège.....63....D1
Tarasp.....85....E3
Tarazona.....69....D2
Tarazona de la Mancha.....75....D1
Tărbărk.....12....C2
Tarbert.....18....A3
Tarbert.....18....B3
Tarbert.....16....B2
Tarbes.....63....D1
Tarbet.....18....C1
Tarbolton.....20....B3
Tarcău.....109....D3
Tarcea.....107....D3
Tarcento.....91....D3
Tarčin.....111....D1

Tardets-Sorholus.....62....B2
Tarhos.....106....C2
Tarifa.....83....E1
Tarland.....19....E2
Tarm.....12....A2
Tarmstedt.....33....D2
Tärnaby.....3....F4
Tarnaméra.....106....B4
Tarnos.....69....E4
Tärnsjö.....10....B2
Tarp.....33....D4
Tarporley.....22....C2
Tarquinia.....97....F3
Tarragona.....70....C2
Tarrant Hinton.....27....E2
Tárrega.....70....B3
Tårs.....12....B3
Tårs.....12....C1
Tarsia.....101....D2
Tarskavaig.....18....B2
Tartas.....62....B3
Tărtăşeşti.....114....C3
Tartorici.....103....D3
Tarutino.....109....F2
Tarvasjoki.....6....B1
Tarvin.....22....C3
Tarvisio.....91....E3
Täsch.....84....B1
Tăşnad.....107....D3
Tåstrup.....12....C2
Tata.....105....E4
Tatabánya.....105....E4
Tataháza.....106....B2
Tătărăştii de Sus.....114....C3
Tatárszentgyörgy.....106....B3
Tatlisu (Akanthou).....122....B2
Tattershall.....23....F2
Tau.....8....A2
Tauberbischofsheim.....41....D1
Taucha.....39....D2
Taufkirchen.....46....C2
Taufkirchen.....86....C4
Taunton.....27....D2
Taunusstein.....40....C2
Tauplitz.....86....C2
Tauriranova.....103....F4
Tauste.....69....E2
Tauves.....59....F2
Tavannes.....84....B3
Tavarnelle Val di Pesa.....94....C2
Tavastkenka.....5....E3
Tavaux.....56....A1
Taverna.....101....D1
Tavernelle.....98....A4
Tavernes.....65....D2
Tavira.....82....C3
Tavistock.....26....C1
Taxenbach.....86....B2
Tayinloan.....15....E4
Taynuilt.....18....C1
Tayport.....19....E1
Tayvallich.....15....E4
Tázlár.....106....B2
Teaca.....108....B3
Teano.....99....D1
Teascu.....114....B3
Tebay.....21....D2
Techendorf.....86....B1
Techirghiol.....115....D1
Tecklenburg.....36....B3
Tecuci.....109....E1
Tegelen.....31....E4
Tegernsee.....46....C1
Teichel.....42....B3
Teignmouth.....27....D2
Teisendorf.....47....D2
Teisko.....6....C2
Teius.....107....E2
Tekeriš.....112....B4
Tekija.....113....D4
Tekirdağ.....119....E3
Telciu.....108....B3
Telese.....99....D1
Telford.....23....D2
Telfs.....85....F3
Telgte.....36....C3
Telheira.....82....B4
Telish.....114....B2
Teliu.....108....C1
Tellingstedt.....33....D3
Telti.....96....B3
Tembleque.....74....B2
Temerin.....106....B1
Temmes.....5....E3
Têmpio Pausânia.....96....B3
Temple Bar.....26....C4
Templecombe.....27....E2
Templemore.....16....C2
Templepatrick.....15....E2
Temple Sowerby.....21....D2
Templetouhy.....17....D2
Templin.....35....D2
Temse.....31....D4
Temska.....113....E2
Tenala (Tenhola).....6....C1
Tenbury Wells.....22....C1
Tenby.....26....C4
Tence.....60....B2
Tende.....65....F3
Tendilla.....74....C3
Tenebrón.....73....D2
Tenevo.....115....D1
Tenhola (Tenala).....6....C1
Tenhult.....13....E2
Tenterden.....25....E1
Tepelenë.....116....C2
Teplá.....43....D2
Teplice.....43....E3
Téramo.....98....C3
Ter Apel.....29....F3
Teregova.....113....D3
Terezín.....43....E3

Terezino Polje .... 105 .... D2
Terkoz .... 119 .... F3
Tèrmini Imerese .... 102 .... C3
Terminillo .... 98 .... B3
Termoli .... 99 .... E2
Termonfeckin .... 17 .... E4
Terneuzen .... 28 .... C1
Terni .... 98 .... B3
Ternitz .... 87 .... E3
Terpan .... 116 .... C2
Terracina .... 98 .... C1
Terradillos de los Templarios .... 68 .... A2
Terråk .... 3 .... E4
Terralba .... 96 .... B2
Terranova di Pollino .... 101 .... D2
Terrassa .... 70 .... C2
Terrasson-la-Villedieu .... 59 .... C2
Tertenia .... 96 .... C2
Teruel .... 75 .... E3
Tervakoski .... 6 .... C2
Tervel .... 115 .... E2
Tervo .... 5 .... F1
Tervuren .... 31 .... D3
Terz .... 87 .... E3
Teslić .... 111 .... D3
Tessay .... 49 .... D1
Tessin .... 34 .... C3
Tét .... 105 .... D4
Tetbury .... 27 .... E3
Teterow .... 34 .... C3
Teteven .... 114 .... E1
Tetovo .... 117 .... D4
Tetovo .... 115 .... D2
Tetrálofon .... 117 .... E4
Tettnang .... 45 .... D1
Teufen .... 85 .... D3
Teulada .... 96 .... B1
Teulada .... 76 .... A1
Teupitz .... 39 .... E3
Teuro .... 6 .... C2
Teuva .... 4 .... C1
Tevaniemi .... 6 .... B3
Tewkesbury .... 27 .... E4
Thale .... 38 .... B2
Thalfang .... 40 .... B2
Thalmässing .... 46 .... B4
Thalwil .... 84 .... C3
Thame .... 27 .... F3
Thann .... 56 .... C2
Thannhausen .... 45 .... E2
Tharandt .... 43 .... E4
Thásos .... 118 .... C3
Thatcham .... 27 .... F3
Thaxted .... 25 .... E3
Theale .... 27 .... F3
The Bungalow .... 20 .... B1
Themar .... 42 .... B3
Thénezay .... 58 .... C4
Thenon .... 59 .... D2
Théoule .... 65 .... E2
Thérma .... 118 .... C2
Thérmi .... 117 .... F2
Thermisia .... 121 .... D2
Thérmon .... 120 .... B4
Thérouanne .... 50 .... B4
Thespiaí .... 121 .... D4
Thessaloníki .... 117 .... F3
Thetford .... 25 .... E3
Theux .... 31 .... E3
Thiaucourt .... 51 .... E1
Thiberville .... 49 .... E1
Thiéblemont-Farémont .... 55 .... F4
Thiendorf .... 39 .... E2
Thiene .... 90 .... C2
Thiers .... 60 .... B3
Thiersee .... 86 .... A2
Thiesi .... 96 .... B3
Thiessow .... 35 .... D4
Thionville .... 51 .... F2
Thíra (Fíra) .... 121 .... F1
Thirsk .... 21 .... E1
Thisted .... 12 .... A3
Thísvi .... 121 .... D4
Thívai .... 121 .... D4
Thivars .... 54 .... B3
Thiviers .... 59 .... D2
Thizy .... 60 .... B3
Thoissey .... 60 .... C3
Tholen .... 120 .... B2
Thomas Street .... 16 .... C4
Thomastown .... 17 .... D2
Thonon .... 61 .... E4
Thorikón .... 121 .... E3
Thornaby .... 27 .... E3
Thornbury .... 27 .... E3
Thorney .... 23 .... F2
Thornhill .... 20 .... C3
Thornhill .... 20 .... C4
Thornton Cleveleys .... 22 .... C4
Thornton Dale .... 21 .... F1
Thorpe-le-Soken .... 25 .... F2
Thorpeness .... 25 .... F3
Thouarce .... 53 .... E1
Thouars .... 53 .... E1
Thouría .... 120 .... C2
Thoúrion .... 119 .... D4
Thrapston .... 23 .... E1
Three Cocks .... 27 .... D4
Threlkeld .... 20 .... C2
Threshfield .... 21 .... D1
Thueyts .... 60 .... B1
Thuir .... 63 .... F1
Thum .... 43 .... D3
Thun .... 84 .... B2
Thürkow .... 34 .... C3
Thurles .... 16 .... C2
Thurlestone .... 26 .... C1
Thurmaston .... 23 .... E2
Thurnau .... 42 .... C2
Thursby .... 20 .... C2
Thurso .... 19 .... D4
Thury-Harcourt .... 49 .... D1

Thusis .... 85 .... D2
Thyborøn .... 12 .... A3
Tiana .... 96 .... B2
Tibana .... 109 .... E3
Tibro .... 13 .... E4
Ticehurst .... 25 .... E1
Ticha .... 115 .... D1
Ticino .... 23 .... D2
Tidaholm .... 13 .... D4
Tidan .... 9 .... F1
Tideswell .... 23 .... D3
Tiefencastel .... 85 .... D2
Tiefensee .... 39 .... E4
Tiel .... 29 .... E2
Tielt .... 30 .... C3
Tiemassaari .... 7 .... E3
Tienen .... 31 .... D3
Tiengen .... 44 .... C1
Tierce .... 53 .... E2
Tierp .... 10 .... C2
Tigănești .... 115 .... D4
Tigharry .... 18 .... A3
Tighnabruaich .... 20 .... B4
Tigmandru .... 108 .... B2
Tignes .... 61 .... E2
Tigveni .... 114 .... B4
Tihany .... 105 .... D3
Tiistenjoki .... 5 .... D1
Tikkakoski .... 5 .... E1
Tikkala .... 5 .... E1
Tilberga .... 10 .... B2
Tilburg .... 29 .... D1
Tilbury .... 25 .... E2
Til-Châtel .... 56 .... A2
Tilisos .... 122 .... B3
Tillicoultry .... 20 .... C4
Tiltrem .... 3 .... D2
Timahoe .... 17 .... D3
Timbákion .... 122 .... B3
Timfristós .... 120 .... C4
Timi .... 122 .... A1
Timișoara .... 106 .... C1
Timișul de Sus .... 108 .... C1
Timmele .... 13 .... D4
Timmendorfer Strand .... 34 .... B3
Timmernabben .... 13 .... F3
Timoleague .... 16 .... B1
Timrå .... 4 .... A1
Tinahely .... 17 .... E2
Tinca .... 107 .... D2
Tinchebray .... 53 .... E4
Tineo .... 67 .... E4
Tingsryd .... 13 .... E2
Tingvoll .... 2 .... C1
Tinos .... 121 .... F3
Tintagel .... 26 .... B2
Tintăreni .... 113 .... E4
Tintern .... 27 .... D3
Tione di Trento .... 90 .... B3
Tipperary .... 16 .... C2
Tiranë .... 116 .... C3
Tirano .... 89 .... E3
Tirgo .... 68 .... C3
Tîrgoviște .... 114 .... C4
Tîrgu Bujor .... 109 .... E1
Tîrgu Cărbunești .... 113 .... E4
Tîrgu Frumos .... 109 .... D3
Tîrgu Jiu .... 113 .... E4
Tîrgu Lăpuș .... 108 .... B3
Tîrgu Mureș .... 108 .... B2
Tîrgu Neamț .... 109 .... D3
Tîrgu Ocna .... 109 .... D4
Tîrgu Secuiesc .... 109 .... D1
Tîrgușor .... 115 .... F3
Tiriolo .... 101 .... D1
Tirmo .... 7 .... D1
Tîrnăveni .... 108 .... B2
Tîrnavos .... 117 .... E1
Tirrénia .... 93 .... E2
Tirschenreuth .... 43 .... D2
Tirstrup .... 12 .... B2
Tisbury .... 27 .... E2
Tismana .... 113 .... E4
Tisvildeleje .... 12 .... C2
Tiszaalpár .... 106 .... B3
Tiszabábolna .... 106 .... C4
Tiszabecs .... 107 .... E4
Tiszacsege .... 106 .... C3
Tiszaföldvár .... 106 .... B3
Tiszafüred .... 106 .... C3
Tiszakécske .... 106 .... B3
Tiszaörs .... 106 .... C3
Tiszaszőlős .... 106 .... C3
Tiszavasvári .... 106 .... C4
Titel .... 112 .... C4
Titești .... 108 .... B1
Titisee .... 44 .... C2
Titograd .... 111 .... E1
Titova Korenica .... 110 .... B4
Titova Mitrovica .... 112 .... C1
Titova Velenje .... 104 .... B2
Titovo Užiče .... 112 .... B3
Titov Veles .... 117 .... E4
Titran .... 2 .... C2
Tittling .... 47 .... E3
Tittmoning .... 47 .... D2
Titu .... 114 .... C3
Titz .... 40 .... A4
Tiukka (Tjöck) .... 6 .... A3
Tivat .... 111 .... E1
Tiverton .... 27 .... D2
Tivoli .... 98 .... B2
Tjåmotis .... 10 .... B1
Tjele .... 12 .... B3
Tjentište .... 112 .... E2
Tjöck (Tiukka) .... 6 .... A3
Tjolmen .... 3 .... A4
Tjønnefoss .... 8 .... C1
Tjøtta .... 3 .... A4
Tkon .... 110 .... B3
Tobarra .... 81 .... E4
Tobercurry .... 14 .... B1

Tobermore .... 15 .... D2
Tobermory .... 18 .... B1
Tocha .... 72 .... B2
Töckfors .... 9 .... E2
Toddington .... 25 .... D2
Todi .... 98 .... B4
Todirești .... 109 .... E3
Todtnau .... 44 .... C1
Tofte .... 9 .... D2
Toftlund .... 12 .... A1
Togher .... 16 .... C3
Tohmajärvi .... 7 .... F3
Toholampi .... 5 .... D2
Toijala .... 6 .... C2
Toivakka .... 5 .... E1
Toivola .... 5 .... D2
Töjby .... 4 .... C1
Tojšići .... 111 .... E3
Toksovo .... 7 .... F1
Tolbukhin .... 115 .... E2
Toledo .... 74 .... B2
Tolentino .... 95 .... E1
Tolfa .... 98 .... A3
Tolga .... 3 .... D1
Tolkinnen (Tolkis) .... 7 .... D1
Tolkis (Tolkkinen) .... 7 .... D1
Tolleshunt D'Arcy .... 25 .... E2
Tolmezzo .... 91 .... E3
Tolmin .... 104 .... A2
Tolna .... 105 .... E2
Tolob .... 19 .... F3
Tolón .... 121 .... D3
Tolosa .... 69 .... D4
Tolve .... 100 .... C3
Tomar .... 78 .... B4
Tomaševo .... 112 .... B2
Tomášikovo .... 105 .... D4
Tomatin .... 19 .... D2
Tomdoun .... 18 .... C2
Tomelilla .... 13 .... D1
Tomelloso .... 74 .... C1
Tomești .... 109 .... E3
Tomintoul .... 19 .... D2
Tømmervåg .... 2 .... C2
Tompa .... 106 .... B3
Tomra .... 2 .... B1
Tomter .... 9 .... D2
Tona .... 71 .... D3
Tonara .... 96 .... B2
Tonbridge .... 25 .... E1
Tondela .... 72 .... B2
Tønder .... 12 .... A1
Tongeren (Tongres) .... 31 .... E3
Tongres (Tongeren) .... 31 .... E3
Tongue .... 18 .... C4
Tonnay-Boutonne .... 58 .... B3
Tonnay-Charente .... 58 .... B3
Tonneins .... 62 .... C4
Tonnerre .... 55 .... E2
Tönning .... 33 .... D4
Tønsberg .... 9 .... D2
Tonstad .... 8 .... B1
Tonypandy .... 27 .... D3
Tonyrefail .... 27 .... D3
Toomyvara .... 16 .... C2
Toormore .... 16 .... B1
Topa de Criș .... 107 .... D3
Topalu .... 115 .... E3
Topchii .... 115 .... D2
Topchin .... 39 .... E3
Topcliffe .... 21 .... E1
Toplet .... 113 .... D4
Toplița .... 108 .... C3
Topola .... 112 .... C3
Topolcani .... 117 .... D3
Topolog .... 115 .... F4
Topolováțu .... 107 .... D1
Topoloveni .... 114 .... C4
Topolovgrad .... 119 .... D4
Topolovnik .... 113 .... D4
Topolovo .... 118 .... C4
Topraisar .... 115 .... F3
Torbole .... 90 .... B2
Torcross .... 27 .... D1
Tordera .... 71 .... D3
Tordesillas .... 73 .... F4
Töre .... 5 .... D4
Töreboda .... 9 .... F1
Torekov .... 13 .... D2
Toreno .... 67 .... D3
Torfyanovka (Yulya Urpala) .... 7 .... E2
Torgau .... 39 .... D2
Torgelow .... 35 .... D2
Torgyle .... 18 .... C2
Torhamn .... 13 .... E2
Torhout .... 30 .... B4
Torigni .... 49 .... D1
Torija .... 74 .... C4
Torino .... 88 .... B1
Torino di Sangro Marina .... 99 .... D3
Torla .... 70 .... A4
Törmänmäki .... 5 .... D3
Tornio .... 5 .... D4
Tornjoš .... 106 .... B1
Torö .... 73 .... F4
Törökszentmiklós .... 106 .... C3
Torone .... 118 .... B2
Torony .... 104 .... C3
Torpo .... 8 .... C2
Torpoint .... 27 .... C1
Torpsbruk .... 13 .... E3
Torquay .... 27 .... D1
Torrance .... 20 .... B4
Torrão .... 78 .... B2
Torre .... 102 .... A1
Torre Annunziata .... 100 .... B3
Torre Baja .... 75 .... D3
Torre Beretti .... 88 .... C1
Torreblanca .... 76 .... A4
Torre Canne .... 101 .... E4
Torre de la Higuera .... 83 .... D2

Torre del Bierzo .... 67 .... E2
Torre del Greco .... 100 .... B3
Torre del Mar .... 80 .... B1
Torredembarra .... 70 .... C2
Torre de Passeri .... 98 .... C3
Torredonjimeno .... 80 .... B3
Torre Faro .... 103 .... E4
Torre Grande .... 96 .... A2
Torre Orsaia .... 100 .... C3
Torregamones .... 73 .... E4
Torrejón de la Calzada .... 74 .... B3
Torrejón el Rubio .... 79 .... E4
Torrelaguna .... 74 .... B4
Torrelapaja .... 69 .... D1
Torrelavega .... 68 .... D4
Torrelodones .... 74 .... B3
Torremaggiore .... 99 .... E2
Torremolinos .... 80 .... A1
Torrenostra .... 76 .... A4
Torrente de Cinca .... 70 .... A2
Torrenueva .... 80 .... B1
Torre Pellice .... 92 .... A4
Torrequemada .... 79 .... D2
Torres Novas .... 78 .... B4
Torres Vedras .... 78 .... A3
Torre Vã .... 82 .... B4
Torrevieja .... 81 .... F3
Torri del Benaco .... 90 .... B2
Torridon .... 18 .... B3
Torríglia .... 92 .... C3
Torrijos .... 74 .... A2
Tørring .... 12 .... B2
Torrington .... 26 .... C2
Torrita di Siena .... 94 .... C1
Torroella de Montgri .... 71 .... E3
Torsåker .... 10 .... B3
Torsås .... 13 .... E2
Torsborg .... 3 .... E1
Torsby .... 9 .... E1
Torshälla .... 10 .... B2
Tørring .... 12 .... A3
Tortinmäki .... 6 .... B1
Tortoli .... 96 .... C2
Tortona .... 92 .... C4
Tortosa .... 70 .... B1
Torup .... 13 .... D3
Torup Strand .... 12 .... B3
Tor Vaiánica .... 98 .... B2
Torver .... 20 .... C2
Torvikbukt .... 2 .... B1
Tørvikbygd .... 8 .... A3
Torvsjö .... 8 .... A3
Torzym .... 390 .... F3
Tosbotn .... 3 .... E4
Toscolano Maderno .... 90 .... B2
Tossa de Mar .... 71 .... D3
Tosse .... 9 .... E1
Tostedt .... 33 .... D2
Tószeg .... 106 .... B3
Totana .... 81 .... E3
Tôtes .... 49 .... F2
Totești .... 107 .... E1
Tótkomlós .... 106 .... C2
Totlandsvik .... 8 .... B2
Totley Rise .... 23 .... D3
Totnes .... 27 .... D1
Tottijärvi .... 6 .... B2
Totton .... 27 .... F2
Toucy .... 55 .... D2
Toul .... 56 .... B4
Toulon .... 65 .... D2
Toulon-sur-Arroux .... 60 .... B4
Toulouse .... 63 .... D2
Tourcoing .... 50 .... C4
Tournai (Doornik) .... 30 .... C3
Tournan .... 55 .... D4
Tournay .... 62 .... C2
Tournon .... 60 .... C1
Tournon-d'Agenais .... 63 .... D4
Tournon-St-Martin .... 59 .... D4
Tournus .... 60 .... C4
Tours .... 54 .... A2
Toužim .... 43 .... D2
Tovarnik .... 111 .... E4
Tøvik .... 2 .... B2
Towcester .... 27 .... F4
Tow Law .... 21 .... D2
Töysä .... 5 .... D1
Trabadelo .... 67 .... D3
Traben-Trarbach .... 40 .... B2
Trabia .... 102 .... C3
Trädet .... 13 .... D4
Trafoi .... 89 .... E3
Tragecete .... 75 .... D3
Traian .... 114 .... C2
Traisen .... 87 .... E3
Traiskirchen .... 87 .... E3
Traismauer .... 87 .... E4
Trakheiá .... 121 .... D3
Trakošćan .... 104 .... C2
Tralee .... 16 .... B2
Tramariglio .... 96 .... A3
Tramelan .... 84 .... A3
Tramonti .... 17 .... D1
Tranås .... 13 .... D1
Tranås .... 13 .... E4
Trancaso .... 72 .... C3
Tranekær .... 12 .... B1
Tranemo .... 13 .... D3
Tranent .... 21 .... D4
Trångsviken .... 3 .... E2
Trani .... 99 .... F1
Trans .... 13 .... D1
Tranum Strand .... 12 .... B3
Tranup .... 102 .... A1
Trapishte .... 115 .... D2
Traquair .... 20 .... C3
Taryd .... 13 .... D2
Träskvik .... 6 .... B3
Träslövsäge .... 12 .... C3
Trassem .... 40 .... A1
Traun .... 86 .... C3

Traunkirchen .... 86 .... C3
Traunreut .... 47 .... D2
Traunstein .... 47 .... D2
Travemünde .... 34 .... B3
Travers .... 84 .... A3
Travnik .... 111 .... D3
Trawsfynydd .... 22 .... B2
Trebarwith .... 26 .... B2
Trebatsch .... 39 .... E3
Trebbin .... 39 .... D3
Trebenice .... 43 .... E3
Trébeurden .... 52 .... B4
Trebinje .... 111 .... D1
Trebisacce .... 101 .... D2
Trebnje .... 104 .... B2
Třebôň .... 47 .... F4
Tréboul .... 52 .... A3
Trebujena .... 83 .... E2
Trecastagni .... 103 .... D3
Trecastle .... 27 .... D4
Tredegar .... 27 .... D3
Treen .... 26 .... B1
Tregaron .... 22 .... B1
Trégastel .... 48 .... A1
Tregony .... 26 .... B1
Tréguier .... 52 .... B4
Treherbert .... 27 .... D3
Treia .... 33 .... D4
Treia .... 95 .... E1
Treignac .... 59 .... E2
Treignat .... 59 .... E2
Treis .... 40 .... B2
Trelleborg .... 13 .... D1
Tremadog .... 22 .... B2
Tremestieri .... 103 .... E3
Tremezzo .... 89 .... D3
Tremošna .... 43 .... E2
Tremp .... 70 .... B3
Trendelburg .... 37 .... D2
Trengereid .... 8 .... A3
Trento .... 90 .... C3
Tresenda .... 89 .... E3
Tresfjord .... 2 .... B1
Trets .... 65 .... D2
Tretten .... 9 .... D4
Treuchtlingen .... 46 .... B3
Treuenbrietzen .... 39 .... D3
Trevi .... 98 .... B4
Treviglio .... 89 .... D2
Trevignano Romano .... 98 .... A3
Treviso .... 91 .... D2
Trévoux .... 60 .... C3
Trgovište .... 113 .... D1
Trhové Sviny .... 47 .... F3
Triaize .... 58 .... B4
Triaucourt .... 51 .... D1
Tribanj Krušćica .... 110 .... B3
Triberg .... 44 .... C2
Tribsees .... 35 .... D3
Tricárico .... 101 .... D3
Tricesimo .... 91 .... E3
Trichiana .... 91 .... D3
Trie .... 62 .... C2
Trieben .... 87 .... D2
Trier .... 40 .... A2
Trieste .... 91 .... E2
Trifești .... 107 .... E1
Trighonan .... 117 .... D3
Trikkala .... 117 .... E1
Trilj .... 110 .... C2
Trim .... 17 .... D4
Trinita d'Agultu .... 96 .... B4
Trinitapoli .... 99 .... F1
Trino .... 88 .... C1
Tripití .... 118 .... B2
Trípolis .... 120 .... C3
Triponzo .... 98 .... B4
Tripótama .... 120 .... C3
Trittau .... 33 .... E2
Trittenheim .... 40 .... B2
Trnovo .... 111 .... E2
Troarn .... 49 .... D1
Trofaiach .... 87 .... D2
Trofors .... 3 .... E4
Trogir .... 110 .... C2
Troia .... 99 .... E1
Tróia .... 78 .... A2
Troina .... 103 .... D3
Trois-Ponts .... 31 .... E2
Trojane .... 104 .... B2
Trollhättan .... 13 .... D4
Trondheim .... 3 .... D1
Troodos .... 122 .... A1
Troon .... 20 .... B3
Tropea .... 103 .... E2
Tropojë .... 112 .... B1
Trosa .... 10 .... C1
Trossachs .... 18 .... C3
Tröstau .... 43 .... D2
Troutbeck .... 21 .... D2
Trouville .... 49 .... E2
Trowbridge .... 27 .... E3
Troyan .... 114 .... C1
Troyanovo .... 115 .... E2
Troyes .... 55 .... E1
Trpanj .... 111 .... D1
Trstenik .... 112 .... C2
Trsteno .... 111 .... D1
Truchtersheim .... 57 .... D4
Trud .... 118 .... C4
Trujillo .... 79 .... E1
Trumpington .... 25 .... F3
Trun .... 113 .... F1
Trŭn .... 113 .... F1
Truro .... 26 .... B1
Trușești .... 109 .... D3
Trustrup .... 12 .... C2
Tryavna .... 114 .... C1
Trzcinno .... 35 .... F1
Trzcińsko Zdój .... 12 .... E2
Trzebiatów .... 35 .... F1
Trzebiel .... 39 .... F2

Trzebież .... 35 .... E3
Tržič .... 104 .... A2
Tsangarádha .... 118 .... A1
Tsarevets .... 114 .... C2
Tschernitz .... 39 .... F2
Tsenovo .... 114 .... C2
Tsotilion .... 117 .... D2
Tuam .... 16 .... C4
Tuamgraney .... 16 .... C3
Tubilla de Agua .... 68 .... A3
Tübingen .... 45 .... D3
Tubre-Taufers .... 89 .... E3
Tučepi .... 110 .... C2
Tüchen .... 34 .... C1
Tuddal .... 8 .... C2
Tudela .... 69 .... E2
Tudela de Duero .... 68 .... A1
Tufești .... 115 .... E4
Tuffe .... 54 .... A3
Tuhkakylä .... 5 .... F3
Tui .... 66 .... B2
Tulare .... 113 .... D1
Tulca .... 107 .... D2
Tulcea .... 109 .... F1
Tulghes .... 108 .... C3
Tulla .... 16 .... C3
Tullamore .... 17 .... D3
Tulle .... 59 .... E2
Tullins .... 61 .... D2
Tulln .... 87 .... E4
Tullow .... 17 .... D2
Tulsk .... 16 .... C4
Tulucești .... 109 .... E1
Tumba .... 10 .... C1
Tummel Bridge .... 19 .... D1
Tunbridge Wells .... 25 .... E1
Tunnerstad .... 13 .... E4
Tunnhovd .... 8 .... C3
Tunstall .... 23 .... D4
Tuohikotti .... 7 .... D2
Tuorila .... 6 .... B3
Tura .... 106 .... B4
Turalići .... 111 .... E3
Turbe .... 111 .... D3
Turckheim .... 56 .... C3
Turégano .... 74 .... B4
Turenki .... 6 .... C2
Türgovishte .... 115 .... D2
Turi .... 101 .... E4
Turia .... 109 .... D2
Turija .... 113 .... D4
Türkeve .... 106 .... C3
Türkheim .... 46 .... B2
Turku (Åbo) .... 6 .... B1
Turlough .... 14 .... B1
Turnberry .... 20 .... B3
Turners Hill .... 25 .... E1
Turnhout .... 31 .... D4
Turnitz .... 87 .... E3
Turnov .... 43 .... F3
Turnu Măgurele .... 114 .... C2
Turnu Severin .... 113 .... E4
Turny .... 105 .... E1
Turrach .... 86 .... C1
Turriff .... 19 .... E2
Turtagrø .... 8 .... C4
Turulung .... 107 .... E4
Tuscánia .... 98 .... A3
Tušilovac .... 104 .... B3
Tušnad .... 108 .... C2
Tutbury .... 23 .... D2
Tutin .... 112 .... B2
Tutjunniemi .... 7 .... E4
Tutrakan .... 115 .... D3
Tuttlingen .... 45 .... D2
Tutzing .... 46 .... C2
Tuukkala .... 7 .... D3
Tuulos .... 6 .... C2
Tuupovaara .... 7 .... F4
Tuusjärvi .... 7 .... E4
Tuusniemi .... 7 .... E4
Tuusula .... 6 .... C3
Tuv .... 8 .... C3
Tuxford .... 23 .... E3
Tuzi .... 111 .... E1
Tuzla .... 111 .... E3
Tuzlata .... 115 .... F2
Tvååker .... 12 .... C3
Tvärålund .... 4 .... A2
Tvedestrand .... 8 .... C1
Tveitsund .... 8 .... C1
Tver .... 12 .... B4
Tvrdošovce .... 105 .... E4
Tvŭrditsa .... 115 .... D2
Twatt .... 19 .... F1
Tweedmouth .... 21 .... D4
Tweedsmuir .... 20 .... C3
Twimberg .... 87 .... D1
Twist .... 36 .... B4
Twistringen .... 36 .... C4
Two Bridges .... 26 .... C1
Twycross .... 23 .... D2
Twyford .... 25 .... D2
Tychevo .... 107 .... F2
Tyfors .... 9 .... F2
Tyholland .... 15 .... D1
Tyin .... 8 .... C4
Tylldal .... 3 .... D1
Tylösand .... 13 .... D1
Tylstrup .... 12 .... B3
Tyndrum .... 18 .... C3
Tynemouth .... 21 .... E1
Tynkä .... 5 .... D3
Tyn nad Vltavou .... 47 .... F4
Tynset .... 3 .... D1
Tyrävaara .... 5 .... F1
Tyringe .... 13 .... D2

Tyrjänsaari ....7.... F4
Tyrnävä ....5.... E3
Tyrrellspass ....17.... D3
Tysse ....8.... B3
Tyssedal ....8.... B3
Tystberga ....10.... C1
Tytherleigh ....27.... D2
Tyulenovo ....115.... F2
Tywyn ....22.... B2
Tzermiádhon ....122.... C3
Tzummarum ....29.... E4

U

Ub ....112.... B3
Úbeda ....80.... C3
Ubergsmoen ....8.... C1
Uberlingen ....45.... D1
Uchte ....37.... D3
Uckange ....51.... F2
Uckfield ....25.... E1
Ucria ....103.... D3
Udbina ....110.... B3
Udbyhøj ....12.... B3
Udbyhøj Vasehuse ...12.... B3
Uddevalla ....12.... C4
Uden ....29.... E1
Udine ....91.... E3
Udovo ....117.... E3
Udvar ....105.... E1
Ueckermünde ....35.... E3
Uelsen ....36.... B3
Uelzen ....33.... E1
Uetersen ....33.... D2
Uetze ....37.... E3
Uffenheim ....41.... E1
Ugento ....101.... F2
Ugijar ....80.... C1
Ugine ....61.... E3
Ugljan ....110.... B3
Ugljane ....110.... C2
Ugrinovci ....112.... C3
Ugúrchin ....114.... B1
Uhlířské Janovice ..43.... F2
Uhřiněves ....43.... F2
Uig ....18.... B3
Uileacu de Criş ...107.... D3
Uileacu Şimleului .107.... E3
Uimaharju ....7.... F4
Uirage-les-Bains ...61.... D2
Uithoorn ....29.... D2
Uithuizen ....29.... F4
Újfehértó ....107.... D4
Újszász ....106.... B3
Ukkola ....7.... E4
Ulbjerg ....12.... B3
Ulcani ....108.... C2
Ulceby ....23.... E3
Ulcinj ....116.... B4
Ulefoss ....8.... C2
Ulëzë ....116.... C4
Ulfborg ....12.... A2
Uljma ....112.... C4
Ullapool ....18.... C3
Ullared ....13.... D3
Ulldecona ....70.... B1
Ulldemolins ....70.... B2
Ullés ....106.... B2
Üllő ....106.... B3
Ulm ....45.... E2
Ulmen ....40.... B2
Ulmeni ....115.... D3
Ulmeni ....115.... D4
Ulnes ....8.... C3
Ulog ....111.... E2
Ulpha ....20.... C1
Ulricehamn ....13.... D4
Ulriksfors ....3.... F2
Ulsberg ....2.... C1
Ulsteinvik ....2.... A1
Ulstrup ....12.... B2
Ulstrup ....12.... C2
Uluabat ....119.... F2
Ulukışla (Marathovouno) ...122.... B2
Ulvália ....9.... E3
Ulverston ....20.... C1
Ulvestad ....8.... B4
Ulvik ....8.... B3
Ulvila ....6.... B2
Umag ....91.... E2
Umberleigh ....26.... C2
Umbertide ....95.... D1
Umbukta ....3.... F4
Umčari ....112.... C4
Umeå ....4.... C2
Ume-Ersmark ....4.... C2
Umfors ....3.... F4
Umhausen ....85.... E3
Umka ....112.... C4
Umurbey ....119.... D2
Unapool ....18.... C4
Undenäs ....9.... F1
Undersåker ....3.... E2
Úněšov ....43.... D2
Ungeny ....109.... E3
Ungheni ....108.... B2
Ungheni ....114.... C3
Ungureni ....109.... D4
Unhošt ....43.... E1
Unirea ....113.... E2
Unirea ....108.... B2
Unna ....36.... B2
Unquera ....68.... A4
Unterach ....86.... B3
Unterlüss ....33.... E1
Unter Pfaffenhausen .46.... C2
Unter-Schleissheim .46.... C2

Unteruhldingen .....45.... D1
Unterwasser ....85.... D3
Unterweissenbach ...87.... D4
Unterwössen ....47.... D1
Upavon ....27.... E3
Upper Brailes ......27.... E4
Upper Tean ....23.... D2
Uppingham ....23.... E2
Upplands Väsby .....10.... C2
Uppsala ....10.... C2
Upton-on-Severn ....27.... E4
Upwey ....27.... E2
Úras ....96.... B2
Urbánia ....95.... D2
Urbino ....95.... D2
Urchfont ....27.... E3
Urdari ....113.... E4
Urdos ....62.... B1
Uriage-les-Bains ...61.... D2
Uricani ....107.... E1
Uriu ....108.... B3
Urjala ....6.... C2
Urk ....29.... E3
Urleasca ....115.... E4
Urlingford ....17.... D2
Urnäsch ....85.... D3
Uroševac ....112.... C1
Ury ....54.... C3
Urziceni ....115.... D4
Urzicuţa ....113.... E3
Usagre ....79.... E2
Uśče ....112.... C2
Usedom ....35.... E3
Usingen ....40.... C3
Usk ....27.... D3
Uskedal ....8.... A3
Uslar ....37.... D2
Ussel ....59.... E2
Usti ....36.... C1
Ustaoset ....8.... C3
Ustaritz ....62.... A2
Ustchorna ....108.... B4
Uste ....7.... F1
Uštěk ....43.... E3
Uster ....81.... D4
Ustibar ....112.... B2
Ústí nad Labem .....43.... E3
Ustipraca ....111.... E2
Ust'-Luga ....7.... E1
Ustrem ....119.... D4
Ustronie Morskie ...35.... D4
Ususău ....107.... D2
Utajärvi ....5.... E3
Utåker ....8.... A2
Utbjoa ....8.... A2
Utiel ....75.... E2
Utne ....8.... B3
Utrecht ....29.... D2
Utrera ....83.... E3
Uttendorf ....86.... B3
Uttendorf ....86.... B2
Utti ....7.... D2
Utting ....46.... B2
Uttoxeter ....23.... D2
Utvik ....8.... B4
Utvorda ....3.... D3
Uurainen ....5.... E1
Uusikaarlepyy (Nykarleby) ...4.... C2
Uusikaupunki ....6.... B1
Uusikylä ....7.... D2
Uusi-Värtsilä ....7.... F3
Uva ....5.... F3
Uvac ....112.... B2
Úvaly ....43.... F2
Uyeasound ....19.... F4
Uzel ....64.... C3
Uzerche ....59.... E2
Uzès ....64.... C3
Uzunköprü ....119.... D3

V

Vå ....8.... B2
Vaajokoski ....5.... E1
Vääkio ....5.... F4
Vääksy ....7.... D2
Vaala ....5.... F3
Vaalimaa ....7.... E2
Väärinmaja ....6.... C3
Vaas ....53.... F2
Vaasa (Vasa) ....4.... C1
Vaassen ....29.... E2
Väätäiskylä ....5.... E1
Vác ....106.... B4
Văcăreni ....106.... E1
Văchartyán ....106.... B4
Väckelsäng ....13.... E4
Väderstad ....13.... E4
Vadheim ....8.... B4
Vado Ligure ....92.... C3
Vadoússa ....119.... D1
Vadstena ....13.... E4
Vadu Izei ....108.... B4
Vadu Oii ....115.... E4
Vaduz ....84.... D3
Vaféíka ....118.... C3
Vågåholmen ....7.... D3
Vågåmo ....8.... C4
Våge ....8.... A3
Våge ....8.... B1
Vaggeryd ....13.... D3
Vagnhärad ....10.... C1
Vagos ....72.... B2
Vägsele ....4.... B3
Vägsjöfors ....9.... E3
Vägslid ....8.... C1
Vahanka ....5.... E1

Vái ....122.... C4
Vaiges ....53.... E3
Vaihingen ....45.... D3
Vailly ....54.... C2
Vailly ....50.... C2
Vâlşoara ....107.... E1
Vaison-la-Romaine ..64.... C3
Vajszló ....105.... D1
Vajta ....116.... C2
Vakarel ....113.... F1
Vaksdal ....8.... B3
Vålådalen ....3.... E1
Valandovo ....117.... E3
Valanídha ....117.... E2
Valbella ....85.... D2
Valberg ....65.... E3
Vålberg ....9.... E2
Valbonnais ....61.... D1
Valcarlos ....69.... E4
Val-Claret ....61.... E2
Valdagno ....90.... C2
Valdahon ....56.... B1
Valdalen ....9.... E4
Val d'Arda ....94.... A4
Valdeltormo ....70.... A1
Valdemarsvik ....13.... F4
Valdemorillo ....74.... B3
Valdenoceda ....68.... B3
Valdepeñas ....80.... C4
Valdėróy ....2.... B1
Val d'Esquières ....65.... E2
Val d'Isere ....61.... E2
Valdobbiádene ......91.... D2
Valdoviño ....66.... C4
Valea Bistrei .....107.... D1
Valea Călugărească 115.... D4
Valea Chioarului ..107.... E3
Valea Cînepei .....115.... E4
Valea Doşului .....107.... E2
Valea lui Mihai ...107.... D3
Valea Lungă ....108.... B2
Valea Mărului .....109.... E1
Valea Sării ....109.... D1
Valea Ursului .....114.... B4
Valea Vinului .....107.... E4
Vale de Açor ....82.... C4
Vale de Cambra .....72.... B3
Vale do Lobo ....82.... B3
Valéggio sul Mincio 90.... B2
Valenca do Minho ...66.... B2
Valençay ....54.... B1
Valence ....60.... C1
Valence ....63.... D3
Valence d'Albigeois 63.... E3
Valencia ....75.... F2
Valencia de Alcántara 78.... C3
Valencia de Don Juan 67.... F2
Valencia de las Torres 79.... E2
Valenciennes ....50.... C3
Văleni ....109.... E2
Vălenii de Munte ..115.... D4
Valensole ....65.... D3
Valentano ....97.... F3
Valenza ....88.... C1
Våler ....9.... D2
Våler ....9.... E3
Valevåg ....8.... A2
Valfábbrica ....95.... D1
Valguarnera Caropepa 103.... C2
Vâlioara ....107.... E2
Vălişoara ....107.... E1
Valjevo ....112.... B3
Valkeakoski ....6.... C2
Valkeala ....7.... D2
Valkenburg ....31.... E3
Valkenswaard ....31.... E4
Valko (Valkom) ......7.... D1
Valkom (Valko) ......7.... D1
Valladó ....67.... D3
Valladolid ....68.... A1
Vållaj ....107.... D4
Vallåkrå ....13.... D2
Vallata ....100.... C4
Valldal ....2.... B1
Valldemosa ....77.... D3
Vall de Uxó ....76.... A3
Valle ....8.... B2
Vallecorsa ....98.... C1
Valle de los Caídos 74.... B3
Vallelunga Pratameno 102.... C3
Vallen ....4.... A2
Vallentuna ....10.... C2
Valleraugue ....64.... B3
Vallet ....53.... D1
Valley ....22.... B3
Vallivana ....76.... A1
Vallo di Lucania ..100.... C3
Valloire ....61.... E2
Vallon-Pont-d'Arc ..64.... C4
Vallorbe ....80.... A3
Vallorcine ....61.... E3
Vallouise ....61.... E1
Valls ....70.... C2
Vallset ....9.... D3
Vallsta ....10.... B4
Valmontone ....98.... B2
Valmorel ....61.... E2
Valognes ....48.... C2
Valpaços ....72.... C4
Valpovo ....105.... D3
Valras-Plage ....64.... A2
Valréas ....64.... C4
Vals ....85.... D2
Valsjöbyn ....2.... C2
Vals-les-Bains .....64.... C1
Valsøybotn ....2.... C2
Val-Suzon ....55.... F2
Váltos ....119.... D4
Valtierra ....69.... C4
Valtournenche ......88.... B2
Valverde del Camino 83.... D3

Valverde del Fresno 73.... D2
Vama ....108.... C3
Vama Veche ....115.... F2
Vamdrup ....8.... A2
Våmhus ....10.... A3
Vammala ....6.... B2
Vámosmikola ....105.... E4
Vámospérce ....107.... D3
Vamosszabadi ......105.... D4
Vampula ....6.... B2
Vanda (Vantaa) ......6.... C1
Vandel ....12.... B2
Vandellós ....70.... B1
Vänersborg ....13.... D4
Vangshylla ....3.... D2
Vangsnes ....8.... B4
Vanhakylä ....6.... B3
Vanjaurfräsk ....4.... B3
Vännacka ....9.... E2
Vännäs ....98.... A3
Vannes ....52.... C2
Vansbro ....9.... F3
Vantaa (Vanda) ......6.... C1
Vanttauskoski ....6.... C1
Vanviken ....3.... D2
Vanyarc ....106.... B4
Vara ....13.... D4
Varades ....53.... D3
Varallo ....88.... C2
Vărăşti ....115.... D3
Văratec ....109.... D3
Varazze ....92.... C3
Varberg ....13.... D4
Vârbilău ....114.... C4
Varces ....61.... D2
Várda ....120.... B3
Varde ....12.... A2
Vardim ....114.... C2
Vårdö ....11.... D2
Várdomb ....105.... D2
Varel ....32.... C2
Varengeville ....49.... F3
Varenna ....89.... D3
Varennes-en-Argonne 51.... D1
Varennes-sur-Allier 60.... A3
Vareš ....111.... E3
Varese ....88.... C2
Varese Ligure ......93.... D3
Vårgårda ....13.... D4
Vargón ....13.... D4
Varhaug ....8.... A1
Vari ....121.... F2
Varilhes ....63.... E2
Varkaus ....7.... E3
Várkiza ....121.... E3
Varna ....112.... B4
Varna ....13.... D3
Várnamo ....13.... D3
Városföld ....106.... B3
Városlöd ....105.... D3
Varpaisjärvi ....7.... D4
Várpalota ....105.... E3
Varpanen ....7.... D2
Varparanta ....7.... E3
Vars ....65.... E4
Vărşand ....106.... C2
Varsseveld ....29.... F2
Vartdal ....2.... B1
Värtsilä ....7.... F3
Varvara ....118.... B4
Varvara ....119.... E4
Varzi ....93.... D4
Varzy ....55.... D1
Vasa (Vaasa) ....6.... B4
Vasankari ....5.... D3
Vásárosnamény .....107.... D4
Vaşcău ....107.... D2
Väse ....9.... E2
Vasilati ....120.... C3
Vasiliká ....117.... F2
Vasiliká ....121.... D4
Vasiliki ....120.... A4
Vasiliki ....120.... B3
Vasilikón ....121.... D4
Vaskio ....6.... B1
Vaskivesi ....6.... C3
Vaslui ....109.... E2
Vassbotten ....9.... D1
Vassenden ....8.... B4
Vassmolösa ....13.... F2
Vassy ....53.... E4
Västeras ....10.... B2
Västerhaninge .....10.... C1
Västermyrriset ......4.... B3
Västervik ....13.... F4
Vasto ....99.... D3
Vasvár ....104.... C3
Vát ....104.... C3
Vatan ....54.... C1
Vaterå ....119.... D1
Vathi ....121.... D4
Vathy Petro ....122.... B3
Vatin ....112.... C4
Vátolakkos ....117.... D2
Vatne ....2.... B1
Vátolalakkos ......117.... D2
Vatra Dornei ......108.... C3
Vatra Moldovitei ..108.... C3
Vaucouleurs ....56.... B3
Vau i Dejës ....116.... C4
Vauldalen ....3.... D1
Vauvert ....64.... C2
Vauvillers ....56.... C2
Vaxholm ....10.... C2
Vaxtorp ....13.... E2
Váyia ....121.... D4
Vayrac ....59.... C1
Veberöd ....13.... D1

Vechta ....36.... C4
Vecinos ....73.... E3
Vecsés ....106.... B3
Vedavågen ....8.... A2
Vedbæk ....12.... C2
Veddige ....12.... C3
Vedea ....114.... B4
Vedea ....114.... C2
Vedersø Klit ....12.... A2
Veendam ....29.... F4
Veenendaal ....29.... E2
Veere ....28.... C1
Vegadeo ....67.... D4
Veggli ....8.... C2
Veghel ....29.... E1
Vegusdal ....8.... B1
Vehkajärvi ....6.... C2
Vehmaa ....6.... B1
Vehu ....5.... E1
Veiano ....98.... A3
Vejen ....12.... A2
Vejer de la Frontera 83.... E1
Vejers Strand ......12.... A2
Vejle ....12.... B2
Velagići ....110.... C3
Vela Luka ....110.... C1
Velbert ....36.... B2
Velburg ....46.... C4
Veldemelen ....3.... D3
Velden ....42.... C1
Velden ....47.... D2
Velden ....86.... C1
Veldhoven ....29.... D1
Velešín ....47.... F3
Velešta ....117.... D3
Velestínon ....117.... F1
Vélez Blanco ....81.... D3
Vélez-Málaga ....80.... B1
Vélez Rubio ....81.... D3
Veličani ....111.... D1
Velico Orăşie .....112.... C3
Velika Gorica .....104.... C1
Velika Kladuša ....104.... B1
Velika Plana ......112.... C3
Veliki Zdenci .....105.... D1
Veliko Gradište ...113.... D4
Veliko Tŭrnovo ....114.... C1
Veli Losinj ....110.... A3
Velingrad ....118.... B4
Veljun ....104.... B1
Velká Hled'sebe ....43.... D2
Velké Březno ....43.... E3
Velkua ....6.... B1
Vel'ky Krtíš ......106.... B4
Vel Lašče ....104.... A2
Velletri ....98.... B2
Vellige ....13.... D1
Velp ....29.... E2
Velpke ....38.... B3
Veltrusy ....47.... E3
Velvary ....43.... E3
Vemb ....12.... A3
Vemdalen ....3.... E1
Vemhån ....3.... E1
Vena ....13.... E3
Venabu ....9.... D4
Venaco ....57.... F3
Venafro ....99.... D2
Venčane ....112.... C3
Vence ....65.... F3
Venda de Galizes ...72.... C2
Venda Nova ....66.... C1
Vendargues ....64.... B3
Vendas Novas ....66.... C1
Vendesund ....8.... D1
Vendeuvre ....55.... E3
Vendôme ....54.... B2
Veneheitto ....5.... D1
Veneskoski ....5.... D1
Venetpalo ....5.... D1
Venets ....115.... D1
Venets ....91.... D1
Venezia ....91.... D1
Venlo ....31.... E4
Vennesla ....8.... B1
Venosa ....100.... C4
Venray ....29.... E1
Venta de Arraco ....69.... C3
Venta de Cardeña ...80.... A3
Ventimiglia ....92.... B2
Ventnor ....27.... E4
Venus ....115.... F3
Venzone ....91.... E3
Vepsä ....5.... E4
Vera ....81.... D2
Vera ....3.... E2
Vera de Bidasoa ....69.... D4
Verbania-Pallanza ..88.... C3
Verberie ....50.... B2
Verbier ....84.... A1
Vercelli ....88.... C2
Verdalsøra ....3.... D2
Verden ....33.... D1
Verdens Ende ....9.... D1
Verdun ....51.... E1
Verfeil ....63.... D2
Vergato ....94.... B3
Vergina ....117.... E2
Vergt ....59.... D1
Verguleasa ....114.... B3
Verín ....67.... D1
Verkhovina ....108.... B4
Verl ....36.... C2
Verma ....2.... B1
Vermenton ....55.... E1
Vermes ....52.... C4
Vermuntila ....6.... B2
Verneşti ....115.... D4
Vernet ....63.... D2
Vernet-les-Bains ...63.... E1
Vernet-les-Bains ...63.... E1
Verneuil ....54.... B4

Vernon ....49.... F1
Verny ....51.... F1
Véroia ....117.... E2
Verona ....90.... B2
Verrabotn ....3.... D2
Verrès ....88.... B2
Versailles ....54.... C4
Versmold ....36.... C3
Versoix ....61.... E3
Verteillac ....58.... C2
Vertus ....55.... E4
Verucchio ....95.... D2
Verviers ....31.... E3
Vervins ....50.... C2
Verwood ....27.... E2
Veryan ....26.... B1
Verzuolo ....92.... B4
Verzy ....51.... D1
Vesanka ....5.... E1
Vesanto ....5.... E1
Vése ....105.... D2
Veselinovo ....115.... E1
Vesivehmaa ....7.... D2
Vesoul ....56.... B2
Vessigebro ....13.... D3
Vestbygd ....8.... B1
Vesterø Havn ....12.... C3
Vestervig ....12.... A3
Vestfossen ....9.... D2
Vestnes ....2.... B1
Vestone ....89.... E2
Vestre Gausdal ......9.... D4
Veszprém ....105.... D3
Veszprémvarsány ...105.... D3
Vésztő ....106.... C3
Veteli ....5.... D2
Vetlanda ....13.... E3
Vetralla ....98.... A3
Vetren ....114.... C1
Vetrino ....115.... E2
Vetschau ....39.... E2
Veules-les-Roses ...49.... F2
Veulettes-sur-Mer ..49.... F2
Veurne (Furnes) ....30.... B4
Vevey ....84.... A2
Vévi ....117.... D3
Veynes ....65.... D4
Veyrier ....61.... D3
Vézelay ....55.... E1
Vézelise ....56.... B3
Vézénobres ....64.... B3
Vezzano ....90.... B3
Viadana ....93.... E4
Viaréggio ....93.... E2
Viais ....53.... D1
Viala ....6.... C2
Viana do Alentejo ..78.... B2
Viana do Bolo ......67.... D2
Viana do Castelo ...66.... B1
Vianen ....29.... D2
Vianne ....62.... C3
Vias ....64.... B2
Viborg ....12.... B3
Viborg ....7.... D1
Vibo Valentia .....103.... F4
Vibraye ....54.... A3
Vic ....60.... A2
Vič ....71.... D3
Viç ....104.... B3
Vicdessos ....63.... D1
Vic-en-Bigorre .....62.... C2
Vicenza ....90.... C2
Vic-Fezensac ....62.... C3
Vichy ....60.... B3
Vickerstown ....20.... C1
Vico ....57.... F2
Vico del Gargano ...99.... F2
Vico Equense ......100.... B3
Vicovaro ....98.... B2
Vic-sur-Aisne ......50.... C2
Vic-sur-Cère ....59.... F1
Victoria ....108.... C1
Vidauban ....65.... E2
Videbæk ....12.... A2
Videle ....114.... C3
Videseter ....2.... B1
Vidigueira ....78.... C1
Vidlin ....19.... F3
Vidra ....115.... D3
Vidra ....109.... D1
Vidsel ....4.... C3
Viechtach ....47.... D4
Viella ....70.... B4
Vielsalm ....31.... E2
Vienenburg ....37.... E3
Vienne ....60.... B3
Vieremä ....5.... F2
Viersen ....36.... A1
Vieru ....7.... D2
Vierumäki ....7.... D2
Vierzehnheiligen ...42.... B2
Vierzon ....54.... C1
Vieste ....99.... F2
Vietri di Potenza .100.... C4
Vietri sul Mare ...100.... B3
Vietsiluoto ....5.... D4
Vieux-Boucau ....62.... A3
Vif ....61.... D1
Vig ....12.... C2
Vigeland ....8.... B1
Vigevano ....88.... C1
Vignanello ....98.... A3
Vigneulles ....51.... E1
Vignola ....94.... C3
Vignory ....55.... F3
Vigo ....66.... B2
Vigrestad ....8.... A1
Vihantasalmi ....7.... D3
Vihanti ....5.... E3

Vihiers....53....E1
Vihtari....7....E4
Vihtasuo....7....E4
Vihti....6....C1
Vihtijärvi....6....C1
Vihtiläjärvi....6....B2
Viiala....6....C2
Viinijärvi....7....E4
Viinikoski....5....E4
Viitajärvi....5....E2
Viitaniemi....7....E4
Viitasaari....5....E2
Vik....8....B4
Vik....3....E4
Vik....13....D1
Vika....10....B3
Vikanes....8....A3
Vikarbyn....10....A3
Vikebukt....2....B1
Vikedal....8....A2
Viken....13....D2
Vikersund....9....D2
Vikeså....8....A1
Vikmanshyttan....10....B2
Viladamar....71....E3
Vila de Rei....78....B4
Vila do Bispo....82....A3
Vila do Conde....72....B4
Vila Flor....73....D3
Vilafranca del Penedès....70....C2
Vila Franca de Xira....78....A3
Vila Fresca de Azeitão....78....A2
Vilagarcía de Arousa....66....B3
Vilamoura....82....B3
Vila Nova da Cerveira....66....B2
Vilanova de Arousa....66....B3
Vila Nova de Foz Côa....73....D3
Vila Nova de Milfontes....82....A4
Vila Nova de Ourem....78....B4
Vila Nova de Paiva....72....C3
Vilanova i la Geltrú....70....C2
Vila Novo de Famalicão....72....B4
Vilanueva de Argaño....68....B2
Vila Pouca de Aguiar....72....C4
Vila Praia de Âncora....66....B1
Vila Real....72....C3
Vilar Formoso....73....D2
Vila-rodona....70....C2
Vila Velha de Ródão....78....C4
Vila Verde de Ficalho....78....C1
Vila Viçosa....78....C2
Vilhelmina....4....A3
Viljakkala....6....B2
Viljolahti....7....E3
Villablino....67....E3
Villacañas....74....C2
Villacarlos....77....F4
Villacarrillo....80....C3
Villacastin....74....A4
Villach....86....C1
Villacidro....96....B2
Villada....67....F2
Villadiego....68....B3
Villafianca Tirrena....103....E4
Villafranca del Bierzo....67....D3
Villafranca del Cid....76....A4
Villafranca de los Barros....79....D2
Villafranca di Verona....90....B2
Villafranca Montes de Oca....68....C2
Villafrati....102....B3
Villa Fruela....68....B2
Villagarcia de Arosa....66....B3
Villaggio Mancuso....101....D1
Villahermosa....80....C4
Villahoz....68....B2
Villaines-la-Juhel....53....E3
Villajoyosa....76....A1
Villala....7....E3
Villalba....66....C4
Villalba....74....B3
Villalba de la Sierra....75....D3
Villalcázar de Sirga....68....A2
Villa Literno....100....A4
Villalón de Campos....67....F2
Villalpando....67....F1
Villamañán....67....F2
Villamanín....67....E3
Villamar....96....B2
Villamartín de Campos....68....A2
Villamassargia....96....B1
Villa Minozzo....93....E3
Villandraut....62....B4
Villandry....53....A1
Villanueva de Argaño....68....B2
Villanueva de Córdoba....80....A4
Villanueva de Gállego....69....E1
Villanueva del Arzobispo....80....C3
Villanueva de la Vera....73....F1
Villanueva del Campo....67....F1
Villanueva del Fresno....78....C2
Villanueva del Huerva....69....E1
Villanova Monteleone....96....A3
Villanueva de la Serena....79....E3
Villanueva de la Sierra....73....D2
Villanueva de los Castillejos....82....C3
Villanueva de los Infantes....80....C4
Villány....105....E1
Villapiance Scalo....101....D2
Villa Potenza....95....E1
Villaputzu....96....C2
Villarcayo....68....B3
Villard-de-lans....61....D2
Villardefrades....67....F1
Villarejo de Salvanés....74....C3
Villarmayor....73....E3
Villarreal de los Infantes....76....A3
Villarreal de San Carlos....73....E1
Villarrobledo....74....C3
Villarroya de la Sierra....69....D1
Villarrubia de los Ojos....74....B1

Villars....56....C1
Villars....65....F3
Villars....84....A1
Villars-les-Dombes....60....C3
Villasalto....96....B2
Villa San Giovanni....103....E4
Villa Santa Maria....99....D2
Villa Santini....91....D3
Villasimius....96....B1
Villasor....96....B1
Villasrubias....73....D2
Villastar....75....E3
Villatobas....74....C2
Villatoro....68....B2
Villatoya....75....E1
Villavelayo....68....C2
Villaviciosa....79....F1
Villaviciosa....67....F4
Villa Vomano....98....C3
Villé....56....C3
Villebois Lavalette....58....C2
Villedieu-les-Poêles....53....D4
Ville-en-Tardenois....50....C1
Villefagnan....58....C3
Villefort....64....B4
Villefranche....65....F3
Villefranche-d'Albigeois....63....E3
Villefranche-de-Lauragais....63....E2
Villefranche-de-Lonchat....58....C1
Villefranche-de-Rouergue....63....E4
Villefranche-du-Périgord....63....D4
Villefranche-sur-Cher....54....B1
Villefranche-sur-Saone....60....C3
Villemur....63....E3
Villena....81....F4
Villenauxe-la-Grande....55....D3
Villeneuve....63....E4
Villeneuve....64....C3
Villeneuve-de-Berg....64....C3
Villeneuve-de-Marsan....62....B3
Villeneuve-l'Archevêque....55....D3
Villeneuve-Loubet....65....F3
Villeneuve-sur-Allier....60....C4
Villeneuve-sur-Lot....63....D4
Villeneuve-sur-Yonne....55....D3
Villeréal....63....D4
Villers....49....E2
Villers Bocage....49....D1
Villers-Bretonneux....50....B2
Villers-Cotterêts....50....B1
Villersexel....56....B2
Villers-St.Georges....55....D4
Villerville....49....E2
Villia....121....D3
Villingen....44....C2
Villoldo....68....A2
Vilntilă Voda....65....F3
Vilppula....6....C3
Vilsbiburg....47....D3
Vilseck....42....C1
Vilshofen....47....D3
Vilsund....12....A3
Vilusi....111....E1
Vimianzo....66....B3
Vimieiro....78....C2
Vimioso....73....D4
Vimmerby....13....E4
Vimoutiers....49....E1
Vimpeli....5....D2
Vimperk....47....E4
Vinac....111....D3
Vinadio....92....A3
Vinaixa....70....B2
Vinaròs....76....B4
Vinatori....108....C2
Vinători....109....E3
Vinay....61....D2
Vinca....71....D4
Vinchiaturo....99....D2
Vinci....94....B2
Vindelgransele....4....B3
Vindeln....4....B2
Vinderup....12....A3
Vindsvik....8....B2
Vinga....106....C1
Vingåker....10....B1
Vingnes....9....D3
Vinhais....67....D1
Vinica....117....E4
Viničani....117....E4
Vinishte....113....E2
Vinje....8....B2
Vinje....8....B3
Vinjeøra....2....C2
Vinje Mare....113....E3
Vinkovci....105....E1
Vinliden....4....B3
Vinogradov....107....C4
Vinon-sur-Verdon....65....D3
Vinslöv....13....D2
Vinstra....9....D4
Vintjärn....10....B3
Vintzelberg....38....C4
Vipereşti....115....D4
Vipiteno-Sterzing....90....C4
Vira....110....C2
Virfurile....107....D2
Virgen....86....A1
Virgen de la Cabeza....80....B3
Vīrghiş....108....C2
Virginia....17....D4
Virieu....61....D2
Virieu-le-Grand....61....D3
Virkby (Virkkala)....6....C1
Virkkala (Virkby)....6....C1
Virklund....12....B2
Virmutjoki....7....E2
Virojoki....7....E2

Virolahti....7....E1
Virovitica....105....D1
Virpazar....112....A1
Virrat....5....D1
Virsbo....10....B2
Virserum....13....E3
Virtasalmi....7....D3
Virtoapele....114....C3
Virton....31....E1
Vîrtopu....113....E3
Virttaa....6....B2
Visagu....107....E2
Visbeck....32....C1
Visby....11....E1
Visé....31....E3
Višegrad....111....E2
Visegrád....105....E4
Viseu....72....C2
Vişeu de Jos....108....B4
Vişeu de Sus....108....B4
Vișina Veche....114....B2
Viskafors....13....D4
Vislanda....13....E3
Viso del Marqués....80....B4
Visoko....111....D3
Visp....84....B1
Vissefjärda....13....E2
Visselhövede....33....D1
Vissenbjerg....12....B1
Visso....98....B4
Vistea de Jos....108....B1
Visuvesi....6....C3
Visz....105....D3
Vitănești....114....C3
Vitanovac....112....C3
Vitemölla....13....D2
Viterbo....98....A3
Vitigudino....73....D3
Vitina....111....D2
Vitina....120....C3
Vitis....87....D4
Vitomirica....112....C1
Vitoria (Gasteiz)....68....C3
Vitré....53....D3
Vitry-le-François....55....E4
Vitsand....9....E3
Vitteaux....55....E2
Vittel....56....B3
Vittjärn....9....E2
Vittória....103....D1
Vittório Veneto....91....D2
Vittsjö....13....D2
Vitznau....84....C3
Vivario....57....F2
Viveiro....66....C4
Vivel del Río Martin....75....E4
Viver....75....F2
Viviers....64....C4
Vivonne....58....C4
Vize....119....E4
Vizhnitsa....108....C4
Vizille....61....D2
Vizinada....104....A1
Vizovice....115....E4
Vizzavona....57....F2
Vizzini....103....D2
Vlaardingen....28....C2
Vlachovo Březi....47....E4
Vlǎdeni....109....E1
Vladičin Han....113....D1
Vladimirescu....106....C2
Vlad Ţepeş....115....D3
Vlagtweede....29....F4
Vlăhița....108....C2
Vlakhióti....120....C2
Vlakhokorasiá....120....C2
Vlas....115....E1
Vlasenica....111....E3
Vlasiá....120....C3
Vlašim....43....F2
Vlasin....114....C3
Vlasina Okruglica....113....D1
Vlasotince....113....D2
Vlíkhón....120....B4
Vlissingen....28....C1
Vlokhós....117....E1
Vlorë....116....B2
Vlotho....37....D3
Vöcklabruck....86....C3
Vodice....110....B2
Voditsa....115....D2
Vodňany....47....E4
Voe....19....F4
Voersä....12....B3
Voghastikón....117....D2
Voghera....88....C1
Vohburg....46....C3
Vohenstrauss....43....D2
Vöhringen....45....E2
Void....56....B4
Voila....108....B1
Voineasa....108....B1
Voinești....114....C4
Voinești....109....E3
Voiron....61....D2
Voise....54....B3
Voislova....107....D1
Voiteg....106....C1
Voitsberg....87....D2
Voix....65....D3
Vojakkala....6....C2
Vojens....12....B1
Vojnić....104....B1
Vojnik....104....B2
Vojtanov....42....C2
Volary....47....E3
Volda....2....B1
Volden....6....C4

Volders....85....F3
Volendam....29....D3
Volimais....120....A3
Volkach....41....E2
Völkermarkt....87....D1
Völklingen....44....B4
Volkmarsen....37....D2
Volkovija....117....D4
Vólos....117....F1
Volosovo....7....F1
Volovo....114....C2
Volterra....94....C1
Voltri....92....C3
Voltti....5....D2
Volturara Appula....99....E2
Volyne....47....E4
Voorschoten....29....D2
Voorst....29....E2
Vörå (Vöyri)....5....D1
Vorau....87....E2
Vorchdorf....86....C3
Vórden....36....E2
Vordernberg....87....D2
Vorderriss....46....C1
Vordingborg....12....C1
Vorë....116....C3
Voreppe....61....D2
Vorey....60....B2
Vormsund....9....D2
Vorniceni....109....D4
Vorokhta....108....B4
Voronet....108....C3
Vorsfelde....38....B3
Voşlobeni....108....C2
Voss....8....B3
Votice....43....F2
Voukolia....122....A4
Vouillé....58....C4
Voúla....121....D3
Vouliagméni....121....D3
Vourkári....121....E3
Voutonári....117....D1
Vouvray....54....A2
Vouzela....72....B3
Vouziers....51....D2
Voves....54....B3
Voxna....10....B4
Voz....104....A1
Vozarci....117....E4
Vrå....12....B3
Vrå....13....D3
Vráble....105....E4
Vračevšnica....112....C3
Vrådel....8....C2
Vråliosen....8....C2
Vrana....110....A4
Vranduk....111....D3
Vranino....115....F2
Vranja....104....A1
Vranje....113....D1
Vranjska Banja....113....D1
Vransko....110....B2
Vratarnica....113....D3
Vratnica....112....D4
Vratno....104....C2
Vratsa....113....E2
Vražogrnac....113....D3
Vrbas....106....B1
Vrbanja....111....D4
Vrbnik....110....A1
Vrboska....110....C2
Vrbovec....104....C2
Vrbovsko....104....B1
Včin....112....C4
Vreden....36....B3
Vrelo....110....B4
Vrena....10....B1
Vresse....31....D2
Vretstorp....9....A1
Vrginmost....104....B1
Vrgorac....110....C3
Vrhnika....104....A2
Vrhpolje....110....C3
Vrigstad....13....E3
Vrisai....122....A4
Vrlika....110....C3
Vron....50....A3
Vroomshoop....29....F3
Vrousina....116....C1
Vroutek....43....E2
Vrpolje....110....C2
Vrpolje....105....E1
Vršac....112....C4
Vršani....111....E4
Vrsar....91....E1
Vrška Čuka....113....D3
Vrtoče....110....C3
Vrův....113....E3
Vsevolozhsk....7....F1
Vučitrn....112....C1
Vught....29....D1
Vuglevtsi....114....C1
Vukovar....105....E1
Vulcan....107....E2
Vûlchedrûm....114....B4
Vulchidol....115....F2
Vulturesti....109....E3
Vuokatti....5....F3
Vuolenkoski....7....D2
Vuolijoki....7....E3
Vuoriniemi....7....E3
Vuotner....4....B4
Vuottolahti....7....D3
Vûrbitsa....115....D3
Vûrshets....113....E2

W

Waabs....33....E4
Waalwijk....29....D2
Wabern....41....D4
Wachow....39....D4
Wächtersbach....41....D2
Wackersdorf....46....C4
Waddesdon....27....F4
Waddington....23....E3
Waddington....17....E2
Wädenswil....84....C3
Wadebridge....26....B1
Wadern....44....B3
Wageningen....29....E2
Waging....47....D2
Wahlwies....45....D1
Wahrenholz....37....E4
Waiblingen....45....D3
Waidhaus....43....D2
Waidhofen-an-der-Thaya....87....D4
Waidhofen-an-der-Ybbs....87....D3
Waidring....86....B2
Wainfleet....25....E4
Waischenfeld....42....C2
Wakefield....23....D3
Walbeck....38....B3
Walberswick....25....F3
Walchensee....46....C1
Walchsee....86....A2
Wald....84....C3
Waldbröl....40....B3
Waldeck....37....D1
Waldenbuch....45....D3
Waldenburg....43....D4
Waldfischbach....44....B4
Waldheim....39....D1
Waldkirchen....47....E3
Waldkraiburg....47....D2
Waldmünchen....43....D1
Waldowice....39....F4
Waldsassen....42....C2
Waldshut....44....C1
Walenstadt....85....D3
Walkenburn....20....C4
Wallasey....22....C3
Walldorf....44....C4
Walldürn....41....D1
Wallenfels....42....C2
Wallersdorf....47....D3
Wallerstein....45....E3
Wallingford....27....F3
Walls....19....F4
Wallsbüll....34....D4
Walmer....25....F1
Walsall....23....D2
Walsrode....33....D1
Waltham-on-the-Wolds....23....E2
Walton....22....C1
Walton-on-the-Naze....25....F2
Waltrop....36....B2
Wanderup....33....D4
Wanfried....37....E1
Wangen....45....E1
Wangenbourg....56....C4
Wangerooge....32....C3
Wängi....84....C3
Wanne-Eickel....36....B2
Wansford....23....E2
Wantage....27....F3
Wanzleben....38....B3
Warboys....23....F1
Warburg....37....D2
Warcop....21....D2
Ware....25....D2
Waregem....30....C3
Wareham....27....E2
Waremme....31....E3
Waren....35....D2
Warendorf....36....C3
Warenford....21....D3
Wargrave....25....D2
Warin....34....C3
Wark....21....D2
Warkworth....21....E3
Warmensteinach....42....C2
Warmington....27....E4
Warminster....27....E2
Warnemünde....34....C2
Warnsveld....29....E2
Warrenpoint....15....E1
Warrington....22....C3
Warslow....23....D3
Warstein....36....C2
Warth....45....E1
Warwick....21....D2
Wasbister....19....F1
Wasdale Head....21....D2
Washington....21....C2
Wasselone....56....C4
Wassen....84....C2
Wassenaar....29....D2
Wasseralfingen....45....E3
Wasserbillig....31....F1
Wasserburg....47....D2
Wassertrüdingen....46....B3

Vyartsilya....7....F3
Vyra....7....F1
Vyšši Brod....47....F3

Wassy....55....F3
Wasungen....41....E4
Watchet....27....D3
Waterbeach....25....E3
Waterford....17....D2
Watergate Bay....26....B1
Watergrasshill....16....C1
Waterhouses....23....D2
Waterloo....31....D3
Waterlooville....27....F2
Waterville....16....A1
Watford....25....D2
Watford....23....E1
Watlington....27....F3
Watten....19....D4
Wattens....84....F3
Watton....25....E4
Watton-at-Stone....25....D2
Wattwil....85....D3
Waulsort....31....D2
Wavre....31....D3
Waxweiler....40....A2
Wearhead....21....D2
Wedel....33....D2
Weedon....23....E1
Weener....32....B2
Weert....31....E4
Weesen....85....D3
Weeze....36....A2
Wegberg....36....A1
Weggis....84....C3
Wegliniec....39....F2
Wegorzyno....35....F3
Wegscheid....47....E3
Wehr....44....C1
Weichshofen....47....D1
Weida....42....C3
Weiden....42....C2
Weidenberg....42....C2
Weikersheim....41....E1
Weil....45....D3
Weilburg....40....C3
Weilheim....46....B2
Weimar....42....B4
Weinfelden....85....D3
Weingarten....45....D1
Weinheim....40....C1
Weinsberg....45....D4
Weismain....42....B2
Weissbriach....86....B1
Weissenbach....85....E3
Weissenburg....46....B3
Weissenfels....38....C1
Weissenhorn....45....E2
Weissenkirchen....87....D4
Weissensee....38....B1
Weissenstadt....42....C2
Weisskirchen....87....D2
Weisswasser....39....F2
Weitendorf....34....C3
Weitra....87....D4
Weiz....87....E2
Welden....45....E3
Weldon Bridge....21....D3
Welford....23....E1
Well....29....E1
Wellaune....39....D2
Welle....33....D2
Wellesbourne....23....D1
Wellin....31....D2
Wellingborough....23....E1
Wellington....27....D2
Wellington....23....D2
Wells....27....D3
Wells-next-the-Sea....25....E4
Welney....25....E3
Wels....86....C3
Welshpool....22....C2
Weltenburg....46....C3
Welwyn....25....D2
Welwyn Garden City....25....D2
Welzheim....45....D3
Wem....22....C2
Wembury....26....C1
Wemding....46....B3
Wemperhaardt....31....E2
Wemyss Bay....20....B4
Wendover....25....D2
Wengen....84....B2
Wengernalp....84....B2
Wenns....85....E3
Wépion....31....D2
Weppersdorf....87....F3
Werben....34....C1
Werbomont....31....E2
Werdau....42....C3
Werder....39....D3
Werdohl....36....C1
Werfen....86....B2
Werl....36....C2
Werlte....32....B1
Wermelskirchen....36....B1
Wernberg....42....C1
Werne....36....B2
Werneck....41....E2
Werneuchen....39....E4
Wernigerode....38....B2
Wertach....45....E1
Werther....36....C3
Werther....41....D2
Wesel....36....A2
Wesenberg....35....D2
Wesendorf....37....E4
Wesentheid....41....E2
Wessobrunn....46....B2
West Auckland....21....D2
West Bay....27....D2
West Bridgford....23....E2

West Bromwich ... 23 ... D2
Westbury ... 27 ... E4
Westbury ... 27 ... E3
West Calder ... 20 ... C4
Westcliffe-on-Sea ... 25 ... E2
Westende-Bad ... 30 ... B4
Westenholz ... 37 ... D4
Westensee ... 33 ... D3
Westerdale ... 19 ... D4
Westerham ... 25 ... E1
Westerholt ... 32 ... B2
Westerland ... 32 ... C4
Westerlo ... 31 ... D3
Westerndorf ... 86 ... A2
Westerstede ... 32 ... C2
Westkapelle ... 28 ... C1
West Kilbride ... 20 ... B4
West Lavington ... 27 ... E3
West Linton ... 20 ... C4
West Lulworth ... 27 ... E2
West Meon ... 27 ... F2
West Mersea ... 25 ... E4
Weston ... 23 ... D2
Weston-on-the-Green ... 27 ... F4
Weston Subedge ... 27 ... E4
Weston-super-Mare ... 27 ... D3
Westport ... 16 ... B4
West Runton ... 25 ... F4
Westruther ... 21 ... D4
West Sandwick ... 19 ... F4
West Tarbert Pier ... 15 ... E4
West-Terchelling ... 29 ... D4
Westward Ho! ... 26 ... C2
West Wittering ... 25 ... D1
West Woodburn ... 21 ... D3
West Wycombe ... 25 ... D2
Wetheral ... 21 ... D2
Wetherby ... 21 ... E1
Wetter ... 36 ... B2
Wetteren ... 30 ... C3
Wettringen ... 36 ... B3
Wetzikon ... 84 ... C3
Wetzlar ... 40 ... C3
Wexford ... 17 ... E2
Weybourne ... 25 ... E4
Weyer-Markt ... 87 ... D3
Weyhausen ... 37 ... E4
Weymouth ... 27 ... E2
Weyregg ... 86 ... C3
Wheathampstead ... 25 ... D2
Wheddon Cross ... 27 ... D2
Whiddon Down ... 26 ... C2
Whipsnade ... 25 ... D2
Whitby ... 21 ... F2
Whitchurch ... 27 ... D4
Whitchurch ... 22 ... C2
Whitchurch ... 27 ... F3
Whitchurch ... 25 ... D2
Whitegate ... 16 ... C1
Whitehall ... 19 ... F1
Whitehaven ... 20 ... C2
Whitehead ... 15 ... E2
Whitehouse ... 15 ... E4
Whiteparish ... 27 ... E2
Whitewell ... 21 ... D1
Whithorn ... 20 ... B2
Whiting Bay ... 20 ... B3
Whitland ... 26 ... C4
Whitley Bay ... 21 ... E3
Whitney-on-Wye ... 27 ... D4
Whitstable ... 25 ... F2
Whittington ... 22 ... C2
Whittlesey ... 23 ... F2
Wick ... 19 ... D4
Wickford ... 25 ... E2
Wickham Market ... 25 ... F3
Wicklow ... 17 ... E3
Wickwar ... 27 ... E3
Widdrington ... 21 ... E3
Widecombe-in-the-Moor ... 26 ... C2
Widemouth ... 26 ... C2
Widnes ... 22 ... C3
Widuchowa ... 35 ... E2
Wiedenbrück ... 36 ... C2
Wiefelstede ... 32 ... C2
Wiehe ... 38 ... C1
Wiek ... 35 ... D4
Wien ... 87 ... E3
Wiener Neustadt ... 87 ... E3
Wierden ... 29 ... F3
Wies ... 46 ... B1
Wiesau ... 42 ... C2
Wiesbaden ... 40 ... C2
Wieselburg ... 87 ... D3
Wiesensburg ... 38 ... C3
Wiesentheid ... 41 ... E2
Wiesloch ... 44 ... C4
Wiesmath ... 87 ... E2
Wiesmoor ... 32 ... C2
Wietze ... 37 ... D4
Wigan ... 22 ... C3
Wigston Magna ... 23 ... E2
Wigton ... 20 ... C2
Wigtown ... 20 ... B2
Wijhe ... 29 ... E3

Wil ... 85 ... D3
Wildalpen ... 87 ... D2
Wildbad ... 44 ... C3
Wildenrath ... 36 ... A1
Wildeshausen ... 32 ... C1
Wildhaus ... 85 ... D3
Wilfersdorf ... 87 ... E1
Wilfersdorf ... 87 ... F4
Wilhelm-Pieck-Stadt-Guben ... 39 ... F3
Wilhelmsburg ... 87 ... E3
Wilhelmshaven ... 32 ... C2
Wilhering ... 86 ... C3
Willebroek ... 31 ... D3
Willemstad ... 29 ... D2
Willerby ... 23 ... E3
Willersley ... 27 ... D4
Willingen ... 36 ... C1
Willingham ... 23 ... F1
Williton ... 27 ... D2
Wilmslow ... 23 ... D3
Wilnsdorf ... 40 ... C3
Wilsontown ... 20 ... C4
Wilster ... 33 ... D3
Wilton ... 27 ... E2
Wiltz ... 31 ... E2
Wimborne Minster ... 27 ... E2
Wimereux ... 50 ... A4
Wimereux ... 50 ... A4
Wincanton ... 27 ... E2
Winchcombe ... 27 ... E4
Winchelsea ... 25 ... E1
Winchester ... 27 ... F2
Windeck ... 40 ... B3
Windermere ... 21 ... D2
Windisch ... 42 ... C2
Windischgarsten ... 86 ... C3
Windsbach ... 46 ... B4
Windsor ... 25 ... D2
Wing ... 25 ... D2
Wingham ... 25 ... F2
Winkleigh ... 26 ... C2
Winklern ... 86 ... B1
Winnenden ... 45 ... D3
Winnigstedt ... 38 ... B3
Winnweiler ... 40 ... C1
Winschoten ... 29 ... F4
Winsen ... 33 ... E2
Winsen ... 37 ... E4
Winsford ... 23 ... D3
Winslow ... 27 ... F4
Winston ... 21 ... E2
Winsum ... 29 ... F4
Winterberg ... 36 ... C1
Winterbourne Abbas ... 27 ... E2
Winterbourne Stoke ... 27 ... E3
Winterfeld ... 38 ... B4
Wintermoor ... 33 ... D2
Winterslow ... 27 ... E2
Winterswijk ... 29 ... F2
Winterthur ... 84 ... C3
Winterton ... 23 ... E3
Winterton-on-Sea ... 25 ... F4
Wipperfürth ... 36 ... B1
Wippra ... 38 ... B2
Wirksworth ... 23 ... D2
Wisbech ... 25 ... E4
Wischhafen ... 33 ... D3
Wiselka ... 35 ... E3
Wishaw ... 20 ... C4
Wismar ... 34 ... B3
Wissant ... 50 ... A4
Wissembourg ... 57 ... D4
Wissen ... 40 ... B3
Witham ... 25 ... E2
Witheridge ... 26 ... C2
Withernsea ... 23 ... F3
Withypool ... 27 ... D2
Witney ... 27 ... F4
Witnica ... 35 ... F1
Wittdün ... 32 ... C4
Witten ... 36 ... B2
Wittenberge ... 34 ... C1
Wittenburg ... 34 ... B2
Wittichenau ... 39 ... E2
Wittingen ... 38 ... B4
Wittlich ... 40 ... B2
Wittmund ... 32 ... C2
Witton-le-Wear ... 21 ... E2
Wittstock ... 34 ... C2
Witzenhausen ... 37 ... E1
Wiveliscombe ... 27 ... D2
Wivenhoe ... 25 ... E2
Woburn ... 25 ... D3
Woburn Sands ... 25 ... D3
Woerden ... 29 ... D2
Wœrth ... 57 ... D4
Wohlen ... 84 ... C3
Woking ... 25 ... D2
Wokingham ... 25 ... D2
Woldegk ... 35 ... D2
Wolfach ... 44 ... C2
Wolfegg ... 45 ... E1
Wolfen ... 38 ... C2
Wolfenbüttel ... 37 ... E3
Wolfhagen ... 37 ... D2

Wolframs-Eschenbach ... 46 ... B4
Wolfratshausen ... 46 ... C2
Wolfsberg ... 87 ... D1
Wolfsburg ... 38 ... B3
Wolfstein ... 40 ... B1
Wolgast ... 35 ... E3
Wolhusen ... 84 ... B3
Wolin ... 35 ... E3
Wolkenstein ... 43 ... D3
Wolkersdorf ... 87 ... F4
Wollaston ... 23 ... C2
Wollaston ... 23 ... E1
Wöllersdorf ... 87 ... E3
Wollin ... 38 ... C3
Wolmirstedt ... 38 ... C3
Wolnzach ... 46 ... C3
Wolsingham ... 21 ... D2
Wolvega ... 29 ... E3
Wolverhampton ... 23 ... D2
Wolvey ... 23 ... E1
Wolviston ... 21 ... E2
Yatton ... 24 ... B2
Woodbridge ... 25 ... F3
Woodenbridge ... 17 ... E2
Woodford ... 16 ... C3
Woodhall Spa ... 23 ... F3
Woodham Ferrers ... 25 ... E2
Woodstock ... 27 ... F4
Woofferton ... 22 ... C1
Wookey Hole ... 27 ... D3
Wool ... 27 ... E2
Woolacombe ... 26 ... C2
Wooler ... 21 ... D3
Woolpit ... 25 ... E3
Woore ... 23 ... D2
Wootton Bassett ... 27 ... E3
Wootton Wawen ... 23 ... D1
Worb ... 84 ... B2
Worbis ... 37 ... E2
Worcester ... 23 ... D1
Worfield ... 23 ... D2
Wörgl ... 86 ... A2
Workington ... 20 ... C2
Worksop ... 23 ... E3
Workum ... 29 ... E4
Wörlitz ... 38 ... C2
Wormerveer ... 29 ... D3
Wormhout ... 50 ... B4
Wormit ... 19 ... E1
Worms ... 40 ... C1
Wörrstadt ... 40 ... C2
Wörth ... 44 ... C3
Wörth ... 41 ... D2
Wörth ... 47 ... D3
Worthing ... 25 ... D1
Wotton-under-Edge ... 27 ... E3
Wragby ... 23 ... F3
Wrawby ... 23 ... E3
Wredenhagen ... 34 ... C2
Wrentham ... 25 ... F3
Wrexham ... 22 ... C2
Wriezen ... 35 ... E2
Writtle ... 25 ... E2
Wroxeter ... 22 ... C2
Wroxham ... 25 ... F4
Wroxton ... 27 ... F4
Wulfen ... 36 ... B2
Wullowitz ... 86 ... C4
Wünnenberg ... 36 ... C2
Wunsiedel ... 42 ... C2
Wunstorf ... 37 ... D3
Wuppertal ... 36 ... B1
Wurzbach ... 42 ... C3
Würzburg ... 41 ... E2
Wurzen ... 39 ... D2
Wust ... 38 ... C4
Wusterhausen ... 33 ... C1
Wüstermarke ... 39 ... E2
Wustrow ... 34 ... C4
Wuustwezel ... 29 ... D1
Wyk ... 32 ... C4
Wylye ... 27 ... E2
Wymondham ... 25 ... E4

Y

Yablanitsa ... 114 ... B1
Yablonov ... 108 ... C4
Yagoda ... 114 ... C1
Yakoruda ... 118 ... B4
Yambol ... 115 ... D1
Yampol ... 109 ... E4
Yarcombe ... 27 ... D2
Yaremcha ... 108 ... B4
Yarm ... 21 ... E2
Yarmouth ... 27 ... F2
Yarrow ... 20 ... C3
Yasen ... 114 ... B2
Yasinya ... 108 ... B4
Yasna Polyana ... 115 ... E1
Yassiviran ... 119 ... F3
Yatağan ... 27 ... D3
Yatton ... 24 ... B2
Yavorets ... 114 ... C1
Ybbs-an-der-Donau ... 87 ... D3
Ybbsitz ... 87 ... D3
Yeadon ... 23 ... D4
Yealmpton ... 26 ... C1
Yecla ... 81 ... E4
Yedintsy ... 109 ... D4
Yéfira ... 117 ... C1
Yelverton ... 26 ... C1
Yenice ... 119 ... E2
Yenierenköy (Yialousa) ... 122 ... C2
Yeniköy ... 119 ... F1
Yenne ... 61 ... D3
Yeoryioúpolis ... 122 ... A4
Yeovil ... 27 ... E2
Yeovilton ... 27 ... D2
Yeráki ... 120 ... C2
Yerakini ... 118 ... A2
Yerolimin ... 120 ... C1
Yeroskipos ... 122 ... A1
Yerville ... 49 ... F2
Yesa ... 69 ... E3
Yeşilköy ... 119 ... F3
Yeste ... 81 ... D4
Yetholm ... 21 ... D3
Yetts o' Muckhart ... 19 ... D1
Yiannitsá ... 117 ... E3
Yiğitler ... 119 ... D2
Yíthion ... 120 ... C2
Yiámaa ... 7 ... E2
Yläne ... 39 ... D3
Ylihärmä ... 5 ... D1
Yli-Kärppä ... 5 ... E4
Ylikiiminki ... 5 ... E4
Yli-Lesti ... 5 ... E2
Yli-Ii ... 5 ... E4
Ylimarkku (Övermark) ... 6 ... A3
Ylistaro ... 5 ... D1
Ylivieska ... 5 ... E3
Ylöjärui ... 5 ... D2
Yngsjö ... 13 ... D2
Yoğuntas ... 119 ... E4
Yordankino ... 113 ... E1
York ... 21 ... E1
Youghal ... 16 ... C1
Youlgreave ... 23 ... D3
Yoxford ... 25 ... F3
Yport ... 49 ... E2
Ypäri ... 5 ... D3
Ypres (Ieper) ... 30 ... B3
Ysbyty Ystwyth ... 22 ... B1
Yset ... 3 ... D1
Yssingeaux ... 60 ... B2
Ystad ... 13 ... D1
Ystalyfera ... 26 ... C4
Yste brød ... 8 ... A1
Ystradgynlais ... 26 ... C4
Ystrad Mynach ... 27 ... D3
Ytre Enebakk ... 9 ... D2
Ytterbyn ... 5 ... D4
Ytterhogdal ... 10 ... B4
Yulya Urpala (Torfyanovka) ... 7 ... F2
Yundola ... 118 ... B4
Yverdon-les-Bains ... 84 ... A2
Yvetot ... 49 ... E2
Yvoire ... 61 ... E4

X

Xanten ... 36 ... A2
Xánthi ... 118 ... C3
Xàtiva ... 75 ... F1
Xeraco ... 76 ... A2
Xeresa ... 76 ... A2
Xertigny ... 56 ... B3
Xhoffraix ... 31 ... E2
Xilaghani ... 118 ... C3
Xilókastron ... 120 ... C3
Xinó Neró ... 117 ... D3
Xinzo de Limia ... 66 ... C2
Xubia ... 66 ... C4

Z

Zaandam ... 29 ... D3
Zábala ... 109 ... D3
Žabalj ... 106 ... B1
Žabari ... 112 ... C3
Žabljak ... 111 ... E1
Žabno ... 104 ... C2
Zabok ... 104 ... C2
Zabrani ... 107 ... D2
Zadar ... 110 ... B3
Zadvarje ... 110 ... C2
Zafirovo ... 115 ... D3
Zafra ... 79 ... D2
Zaga ... 91 ... E3

Zagan ... 39 ... F2
Zaglavak ... 112 ... B3
Zagon ... 109 ... D1
Zagorá ... 117 ... F1
Zagorje ... 104 ... B2
Zagreb ... 104 ... C1
Žagubica ... 113 ... D3
Zagvozd ... 110 ... C2
Zahara de los Atunes ... 83 ... E1
Zahna ... 39 ... D3
Záhony ... 117 ... D4
Zajas ... 117 ... D4
Zaječar ... 113 ... D3
Zakháro ... 120 ... B3
Zákinthos ... 120 ... B3
Zákros ... 122 ... C3
Zákupy ... 43 ... F3
Zalaapáti ... 105 ... D3
Zalabaksa ... 104 ... C3
Zalabér ... 105 ... D3
Zalaegerszeg ... 104 ... C3
Zalakomár ... 105 ... D2
Zalalövö ... 104 ... C3
Zalamea de la Serena ... 79 ... E2
Zalamea la Real ... 83 ... D4
Zalaszentbalázs ... 105 ... D2
Zaläu ... 107 ... E3
Zaltbommel ... 29 ... D2
Zalužnica ... 110 ... B4
Zamárdi ... 105 ... D3
Zambrana ... 68 ... C3
Zambujeira do Mar ... 82 ... A3
Zamora ... 73 ... E4
Zandvoort ... 29 ... D3
Zaostrog ... 111 ... D2
Zapfendorf ... 42 ... B2
Záppion ... 117 ... E1
Zapponeta ... 99 ... F2
Zaprešić ... 104 ... C2
Zaragoza ... 69 ... E1
Zárakes ... 121 ... E3
Zárand ... 107 ... D2
Zarautz ... 69 ... D4
Zárkos ... 117 ... E1
Zárnesti ... 108 ... C1
Zárrentin ... 34 ... B2
Zary ... 39 ... F2
Zasieki ... 39 ... F2
Zátreni ... 114 ... B4
Zăreni ... 107 ... D3
Zauchwitz ... 39 ... D3
Zău de Cimpie ... 108 ... B2
Zavet ... 115 ... D2
Závideni ... 114 ... B4
Zavidovići ... 111 ... D3
Zavlaka ... 112 ... B3
Závoaia ... 115 ... E4
Zawada ... 39 ... F3
Zawidów ... 39 ... F1
Žažina ... 104 ... C1
Zbraslav ... 43 ... F2
Zbraslavice ... 43 ... F2
Zdiby ... 43 ... F3
Zdice ... 43 ... E2
Zebrzdowa ... 39 ... F2
Žednik ... 106 ... B1
Zeebrugge ... 28 ... B1
Zefiría ... 121 ... E2
Zehdenick ... 35 ... D2
Zeist ... 29 ... D2
Zeitz ... 42 ... C4
Zelenika ... 111 ... E1
Zelenogorsk ... 7 ... F1
Železná Ruda ... 47 ... D4
Železnik ... 112 ... C4
Železný Brod ... 43 ... F3
Želiezovce ... 105 ... E4
Želin ... 104 ... A2
Zelina ... 104 ... C2
Zell ... 40 ... B2
Zell ... 44 ... C1
Zell ... 86 ... C2
Zella-Mehlis ... 42 ... B3
Zell am See ... 86 ... B2
Zell am Ziller ... 86 ... A2
Želnava ... 47 ... E3
Zeltweg ... 87 ... D2
Zelzate ... 30 ... C4
Zemen ... 113 ... E1
Zenica ... 111 ... D3
Zennor ... 26 ... B1
Zepče ... 111 ... D3
Zerbst ... 38 ... C3
Zerf ... 40 ... A1
Zerind ... 107 ... D2
Zermatt ... 84 ... B1
Zernez ... 85 ... E2
Zernien ... 34 ... B2
Zerqan ... 116 ... C4
Zetea ... 108 ... C2
Zetel ... 32 ... C2
Zeulenroda ... 42 ... C3
Zeven ... 33 ... D2
Zevenaar ... 29 ... E2

Zeytindağ ... 119 ... E1
Zgorzelec ... 39 ... F2
Zheleznitsa ... 113 ... E1
Zicavo ... 57 ... F2
Zickhusen ... 34 ... B3
Zidani Most ... 104 ... B2
Ziegenrück ... 42 ... C3
Zielona Góra ... 39 ... F3
Zierikzee ... 28 ... C2
Zierzow ... 85 ... E4
Ziersdorf ... 34 ... C2
Ziesar ... 38 ... C3
Ziethen ... 35 ... D3
Zijpe ... 28 ... C2
Zimandu Nou ... 106 ... C2
Zimbor ... 107 ... E3
Zimnicea ... 114 ... C2
Zimnitsa ... 115 ... D1
Zinal ... 84 ... B1
Zingst ... 34 ... C4
Zinnowitz ... 35 ... E3
Zinnwald-Georgenfeld ... 43 ... E3
Zirc ... 105 ... D3
Zirchow ... 35 ... E3
Žiri ... 104 ... A2
Zirl ... 85 ... F3
Ziros ... 122 ... C3
Zistersdorf ... 87 ... F3
Žitište ... 111 ... C1
Zitomislići ... 111 ... D2
Žitoradja ... 113 ... D2
Zitsa ... 117 ... D1
Zittau ... 43 ... F3
Živaja ... 104 ... C1
Zivinice ... 111 ... D3
Zizers ... 85 ... D2
Zlalar Bistrica ... 104 ... C2
Zlatar ... 111 ... D2
Zlatari ... 112 ... C2
Zlatitsa ... 114 ... B1
Zlatna ... 107 ... E2
Zlatna Panega ... 114 ... B1
Zlatni Pyasŭti ... 115 ... E2
Zlatograd ... 118 ... C3
Žljebovi ... 111 ... E3
Zlonice ... 43 ... E3
Žlutice ... 43 ... D2
Žminj ... 104 ... A1
Zoetermeer ... 29 ... D2
Zofingen ... 84 ... B3
Zolder ... 31 ... E3
Zomba ... 105 ... D2
Zöni ... 111 ... D4
Zonza ... 57 ... F2
Zörbig ... 38 ... C2
Zorge ... 38 ... B2
Zorita ... 79 ... E3
Zorleni ... 109 ... E2
Zorneding ... 46 ... C2
Zornitsa ... 115 ... D1
Zornotza ... 68 ... C3
Zossen ... 39 ... D3
Zoutkamp ... 29 ... E1
Zrenjanin ... 106 ... B1
Zrze ... 112 ... C1
Zsadány ... 106 ... C3
Zsana ... 106 ... B2
Zschopau ... 43 ... D3
Zubin Potok ... 112 ... C1
Zubiri ... 69 ... E3
Zudar ... 35 ... D4
Zuera ... 69 ... E3
Zug ... 84 ... C3
Zuidhorn ... 29 ... F4
Zuidlaren ... 29 ... F4
Zülpich ... 40 ... A3
Zumaia ... 69 ... D4
Zundert ... 29 ... D1
Zuoz ... 85 ... D2
Županja ... 111 ... E4
Žur ... 117 ... D4
Zürich ... 84 ... C3
Zürs ... 85 ... E3
Zurzach ... 84 ... C3
Zusmarshausen ... 46 ... B2
Züsow ... 34 ... C3
Žuta Lokva ... 110 ... B4
Zutphen ... 29 ... E2
Žužemberk ... 104 ... B2
Zvezdel ... 119 ... C4
Zvezdets ... 119 ... E1
Zvorištea ... 109 ... D4
Zvornik ... 111 ... E3
Zweibrücken ... 44 ... B4
Zweifalten ... 45 ... D2
Zweisel ... 47 ... D3
Zweisimmen ... 84 ... B2
Zwettl ... 87 ... D4
Zwettl-an-der-Rodl ... 86 ... C4
Zwickau ... 43 ... D3
Zwijndrecht ... 29 ... D2
Zwingenberg ... 41 ... D1
Zwolle ... 29 ... E3
Zyyi ... 122 ... B1